T0184184

Communications
in Computer and Information Science 1027

Commenced Publication in 2007
Founding and Former Series Editors:
Phoebe Chen, Alfredo Cuzzocrea, Xiaoyong Du, Orhun Kara, Ting Liu,
Krishna M. Sivalingam, Dominik Ślęzak, Takashi Washio, and Xiaokang Yang

Editorial Board Members

Simone Diniz Junqueira Barbosa
Pontifical Catholic University of Rio de Janeiro (PUC-Rio),
Rio de Janeiro, Brazil
Joaquim Filipe
Polytechnic Institute of Setúbal, Setúbal, Portugal
Ashish Ghosh
Indian Statistical Institute, Kolkata, India
Igor Kotenko
St. Petersburg Institute for Informatics and Automation of the Russian
Academy of Sciences, St. Petersburg, Russia
Junsong Yuan
University at Buffalo, The State University of New York, Buffalo, NY, USA
Lizhu Zhou
Tsinghua University, Beijing, China

More information about this series at http://www.springer.com/series/7899

Lorna Uden · I-Hsien Ting ·
Juan Manuel Corchado (Eds.)

Knowledge Management in Organizations

14th International Conference, KMO 2019
Zamora, Spain, July 15–18, 2019
Proceedings

 Springer

Editors
Lorna Uden
University of Staffordshire
Stoke-on-Trent, UK

I-Hsien Ting
National University of Kaohsiung
Kaohsiung, Taiwan

Juan Manuel Corchado 🆔
University of Salamanca
Salamanca, Spain

ISSN 1865-0929   ISSN 1865-0937 (electronic)
Communications in Computer and Information Science
ISBN 978-3-030-21450-0   ISBN 978-3-030-21451-7 (eBook)
https://doi.org/10.1007/978-3-030-21451-7

© Springer Nature Switzerland AG 2019
This work is subject to copyright. All rights are reserved by the Publisher, whether the whole or part of the material is concerned, specifically the rights of translation, reprinting, reuse of illustrations, recitation, broadcasting, reproduction on microfilms or in any other physical way, and transmission or information storage and retrieval, electronic adaptation, computer software, or by similar or dissimilar methodology now known or hereafter developed.
The use of general descriptive names, registered names, trademarks, service marks, etc. in this publication does not imply, even in the absence of a specific statement, that such names are exempt from the relevant protective laws and regulations and therefore free for general use.
The publisher, the authors and the editors are safe to assume that the advice and information in this book are believed to be true and accurate at the date of publication. Neither the publisher nor the authors or the editors give a warranty, expressed or implied, with respect to the material contained herein or for any errors or omissions that may have been made. The publisher remains neutral with regard to jurisdictional claims in published maps and institutional affiliations.

This Springer imprint is published by the registered company Springer Nature Switzerland AG
The registered company address is: Gewerbestrasse 11, 6330 Cham, Switzerland

Preface

The 14th International Conference on Knowledge Management in Organizations, with the theme of "The Synergistic Role of Knowledge Management in Organizations," was held at the University of Salamanca, Zamora, Spain, during July 15–18, 2019.

The conference was preceded by one day of free tutorials for participants who wished to learn about state-of-the-art of research relating to the topics of KMO. The tutorials were held on July 15, 2019. The conference itself commenced on July 16, 2019.

Knowledge has been identified as a key organizational resource for generating competitive advantage over other firms. It is the transformative catalyst that will get us into the knowledge age. The world is undergoing constant technological and knowledge revolutions. Technologies such as big data, the Internet of Things (IoT), artificial intelligence (AI), and blockchain are increasingly transforming the way we live and work.

Knowledge management (KM) refers to how well an organization leverages its knowledge internally and externally. In this age of big data, analytics, AI, IoT, blockchain, machine learning, and cognitive computing, KM can play synergistic roles. For example, KM can serve a fundamental role in managing the governance of big data and resulting analytics. KM is closely linked to AI and machine learning in terms of knowledge acquisition, knowledge representation, and knowledge generation. In addition, KM is a close cousin with project management and risk management.

There are many other new trends such as the use of social media for KM. Employees in organizations need to access the organization's knowledge management system (KMS) while they are on the go. Consequently, mobile technology and KM software will soon be inseparable.

Another role of KM is to create, build, and maintain competitive advantage through utilization of knowledge and through collaboration practices in innovation. KM systems should allow for external integration so that internal and external parties can share information more easily. Collaboration between individuals, teams, divisions, and organizations is essential, and organizations must develop the skills and culture that enable high-value collaboration. Besides collaboration, there are also issues of trust and cultures to be taken into account.

KM is also facing a challenging time with the advance of big data and IoT as well as cognitive learning. There is the issue of the relationship between innovation, technology, and KM. It is not only limited to technology, but it is the integration of business strategy and process, organizational community and culture, expertise and technology. To understand this relationship this requires that we investigate the new emerging discipline of service science, especially service dominant logic. Co-creation of value is essential to provide services and products that will offer value to users.

KMO 2019 aimed to encourage research into the various aspects of KM so as to address many of the challenges facing organizations. The intent is to create a better understanding of KM practices, research, and practical applications.

These proceedings consist of 46 papers covering various aspects of KM. All published papers have undergone a rigorous review process involving at least four reviewers. Authors of these papers come from 23 different countries including, Algeria, Austria, Brazil, Chile, China, Colombia, Ecuador, Finland, Germany, Hong Kong, India, Italy, Japan, Morocco, New Zealand, Oman, Pakistan, Russia, Spain, Taiwan, Tunisia, UAE, and UK.

The papers are organized into the following thematic sections as:

Knowledge Management Models and Analysis
Knowledge Transfer and Learning
Knowledge and Service Innovation
Knowledge and Organization
Information Systems and Information Science
Data Mining and Intelligent Science
Social Networks and Social Aspects of KM
Big Data and IOT
New Trends in KM and IT

Besides the papers, we also had invited keynote speakers and four tutorials.

We would like to thank our authors, reviewers, and Program Committee for their contributions and the University of Salamanca for hosting the conference. Special thanks to the authors and participants at the conference. Without their efforts, there would be no conference or proceedings.

We hope that these proceedings will be beneficial for your reference and that the information in this volume will be useful for further advancements in KM in both research and industry.

May 2019

Lorna Uden
Juan M. Corchado
I-Hsien Ting

Organization

Conference Chair

Lorna Uden   Staffordshire University, UK

Program Chairs

I-Hsien Ting   National University of Kaohsiung, Taiwan
Juan M. Corchado   University of Salamanca, Spain

Local Chair

Fernando De la Prieta   University of Salamanca, Spain
  Pintado

Program Committee

Reinhard C. Bernsteiner   Management Center Innsbruck, Austria
Dario Liberona   Universidad Santa Maria, Chile
Derrick Ting   National University of Kaohsiung, Taiwan
Akira Kamoshida   Yokohama City University, Japan
Costas Vassilakis   University of the Peloponnese, Greece
Dai Senoo   Tokyo Institute of Technology, Japan
Eric Kin-Wai Lau   City University, Hong Kong, SAR China
George Karabatis   University of Maryland, Baltimore County, USA
Lorna Uden   Staffordshire University, UK
Luka Pavlič   University of Maribor, Slovenia
Marja Naaranoja   Vaasa University of Applied Sciences, Finland
Marjan Heričko   University of Maribor, Slovenia
Remy Magnier-Watanabe   University of Tsukuba, Tokyo, Japan
Stefania Marrara   Consorzio C2T, Milano, Italy
Victor Hugo Medina Garcia   Universidad Distrital Francisco José de Caldas,
                        Colombia
Yuri Zelenkov   Higher School of Economics, Moscow, Russia
K. Chandrasekaran   National Institute of Technology Karnataka (NITK)
                        Mangalore, India
Marta Silvia Tabares   Universidad EAFIT, Medellín, Colombia
Ruben González Crespo   Universidad Internacional de La Rioja, Spain
Gan Keng Hoon   Universiti Sains Malaysia, Malaysia
Stephan Schlögl   MCI Management Center Innsbruck, Austria
Weigang Li   University of Brasilia, Brazil
Cristian Koliver   Federal University of Santa Catarina, Brazil

Houn-Gee Chen	National Taiwan University, Taiwan
William Wang	University of Waikato, New Zealand
Jari Kaivo-Oja	University of Turku, Finland
Christian Ploder	MCI Management Center Innsbruck, Austria
Hércules Antonio do Prado	Catholic University of Brasília, Brazil
Vesa Tapani Nissinen	Finnish Defence Research Agency, Finland
Mariusz Kostrzewski	Warsaw University of Technology, Poland
Kamoun-Chouk Souad	Manouba University, ESCT, LIGUE, Tunisia
Sandeep Kumar	Indian Institute of Technology Roorkee, Uttarakhand, India
Iraklis Varlamis	Harokopio University of Athens, Greece
Furen Lin	National Tsing Hua University, Taiwan
Jinfeng Wang	Zhengzhou University, China

Local Organizing Committee

Juan Manuel Corchado Rodríguez	University of Salamanca, Spain
Galo Sánchez	University of Salamanca, Spain
Fernando De la Prieta Pintado	University of Salamanca, Spain
Sara Rodríguez González	University of Salamanca, Spain
Javier Prieto Tejedor	University of Salamanca, Spain
Juan Carlos Matos Franco	University of Salamanca, Spain
José Escuadra Burrieza	University of Salamanca, Spain
José Luis Pérez Iglesias	University of Salamanca, Spain
María Luisa Pérez Delgado	University of Salamanca, Spain
Pablo Chamoso Santos	University of Salamanca, Spain
Alfonso González Briones	University of Salamanca, Spain
Jesús Angel Román Gallego	University of Salamanca, Spain
Manuel Pablo Rubio Cavero	University of Salamanca, Spain
Alberto Rivas Camacho	University of Salamanca, Spain
Roberto Casado Vara	University of Salamanca, Spain
Elena Hernández	University of Salamanca, Spain
Ines Sitton	University of Salamanca, Spain
María Cruz Sánchez Gómez	University of Salamanca, Spain
Antonio Sánchez Martín	University of Salamanca, Spain
Iago Ramos Fernández	University of Salamanca, Spain
María Victoria Martín Cilleros	University of Salamanca, Spain
Eva González Ortega	University of Salamanca, Spain

Contents

Knowledge Management Models and Analysis

Data Mining and Intelligent Science

Knowledge and Service Innovation

Knowledge and Organization

Data Mining and Intelligent Science/Big Data and IOT

Knowledge and Organization/Social Network and Social Aspect of KM

Big Data and IOT

Knowledge Transfer and Learning

Information Systems and Information Science

New Trends in KM and IT

Knowledge Management Models and Analysis

Enabling Technologies of Industry 4.0 and Their Global Forerunners: An Empirical Study of the Web of Science Database

Mikkel Stein Knudsen[1(✉)], Jari Kaivo-oja[1,2], and Theresa Lauraeus[1,2]

[1] Finland Futures Research Centre, University of Turku, 20014 Turku, Finland
{Mikkel.knudsen,Jari.kaivo-oja,
Theresa.lauraeus}@utu.fi
[2] Kazimieras Simonavicius University, 02189 Vilnius, Lithuania

Abstract. Knowledge management in organizations brings many benefits for R&D operations of companies and corporations. This empirical study demonstrates the power of large database analyses for industrial strategies and policy. The study is based on the Web of Science database (Core Collection, ISI) and provides an overview of the core enabling technologies of Industry 4.0, as well as the countries and regions at the forefront of the academic landscape within these technologies. The core technologies and technologies of Industry 4.0 and Manufacturing 4.0 are: (1) Internet of Things and related technologies (2) Radio Frequency Identification (RFID), (3) Wireless Sensor Network (WSN), and (4) ubiquitous computing. It also covers (5) Cloud computing technologies, including (6) Virtualization and (7) Manufacturing as a Service (MaaS), and new (8) Cyber-physical systems, such as (9) Digital Twin-technology and (10) Smart & Connected Communities. Finally, important for the manufacturing integration Industry 4.0 enabling technologies are (11) Service Oriented Architecture (SOA), (12) Business Process Management (BPM), and (13) Information Integration and Interoperability. All these key technologies and technology drivers were analysed in this empirical demonstration of knowledge management.

Keywords: Industry 4.0 · Web of Science · Technology foresight

1 Introduction

In order to remain successful, organizations today must face the challenges and opportunities provided by digitalization, automation, and other rapidly emerging new technologies. In the context of manufacturing firms, this rapid transformation is captured by the term Fourth Industrial Revolution [1], or, in short, Industry 4.0 [2, 3].

The concept of Industry 4.0 has received very broad attention in recent years from all parts of the innovation Triple Helix: Industries, governments, and academia. It is also clear that Industry 4.0 has very important implications for knowledge management. Some scholars have even begun to talk of 'Knowledge Management 4.0' [4–6].

However, it appears still difficult to pin down an exact and commonly accepted definition of the term Industry 4.0 [7]. Similarly, a number of studies have attempted to elaborate various definitions of what 'Industry 4.0' constitutes [8–11].

© Springer Nature Switzerland AG 2019
L. Uden et al. (Eds.): KMO 2019, CCIS 1027, pp. 3–13, 2019.
https://doi.org/10.1007/978-3-030-21451-7_1

Elaborating the constituting elements of Industry 4.0 is not only relevant in order to settle academic debates. It will also be a helpful element in order to prepare real-world organizations for their own changing landscapes. If organizational decision-makers have hard times grasping the meaning of the concept, they will also have hard times using the terminology as guidance for decisions on their organizations' strategy, business model, or production system. In that case, 'Industry 4.0' might remain as little more than an academic and business consulting catchphrase.

For adapting organizational knowledge management to this new emerging business environment, it is therefore paramount not only to understand the general concepts of Manufacturing 4.0 and Industry 4.0, but also to explore their core enabling technologies.

This article draws on several key survey articles in order to establish a list of core technologies of Industry 4.0. This answers our first important research question:

R1: *What are the core enabling technologies of Industry 4.0?*

Thereafter an empirical study is performed in the *Web of Science-database* for peer-reviewed academic articles on these core technologies, identifying more than 100,000 published articles featuring these technologies either in the title or as topic keywords. Based on this large-scale literature search, we then perform analyses answering to two additional important Industry 4.0 research questions breaking down the geographical, technological, and temporal dimensions of the Industry 4.0 technology waves:

R2: *Where in the world are the forerunners of Industry 4.0?*
R3: *Where in the world are the forerunners of the individual core enabling technologies of Industry 4.0?*

This empirical study provides important empirical insights into the driving forces of Industry 4.0, as well as the state of the art of the field. Simultaneously, it also demonstrates the power of large database analyses for industrial strategies and policy. This is a pertinent point for developing R&D knowledge management methods in organizations.

2 Core Enabling Technologies of Industry 4.0

Despite increasing interest about Industry 4.0, it is still a non-consensual concept [10]. There are differences in the understanding of the definition, the vision, the implications, and also of the important driving technologies behind Industry 4.0. In a survey article from 2017 [8], Lu identifies 20 different research articles on key technologies of Industry 4.0. Since then, the number has likely grown significantly. From a technical point of view, Industry 4.0 has been described as the increasing digitization and automation of the manufacturing environment, as well as the creation of a digital value chain enabling communication between products, their environments and business partners [12]. In practice, numerous technologies related to automation, digitization, and increased connectivity are therefore used to implement elements of Industry 4.0.

Lichtblau et al. [13] and Oztemel and Gursev [14] lists as basic components of Industry 4.0: i. *IoT platforms*, ii. *Location detection technologies*, iii. *Advanced human-machine interfaces*, iv. *Authentification & fraud detection*, v. *3D printing*, vi. *Smart sensors*, vii. *Big data analytics and advanced algorithms*, viii. *Multilevel customer interaction and customer profiling*, ix. *Augmented reality/wearables*, and x. *Cloud computing*.

Using more general concept terms, Posada et al. [15] lists the technologies of Industry 4.0 as related to: i. *Semantic technologies*, ii. *Internet of Things, Industrial Internet, cloud technologies*, iii. *Product life-cycle management*, iv. *Visual computing*, v. *Industrial automation*, vi. *Intelligent robotics*, vii. *Cybersecurity*, and viii. *Industrial big data*.

Cheng et al. [16] talks of "*Industry 4.0's nine pillars of technology, including virtual reality, artificial intelligence, industrial internet, industrial big data, 3D printing, cloud computing, knowledge work automation, and industrial network security*".

This article uses the operationalization of Xu et al. [17], as illustrated in Figure 1. This is explicitly not an exhaustive list, but it does function as a guide to "*selected technologies that are particularly significant for Industry 4.0*". The technologies also relate to the four main features of Industry 4.0: Interconnectivity, data, integration, and innovation [16].

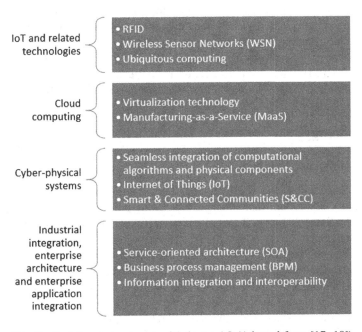

Fig. 1. Enabling technologies of Industry 4.0 (Adapted from [17, 18])

The first category of technologies is related to '*IoT and related technologies*'. The first foundation for Internet-of-Things (IoT) can be considered as a global network infrastructure composed of connected devices relying on sensory, communication, networking and information processing technologies. The aim of IoT is to interconnect all objects across different purposes, types and locations [19]. Several communication technologies has helped paved the way for a new ICT environment allowing for

Industry 4.0. These key enabling technologies are (1) *Internet-of-Things*, (2) *Radio Frequency Identification (RFID)*, (3) *Wireless sensor networks (WSN)*, and (4) *Ubiquitous computing*.

The second category of Industry 4.0-technologies is related to (5) *Cloud Computing* which allows high performance computing cost-effectively. Enabling technologies within this framework are (6) *Virtualization* technologies, and new technological and business model opportunities provided by (7) *Manufacturing-as-a-Service*. Service-orientation is an effective mean of enabling large-scale manufacturing collaboration, smart manufacturing [20].

The third category is the development of (8) *Cyber-Physical Systems*. This is perhaps the most central element of the Industry 4.0-concept [21]. Part of Cyber-Physical Systems is the seamless integration between the virtual and the physical world, and an important enabler for this is (9) *Smart and Connected Communities (S&CC)*. Another important enabling technology for this is (10) *Digital Twin*-technology [20, 21].

The final important category relates to the dimension of industrial integration and covers manufacturing and enterprise architecture. In some of the originating work on Industry 4.0 [10, 22], the whole concept rested primarily on three dimensions of integration: (1) Horizontal integration in value networks, (2) Vertical integration within manufacturing systems, and (3) End-to-end digital integration of engineering across the full value chain. Among important supportive building blocks for these integration mechanisms are (11) *Service-oriented architecture (SOA)*, and (12) *business process management* (BPM). The research area of industrial integration is covered by the technology term (13) *Information integration and interoperability* (III).

3   Methodology

3.1   Web of Science Database

The Web of Science-database was inaugurated in 2004 by Thomson Scientific, a part of the Thomson Corporation, and it quickly came to dominate the field of academic reference [23]. Since 2016, the database has been part of the then-established company Clarivate Analytics.

Web of Science has a quick basic search (by entering a topic), a cited reference search, an advanced search, an author search, and a structure search. Results can be restricted by languages (51 different languages are available at the time of writing), by timespan (from 1900 onwards), by document types, or by various Web of Science Core Collection: Citation Indexes. For advanced searches, a range of Field Tags are available, e.g. topic, title, research area, and DOI. It also is possible to use Boolean operators (AND, OR, NOT, SAME, NEAR).

Advanced searches allow for numerous opportunities of refining the results as well as several visualization tools. This makes the database very useful for researchers and knowledge managers who want to perform targeted literature searches in which scientific areas (broad or narrow) are swiftly broken down into analytical or operational elements.

3.2   Literature Search

The literature search is performed as advanced search in the Web of Science-database with the use of Field Tags, Boolean operators and truncated search strings. Field tags ensures that all results including the truncated search strings in either the publication topic (TS) or title (TI) are identified. For certain technologies both the name of the technology and commonly accepted abbreviations thereof are used. In other cases, testing shows too many false positives related to e.g. other scientific fields, wherefore only names of the technology are used.

All searches were performed in December 2018 and results limited to a period ending in 2017.

Table 1. Web of Science Industry 4.0 literature search

Technology	Search strings	Results
Internet-of-Things	TS="Internet-of-Things" OR TI="Internet-of-Things"	23,053
Radio Frequency Identification (RFID)	TS="Radio Frequency Identification" OR TI="Radio Frequency Identification" OR TS=RFID OR TI=RFID	22,427
Wireless Sensor Network (WSN)	TS="Wireless Sensor Network" OR TI="Wireless Sensor Network"	24,417
Ubiquitous computing	TS="Ubiquitous comp*" OR TI="Ubiquitous comp*"	7,337
Cloud computing	TS="Cloud comput*" OR TI="Cloud comput*"	34,766
Virtualization technologies	TS=Virtualization OR TI=Virtualization OR TS=Virtuliasation OR TI=Virtualisation	12,461
Manufacturing as a Service (MaaS)	TS="Manufacturing-as-a-service" OR TI="Manufacturing-as-a-service"	14
Cyber-physical systems (CPS)	TS="Cyber-physical syst*" OR TI="Cyber-physical syst*"	594
Digital Twin (DT)	TS="Digital Twin*" OR TI="Digital twin*"	182
Smart and Connected Communities (S&CC)	TS="Smart and Connected Communities" OR TI="Smart and Connected Communities" OR TS=S&CC OR TI=S&CC	349
Service Oriented Architecture (SOA)	TS="Service Oriented Architecture" OR TI="Service Oriented Architecture"	6,684
Business Process Management (BPM)	TS="Business Process Management" OR TI="Business Process Management"	2,995
Information Integration and Interoperability (III)	TS="Information integration and interoperability" OR TI="Information Integration and Interoperability"	13

(continued)

Table 1. (*continued*)

Technology	Search strings	Results
All Industry 4.0 enabling technologies	TS="Internet-of-Things" OR TI="Internet-of-Things" OR TS="Radio Frequency Identification" OR TI="Radio Frequency Identification" OR TS=RFID OR TI=RFID OR TS="Wireless Sensor Network" OR TI="Wireless Sensor Network" OR TS="Ubiquitous comp*" OR TI="Ubiquitous comp*" OR TS="Cloud manufactur*" OR TI="Cloud manufactur*" OR TS=Virtualization OR TI=Virtualization OR TS=Virtualisation OR TI=Virtualisation OR TS="Manufacturing-as-a-service" OR TI="Manufacturing-as-a-service" OR TS="Cyber-physical syst*" OR TI="Cyber-physical syst*" OR TS="Digital Twin*" OR TI="Digital twin*" OR TS="Smart and Connected Communities" OR TI="Smart and Connected Communities" OR TS=S&CC OR TI=S&CC OR TS="Service Oriented Architecture" OR TI="Service Oriented Architecture" OR TS="Business Process Management" OR TI="Business Process Managament" OR TS="Information integration and interoperability" OR TI="Information Integration and Interoperability"	119,634

Table 1 shows the total literature search for Industry 4.0-technologies with almost 120,000 published articles by the end of 2017, even when search terms are limited to titles and topics. This amount of articles is clearly too large for any comprehensive human-based literature review, but it provides a great framework for further analysis through systematic use of data analytics. With modern methods of text mining and machine learning, knowledge managers have new options of combing through this large accumulation of knowledge in order to obtain targeted information. The example in [12] of frequency analysis within Industry 4.0 may serve as a rather simple inspiration.

Table 1 also shows the developed 'global' search string, which can underpin more targeted searches in specific organizational contexts. To use examples from the largest manufacturing operations of the region of Southwest Finland [24], shipbuilding and the automotive industry, knowledge managers can assess the state of the art of Industry 4.0-technologies by combining the global search string with AND (TS=shipbuild* OR TI=shipbuild*) or (TS=automotive OR TI=automotive). Again limiting to the end of 2017, these searches provide 16 results within the shipbuilding industry compared to 529 results in the automotive industry, showing also the close connections between the development of concepts of Industry 4.0 and the manufacturing of cars.

4 Global Forerunner Regions of Industry 4.0

Using tools directly available in Web of Science, we now analyze the geographical distribution of the almost 120,000 articles by sorting them by countries of origin. For this Web of Science distributes by locations of the organizations submitted by article authors (in the case of international collaboration, articles are attributed to several countries).

Table 2. Regional shares of total articles on Industry 4.0 enabling technologies

Region share of total	-2005	2006	2007	2008	2009	2010	2011
Total no. of articles	4,059	2,657	4,061	4,882	6,202	5,454	6,594
Europe	32,6 %	27,0 %	30,8 %	30,9 %	36,5 %	38,6 %	36,0 %
USA	32,3 %	24,7 %	23,1 %	19,0 %	17,7 %	20,4 %	17,9 %
Japan, South Korea, Taiwan	17,8 %	24,9 %	23,1 %	19,2 %	15,9 %	15,8 %	14,6 %
China	6,4 %	13,5 %	14,8 %	21,1 %	21,2 %	19,1 %	24,4 %
India	1,2 %	2,2 %	1,8 %	2,3 %	2,7 %	2,8 %	4,3 %
CELAC	1,3 %	1,5 %	1,2 %	2,3 %	1,6 %	2,4 %	2,3 %
ASEAN	1,1 %	2,1 %	2,1 %	2,8 %	2,9 %	2,5 %	2,7 %
Africa	0,4 %	0,3 %	0,5 %	0,5 %	1,0 %	1,2 %	1,1 %

Region share of total	2012	2013	2014	2015	2016	2017
Total no. of articles	8,665	11,013	13,073	15,876	18,189	18,833
Europe	32,6 %	32,9 %	35,2 %	35,7 %	36,3 %	36,1 %
USA	16,6 %	15,7 %	15,6 %	14,7 %	15,2 %	15,7 %
Japan, South Korea, Taiwan	13,3 %	11,9 %	11,3 %	10,3 %	10,1 %	10,2 %
China	25,7 %	25,7 %	24,4 %	22,7 %	23,1 %	22,1 %
India	5,6 %	6,7 %	9,5 %	11,7 %	12,4 %	12,5 %
CELAC	2,5 %	2,9 %	3,3 %	3,9 %	3,4 %	2,8 %
ASEAN	3,3 %	4,0 %	4,5 %	3,6 %	4,2 %	4,6 %
Africa	1,9 %	2,3 %	3,0 %	3,4 %	3,9 %	4,5 %

Our hypothesis here is that those countries supplying the largest share of these publications at any given time can be considered among the (academic, at least) forerunners of Industry 4.0 at this given time.

Table 2 provides an overview of this analysis. For the purpose of clarity, countries are grouped together in regions, and not all countries or regions are represented. All categories (regions) were created after data analysis on country level.

Europe here refers to countries part of the European Research Area which is broader than the European Union, while ASEAN and CELAC refers to countries which are members of these two international organizations.

Several conclusions can immediately be drawn from reading Table 2. First, Europe consistently remains the world's leading region for Industry 4.0-technologies (although in relative terms the region's totals is likely boosted by double counting of intra-European international collaborations). Secondly, the East Asian countries of Japan, South Korea, and Taiwan appear to have lost ground over the past decade. Thirdly, the rapid rise of China from a minor player prior to 2006 to overtaking the United States of America as the world's largest national contributor of Industry 4.0 enabling technology publications in 2009. China's share has remained relatively stable within the latest decade, while, fourthly, India is now becoming a major player. Since 2015 the contribution of India has exceeded the combined contributions of Japan, South Korea, and Taiwan. 15–20 years ago this would have been probably have been almost unthinkable. Finally, the contributions from other regions of the world such as Southeast Asia, Caribbean and Latin America, and Africa are growing in absolute and relative terms. Africa, in particularly, has witnessed a major growth in publications over the past four years.

5 Variations of Forerunners Across Technologies

Unsurprisingly, there are major variations between different major players in terms of shares of published articles of given technologies. Table 3 illustrates these differences by ranking the six largest country contributors in the dataset, China, USA, India, South Korea, Germany, and Italy.

Again, several conclusions are easily drawn from these data. First, the rise of India concerns particularly the *interconnectivity* dimension of Industry 4.0. For communication technologies India is among the world leaders. When it comes to other innovation and integration elements of Industry 4.0, the Indian share of global publications is much less. One might summarize the data in such a way that India is a world leader in the ICT technologies underpinning the fourth industrial revolution, but still lacking behind in technologies more closely connected with industrial manufacturing. For Germany, the situation is almost exactly the opposite. The German share of global publications on ICT is relatively small, but for manufacturing integration tools and cyber-physical systems, the country is a titan. For the emerging Digital Twin-technology, Germany is the clear global forerunner.

Another remarkable feature is the South Korean stronghold in ubiquitous computing in which the country is second only to the USA globally. For ubiquitous computing South Korea significantly distances both European and other Asian competitors.

Table 3. Share of total publications within various technology fields

China		USA		India	
Technology	*Share*	*Technology*	*Share*	*Technology*	*Share*
Wireless Sensor Network (WSN)	28,6 %	CPS	34,0 %	S&CC	15,3 %
Cloud Computing (CC)	25,3 %	DT	27,5 %	WSN	13,8 %
Information, Integration and Interoperability (III)	25,0 %	III	25,0 %	CC	12,0 %
Internet-of-Things (IOT)	22,5 %	VT	21,1 %	IoT	8,3 %
Radio Frequency Identification (RFID)	21,5 %	S&CC	18,6 %	VT	6,2 %
Virtualization Technology (VT)	19,8 %	UC	18,4 %	SOA	4,8 %
Cyber-Physical Systems (CPS)	18,7 %	MaaS	18,2 %	RFID	3,9 %
Manufacturing-as-a-Service (MaaS)	18,2 %	SOA	16,8 %	UC	2,9 %
Service Oriented Architecture (SOA)	17,8 %	CC	16,7 %	CPS	2,8 %
Business Process Management (BPM)	9,8 %	RFID	16,3 %	BPM	1,1 %
Smart and Connected Communities (S&CC)	7,8 %	IoT	14,3 %	DT	1,1 %
Ubiquitous computing (UC)	6,9 %	WSN	14,3 %	MaaS	0
Digital Twin (DT)	5,5 %	BPM	9,0 %	III	0

South Korea		Germany		Italy	
Technology	*Share*	*Technology*	*Share*	*Technology*	*Share*
UC	14,7 %	DT	33,0 %	S&CC	7,2 %
RFID	7,8 %	BPM	19,3 %	IoT	6,3 %
IoT	6,1 %	CPS	12,7 %	DT	5,5 %
VT	4,6 %	SOA	9,2 %	VT	5,2 %
CC	3,5 %	MaaS	9,1 %	CPS	5,1 %
BPM	3,4 %	III	8,3 %	RFID	4,7 %
CPS	3,4 %	VT	7,8 %	SOA	4,3 %
DT	3,3 %	S&CC	7,5 %	BPM	3,8 %
SOA	2,4 %	UC	7,5 %	CC	3,8 %
WSN	1,9 %	IoT	5,1 %	UC	3,6 %
S&CC	1,2 %	RFID	4,8 %	WSN	3,3 %
MaaS	0	CC	3,9 %	MaaS	0
III	0	WSN	1,9 %	III	0

For organizations interested in the prospects of various elements of Industry 4.0, Table 3 provides guidance to where in the world the expertise most promisingly exists. This might be beneficial for strategic decisions on locations, markets and possible partnerships. The conclusion has the forefront of R&D within ICT-sectors has shifted to Asia – primarily China and India – might not come as a surprise, but the analysis highlights the prime role of these countries for emerging manufacturing technology fields.

6   Conclusions

This article has examined the main technologies driving the development of Industry 4.0. A total of thirteen main technologies were analyzed in the database Web of Science, revealing almost 120,000 academic publications by the end of 2017. This impressive amount of scholarly work would be even greater, had the literature search not been limited to publication titles and keywords. Web of Science is therefore an effective method of detecting massive amounts of information - and for targeting context-relevant information within this population.

The large-scale literature search identified shifting global Industry 4.0 frontrunner regions. While Europe (when seen as a whole) remain a global leader of Industry 4.0 technologies, China has risen provide the largest national share of publications. Indeed, the data shows a very rapid academic rise of China in this research arena during the period 2006–2009. Over the past five years (2013–2017), also India has experienced a very rapid rise; in some Industry 4.0-technological fields even to the world's forefront. On the other hand the combined shares of East Asian tigers Japan, South Korea and Taiwan has decreased from almost 25% of global publications in 2006 to a consistent level of around 10% of global publications in 2015–2017. Finally, there are signs of emerging academic powers of African and ASEAN-countries related to Industry 4.0.

Thus the empirical study allows us both to provide robust conclusions about the development and distribution of Industry 4.0, and it can serve as a demonstration of the value large database analyses can have as a R&D knowledge management method for organizations in support of decisions on industrial strategies and policy.

References

1. World Economic Forum: The future of jobs: employment, skills and workforce strategy for the Fourth Industrial Revolution. World Economic Forum, Geneva, Switzerland (2016)
2. Brettel, M., Friederichsen, N., Keller, M., Rosenberg, M.: How virtualization, decentralization and network building change the manufacturing landscape: an Industry 4.0 perspective. Int. J. Inf. Commun. Eng. **8**(1), 37–44 (2014)
3. Zezulka, F., Marcon, P., Vesely I., Sajdl, O.: Industry 4.0 – an introduction in the phenomenon. IFAC PapersOnLine 49-25, 008-012 (2016)
4. Roblek, V., Mesko, M., Krapez, A.: A complex view of Industry 4.0. SAGE Open **6**, 1–11 (2016)
5. Di Fatta, D., Roblek, V., Dominici, G.: Knowledge management in cyberphysical systems: determining the quality requirements for health systems with the KANO model. Int. J. Mark. Bus. Syst. **3**(2), 163–180 (2018)

6. Foresti, F., Varvakis, G.: Ubiquity and Industry 4.0. In: North, K., Maier, R., Haas, O. (eds.) Knowledge Management in Digital Change. Progress in IS, pp. 343–358. Springer, Cham (2018). https://doi.org/10.1007/978-3-319-73546-7_21

7. Müller, J.M., Buliga, O., Voight, K.-I.: Fortune favors the prepared: how SMEs approach business model innovations in Industry 4.0. Technol. Forecast. Soc. Change **132**, 2–17 (2018)

8. Lu, Y.: Industry 4.0: a survey on technologies, applications and open research issues. J. Ind. Inf. Integr. **6**, 1–10 (2016)

9. Hoffman, E., Rüsch, M.: Industry 4.0 and the current status as well as future prospects on logistics. Comput. Ind. **89**, 23–34 (2017)

10. Pereira, A.C., Romero, F.: A review of the meanings and implications of the Industry 4.0 concept. Procedia Manuf. **13**, 1206–1214 (2017)

11. Muhuri, P.K., Shukla, A.K., Abraham, A.: Industry 4.0: a bibliometrics analysis and detailed overview. Eng. Appl. Artif. Intell. **79**, 218–235 (2019)

12. Oesterreich, T.D., Teuteberg, F.: Understanding the implications of digitisation and automation in the context of Industry 4.0: a triangulation approach and elements of a research agenda for the construction industry. Comput. Ind. **83**, 121–139 (2016)

13. Lichtblau, K., Stich, V., Bertenrath, R., Blum, R., Bleider, M., Millack A., et al.: IMPULS, Industry 4.0 readiness. VDMA (2016)

14. Oztemel, E., Gursev, S.: Literature review of Industry 4.0 and related technologies. J. Intell. Manuf. 1–56 (2018, in press)

15. Posada, J., et al.: Visual computing as a key enabling technology for Industrie 4.0 and industrial internet. IEEE Comput. Graph. Appl. **35**(2), 26–40 (2015)

16. Cheng, G., Liu, L., Qiang, X., Liu, Y.: Industry 4.0 development and application of intelligent manufacturing. In: International Conference on Information Systems and Artificial Intelligence (ISAI). IEEE Xplore (2016)

17. Xu, L.D., Xu, E.L., Li, L.: Industry 4.0: state of the art and future trends. Int. J. Prod. Res. **56**(8), 2941–2962 (2018)

18. Knudsen, M.S., Kaivo-oja, J.: Are we in the midst of a fourth industrial revolution? New Industry 4.0 insights from future technology analysis professionals. FFRC-blog, 20 August 2018. https://ffrc.wordpress.com/2018/08/20/are-we-in-the-midst-of-a-fourth-industrial-revolution/

19. Molano, J.I.R., Lovelle, J.M.C., Montenegro, C.E., Granados, J.J.R., Crespo, R.G.: Metamodel for integration of Internet of Things, social networks, the cloud and Industry 4.0. J. Ambient Intell. Hum. Comput. **9**, 709–723 (2018)

20. Qi, Q., Tao, F.: Digital twin and big data towards smart manufacturing and Industry 4.0: 360 degree comparison. IEEE Access **6**, 3585–3593 (2018)

21. Kagermann, H., Helbig, J., Hellinger, A., Wahlster, W.: Recommendations for implementing the strategic initiative INDUSTRIE 4.0, Munich (2013)

22. Grieves, M., Vickers, J.: Digital twin: mitigating unpredictable, undesirable emergent behavior in complex systems. In: Kahlen, F.-J., Flumerfelt, S., Alves, A. (eds.) Transdisciplinary Perspectives on Complex Systems, pp. 85–113. Springer, Cham (2017). https://doi.org/10.1007/978-3-319-38756-7_4

23. Falagas, M.E., Pitsouni, E.I., Malietzis, G.A., Pappas, G.: Comparison of PubMed, web of science, and Google Scholar: strengths and weaknesses. FASEB J. **22**, 338–342 (2008)

24. Kaivo-Oja, J., Knudsen, M.S., Lauraeus, T.: Reimagining Finland as a manufacturing base: the nearshoring potential of Finland in an Industry 4.0 perspective. Bus. Manage. Educ. **16**, 65–80 (2018)

Scientometric Analysis of Knowledge in the Context of Project Management

Subject Area: (Knowledge Management and Project Management)

César Rincón-González[1]([⊠]) and Flor Nancy Díaz-Piraquive[2]([⊠]) [iD]

[1] Faculty of Engineering, EAN University, Bogotá, Colombia
cesarrincong@yahoo.com,
crincon2.d@universidadean.edu.co
[2] Faculty of Engineering, Catholic University of Colombia, Bogotá, Colombia
fndiaz@ucatolica.edu.co

Abstract. This research work carried out a meticulous scientometric analysis about the knowledge management in the context of project management, in order to build a detailed state of the art about the matter of study, allowing the identification of main elements investigated on the scientific literature about the knowledge on this context. Firstly; a theoretical framework was build, allowing the identification of concepts about knowledge management and scientometric analysis. Secondly; a methodology was constructed, by integrating analytics and measurement tools, 881 publications related to the knowledge management on projects were identified on the main databases, later, detailed bibliometric analysis were conducted in order to highlight the most investigated topics, main authors (Gemino, Carrillo and Reich) and sources with higher amount of documents and quotes on the scientific literature about the matter of study (International Journal of Project Management, Project Management Journal and Journal of Knowledge Management). Afterwards; the results of the scientometric analysis about the knowledge on projects were documented. And finally; conclusions were established and as future lines of research were identified the impact of knowledge management on project performance, leadership, management, and innovation.

Keywords: Scientometric analysis · Knowledge management · Project management

1 Introduction

Several scholars had conducted studies about knowledge management in the context of projects, mainly, from an exploratory perspective. This research work developed a meticulous state of the art about knowledge in the context of projects, by conducting a detailed scientometric analysis of this matter of study.

© Springer Nature Switzerland AG 2019
L. Uden et al. (Eds.): KMO 2019, CCIS 1027, pp. 14–24, 2019.
https://doi.org/10.1007/978-3-030-21451-7_2

The main objective of this research is to develop a detailed scientometric analysis of knowledge management in the context of project management. As specific objectives of this study, were defined:

- Develop a theoretical framework about main concepts related to knowledge management and project management as well as scientometric.
- Define a research methodology in order to develop a meticulous scientometric analysis about knowledge management in the context of project management.
- Conduct comprehensive bibliometric analysis about main authors, topics of study and sources about knowledge on project management.
- Document the findings about the scientometric analysis on knowledge in the context of project management.
- Identify conclusions, and define future lines of research about knowledge management and project management as a topic of study.

2 Theoretical Framework

On this paper, main concepts related to knowledge management in the context of project management as well as scientometric were defined. These elements were included on the research methodology of this study.

2.1 Terms Related to Knowledge Management in the Context of Project Management

The main meaning of knowledge, as a noun, is "facts, information, and skills acquired through experience or education; the theoretical or practical understanding of a subject" [1]. Nevertheless, when investigating this term in the context of project management, it is defined as "a mixture of experience, values and beliefs, contextual information, intuition, and insight that people use to make sense of new experiences and information [to manage a project properly]" [2; p. 709]. Knowledge had been also defined as "the collection of information and experience that an individual possesses. For example, understanding the concept of a Gantt chart might be considered knowledge" [3; p. 15].

Project management is defined as "the application of knowledge, skills, tools, and techniques to project activities to meet the project requirements" [2; p. 10].

Organizational knowledge repositories are defined as [2]:

- Organizational standards, policies, procedures, and any project document;
- Financial data of projects;
- Historical information and lessons learned knowledge repositories;
- Issues and defects data;
- Data repositories; and
- Files from previous projects.

Other definition of project management is "the application of processes, methods, knowledge, skills and experience to achieve project objectives" [4; p. 241].

In order to provide leadership, planning, and coordination through communication, the project manager should possess project management knowledge, technical knowledge, and understanding and experience [2], this indicates that knowledge is a key element when managing projects.

Manage project knowledge is defined as "the process of using existing knowledge and creating new knowledge to achieve the project's objectives and contribute to organizational learning" [2; p. 70]. On the other hand, project integration management it's about "ensuring the creation and the use of the appropriated knowledge to and from the project as necessary" [2; p. 72].

Knowledge management is "the systematic management of information and learning. It turns personal information and experience into collective knowledge that can be widely shared throughout an organization and a profession" [4; p. 238]. A related term is professionalism defined as "the application of expert and specialized knowledge within a specific field and the acceptance of standards relating to the profession" [4; p. 240]. Ability, is another related term as "the effective delivery of knowledge and skills in a given context [for instance projects]" [3; p. 15].

The benefits of manage project knowledge are "that prior organizational knowledge is leveraged to produce or improve the project outcomes, and knowledge created by the project is available to support organizational operations and future projects" [2; p. 98].

"Knowledge management tools and techniques connect people so they can work together to create new knowledge, share tactic knowledge, and integrate the knowledge of diverse teams members" [2; p. 102]. The outputs of manage project knowledge are lessons learned from the project, project management plan updates and new knowledge for future projects [2].

There are several kinds of knowledge that must be considered when managing projects such as: the explicit knowledge "knowledge that can by codified using symbols such as words, numbers, and pictures" [2; p. 706]; lesson learned "the knowledge gained during a project which shows how project events were addressed or should be addressed in the future for the purpose of improving future performance" [2; p. 709]; organizational learning "a discipline connected with the way individuals, groups, and organizations develop knowledge" [2; p. 712]; organizational process asset "plans, processes, procedures, and knowledge bases that are specific to and used by the performing organization [when doing projects]" [2; p. 712]; and the tactic knowledge "personal knowledge that can be difficult to articulate and share such as beliefs, experience, and insights" [2; p. 724].

2.2   Terms Related to Scientometric Analysis

Scientometric is the "the branch of information science concerned with the application of bibliometrics to the study of the spread of scientific ideas; the bibliometric analysis of science" [5]. Bibliometric is the "statistical analysis of books, articles, or other publications" [6].

Scientific information analysis tools "allows the researcher to obtain scientometric data, as the most relevant information about authors and articles quoted as well as the ranking of journals worldwide" according to the matter of study under investigation [7].

3 Methodology

In this section, an exploratory methodology was defined based on the scientometric and bibliometric analyses, the components used on this research work were: (a) search of the terms knowledge, knowledge management and project management on the main scientific information analysis tools; (b) identification of 881 scientific publications between 1998 and 2018 (December), related to the matter of study (Fig. 2); (c) depuration of the data from the selected publications; (d) construction of the loading information files; (e) exportation of the selected publications information in to the bibliometric analysis tool; (f) conduct the bibliometric analysis of main topics of investigation about knowledge management in the context of project; (g) definition of key authors; (h) determination of the principal sources (journals), and (i) documentation of the scientometric analysis results about knowledge management in the context of project management. The methodology of research is show in the Fig. 1.

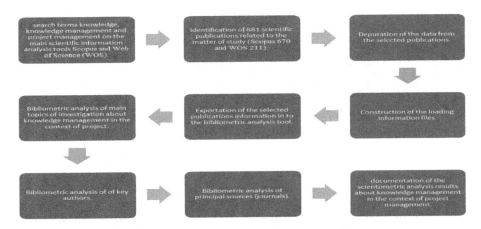

Fig. 1. Methodology of research. Source: The authors

The construction of the graphs analyzed from the topics related to knowledge management in the context of project management, was done with the software VOSviewer 1.66.

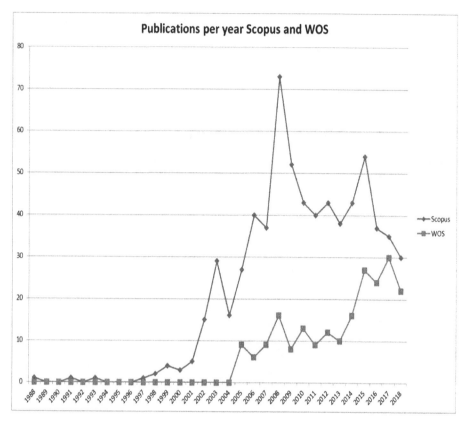

Fig. 2. Publications per year (1988–2018) about knowledge management and project management on mail journal. Source: The authors with information from Scopus and Web of Science (December 2018).

4   Results

After the exploration of the scientometric information associated to the scientific publications related with knowledge management in the context of project management, a detailed bibliometric analysis was conducted about the matter of study. Firstly, main topics of research of knowledge management in projects were identified (Fig. 3). Secondly, key authors, whit more citation and publications were acknowledged (Fig. 4). Afterwards, principal sources, with large numbers of scientific publication related to knowledge management in projects were highlighted (Fig. 5). Finally, scientific analysis results from the research were documented (Table 1).

In Fig. 3, a strong correlation is identified between the topics studied on project management and knowledge management, this is because the projects went from being a tool of simple execution and control, to start being a discipline that generates knowledge through of the storage of the lessons learned and their best practices in their information repositories, such as learning in the execution of other projects.

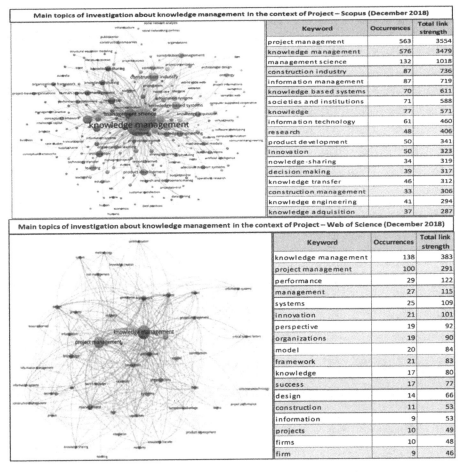

Main topics of investigation about knowledge management in the context of Project – Scopus (December 2018)		
Keyword	Occurrences	Total link strength
project management	563	3554
knowledge management	576	3479
management science	132	1018
construction industry	87	736
information management	87	719
knowledge based systems	70	611
societies and institutions	71	588
knowledge	77	571
information technology	61	460
research	48	406
product development	50	341
innovation	50	323
nowledge-sharing	34	319
decision making	39	317
knowledge transfer	46	312
construction management	33	306
knowledge engineering	41	294
knowledge adquisition	37	287

Main topics of investigation about knowledge management in the context of Project – Web of Science (December 2018)		
Keyword	Occurrences	Total link strength
knowledge management	138	383
project management	100	291
performance	29	122
management	27	115
systems	25	109
innovation	21	101
perspective	19	92
organizations	19	90
model	20	84
framework	21	83
knowledge	17	80
success	17	77
design	14	66
construction	11	53
information	9	53
projects	10	49
firms	10	48
firm	9	46

Fig. 3. Bibliometric analysis of main topics of investigation about knowledge management in the context of projects. Source: The authors.

Figure 4 shows that more and more authors are finding in project management a collaboration tool that is propitiating the appropriation of knowledge that gives a high citation in response. Especially Carrillo and Lindner, who have the highest citations in the studies, for conducting project management analysis as a mechanism to increase collaboration and knowledge in management.

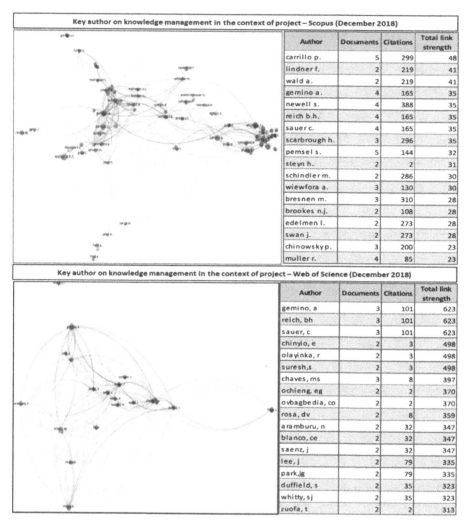

Fig. 4. Bibliometric analysis of key authors on knowledge management in the context of projects. Source: The authors.

Figure 5 shows the bibliometric analysis shows the relationship of the main sources of knowledge management publication in the context of projects, finding magazines as important for their citation as the international journal of project management and organization science.

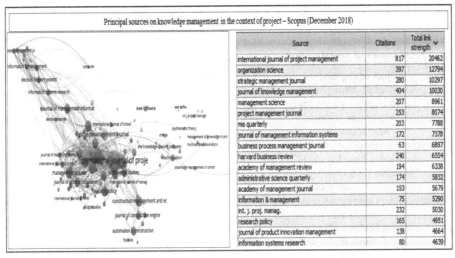

Principal sources on knowledge management in the context of project – Scopus (December 2018)		
Source	Citations	Total link strength v
international journal of project management	817	20462
organization science	397	12794
strategic management journal	280	10297
journal of knowledge management	404	10030
management science	207	8961
project management journal	253	8074
mis quarterly	203	7788
journal of management information systems	172	7378
business process management journal	63	6897
harvard business review	240	6554
academy of management review	194	6338
administrative science quarterly	174	5832
academy of management journal	153	5679
information & management	75	5290
int. j. proj. manag.	232	5030
research policy	165	4951
journal of product innovation management	138	4664
information systems research	80	4639

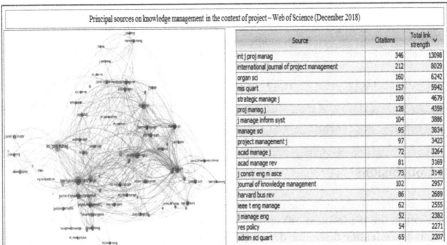

Principal sources on knowledge management in the context of project – Web of Science (December 2018)		
Source	Citations	Total link strength v
int j proj manag	346	13098
international journal of project management	212	8029
organ sci	160	6242
mis quart	157	5942
strategic manage j	109	4679
proj manag j	128	4359
j manage inform syst	104	3886
manage sci	95	3834
project management j	97	3423
acad manage j	72	3264
acad manage rev	81	3169
j constr eng m asce	73	3149
journal of knowledge management	102	2957
harvard bus rev	86	2689
ieee t eng manage	62	2555
j manage eng	52	2382
res policy	54	2271
admin sci quart	65	2207

Fig. 5. Bibliometric analysis of principal sources on knowledge management in the context of projects. Source: The authors.

The results of the scientometric analysis on knowledge management in the context of projects, show that the authors analyzed, especially Carrillo P., Gemino A., Reich B., Sauer C. and Chinyio E., share their studies in the main management issues related to project management, administrative knowledge, performance/successes, management science, administration and information management, among others, and that the main management journals are publishing them due to their importance and to increase management of knowledge. See Table 1.

Table 1. Results of the scientometric analysis on knowledge management in the context of projects.

Main topics of investigation	Key authors	Principal sources
Project management. Knowledge management. Performance / successes. Management science. Management. Information management / systems / knowledge based systems / information technology. Innovation / perspective. Knowledge – sharing / Knowledge transfer. Organizations / firms. Models. Frameworks. Knowledge acquisition. Knowledge engineering.	Carrillo P. Gemino A. Reich B. Sauer C. Chinyio E.	International Journal of Project Management. Project Management Journal. Journal of Knowledge Management. Organizational Science. Strategic Management Journal. Journal of Management Information Systems. Management Science. Harvard Business Review. Academy of Management Review. Academy of Management Journal. Research Policy. Journal of Management in Engineering.
Main publication of key authors		
Carrillo P.	Gemino A., Reich B. & Sauer C.	Reich B., Gemino A. & Sauer C.	Chinyio E.
[8, 9, 10, 11, 12, 13, 14, 15, 16]	[17, 18]	[19, 20]	[21, 22]

Source: The authors.

5   Conclusions

The theoretical framework identified the main concepts related to the knowledge management in the context of project management, as well as the scientometric analysis as a scientific discipline dedicated to the study of science. Those elements were incorporated into the research methodology.

The research methodology allowed to identify the search, identification and depuration elements needed, also the use of scientific scoring and analysis tools required, same as the bibliometric software in order to conduct a detailed scientometric analysis about the knowledge management in the context of projects.

The meticulous bibliometric analysis about the knowledge management within the discipline of managing projects identified the most investigated topics, key authors and principal sources with the majority of quotations and documents.

The scientometric analysis established a precise state of the art about the matter of study. As main topics arisen: project management; knowledge management; project performance and success; information technology (information management, systems, knowledge based systems); innovation and perspective; knowledge – sharing and knowledge transfer; organizations and firms; models and frameworks; knowledge acquisition; and knowledge engineering.

As key authors emerged: Carrillo P.; Gemino A.; Reich B.; Sauer C.; and Chinyio E. and finally, as principal sources, with the larger number of articles and citations appeared: International Journal of Project Management; Project Management Journal; Journal of Knowledge Management; Organizational Science; Strategic Management Journal; Journal of Management Information Systems; Management Science; Harvard Business Review; Academy of Management Review; Academy of Management Journal; Research Policy and Journal of Management in Engineering.

Definitely the most researched topics in the context of projects, is how to appropriate knowledge from error, to document the lessons learned and best practices, to be used precisely in the execution of future projects.

More and more knowledge management facilitators are being used in the execution of the projects, to improve the transmission of information, forming repsoitories of information that are then used by the members of the project team [23].

As future lines of research, it was proposed to develop applied studies in order to determinate the impact of knowledge management on project performance, leadership, management, and innovation.

References

1. Oxford: Oxford dictionaries (2018). https://en.oxforddictionaries.com/definition/knowledge. Accessed December 2018
2. Project Management Institute (PMI). A guide to the Project Management Body of Knowledge - PMBOK® Guide - Sixth Edition, Pennsylvania, USA (2017)
3. International Project Management Association (IPMA). Individual Competency Baseline ICB 4 (2015)
4. Association for Project Management (APM). APM Body of Knowledge, 6th edition (2012)
5. Oxford. Oxford dictionaries (2018). https://en.oxforddictionaries.com/definition/scientometrics. Accessed December 2018
6. Oxford. Oxford dictionaries (2018). https://en.oxforddictionaries.com/definition/bibliometrics. Accessed December 2018
7. EAN. Herramientas de Análisis y Medición (2018). https://universidadean.edu.co/es/biblioteca/recursos-de-apoyo-al-investigador/herramientas-de-analisis-y-medicion. Acceseed December 2018
8. Al-Ghassani, A.M., Kamara, J.M., Anumba, C.J., Carrillo, P.M.: A tool for developing knowledge management strategies. Electronic J. Inf. Technol. Constr. **7**, 69–82 (2002). https://www.scopus.com/inward/record.uri?eid=2-s2.0-3042552726&partnerID=40&md5=960a5d922e8191a4aaa311f380fc8514
9. Al-Ghassani, A.M., Kamara, J.M., Anumba, C.J., Carrillo, P.M.: An innovative approach to identifying knowledge management problems. Eng. Constr. Arch. Manag. **11**(5), 349–357 (2004). https://doi.org/10.1108/09699980410558548
10. Carrillo, P.: Managing knowledge: lessons from the oil and gas sector. Constr. Manag. Econ. **22**(6), 631–642 (2004). https://doi.org/10.1080/0144619042000226289
11. Carrillo, P.: Lessons learned practices in the engineering, procurement and construction sector. Eng., Constr. Arch. Manag. **12**(3), 236–250 (2005). https://doi.org/10.1108/0969998-0510600107

12. Carrillo, P., Chinowsky, P.: Exploiting knowledge management: the engineering and construction perspective. J. Manag. Eng. **22**(1), 2–10 (2006). https://doi.org/10.1061/(ASCE) 0742-597X(2006)22:1(2)
13. Carrillo, P., Ruikar, K., Fuller, P.: When will we learn? Improving lessons learned practice in construction. Int. J. Proj. Manag. **31**(4), 567–578 (2013). https://doi.org/10.1016/j.ijproman. 2012.10.005
14. Chinowsky, P., Carrillo, P.: Knowledge management to learning organization connection. J. Manag. Eng. **23**(3), 122–130 (2007). https://doi.org/10.1061/(ASCE)0742-597X(2007)23: 3(122)
15. Tan, H.C., Carrillo, P.M., Anumba, C.J.: Case study of knowledge management implementation in a medium-sized construction sector firm. J. Manag. Eng. **28**(3), 338–347 (2012). https://doi.org/10.1061/(ASCE)ME.1943-5479.0000109
16. Udeaja, C.E., et al.: A web-based prototype for live capture and reuse of construction project knowledge. Autom. Constr. **17**(7), 839–851 (2008). https://doi.org/10.1016/j.autcon.2008. 02.009
17. Gemino, A., Reich, B.H., Sauer, C.: A temporal model of information technology project performance. J. Manag. Inf. Syst. **24**(3), 9–44 (2007). https://doi.org/10.2753/MIS0742-1222240301
18. Gemino, A., Reich, B.H., Sauer, C.: Plans versus people: comparing knowledge management approaches in IT-enabled business projects. Int. J. Proj. Manag. **33**(2), 299–310 (2015). https://doi.org/10.1016/j.ijproman.2014.04.012
19. Reich, B.H., Gemino, A., Sauer, C.: Knowledge management and project-based knowledge in it projects: a model and preliminary empirical results. Int. J. Proj. Manag. **30**(6), 663–674 (2012). https://doi.org/10.1016/j.ijproman.2011.12.003
20. Reich, B.H., Gemino, A., Sauer, C.: How knowledge management impacts performance in projects: an empirical study. Int. J. Proj. Manag. **32**(4), 590–602 (2014). https://doi.org/10. 1016/j.ijproman.2013.09.004
21. Olayinka, R., Suresh, S., Chinyio, E.: Impact of knowledge management on the cost of poor quality. Proc. Inst. Civ. Eng.: Manag. Procure. Law **168**(4), 177–188 (2015). https://doi.org/ 10.1680/mpal.1400035
22. Suresh, S., Olayinka, R., Chinyio, E., Renukappa, S.: Impact of knowledge management on construction projects. Proc. Inst. Civ. Eng.: Manag. Procure. Law **170**(1), 27–43 (2017). https://doi.org/10.1680/jmapl.15.00057
23. Díaz-Piraquive, F.N., Martínez, O.S., Crespo, R.G.: Knowledge management model for project management KM+PMTIC. In: Hall, K. (ed.) Construction Projects. Nova Science Publishers, Inc, EEUU, New York, pp. 55–92 (2017). https://www.novapublishers.com/ catalog/product_info.php?products_id=60711&osCsid=7dc791a61a83517739bc4d70b6bc5 e88. ISBN 978-1-53610-742-5

Modeling the Colombian Swine Supply Chain from a Knowledge Management Perspective

Johanna Trujillo-Diaz[1,2]([✉]) [iD], Flor Nancy Diaz-Piraquive[3]([✉]) [iD],
Milton M. Herrera[4]([✉]) [iD], and Jairo Gómez Acero[5]([✉])

[1] Escuela Colombiana de Ingeniería Julio Garavito, Bogotá, Colombia
johanna.trujillo@escuelaing.edu.co
[2] Strategic Planning and Technological Management, Universidad Popular
Autónoma del Estado de Puebla (UPAEP), Puebla, Mexico
[3] Universidad Católica de Colombia, Bogotá, Colombia
fndiaz@ucatolica.edu.co
[4] Universidad Militar Nueva Granada, Bogotá, Colombia
Milton.herrera@unimilitar.edu.co
[5] Fundación Universitaria Cafam, Bogotá, Colombia
jairo.gomez@unicafam.edu.co

Abstract. The Colombian swine supply chain (CSSC) has a low level of national competitiveness compared to other supply chains such as coffee and fruit. While consumption of pork has raised in Colombia, most dealers are importing it from The United States and Canada, since farmers in those countries have received agricultural incentives to breed and commercialize pigs. Additionally, agribusiness have received technological developments to share information and develop the swine sector. This article aims to state theoretical Knowledge Management (KM) dimensions for CSSC that were built under authors' assumptions on the literature. These were proposed to identify the competitiveness level in CSSC, because only two different kinds of measuring for swine competitiveness were found, but on the other hand, no model about Swine Supply Chain (SSC) was found. Perspectives of researching KM in CSSC would integrate stakeholders using a technological web platform which allows interchange of information among them.

Keywords: Swine supply chain · Colombian swine sector ·
Knowledge management model · Theoretical model · Knowledge sharing ·
Competitiveness

1 Introduction

1.1 Background

The swine sector is very attractive for Colombian economy, because it generates employment [1]. However, it does not have enough technology and knowledge transfer, specialized transportation, or government subsidies. Furthermore, swine smallholders and technified producers are searching to lower its cost, because pork consumption in Colombia has been growing for the last ten years according to statistics from the

© Springer Nature Switzerland AG 2019
L. Uden et al. (Eds.): KMO 2019, CCIS 1027, pp. 25–35, 2019.
https://doi.org/10.1007/978-3-030-21451-7_3

Federation of Cattle Ranchers - FEDEGAN (acronym in Spanish), but demand is not enough. In 2017, swine consumption was 7.1 kg per inhabitant [2], but the productive cost is between 60% and 70% of the total cost which includes disease and pest prevention, high quality, health and safety, and the lack of livestock policies [3].

Pork is the most consumed type of meat worldwide [4]. The United States of America is the second largest pork producer in the world after China, which has almost half of the world's total production [4]. Additionally, 60% of meat consumed in China is pork [5]. According to projections of The United States Department of Agriculture (USDA), Brazil will become the world's largest pork exporter by 2021 [6].

The most competitive countries in Swine Supply Chain, such as China, have implemented laws in the last 20 years to guarantee innocuousness in pigs' slaughter houses centralizing butchers [5]. Moreover, some countries have been controlling prices, whose increase is proportional to food, market speculation, safety, etc. [7]. Alternatively, some countries have made associations to share information and develop competitive strategies, InterPIG, for instance, which is composed by seventeen countries [8].

In Latin-American countries, Brazil has established coordination strategies and governance structures in pork slaughterhouses and processors, including contracts, alliances, cooperatives, and vertical integration to comply with public quality regulation [9–11]. The livestock sector in Latin America has grown at an annual rate (3.7%), higher than the global average growth rate (2.1%) [3]. In 2018, Colombia's agriculture and livestock sectors increased 5.9% higher than in 2017. In addition, in Colombia, agricultural crops and its related activities have incremented 6.0%, livestock 5.8%, growth of the pig's sector is more than double with 8.8%, while cattle was only 4.2% [12].

In the second quarter of 2018, Colombia's Gross Domestic Product (GDP) was 2.8% higher than in 2017 [12]. Furthermore, during 2017 the GDP was 1.8%, which was led by the agricultural and financial services sectors. Colombia has a large rural sector extended throughout its geographical territory; agricultural and livestock activities take place all over it. In fact, livestock is classified in bovine, swine, poultry, among others. Historically, agriculture has allowed the evolution of the country's economy, it has also allowed to accumulate capital to develop other sectors, for instance the technology and services sector [13]. Currently, the Colombian agricultural GDP is 6.5% [14, 15] which exceeded 2017's world average of 3.5% [16].

Carcass meat imports in Colombia have been growing since 2008. In 2017, the most important exporting countries of pork were: United States, Germany, Spain, Denmark, Canada, Netherlands, and Brazil. In contrast, leading exporters of pigs were Denmark, Netherlands, China, Canada, Germany, and Belgium [17]. On the other hand, Colombian imports were made up of (a) breeding pigs; (b) fresh, chilled or frozen pork; and (c) edible offal in 2017, which sum USD$ 177,007,661. Notably, 91.2% of pork importations are from The USA, followed by Canada (5.1%), Chile (3.7%) and other countries such as Denmark, Portugal, and Spain (0.1%) [17]. In Colombia, those imports go to Bogotá, Valle del Cauca, and Bolívar [18].

CSSC's production of pork covers only the domestic demand, it is located mainly in Antioquia, Valle del Cauca, Cundinamarca, Meta, and Córdoba. That sector is the second most important in livestock, it represents around 17% of national production [9]. CSSC's products include reproductive male, pregnant sows, lactating, non-lactating, replacement, backyard-pigs, and prime pigs [19] (see Fig. 1). Its average productive cycle is 296 days, it includes 142 days for raising farms and 154 days for fattening up farms.

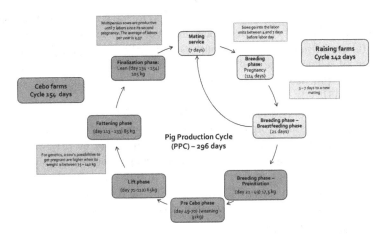

Fig. 1. Pig production cycle

In 2017, total bovine, swine, and poultry sectors production was 3,377,833 tons [15] which are represented by: poultry 46%, bovine 43%, and swine 11%. In addition, 458 thousand tons of pigs were slaughtered [20]. For the second quarter of 2018, the record of pigs slaughtered was 1,075,697, it showed an increase of 9% compared to the same period in 2017 [21]. On average, more males are slaughtered than females. For instance, in the second quarter of 2018 in Colombia, slaughter levels for males are higher than females, that is, 67% male and 33% female pigs [21].

What are the dimensions or key indicators of knowledge management that CSSC needs for increasing its competitiveness?

CSSC's background and problematics are explained on the first part of the article. Secondly, applications of knowledge management in supply chains found in the literature are described. The model and its dimensions are explained at the third part of the article.

1.2   Related Works in KM in Supply Chains

Knowledge management (KM) is defined by [22] as a systematic process to add value [22, 23]. To obtain competitive advantage [24, 25], a KM model must be accessible [26], validated [27], materialized [28], and improved or updated [24, 29, 30]. Some benefits in the use of KM practices into a SC are cooperation [31–34], integration [35–40], dissemination of good practices [33], and decision-making support [41–43]. Nevertheless, the main objectives of KM are both social capital and intellectual capital, that is, people knowledge and learning [28, 44–47]. Thus, KM processes are knowledge creation [27, 48], knowledge storage [29, 30, 49], knowledge transfer [29, 30, 49], and knowledge application [27, 29, 30, 48, 50].

There are few models found in the literature about KM models for improving efficiency or competitiveness applied to organizations like: supply chains, clusters, industrial groups, etc. On the contrary, there are several models found in the literature applied to firms. Those models complement each other, so:

(i)   The model developed by [28] is considered to be the cornerstone of KM models [50]. This model explains the processes involved in knowledge transfer, those are: (a) *socialization* or interaction; (b) *externalization*, defined as the formalization of a knowledge body; (c) *internalization*, described as the change of theory into practice; and (d) *combination*, explained as the unification of existing theories [45].

(ii)   An adaptation of Nonaka's model was made by [51] who classified knowledge into individual, group, organizational and inter-organizational levels.

(iii) Another adaptation of Nonaka's model was carried out by [51] who classified knowledge into codified and uncodified knowledge (depending on the ability of preparation for sharing purposes), and into diffused and undiffused knowledge (depending on sharing speed), moreover, the author adds a new knowledge catalogue: patented, public, personal, and common sense.

Different catalogues of KM models were found in the literature review: (a) according to knowledge definition [28, 45, 48, 52, 53], (b) intellectual capital models [45, 52–54], (c) models constructed under social objectives [45, 55], (d) networks and communities of people models [48, 52, 53], (e) scientific and technological [53, 55], where the main driving force for knowledge creation are IT tools, (f) quantitative models [52], (g) philosophical models [52, 53, 56], based on epistemology, and (h) holistic models [53]. Regarding knowledge definitions, the following were found: tacit [57, 58], explicit [57, 58], programmed [59], acquired [59], codified/uncodified [51], diffused/undiffused [51], public [51, 60], registered or patented [51, 59], and personal [51, 60].

2 Methodology

This article is an exploratory study about CSSC where collected variables for building KM determinants are summarized and represented in the model proposed. To answer the research question, first, background was collected from primary sources; it summarized the most important issues for the Colombian swine sector that have had an impact on economy. In this part, transversal information from 10 years until the present day was used.

The literature review has four issues, namely: (a) global information about competitiveness and its main targets; (b) KM; and (c) KM in CSSC. These were done consulting papers on SCOPUS and all collections from WoS database. This search was made using the following query: "Knowledge Management" AND (pig OR swine OR pork) AND ("supply chain" OR "swine sector"). Therefore, this model is proposed based on previously written frameworks which have elements from knowledge management models, either applications of KM to supply chains or other sectors.

Information analysis and assessment for papers were obtained through a hypothetic-deductive method in which the information was identified and classified by dimensions, constructs, and variables.

3 Proposed KM Model in CSSC

CSSC represents the flow of information and swine products across stakeholders (see Fig. 2). In this figure, CSSC has eight steps, depicted in gray, and market segments, in yellow. CSSC's information and products flow is set up as: (a) suppliers that include genetic providers, veterinary products, medicines and vaccines, food, machinery and equity, and supplies; (b) primary production composed by breeding, fattening or complete cycle farms; those farms could be technified, non-technified or traditional; (c) standing pigs trade gathered by formal and informal transporters; (d) pig slaughter, either technified in plants or performed informally; (e) pork slaughter done by wholesalers and retailers; (f) sausage processing plants; (g) wholesale and large surfaces; and finally (h) retail trade, which includes institutional channels, specialized expenses, stores and supermarkets, meat stores, and restaurant expenses.

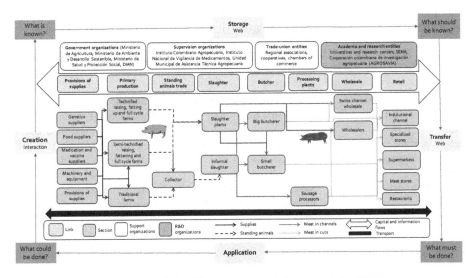

Fig. 2. Knowledge Management model proposed for CSSC

In addition, CSSC has been linked to government, union, and supervision organizations. However, in this proposed KM model academic organizations involved in innovation, research, and development are included. Those organizations in the figure are represented in a green box on the upper right corner.

In Fig. 2, knowledge management processes involve the whole CSSC, and are represented by the blue boxes. Those boxes show the creation, storage, transfer, and knowledge application stages; those are jointly generating a continuous improvement cycle. Since the KM model at this stage is a proposal, and the CSSC currently has a level of tacit knowledge, the indicators of interest and good practices throughout it are identified through literature that would allow CSSC to increase its competitiveness.

There are global indexes such as the Global Competitiveness Report or Annual Global Competitiveness Book. However, swine competitiveness indexes are few, this research has been partially addressed in France [61], Denmark [62], and The United Kingdom [63] as shown in Table 1.

Table 1. Dimensions or key indicators to develop a KM model in CSSC

Strategic		
Pork imports Number of direct connections with industry, government, unions, and research centers [61] Laws and regulations for price protection		
Supply pig farms	Swine breeding farms	Pig fattening farms
Utility per national package of sold food Utility per imported bulk of sold food Utility per sold vaccines Proximity to breeding and fattening points	Productivity of sows [61] Utility per pig sold [61, 63] Loss due to stillborn pigs Labor, food, transportation, and indirect costs [63] Available and occupied capacity (pigs) [61] Number of pigsties [61] Automation level Investment infrastructure and RD&I [61]	Utility per pig sold [61, 63] Labor, food, transportation and indirect costs [63] Available and occupied capacity (pigs) [61] Number of pigsties [61] Proximity to slaughter points Automation level
Slaughter companies	Swine stripping companies	Distribution
Sales volume [61, 63] Utility [61, 63] Labor, storage, transportation, and indirect costs [63] Proximity to deboning zone	Utility [61, 63] Labor, storage, transportation and indirect costs [61, 63] Automation level [61] Cutting standardization [61] Sales volume [61, 63] Investments infrastructure and RD&I[61] Proximity to distribution area [61]	Labor, storage, transportation and indirect costs [63] Sales volume [61, 63] Utility [61, 63] Sales force [61] Quantity of employees [61]

4   Conclusions

In the literature, the proposed KM model is original for CSSC, because it is at a stage of tacit knowledge [57, 58], this research hopes to share this knowledge through a web platform in which CSSC's stakeholders can interact. That web platform expects to have all phases of knowledge management models: creation, storage, transfer, and application. Thus, stakeholders can share their key indicators and good practices. The proposed KM model validation would be done using a competitiveness index built and fed by stakeholders' interactions on a web-platform designed for that purpose.

Competitiveness can be seen as a legislative, political, economic, and social advantage between two different systems [64], it involves the transformation of granted and produced goods which represent an economic profit [65] and added value in agroindustry [66–69]. The low technological level in CSSC is the main obstacle in developing competitiveness [70–72]. Other obstacles are the lack of (a) production capacity [70, 71, 73], (b) innovation [73], research and development (R&D) [70, 71], (c) exports [71, 74, 75], (d) product quality, (e) strong government policies in terms of price fixing and market protection [70, 71], and (f) tax incentives to specific industries [70, 71]. Thus, the proposed model in KM would be used to encourage industrial cooperation [76, 77], to share information, knowledge, and raise CSSC competitiveness.

There is no evidence of platforms which integrate the different actors involved into CSSC, so there is a need for high technological capabilities in both human resources and infrastructure to develop a strong upstream and downstream communication in all stages of CSSC.

Low technological development and a lack of interest from SC stakeholders seem to be the main barriers in the development of a KM model in CSSC.

KM and SCM's practices should be taken into consideration as strategic rather than operational factors due to their high impact through all SC and their importance for decision making and planning.

Stakeholders, such as government, public institutions, and universities, must become involved in the SC to create a "knowledge region", stimulate the demand, and obtain both cluster policies from government and incentives from public institutions.

Acknowledgments. The authors would like to thank the anonymous reviewers for their comments that helped improve the content of the article. The authors thank ECIJG (DII/C008 CIJI2019), UMNG (INV-ECO-3008), UCC, and UNICAFAM for providing financial support to this research.

References

1. DNP: Bases del Plan Nacional de Desarrollo 2018–2022, 6 March 2018. https://colaboracion.dnp.gov.co/CDT/Prensa/PND-2018-2022.pdf
2. FEDEGAN: Estadísticas – Consumos, 22 August 2018. http://www.fedegan.org.co/estadisticas/consumo-0
3. FAO: Producción pecuaria en América Latina y el Caribe, 24 August. http://www.fao.org/americas/prioridades/produccion-pecuaria/es/
4. AGMRC: Pork International Markets Profile, 2 February 2018. https://www.agmrc.org/commodities-products/livestock/pork/pork-international-markets-profile
5. Chen, Y., Yu, X.: Does the centralized slaughtering policy create market power for pork industry in China? China Econ. Rev. **50**, 59–71 (2018)
6. USDA: Agricultural Baseline Projections, 19 February 2018. https://www.ers.usda.gov/topics/farm-economy/agricultural-baseline/
7. Yu, X.: Meat consumption in China and its impact on international food security: status quo, trends, and policies. J. Integr. Agric. **14**, 989–994 (2015)

8. Hoste, R.: International comparison of pig production costs 2015 (2017). https://library.wur.nl/WebQuery/wurpubs/fulltext/412970
9. Ménard, C.: The economics of hybrid organizations. J. Inst. Theor. Econ. JITE **160**, 345–376 (2004)
10. Raynaud, E., Sauvee, L., Valceschini, E.: Alignment between quality enforcement devices and governance structures in the agro-food vertical chains. J. Manag. Governance **9**, 47–77 (2005)
11. Martins, F.M., Trienekens, J., Omta, O.: Differences in quality governance: the case of the Brazilian pork chain. Br. Food J. **119**, 2837–2850 (2017)
12. DANE: Boletín técnico - Producto Interno Bruto, 22 August 2018. https://www.dane.gov.co/files/investigaciones/boletines/pib/bol_PIB_IItrim18_producion_y_gasto.pdf
13. DANE: Cuenta Satélite Piloto de la Agroindustria (CSPA): Procesos de cría de ganado bovino y porcino y su primer nivel de transformación industrial (Resultados preliminares 2005–2011), 28 June 2013. https://www.dane.gov.co/files/investigaciones/pib/agroindustria/metodologia_CSPA_Ganado_bovino_porcino_23_2013.pdf
14. DANE: Cuentas Trimestrales - Colombia Producto Interno Bruto (PIB): Primer Trimestre de 2015, 22 August 2018. http://www.dane.gov.co/index.php/52-espanol/noticias/noticias/4174-producto-interno-bruto-pib-i-trimestre-2017
15. SAC: Estadísticas > Producción Agropecuaria desde 2000 > Producción pecuaria, 22 August 2018. http://sac.org.co/es/estudios-economicos/estadisticas.html
16. BM: Indicadores > Agricultura, valor agregado (% del PIB) Colombia (Banco Mundial ed.), 22 August 2018. https://datos.bancomundial.org/indicador/NV.AGR.TOTL.ZS?locations=CO
17. UN-COMTRADE: Base de datos Estadísticas sobre las Naciones Unidas sobre el comercio de mercancías, 22 August 2017. http://comtrade.un.org/data/
18. SIEX: Importaciones - Supartida arancelaria - Departamento de destino (Sistema Estadístico de Comercio Exterior (SIEX) - Dirección de Impuestos y Aduanas Nacionales (DIAN) ed.), 25 August 2018. http://websiex.dian.gov.co/
19. DANE: Tercer Censo Nacional Agropecuario (Departamento Administrativo Nacional de Estadística (DANE) ed.), 20 August 2018. https://www.dane.gov.co/files/images/foros/foro-de-entrega-de-resultados-y-cierre-3-censo-nacional-agropecuario/CNATomo2-Resultados.pdf
20. DANE: Encuesta de sacrificio de ganado (ESAG), 25 August 2018. http://www.dane.gov.co/index.php/estadisticas-por-tema/pobreza-y-condiciones-de-vida/encuesta-nacional-del-uso-del-tiempo-enut?id=131&phpMyAdmin=3om27vamm65hhkhrtgc8rrn2g4
21. DANE: Boletín técnico > Encuesta de Sacrificio de Ganado - ESAG, 27 August 2018. http://www.dane.gov.co/files/investigaciones/boletines/sacrificio/bol_sacrif_IItrim18.pdf
22. Choo, C.W.: The knowing organization: How organizations use information to construct meaning, create knowledge and make decisions. Int. J. Inf. Manag. **16**, 329–340 (1996)
23. De Jarnett, L.: Knowledge the latest thing, Information Strategy. Executives J. **12**, 3–5 (1996)
24. Bukowitz, W.R., Williams, R.L.: The Knowledge Management Fieldbook. Financial Times/Prentice Hall (2000)
25. Wigg, K.: Knowledge management foundations (1993)
26. Muñoz-Avila, H., Gupta, K., Aha, D.W., Nau, D.: Knowledge-based project planning. In: Dieng-Kuntz, R., Matta, N. (eds.) Knowledge Management and Organizational Memories. Springer, Boston (2002). https://link.springer.com/chapter/10.1007/978-1-4615-0947-9_11#citeas
27. Johnston, R., Blumentritt, R.: Knowledge moves to center stage. Sci. Commun. **20**, 99–105 (1998)

28. Nonaka, I., Takeuchi, H.: The knowledge-creating company: how Japanese companies create the dynamics of innovation. Long Range plann. **4**, 592 (1996)
29. Meyer, M., Zack, M.: The design and implementation of information products. Sloan Manag. Rev. **37**, 43–59 (1996)
30. Zack, M.H.: Managing codified knowledge. Sloan Manag. Rev. **40**, 45–58 (1999)
31. Zhang, M., Zhao, X., Lyles, M.A., Guo, H.: Absorptive capacity and mass customization capability. Int. J. Oper. Prod. Manag. **35**, 1275–1294 (2015)
32. Kant, R., Singh, M.: An integrative framework of knowledge management enabled supply chain management. In: IEEE International Conference on Industrial Engineering and Engineering Management, IEEM 2008, pp. 53–57 (2008)
33. Peng Wong, W., Yew Wong, K.: Supply chain management, knowledge management capability, and their linkages towards firm performance. Bus. Process Manag. J. **17**, 940–964 (2011)
34. Croom, S.R.: The impact of e-business on supply chain management: an empirical study of key developments. Int. J. Oper. Prod. Manag. **25**, 55–73 (2005)
35. Yu, W., Jacobs, M.A., Salisbury, W.D., Enns, H.: The effects of supply chain integration on customer satisfaction and financial performance: an organizational learning perspective. Int. J. Prod. Econ. **146**, 346–358 (2013)
36. Angeles, R.: RFID critical success factors and system deployment outcomes as mitigated by IT infrastructure integration and supply chain process integration. Int. J. Value Chain Manag. **6**, 240–281 (2012)
37. Cheung, C.F., Cheung, C., Kwok, S.: A knowledge-based customization system for supply chain integration. Expert Syst. Appl. **39**, 3906–3924 (2012)
38. Li, Y., Tarafdar, M., Subba Rao, S.: Collaborative knowledge management practices: theoretical development and empirical analysis. Int. J. Oper. Prod. Manag. **32**, 398–422 (2012)
39. Nikabadi, M.S.: A multidimensional structure for describing the influence of supply chain strategies, business strategies, and knowledge management strategies on knowledge sharing in supply chain. Int. J. Knowl. Manag. (IJKM) **8**, 50–70 (2012)
40. Ayoub, H.F., Abdallah, A.B., Suifan, T.S.: The effect of supply chain integration on technical innovation in Jordan: the mediating role of knowledge management. Benchmarking Int. J. **24**, 594–616 (2017)
41. Chong, A.Y.-L., Bai, R.: Predicting open IOS adoption in SMEs: an integrated SEM-neural network approach. Expert Syst. Appl. **41**, 221–229 (2014)
42. Revilla, E., Knoppen, D.: Building knowledge integration in buyer-supplier relationships: the critical role of strategic supply management and trust. Int. J. Oper. Prod. Manag. **35**, 1408–1436 (2015)
43. Davis-Sramek, B., Germain, R., Krotov, K.: Examining the process R&D investment–performance chain in supply chain operations: the effect of centralization. Int. J. Prod. Econ. **167**, 246–256 (2015)
44. Butter, M.C., Veloso, A.A.: Modelo de gestión del conocimiento basado en la integración curricular de tecnologías de información y comunicación (tic) en la docencia universitaria (GC + TIC/DU). REXE: Revista de Estudios y Experiencias en Educación **5**, 55–74 (2006)
45. McAdam, R., McCreedy, S.: A critical review of knowledge management models. Learn. Organ. **6**, 91–101 (1999)
46. López, M., Hernández, A., Marulanda, C.E.: Procesos y prácticas de gestión del conocimiento en cadenas productivas de Colombia. Información tecnológica **25**, 125–134 (2014)
47. González, M.R.: El negocio es el conocimiento: Ediciones Díaz de Santos (2006)

48. Swan, J., Newell, S.: Linking knowledge management and innovation. In: ECIS 2000 Proceedings, p. 173 (2000)
49. Jordan, J., Jones, P.: Assessing your company's knowledge management style. Long Range Plann. **30**, 392–398 (1997)
50. Morales, F.J.L., Gutiérrez, H.A.: La gestión del conocimiento: Modelos de comprensión y definiciones. Revista de investigación en ciencias estratégicas **2**, 84–111 (2015)
51. Boisot, M.: Information and Organizations: The Manager as Anthropologist. Fontana, London (1987)
52. Kakabadse, N.K., Kakabadse, A., Kouzmin, A.: Reviewing the knowledge management literature: towards a taxonomy. J. Knowl. Manag. **7**, 75–91 (2003)
53. Barragán Ocaña, A.: Aproximación a una taxonomía de modelos de gestión del conocimiento (2009)
54. Sánchez Díaz, M.: Breve inventario de los modelos para la gestión del conocimiento en las organizaciones. Acimed **13**, 0 (2005)
55. Rodríguez Gómez, D.: Modelos para la creación y gestión del conocimiento: una aproximación teórica. Educar **37**, 025–039 (2006)
56. Polanyi, M.: Personal Knowledge: Towards a Post-critical Philosophy. University of Chicago Press, Chicago (1958)
57. Nonaka, I.: The Knowledge-Creating Company. Harvard Business Review Press (2008)
58. Hedlund, G.: A model of knowledge management and the N-form corporation. Strateg. Manag. J. **15**, 73–90 (1994)
59. McLaughlin, H., Thorpe, R.: Action learning-a paradigm in emergence: the problems facing a challenge to traditional management education and development. Br. J. Manag. **4**, 19–27 (1993)
60. Wiig, K.: Knowledge Management Foundations: Thinking About-How People and Organizations Create, Represent, and Use Knowledge. Schema, Arlington (1993)
61. Duflot, B., Roussillon, M., Rieu, M.: A competitiveness index for national pork chains in Europe: for the years 2010, 2011 and 2012, Cahiers de l'IFIP, vol. 1, pp. 29–45 (2014)
62. Selva, G.: "Analysis of the Competitiveness of the Pork Industry in Denmark. In: 99th seminar of the EAAE "The Future of Rural Europe in the Global Agri-Food System", Copenhagen, Denmark, pp. 24–27, August 2005
63. AHDB and BPEX: Profitability in the pig supply Chain (2011). https://pork.ahdb.org.uk/media/2338/profitability_in_the_pig_supply_chain.pdf
64. Porter, M.E.: Competitive Advantage of Nations: Creating and Sustaining Superior Performance. Simon and Schuster (2011)
65. Dwyer, L., Kim, C.: Destination competitiveness: development of a model with application to Australia and the Republic of Korea. Department of Industry Science and Resources, Canberra (2001)
66. Mugera, A.W.: Sustained competitive advantage in agribusiness: Applying the resource-based theory to human resources. Int. Food Agribusiness. Manag. Rev. **15**(1030–2016-82811), 27–48 (2012)
67. Pérez-Mesa, J.C., Galdeano-Gómez, E.: Agrifood cluster and transfer of technology in the Spanish vegetables exporting sector: the role of multinational enterprises. Agric. Econ. **56**, 478–488 (2010)
68. Pitts, E., Lagnevik, M.: What determines food industry competitiveness. In: Competitiveness in Food Industry, London, pp. 1–34 (1998)
69. Boyle, G., Kearney, B., McCarthy, T., Keane, M.: The competitiveness of Irish agriculture: Irish Farmers Journal Dublin, (2002)
70. Amin, S., Hagen, A.: Strengthening American international competitiveness: a recommended strategy. Am. Bus. Rev. **16**, 94 (1998)

71. Fagerberg, J., Srholec, M., Knell, M.: The competitiveness of nations. Presented at the DRUID Tenth Anniversary Summer Conference, Aalborg, Denmark (2005)
72. Trujillo-Diaz, J., Rojas, M.M., Franco, C.F., Contreras, A.T.V., Bolivar, H., Gonzalez, J.F. P.: Criteria for decision-making in transportation logistics function. Presented at the IEOM 2015 - 5th International Conference on Industrial Engineering and Operations Management, Proceeding, United Arab Emirates (2015)
73. Porter, M.E., Ketels, C.H.: UK competitiveness: moving to the next stage (2003)
74. Adams, G., Gangnes, B., Shachmurove, Y.: Why is China so competitive? Measuring and explaining China's competitiveness. World Econ. **29**, 95–122 (2006)
75. Waheeduzzaman, A.: Competitiveness and convergence in G7 and emerging markets. Competitiveness Rev. Int. Bus. J. **21**, 110–128 (2011)
76. Sölvell, Ö., Lindqvist, G., Ketels, C.: The Cluster Initiative Greenbook. Ivory Tower Stockholm (2003)
77. Boekholt, P., Thuriaux, B.: Public policies to facilitate clusters: background, rationale and policy practices in international perspective. Boosting innovation: the cluster approach, pp. 381–412 (1999)

Entrepreneurship Knowledge Insights in Emerging Markets Using a SECI Model Approach

Dario Liberona[1]([⊠]), Aravind Kumaresan[2], Lionel Valenzuela[1],
Cristian Rojas[1], and Roberto Ferro[3]

[1] Department of Business Administration,
Universidad Técnica Federico Santa Maria, Valparaíso, Chile
{Dario.liberona,Lionel.valenzuela}@usm.cl,
cristian.rojas.12@sansano.usm.cl
[2] University of Vaasa, Vaasa, Finland
Aravind.kumaresan@gmail.com
[3] Universidad Distrital Francisco José de Caldas, Bogotá, Colombia
rferro@udistrital.edu.co

Abstract. Entrepreneurship is an engine for economic growth, but generally the success rates are low [8, 10, 19], and they are even lower in developing countries where the relative cost of failure is even higher than in develop countries. There is little specific Latin American knowledge that has been incorporated to help reducing this failure rate, most of the entrepreneurial models have been developed for economies with advanced entrepreneurial ecosystems such has Silicon Valley, with economies and cultures that differ from developing economies, there is a lack of data and research on this topic. This research aims to use the SECI model approach in order to identify entrepreneurial practices for emerging countries that could improve the chances of success and to transfer these practices.

The study shows that the use of a SECI model approach is very successful at an ecosystem level and that the entrepreneurial knowledge is related to the actual stage of the entrepreneurial journey of startups, also that there are significant differences in access to venture capital funds and angel investors in the Latin American Market and also a much less tolerance to failure in Chile and the region.

Keywords: SECI model · Startups · Entrepreneurship practices ·
Entrepreneurship ecosystem · Knowledge transfer

1 Introduction

1.1 Origins of Entrepreneurship, Evolution and the New Entrepreneurs

Entrepreneurship has become a trending topic since the 20th century, with the appearance of the digital Era and the strong technology evolution and the success of the so called "digital unicorns" [12]. Even though, the terminology can be track back as old as the formal discipline of economic activity [22]. It was first introduced by Richard Cantillon in 1755, with a lot of controversy from theoreticians and academics, he stated

© Springer Nature Switzerland AG 2019
L. Uden et al. (Eds.): KMO 2019, CCIS 1027, pp. 36–47, 2019.
https://doi.org/10.1007/978-3-030-21451-7_4

that "Entrepreneurs work on uncertain wages, whether they establish with or without capital." In 1928 Schumpeter revolutionized the field of Economics by introducing the concept of Creative Destruction, innovation made in Entrepreneurship. He defined Entrepreneurship as an innovative, disruptive and new combinations of production factors to create a new business. In the other hand, Hayek focused on information and knowledge rather than the issue of entrepreneurial decision making [11]. He tried to understand how individuals successfully coordinate their actions, involved in complex expanding division of labor with only local and idiosyncratic knowledge. An important element of his thought on the learning process was the problem of division of knowledge [11]. One of the latest definitions came from the Economist D. H. Harper, who stressed rational and critical aspects of entrepreneurship, which are fundamental to acquire new knowledge. He defined Entrepreneurship as "profit seeking activity aimed at identifying and solving specific problems, structurally uncertain and complex situations. It another hand, Hayek refers to a startup has a newly formed organization [13].

It is hard to agree on a single definition of entrepreneurship, but we can acknowledge that the importance of startups is growing in the economies [5], especially in Chile and Colombia, Steve Blank [3, 6] referred to them as a temporary organization that is searching for a repeatable and scalable business model, he and other authors have attempted to create clear guidelines for the next generation of entrepreneurs. Thanks to the internet and digital revolution, entrepreneurship has evolved to be an innovative, disruptive and creative way of creating a new business that is able to scale dynamically and able to transform rapidly, adapt and evolve continuously over time, in a process where knowledge transfer is fundamental [2]. Regarding the Startup concept, it is consider a venture or business that has a large technological component in its business model and the ability to rapidly scale at a global domain [20].

1.2 Main Issues Affecting Entrepreneurship and the Correct Development

Nowadays, there is a lack of information regarding the rate of success or failure of Startups in a global scale, some studies show that 50% of Startups fail during their first year of operation, others say 7 out of 10 survive the first year, but the reality is that more likely in Latin America and emerging countries there is a higher failure rate, with an estimated than close to 8 out of 10 Startups disappearing after the first year and 9 out of 10 in three years [1, 8].

Some of the main issues that trigger this problem are related to adoption of technology, lack of connection with research centers and very little knowledge transfer among the ecosystem according to successful founders in Chile and other Latin American countries, that also mentioned the scarcity of private investing and a organized and collaborative entrepreneurial ecosystem [8, 10, 15, 21, 23].

1.3 Entrepreneurship in the Region

Research have shown that majority of start-ups fails [18, 21, 23]. Some of the reasons can be expressed as follows: lack of entrepreneurial knowledge and experience, premature scaling, poor product development, ignoring local opportunities, among other that have been studied. One of the main factors of failure in emerging countries is caused by the lack of entrepreneurial skills and entrepreneurial Knowledge of founders and their co-workers. Over the last decade or so more interest in being entrepreneurs have been on the rise in Chile and Guatemala, Peru, Colombia and Brazil being some of the most entrepreneurial countries in the world in terms of early stage entrepreneurial activity according to the last GEM report, a study that profiles 49 economies and reports the looks outward at the environment for entrepreneurship [4] (Fig. 1).

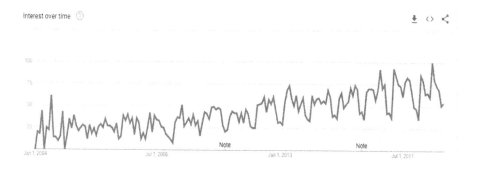

Fig. 1. Grow of interest in Entrepreneurship in Chile (2004–2018, google trends).

Meanwhile in the world the Startups has been growing and with that a lot of research and publications have been develop over the last decade, however regardless of the many guides, methodologies, knowledge transfer and experiential publications available (Table 1), the success factor rates have not really improved in Chile or Latin American.

Table 1. Some methodologies use in Startups. (Source: own elaboration)

Theory/Approach/Methodology	Author	Since/Year
Traditional Business Models	Various Authors	1980/2018
Canvas Business Model	Alexander Osterwalder	2004
Blue Ocean Strategy	W. Chan Kim	2005
Lean Startup	Eric Ries	2010
The Silicon Valley Way	Elton Sherwin	2010
Startup Business Owner	Steve Blank	2011
Harvard u. Startup Guide	Isaac Kohlberg	2011
Disciplined Entrepreneurship	Bill Aulet	2013
Scaling Up Excellence	Robert Sutton	2014
Lean Canvas	Ash Maurya	2009

Most of this methodology (Table 1) are widely used in emerging markets startup ecosystems, with still very low success rates and a clear indication that the main premise that spillover and application of entrepreneurship theory has more limitations in the context of developing economies [9].

Creating a favorable startup ecosystem requires cooperation of many stakeholders such as companies, public institutions (universities, self-governing regions, research centers, incubators, co-work spaces) as well as enthusiastic individuals. Universities play a crucial role in the ecosystem creation and development of entrepreneurial knowledge and skills.

The Chilean government through its entrepreneurial branch Corfo, has been helping to enrich the ecosystem in the country with policies and incentives to help improve the success rate, in Colombia there are many different efforts to support the entrepreneurial ecosystem, but they are not consistent and permanent over time.

In order to find relevant entrepreneurial knowledge for emerging countries, a series of surveys and interviews were conducted in order to find some of the local success factor practices, and then develop ways of sharing the findings, this was in collaboration with the Ministry of Economy of Chile and its entrepreneurship branch CORFO, a government entity that was created to help the recovery of industry in Chile after the 1960 big earthquake, the biggest earthquake register in the world a mega thrust earthquake that heavily impacted the Chilean economy.

2   Methodology

2.1   The SECI Model

In order to collaborate in the challenge of helping to improve the success rate of startups in the Region, we used a SECI model approach for entrepreneurial knowledge transfer, there are many applications for the model inside companies, but not attempts to use it at an ecosystem level. The SECI model was selected since is one of the fundamental models in Knowledge Management theory [14], and since the problem was to identify local entrepreneurial success practices and sharing them with entrepreneurs.

Our research based on the SECI Model [14, 17], as can be seen on Fig. 2, consist on applying the model in order to transfer Knowledge through a sequence of tacit and explicit processes involving Socialization, externalization, combination and internalization.

The first one, **Socialization**, is about an informal sharing of experience (e.g. between master and apprentice), for this process a serious of personal interviews were conducted with around 60 successful technological and innovative entrepreneurs in Chile most of them operated at a Latin American scale or at least in more than two Latin American Countries. Also, a series of visits to incubators with interviews were developed during a 9 months period. A previous work was done in order to identify successful startups and finding a local definition of success.

During this stage the question of what will be considered a successful startup was a key starting point, after the analysis we found and agreement among 189 founders that there were three basic goals that startups try to achieve during a three-year period and identify five stages of the startup journey during its first five to six years (Fig. 3), this success factors were level of sales, achieving break even and obtaining private investment.

There was observation of tremendous interaction and socialization process in the Co-work spaces and business incubators that provided co-work environments, in Chile, during this process many entrepreneurs learn from other founders and team members. Since 2014 Corfo has develop funds to support this entrepreneurial socialization centers.

During this stage we also learn about the experiences of successful founders, about the stages of entrepreneurial journey and were able to meet most of the members of the startup ecosystem.

The second key process in the model, **Externalization**, is about the formalization of tacit knowledge, here the interviews helped to identify and document a series of practices and the general process of developing and startup which was denominated the Startup Journey process. In this stage we were able to conduct a survey with more than 900 participants (Startups founders). In this case the results of the surveys an interviews were built into an online course that was made available for entrepreneurs. The aim was to publish and articulate the tacit knowledge, so a public Web Site was developed in order to connect the entrepreneurial community and share some of the findings and information.

The third process in the SECI model implemented was **Combination**, related to the construction of explicit knowledge from tacit knowledge, a series of practices were identified, and a series of surveys with the participation of more than a thousand founders of startups in Chile permitted to validate and weighted the practices that were identified during the socialization and externalization process. During this process CORFO was able to develop policies, programs and incentives that helped to mature and made more efficient the ecosystem and combined programs with successful practices such as the development of a program that promoted the relationship among funders and mentors (Table 2).

Table 2. Number of full survey participants startups and their industry (Own elaboration)

Industry	Startups	Percentage
IT & Enterprise Software	85	14,1%
Tourism	47	7,8%
Agro-Industry	45	7,5%
Retail	41	6,8%
Health and Biotechnology	39	6,5%
Professional Services	38	6,3%
Education	37	6,2%
Food-Restaurant	36	6,0%
Online Retail	36	6,0%

(*continued*)

Table 2. (*continued*)

Industry	Startups	Percentage
Services	29	4,8%
Energy and Clean Technologies	27	4,5%
Social Networks	17	2,8%
Construction - Building	17	2,8%
Social Companies	12	2,0%
Mining	11	1,8%
Wireless and Mobile	10	1,7%
Other	74	12,3%

The combination process was considered by the team has the most complex since it requires that new knowledge will be created from previous findings and the combination of a series of process and knowledge, during this process there were the combination of the startup journey stages and the SECI model, during this stage the recognition of different competences and knowledge were identify and structured, for example previous to the launching of the a project, in the stage of preparation it is important to define and establish the correspondent participation of founders, generally founders lack of experience and usually only divide the company among them in equal participations, this often end up has a problem among them, with investors, and potential partners since does not recognized the contributions of each founder, and the possible participation of future partners in the ownership, here the combination of knowledge for example with the Slicing Pie methodology [16] is a set of knowledge that should be tough previous to the launching of the startup.

The fourth one, **internalization**, is the transformation of explicit knowledge into tacit knowledge through the creation of a documents, information and practices and through the match of financial support instruments for startups at different stages into a government program also denominated Startup Journey, with the work a Corfo Team and collaborators. This stage has considered the development of a process to certify entrepreneurs with entrepreneurial skills with a program and a "journey" meant to be followed by entrepreneurs, with knowledge (courses, certifications), some financial support divided in stages, idea development, starting the company, and scaling. Later with the development of a public data base of complex entrepreneurial information that could be use by different researches and could be a monitoring system of the effects of policies and public investment.

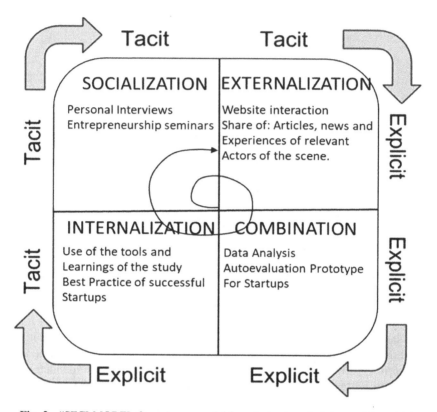

Fig. 2. "SECI MODEL for entrepreneurial knowledge transfer" (own elaboration)

3   Findings and Discussion

3.1   Startups Life Cycle Stages

One of main findings was the recognition of the stages in the journey of entrepreneurs, during this stages different knowledge, incentives and support is needed in order to improve the survival results of startups (Success rates) according to successful startups founders.

We recognized five stages for an emerging Startup, there are four initial stages, the time in which the companies pass through his stages varies among different industries and different Startups, but we consider that a sixty months is the normal period of startup development and in some cases upto seventy two months since the beginning of the operations. This time frame will fairly represent the initial stages of the projects in Latin America. In the case of develop economies the startup genome report [15] defines a period that varies between thirty-six to forty-eight months, so Latin American startups takes one or two extra years to scale up or find and exit (Merge, sale, or other growth strategy). One of the reasons to explain this is the venture capital development in this develop economies is scarce.

There have been many ways in literature that define the startup stages, some of them are the years since launch, number of employees, product stage, revenues, market capitalization or the number of shareholders within the company. This proposed frame will consider the time since launching and will define five initial stages.

a. Preparation Stage (Anticipate)
b. Launch-Initial operations (Activate)
c. Survival (Acknowledge)
d. Break Even (Adapt)
e. Exit (Scale, Sale, Merge, close the project, other strategy)

The stages one to four are usually cover in five years, and the final stage the "Exit", refers to the plan that the founders have for the growth or development of the company and can last many years.

The different stages helped to develop a incremental learning program with topics that were identify by the experts interviews, this programs are in the implementation stages and Corfo is looking to make an official list with certified providers of this courses.

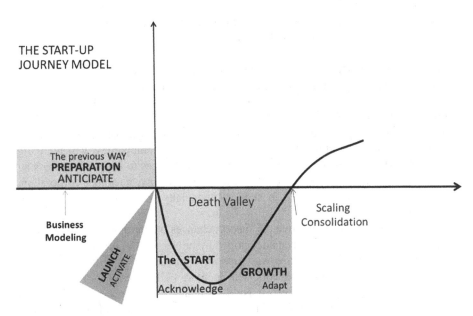

Fig. 3. The Startup Journey stages in emerging economies (Own elaboration with Wessner work [25])

3.2 What is a Successful Startup Company?

This is a very important question, an even that it seems very simple, we found out that there is not a clear definition or standards of success, other than the general concept of a Unicorns [12], that are companies with a market valuation of over a billion dollars in a short period of time, however there are very few companies in Latin America that has been able to go to the stock markets and become public investment companies, so in develop markets success is achieve in terms of market valuation or traction being a fast ability to grow users and market penetration, this usually helped with massive rounds of investments.

In terms of Latin American startups there are three main factors to consider for success, the first is to achieve the breakeven stage, to have sales among Us$ 300.000 to Us$ 1.000.000 in the first three years, and to have a round of investment from private funds.

With the results of the survey and interviews from close to a thousand founders, we manage to find entrepreneurial practices that are recognized among different successful Startups:

1. Designed to Stay: Startups that have leaders that work and dedicate their 100% on the business are more likely to succeed. They must look at the big picture and work on long run goals (5–6 years results). this consideration has led to the growth in the number of team founders in the startups over the year, coming from a "solo" founder to an average of 2,5 founders (Preparing and Launching stages).
2. Focus on Survival: The lack of capital and private funding, on emerging markets indicates the importance of achieving of financial breakeven. The common Silicon Valley practice of "Fail fast, fail often" [2] does not apply to for Startups on emerging markets (Start and Growth stage)
3. Emerging Timing: The Launching of the product is key to success. Finding the right moment, time and place, according to the realities of the country, taking in count that the demand on emerging economies is not the same as in developed once (Launch stage)
4. Financing and support from mothership companies: Because of the low venture capital availability, Startups should seek for "mothership companies" which are big companies able to provide sustained funding and resources to support the crossing of the Death Valley, this entity could be a large company, customer corporation, partners, any organization able to support financially the Startups (Growth and Scale stages).
5. Mentors are important to improve the success chances of startups, so in the last few years Mentors networks have been developed by universities in order to collaborate with founders. Also, this practice was supports by means of specific small grants that supported the collaborative work with mentors (All stages).
6. The number of founders has also a good correlation with success, and we can observe a growth in the number of team founders in the startups over the years, coming from a "solo" founder to an average of 2,5 founders. (Preparation and Launch stages).
7. Another problem that was identify during the socialization and combination is the lack of basic entrepreneurial knowledge in terms of methodologies, knowledge about the local entrepreneurial ecosystem, and knowledge of best entrepreneurial practices among the founders (All stages).

4 Conclusions

Usually the SECI model approach has been use inside companies, and has been related to internal organizational culture, in this case we have use a SECI model approach in an entire ecosystem with multiple organizations, this has the complexity of interacting with different non related organizations and players, the results of this experience was very positive and useful and has proven to be an effective methodology outside de domain of a single organization, to follow the process was an excellent guideline to improve the results of finding and disseminating local entrepreneurial knowledge in the Chilean ecosystem, the monitoring of the process spiral was resolve with the creation of a website with open access with the collected data of all startups that have been supported with entrepreneurial incentives by all the government entrepreneurial incentive programs (Corfo) since year 2010 and ongoing.

The Socialization stage is very intuitive and natural process of knowledge transfer, finding out the relevant knowledge for the next steps, in the case of socialization in a company is a very strait forward process, however in the case of an entire Ecosystem is not, finding the right collaborators in order to have more impact is fundamental, to develop a web site with the information and an e-learning program course to dispose entrepreneurial knowledge is not enough to improve the success factor of startups, here the support of the government and the alignment of incentives with the experiential knowledge acquire was fundamental, as in the case of single companies having the support of the upper management in key, in this case having the support of the government agency dedicated to entrepreneurship was fundamental in order to be successful, they set the right incentives for entrepreneurs to motive founders to participate and use the teaching programs that were develop plus provide a monitoring platform of the advances, also letting Universities or research centers to help on the task of analysis and creating new insights on an spiral fashion.

The aim of the study and Corfo was using and applying a methodology to support the entrepreneurial ecosystem, with the development of a training program and a platform to connect and interact with the startup founders. The SECI Model is a process model, and a continuous spiral model, in this case the approach of the process done by the Corfo Team has been consistent and even though it has taken many years of learning and implementing, it is proving to be the right approach. Not only a lot of information related to the startup ecosystem was classified but also made available with the launch of a open entrepreneurial data web site "dataemprendimiento.corfo.cl" (Entrepreneurship Data) to monitor the effect of the knowledge transfer process and inviting others to participate in the knowledge transfer process on a continuous fashion.

Even that there has been some criticism at Nonaka's SECI model [14, 24], this empirical approach has been very helpful in the process of helping to improve the entrepreneurial ecosystem in Chile.

We can assess the importance of the spiral of knowledge involved in the model, where the explicit and tacit knowledge interact with each other in a continuous process that will growth in terms of volume and participants, something that was not considered at the time the model was develop is the rol of technology and the ability of open platforms that are the ones that allow this process not only inside companies, but in an whole ecosystem like the entrepreneurial one. The central thought of the model is that knowledge held by individuals is shared with other individuals, so it interconnects to a new knowledge, in this case there is a proposal learning program and the incentives for founders to follow and certified their projects in order to easy the access to government supporting funds.

Since the spiral of knowledge or the amount of knowledge so to say, grows all the time when more rounds are done in the model, we can expect an increase in the learning curve of the ecosystem through the implemented systems and incentives, the findings of this research highlight the supportive and significant role of knowledge management models for startups success, generally this methodologies are not considered since they are long term process and the startups generally focus on short terms priorities.

References

1. Andersen, D.: Steve Blank Teaches Entrepreneurs How to Fail Less. Tech Crunch (2012). https://techcrunch.com/2012/04/15/steve-blank-teaches-entrepreneurs-how-to-fail-less/. Accessed 2 Nov 2016
2. Babineaux, R., Krumboltz, J.: Fail Fast, Fail Often. How Losing Can Help You Win. Penguin Random House Company, New York (2013)
3. Blank, S., Dorf, B.: The Startup Owner's Manual: The Step-By-Step Guide for Building a Great Company. K and S Ranch Press, Pescadero (2012)
4. Bosma, N., Kelley, D.: Global Entrepreneurship Monitor, 2018/2019 Global Report. Gráfica Andes, Chile (2019)
5. Carrera, M., Thurika, A.: The Impact of Entrepreneurship on Economic Growth. Centre for Advanced Small Business Economics (CASBEC) at Erasmus University Rotterdam EIM Business and Policy Research, Zoetermeer Faculty of Economics and Business Administration, University of Maastricht, July 2002
6. Cook, J.: Q&A with Silicon Valley "Godfather" Steve Blank. Reuters (2012). http://blogs.reuters.com/small-business/2012/10/09/qa-with-silicon-valley-godfather-steve-blank/. Accessed 21 Oct 2016
7. Drucker, P.: Landmarks of Tomorrow. Harper & Brothers, New York (1959)
8. Feinleib, D.: Why Startups Fail: And How Yours Can Succeed. Springer, New York (2011). https://doi.org/10.1007/978-1-4302-4141-6s
9. González-Pernía, J.L., Jung, A., Peña, I.: Innovation-driven entrepreneurship in developing economies. Entrepreneurship Reg. Dev. **27** (9–10), 555–573 (2015)
10. Green, A.: Why 90% of Startups FAIL? Entrepreneurial Books, Kindle Edition. Amazon Digital Services (2014)
11. Hayek, F.A.: Economics and Knowledge. A presidential address to the London Economic Club, 10 November 1936. First published in Economica, February 1937
12. Lee, A.: Welcome To The Unicorn Club: Learning From Billion-Dollar Startups (2013). https://techcrunch.com/2013/11/02/welcome-to-the-unicorn-club/. Accessed 27 Oct 2017
13. Luger, M.I., Koo, J.: Defining and tracking business startups. Small Bus. Econ. **24**(1), 17–28 (2005)
14. McAdam, R., McCreedy, S.: A critical review of knowledge management models. Learn. Organ. **6**(3), 91–100 (1999)

15. Marmer, M., Hermann, B., Berman, J.: The Startup Genome: A new framework for understanding why startups succeed (2011). https://s3.amazonaws.com/startupcompass-public/StartupGenomeReport1_Why_Startups_Succeed_v2.pdf. Accessed 2 Dec 2015
16. Moyer, M.: Slicing Pie Handbook. Eureka. Paper back, 21 September 2016
17. Nonaka, T.: The knowledge creating company: how Japanese companies create the dynamics of innovation, p. 284. Oxford University Press, New York (1994)
18. Patel, N.: 90% Of Startups Fail: Here's What You Need To Know About The 10%. Forbes.com (2015). https://www.forbes.com/sites/neilpatel/2015/01/16/90-of-startups-willfail-heres-what-you-need-to-know-about-the-10/#5e728d8b6679. Accessed 17 Mar 2017
19. Pride, J.: Unicorn Tears: Why Startups Fail and How To Avoid It. Wiley, Australia (2018)
20. Robehmed, N.: What Is A Startup? Forbes Magazine (2013). http://www.forbes.com/sites/natalierobehmed/2013/12/16/what-is-a-startup/
21. Shorewala, P., Chaudhary, P.: Why indian startups fail?-do's and don'ts. IOSR J. Bus. Manage. (IOSR-JBM) 18(2), 12–16 (2016). www.iosrjournals.org. e-ISSN: 2278-487X, p-ISSN: 2319-7668
22. Schumpeter, J.: Economic Problems in Essays. Port Washington, New Jersey (1951)
23. Silas, T.: Key Reasons Why Small Businesses Fail. Commissioned by IIB-Business Support Americas (2004). http://www.summitbusinesssolutions.ws/docs/reasons_biz_fail.pdf. Accessed 10 Feb 2017
24. Tsoukas, H.: Do we really understand tacit knowledge? In: Easterby-Smith, M., Lyles, M.A. (eds.) Handbook of Organizational Learning and Knowledge, pp. 410–427. Blackwell, Oxford (2003)
25. Wessner, C.W.: Driving innovations across the valley of death. Res. Technol. Manage. 48(1), 9–12 (2005)

Data Mining and Intelligent Science

Efficient Estimation of Ontology Entities Distributed Representations

Achref Benarab[1](✉)(iD), Jianguo Sun[1], Allaoua Refoufi[2], and Jian Guan[1]

[1] College of Computer Science and Technology,
Harbin Engineering University, Harbin, China
{achref.benarab,sunjianguo,j.guan}@hrbeu.edu.cn
[2] Computer Science Department, University of Sétif-1, Sétif, Algeria
allaoua.refoufi@univ-setif.dz

Abstract. Ontologies have been used as a form of knowledge representation in different fields such as artificial intelligence, semantic web and natural language processing. The success caused by deep learning in recent years as a major upheaval in the field of artificial intelligence depends greatly on the data representation, since these representations can encode different types of hidden syntactic and semantic relationships in data, making their use very common in data science tasks. Ontologies do not escape this trend, applying deep learning techniques in the ontology-engineering field has heightened the need to learn and generate representations of the ontological data, which will allow ontologies to be exploited by such models and algorithms and thus automatizing different ontology-engineering tasks. This paper presents a novel approach for learning low dimensional continuous feature representations for ontology entities based on the semantic embedded in ontologies, using a multi-input feed-forward neural network trained using noise contrastive estimation technique. Semantically similar ontology entities will have relatively close corresponding representations in the projection space. Thus, the relationships between the ontology entities representations mirrors exactly the semantic relations between the corresponding entities in the source ontology.

Keywords: Ontology entities distributed representations ·
Continuous vector representations · Feature representation ·
Concept embeddings · Neural networks

1 Introduction

Ontologies are a powerful paradigm for knowledge representation and exchange, they provide a specific vocabulary to a knowledge domain, and according to a variable degree of formalization, they set the sense of the concepts and relationships uniting them. Gruber defines the term ontology as: "An ontology is an explicit specification of a conceptualization" [1]. Ontologies not only allow us to

© Springer Nature Switzerland AG 2019
L. Uden et al. (Eds.): KMO 2019, CCIS 1027, pp. 51–62, 2019.
https://doi.org/10.1007/978-3-030-21451-7_5

represent concepts that completely describe a knowledge domain, but also represent the semantics associated with them. The concepts are linked to each other by taxonomic and semantic relationships forming a semantic network. Ontologies have been used in several fields, such as engineering and knowledge management systems, natural language processing, semantic web, intelligent integration of information etc. The aim is to facilitate knowledge sharing and reuse [2].

In front of the huge success of deep learning techniques, until recently these techniques did not get enough interest in the ontology-engineering field because of the nature of the ontological data. However, representing ontological entities in a low dimensional continuous vector space provides generic representations for most machine learning and deep learning tasks, allowing the ontology-engineering field to benefit from these techniques. Representing ontology entities as continuous vector representations allows also applying several operations to manipulate representations: measures of similarity or distance, addition, subtraction etc. Our contribution in this paper is the proposition of a model capable of generating low dimensional continuous vector representations for ontology entities (concepts, individuals and semantic relationships) using multi-input feed-forward neural networks trained using noise contrastive estimation technique, where the training samples are generated on the basis of the different taxonomic, semantic relationships and restrictions.

The rest of the paper is organized as follows. In Sect. 2 we give an overview of related work. In Sect. 3 we present the technical details and the different methods used to generate the continuous vector representations for ontology entities in our approach. We evaluate and discuss the obtained results using several real world ontologies in Sect. 4. In Sect. 5, we give the conclusion, and highlight some directions and perspectives for future work.

2   Related Work

Conventional natural language processing tasks often use the one-hot or the bag of words representations. However, these simple words representations face several limitations, where they are very expensive i.e. the vectors are of high dimension, another limitation is that they cannot capture relations between words, even if there is a strong semantic or syntactic correlation between some of them. Continuous vector representations have been proposed for the first time for language modeling in [3], the model consists to train a feed-forward neural network to estimate the probability of the next word, based on the continuous representation of the previous words. These representations are called word embeddings, neural embeddings or prediction-based embeddings, they have been introduced through the construction of neural language models [4,5]. Word embeddings are a projection of a vocabulary words into a low dimensional space in order to preserve semantic and syntactic similarities. Thus, if the word vectors are close to one another in terms of distance in the projection space, the words must be semantically or syntactically close. Each dimension represents a latent characteristic of the word, which can capture syntactic and semantic properties.

The currently most popular word embeddings in the literature are provided by the Word2vec toolkit [6,7]. The authors proposed two architectures CBOW (Continuous Bag Of Words) and Skip-gram model for learning word embeddings that are less expensive in terms of computing time than previous models. The authors in [8] have shown that word embeddings created by a recurrent neural network capture the similarities between words and word pairs. Another recent approach is called GloVe [9], which combines two approaches: count-based matrix factorization and predictive or neural models. This approach relies on the construction of a global co-occurrence matrix of words, treating the whole corpus using a sliding window. GloVe is a model of unsupervised learning that takes into account all the information carried by the corpus and not only the information carried by a sliding window of words.

Several algorithms have been proposed to solve the problem of dimensionality reduction for graph representations such as [10–13] that were based on Principal Component Analysis and Multi-Dimensional Scaling. Authors in [14] proposed a semi-supervised algorithm to learn continuous feature representations for nodes in networks based on random walks algorithm and motivated by the previous work [6] on natural language processing. Authors in [15,16] proposed a method for representing RDF (Resource Description Framework) nodes in linked open data using language modeling approaches for unsupervised feature extraction from sequences of words based on deep walk and deep graph kernels approaches.

Embeddings evaluation techniques can be classified into two major families, extrinsic and intrinsic evaluations [17]. Extrinsic evaluation aims to evaluate the continuous vector representations on real applications of the use of embeddings for specific task. The intrinsic evaluation aims to evaluate semantic and syntactic relations between words or concepts [18], it is an inexpensive method and it gives a good estimation of a model that works or not. It uses the cosine similarity, Euclidean distance, human judgment, etc. Continuous vector representations models showed a good behavior and achieved good results in language modeling tasks. They are rapid, efficient and easy to train, meanwhile, they need few manipulations to have a model that works well and can be easily integrated into the input of deep learning systems for example.

3   The Proposed Approach

The purpose of our approach is to encode ontology concepts, individuals and semantic relations in a low dimensional space, so that the similarity in the embedding space can be used to approximate the semantic similarity in the ontology. It aims to learn low dimensional embedded vectors for ontology entities using multi-input feed-forward neural network to report semantics contained in ontologies. This method allows us to represent each ontology entity by a corresponding real number vector in $\mathbb{R}^n$. Another objective of our approach lies in putting the information and data contained in ontologies at the disposal of machine learning and deep learning algorithms. The ontology can be seen as a set of triples (subject, predicate and object), it is built from conceptual models that are semantically richer due to the explicit definition of associations and relationships between entities in the conceptual schema. Therefore, in our approach, we take benefit from these characteristics and exploit the semantic relations in the ontologies to generate the embeddings.

3.1 The Ontological Approach

Our contribution aims to use several approaches to generate the ontology entities distributed representations based on the different taxonomic and semantic relationships in the ontology.

Taxonomic Relationships. Taxonomic relations are the main mode of structuring an ontology. We assume two concepts are similar if they have the same super class. Let us consider the concepts $C_1, C_2, C_3 \sqsubseteq \top$ in an ontology O, then:

$$C_1 \sqsubseteq C_2 \wedge C_3 \sqsubseteq C_2 \Rightarrow C_1 \simeq C_3 \tag{1}$$

Non-taxonomic Relationships and Restrictions. Based on the non-taxonomic semantic relationships (object properties), we assume two concepts are semantically close if they have similar structural roles and they share semantic relations or restrictions with the same concepts:

$$\alpha C_1.r(C_2) \wedge \beta C_3.r(C_2) \Rightarrow C_1 \simeq C_3 \tag{2}$$

where r is a semantic relation and $\alpha, \beta \in \{\forall, \exists, \leqslant_n, \geqslant_n\}$.

Instances. For the ontology individuals (instances), we have applied three approaches to identify the similar individuals:

– We assume two individuals x and y are similar if they are instantiated from the same class:
$$C_1(x) \wedge C_1(y) \Rightarrow x \simeq y \tag{3}$$

– The second approach is based on the relations between the individual's concepts:
$$C_1(x) \wedge C_2(y) \wedge \alpha C_1.r(C_3) \wedge \beta C_2.r(C_3) \Rightarrow x \simeq y \tag{4}$$

– The third approach is based on the relations between the instances themselves. x, y and z are ontology individuals and r is an ontology role, then:

$$\alpha x.r(y) \wedge \beta z.r(y) \Rightarrow x \simeq z \tag{5}$$

3.2 The Neural Network Model

We have proposed a feed-forward multi-input neural network model, it aims to predict an object o, given a subject s and a relation r in an ontology O i.e. $G(s, r) \longrightarrow o$. The training set is a sequence of triples $(subject, predecate, object)$ defined as $\langle (s_1, r_1, o_1), \cdots, (s_k, r_l, o_k) \rangle$ where $k = |C|$, $l \in \{1, 2, \cdots, |R|\}$ and C is the set of the concepts and instances in the ontology O. The objective is to learn a model $g(s, r, o) = P(o|r, s)$ where g can be decomposed into three parts:

- A mapping M to a vector for ontology entity s in O.
- A mapping M' to a vector for each semantic relation r.
- The probability function P over the ontology entities in O.

The neural network model consists of two separated input layers, two separated projection layers and an output layer (see Fig. 1).

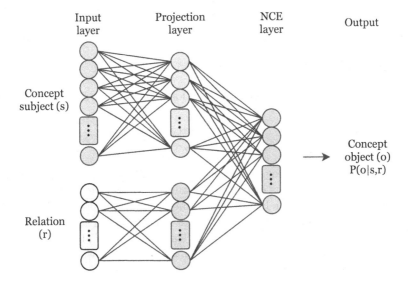

Fig. 1. The proposed neural network model architecture.

The neural probabilistic model specifies the distribution for the target concept o given a subject s and a relation r using the scoring function f:

$$P_\theta(o|s, r) = \frac{exp(f_\theta(v_o, v_s, v_r))}{\sum_{i=1}^{|C|} exp(f_\theta(v_{c_i}, v_s, v_r))} \tag{6}$$

where θ represents the model parameters, c_i is an entity (concept or instance) from the ontology O and v_o, v_s, v_r, v_{c_i} represent the vectors of o, s, r, c_i respectively. The scoring function f requires normalizing over the entire ontology entities, which is impractical and computationally expensive [19,20] when dealing with large ontologies. The noise contrastive estimation (NCE) [21] method has been used to train the model to reduce the density estimation to a probabilistic binary classification. The condition likelihood becomes:

$$P(D = 0|s, r, o) = \frac{k \times q(v_o)}{exp(f_\theta(v_o, v_s, v_r)) + k \times q(v_o)} \tag{7}$$

$$P(D = 1|s, r, o) = \frac{exp(f_\theta(v_o, v_s, v_r))}{exp(f_\theta(v_o, v_s, v_r)) + k \times q(v_o)} \tag{8}$$

where k represents noise samples from q. $D = 0$ means that it is a noise sample, whereas $D = 1$ defines true distribution sample. We can summarize the learning process as follows:

– Each ontology entity c is associated with a vector $v \in \mathbb{R}^n$ initialized randomly.
– For each couple s, r in a triple (s, r, o) from O as an input, the element o is taken into account as an output.
– $P(D = 1|s, r, o)$ represents the probability that an ontology entity s is the subject of a relation (predicate) r, which o is its object.
– $P(D = 0|s, r, o)$ the probability that s is not the subject of a relation r, which o is its object.
– The optimization objective function is defined as follows:

$$L(V) = arg\ max \sum_{s, o \in C, r \in R} \log P(D = 1|s, r, o) +$$

$$\sum_{s', o \in C, r \in R} \log P(D = 0|s', r, o) \tag{9}$$

It defines the sum of the logarithms of the probabilities $P(D = 1|s, r, o)$ for all the ontology elements o as objects, s as subjects, r as a relation in the set of triples, and the sum of the logarithms of the probabilities $P(D = 0|s', r, o)$ for all the elements o and r in the set of triples and a random sample of elements s' out of their triples. The symbol V indicates the set of all the vectors v of the elements which represents our model, and of which we try here to look for the optimal values in order to maximize the objective function $L(V)$. The gradient descent approach is used to find the optimal values of all vectors v corresponding to the ontology elements.

This approach allows us to find the vectors that bring together the semantically close ontology entities and can keep the semantically distant entities away.

4   Evaluation

In order to evaluate the performance of the proposed model, we have used several ontologies from different domains obtained from The Open Biological and Biomedical Ontologies (OBO[1]) Foundry [22] and BioPortal[2] repository [23].

---

[1] http://obofoundry.org.
[2] https://bioportal.bioontology.org.

4.1 Evaluation Metrics

To evaluate the quality of the ontology entities representations generated for each ontology, three different approaches have been used: the projection onto a two or three-dimensional map, cosine similarity and the Euclidean distance. Then we compare these representations with their corresponding ontology entities based on the semantic relations, restrictions and axioms using the Jaccard similarity. This task aims to measure the degree of similarity of the close concepts and instances in the ontology. The Jaccard index between two sets A and B is defined as follows:

$$Jaccard(A, B) = \frac{|A \cap B|}{|A \cup B|}$$

For two vectors x and y, the cosine similarity and the Euclidean distance are defined as follows:

$$Cosine\_similarity(x, y) = \frac{x \cdot y}{\| x \| \cdot \| y \|}$$

$$Euclidean\_distance(x, y) = \sqrt{\sum_{i=1}^{n} (x_i - y_i)^2}$$

The similarity values obtained from the generated representations and those obtained from the corresponding concepts and instances in the ontologies are evaluated using the standard metrics: Precision, Recall and F-measure. Given a set of similar concepts B, the precision (P) of the generated similar vector representations A is the ratio of the correct matches found and the total number of matches:

$$P(A, B) = \frac{|A \cap B|}{|A|}$$

The recall (R) computes the ratio of the correct matches found and the total number of expected connections in the ontology:

$$R(A, B) = \frac{|A \cap B|}{|B|}$$

The metric F-measure (F_1) is a harmonic measure, it combines both measures of Precision and Recall:

$$F_1(A, B) = 2 \times \frac{P(A, B) \times R(A, B)}{P(A, B) + R(A, B)}$$

4.2 Results and Discussion

For the visualization of the generated vectors in a two or three-dimensional map, we have employed the t-Distributed Stochastic Neighbor Embedding (t-SNE) technique [24], which is a non-linear dimension reduction technique particularly suitable for projecting high dimensional data onto a two or three-dimensional space. These representations can be viewed as a scatter plot, Fig. 2 illustrates a 2D representation of some concept embeddings obtained using our approach on The Human Ancestry Ontology [25]. The countries that belong to the same geographic region have close vector representations: Northern Africa countries, South-Central Asia, Western Europe, Central America, Northern Europe and the concepts representing the geographical regions as well.

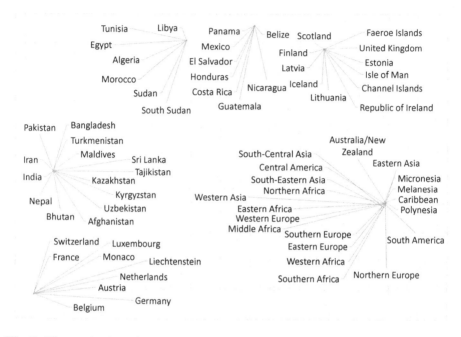

Fig. 2. The projection of some concept vectors obtained from The Human Ancestry Ontology.

We can see that the concepts that are semantically close tend to have close vector representations in the embedding space. The neural network learned also to layout the corresponding concept vector representations hierarchically in the embedding space based on the ontology taxonomic and semantic relationships between concepts from general to the most specific relationships. Initially, the entirety of the concept-vector-representations are seen as some initial concept islets. By drilling down, we can visualize the next hierarchical level that displays the respective concepts which increases the amount of information displayed locally for that particular islet.

We have applied two qualitative methods for the similarity measures, the cosine similarity and the Euclidean distance to identify the closest concepts (similar) of a given concept. The concepts considered similar based on the generated vector representations (using the cosine similarity and the Euclidean distance) are then compared to the set of similar concepts obtained from the ontology using the Jaccard index based on the taxonomic and semantic relationships. The three standard criteria: precision, recall and f-measure values are calculated for each ontology based on the cosine similarity (see Table 1) and the Euclidean distance (see Table 2).

Table 1. Values of precision, recall and f-measure for each ontology obtained using the cosine similarity.

Ontology	Precision	Recall	F-measure
HANCESTRO	0.99	0.99	0.99
SPD	0.91	0.99	0.95
UO	1.00	1.00	1.00
MF	0.99	1.00	0.99
BNO	1.00	1.00	1.00
NPI	1.00	1.00	1.00
BP	0.96	0.97	0.97
AO	1.00	1.00	1.00
BCTT	1.00	1.00	1.00
ADMIN	1.00	1.00	1.00
BFO	1.00	1.00	1.00
FAO	1.00	1.00	1.00
FHHO	0.99	1.00	0.99
SYMP	0.99	1.00	0.99
Average	0.99	0.99	0.99

From what preceded, and based on the values of the precision and recall, the generated vector representations using our approach mimic to a large degree the semantic properties of the corresponding ontology entities, where the semantically close concepts have close vector representations in the projection space (an average of 99% for cosine similarity and Euclidean distance).

Another behavior have been observed concerning the generated representations, where we have found that the semantic relationships don not have the same influence on the generated vector representations (the way that the generated vector representations are grouped in the projection space). We have found that the relationships that are frequently used in the ontology have more influence on the generated vector representations than those that are less used. That gives our method more expressiveness and an ability to better represent the concepts. For the concepts: $C_1, C_2, C_3, C_4, C_5 \sqsubseteq \top$, and the ontology roles r_1 and r_2, the relation r_1 is widely used in the ontology O than r_2, then:

$$\alpha C_1.r_1(C_2) \wedge \beta C_3.r_1(C_2) \wedge \gamma C_1.r_2(C_4) \wedge \delta C_5.r_2(C_4) \Rightarrow C_1 \simeq C_3 \qquad (10)$$

where $\alpha, \beta, \gamma, \delta \in \{\forall, \exists, \leqslant_n, \geqslant_n\}$. Thus, the concept C_1 is more similar to C_3 compared to C_5.

Table 2. Values of precision, recall and f-measure for each ontology obtained using the Euclidean distance.

Ontology	Precision	Recall	F-measure
HANCESTRO	0.99	0.99	0.99
SPD	0.91	0.98	0.94
UO	1.00	1.00	1.00
MF	0.99	1.00	0.99
BNO	1.00	1.00	1.00
NPI	1.00	1.00	1.00
BP	0.95	1.00	0.97
AO	1.00	1.00	1.00
BCTT	1.00	1.00	1.00
ADMIN	1.00	1.00	1.00
BFO	1.00	1.00	1.00
FAO	1.00	1.00	1.00
FHHO	1.00	1.00	1.00
SYMP	0.99	1.00	0.99
Average	0.99	0.99	0.99

The proposed model generates distributed vector representations in $\mathbb{R}^n$ for each entity in the ontology, these vectors express the probability function of the semantic relations in the ontology. The probability function is expressed as the product of conditional probabilities of the object given the subject and the predicate in the ontology triples. A low dimensional space makes it possible to group semantically similar elements together where the position (the distance and the direction) in the vector space makes it possible to encode the semantics embedded in ontologies in a suitable continuous vector representation.

5   Conclusion

In this paper, we have presented a novel approach for learning low dimensional continuous vector representations for ontology entities, based on taxonomic, semantic relations and restrictions. A multi input feed-forward neural network model have been proposed and used to generate ontology entities vector representations, trained using noise contrastive estimation technique. This research gives a glimpse of the potential of the neural networks and embedding approaches to identify relationships between concepts and instances in ontologies, where the geometric relationships between the generated vector representations in the vector space fully reflect the semantic relations between the corresponding entities in the source ontology. Summing up the results, it can be concluded that the continuous vector representations model is relatively simple to grasp (linear algebra) and easy to implement. It makes it possible to find semantically equivalent entities in an ontology. Experiments also showed that its effectiveness depends for a large part on the quality of the representations in ontologies (concepts and semantic relations between them). In this paper, we have only examined different semantic relationships between concepts and instances. More broadly, we intend to concentrate on exploring different characteristics of the data types properties as well. Further studies are needed to apply the results of our approach in the ontology-engineering field tasks.

Acknowledgments. This paper is funded by the International Exchange Program of Harbin Engineering University for Innovation-oriented Talented Cultivation.

References

1. Gruber, T.R.: A translation approach to portable ontology specifications. Knowl. Acquisit. **5**(2), 199–220 (1993)
2. Gómez-Pérez, A., Corcho, O.: Ontology languages for the semantic web. IEEE Intell. Syst. **17**(1), 54–60 (2002)
3. Bengio, Y., Ducharme, R., Vincent, P., Jauvin, C.: A neural probabilistic language model. J. Mach. Learn. Res. **3**(Feb), 1137–1155 (2003)
4. Schwenk, H., Dchelotte, D., Gauvain, J.-L.: Continuous space language models for statistical machine translation. In: Proceedings of the COLING/ACL on Main Conference Poster Sessions, pp. 723–730. Association for Computational Linguistics (2006)
5. Schwenk, H.: CSLM-a modular open-source continuous space language modeling toolkit. In: INTERSPEECH, pp. 1198–1202 (2013)
6. Mikolov, T., Chen, K., Corrado, G., Dean, J.: Efficient estimation of word representations in vector space. arXiv preprint arXiv:1301.3781 (2013)
7. Mikolov, T., Sutskever, I., Chen, K., Corrado, G.S., Dean, J.: Distributed representations of words and phrases and their compositionality. In: Advances in Neural Information Processing Systems, pp. 3111–3119 (2013)
8. Mikolov, T., Yih, W., Zweig, G.: Linguistic regularities in continuous space word representations. In: Proceedings of the 2013 Conference of the North American Chapter of the Association for Computational Linguistics: Human Language Technologies, pp. 746–751 (2013)
9. Pennington, J., Socher, R., Manning, C.: GloVe: global vectors for word representation. In: Proceedings of the 2014 Conference on Empirical Methods in Natural Language Processing (EMNLP), pp. 1532–1543 (2014)
10. Roweis, S.T., Saul, L.K.: Nonlinear dimensionality reduction by locally linear embedding. Science **290**(5500), 2323–2326 (2000)
11. Tenenbaum, J.B., De Silva, V., Langford, J.C.: A global geometric framework for nonlinear dimensionality reduction. Science **290**(5500), 2319–2323 (2000)
12. Yan, S., Xu, D., Zhang, B., Zhang, H.-J.: Graph embedding: a general framework for dimensionality reduction. In: IEEE Computer Society Conference on Computer Vision and Pattern Recognition, CVPR 2005, vol. 2, pp. 830–837. IEEE (2005)
13. Yan, S., Xu, D., Zhang, B., Zhang, H.-J., Yang, Q., Lin, S.: Graph embedding and extensions: a general framework for dimensionality reduction. IEEE Trans. Pattern Anal. Mach. Intell. **29**(1), 40–51 (2007)

14. Grover, A., Leskovec, J.: node2vec: scalable feature learning for networks. In: Proceedings of the 22nd ACM SIGKDD International Conference on Knowledge Discovery and Data Mining, pp. 855–864. ACM (2016)
15. Ristoski, P., Rosati, J., Di Noia, T., De Leone, R., Paulheim, H.: Rdf2Vec: RDF graph embeddings and their applications. Semant. Web (Preprint), 1–32 (2018)
16. Cochez, M., Ristoski, P., Ponzetto, S.P., Paulheim, H.: Global RDF vector space embeddings. In: d'Amato, C., et al. (eds.) ISWC 2017. LNCS, vol. 10587, pp. 190–207. Springer, Cham (2017). https://doi.org/10.1007/978-3-319-68288-4_12
17. Bakarov, A.: A survey of word embeddings evaluation methods. CoRR, abs/1801.09536 (2018)
18. Schnabel, T., Labutov, I., Mimno, D., Joachims, T.: Evaluation methods for unsupervised word embeddings. In: Proceedings of the 2015 Conference on Empirical Methods in Natural Language Processing, pp. 298–307 (2015)
19. Mnih, A., Kavukcuoglu, K.: Learning word embeddings efficiently with noise-contrastive estimation. In: Advances in Neural Information Processing Systems, pp. 2265–2273 (2013)
20. Dyer, C.: Notes on noise contrastive estimation and negative sampling. arXiv preprint arXiv:1410.8251 (2014)
21. Gutmann, M., Hyvärinen, A.: Noise-contrastive estimation: a new estimation principle for unnormalized statistical models. In: Proceedings of the Thirteenth International Conference on Artificial Intelligence and Statistics, pp. 297–304 (2010)
22. Smith, B., et al.: The OBO foundry: coordinated evolution of ontologies to support biomedical data integration. Nat. Biotechnol. 25(11), 1251 (2007)
23. Whetzel, P.L., et al.: BioPortal: enhanced functionality via new web services from the national center for biomedical ontology to access and use ontologies in software applications. Nucleic Acids Res. 39(suppl_2), W541–W545 (2011)
24. van der Maaten, L., Hinton, G.: Visualizing data using t-SNE. J. Mach. Learn. Res. 9(Nov), 2579–2605 (2008)
25. Morales, J., et al.: A standardized framework for representation of ancestry data in genomics studies, with application to the NHGRI-EBI GWAS catalog. Genome Biology. 19(1), 21 (2018)

Automatic Sleep Staging Based on Deep Neural Network Using Single Channel EEG

Yongfeng Huang, Yujuan Zhang[✉], and Cairong Yan

School of Computer Science and Technology,
Donghua University, Shanghai 201620, China
yfhuang@dhu.edu.cn, 13262577380@163.com

Abstract. Sleep staging is the first step for sleep research and sleep disorder diagnosis. The present study proposes an automatic sleep staging model, named ResSleepNet, using raw single-channel EEG signals. Most of the existing studies utilize hand-engineered features to identify sleep stages. These methods may ignore some important features of the signals, and then influence the effect of sleep stage classification. Instead of hand-engineering features, we combine feature extraction and classification into an algorithm based on residual network and bidirectional long short-term memory network. In the proposed method, we develop a 22-layer deep network to automatically learn features from the raw single-channel EEG and classify sleep stages. Residual network can learn time-invariant features, and bidirectional long short-term memory can add learned transition rules among sleep stages to the network. The model ResSleepNet is tested on the Sleep-EDF database. We perform 10 experiments and get average overall accuracy of 90.82% and 91.75% for 6-state and 5-state classification of sleep stages. Experimental results show the performance of our model is better than the state-of-the-art sleep staging methods, and it yields high detection accuracy for identifying sleep stage S1 and REM. In addition, our model is also suitable for extracting features from other signals (EOG, EMG) for sleep stage classification.

Keywords: Residual network · Bidirectional long short-term memory ·
Sleep stage classification · Deep learning · Single channel EEG

1 Introduction

Sleep is an essential physiological process, which can eliminate fatigue and promote the body's recovery and growth. Insufficient sleep and insomnia are very harmful to the human body. Sleep staging is the basis for assessing sleep quality and diagnosing sleep related ailments [1] such as hypersomnia, sleep apnea syndrome and narcolepsy. Rechtschaffen and Kales (R&K) divided sleep stages into Wakefulness (W), Rapid Eye Movement (REM) and Non-Rapid Eye Movement (NREM) stage according to Electroencephalogram (EEG), Electrooculogram (EOG) and Electromyogram (EMG) recordings during sleeping of human beings [2] in 1968. The NREM sleep was further divided into S1, S2, S3 and S4 stage. The American Academy of Sleep Medicine (AASM) revised R&K standard in 2007, merging S3 and S4 into N3 (S1 and S2 were

© Springer Nature Switzerland AG 2019
L. Uden et al. (Eds.): KMO 2019, CCIS 1027, pp. 63–73, 2019.
https://doi.org/10.1007/978-3-030-21451-7_6

also called N1, N2) [3]. Sleep staging is generally performed based on Polysomnographic (PSG) recordings (including EEG, EOG and EMG) [4, 5]. Traditionally, overnight PSG recordings are visually staged by experts in accordance with the guidelines of R&K or a set of recommendations developed by AASM. Manual sleep staging, because of its time-consuming and human error, is not suitable for processing large data-sets [1]. Therefore, it is obvious that various automatic sleep staging methods have been proposed. Most of prior studies have demonstrated that EEG signals are very suitable for the data of sleep analysis [6]. There is gradually a great demand of a wearable and portable at-home sleep monitoring device integrating an automatic sleep staging scheme with less signals. Therefore, the majority of studies [7, 8] focus on employing single-channel EEG signals to identify sleep stages.

Previous approaches for automatic sleep stage classification generally extract some features from raw signals, and then use machine learning classification algorithms, which take advantage of these features to train models of identifying sleep stages [9]. Hassan et al. [10] used four statistical moments of single-channel EEG signals as features, based on tunable-Q wavelet transform (TQWT), and utilized bootstrap aggregating (Bagging) classifier to classify sleep stages. Zhu et al. [11] extracted nine features from Visibility Graph (VG) and Horizontal VG generated from single channel EEG, and support vector machine as the classifier.

Recently, in the field of deep learning, convolutional neural networks (CNNs) have made great breakthroughs in image classification [12] and speech recognition [13]. There is recently a trend of growth in using CNNs for processing one-dimensional biological signals (e.g. EEG, ECG, EMG) [14]. CNNs can learn the features of the signals with highly local correlation well. For instance, Tsinalis et al. [14] trained a 2-layer convolutional neural network to classify 5-state sleep stages. The advantage of deep networks is naturally integrating feature extraction and classification in an end-to-end multi-layer fashion, and the "levels" of features can be enriched by the depth of networks (the number of layers) [15]. Many studies [16, 17] show that the depth of network is crucial. For plain networks such as CNNs, with the depth of network increasing, the accuracies of the network models on the training set and test set begin to decline. It is difficult to train plain deeper network. He et al. [15] put forward residual network to ease the training of networks. The experiments show deep residual networks are easy to optimize, and ensure the improvement of accuracy from greatly increased depth. Ng et al. [18] trained a 34-layer residual network to detect 14-class arrhythmias from single-lead ECG signals. The experiments demonstrate their model exceeds the performance of cardiologist.

The literature on using recurrent neural networks (RNNs) for sleep staging is still rare. RNNs has a strong ability to express temporal and semantic information of sequential data. For instance, in natural language processing, RNNs can be used to predict next word based on the previous information. The advantage of RNNs is that they can be trained to extract time-related features of EEG signals. Sleep experts believe temporal information of previous sleep stages is an important factor to identify next sleep stage [19].

In this article, ResSleepNet, an automatic sleep staging model using raw single-channel EEG signals is proposed. We train a 22-layer deep network to classify sleep stages, which is different from the existing methods using hand-engineered features.

Instead of hand-engineering features, our network model integrates feature extraction and classification into an algorithm. CNN can learn the local features of the raw EEG signal. The introduction of shortcut connections into the network can further deepen the network, which enables model to learn more subtle features of the signals. Bidirectional long short-term memory (Bi-LSTM) can learn temporal information among sleep stages. When adding Bi-LSTM to the model, the classification accuracy is further improved. We train and test our model on Sleep-EDF database. The performance of the proposed model is compared with those of state-of-the-art methods using the same dataset. The experiments demonstrate that our model achieves better accuracy than the existing methods for the classification of 5-state and 6-state sleep stages. The rest of the paper is organized as follows: the proposed ResSleepNet model are introduced in Sect. 2. Section 3 describes experiments and results in detail. The discussion and conclusion are described in Sect. 4.

2 ResSleepNet

We train a 22-layer deep neural network, named ResSleepNet for this end-to-end learning task. The architecture of the ResSleepNet is shown in Fig. 1. The inputs of the network are 30-s epochs (one dimensional matrixs of 1 * 3000) of the raw single channel EEG signals, and the outputs are the predicted sleep stages. The first layer of the network is a convolutional layer. The middle consists of 8 residual blocks with 2 convolutional layers per block and 2 Bi-LSTM layers. The end of the network is 2 fully-connected layers and the softmax activation layer, which outputs a distribution over the 5/6 states of sleep staging for each epoch.

Residual network is mainly used to extract time-invariant features from single 30-s EEG epoch. In order to speed up the convergence of the ResSleepNet model and avoid gradient explosion/disappearance [20], in the residual blocks, we apply batch normalization (BN) [21] after each convolutional layer and before activation. To prevent overfitting, we also adopt dropout [22] between convolutional layers and after activation. The activation function utilized is rectified linear unit (ReLU). Because ReLU function has fast convergence and simpler implementation [23]. For shortcut connections, when the input and output has the same dimensions, identity shortcuts be utilized directly. While the dimensions of the outputs increase, we still perform identity shortcuts, with all zero padding that does not introduce extra parameters for increasing dimensions.

The first convolutional layer of the model have a filter length of 9. The length of filters of the other convolutional layers all are 5 in the residual blocks, and they are conducted using a stride of 1. The subsample layers use the Max Pooling operation with the filter length of 5 and the stride of 5. The initial value of the bias is set to 0.

After residual blocks, we apply a 2-layer Bi-LSTM to add learned temporal information between several adjacent sleep stages to sequences of extracted features of residual network. The Bi-LSTM is composed of two LSTMs with opposite directions, and so it can make full use of the past and future contextual information to judge the current state. Hidden sizes of forward and backward LSTMs are shown in each Bi-LSTM block.

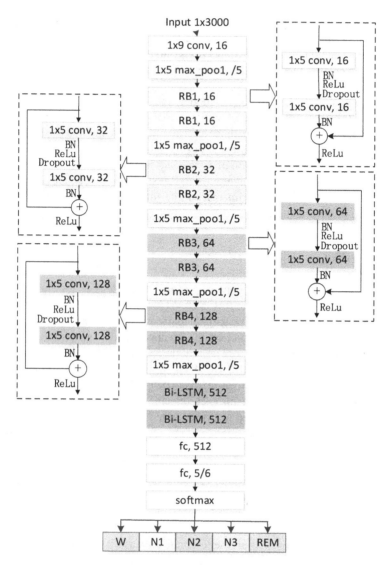

Fig. 1. The architecture of ResSleepNet for sleep staging. The RB refers to a residual block. The dotted rectangles are detailed description of the residual blocks, which contain two convolutional layers.

3   Experiments and Results

3.1   Data

The dataset that we utilized to perform the experiments is publicly available from the Sleep-EDF database at Physionet [24]. There are 61 PSG recordings in the database. In our work we use 39 PSGs which consist of the recordings of 10 males and 10 females

Table 1. Number of epochs for each sleep stage from Sleep-EDF database

	W	S1	S2	S3	S4	REM	Total
Train epochs	33441	2384	14850	2861	2017	6603	62156
Test epochs	5150	419	2949	509	316	1115	10458

(25–34 years old) numbered 00 through 19, without any sleep-related medication. The PSG recordings contain EEG (from Fpz-Cz and Pz-Oz electrode locations), EOG (horizontal), submental chin EMG, and an event marker [4]. The EOG and EEG signals were each sampled at 100 Hz. The EEG Pz-Oz signals was used as the single-channel EEG in our study. The length of each EEG recording is approximately 20 h. Each EEG epoch duration is 30 s (or 3000 samples), and it was manually classified by well-trained technicians into one of the eight classes: W, REM, 1, 2, 3, 4, M (Movement time) and ? (not scored). In the pre-processing, we exclude Movement time and not scored stages, because they are not part of sleep stages. Each recording has long periods of stage W at the beginning, in which a subject is awake. We just use part of such periods. Table 1 shows the number of epochs of each sleep state for all subjects in this study.

3.2 Implementation

Pre-processing. The PSG recordings contain EEG Fpz-Cz, EEG Pz-Oz and other signals, only the EEG Pz-Oz signals is used for our experiments. We download the PSG recordings and their corresponding sleep stages (labels) from the Sleep-EDF database. Then we separate EEG Pz-Oz signals from PSGs using blockEdfLoad function by MATLAB R2014b. Finally, the EEG signals are processed into epochs of 30 s, and the corresponding label of sleep stage is attached to each epoch. Table 1 shows the amount of data used to train and test the model.

Classifying. We implement our model using Google TensorFlow 1.2. It is an open source software library for numerical computation using dataflow graphs. TensorFlow has the advantages of good scalability, cross platform, rich interface and easy deployment. It can support CPUs, GPUs and mobile phones. We deploy the training and testing tasks of our ResSleepNet model to GPU. The type of GPU we used is NVIDIA Tesla K40c.

Table 2. Confusion matrix for 6-state sleep staging

True class	Predicted class						Sen
	S1	S2	S3	S4	W	REM	
S1	173	118	0	1	45	82	41.29%
S2	31	2745	72	2	12	87	93.08%
S3	0	84	317	108	0	0	62.28%
S4	0	1	42	273	0	0	86.39%
W	54	25	5	4	5043	19	97.92%
REM	45	111	0	0	12	947	84.93%

Table 3. Confusion matrix for 5-state sleep staging

True class	Predicted class					Sen
	N1	N2	N3	W	REM	
N1	173	115	1	68	62	41.29%
N2	46	2795	163	18	77	93.08%
N3	0	117	705	3	0	85.45%
W	40	25	1	5077	7	98.58%
REM	75	109	0	36	895	80.30%

3.3   Performance Analysis

Table 2 exhibits confusion matrix for 6-state classification on the test dataset. From the table we can see that W stage has the highest sensitivity of 97.92%, but the sensitivity of S1 stage is a little low. Actually, the epochs of S1 stage are easily misclassified into REM stage. And visual observation basically can not distinguish between them. The common drawback of existing methods is their poor ability to identify S1 and REM stage. The main reason is that the waveforms of the signals of stage S1 and REM are very similar. Besides, imbalance-class dataset may also lead to this problem. A sensitivity of 18.5% and 37.42% for S1 stage respectively are reported in [8] and [10] in 6-state classification. The identification of S1 stage of our model is better and yields a higher sensitivity of 41.29%. Furthermore, for the sensitivity value of REM and S2 stage, the proposed method gives 84.93% and 93.08% which are higher than [1, 8, 10]. The case of 5-state sleep stages is shown in Table 3, its performance comparison is similar to 6-state classification. In particular, the detection accuracy of S3-S4 (refers to N3) phase is better than most methods [6, 10, 11, 25].

3.4   Comparison with Plain Network

To prove the advantages of residual network for sleep staging, we build the other three different networks to compare with 20-layer residual network that we use in the ResSleepNet. The first is a plain network, except that shortcut connections are not introduce into the net, the rest of structure are exactly the same as our 20-layer residual network. The second is a 12-layer residual network, it consists of four residual blocks, the initial convolutional layer, the final two fully-connected layers and the softmax layer. The third is a plain network of 12 layers. For meaningful comparison, the four network models have the same hyper-parameters.

Figure 2 depicts the curves of error rates of sleep staging of the four networks on the test dataset along with the number of iterations. It is perfectly clear that as the number of iterations increases, the testing error rates of the four models are on clear downward trend, decreasing rapidly from the beginning and then tend to be steady. For 6-state sleep classification, we can see from (a) that for the plain neural networks, with increasing of network depth, the error rate of 20-layer model is higher than that of 12-layer. The result is not what we have expected: deeper networks can learn richer features for better results. This further illustrates that if the plain network is too deep,

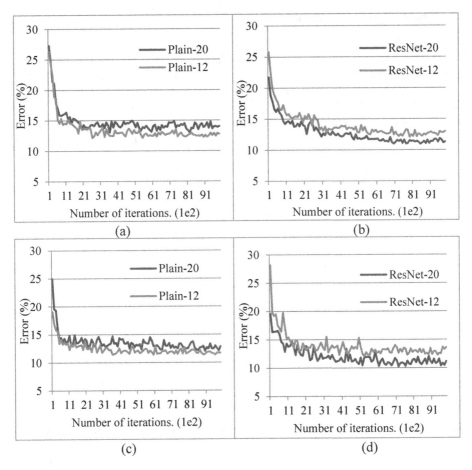

Fig. 2. Performance comparison of plain and residual networks with different network depth. (a) Comparison of the error rate of two plain networks for 6-state sleep staging. (b) Comparison of the error rate of two residual networks for 6-state sleep staging. (c) Comparison of the error rate of two plain networks for 5-state sleep staging. (d) Comparison of the error rate of two residual networks for 5-state sleep staging.

the accuracy will decline. The results are shown in (b) after introducing residual blocks into plain networks. We can see that the error rate of 20-layer residual network is lower than that of the 12-layer. The introduction of residual blocks can ensure that deeper network can get higher accuracy. For 5-state sleep stage classification, it can be seen from (c) and (d) that shallow residual network does not perform as well as plain network. However, the deeper 20-layer residual network has a lower error rate than 12-layer plain network. We can conclude that the 20-layer residual network achieves better results for 5-state and 6-state sleep classification.

3.5   The Analysis of Different Model

We train a 2-layer Bi-LSTM network for sleep stage classification to compare with our ResSleepNet and the 20-layer residual network. Figure 3 presents the box plot of the accuracies of these three model for 5-state sleep staging. The first is 2-layer Bi-LSTM with a lowest accuracy. When we try to increase the depth of this model, it has a lower accuracy. We argue that the model can not learn enough features from single EEG epoch when we only use Bi-LSTM. The second model is 20-layer residual network which achieves a better overall accuracy of 89%. When Bi-LSTM is added to the second model, the accuracy increases significantly. This proves that temporal correlation information among sleep stages learned by Bi-LSTM is useful for identify sleep stages.

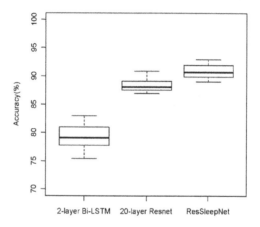

Fig. 3. The box plot of the accuracies of 2-layer Bi-LSTM, 20-layer Resnet and ResSleepNet model for 5-state sleep staging.

3.6   Comparison with Existing Methods

To assess the performance of our model, we compare our approach with the existing automated sleep staging methods. These methods all use the same EEG signals and Physionet's Sleep-EDF dataset. Table 4 shows the values of overall accuracy of some existing methods. Hassan et al. [25, 26] utilized hand-engineered features from the raw single channel signal to classify 6-state and 5-state sleep stages. Tsinalis et al. [27] used ensemble learning with an ensemble of stacked sparse autoencoders to classify 5-state sleep stages. Tsinalis et al. [14] only used a 2-layer convolutional neural network to identify 5 sleep stages, and achieved a lower accuracy. We think this is because the network is too shallow to fully learn the features of the signal. Deeper 16-layer VGG-FT model [28] got good results. All the accuracy values in the table are the best results for this method. Clearly, our method performs better than the other methods for both 5-state and 6-state sleep stage classification.

Table 4. Performance comparison of various methods on Sleep-EDF database. The highest accuracy value of each method is reported

Methods	6-state	5-state
Moment based features and adaptive boosting [26]	80.34%	82.03%
Statistical features, bagging [25]	85.57%	86.53%
Stacked sparse autoencoders [27]	–	82%
2-layer CNN [14]		76%
VGG-FT [28]	–	86%
Proposed method	**90.82%**	**91.75%**

3.7 Visualization of the Features

To better understanding how ResSleepNet classifies 30-s raw EEG epochs, we compare and analyze visualization of the features for 5-state sleep stage classification. To make the feature of each sleep stage clearer (not need to add temporal correction information among sleep stages to the model), we only use the part of model excluding 2-layer Bi-LSTM to extract the features of each sleep stage. Formally, suppose extracted features of the sleep stage c by our model can be represented as $\{X_1, \ldots X_n\}$. The average of the features for the sleep stage c can be $\{Z_1, \cdots, Z_n\}$, which is computed as follows:

$$Z_i = \frac{\sum_{i=1}^{N_{y_{pred}=c}} X_i}{N_{y_{pred}=c}} \tag{1}$$

where $N_{y_{pred}=c}$ is the number of 30-s EEG epochs that are predicted as sleep stage c by the model. We compute the average features of all sleep stages in the training for 5-stage sleep staging according to Eq. (1), and then we do the feature visualization. Figure 4 shows an example of features visualization of 5 sleep stages when the dimension n is set to 32. From the first row to the last row, each row corresponds to the 32-dimension vector. 0 to 4 indicate sleep stage W, N1, N2, N3 and REM respectively. We can see from the Fig. 4 that sleep stage W, N2 and N3 have obvious differences in their features, so they are easy to distinguish for the model. However, for stage N1 and REM, their features are very similar. It is difficult for the model to identify them. Besides, imbalance-class dataset also cause misclassification of sleep stages. We can draw conclusion from visual analysis, improving accuracy of identifying sleep stage N1 and REM is crucial for the improvement of overall accuracy.

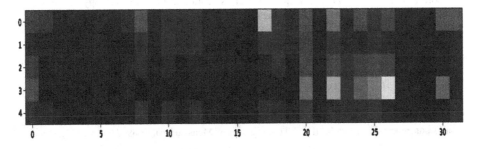

Fig. 4. The example of feature visualization for 5-state sleep staging.

4   Discussion and Conclusion

Compared with the state-of-the-art methods, our model can automatically learn features from raw EEG signals for sleep staging. The introduction of residual blocks optimizes the performance of the ResSleepNet model well. The depth of the network and the choice of hyper-parameters are both important factors that affect the performance of our model. More importantly, adding Bi-LSTM that can learn time-related features among adjacent sleep stages to the model helps to further improve classification accuracy. Even though the results 'are encouraging, our proposed model is still subject to several limitations. Actually, imbalance-class problem exists in dataset. It can be seen from Table 1 that the epochs of different sleep stages in number varies greatly. Stage W has the largest amount of data. The number of epochs of S1, S3 and S4 stage are relatively small compared to the rest of sleep stages. Class-imbalance might influence the performance of our model for automatic sleep staging to some extent.

In this paper, we train a 22-layer deep neural network model, named ResSleepNet, for automatic sleep staging based on raw single-channel EEG. Unlike the methods of hand-engineered features, our model can automatically learn features from one-dimensional original EEG epochs, and classify it into the corresponding sleep stage according to the learned features. Residual network is trained to deepen the depth of network to extract more abundant features from single EEG epoch, and 2-layer Bi-LSTM is used to learn time-related information among sleep stages from a sequence of EEG epochs. The experimental results demonstrated that the proposed model is efficient and effective. In addition, we compared and analyzed ResSleepNet and plain networks. The results proved that our model has a good performance on the Sleep-EDF database. In the future, we can apply this model to classify other biological signals such as ECG and EMG signals.

References

1. Hassan, A.R., Bhuiyan, M.I.H.: Computer-aided sleep staging using complete ensemble empirical mode decomposition with adaptive noise and boot strap aggregating. Biomed. Signal Process. Control **24**, 1–10 (2016)
2. Hsu, Y.L., Yang, Y.T., Wang, J.S., Hsu, C.Y.: Automatic sleep stage recurrent neural classifier using energy features of EEG signals. Neurocomputing **104**, 105–114 (2013)
3. Berry, R.B.: Rules for scoring respiratory events in sleep. J. Clin. Sleep Med. JCSM Off. Publ. Am. Acad. Sleep Med. **8**(5), 597–619 (2012)
4. Osorioforero, A.: Automatic sleep stages classification using EEG entropy features and unsupervised pattern analysis techniques. Entropy **16**(12), 6573–6589 (2014)
5. Lan, K.C., Chang, D.W., Kuo, C.E., Wei, M.Z.: Using off-the-shelf lossy compression for wireless home sleep staging. J. Neurosci. Methods **246**, 142–152 (2015)
6. Hassan, A.R., Bhuiyan, M.I.H.: Automatic sleep scoring using statistical features in the EMD domain and ensemble methods. Biocybern. Biomed. Eng. **36**(1), 248–255 (2016)
7. Imtiaz, S.A., Rodriguez-Villegas, E.: A low computational cost algorithm for REM sleep detection using single channel EEG. Ann. Biomed. Eng. **42**(11), 2344–2359 (2014)
8. Liang, S.: Automatic stage scoring of single-channel sleep eeg by using multiscale entropy and autoregressive models. IEEE Trans. Instrum. Meas. **61**(6), 1649–1657 (2012)

9. Aboalayon, K.A.I., Faezipour, M., Almuhammadi, W.S., Moslehpour, S.: Sleep stage classification using EEG signal analysis: a comprehensive survey and new investigation. Entropy **18**(9), 272 (2016)
10. Hassan, A.R., Subasi, A.: A decision support system for automated identification of sleep stages from single-channel EEG signals. Knowl.-Based Syst. **128**, 115–124 (2017)
11. Zhu, G., Li, Y., Wen, P.P.: Analysis and classification of sleep stages based on difference visibility graphs from a single-channel eeg signal. IEEE J. Biomed. Health Inf. **18**(6), 1813–1821 (2014)
12. Jia, X., Shen, L., Zhou, X., Yu, S.: Deep convolutional neural network based HEp-2 cell classification. In: International Conference on Pattern Recognition, pp. 77–80 (2017)
13. Xiong, W., Droppo, J., Huang, X., Seide, F., Seltzer, M., Stolcke, A.: Achieving human parity in conversational speech recognition. IEEE/ACM Trans. Audio Speech Lang. Process. **PP**(99)
14. Tsinalis, O., Matthews, P.M., Guo, Y., Zafeiriou, S.: Automatic sleep stage scoring with single-channel EEG using convolutional neural networks
15. He, K., Zhang, X., Ren, S., Sun, J.: Deep residual learning for image recognition. In: Proceedings of the IEEE Conference on Computer Vision and Pattern Recognition, pp. 770–778 (2015)
16. Simonyan, K., Zisserman, A.: Very deep convolutional networks for large-scale image recognition. Comput. Sci.
17. Szegedy, C., Liu, W., Jia, Y., Sermanet, P., Reed, S.: Going deeper with convolutions. In: Proceedings of the IEEE Conference on Computer Vision and Pattern Recognition, pp. 1–9 (2014)
18. Rajpurkar, P., Hannun, A.Y., Haghpanahi, M., Bourn, C., Ng, A.Y.: Cardiologist-level arrhythmia detection with convolutional neural networks
19. Supratak, A., Dong, H., Wu, C., Guo, Y.: DeepSleepNet: a model for automatic sleep stage scoring based on raw single-channel EEG. IEEE Trans. Neural Syst. Rehabil. Eng. **25**(11), 1998–2008 (2017)
20. Glorot, X., Bengio, Y.: Understanding the difficulty of training deep feed-forward neural networks. J. Mach. Learn. Res. **9**, 249–256 (2010)
21. Ioffe, S., Szegedy, C.: Batch normalization: accelerating deep network training by reducing internal covariate shift, pp. 448–456 (2015)
22. Hinton, G.E., Srivastava, N., Krizhevsky, A., Sutskever, I., Salakhutdinov, R.R.: Improving neural networks by preventing co-adaptation of feature detectors. Comput. Sci. **3**(4), 212–223 (2012)
23. Krizhevsky, A., Sutskever, I., Hinton, G.E.: ImageNet classification with deep convolutional neural networks. In: International Conference on Neural Information Processing Systems, pp. 1097–1105 (2012)
24. Goldberger, A.L., Amaral, L.A., Glass, L., Hausdorff, J.M., Ivanov, P.C.: PhysioBank, PhysioToolkit, and PhysioNet: components of a new research resource for complex physiologic signals. Circulation **101**(23), E215 (2000)
25. Hassan, A.R., Bashar, S.K., Bhuiyan, M.I.H.: On the classification of sleep states by means of statistical and spectral features from single channel electroencephalogram. In: International Conference on Advances in Computing, Communications and Informatics (2015)
26. Hassan, A.R., Bashar, S.K., Bhuiyan, M.I.H.: Automatic classification of sleep stages from single-channel electroencephalogram. In: India Conference (2016)
27. Tsinalis, O., Matthews, P.M., Guo, Y.: Automatic sleep stage scoring using time-frequency analysis and stacked sparse autoencoders. Ann. Biomed. Eng. **44**(5), 1587–1597 (2015)
28. Vilamala, A., Madsen, K.H., Hansen, L.K.: Deep convolutional neural networks for interpretable analysis of EEG sleep stage scoring, pp. 1–6 (2017)

Evolving Fuzzy Membership Functions for Soft Skills Assessment Optimization

Antonia Azzini, Stefania Marrara$^{(\boxtimes)}$, and Amir Topalović

Consortium for the Technology Transfer (C2T),
via Nuova Valassina, Carate Brianza, MB, Italy
{antonia.azzini,stefania.marrara,amir.topalovic}@consorzioc2t.it

Abstract. This work proposes the design of a decision support tool able to guide the choices of any company HR manager in the evaluation of the profiles of PhD candidates. This paper is part of an ongoing research in the field of PhD profiling. The novelty here is an evolutionary fuzzy model, based on the Membership Functions (MFs) optimization, used to obtain the soft skills candidate profiles. The general aim of the project is the definition of a set of fuzzy rules that are very similar to those that a HR expert would otherwise have to calculate each time for each selected profile and for each individual skill.

Keywords: Fuzzy logic · Evolutionary algorithms ·
Membership function optimization

1 Introduction

Since many years, those who have been facing a PhD course in Europe have been aware that a good percentage of them will not find a permanent position in the Academy, but will have to migrate to companies and public/private organizations that are not always ready to understand and enhance the research experience [6].

One of the problems at the basis of this misunderstanding between PhDs and companies is encountered during the recruitment phase. Most job matching portals are based on keyword searches in a candidate's CV, but the taxonomy used in job offers (also called *job vacancies*) is set on employers' vocabulary and usually does not match the words that a PhD would use to describe her experience. Consequently, it is widely recognized that there is a need to define a system that can support an Human Resources (HR) team in recruiting doctoral candidates.

In the analysis of the profiles of possible candidates for a job vacancy, the identification of skills is a very important but costly activity in terms of time for the HR team. To overcome this problem, some works in the literature adopt machine learning and fuzzy based approaches to manage, for example, employability [10], which, together with skills, takes into account personal attributes for the development of teaching strategies.

© Springer Nature Switzerland AG 2019
L. Uden et al. (Eds.): KMO 2019, CCIS 1027, pp. 74–84, 2019.
https://doi.org/10.1007/978-3-030-21451-7_7

This work is part of the project *"SOON - Skills Out of Narrative"*, which aims at designing a decision support tool able to guide the choices of any company HR manager in the evaluation of the profiles of PhD candidates.

The novelty of this work, compared to previous works in the same project [3–5], is focused on obtaining the soft skills candidate profiles by using an evolutionary fuzzy approach.

Since fuzzy models highly depend on the sets of terms underlying each variable and the fuzzy inference method adopted, although easy to design, they are often difficult to be tuned.

In this direction the evolutionary algorithm employed in this work aims at optimizing the Fuzzy Inference System (FIS) model by creating the population of Membership Functions (MFs). The interval values representing the MFs are encoded in the chromosome of the evolutionary algorithm as real numbers. The chromosome of each individual represents the diffusion of the MFs generated.

This approach is in fact able to compute a set of fuzzy rules that are very similar to those that a HR expert would otherwise have to calculate each time for each selected profile and for each individual skill.

The core of this work is the definition of an evolved model, whose behavior will be completely customized because computed on a dataset of pairs (profile, set of soft skills) that represents the decision-making behavior of a certain HR Manager rather than another.

The remaining of the paper is organized as follow. After a brief summary of the related works in Sect. 2, while the taxonomy is defined into Sect. 3. The soft skills profiles are defined into Sect. 4. Then, the evolutionary encoding of the MFs, together with the overall architecture of the approach and the details of the evolutionary algorithm, are reported into Sect. 5. Preliminary experiments are presented and discussed, together with the obtained results, in Sect. 6, while final remarks are reported in Sect. 7.

2   Related Work

The automatic extraction of meaningful information from unstructured texts has been mainly devoted to support the e-recruitment process [12], e.g., to help human resource departments to identify the most suitable candidate for an open position from a set of applicants or to help a job seeker in identifying the most suitable open positions. For example, the work described in [16] proposes a system which aims to analyze candidate profiles for jobs, by extracting information from unstructured resumes through the use of probabilistic information extraction techniques as Conditional Random Fields [11].

Differently, in [18] the authors define Structured Relevance Models (SRM), a context based extension of relevance-based language models for modeling and retrieving semi-structured documents, and describe their use to identify job descriptions and resumes vocabulary, while in [4], a methodology based on machine learning aimed at extracting the soft skills of a PhD from a textual, self-written, description of her competencies is described. In that paper a neuro-fuzzy controller defining a set of inference rules, similar to those setted by a HR expert, is proposed. Anyway, in that case the most critical aspect refers to the definition of the fuzzy MFs.

In fact, MFs are a crucial part of the definition as they define the mappings to assign meaning to input data. The MFs map crisp input observations of linguistic variables to degrees of membership in fuzzy sets to describe properties of the linguistic variables. Kroeske, for example, explains in [9] how suitable MFs are designed depending on the specific characteristics of the linguistic variables as well as peculiar properties related to their use in optimization systems.

Other works have been presented in this direction. Some of them consider the evolution of fuzzy rules, while some others are focused on the MFs deployment. A last set of approaches consider the optimization of both memberships and rules: in [8] the authors present a genetic algorithm to optimize the MFs used in determining fuzzy association rules. On the other hand, the genetic tuning algorithm implemented in [14] aims at optimizing both MFs and rules for the optimization of a fuzzy temperature controller. Herrera [7] proposes a review of classical models compared with the most recent trends for Genetic Fuzzy Systems, while an approach based on the fuzzy rules evolution has been more recently explained by Mankad and colleagues [13].

Other examples of evolutionary algorithms, as Differential Evolution and Evolutionary Strategies, are instead more natural for continuous optimization. In the work carried out in [17], two kinds of computational intelligence techniques were used to create the framework: a fuzzy logic system (FS) as the decision maker and evolutionary computation as the model parameter optimizer. In particular, FS membership function parameters have been optimized by using a differential evolution (DE) algorithm to find optimal model parameters. Also Adhikari and colleagues presented in their work [1] a fuzzy adaptive differential evolution (DE) for path planning. The path-planning problem was formulated as a multi-objective unconstrained optimization problem, with the aim of minimizing the costs as well as finding the shortest path. DE has been used for optimization with a fuzzy logic controller used to find the parameter values of DE during the optimization process. Evolutionary Strategies are then proposed by Santika and colleagues in [15] was based on an Evolution Strategy method to determine the appropriate rules for Sugeno FIS having the minimum forecasting error. Near to the work carried out into this project, the Mean Square Error (MSE) has been used to evaluate the goodness of the result (in their case a forecasting). The numerical experiments showed the effectiveness of the proposed optimized Sugeno FIS for several test-case problems, as well as the capability to produce the lower MSE comparable to those achieved by other well-known methods in the literature.

3   The Soft Skills Taxonomy

In the last years, recognizing, evaluating and in case enhancing soft skills in employees has been a hot topic in literature. *Soft or Transferable skills* enhance people future employability, adaptability and occupational mobility. Since FYD's mission is to promote researchers employment in companies, the core of the project is identifying the skills that can be transferred from the Academy experience. There is a lack of consistent theory for defining and classifying various skills, and there is no generally accepted transferable skills taxonomy. The European project team decided to distinguish three categories of skills: (1) soft skills; (2) generic hard skills; (3) specific hard skills. Specific hard skills are characterized by their lower level of transferability, whereas soft skills and generic hard skills are skills with high transferability across sectors and occupations and can be identified as transversal skills. Focusing on researchers our attention was centered on capturing the soft skills that support the innovation activity. Having these skills, which can be transferred from one context to another, is a good basis for accumulation of specific skills required by a given job expected in managing a robust innovation pipeline and portfolio to deliver new growth opportunities.Therefore, our approach classifies the researcher soft skills into 6 categories: *carefulness*, i.e., the candidate is careful to look at or consider every part of something to make certain it is correct or safe; *creativity*, i.e., the ability to produce original and unusual ideas, or to make something new or imaginative; *unexpected/emergency* i.e., the ability to deal in an effective way with something that happens suddenly or expectantly and needs fast action in order to avoid harmful results; *uncertainty*, i.e., the ability to deal with a situation in which something is not known, or with something that is not known or certain; *communication*, i.e., the ability to communicate with people; and *networking*, i.e., the process of meeting and talking to a lot of people, esp. in order to get information that can help you.

Each skill category is divided into several classes, each class representing a particular soft skill. A detailed description of the taxonomy is available in [4].

4 PhDs Profiles Definition

As described in [1,2], in the *"SOON - Skills Out of Narrative"* project each PhD is required to provide two textual descriptions of her experience, the *curriculum vitae (CV)* and a questionnaire composed by 13 free text questions called *experience pills*, or simply *pills*, in which she is loosely guided to describe her soft skills. The approach extracts the skills from the text provided by cv and pills and creates a formal representation of the researcher, the profile.

In literature several techniques that can be applied to create the PhD profile are presented, at present the vector based representation developed by the Information Retrieval researchers for documents representation is adopted. In the vector based model a document D is represented as an *m-dimensional* vector, where each dimension corresponds to a distinct term and m is the total number of terms used in the collection of documents.

From this basis, in this approach a profile RP is composed by two vectors, $RP = (H, S)$ where H is the vector representing the hard skills of the PhD, while S represents her soft skills. The hard skills vector H is not focus of this paper (see [4]). The soft skills vector S is written as $(x_1, ..., x_n)$, where x_j is the weight of skill s_j and n is the number of skills defined in the soft skills proprietary taxonomy described in [4]. If the profile does not contain a skill then the corresponding weight is zero.

PhD Soft Skills Representation. Every item of the vector S is a linguistic 2-tuple value [7] representing the degree the PhD possesses that soft skill. Note that a positional notation is used: $S = (s_1, s_2, .., s_k)$, where $s_j \in S$, with $j = \{1, ..., 60\}$, describes the linguistic degree assigned to the $j - th$ skill of the PhD.

The vector of soft skills S is computed by taking into account two contributions. The first contribution to S is a vector HR of 60 skills, which represents the assessment the HR operator performs during an interview with the candidate. To allow a flexible assessment, but avoiding at the same time an excessive overhead for the HR operator, this vector adopts a representation with 5 labels (L^5) plus the NC value (NC =not classified) to describe each skill. Note that during an interview the HR operators explicitly assess only a few skills (usually 6 or 7), all other skills are set to NC by default.

- $L^5 = \{l_0 = VeryLow = VL, l_1 = Low = L, l_2 = Medium = M, l_3 = High = H, l_4 = Full = F\}$

The second contribution to S is the vector ML of 60 skills that represents the automatic assessment of the candidate performed by the machine learning based classifier, presented in [3,4] . After a preprocessing phase in which the raw text is divided into sentences, each sentence is analyzed to extract the skills. The ML classifier analyses the textual self description each PhD is required to provide when she enrolls to the project. In order to allow a high flexibility for the ML vector we adopt a representation with 11 labels (L^{11}) to assess each skill (s_j).

- $L^{11} = \{L_0 = Null = N, l_1 = VeryVeryLow = VVL, l_2 = VeryLow = VL, l_3 = Low = L, l_4 = AlmostMedium = AM, l_5 = Medium = M, l_6 = MoreThanMedium = MM, l_7 = AlmostHigh = AH, l_8 = High = H, l_9 = VeryHigh = VH, l_{10} = Full = F\}$

The final vector S employs 11 labels as the vector ML.

The result obtained from the vector product of the labels of the two HR and ML vectors (added to the null case rule, i.e. $(5 * 11) + 1$) represents the total number of rules that are generated and then evaluated by a FIS model.

5   The Approach

The architecture of the tool able to extract the soft skills profiles for a PhD is shown in Fig. 1.

The PhD registering to the project is asked to provide a textual description of her transverse competencies: the questionnaire called "pills".

The *Text Preprocessing & Skills ML Extraction* module is in charge to extract a soft skills vector (in Figure is the *Soft-Skills ML Vector*) from the textual content of the "pills". In this approach the HR Operator, during the interview, compiles a report regarding her evaluation of the soft skills of the candidate via a simple interface (in Figure *HR Interface*) that guides the compilation of the *Soft-Skills HR Vector*. Please note that even if a complete evaluation of the candidate would require an assessment of each of the 60 soft skills available in the adopted taxonomy, this is not necessary here, and the operator is required to give an explicit assessment only to the few skills (usually 6/7) he really saw during the interview. The others skills in the *Soft-Skills HR Vector* are automatically set to NC (*not classified*).

The two soft skills vectors are used by the *Evolutionary Module* to compute the final *Soft Skills RP Vector* that composes the Researcher Profile (RP). Section 5.2 detail how the *Evolutionary Module* works.

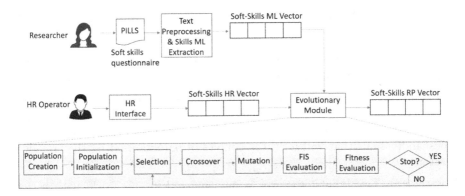

Fig. 1. Architecture of the HR supporting tool.

5.1 Evolutionary Encoding of Fuzzy Membership Functions

In the evolutionary module an individual represents the overall space coverage as its chromosome encodes the MFs associated to the different linguistic degrees in the fuzzy partition considered by the FIS module. In particular each individual chromosome encodes the MFs for each of the two input vectors that define a candidate soft skills profile, i.e., the *ML* and the *HR* vector.

Each MF is represented in the chromosome by the triple (a, c, b), where (a, b) represent the edges of the triangle base, while c represents triangle center. Note that almost all the MFs are represented by non-symmetric triangles. An example of an individual encoding is shown in Fig. 2. All the MFs are randomly initialized in $[-0.5, 0.5)$.

5.2 Evolutionary Algorithm

The evolutionary phase of the algorithm starts with a population of N individuals, with randomly generated chromosomes, and, on the basis of a first fitness evaluation, the individuals are evolved by the evolutionary cycle till the stop condition is reached, as shown in the grey selection of Fig. 1.

In each generation the worst individuals of the population are replaced with the new ones generated after crossover and mutation. The obtained results are used to calculate the performances (i.e. the fitness) of the individuals. The evolutionary process is stopped accordingly to one of these conditions: (1) no new

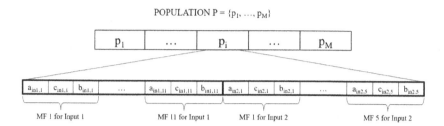

Fig. 2. Individual chromosome representation.

best value was given in the past n iteration; where n is set to 25, or (2) the maximum number of generations is reached.

Selection: the Tournament Selection is implemented by choosing the best individual among a group of x individuals, randomly selected, from the overall population. In this work x is set to 15. The selection is repeated in order to obtain the 10 best individuals that will form the couples of parents used by the crossover operator.

Crossover: a Two-Point Crossover is implemented in this work, with *pcross* probability. It's applied over the five couples of individuals obtained from the selection operator. The two-point crossover is carried out by considering two different cutting points, one for each of the inputs, respectively the ML and the HR vectors, applied over each chromosome of the two parents.

Mutation: is applied, with a probability *pmut*, to each MF of the offspring generated from the crossover operator. The elements involved in the mutation are, hence, the vectors $<a, b, c>$ that define each MF. The mutation is applied with the same probability on each element of the vector and on their respective combinations with a mutation rate $pmut_{rate}$.

After each mutation all MFs are checked and those that are included into larger ones and, with centers c_1 and c_2 shifted by a small distance δ, are deleted, since their contribution becomes negligible with respect to the overall individual behavior (Delete Mutation).

Fitness Evaluation: the fitness of each individual, $fitness = \frac{1}{MSE}$, refers to a maximization problem, and it is calculated over the result produced by the FIS Evaluation module according to the Mean Square Error (MSE). MSE measures the similarity between the estimated model (the soft skill S vector) and the expected one (created by hand by the HR team and modeled as a Mamdani fuzzy system) as explained by the Eq. 1.

$$MSE = \frac{1}{N} \sum_{j=1}^{N} (S_j - O_j)^2 \tag{1}$$

N corresponds to the population dimension, S_j is the output calculated by the evolving fuzzy approach, while O_j is the output defined by the fuzzy system modeled by hand.

6   Preliminary Experiments and Discussion

This approach represents the first step of an ongoing research project that aimed at defining an automatic approach for the representation of the human expert knowledge in the recruiting process. A first set of experiments has been carried out in order to test the defined architecture.

A benchmark dataset was prepared by analyzing about 600 questionnaires gathered by the HR team cooperating with the project, by dividing each questionnaire answer in sentences, and by labeling each sentence with the most appropriate soft skill. This analysis step gathered around 15,000 labeled sentences. Unfortunately not all the soft skills categories detailed in the taxonomy were populated enough to perform a classifier training task. The most populated category was "communication" with around 5000 sentences randomly partitioned in the 9 soft skills belonging to this area, and stating the classes of the ML classifiers.

For this reason a preliminary evaluation was performed only on this area, with the aim to assess the benefits of using an evolutionary approach applied to a fuzzy system in this context. The benchmark creation activity is currently an ongoing work, with the aim to complete the labeling of all questionnaires available now in the full collection.

The evolutionary process runs over a population of 50 individuals randomply created, for 200 generations, while the dataset was used to evolve. After the selection of the best 5 couples individuals, chosen by the tournament, the crossover is applied to the selected parents with a *pcross* probability set to 0.5. The mutation of the generated offspring is applied with a *pmut* probability set to 0.2., with a $pmut_{rate}$ set to 0.14. The fitness curve of the best individual resulting from the application of the fuzzy evolutionary approach over the test set is reported into Fig. 3. It is possible to observe how the function, which is a maximization, results to be increasing over the execution time, until the maximum number of generations is reached.

The output has been validated by comparing the results obtained by the evolving fuzzy approach with a Mamdani fuzzy system manually defined by the HR manager as shown in Table 1. The input values correspond respectively, to the encoding of the labels reported into the ML and HR input vectors, while the output produced corresponds to the ownership intensity of the analyzed soft skills.

The obtained results suggest that the Evolving Fuzzy approach follows the behaviour of the HR expert whenever she is not available, with an accuracy of the best individual equal to 93.9% and an averaged MSE equal to 6.1%, thus representing a good automation of her reasoning when assessing profiles.

Moreover, the evaluations carried out on the skills by the evolving fuzzy approach show a cautious and prudent attitude, especially when the assessment made by the human expert is really different from that made by the evolutionary approach.

Moreover, the experiments carried out in this work highlight that, as shown by comparing Figs. 4 and 5, the elimination of all the MFs with a negligible behavior, allows to reduce the overall number of rules that have to be evaluated

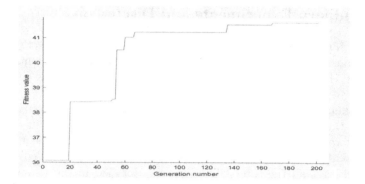

Fig. 3. Fitness function of the best individual calculated over the test set.

Table 1. Comparative results between the mamdani and the evolutionary fuzzy approach.

Output	Inputs (ML, HR)								
	$(-0.3, -0.3)$	$(-0.3, 0)$	$(-0.3, 0.3)$	$(0, -0.3)$	$(0, 0)$	$(0, 0.3)$	$(0.3, -0.3)$	$(0.3, 0)$	$(0.3, 0.3)$
Mamdani	-0.2241	-0.2000	0.0009	-0.1000	0.0009	0.1000	0.0545	0.1545	0.3241
Evo-fuzzy	-0.2040	-0.2000	-0.0907	-0.0356	-0.0339	0.0410	0.1679	0.1419	0.2731

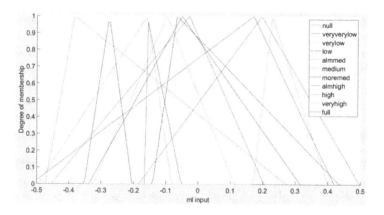

Fig. 4. Triangular evolved membership functions distribution without delete mutation.

each time by the fuzzy system, by also reducing the computational costs of the entire approach. In this case the total number of triangles was reduced from 11 to 8, and the total number of FIS rules from 56 to 41. The evolutionary approach has also allowed the triangular MFs not to saturate at the extremes of the crisp values, but to obtain discrete values.

Preliminary evaluations show that MFs mostly disappear in the set of ML inputs, by simplifying the corresponding individual encoding. In this sense the evolutionary algorithm is able to optimize the MFs by approximating the behavior of a human expert.

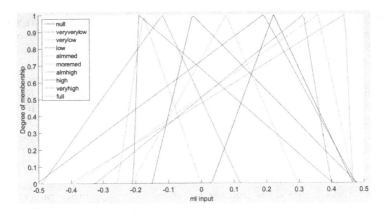

Fig. 5. Triangular evolved membership functions distribution with delete mutation.

With respect to our previous work [5], in which it was necessary to have knowledge of the output of the Neuro-Fuzzy model in order to build the FIS model, the evolutionary fuzzy approach here presented requires only an expected profile of the PhD (manually created by the HR team), while the FIS model is built by means of an evolutionary algorithm. Moreover, a smaller number of MFs reduces the computational complexity of the FIS model.

7 Conclusion

In this paper an evolutionary fuzzy approach is used to compute the vector of soft skills that composes a profile. The vector is the output of two contributes: one obtained by human assessment, and one obtained by extracting the soft skills from a textual self description. The evolutionary tuning algorithm employed in this works aims at optimizing the fuzzy membership functions. Preliminary results show that the evolutionary fuzzy approach well approximates the reasoning of a human expert when assessing profiles. Moreover, differently from the previous approach [4], the evolutionary approach allows to automatically define the FIS system without any previous knowledge of the desired output. Future work will investigate the application of the proposed approach in other contexts of HR recruitment, besides PhD, thus collecting more datasets to better test the hypothesis of creating a good "HR manager bot".

References

1. Adhikari, D., Kim, E., Reza, H.: A fuzzy adaptive differential evolution for multi-objective 3D uav path optimization. In: Proceedings of the IEEE Conference on Evolutionary Computation (CEC), June 2017
2. Azzini, A., Galimberti, A., Marrara, S., Ratti, E.: A taxonomy of researchers soft skills (2017)

3. Azzini, A., Galimberti, A., Marrara, S., Ratti, E.: A classifier to identify soft skills in a researcher textual description. In: Sim, K., Kaufmann, P. (eds.) EvoApplications 2018. LNCS, vol. 10784, pp. 538–546. Springer, Cham (2018). https://doi.org/10.1007/978-3-319-77538-8_37

4. Azzini, A., Galimberti, A., Marrara, S., Ratti, E.: SOON: supporting the evaluation of researchers' profiles. In: Uden, L., Hadzima, B., Ting, I.-H. (eds.) KMO 2018. CCIS, vol. 877, pp. 3–14. Springer, Cham (2018). https://doi.org/10.1007/978-3-319-95204-8_1

5. Azzini, A., Marrara, S., Topalovic, A.: A neuro-fuzzy approach to assess the soft skills profile of a PhD. In: Fullér, R., Giove, S., Masulli, F. (eds.) WILF 2018. LNCS (LNAI), vol. 11291, pp. 134–147. Springer, Cham (2019). https://doi.org/10.1007/978-3-030-12544-8_11

6. Box, S.: Transferable skills training for researchers supporting career development and research: supporting career development and research. OECD Publishing (2012)

7. Herrera, F.: Genetic fuzzy systems: status, critical considerations and future directions. Int. J. Comput. Intell. Res. **1**(1), 59–67 (2005)

8. Kaya, M., Alhajj, R.: Utilizing genetic algorithms to optimize membership functions for fuzzy weighted association rules mining. Appl. Intell. **24**(1), 7–15 (2006)

9. Kroeske, J., Ghandar, A., Michalewicz, Z., Neumann, F.: Learning fuzzy rules with evolutionary algorithms—an analytic approach. In: Rudolph, G., Jansen, T., Beume, N., Lucas, S., Poloni, C. (eds.) PPSN 2008. LNCS, vol. 5199, pp. 1051–1060. Springer, Heidelberg (2008). https://doi.org/10.1007/978-3-540-87700-4_104

10. Kumar, S., Kumari, R., Sharma, V.: Adaptive neural fuzzy inference system for employability assessment. Int. J. Comput. Appl. Technol. Res **3**, 159–164 (2014)

11. Lafferty, J., McCallum, A., Pereira, F.: Conditional random fields: probabilistic models for segmenting and labeling sequence data. In: Proceedings of the Eighteenth International Conference on Machine Learning, ICML, vol. 1, pp. 282–289 (2001)

12. Lee, I.: Modeling the benefit of e-recruiting process integration. Decis. Support Syst. **51**(1), 230–239 (2011)

13. Mankad, K., Sajja, P., Akerkar, R.: Evolving rules using genetic fuzzy approach - an educational case study. Int. J. Soft Comput. IJSC **2**(1), 35–44 (2011)

14. Mudholkar, R., Somnatti, V.: Genetic tuning of fuzzy inference system for furnace temperature controller. Int. J. Comput. Sci. Inf. Technol. **6**(4), 3496–3500 (2015)

15. Santika, G., Mahmudy, W., Naba, A.: Rule optimization of fuzzy inference system sugeno using evolution strategy for electricity consumption forecasting. Int. J. Electr. Comput. Eng. **7**, 2241–2252 (2017)

16. Singh, A., Rose, C., Visweswariah, K., Chenthamarakshan, V., Kambhatla, N.: PROSPECT: a system for screening candidates for recruitment. In: Proceedings of the 19th ACM International Conference on Information and Knowledge Management, pp. 659–668. ACM (2010)

17. Vorachart, V., Takagi, H.: Evolving fuzzy logic rule-based game player model for game development. Int. J. Innov. Comput. Inf. Control **13**(6), 1941–1951 (2017)

18. Yi, X., Allan, J., Croft, W.B.: Matching resumes and jobs based on relevance models. In: Proceedings of the 30th Annual International ACM SIGIR Conference on Research and Development in Information Retrieval, pp. 809–810. ACM (2007)

Unsupervised Deep Clustering
for Fashion Images

Cairong Yan[✉], Umar Subhan Malhi, Yongfeng Huang,
and Ran Tao

School of Computer Science and Technology,
Donghua University, Shanghai, China
cryan@dhu.edu.cn

Abstract. In many visual domains like fashion, building an effective unsupervised clustering model depends on visual feature representation instead of structured and semi-structured data. In this paper, we propose a fashion image deep clustering (FiDC) model which includes two parts, feature representation and clustering. The fashion images are used as the input and are processed by a deep stacked autoencoder to produce latent feature representation, and the output of this autoencoder will be used as the input of the clustering task. Since the output of the former has a great influence on the later, the strategy adopted in the model is to integrate the learning process of the autoencoder and the clustering together. The autoencoder is trained with the optimal number of neurons per hidden layers to avoid overfitting and we optimize the cluster centroid by using stochastic gradient descent and backpropagation algorithm. We evaluate FiDC model on a real-world fashion dataset downloaded from Amazon where images have been extracted into 4096-dimensional visual feature vectors by convolutional neural networks. The experimental results show that our model achieves state-of-the-art performance.

Keywords: Unsupervised clustering · Representation learning · Autoencoder · Fashion images

1 Introduction

Fashion is a hot topic in computer vision domain, and it gives many challenging problems to fundamentals of computer vision task - cross image matching [1, 2], recognition [3], human body parsing [4, 5]. At the same time research agenda forecasting fashion trends require unsupervised fashion images clustering for discovering fashion trends based on visual appearance [6]. In literature, limited research explores fashion clustering which motivates us to perform unsupervised deep clustering on real-world fashion dataset.

Unlike supervised classification, an unsupervised classifier is trained to find a representation of image features without labelling data which leads to perform unsupervised clustering. While in clustering task, widely used algorithms are K-means [7], Spectral clustering and Gaussian mixture model [8]. All these algorithms utilize

© Springer Nature Switzerland AG 2019
L. Uden et al. (Eds.): KMO 2019, CCIS 1027, pp. 85–96, 2019.
https://doi.org/10.1007/978-3-030-21451-7_8

distance base similarity to make clusters. While in high dimensional data space distance base similarity becomes ineffective because of "curse of dimensionality" problem [9].

To tackle the curse of dimensionality problem most of literature studies give a solution to convert high dimension data to low dimensions called latent space. Afterwards, clustering assignment on latent space representation will be performed [10–12]. There are two possible ways to perform clustering assignment on latent space. First, we can reduce dimension independently and perform clustering direct on latent space. Second, we can jointly perform latent features learning and clustering.

In a case in which no additional clustering loss is used may have worse latent representation or it will breakdown clustering assignment because of independent latent space representation learning [13]. On the hand recent work of deep clustering add priori knowledge to learn better latent representation [14, 15]. Second way which we adopt, perform clustering assignment and latent representation leaning simultaneously under the same network which transforms input x to reconstruction output z and minimum reconstruction loss ensure that we didn't lose any important information during latent representation learning. In such case we also used target distribution information which leads to learn meaningful latent representation [16].

In a specific domain like fashion, most of the research work utilizes text based nonvisual attribute to perform clustering task. In such case, we have to describe visual representation of a product manually according to their pattern, color, material which is quite expensive task. Practically we utilize these nonvisual attribute to perform article mapping, retrieve products, describe fashion as well as for clustering task [6]. Unlike prior work we perform fashion images clustering based on visual appearance without any label information.

In this paper, we adopt a technique which learns clustering-friendliness latent representation space. Initially, we perform initial clustering assignment on latent dimension. Afterwards, we optimize it by minimizing the Kullback-Leibler divergence loss to improve feature representation and data distribution with auxiliary target distribution.

To evaluate our model FiDC efficiency, we perform our experiments on real-world fashion dataset downloaded from Amazon. For experiments we preprocess dataset which consists image feature extracted from CNN and ground truth label. In such a way that we train our network to discover similar visual space without looking at any training sample.

This paper is structured as follows. In Sect. 2 we will describe the network that yields the fashion images deep clustering (FiDC) Model. Additionally, we expand our framework explanation into Sect. 3 which clarify how autoencoder and clustering layer work simultaneously. In experimental Sect. 4, we will introduce a real-world fashion data set, a feature extraction method and evaluation of the algorithm. In the last section, we will conclude our work and discuss future direction.

2 Fashion Clustering Framework Based on Deep Autoencoder

Fashion images deep clustering (FiDC) framework is established on deep stacked autoencoder. In this section we will clarify FiDC architecture and autoencoder configuration to learn better feature representation. Moreover we will explain how Clustering layers and optimization technique work under the same network.

Figure 1 explains the architecture of FiDC. This network is trained on fashion images data where visual feature of each image extracted by CNN, i.e. F = 4096 vector dimension explained in Sect. (4.2). In such high dimensional data space Euclidean distance become ineffective because of the curse of dimensionality [9], so instead of performing clustering algorithm direct on data space X. we transform data to low dimension, i.e. Y = 256 node called latent feature space.

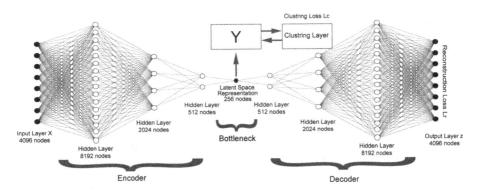

Fig. 1. The architecture of fashion images deep clustering model

Additionally, we adopt deep stacked autoencoder to learn useful features representation which makes our classifier flawless by following [17] work to learn useful Representations in a Deep Network. We train our model in such a way that which initialize with an appropriate weight—first input layer trained on noised input data and remaining layers on original input data.

For pre-training of the network, we initialize with the optimal parameter which discovers interesting representation of data by layer-wise training of deep stacked autoencoder. In this kind of network configuration number of hidden layers, nodes per hidden layer and deviation of noise are susceptible [18]. While to avoid overfitting of our model we initiate first hidden layer in the stack with 8192 nodes and this value is much larger than the input dimension 4096 [19, 20]. In general, for compression of data overfitting doesn't matter but to find a meaningful pattern for data distribution it becomes essential [20]. Most of recent work Parametric t-SNE, DEC, IDEC [11, 12] follow experimental setup employed by Salakhutdinov and Hinton work [21] which used (input − 500 − 500 − 2000 − d) network dimension which perform worst behavior in our dataset. In our model bottleneck is the significant point which is obtained by passing through the whole network, forced to learn a small representation of high dimensional data. We discover 256 node representation allows much more accurate performance [19].

A clustering layer is put at the top of bottleneck point, thus in the supervised way we optimize our network using Stochastic Gradient Descent (SGD) and backpropagation.

3   Clustering Method

3.1   Latent Space Learning Using Deep Stacked Autoencoder

An autoencoder is a neural network for unsupervised learning which implies back propagation, in which we trained network in a way that reduced representation should be equal to input values as close as possible i.e. $y^i \approx x^i$.

In our model, by getting motivation from Denoising autoencoder (DAE), we train autoencoder in which input value x and Output Value z are not same as like simple mapping which just memorizes data. We input to NN a stochastically corrupting data $\tilde{x}$ which contain slight noise on original data x. Then autoencoder is trained against original data and predicts missing input data. See Fig. 2.

$$y = f_e(W\tilde{x} + b) \tag{1}$$

where y donate feature representation code, W is input to hidden layer weight, b as bias, $W\tilde{x} + b$ referred input to the hidden layer and f_e is rectified linear unit (relu) as activation function [22] for all hidden layers of encoder and decoder part.

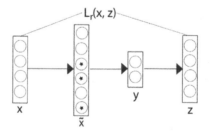

Fig. 2. Denoising autoencoder

The reconstruction z is obtained by using the mapping function f_d

$$z = f_d(W'^{\tilde{x}} + b') \tag{2}$$

where W' donate as tied weights and f_d represent decoding function.

Figure 1 shows that the FiDC model contains three hidden layers in both encoding and decoding part. The resultant value of the first encoding layers will be the input of the next encoding layer. Suppose we have L hidden layers and k referred activation and decoding function of the kth layer. Then activation and decoding function of the kth encoding layer will be defined as

$$y^{(k+1)} = f_e\left(Wy^k + b^{(k+1)}\right) \tag{3}$$

$$z^{(k+1)} = f_d\left(W^{(L-K)^T}Z^k + b'^{(k+1)}\right) \tag{4}$$

where k initialize from 0, $y^{(0)}$ is original data and $y^{(L)}$ refer to the last encoding layer, $z^{(0)}$ first decoding layer, $z^{(L)}$ is last decoding layer and T donate to transform matrix.

Cross-entropy loss $L_r(x, z)$ which is a loss between input value x and reconstructed value z that is utilized as an objective function for updated weight in stochastic gradient descent.

$$\begin{aligned} L_r(\mathbf{x}, \mathbf{z}) =& \alpha\left(-\sum_{J \in J(\tilde{x})} \left[x_j log z_j + (1 - x_j) \log(1 - z_j)\right]\right) \\ &+ \beta \sum_{J \notin J(\tilde{x})} \left[x_j log z_j + (1 - x_j) \log(1 - z_j)\right] \end{aligned} \tag{5}$$

Where $J\tilde{x}$ is referred to the index of corrupted data from x.

3.2 Clustering Layer

Clustering layer convert original input feature x to soft label q_{ij} suppose we have n data points, k number of clusters and initial cluster center μ_j i.e. calculated by K means, where j = 1..., k. we perform clustering assignment on Y latent feature representation space which is much more smaller than original input x. First, we utilize Student's t-distribution [11, 12, 23] to calculate the probability between cluster centers μ_j and embedded points y_j (corresponding to x_j) i.e. soft assignment q_{ij}. While in second step by using an auxiliary target distribution, we refine our cluster's center by learning from high confidence assignments.

$$q_{ij} = \frac{\left(1 + \|y_i - \mu_i\|^2\right)^{-1}}{\sum_j \left(1 + \|y_i - \mu_i\|^2\right)^{-1}} \tag{6}$$

And p_{ij} target distribution defined as

$$p_{ij} = \frac{q_{ij}^2 / \sum_j q_{ij}}{\sum_j q_{ij}^2 / \sum_j q_{ij}} \tag{7}$$

The encoder is fine-tuned by optimizing the following objective and predicts the label for x_i is arg $max_i q_{ij}$

$$L = KL(P|Q) = \sum_i \sum_j p_{ij} log \frac{p_{ij}}{q_{ij}} \tag{8}$$

where L represent KullbackLeibler divergence loss that measures the non-symmetric difference between target distributions p_i and soft assignment q_i.

3.3   Optimization

We fine-tune weights using stochastic gradient descent (SGD) and backpropagation algorithms. The gradient of L corresponding to each embedding point y_i and each cluster center μ_j are calculated as reference [10].

$$\frac{\partial L}{\partial y_j} = \sum_j \left(1 + \|y_i - \mu_j\|^2\right)^{-1} \times \left(P_{ij} - q_{ij}\right)\left(y_i - \mu_j\right) \tag{9}$$

$$\frac{\partial L}{\partial u_j} = -\sum_i \left(1 + \|y_i - \mu_j\|^2\right)^{-1} \times \left(P_{ij} - q_{ij}\right)\left(y_i - \mu_j\right) \tag{10}$$

The cluster centroids are updated by the following setting: learning rate $\lambda = 0.001$ the coefficient of clustering $\gamma = 0.1$ batch size m = 256

$$\mu_j = \mu_j - \frac{\lambda}{m} \sum_{i=1}^m \left(\frac{\partial L_c}{\partial \mu_j}\right) \tag{11}$$

The autoencoder and decoder weights are updated by the following formulation.

$$W = W - \frac{\lambda}{m} \sum_{i=1}^m \left(\frac{\partial L_r}{\partial W} + \gamma \frac{\partial L_c}{\partial W}\right) \tag{12}$$

$$W' = W' - \frac{\lambda}{m} \sum_{i=1}^m \left(\frac{\partial L_r}{\partial W}\right) \tag{13}$$

where L_r donate reconstruction loss, L_c donate clustering loss, m is the batch size, and λ is the learning rate. We stop optimization when it reaches a tolerance threshold.

We conclude overall process to perform deep clustering in Algorithm 1.

Algorithm 1: Deep Clustering
Input: fashion images
Output: clusters
Begin
    For each image, extract the CNN feature i.e. X=4096; //Explained in section 4.2
    Learn latent feature representation;
    Initialize cluster centroid μ_j, encoder weight W and decoder weight W';
    Set t=0;
    Repeat
        Compute all latent points Y;
        Assign labels l to x_i as $\arg\max_j qij$;
        Update target distribution p_{ij}, which is derived from q_{ij} using eq. (6) and eq.
(7);
        Update all latent representation points y_i;
        Save last labels as $l_{last} = l$;
        Compute new labels l for x_i;
        If $(sum(\,l_{last} \neq l)$ or $n < \delta)$ // δ is the stopping threshold
                Stop training;
        Update cluster centroid μ_j, encoder weight W and decoder weight W';
        Using eq. (11) (12) (13);
        t=t+1;
    Until (t < MaxIteration)
End

4   Experiments

4.1   Dataset

To evaluate the ability of our approach at capturing fashion dynamics, we are interested in a real-world dataset with high dimension visual features to compete with the curse of dimensionality problem. We preprocess dataset to fulfil our model requirement based on Amazon store. Amazon review dataset was introduced in [24] which consists product's images, description, tags etc. First, we split "Clothing, Shoes and Jewelry" dataset to (Men, Women, Kids, girls, Boys). Further for deep clustering evaluation, we split the main categories to subcategories (shirts, Dresses, Jackets, pants etc.). See Fig. 3 the illustration of experimental dataset.

For experiments, we consider 8 classes in which each product consist of image feature for unsupervised deep clustering and label to evaluate the clustering performance of the model. By this way, we train/test our model without seeing any image or tag from the training dataset, unlike supervised or semi-supervised task.

MNIST: we also evaluate our model performance on MNIST Handwritten digits dataset which have 10 classes.

4.2 Feature Extraction

We used visual features of each image extracted by deep CNN. In our experiments, we employ a pre-trained CNN called Caffe [25] reference model 3 for better fitting the multi-view fashion domain with 5 convolutional layers followed by 3 fully-connected layers, which has trained in more than 1 million ImageNet images database [26] We use the output of FC7 feature extracted from the last hidden layer, the second fully-connected layer, which results in a feature 1 vector of length F = 4096 [24, 27].

4.3 Evaluation Matrices

We consider most commonly used matrices to measure deep clustering performance. During these experiments, we employ the three metrics Clustering Accuracy (ACC), normalized mutual information (NMI) and Adjusted Rand Index (ARI) [28]. NMI and ACC matrices range lie between zero and one, higher values considered as good performance while zero will be worst. ARI values lie between −1 to 1, a higher value considered as good results same as above.

$$ACC = \max_m \frac{\sum_{i=j}^n 1(c_i = m(c_i'))}{N} \tag{14}$$

$$NMI = \frac{I(c, c')}{(H(c) + H(c'))/2} \tag{15}$$

$$ARI = \frac{\sum_{ij}\binom{n_{ij}}{2} - \left[\sum_i\binom{a_i}{2}\sum_j\binom{b_j}{2}\right]/\binom{n}{2}}{\frac{1}{2}\left[\sum_i\binom{a_i}{2}\sum_j\binom{b_j}{2}\right] - \left[\sum_i\binom{a_i}{2}\sum_j\binom{b_j}{2}\right]/\frac{n}{2}} \tag{16}$$

Where c_i ground-truth class and c_i' is the clustering assignment, m $(\cdot)$ all possible one-to-one mapping between labels and clusters and $1(\cdot)$ is an indicator function, In NMI H is, the entropy and, $I(\cdot)$ is the mutual information metric. In ARI n_{ij}, a_i, a_{ji} are values from the contingency table [29].

In addition to measure the effectiveness of model we demonstrate true and predicted class using confusion matrix in Fig. 4.

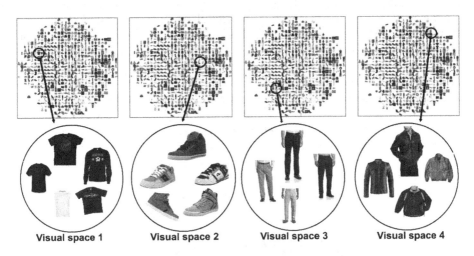

Fig. 3. The illustration that summarizes view of amazon dataset by t-SNE, which maps data to 2-d. The following 4 visual space is extracted from our experimental dataset in which each visual space represents a single class.

4.4 FiDC Performance

While so far we have established the ability of our model to make clusters of real-world fashion images in an unsupervised way. To evaluate our model performance we compare experiments results of our method with other approaches from literature. First one is K means which implemented on raw CNN feature. Secondly, Conventional autoencoder based clustering and the last one Deep Embedding clustering by using same number of neurons in latent space used in our experiments. The results are shown in Tables 1 and 2.

Table 1. MINST digit dataset performance comparison

Model	MNIST dataset		
	ACC	NMI	ARI
K-means	0.532	0.499	0.365
Conv. AE + K-means	0.815	0.785	0.720
DEC	0.865	0.827	0.740
FiDC (ours)	**0.940**	**0.887**	**0.893**

Table 2. Amazon dataset performance comparison

Model	Amazon data		
	ACC	NMI	ARI
K-means	0.587	0.705	0.481
Conv. AE + K-means	0.749	0.765	0.617
DEC	0.780	0.678	0.590
FiDC (ours)	**0.843**	**0.756**	**0.694**

For experiments we consider eight unbalanced classes which consist of 21 thousand total images in amazon dataset, our model achieves 84% accuracy over amazon fashion images. It also gets better results over all other evaluation matrices. For baseline testing, we also implement the same network with optimal parameters on MNIST handwritten dataset and achieve 94% accuracy.

We observe that our model FiDC results are better as par all other approaches used in our experiments. Overall, the performance of FiDC is strong enough while the dimension of the latent space representation dimension is very low as compare to the original input. We conclude FDA outperforms because of better feature learning, more compact latent space feature representation and their distribution. Our model FiDC convergence is steady and fast. Our model achieves state-of-the-art performance after 100 epochs.

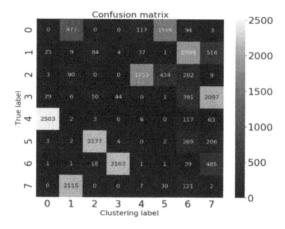

Fig. 4. Confusion/Error matrix of FiDC model over Amazon dataset

To visualize the summary of deep clustering performance, we utilized confusion matrix also known as error matrix where each row of Confusion matrix represents true labels while column represents the clustering labels. Find the results in Fig. 4.

5   Conclusion and Future Work

In this paper, we present a deep clustering model for fashion images in a fully unsupervised way. We implement our experiments in real-world data downloaded from Amazon and deep CNN is used to extract the visual feature vectors of fashion images in advance. By pre-training the deep stacked autoencoder, the model can obtain the latent feature representations of these vectors and then perform initial clustering assignment in latent space. Moreover, we refine the cluster's centre by using auxiliary target distribution and fine-tune until it reaches a tolerance threshold. As a result, we saw our method outperformed because of the more compact feature representation and distribution.

In the future, we will employ this research work to detect and forecast fashion trend based on visual appearances unlike previous work based on metadata.

Acknowledgments. This research was partly funded by the National Natural Science Foundation of China (No. 61402100).

References

1. Kiapour, M.H., Han, X., Lazebnik, S., Berg, A.C., Berg, T.L.: Where to buy it: matching street clothing photos in online shops. In: ICCV, Santiago (2015)
2. Chen, Q., Huang, J., Feris, R., Brown, L.M., Dong, J., Yan, S.: Deep domain adaptation for describing people based on fine-grained clothing attributes. In: CVPR, Boston (2015)
3. Liu, Z., Luo, P., Qiu, S., Wang, X., Tang, X.: DeepFashion: powering robust clothes recognition and retrieval with rich annotations. In: CVPR, Las Vegas (2016)
4. Yamaguchi, K., Kiapour, M.H., Ortiz, L.E., Berg, T. L.: Parsing clothing in fashion photographs. In: CCPR, pp. 3570–3577 (2012)
5. Yamaguchi, K., Kiapour, M.H., Ortiz, L.E., Berg, T.L.: Retrieving similar styles to parse clothing. IEEE Trans. Pattern Anal. Mach. Intell. **37**(5), 1028–1040 (2015)
6. Al-Halah, Z., Stiefelhagen, R., Grauman, K.: Fashion forward: forecasting visual style in fashion. In: IEEE International Conference on Computer Vision (ICCV), Venice, Italy (2017)
7. MacQueen, J.: Some methods for classification and analysis of multivariate observations. In: Berkeley Symposium on Mathematical Statistics and Probability, vol. 1, pp. 281–297 (1967)
8. Bishop, C.M.: Pattern Recognition and Machine Learning. Springer, Heidelberg (2006)
9. Eamonn, K., Abdullah, M.: Curse of dimensionality. In: Liu, L., Özsu, M.T. (eds.) Encyclopedia of Machine Learning and Data Mining. Springer, Boston (2017). https://doi.org/10.1007/978-0-387-39940-9
10. Hinton, E., Salakhutdinov, R.R.: Reducing the dimensionality of data with neural networks. Science **313**, 504–507 (2006)
11. Xie, J., Girshick, R., Farhadi, A.: Unsupervised deep embedding for clustering analysis. In: International Conference on Machine Learning, New York (2017)
12. Guo, X., Gao, L., Liu, X., Yin, J.: Improved deep embedded clustering with local structure preservation. In: IJCAI (2017)
13. Yang, B., Fu, X., Sidiropoulos, N.D., Hong, M.: Towards k-means-friendly spaces: simultaneous deep learning and clustering. In ICML (2016)
14. Tian, F., Gao, B., Cui, Q., Chen, E., Liu, T.-Y.: Learning deep representations for graph clustering. In: AAAI (2014)
15. Peng, X., Xiao, S., Feng, J., Yau, W.-Y., Yi, Z.: Deep subspace clustering with sparsity prior. In: IJCAI (2016)
16. Hsu, C.-C., Lin, C.-W.: Cnn-based joint clustering and representation learning with feature drift compensation for large-scale image data. IEEE Trans. Multimed. **20**(2), 421–429 (2017)
17. Vincent, P., Larochelle, H., Lajoie, I., Bengio, Y., Manzagol, P.-A.: Stacked denoising autoencoders: learning useful representations in a deep network with a local denoising criterion. J. Mach. Learn. Res. **11**, 3371–3408 (2010)
18. Chowdhury, A.M.S., Rahman, M.S., Khanom, A., Chowdhury, T. I., Uddin, A.: On stacked denoising autoencoder based pre-training of ANN for isolated handwritten Bengali numerals dataset recognition. In: ICERIE, Sylhet (2017)

19. Krizhevsky, A., Hinton, G.E.: Using very deep autoencoders for content-based image retrieval. In: ESANN (2011)
20. Sarle, W.S.: Stopped training and other remedies for overfitting. In: Proceedings of the 27th Symposium on the Interface of Computing Science and Statistics (1995)
21. Hinton, G., Salakhutdinov, R.: Learning a non-linear embedding by preserving class neighbourhood structure. In: International Conference on Artificial Intelligence and Statistics (2007). http://proceedings.mlr.press/v2/salakhutdinov07a.html
22. Glorot, X., Bordes, A., Bengio, Y.: Deep sparse rectifier neural networks. In: AISTATS (2011)
23. van der Maaten, L., Hinton, G.E.: Visualizing data using t-SNE. J. Mach. Learn. Res. **9**, 2579–2605 (2008)
24. McAuley, J., Targett, C., Shi, Q., van den Hengel, A.: Image-based recommendations on styles and substitutes. In: SIGIR, New York (2015)
25. Shelhamer, E., Donahue, J., Jia, Y., Darrell, T.: Caffe: convolutional architecture for fast feature embedding. In: ACM (2014)
26. Krizhevsky, A., Sutskever,I., Hinton, G.E.: ImageNet classification with deep convolutional neural networks. In: Advances in Neural Information Processing Systems, vol. 25 (2012)
27. He, R., McAuley, J.: Ups and downs: modeling the visual evolution of fashion trends with one-class collaborative filtering. In: IW3C2 (2016)
28. Cai, D., He, X., Han, J.: Locally consistent concept factorization for document clustering. IEEE Trans. Knowl. Data Eng. **23**(6), 902–913 (2011)
29. Santos, J.M., Embrechts, M.: On the use of the adjusted rand index as a metric for evaluating supervised classification. In: Alippi, C., Polycarpou, M., Panayiotou, C., Ellinas, G. (eds.) ICANN 2009. LNCS, vol. 5769, pp. 175–184. Springer, Heidelberg (2009). https://doi.org/10.1007/978-3-642-04277-5_18

A FCM, Grey Model, and BP Neural Network Hybrid Fashion Color Forecasting Method

Ran Tao, Jie Zhang$^{(\boxtimes)}$, Ze-Ping Lv, You-Qun Shi,
and Xiang-Yang Feng

School of Computer Science and Technology,
Donghua University, Shanghai 201620, China
{taoran,yqshi,fengxy}@dhu.edu.cn, 644864976@qq.com,
1025999102@qq.com

Abstract. In view of the low prediction accuracy of the existing fashion color prediction methods, this paper propose a fashion color forecasting method used the spring and summer women's fashion color data released by the International Fashion Color Committee from 2007 to 2013. In preprocess stage, the Pantone color system is used as the color quantization basis, the fuzzy c-means is used to cluster the sample data at first, and a FCM algorithm is used to statistic the color categories in different time series. In forecasting stage, both the grey model and BP neural network are used respectively to construct the fashion color hue prediction model from the statistical results generated from FCM. In evaluation stage, the mean square error is used to compare the prediction effect. The results show that the grey model based on FCM has the smallest error and has the best prediction effect. The proposed model can be used to predict the future fashion color, which can help the apparel industry stakeholders to grasp the trend of the future fashion color and make design and production plan more effectively. The FCM and grey model hybrid prediction method shown in this model also can be used in other small sample data prediction scenario.

Keywords: Clothing fashion color prediction · Fuzzy c-means · Grey model · BP neural network

1 Introduction

Color is an important factor to improve the competitiveness of commodities in the textile and garment industry [1]. Studies show that appropriate color design can bring 10%–25% added value to the product without increasing the cost [2]. Popular color refers to the color that is generally welcomed by people in a certain period and a certain consumer group. It is the direction of fashion and plays an important role in product marketing [3]. Stakeholders in the apparel industry need to participate in the design, sample, ordering, marketing and sales of clothing according to the predicted fashion color. Establishing a high-precision and objective fashion color prediction model is a major research topic in the apparel industry [4].

Color research institutions, such as Inter Color, Pantone, Merck, etc., are specialized in the research, prediction and release of popular colors. However, the

© Springer Nature Switzerland AG 2019
L. Uden et al. (Eds.): KMO 2019, CCIS 1027, pp. 97–109, 2019.
https://doi.org/10.1007/978-3-030-21451-7_9

confidentiality of popular colors hinders the spread of prediction techniques, methods and finalization, and restricts the embodiment of economic value of popular colors. For example, the international fashion color can only be shared directly in the member states and is not open to the public, and the prediction process has not been made publicly. For most non-member companies, the timeliness and accuracy of the clothing trend information is still an urgent problem to be solved [5].

At present, the research theories applied to predict the trend of popular colors mainly include grey system theory [3], neural network [6], grey neural network [7], multi-swarm cooperative evolutionary algorithm [8], and other combination theories [9]. These research methods provide an important reference for the prediction of popular colors, but the research on fashion color is still in the exploration stage, and the prediction performance of color is still insufficient and controversial [10].

Aiming at the low prediction accuracy of fashion color, we proposed a FCM, grey model, and BP neural network hybrid fashion color forecasting method, and using the mean square error (MSE) as the comprehensive evaluation index of prediction effect.

The rest of the paper is organized as follows: The second part summarizes the research status of popular color trend prediction, FCM algorithm, grey model and BP neural network. The third part introduces the process of fashion trend forecasting and theoretical analysis. The fourth part shows the experimental process comparative analysis. The conclusion and the future research were given in the last part.

2   Related Literature Review

The quantification and classification of color is the basis for the study of fashion color prediction and is an important factor affecting the accuracy of prediction [11]. The determination of boundary value of hue interval is an important basis for realizing the statistics of hue quantization data. Pantone color system uses the color coding of six numbers to indicate the value of lightness, hue and purity attributes of the color. The hue is represented by a circle, and the hue value ranges from 1 to 64. However, there is no labeling of color classification in the Pantone color system. Therefore, the determination of boundary values of 10 types of color intervals in Pantone phase ring is an important basis for the prediction of fashion color. Chang [5] proposed a color quantization method and classification standard based on the Pantone color system and they have been applied to the literature [12] and so on. However, in the literature [12], the final spring-summer color reproduction accuracy is 60%, and the result is not satisfactory. Therefore, this paper proposes to quantify the data using the Pantone color space and classify the data using the FCM-based method.

FCM algorithm is an unsupervised fuzzy clustering algorithm, which uses initialization to determine the number of initial clustering centers, and iteratively changes the clustering center to make the spacing between clustering centers less than the given constraint conditions, so as to obtain the minimum value of the objective function [13]. At present, the FCM algorithm has been effectively applied in the fields of medical imaging, digital watermarking, target recognition and image separation [14]. This paper creatively applies the FCM algorithm to the data processing stage of color prediction.

The grey prediction model is a dynamic prediction model based on the grey system theory. The most widely used model is the GM(1,1) model. The grey prediction model is suitable for the prediction of social and economic systems with large factors, complex structure, wide coverage, and comprehensiveness, as well as the main behavioral characteristics, such as total population, total output, national income, consumption level, and productivity [15]. The factors influencing the change in fashion colors are uncertain, and the relationship between fashion colors is uncertain. Therefore, it is feasible to apply the grey model to the prediction of fashion colors.

The Back Propagation (BP) neural network was proposed by the team of scientists led by Rumelhart and McClelland in 1956. It is widely used in many fields such as finance, medicine, and electric power, and has important research value. The Kolmorov continuity theorem in neural network theory shows that the BP neural network can approximate a non-linear continuous function with any accuracy [16], which indicates that the prediction of fashion color by applying it is based on theory.

In terms of clothing color prediction, YZ Wu and others from Donghua University discussed the application of the grey model and BP neural network model in the study of clothing color [17], the study used the spectrophotometer to quantify the color classification, and then adopt the grey model and BP neural network and improve the combination grey BP network, studies show that grey BP model prediction effect is best, the study further developing the color prediction research train of thought; LY Chang of Jiangnan University and others proposed the quantification and prediction of fashion color, and compared the prediction efficiency of the model by changing the length of the time series, and also realized the color brightness and purity [5].

3   A FCM, Grey Model, and BP Neural Network Hybrid Fashion Color Forecasting Method

3.1   Research Process

In order to predict future fashion color from small sample data, we designed this hybrid fashion color forecasting method, shown as Fig. 1.

The input of this process is the historical fashion color released by the International Fashion Color Committee, and the output is the predicted hue ratio of future fashion color. There are 6 steps in this process, shown as follows:

Step 1: Collecting the historical fashion color data in the form of the Pantone color;

Step 2: Extracting the hue H value from the collected Pantone color data;

Step 3: Clustering the H values with the use of FCM algorithm, the results are various cluster centers and a membership matrix;

Step 4: Calculating the hue ratio for each color class in different years from the results of 3;

Step 5a: Predicting the future fashion color with the use of the grey model and calculating the MSE;

Step 5b: Predicting the future fashion color with the use of the BP neural network and calculate the MSE;

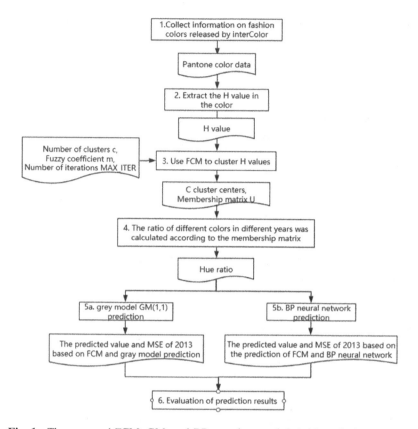

Fig. 1. The proposed FCM, GM, and BP neural network hybrid prediction process.

Step 6: Evaluating the prediction results.
The FCM algorithm, grey model and BP neural network are the main steps in this process, discussing as follows.

3.2 FCM Algorithm

The FCM divides the n hue samples x_i (i = 1, 2, ..., n) into c fuzzy groups, then finds the cluster center of each group of colors so that the objective function of the non-similarity index is minimized. The total membership degree of all samples is 1. As shown in Formula (1), u_{ij} indicates the membership degree of the sample I to the clustering center j.

$$\sum_{i=1}^{c} u_{ij} = 1, \forall j = 1, \ldots, n \tag{1}$$

The generalized form of the objective function of FCM is shown as Formula (2), c_i represents the clustering center of the class i; The distance $d_{ij} = \left\| c_i - x_j \right\|^2$ represents the cluster center of the samples i and j, m is the weighted index, and U is the membership matrix.

$$J(U, c_1, c_2, \ldots, c_c) = \sum_{i=1}^{c} J_i = \sum_{j=1}^{n} \sum_{i=1}^{c} u_{ij}^m \left\| c_i - x_j \right\|^2 \tag{2}$$

The specific steps of the FCM clustering algorithm are as follows:

Step 1: Set the number of clusters c, the fuzzy coefficient m (usually taken as 2), the maximum number of iterations MAX_ITER, and the minimum error δ;

Step 2: The membership matrix U is initialized so that it satisfies the condition in Formula (1). Where U = c×n, where c is the number of cluster centers and n is the total number of samples;

Step 3: Use Formula (3) to calculate the color clustering center ci, i = 1,2,…, c;

$$c_i = \sum_{j=1}^{n} u_{ij}^m x_j \Big/ \sum_{j=1}^{n} u_{ij}^m \tag{3}$$

Step 4: Use Formula (4) to calculate the distance matrix from each sample point to the cluster center and obtain a new membership matrix.

$$u_{ij} = 1 \Big/ \sum_{k=1}^{c} \left(d_{ij} / d_{kj} \right)^{2/(m-1)} \tag{4}$$

Step 5: Calculate the objective function value J according to Formula (2) and evaluate whether the iterative process is terminated. Set the minimum error to $\delta = |J_t - J_{t-1}| / J_t$. If the value is less than the given convergence precision δ or the number of iterations exceeds MAX_ITER then the algorithm stops, otherwise it returns to the third step.

The hue is clustered by FCM, and ten cluster centers i (i = 1, 2, …, 10) and the membership matrix U are returned. Cluster the hue through FCM, and return ten clustering centers i (i = 1, 2, …,10) and the membership matrix U. By processing the membership matrix, the hue value interval of each class of colors can be obtained [mini, maxi], where i represents the class i in the clustering center of class 10. mini represents the minimum hue value of the clustering center of class i, and maxi represents the maximum hue value of the clustering center of class i. Individual unclassified hue values are automatically assigned to the adjacent interval with a larger span of hue values. The frequency of each color phase in different years can be obtained through statistics, and the proportion of each color phase can be calculated through Formula (5):

$$R_i = \frac{v_i}{V} \times 100\%, i = 1, 2, \ldots, 10 \tag{5}$$

In Formula (5), Ri represents the proportion of the ith color in different years, vi represents the number of colors appearing as the cluster center of the ith class; i represents the ith class in the 10-type cluster center; V represents the total number of colors contained in the finalization of fashion colors in a certain year.

The pseudo code for the FCM algorithm is as follows:

Algorithm: FCM algorithm
Data: hue sample set N, objective function precision δ, number of clusters c, blur coefficient m (usually 2), maximum iteration number MAX_ITER
Result: c cluster centers, belonging to the matrix U
1   Begin
2   Call pd.read_csv to read the sample data x.csv
3   Set c, m, MAX_ITER, δ
4   Membership_mat = initializeMembershipMatrix()   // Initialize the membership matrix

5   While iterations <= MAX_ITER or precision <δ do
 Cluster_centers=calculateClusterCenter(membership_mat)
                           //Calculation Cluster Center
 Membership_mat,data=updateMembershipValue(membership _mat,cluster_centers)
 //Update membership getClusters(membership_mat)
 //Get clustering results

6   End
7   Foreach cluster_centers   Find the maximum value max, minimum min   // various color intervals
8   End

3.3   Grey Model

The idea of the grey model is to directly transform the time series into differential equations, thus establishing a dynamic model of the evolution of the abstract system. This method is mainly used for single-sequence first-order linear dynamic models, namely Grey model(1,1), referred to as GM(1,1), which represents a first-order, one-variable differential equation model. The main steps of clothing color prediction based on the GM(1,1) grey model are shown in Fig. 2:

In the process of modeling the popular color prediction based on the grey model, it is necessary to establish a grey model for each type of color data, and set the original color sequence of a certain color to $x(0)(t)$, $x(0)(t)$ represents data of a certain type of color in different years; generates a sequence $x(1)(t)$ by accumulating formula (2),the accumulation process can weaken the randomness of the original data, so that it presents a more obvious characteristic law; establish a first-r differential equation for the generated sequence, such as formula (3), that is, the GM model, where a is the whitening coefficient, which reflects the variable Development trend, $a \in [0, 1]$, b is the endogenous control grey; solve the differential equation to get the predicted value of a certain color $\hat{x}^{(1)}(t+1)$; Since the predicted value at this time is a sequence generated by accumulation, it needs to be reduced, as in formula (5), and finally obtained

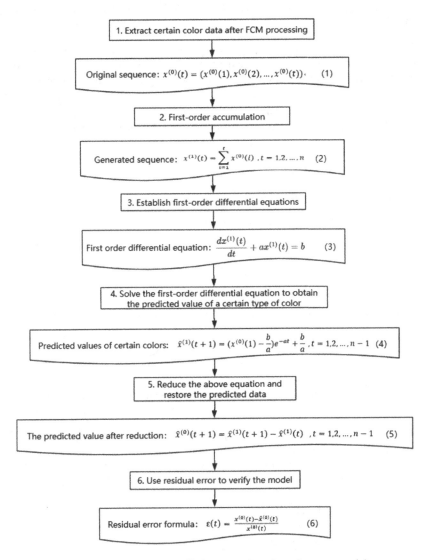

Fig. 2. Fashion color prediction steps based on the grey model.

$\widehat{x}^{(0)}(t+1)$, that is, the predicted value of the color of the class; the other types of colors are separately predicted according to the above steps. Calculate the relative error by Eq. (6), if the relative error of each type of color $|\varepsilon(t)| < 0.1$, that is, to achieve higher accuracy if all kinds of colors $|\varepsilon(t)| < 0.2$, it is considered to meet the general requirements.

3.4 BP Neural Network

The BP neural network is a one-way propagation multi-layer feedforward network. Through the training of sample data, the network weight and threshold are continuously corrected to make the error function fall in the negative gradient direction, approaching the expected output, from the input layer, output layer and hidden. Contains layer composition. Since the fashion color data is less, and the results of the prediction of the popular color are separately analyzed by using different network structures, a 4-7-1 network structure is used for prediction (See Fig. 3).

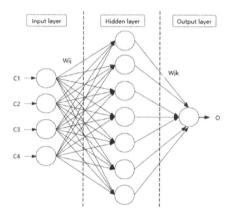

Fig. 3. Topological structure of clothing fashion color based on bp neural network (4-7-1).

The C1, C2, C3, C4 are used to represent the first n years of a certain color respectively. The model is used to predict the color data of the next year. The O is used to represent the target value. Other parameters are discussed in Sect. 4.3.

4 Experiment and Analysis

4.1 Data Selection and Evaluation Criteria

The InterColor's 2007–2013 international spring and summer women's fashion color is used as the research data, and 288 color data are collected.

By extracting the hue information in the Pantone color card, 10 cluster centers are found by FCM. Firstly, set the number of clusters $c = 10$, the fuzzy coefficient $m = 2$, the maximum number of iterations MAX_ITER = 1000, the minimum error $\delta = 10\text{-}5$, the initial cluster center is randomly generated using the random() function, and then the Eq. (3) is used to update it. In addition, the membership matrix is updated using Eq. (4). Finally, after the iteration is completed, a more stable color clustering result was obtained. The classified results and classification intervals after processing are shown in Table 1:

Table 1. 10 cluster centers and 10 hue intervals

Hue classification	Class i	Class ii	Class iii	Class iv	Class v	Class vi	Class vii	Class viii	Class ix	Class x
Cluster center	2	6	10	13	17	26	39	44	53	61
Hue value interval	[1, 4]	[5, 8]	[9, 11]	[12, 15]	[16, 21]	[22, 30]	[31, 40]	[42, 48]	[49, 57]	[59, 64]

The color data obtained from the membership matrix returned by the FCM algorithm and obtained by the formula (4) is as shown in Table 2:

Table 2. 2007–2013 international spring and summer women's fashion color hue ratio

Years	Class i	Class ii	Class iii	Class iv	Class v	Class vi	Class vii	Class viii	Class ix	Class x
2007	0.172	0.069	0.103	0.138	0	0.069	0.069	0.103	0.103	0.172
2008	0.279	0.07	0.07	0.186	0.047	0.047	0.023	0.093	0.047	0.14
2009	0.13	0.196	0.087	0.109	0.087	0.087	0.022	0.043	0.087	0.152
2010	0.113	0.151	0.075	0.094	0	0.094	0.019	0.264	0.113	0.075
2011	0.098	0.146	0.122	0.146	0.024	0.073	0.024	0.146	0.098	0.122
2012	0.167	0.167	0.111	0.111	0.028	0.083	0.028	0.111	0.083	0.111
2013	0.075	0.225	0.125	0.1	0.05	0.05	0.05	0.15	0.075	0.1

The mean square error (MSE) was used to judge the prediction result. The MSE formulas are as follows:

$$\text{Absolute error: } e_i = |\widehat{x}_i - x_i| \tag{6}$$

$$\text{Relative error: } \varepsilon_i = e_i/x_i \tag{7}$$

$$\text{Mean square error: MSE} = \frac{1}{n}\sum_{i=1}^{n} e_i^2 \tag{8}$$

among them, xi represents true value, $\widehat{x}_i$ represents prediction value, n represents the sample number. Smaller MSE means better prediction efficiency.

4.2   Prediction of GM(1,1) Based on FCM

Taking the hue data of 2007–2012 (See Table 2) as the training sample, the grey model was used to predict the 2013 fashion color hue ratio (See Table 3).

Table 3 shows that the MSE value obtained the FCM and grey models is between 0.000004 and 0.001296. The overall MSE, calculated by the Formula (8), is 0.00028.

The comparison between the forecast results of the grey model based on FCM the finalized information on the 2013 fashion color data is shown in Fig. 4, which shows that the predicted values fit the true values very accurately.

Table 3. Prediction results of 2013 fashion color based on FCM grey model.

Category	Original value in 2013	Predictive value in 2013	Absolute error e	Relative error ε	MSE
Class i	0.075	0.077	0.002	0.027	0.000004
Class ii	0.225	0.189	0.036	0.160	0.001296
Class iii	0.125	0.133	0.008	0.064	0.000064
Class iv	0.1	0.095	0.005	0.050	0.000025
Class v	0.05	0.038	0.012	0.240	0.000144
Class vi	0.05	0.061	0.011	0.220	0.000121
Class vii	0.05	0.042	0.008	0.160	0.000064
Class viii	0.15	0.168	0.018	0.120	0.000324
Class ix	0.075	0.102	0.027	0.360	0.000729
Class x	0.1	0.095	0.005	0.050	0.000025

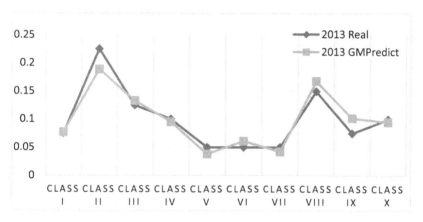

Fig. 4. Comparison the forecast results of the grey model based on FCM and actual values.

4.3   Prediction of BP Neural Network Based on FCM

In this study, we used a 4-7-1 network structure shown as Fig. 3, set the excitation function to relu function, use the adam function to train the data, set the maximum number of iterations to 1000, and the iteration error is 10-4. The original quantitative data from 2007 to 2010 is constructed as the input of the BP neural network, the output is the predicted data of 2011. Then, the data of 2008–2011 is used to predicted data of 2012. Finally the forecast data for 2013 is achieved (See Table 4).

The overall MSE, calculated by the Formula (8), is 0.0036. The comparison of the prediction results with the 2013 finalization information is shown in Fig. 5.

Table 4 shows that the obtained MSE value is small, between 0.000484 and 0.011025, and the overall MSE is 0.0036. The accuracy of this model is lower than that of the gray model. The possible reason is that the gray model is more suitable for small sample data than the BP neural network.

Table 4. Prediction results of BP neural network based on FCM.

Color	Original value in 2013	Predictive value in 2013	Absolute error e	MSE
Class i	0.075	0.169	0.094	0.008836
Class ii	0.225	0.12	0.105	0.011025
Class iii	0.125	0.181	0.056	0.003136
Class iv	0.1	0.157	0.057	0.003249
Class v	0.05	0.027	0.023	0.000529
Class vi	0.05	0.077	0.027	0.000729
Class vii	0.05	0.024	0.026	0.000676
Class viii	0.15	0.128	0.022	0.000484
Class ix	0.075	0.133	0.058	0.003364
Class x	0.1	0.166	0.066	0.004356

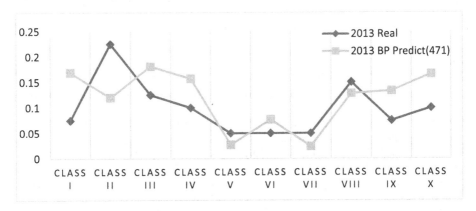

Fig. 5. Comparison of predicted and actual values of FCM-based bp neural network in 2013.

4.4   Performance Comparison with Other Fashion Color Predictions

In order to comprehensively analyze the superiority of the FCM -based fashion color prediction model, the comparison is based on the prediction model based on the traditional classification method: grey model [10], BP neural network [17]. Taking the mean square error as the evaluation index, the fashion color pairs of various models are shown in Table 5:

Table 5. Accuracy comparison with other fashion color prediction models.

Comparative literature	MSE
FCM-based grey model	0.00028
FCM-based BP neural network	0.0036
Literature [10] grey model	0.0071
Literature [17] BP neural network	0.00067

Table 5 shows that the grey model based on FCM has the smallest MSE value, and its prediction effect is optimal.

5 Conclusion

In order to predict future fashion color from historical fashion color data, we proposed a FCM, grey model, and BP neural network hybrid fashion color forecasting method. By comparing the MSE between them and other prediction methods, we found that the FCM and grey model hybrid forecasting method has highest prediction accuracy. This method can help apparel industry stakeholders to master the future fashion color trends and participate in the apparel ecosystem more effectively, it also can be used in other small sample data prediction scenario.

In the future, other unstructured and semi-structured fashion consultations from social media can be used to improve the prediction accuracy of the FCM and BP neural networks hybrid method.

References

1. Diane, T., Cassidy, T.: Colour Forecasting, pp. 6–23. Blackwell Publishing Ltd., Oxford (2005)
2. Li L.Z.: Color economy and marketing strategy. In: Academic Papers of China Fashion Color Association Academic Annual Conference, pp. 66–71 (2012)
3. Lin, J.J., Sun, P.T., Chen, J.J., et al.: Applying gray model to predicting the trend of textile fashion colors. J. Text. Inst. **101**(4), 360–368 (2010)
4. Liu, G.L., Jiang, Y.: Research on the sensibility of clothing style based on the perceptual cognition of the wearer. J. Text. Res. **11**, 101–105 (2007)
5. Chang, L.X. Quantification and prediction of fashion color. Jiangnan University (2013)
6. Di, H.J., Liu, D.Y., Wu, Z.M.: Prediction of popular color in spring and summer women based on bp neural network. J. Text. Res. **32**(7), 111–116 (2011). 126
7. Choi, T.M., Hui, C.L., Ng, S.F., et al.: Color trend forecasting of fashionable products with very few historical data. Syst. Man Cybern. **42**(6), 1003–1010 (2012)
8. Zhao, L., Yang, L.H., Huang, X.: Prediction of fashion color of clothing using multi-bee colony cooperative evolution algorithm. J. Text. **39**(03), 137–142 (2018)
9. Hu, Z.Q.: Research on the application of trend forecasting of home textile fashion based on grey Markov model and support vector machine. Wuhan Textile University (2018)
10. Chang, L.X., Gao, W.D., Pan, R.R., Liu, J.L.: Application of grey GM(1,1) model in the prediction of popular color hue in international spring and summer women. J. Text. Res. **36**(04), 128–133 (2015)
11. Schwarz, M.W., Cowan, W.B., Beatty, J.C.: An experimental comparison of RGB, YIQ, LAB, HSV, and opponent color models. ACM Trans. Graph. **6**(2), 123–158 (1987)
12. Han, W.: Quantitative analysis, prediction, and application of women's fashion color. Donghua University (2017)
13. Bezdek, J.C.: Pattern Recognition with Fuzzy Objective Function Algorithms. Plenum, New York (1981)
14. Deng, J.L.: Control problems of grey systems. Syst. Control Lett. **1**(5), 288–294 (1982)

15. Wang, X.M.: Grey System Analysis and Practical Calculation Program, pp. 50–54. Huazhong University of Science and Technology Press, Hubei (2001)
16. Yang, C.B.: Improved combined forecasting model based on grey model and artificial neural network and its application [Master's thesis]. Shandong Normal University, Jinan (2009)
17. Chang, L.X., Gao, W.D.: Short-term prediction of international fashion color based on bp neural network. Woolen Technol. **46**(02), 87–91 (2018)

Discovering Emerging Research Topics Based on SPO Predications

Zhengyin Hu[1(✉)], Rong-Qiang Zeng[1,2], Lin Peng[1], Hongseng Pang[3], Xiaochu Qin[4], and Cheng Guo[4]

[1] Chengdu Library and Information Center, Chinese Academy of Sciences, Chengdu 610041, Sichuan, People's Republic of China
{huzy, pengl}@clas.ac.cn
[2] School of Mathematics, Southwest Jiaotong University, Chengdu 610031, Sichuan, People's Republic of China
zrq@swjtu.edu.cn
[3] Shenzhen University, Shenzhen 518060, Guangdong, People's Republic of China
phs@szu.edu.cn
[4] Guangzhou Institutes of Biomedicine and Health, Chinese Academy of Sciences, Guangzhou 510530, Guangdong, People's Republic of China
{qin_xiaochu, guo_chen}@gibh.ac.cn

Abstract. With the rapid growth of scientific literatures, it is very important to discover the implicit knowledge from the vast information accurately and efficiently. To achieve this goal, we propose a percolation approach to discovering emerging research topics by combining text mining and scientometrics methods based on Subject-Predication-Object (SPO) predications, which consist of a subject argument, an object argument, and the relation that binds them. Firstly, SPO predications are extracted and cleaned from content of literatures to construct SPO semantic networks. Then, community detection is conducted in the SPO semantic networks. Afterwards, two indicators of Research Topic Age (RTA) and Research Topic Authors Number (RTAN) combined by hypervolume-based selection algorithm (HBS) are chosen to identify potential emerging research topics from communities. Finally, scientific literatures of stem cells are selected as a case study, and the result indicates that the approach can effectively and accurately discover the emerging research topics.

Keywords: Emerging research topics · Subject-Predication-Object · Community detection · Hypervolume-based selection · Stem cell

1 Introduction

Emerging research topics represent the new areas of science and technology (S&T) in which the scientists are highly concerned. Actually, it is of great significance to mine these topics through S&T literatures for scientific research and policy making [1]. With the rapid growth of S&T literatures, it has become a big challenge to efficiently and accurately discover implicit knowledge from the vast literatures in a credible way. Then, Knowledge Discovery in Literature (KDiL) has become an important research

© Springer Nature Switzerland AG 2019
L. Uden et al. (Eds.): KMO 2019, CCIS 1027, pp. 110–121, 2019.
https://doi.org/10.1007/978-3-030-21451-7_10

area. Indeed, it is very interesting and useful to combine text mining with sciento-metrics methods for KDiL.

SPO predication represents the semantic relationships among knowledge units, which consists of a subject argument (noun phrase), an object argument (noun phrase) and the relation that binds them (verb phrase) [2]. In fact, the SPO predication can be considered as a kind of semantic network widely used in KDiL, which can reflect research topics of literatures with semantic information and represent S&T information with more details.

In this paper, we propose a percolation approach to discovering emerging research topics based on SPO predications combining text mining and scientometrics methods. Firstly, SemRep [2] which is a Unified Medical Language System (UMLS)-based information extraction tool and Semantic MEDLINE [3] which is a SPO database generated by SemRep based on PubMed, are used to get SPO predications from biomedical text. The subject and object arguments of each SPO are the concepts from the UMLS Metathesaurus, and the Predicate is a relation from the UMLS Semantic Network [2, 3]. For example, from the sentence "We used hemofiltration to treat a patient with digoxin overdose that was complicated by refractory hyperkalemia", SemRep extracts four predications as follows: "Hemofiltration-TREATS-Patients, Digoxin overdose-PROCESS_OF-Patients, hyperkalemia-COMPLICATES-Digoxin overdose, Hemofiltration-TREATS (INFER)-Digoxin overdose" [2, 3].

Then, community detection is conducted in the SPO semantic networks, and a community containing SPO predications can be considered as a research topic. Afterwards, two scientometrics indicators of RTA and RTAN combined by HBS algorithm are chosen to find potential emerging research topics from communities. Finally, S&T literatures of stem cells are selected as a case study. The result indicates that the approach can effectively and accurately discover emerging research topics.

The rest of this paper is organized as follows. Section 2 briefly describes the previous works related to the discovery of emerging research topics. In Sect. 3, we present a percolation approach to discovering research topics based on SPO predica-tions. Afterwards, we conduct a case study in Sect. 4. The conclusion and discussion about further research are given in the last section.

2 Literature and Review

In this section, we investigate the literature reviews concentrating on discovering emerging research topics. Generally, they are divided into scientometrics methods and text mining methods.

The scientometrics methods usually use indicators analysis to discover emerging research topics based on citation or co-occurrence relationship. In [4], the authors proposed a multi-level structural variation approach, which is motivated by an explanatory and computational theory of transformative discovery. With the novel structural variation metrics derived from the theory, they integrated the theoretical framework with a visual analytic process, which enables an analyst to study the lit-erature of a scientific field across multiple levels of aggregation and decomposition, including the field as a whole, specialties, topics and predicates.

In [5], according to the co-cited networks of regenerative medicine literatures based on a combined dataset of 71,393 relevant papers published between 2000 and 2014, the authors presented a snapshot of the fast-growing fields and identified the emerging trends with new developments. Actually, the structural and temporal dynamics are identified in terms of most active research topics and cited references. New developments are identified in terms of newly emerged clusters and research areas, while disciplinary-level patterns are visualized in dual-map overlays.

In [6], the authors proposed a method of discovering research fronts, which compares the structures of citation networks of scientific publications with those of patents by citation analysis and measures the similarity between sets of academic papers and sets of patents by natural language processing. In order to discover research fronts that do not correspond to any patents, they performed a comparative study to measure the semantic similarity between academic papers and patents. As a result, cosine similarity of term frequency-inverse document frequency (tfidf) vector was found to be a preferable way of discovering corresponding relationships.

The text mining methods usually conduct content-analysis using domain ontology, semantic network, and community detection etc. to mine emerging research topics from the contents of literatures. In [7], based on Human Phenotype Ontology (HPO), the authors presented a method named RelativeBestPair to measure similarity from the query terms to hereditary diseases and rank the candidate diseases. In order to evaluate the performance, they carried out the experiments on a set of patients based on 44 complex diseases by adding noise and imprecision to be closer to real clinical conditions. In comparison with seven existing semantic similarity measures, RelativeBestPair significantly outperformed all other seven methods in the simulated dataset with both noise and imprecision, which might be of great help in clinical setting.

In [8], the authors proposed a multi-phase gold standard annotation approach, which was used to annotate 500 sentences randomly selected from MEDLINE abstracts on a wide range of biomedical topics with 1371 semantic predications. According to the UMLS Metathesaurus for concepts and the UMLS Semantic Network for relations, they measured inter-annotator agreement and analyzed the annotations, so as to identify some of the challenges in annotating biomedical text with relations based on ontology or terminology.

In [9], according to some semi-supervised learning methods named Positive-Unlabeled Learning (PU-Learning), the authors proposed a novel method to predict the disease candidate genes from human genome, which is an important part of nowadays biomedical research. Since the diseases with the same phenotype have the similar biological characteristics and genes associated with these same diseases tend to share common functional properties, the proposed method detects the disease candidate genes through gene expression profiles by learning hidden Markov models. The experiments were carried out on a mixed part of 398 disease genes from 3 disease types and 12001 unlabeled genes, and the results indicated a significant improvement in comparison with the other methods in literatures.

In [10], based on Formal Concept Analysis (FCA), the authors proposed a method named FCA-Map to incrementally generate five types of formal contexts and extract mappings from the derived lattices, which is used to identify and validate mappings across ontologies, including one-to-one mappings, complex mappings and correspondences between object properties. Compared with other FCA-based systems, their proposed method is more comprehensive as an attempt to push the envelope of the FCA formalism in ontology matching tasks. The experiments on large, real-world domain ontologies show promising results and reveal the power of FCA.

Both of the above-mentioned methods face specific challenges. Scientometrics methods are mature, but require that there are complete citation networks or high co-occurrence. If the citation networks are incomplete or not available, for example, the citation networks between papers and patents usually are very weak, the scientometrics methods cannot produce reasonable results. Text mining methods, which analysis fine-grained knowledge units such as keywords, SPO predications, and topics, do not need complete citation networks. However, usually the number of knowledge units is large and it is hard to clean and select the right ones without scientometrics methods.

3 Methodology

In our research, we propose a percolation approach to discovering emerging research topics based on SPO predications, which constructs a three-level SPO-based semantic network. First, we present an introduction to the construction of SPO-based semantic network. Then, we investigate a percolation approach to detecting communities in the network. Afterwards, we take the HBS algorithm on two indicators, RTA and RTAN, to identify potential emerging research topics from the communities.

3.1 SPO-Based Semantic Network Construction

After getting required literatures set, SPO predications can be extracted from content of literatures by SemRep. Then, these SPO predications need to be cleaned by Term Clumping which includes general cleaning and pruning processes [11]. General cleaning will remove some common academic/scientific subjects or objects such as "cells," "organ." Some predicates such as "LOCATION_OF," "PART_OF" that reflect hierarchy or position relationship and are meaningless for mining emerging research topics will also be removed. The pruning process helps with further cleaning by discarding the very low frequency and the meaningless subjects, predicates, objects or SPO. After that, each literature is represented as an exchangeable bag-of-SPO.

Based on four basic principles proposed by M. Fiszman et al., which are relevancy, connectivity, novelty and saliency, a SPO-based semantic network is constructed to detect the communities [12]. An example of SPO-based semantic network is illustrated in Fig. 1, which is composed of thousands of nodes and edges. In Fig. 1, the vertices with different colors denote the different SPO predications, and the size of the vertex denotes the frequency of SPO predication. Actually, many vertices can be both the subjects and the objects so that it makes the whole network become very complicated [13]. Therefore, it is very difficult for the experts to recognize the valuable topics from a SPO-based semantic network directly.

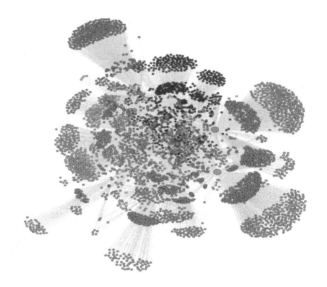

Fig. 1. An example of SPO-based semantic network

3.2 Community Detection

In order to effectively find the communities from a SPO-based semantic network, we propose a percolation approach to achieve the community detection, which employs the widely used modularity function defined as follows [14]:

$$Q = \frac{1}{2m} \sum_{vw} \left[A_{vw} - \frac{k_v k_w}{2m} \right] \delta(C_v, C_w) \tag{1}$$

Suppose that the vertices are divided into different communities such that the vertex v belongs to the community C denoted by C_v. In Formula 1, A is the adjacency matrix of the network G. $A_{vw} = 1$ if one vertex v is connected to another vertex w, otherwise $A_{vw} = 0$. The δ function $\delta(i, j)$ is equal to 1 if $i = j$ and 0 otherwise. The degree k_v of a vertex v is defined to be $k_v = \sum_v A_{vw}$, and the number of edges in the network is $m = \sum_{wv} A_{wv}/2$.

Furthermore, the modularity function can be presented in a simple way, which is formulated below [14]:

$$Q = \sum_i \left(e_{ii} - a_i^2 \right) \tag{2}$$

where i runs over all communities in the network, e_{ii} and a_i^2 are respectively defined as follows [14]:

$$e_{ij} = \frac{1}{2m} \sum\nolimits_{vw} A_{vw} \delta(C_v, i) \delta(C_w, j) \qquad (3)$$

which is the fraction of edges that join vertices in community i to vertices in community j, and

$$a_i = \frac{1}{2m} \sum\nolimits_{v} k_v \delta(C_v, i) \qquad (4)$$

which is the fraction of the ends of edges that are attached to vertices in community i.

Based on the modularity function optimization [15], the percolation approach is a heuristic method to extract the community structure of large networks, which is presented in Algorithm 1.

Table 1. The percolation algorithm to extract community structure

Algorithm 1. Percolation Algorithm
1: **Input**: SPO-based semantic relation network G
2: **Output**: Sequence of communities
3: Initialization (G)
4: Calculating the average weighted degree d of G
5: Calculating the weight of each edge of G multiplies by a random number with the probability $1 - 1/d$
6: $P = \{x_1, \ldots, x_p\} \leftarrow$ Random Initialization (P)
7: **repeat**
8: $x_i \leftarrow$ Local Search (x_i)
9: **until** a stop criterion is met

In this algorithm, we initialize the network into a directed weighted graph according to the SPO-based semantic relation. Then, we calculate the average weighted degree d of this graph. Afterwards, the weight of each edge multiplies by a random number with the probability $1 - 1/d$. Based on the modularity function value, the local search procedure is executed until the modularity does not improve any more. Then, we obtain the communities of the considered network. An example of the communities in a semantic network detected by the algorithm is illustrated in Fig. 2, in which the communities are represented in different colors.

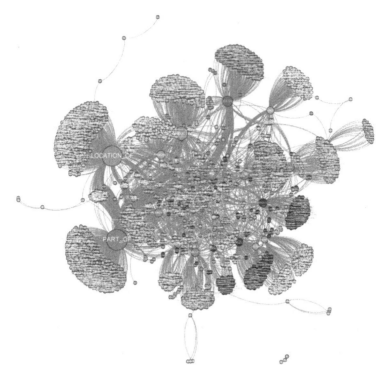

Fig. 2. An example of the communities in SPO-based semantic network

3.3   Hypervolume-Based Selection

After finding communities in the SPO-based semantic network, we aim to select emerging research topics from these communities based on two scientometrics indicators, which are RTA and RTAN proposed in [16]. Specifically, RTA refers to time span of research topics, the larger RTA value is, the wider the time span of distribution of topics is. While RTAN refers to academic attentiveness, the larger RTAN value is, the hotter the topics are. Therefore, we prefer to select the topics with smaller values of RTA and larger values of RTAN as candidates of emerging research topics. RTA and RTAN are defined by the formulas below:

$$f_1 = RTA(topic_i) = \sum_{i=1}^{n} Y_{kw} \frac{n_i}{N} \tag{5}$$

where n_i refers to the number of terms in topic of the time span, N refers to the total number of terms in all topics of the time span and Y_{kw} refers to age of each term.

$$f_2 = RTAN(topic_i) = \frac{n_i}{N} \times 100\% \tag{6}$$

where n_i refers to the number of authors in $topic_i$ of the time span, and N refers to the total number of authors in all topics of the time span.

$$Y_{kw} = \sum_{i=1}^{n} \left(Year_{cur} - Year_i\right) \times tfidf_i / \left(\sum_{j=1}^{n} tfidf_j\right) \qquad (7)$$

where $Year_{cur}$ refers to the last year of the time span, $Year_i$ refers to the year of the time span in all topics and $tfidf_i$ refers to the TF/IDF value of the ith term.

According to the two objective values of f_1 and f_2, we select topics among the communities with the HBS algorithm, which is presented in Algorithm 2 below [17].

Table 2. The hypervolume-based selection algorithm

Algorithm 2. Hypervolume-Based Selection Algorithm

1: calculate two objective values of $topic_i$
2: calculate the fitness value of $topic_i$ with the HC indicator
3: select the topics based on the fitness values

In Algorithm 2, $topic_i$ denotes the ith topic in the semantic relation network. First, we calculate the two objective values of $topic_i$. Then, we calculate the fitness value of $topic_i$ with the HC indicator defined as follows:

$$HC(x) = (f_1(y_1) - f_1(x)) \times (f_2(y_0) - f_2(x)) \qquad (8)$$

As is shown in Fig. 3, the fitness value of $topic_i$ denoted by x corresponds to the size of the red area, where y_0 and y_1 refer to other topics, which are the neighbours of $topic_i$ in the objective space. Thus, we can select a designated number of research topics with high fitness values.

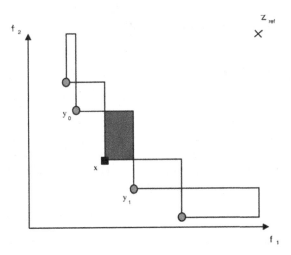

Fig. 3. An example of fitness value calculation

4 Case Study

Stem Cells, which are a group of cells that are capable of self-renewal and multidi-rectional differentiation, are important research objects in biomedical area. Due to their important value and tremendous development prospects in the treatment of diseases and regenerative medicine, stem cells have drawn the worldwide attention and become the hot point of life science and medical research [18]. In this section, stem cells scientific papers are selected as the case study to demonstrate the approach.

4.1 Data Information

Initially, we selected PubMed as the data source, and made retrieval strategy as follow: "(stem cells [MeSH Major Topic]) AND ("2008-01-01"[Date - Publication]: "2017-12-31"[Date - Publication])", and 86,452 records were obtained. After excluding some non-technical papers such as "Clinical Trial," "Dataset", SPO predications were extract from the *title* and *abstract* fields of each paper. Then, the general cleaning and pruning processes were applied to clean these SPO predications. After that, the SPO-based semantic network of stem cell was constructed according to the above method.

4.2 Experimental Results

In this subsection, we presented the experimental result. Some communities from the semantic networks are respectively illustrated in Fig. 4. In the figure, the different communities are represented in different colors, which are composed of subjects, objects and the corresponding predications, and the frequency of the SPO predications is proportional to the size of the vertex. From Fig. 4, we can observe that the predications "AFFECT, STIMULATE, COEXISTS_WITH" etc. are higher frequency. Some communities with these three predications are summarized in Table 3. In this table, we do not present all the found communities in the network but to provide parts of three different communities according to the HBS process, which are considered as emerging research topics in stem cell by experts.

Table 3. Some emerging research topics in stem cell

Predication	Subject	Object
Affect	Genes, MicroRNAs, Transcription Factor, ...	Gene Expression, Cell Proliferation, stem cell division, ...
	Signal Transduction Pathways, Signaling Molecule, ...	Neuronal Differentiation, Cell Survival, Signal Transduction, ...
	Proteins, Bone Morphogenetic Proteins, Therapeutic procedure, ...	Growth, Wound Healing, Chondrogenesis, ...

(continued)

Table 3. (*continued*)

Predication	Subject	Object
Stimulate	Fibroblast Growth Factor, Transforming Growth Factor, ...	Mitogen-Activated Protein Kinases, Collagen, Reactive Oxygen Species, ...
	Erythropoietin, VEGF protein, bone morphogenetic protein, ...	Osteogen, NOS3 protein, Granulocyte Colony-Stimulating Factor, ...
	Transplantation, agonists, Antibodies, ...	Blood flow, Antigens, Recovery, ...
Coexists_With	Functional disorder, Endothelial dysfunction, Injury, ...	Cardiovascular Diseases, Hypertensive disease, Diabetes, ...
	Pathologic Neovascularization, Malignant Neoplasms, ...	Myocardial Ischemia, Neoplasm, Obesity, ...
	Down-Regulation, Fibrosis, Application procedure, ...	Replacement therapy, Tissue Engineering, Cell Therapy, ...

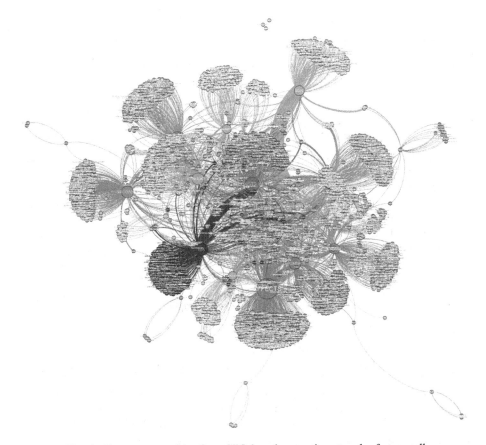

Fig. 4. Some communities from SPO-based semantic network of stem cell

5 Conclusion

In this work, we investigated a percolation approach to discovering emerging research topics from the SPO-based semantic network. Then, we perform the experiments in the research area of stem cells. The results indicate that it can help significantly discover the emerging research topics in the considered area.

However, there are some challenges in the processes. First, there are so many noises in the "Subjects, Objects, Predicates and SPO predications" from the papers and the general cleaning and pruning processing deeply depend on experts' opinions. Secondly, the SPO predications are extracted only from the *title* and *abstract* fields. Maybe it is not enough. Thirdly, the topics should be described in a more understandable way.

In the future, we intend to make more specific general cleaning and pruning rules to help conduct more objective data cleaning. In addition, we will directly extract SPO predications from full texts of papers by SemRep to get more SPO predications. Moreover, further research such as attaching understandable labels to topics, mining the linkages between topics, and discovering topics evolution are ongoing.

Acknowledgments. The work in this paper was supported by the Informationization Special Project of Chinese Academy of Sciences "E-Science Application for Knowledge Discovery in Stem Cells" (Grant No: XXH13506-203) and the Fundamental Research Funds for the Central Universities (Grant No. A0920502051815-69).

References

1. Swanson, D.R.: Medical literature as a potential source of new knowledge. Bull. Med. Libr. Assoc. **78**(1), 29–37 (1990)
2. Rindflesch, T.C., Fiszman, M.: The interaction of domain knowledge and linguistic structure in natural language processing: interpreting hypernymic propositions in biomedical text. J. Biomed. Inform. **36**(6), 462–477 (2003)
3. Rindflesch, T.C., et al.: Semantic MEDLINE: an advanced information management application for biomedicine. Inf. Serv. Use **31**, 15–21 (2011)
4. Chen, C.: Hindsight, insight, and foresight: a multi-level structural variation approach to the study of a scientific field. Technol. Anal. Strat. Manag. **25**(6), 619–640 (2013)
5. Chen, C., Dubin, R., Kim, M.C.: Emerging trends and new developments in regenerative medicine: a scientometric update (2000–2014). Expert. Opin. Biol. Ther. **14**(9), 1295–1317 (2014)
6. Shibata, N., Kajikawa, Y., Sakata, I.: Detecting potential technological fronts by comparing scientific papers and patents. Foresight **13**(5), 51–60 (2011)
7. Gong, X., Jiang, J., Duan, Z., Lu, H.: A new method to measure the semantic similarity from query phenotypic abnormalities to diseases based on the human phenotype ontology. BMC Bioinform. **19**(4), 111–119 (2018)
8. Kilicoglu, H., Rosemblat, G., Fiszman, M., Rindflesch, T.C.: Constructing a semantic predication gold standard from the biomedical literature. BMC Bioinform. **12**(1), 1–17 (2011)
9. Nikdelfaz, O., Jalili, S.: Disease genes prediction by HMM based PU-learning using gene expression profiles. J. Biomed. Inform. **81**, 102–111 (2018)

10. Zhao, M., Zhang, S., Li, W., Chen, G.: Matching biomedical ontologies based on formal concept analysis. J. Biomed. Semant. **9**(11), 1–27 (2018)
11. Zhang, Y., Porter, A.L., Zhengyin, H., et al.: "Term clumping" for technical intelligence: a case study on dye-sensitized solar cells. Technol. Forecast. Soc. Chang. **85**, 26–39 (2014)
12. Fiszman, M., Rindflesch, T.C., Kilicoglu, H.: Abstraction summarization for managing the biomedical research literature. In: Proceedings of the HLT-NAACL Workshop on Computational Lexical Semantics, pp. 76–83 (2004)
13. Hu, Z.-Y., Zeng, R.-Q., Qin, X.-C., Wei, L., Zhang, Z.: A method of biomedical knowledge discovery by literature mining based on SPO predications: a case study of induced pluripotent stem cells. In: Perner, P. (ed.) MLDM 2018. LNCS (LNAI), vol. 10935, pp. 383–393. Springer, Cham (2018). https://doi.org/10.1007/978-3-319-96133-0_29
14. Newman, M.E.J., Girvan, M.: Finding and evaluating community structure in networks. Phys. Rev. E **69**(2), 026113 (2004)
15. Blondel, V.D., Guillaume, J., Lambiotte, R., Lefebvre, E.: Fast unfolding of communities in large networks. J. Stat. Mech.: Theory Exp. **2008**(10), P10008 (2008)
16. Xu, X.Y., Zheng, Y.N., Liu, Z.H.: Study on the method of identifying research fronts based on scientific papers and patents. Libr. Inf. Serv. **60**(24), 97–106 (2016)
17. Basseur, M., Zeng, R.-Q., Hao, J.-K.: Hypervolume-based multi-objective local search. Neural Comput. Appl. **21**(8), 1917–1929 (2012)
18. Wei, L., Hu, Z.Y., Pang, H.S., et al.: Study on knowledge discovery in biomedical literature based on SPO predications: a case study of induced pluripotent stem cells. Digit. Libr. Forum **9**, 28–34 (2017)

Top-N Collaborative Filtering Recommendation Algorithm Based on Knowledge Graph Embedding

Ming Zhu, De-sheng Zhen[✉], Ran Tao, You-qun Shi,
Xiang-yang Feng, and Qian Wang

School of Computer Science and Technology,
Donghua University, Shanghai 201620, China
{zhuming,taoran,yqshi,fengxy}@dhu.edu.cn,
2397646126@qq.com, 2171834@mail.dhu.edu.cn

Abstract. The traditional collaborative filtering recommendation algorithm only uses the item-user rating matrix without considering the semantic information of the item itself, resulting in a problem that the recommendation accuracy is not high. This paper proposes a Top-N collaborative filtering recommendation algorithm based on knowledge graph embedding. The knowledge graph embedding is used to learn a low-dimensional vector for each entity and relationship in the knowledge graph, while maintaining the structure and semantic information of the original graph in the vector. By calculating the semantic similarity between items, the semantic information of the item itself is incorporated into the collaborative filtering recommendation. The algorithm makes up for the defect that the collaborative filtering recommendation algorithm does not consider the knowledge information of the item itself, and enhances the effect of collaborative filtering recommendation on the semantic level. The experimental results on the MovieLens dataset show that the algorithm can get higher values on precision, recall and F1 measure.

Keywords: Collaborative filtering · Knowledge graph embedding ·
Recommendation algorithm · Semantic similarity

1 Introduction

Collaborative filtering recommendation algorithm is one of the most widely used algorithms in recommender system, and has been successfully applied in e-commerce [1], news media [2] and other fields, and has been receiving much attention in the academic community. The collaborative filtering algorithm discovers the user's preferences by mining the user's historical behavior data, and classifies the users based on different preferences and recommends similar products. Collaborative filtering algorithms fall into two categories, namely user-based collaborating algorithm [3] and item-based collaborative filtering [4]. Literature [5] proposes a collaborative filtering algorithm based on user characteristics and expert opinions. The algorithm analyzes user characteristics, compares the similarity between users and experts, and then calculates the similarity matrix to reduce the sparseness of the data set and improve the prediction

© Springer Nature Switzerland AG 2019
L. Uden et al. (Eds.): KMO 2019, CCIS 1027, pp. 122–134, 2019.
https://doi.org/10.1007/978-3-030-21451-7_11

accuracy. In literature [6], an improved cluster-based collaborative filtering algorithm is proposed, which uses clustering algorithm to cluster users and projects respectively, and then uses improved similarity measure to find the nearest neighbors of users and clusters. Finally the candidate set recommended by the project. The algorithm effectively solves the problem of new users, and can also reflect the user's interest changes through multi-dimensional user images. Literature [7] proposes a project-based collaborative filtering algorithm with low time and space complexity. Then interactive iterations are introduced to reflect the user's latest preferences and improve user satisfaction. Compared with the traditional project-based CF algorithm, it has better recall and precision. The existing various collaborative filtering algorithms basically use information such as user explicit feedback datas (such as user ratings) and user implicit feedback datas (such as browsing logs) to recommend the items required by the user to the other party. These algorithms mainly use the items-users rating matrix information, and do not fully consider the semantic information of the items itself.

The knowledge graph contains rich semantic associations between entities, providing a potential source of auxiliary information for the recommendation system. A generic feature-based method was represented by LibFM [8]. This type of method uniformly uses the attributes of users and items as input to the recommendation algorithm. It is not specifically designed for knowledge graph, so it is not possible to efficiently use all the information of the knowledge graph. Path-based methods were represented by PER [9] and MetaGraph [10]. These type of methods treat the knowledge graph as a heterogeneous information network and then constructs meta-path or meta-graph based features between items. The advantage of these type of methods are that they fully and intuitively utilizes the network structure of the knowledge graph. The disadvantage is that manual design of meta-path or meta-graph is required, which is difficult to achieve optimally in practice. This paper proposes a Top-N collaborative filtering algorithm based on knowledge graph embedding. Through the knowledge graph embedding, a low-dimensional vector is obtained for each entity and relationship learning, and the structure and semantic information of the original graph are maintained in the vector. By calculating the semantic similarity between items, the semantic information of the items is incorporated into the recommendation process, and the user is better recommended.

2 Definition

The collaborative filtering recommendation based on knowledge graph establishes a rating matrix according to the user's rating information of the item, calculates the similarity between the items, and then fuses the semantic similarities learned by the knowledge graph embedding to generate an item similarity matrix. Then each user is calculated a predicted rating for the item for which the behavior has not occurred. Based on these predicted ratings, a list of recommended items is generated for user, and finally an appropriate evaluation indicator is selected to measure the accuracy of the recommendation algorithm. The following are concepts related to the algorithm proposed in this paper.

Definition 1 Knowledge graph: Describing the various entities or concepts and their relationships that exist in the real world. It constitutes a huge semantic network graph. Nodes represent entities or concepts, while edges are composed of attributes or relationships. Based on the triplet, which is a general representation of the knowledge graph [11], denoted as (h, r, t).

Definition 2 User: Let sets U be the collection of all users. Where the number of user sets u are expressed as m.

Definition 3 Item: Let sets I be a collection of all items that can be recommended to all users. Where the number of item sets I are expressed as n.

Definition 4 Rating matrix: Each user may generate a rating for each item, and its value constitutes the users-items rating matrix $R_{m \times n}$. $R_{ij}(1 \leq i \leq m, 1 \leq j \leq n)$ is the rating of the item I_j by the user U_i, and the rating represents the degree of preference of the user i for the item j.

Definition 5 Similarity measure: The item-based collaborative filtering algorithm is generally composed of two parts, first calculating the similarity between items, and then generating a recommendation list for the user according to the similarity of the items and the historical preference of the user. The core of this process is the calculation of item similarity. This paper uses Pearson correlation to calculate the similarity between items. The Pearson correlation formula is as follows:

$$PC(I_i, I_j) = \frac{\sum_{e \in I_{i,j}} (R_{i,e} - \overline{R}_i)(R_{j,e} - \overline{R}_j)}{\sqrt{\sum_{e \in I_{i,j}} (R_{i,e} - \overline{R}_i)^2} \sqrt{\sum_{e \in I_{i,j}} (R_{i,e} - \overline{R}_j)^2}} \tag{1}$$

Where $R_{i,e}$ and $R_{j,e}$ represent the ratings of the user u_i and the user u_j for the item i_e, respectively; $\overline{R}_i$ and $\overline{R}_j$ represent the average ratings of the items by the users u_i and u_j, respectively.

Definition 6 Evaluation indicators: This paper uses the recall, precision, and F1 to measure the prediction accuracy of the recommendation algorithm. The recall represents how many of the test sets are in the user's recommendation list. The precision represents the proportion of items that are recommended to the user and belongs to the test set. The F1 is the weighting of the accuracy rate and the recall rate, which evenly reflects the recommended effect.

3 Top-N Collaborative Filtering Recommendation Algorithm Based on Knowledge Graph Embedding

This paper proposes a Top-N collaborative filtering recommendation algorithm based on knowledge graph embedding (denoted as CTransR-CF algorithm), which combines knowledge graph and collaborative filtering algorithm. By introducing the rich content information of the item in the collaborative filtering algorithm, the defect of the collaborative filtering algorithm ignoring the content information of the item itself is effectively compensated, thereby alleviating the problem of data sparsity. The specific idea of the CTransR-CF algorithm is to use the knowledge graph embedding algorithm to embed the items into a low-dimensional space, then calculate the semantic similarity between the items, generate a semantic similarity matrix, and finally obtain the semantic neighbors of the items. At the same time, by adjusting the fusion ratio, the similarity of the items obtained by the semantic neighbor and the item-based collaborative filtering algorithm are proportionally combined to obtain the final recommendation set. The framework process is shown in Fig. 1.

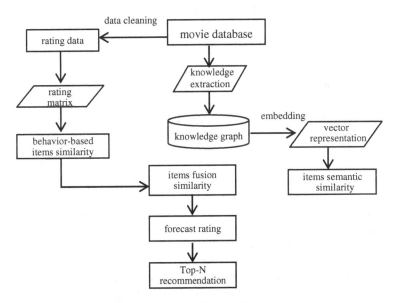

Fig. 1. CTransR-CF algorithm flow

3.1 Construction of Knowledge Graph

Since the constructed knowledge graph is a follow-up recommendation service, and the recommendation algorithm proposed in this paper uses the data set in the movie field, this section builds a knowledge graph in the movie field. Building a knowledge graph in the field of movie requires relevant data support in the movie field. Considering the integrity of the required movie data and the difficulty of data acquisition, this article uses the data provided by the "The Movie Database (TMDb)" website [13], the extracted data. Stored in the form of a triple. Through the analysis and research of the relevant knowledge in the movie field, several elements of the knowledge graph in the movie field are determined. The knowledge of the movie field includes the basic elements of the movie, the basic information of the actors, and the basic information of the director and the screenwriter. Where movie information provides the type, name, introduction, date of film release, language of the movie, and rating information for the movie. The director's elements, scriptwriters, and actor elements provide the names, profiles, births and deaths, and birthplace information of the respective characters.

The ontology [12] belongs to the conceptual layer in the knowledge graph. The ontology establishes an abstract model of the real world by describing concepts in the knowledge graph. The ontology library of the film knowledge graph is constructed in a top-down manner, abstracting the three concepts of "movie", "person" and "type", and defining the classes of related concepts in the domain, the attributes of the entities and their value ranges. Create an instance of the ontology. Through the above steps, the ontology library construction in the movie field is completed. Then the ontology is instantiated, the data layer in the knowledge graph is filled, and the knowledge graph is finally constructed. This paper builds a knowledge map of the movie field, and the knowledge of entities and their attributes is extracted from the structured data.

3.2   Vector Representation of Items Based on CTransR Algorithm

In order to obtain the embedded vector of the entity and relation, in particular the vector of the corresponding item entity in the recommendation system. Entity and relationship embedding are established by translating models like TransE [14] and TransH [15] as de novo entities to tail entities. Entities and relationships are embedded in the same space, thus enhancing the user rating matrix in the collaborative recommendation algorithm. Semantic information about the item. The models mentioned above, including TransR, learn the individual vectors of each relationship. Under this relationship, this low expressiveness may not apply to all pairs of entities, because these relationships are usually diverse. In order to better model these relationships, this paper uses the idea of piecewise linear regression combined with TransR.

The basic idea is that for a triple (h, r, t) in the knowledge graph S, the input instances are first divided into groups. Formally, for a particular relationship r, all pairs of entities (h, t) are clustered into groups, and the pairs of entities in each group exhibit a similar relationship r. All entity pairs are clustered by their vector difference $(h - t)$. A separate relationship vector r_c is then learned for each cluster, and the matrix Mr is learned for each relationship. The projection vectors defining the entities are $h_{r,c} = hMr$ and $t_{r,c} = tMr$. The formula of the rating function is as follows:

$$f_r(\text{h,t}) = \left\|h_{r,c} + r_c - t_{r,c}\right\|_2^2 + \alpha\left\|r_c - r_2^2\right\| \tag{2}$$

Where closer the head entity vector is to the tail entity vector after adding the relation vector, the more accurate the embedding, $\left\|r_c - r_2^2\right\|$ ensures that the clustering vector r_c of a particular relationship is not too far from the original relation vector r, and α plays a role in controlling this limitation. For the rating function of the single triple above, we define a marginal-based rating function as the goal to train, the cost function is as follows:

$$L = \sum_{(h,r,t)\in S} \sum_{(h',r,t')\in S'} \max(0, f_r(\text{h,t}) + \gamma - f_r(h', t')) \tag{3}$$

Where S is a positive triplet set, we believe that all triples in the knowledge graph are correct. S' represents the generated negative triplet set. The negative triplet needs to be constructed by itself. When facing a one-to-many, many-to-one or many-to-many relationship triplet, replace the head and tail entities with different probabilities. Max(x, y) represents the maximum value in x and y, and the cost function is such that each accumulated child value is not less than zero. γ represents the size of the spacing and is used to control the distance between positive and negative samples, typically set to 1. In the learning process, the cost function is optimized by stochastic gradient descent, and the final training result is that the semantically similar entities in the knowledge graph are mapped to the corresponding positions in the vector space. And can make these vectors retain the semantic information of the item entity. Model training algorithm 1 is as follows:

Algorithm 1:The Learning Algorithm Of CTransR

Input: An scoring function $f_r(h,t)$,training set S={(h,r,t)} ,entity set ε(h or t) and relation set R, margin γ,learning rate λ,embedding dimensions k, batch quantity m.

Output: All the enbeddings of e and r,where e$\in\varepsilon$ and r$\in$R

Initizlize parameter θ;

Loop

e$\leftarrow$e/$\|$e$\|$ for each entity

   $S_{batch}\leftarrow$sample(S,m)

   $T_{batch}\leftarrow\emptyset$ //initialize set of pairs

   foreach (h,r,t) $\in T_{batch}$ do

      $(h',r,t')\leftarrow$negSample $\in$ **S** //sample negative triplet with "unif"

      $T_{batch}\leftarrow T_{batch}$ $\cup$((h,r,t),(h',r,t'))

      (h,r',t) $\leftarrow$negSample $\in$ **S** //sample negative triplet by corrupting relation

   $T_{batch}\leftarrow T_{batch}$ $\cup$((h,r,t),(h,r',t))

      Update parameter $\theta\leftarrow\frac{1}{m}\sum_1^m\frac{\partial f}{\partial\theta}$

      Update embedding w.r.t L=$\sum_{((h,r,t),(h',r,t'))\in T_{batch}}\nabla[f_r(h,t)+\gamma-f_r(h',t')]_+$

End loop

3.3 Semantic Similarity Measure

Through the vectorized representation of the items given in the previous section, the vector of the item in the high-dimensional space is finally obtained. It is therefore possible to calculate the semantic similarity of an item based on the embedded vector of the item. We map the item entities and relationships in the knowledge graph to the k-dimensional space. The item I_i is embedded as a k-dimensional vector with the following formula:

$$I_i = (E_{1i}, E_{2i}, \ldots, E_{ki})^T \tag{4}$$

Where E_{ki} represents the value of the embedded vector of the item I_i in the k-dimensional. The rating function used is calculated based on the Euclidean distance when embedding entities and relationships in the knowledge graph. Therefore, this paper uses the Euclidean distance to measure the similarity of the item entities. The final semantic similarity measure is as follows:

$$sim_{kg}(I_i, I_j) = \frac{1}{1 + \sqrt{\sum_{d=1}^k (E_{di} - E_{dj})^2}} \tag{5}$$

It can be seen from the above formula that the closer the result of $\text{sim}_{kg}(I_i, I_j)$ is to 1, the more similar the two entity vectors are, that is, the closer the relationship between the two is in the knowledge graph. When this value is close to zero, we think that the two entities are almost completely different. Therefore, using this semantic neighbor, the collaborative filtering neighbor set based on collaborative filtering recommendation is replaced by semantic fusion, and finally the required recommendation list is obtained.

3.4 Similarity Fusion

Based on the embedded vector of the items in the knowledge graph, the similarity of the items based on the knowledge graph $\text{sim}_{kg}(I_i, I_j)$ is obtained. Based on the user's rating matrix for the item, the similarity of the item based on the user behavior $\text{sim}_{ub}(I_i, I_j)$ is obtained by using Eq. 1. Assume that I is a collection of items that a collaborative filtering algorithm will recommend to the user. The forecast ratings of each object $i \in I$ are sorted to generate a corresponding ordered sequence L. Similarly, an ordered sequence K to be replaced is generated for the semantic neighbor set T. Assuming that the length of the sequence L is ρ and the fusion ratio is p:q, the number of substitutions is $n = \rho \times \frac{p}{p+q}$, and the fusion process is as shown in Algorithm 2:

Algorithm 2:Similarity Fusion Algorithm
Input: Collaborative filtering of neighbor sets I, semantic neighbor set
Output: Recommended set C
Begin
Set L = list(I),K = list(T)
for $L_i \in \{L_{1-n}, L_{1-n+1}, \ldots, L_1\}$ do;
for $K_j \in \{K_1, K_2, \ldots, K_n\}$ do;
$\mathbf{L_i = K_j}$
end do
end do
Set C = set(L)
End

3.5 Forecast Rating

This paper uses p_{ui} to represent the forecasted user u's rating on the item i. The calculation formula of p_{ui} is as follows:

$$p_{ui} = \frac{\sum_{j \in N(u) \cap S(i,k)} \left(S_{ij} \times R_{uj}\right)}{\sum_{j \in N(u) \cap S(i,k)} S_{ij}} \tag{6}$$

Where S_{ij} represents the similarity of the item I_i and the item I_j, R_{uj} represents the rating of the item u in the existing rating matrix, and N(u) represents the set of items that the user u has scored, and S(i, k) represents the collection of the most similar k items of items i. The meaning of this prediction formula is that the set of items that the user u scored and the set of k items most similar to the item i are first as an intersection, and a reference set is generated, and the rating of the item i is referred to the set. In the reference item set each item generates a weight, and the item weight indicates the proportion of the similarity of the item in the similarity of all items. The final user's forecast rating on the item is expressed as a weighted sum of the user's ratings on all items in the reference items set, such as Algorithm 3 shows:

Algorithm 3: Forecast Rating Algorithm

Input: Rating matrix R, items similarity matrix S
Output: User u's predicted rating for I
Begin
    I_1 = GetTopSimItem(S,i,k); //Find the set of k items most similar to item I
    I_2 = GetRatingItem(N,u); //Find the sets of items that user u has scored
    I = $I_1 \cap I_2$; //Refer to the sets
    P= PredictRatingItem(I,j,u,S,R);
Output p;
End

3.6   Recommendation List Generation

In the TOP-N recommendation system, we generate a list of recommendations for each user that contains N items. We recommend the user based on the following assumptions: The higher the user's forecast rating for the item, the more interesting the user is to the item, the more the recommendation system should recommend the item to the user. To put it simply, for each user in the recommendation system, first forecast its rating of the item by Eq. 6, then sort the items in descending order according to their forecast ratings, and use the top N items of the sorted sequence as the item recommendation list is recommended to the user. The specific process is shown in Algorithm 4:

Algorithm 4: Top-N Recommend List Algorithm

Input: Initial recommendation list topNu for user u, recommended number n
Output: User u final recommendation list topNu_New
Begin
for all i∈topNu do
    if i ∈all items
        topNu_New =   ForecastRatingDescend(topNu);
    else
        P = ForecastRatingItem(I,j,u,S,R);
        topNu_New = topNu_New ∪ N;
    end do
End

---

4 Experimental Settings and Results

4.1 Dataset

This section mainly validates and evaluates the effectiveness of the proposed CTransR-CF algorithm. The experimental data set uses MovieLens-1M, which contains 1000209 ratings, involving 6040 users and 3900 movies. The MovieLens dataset has been widely used in academia. At the same time, in order to match the movie in the MovieLens-1M data set and the movie entity extracted from the TMDb movie database, this paper uses the entity link method to map each movie in the MovieLens-1M data set to the knowledge graph. After mapping, it finally matches 3634. In the movie entity data, 93% of Movies in MovieLens-1M can be accurately mapped into the knowledge graph, which is enough for subsequent work. This paper divides the rating data set, with 70% as the train set and 30% as the test set.

4.2 Experimental Results

(1) Determination of mixing ratio

The recommendation algorithm proposed in this paper combines the similarity of items based on knowledge graph and the similarity of items based on user behavior, and finds n neighboring movies for each user. When the fusion ratio is different, the recommended effects are different. The number of Top-N neighbors selected by the experiment is 50. In order to determine the optimal fusion ratio of CTransR-CF, we select the fusion ratio of similarity in the interval [0, 1].When p:q is 0:10, the whole recommendation algorithm is an item-based collaborative filtering algorithm; when p:q is 10:0, the whole algorithm is a recommendation algorithm based on the content of the knowledge map item. The following is the experimental results of the algorithm in the test set with different degrees of convergence given in Fig. 2. It can be seen from the figure that as the proportion of fusion increases, the accuracy, recall rate and F value increase, and reach a peak at a ratio of 5:5. For the case of N = 50, the fusion ratio is 5:5, which works best.

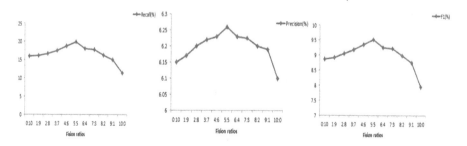

Fig. 2 Recall, precision, F1 under different fusion ratios

(2) Embedded dimension

Knowledge graph embedding embeds the knowledge graph into a low-latitude space, and different recommendation effects for different dimensions are selected for the dimensions embedded in the project entity. Experiments were selected from 100 to 500 dimensions, and it is concluded from Fig. 3 that the best is achieved when 200-dimensional is selected.

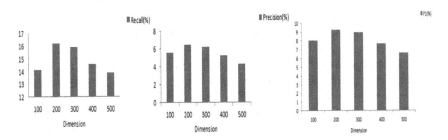

Fig. 3. Recall, precision, F1 under different embedding dimensions

(3) Algorithm performance

Here, the fusion ratio with the highest F1 is selected, and the embedded dimension is 200, and the neighbor number is 30–110. Figure 4 shows that the CTransR-CF algorithm proposed in this paper has a recall of 13%–25%, an precision of 3%–7%, and an F1 of 6%–9%.

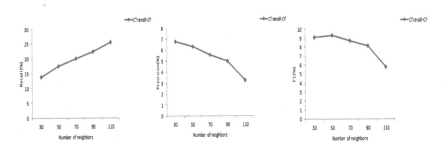

Fig. 4. Recall, precision, F1 under different neighbors

5 Discussion

In this paper, the traditional collaborative filtering recommendation algorithm does not consider the semantic information of the items itself, which leads to the problem that the recommendation accuracy is not high. The article in the knowledge graph is vectorized and introduced into the item-based collaborative filtering recommendation algorithm, and other Compared with the algorithm, CTransR-CF algorithm proposed in this paper has the following advantages:

(a) Using the knowledge graph as auxiliary information, the item semantic information is fully utilized, and the traditional item-based collaborative filtering
algorithm is not semantically compensated for by the items. As can be seen in
Fig. 5, the collaborative filtering algorithm based on pearson correlation has the
worst recommendation effect, and the knowledge graph is introduced into the
collaborative filtering algorithm, and the recommendation performance is significantly improved.

(b) The semantic similarity matrix of the article based on the knowledge graph is
merged with the object similarity matrix based on the user behavior, and the final
similarity of the article is obtained by adjusting the dimension and fusion ratio of
the knowledge graph embedding.

(c) The clustering-based TransR (CTransR) knowledge graph item vectorization
model is integrated into the collaborative filtering algorithm. In the experiment, it
is compared with the TransE and TransH models, because CTransR groups the
clusters by different head-to-tail entities. Learning the relationship vector of each
group can better model the relationship. By comparing several algorithms,
CTransR-CF algorithm has improved recall, precision and F1, which is superior to
other algorithms.

This paper only considers the connotation knowledge of the item itself. The user's
potential relationship information is also an important potential factor in the recommendation system. Therefore, the next research focus is to further improve and integrate the user's potential information in the proposed algorithm. In addition, it will also
be devoted to the research of text representation and semantic entity analysis, and apply
this algorithm to other fields for recommendation and further optimize recommendation
performance.

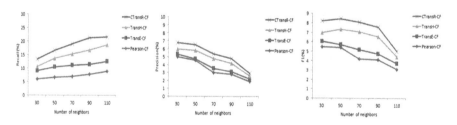

Fig. 5. Performance comparison with other algorithms

6   Conclusion

This paper proposes a Top-N collaborative filtering recommendation algorithm that
integrates knowledge graph embedding, namely CTransR-CF algorithm. Compared
with the traditional recommendation algorithm that only uses the item-user rating
information, the CTransR-CF algorithm can fully utilize the semantic information
inherent in the item itself, and uses the external rating matrix of the item to reflect the
attributes of the item more comprehensively. The algorithm uses knowledge graph

embedding to embed the entity into the low-dimensional space, computes the semantic similarity between the entities, and integrates it into the item-based collaborative filtering recommendation algorithm. To some extent, the effect of collaborative filtering recommendation is enhanced, and the problem that collaborative filtering recommendation does not consider semantics is solved. At the same time, using semantic information, the problem of data sparsity is alleviated to some extent. The experimental results verify that the CTransR-CF algorithm proposed in this paper effectively improves the accuracy of the recommended effect.

7 Acknowledgement

This research is supported by the Dongguan professional town innovation service platform construction project, Dongguan Humen garment collaborative innovation center, and the Guangdong provincial cooperation innovation and platform environment construction special funds (Grant No. 2014B090908004).

References

1. Wang, C.D., Deng, Z.H., Lai, J.H., et al.: Serendipitous recommendation in e-commerce using innovator-based collaborative filtering. IEEE Trans. Cybern. **PP**(99), 1–15 (2018)
2. Huang, X.Y., Xiong, L.Y., Qin-Dong, L.I.: Personalized news recommendation technology based on improved collaborative filtering algorithm. J. Sichuan Univ. **55**(01), 49–55 (2018)
3. Wu, Q., Huang, M., Mu, Y.: A collaborative filtering algorithm based on user similarity and trust. In: IEEE Web Information Systems and Applications Conference, pp. 263–266 (2018)
4. Li, D., Chen, C., Lv, Q., et al.: An algorithm for efficient privacy-preserving item-based collaborative filtering. Futur. Gener. Comput. Syst. **55**(C), 311–320 (2016)
5. Gao, F.Z., Huang, M.X., Zhang, T.T.: Collaborative filtering recommendation algorithm based on user characteristics and expert opinions. Computer Science (2017)
6. Liu, X.: An improved clustering-based collaborative filtering recommendation algorithm. Clust. Comput. **20**(2), 1–8 (2017)
7. Ji, Z., Zhang, Z., Zhou, C., Wang, H.: A fast interactive item-based collaborative filtering algorithm. In: Du, D., Li, L., Zhu, E., He, K. (eds.) NCTCS 2017. CCIS, vol. 768, pp. 248–257. Springer, Singapore (2017). https://doi.org/10.1007/978-981-10-6893-5_19
8. Rendle, S.: Factorization machines with libFM. ACM Trans. Intell. Syst. Technol. **3**(3), 1–22 (2012)
9. Yu, X., Ren, X., Sun, Y., et al.: Personalized entity recommendation: a heterogeneous information network approach. In: Proceedings of the 7th ACM International Conference on Web Search and Data mining. ACM (2014)
10. Zhao, H., Yao, Q., Li, J., et al.: Meta-graph based recommendation fusion over heterogeneous information networks. In: ACM SIGKDD International Conference on Knowledge Discovery & Data Mining. ACM (2017)
11. Zeng-Lin, X.U., Yong-Pan, S., Li-Rong, H.E., et al.: Review on knowledge graph techniques. J. Univ. Electron. Sci. Technol. China **45**, 589–606 (2016)
12. Chah, N.: OK Google, What Is Your Ontology? Or: Exploring Freebase Classification to Understand Google's Knowledge Graph. University of Toronto, Faculty of Information (2018)

13. The Movie Database. The Movie Database [EB/OL], 27 October 2017. https://www.themoviedb.org/
14. Feng, J., Zhou, M., Hao, Y., et al.: Knowledge graph embedding by flexible translation, **2015**, 557–560 (2015)
15. Wang, Z., Zhang, J., Feng, J., et al.: Knowledge graph embedding by translating on hyperplanes. In: Twenty-Eighth AAAI Conference on Artificial Intelligence, pp. 1112–1119. AAAI Press (2014)

Talents Evaluation Modeling Based on Fuzzy Mathematics

Xiangyang Feng, Zhu Liang[✉], Ran Tao, Youqun Shi, and Ming Zhu

College of Computer Science and Technology, Donghua University,
Shanghai, China
{fengxy, taoran, shiyouqun, zhuming}@dhu.edu.cn,
2469607668@qq.com

Abstract. Fuzzy synthetic evaluation is a comprehensive assessment method based on fuzzy mathematics. Using the jurisdiction degree theory in fuzzy mathematics, it transforms qualitative evaluation into quantitative evaluation, and has been widely applied in many fields. In order to make the recruitment process of HRM (Human Resource Management) more systematic and rational, this paper introduces a method to evaluate talents by applying fuzzy synthetic evaluation, and discussed how to implement such mathematical model in our prototype system based on J2EE. Furthermore, the enterprise evaluation process with customizable resume is also proposed in this paper.

Keywords: Fuzzy mathematics · Fuzzy synthetic evaluation ·
Talent evaluation · HRM · Customizable resume · Recruitment

1 Introduction

Under the increasingly fierce talent competition environment, there is agreement on developing and recruiting talents for major enterprises and companies. The essence of enterprise competition is the competition of human resources. The quality and quantity of talents determine the level and future development of an enterprise. Enterprises need stable talent reserve to survive, while talents need to reflect their self-worth by standing out from many competitors. How to find and employ talents accurately has become the common focus on HRM in recent years.

In order to make HRM more efficient, scientific and systematic, relevant research has been done by domestic and overseas scholars for many years. In the early twentieth century, behavior science theory on HRM grew up with the rapid development of Western industrial society. Labor efficiency evaluation was mainly related to laborer's behavior indicators, such as emotions, needs satisfaction and so on. In the mid-twentieth century, the scope and indicators of talent evaluation were constantly extended and refined based on various test, including intelligence test, ability test, sexual orientation test and achievement test. For instance, Kristof integrated the concepts of human-job matching and proposed an integrated matching model according to the theoretical study of job matching and competency model [1]. Ruban studied how to test whether students' learning abilities are hindered by obstacles through their characteristics, so as to educate different students separately [2]. Kroner et al. used some

© Springer Nature Switzerland AG 2019
L. Uden et al. (Eds.): KMO 2019, CCIS 1027, pp. 135–145, 2019.
https://doi.org/10.1007/978-3-030-21451-7_12

correlation indices to study the validity and reliability of computer simulated intelligence tests [3]. Goodman and Svyantek studied the matching between human and organization from the perspective of organizational performance [4]. Price and others put forward the human resource scale as human resource allocation [5].

In other application areas, such as software evaluation, information security risk assessment, project acceptance assessment, etc., different models have been widely used to evaluate. Evaluation model is the core of evaluation activities. The existing evaluation models mainly include hierarchical decomposition model, threat tree model, intelligent evaluation model and mathematical evaluation model. Mathematical evaluation model quantifies qualitative indicators through fuzzy theory, which solves the problems of single index and vague original information in existing evaluation models. Beynon combined analytic hierarchy process (AHP) and evidence theory to propose a multi-attribute decision-making model of DSAHP, which can not only reduce the number of pairwise judgments and consistency checks, but also solve the decision-making problem under incomplete information [6]. On this basis, Hua et al. further proposed the measurement method of unknown information and decision rule setting strategy of DS-AHP model, and analyzed the specific decision-making effect [7]. On the other hand, three consistency indicators are proposed in paper [8]. By comparing the individual overall preference values with the collective ones, the three indices cannot only provide a reference for judging the decision-making effect of each decision maker, but also reflect the effect of group decision-making to a certain extent.

With the development of computer network technology and database technology, human resource management has become an important part of enterprise information management. In this process, talent evaluation is an important intermediate link and basic work. Talent evaluation is not only a hot issue of concern to enterprises, especially human resources departments, but also a difficult problem faced by human resources departments. Therefore, in view of the effective application of mathematical evaluation model in other fields, it is also of great significance to use mathematical model for human resource management.

In recent years, there have been some advances in talent evaluation methods, and these evaluation index systems and methods are different. In the paper [9], the researcher constructed a new evaluation model of managerial talents for the evaluator. Using the Fuzzy Analytic Hierarchy Process (FAHP) to evaluate, we can obtain information in a more systematic and effective way, and assist related management activities. According to the actual needs of human resources management, along with the gradual maturity of web development technology and database technology, the paper [10] designed and implemented a set of human resources management system based on Struts 2 + Spring + Hibernate (SSH) integrated technology framework.

This paper first discussed the basic concepts of the fuzzy comprehensive evaluation method, then used this method to modelled the talent evaluation and gave the formal definition of the talent evaluation model. This model is also designed and implemented in a software system. In addition, considering the differences of different talents, this model has been improved in the process of implementation, that is to say, enterprises can use self-defined indicators to select the required talents.

2   Fuzzy Synthetic Evaluation

2.1   Basic Concept

Fuzzy mathematics is a mathematical theory and method to study and deal with the phenomenon of fuzziness. The mainstream of the development of fuzzy mathematics is its application. The process of judgment, evaluation, reasoning, decision-making and control by using concepts can be described by means of fuzzy mathematics. For example, fuzzy clustering analysis, fuzzy pattern recognition, fuzzy prediction, fuzzy control and so on. These methods constitute a kind of fuzzy system theory.

Fuzzy synthetic evaluation is a very effective multi-factor decision-making method to make a comprehensive evaluation of things. Fuzzy synthetic evaluation is usually divided into two steps: the first step is single factor evaluation, and the second step is comprehensive evaluation according to all factors. Its advantage is that the mathematical model is simple, easy to grasp, and the evaluation effect of complex problems with multiple factors and multiple levels is better. The characteristic of the fuzzy synthetic evaluation method is that it has a unique evaluation value for the evaluated object and is not affected by the set of objects in which the evaluated object is located. The steps of the model are as follows.

(1)   Determining the set of indicators

If each factor u_i makes a single judgment $f(u_i)$, it can be regarded as a U-V fuzzy mapping f, that is:

$$f : U \rightarrow H(V) \tag{1}$$

$$u_i| \rightarrow f(u_i) \in H(V) \tag{2}$$

From f, a fuzzy linear transformation T_f from U to V can be induced, which is regarded as a mathematical model for the comprehensive evaluation of B by weight W. Therefore, the fuzzy mapping f can induce the fuzzy relation $R_f \in H(U \times V)$, that is, $R_f(u_f, v_h) = f(u_i)(v_h) = r_{ih}$. R_f can be expressed by a fuzzy matrix $R \in u_{m \times k}$:

$$R = \begin{bmatrix} r_{11} & r_{12} & \cdots & r_{1k} \\ r_{21} & r_{22} & & r_{2k} \\ & \vdots & \ddots & \vdots \\ r_{m1} & r_{m2} & \cdots & r_{mk} \end{bmatrix} \tag{3}$$

R is called single factor evaluation matrix. Among them, r_{ih} refers to factor x_i, which can be evaluated as the degree of membership of v_i. Specifically, r_{ih} denotes the frequency distribution of factor x_i on comment v_h, which is normalized to satisfy $\sum_{h=1}^{k} r_{ih} = 1$.

(2) Calculating the Value of Fuzzy Comprehensive Evaluation

The fuzzy relation R_f can induce the fuzzy linear transformation T_f from U to V. Thus, (U, R, V, W) constitutes a fuzzy comprehensive evaluation model. In order to comprehensively consider the role of each index, the weighted average model is used to calculate the weight W and the fuzzy matrix R. That is, the model M $(\cdot, +)$ is used to calculate the weight W and the fuzzy matrix R. The comprehensive evaluation formula is as follows:

$$B = W \bullet R \qquad (4)$$

The function of Formula 4 is similar to a converter, as shown in the figure:

$$\xrightarrow{W \in \wp(U)} \boxed{R_f \in \wp(U \times V)} \xrightarrow{B = W \cdot R \in \wp(V)}$$

If a weight $W \in H(U)$ is input, a comprehensive judgement is output:

$$B = W \cdot R \in H(V) \qquad (5)$$

When $\sum_{h=1}^{k} b_h \neq 1$, it is normalized and $B = (b_1, b_2, \cdots, b_k)$. Each b_k here represents the membership strength corresponding to each evaluation level v_k.

2.2   Formal Representation of Talent Evaluation

In this paper, when fuzzy evaluation is applied to talent evaluation in human resource management, the evaluation process here is usually divided into three steps: first, a set of perfect evaluation index system is established; then, the initial semantic evaluation values of each index are obtained by expert evaluation, test analysis and other methods; finally, the evaluation results are given by calculating the evaluation values of each index. Based on the previous description, this paper formalizes the evaluation problem as follows:

$$E = (U, R, V, W)$$

(1) Factor Set of Talent Evaluation
    The factor set of talent evaluation can be set to $U = (u_1, u_2, \cdots, u_n)$, in which u_i is the factor affecting the evaluation object, $i = 1, 2, \cdots, n$. If there are secondary factors, you can set $U_i = (u_{i1}, u_{i2}, \cdots, u_{im})$ for each u_i in U. Apparently m is the number of secondary factors in each category.
(2) Establishing a collection of comments on talent evaluation
    Set the comment set to $V = (v_1, v_2, \cdots, v_k)$, in which each v_j is evaluated by one or all factors. Each numerical response in the comprehensive evaluation vector B is the membership strength in different comments.

(3) Fuzzy evaluation transformation matrix

Through the judgment of each factor, the evaluation grade of each factor is given, thus the relationship between evaluation factor and evaluation grade is established, that is, the fuzzy relationship from U to V, which can be described by the fuzzy evaluation transformation matrix R mentioned above.

(4) Weight distribution of each evaluation factor

Let $W = (w_1, w_2, \cdots, w_n)$ is a fuzzy subset of U, which is called weight allocation set, $\sum_{i=1}^{n} w_i = 1$, $w > 0$, w_i indicates the importance of comprehensive evaluation.

3 Model Implementation

3.1 Realization of Self-defined Evaluation Index

Evaluation factor U is a very important link in the whole evaluation process. The factor set mentioned here is the index set that we want to evaluate, with $U = (u_1, u_2, \cdots, u_n)$ denotes the aspects in which we judge and describe what is being evaluated. It is characterized by a set of several factors and secondary factors. The ultimate goal of the paper's fuzzy evaluation system is to synthetically evaluate the talents through feedback information of job seekers. Therefore, it is necessary to consider the contribution of all the underlying factors to the overall goal.

Enterprises need all kinds of positions in the recruitment process, so the quality of the required talents is different. Even if some studies can give a set of factors and weights, it is difficult to adapt to the differences in different locations. In addition, in the process of fuzzy calculation, if a set of fixed weights is used to calculate, it obviously can not meet the actual situation, so it is difficult to use a set of fuzzy factors and weights to meet the needs of different positions in different enterprises. Therefore, this paper considers the practicability of the system and proposes a customizable fuzzy calculation model.

Taking the recruitment process as an example, in order to avoid evaluating all the objects with a specific evaluation model E (that is, U, R, V and W in E are specific values), we can design a self-customized model of tree structure in the system to achieve fuzzy evaluation. In the three-tier tree structure shown in Fig. 1, enterprise user enterprise constitutes the root node of the tree structure. Because an enterprise can publish many different positions, the child node position of the root node means the different positions belonging to the same enterprise. Each position node has only one child node model. Each model node here represents a complete fuzzy evaluation model E(U, R, V, W). Participants will calculate their own evaluation according to different job types selected, and the corresponding data will be stored separately. Enterprises can design their own set of factors when publishing each location. If the tree structure of Fig. 1 is regarded as the tree structure of the first level, Fig. 2 shows the tree structure nested at the second level in each node model of Fig. 1. As shown in Fig. 2, for each model, it will be customized by enterprise users before it can be used. For each factor, they can also design their own importance, that is, weight values. All applicants for positions can fill in information and participate in the evaluation according to the setting of the enterprise.

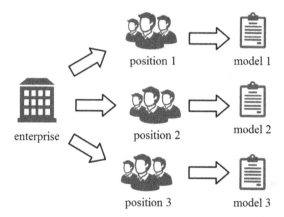

Fig. 1. Customizable model

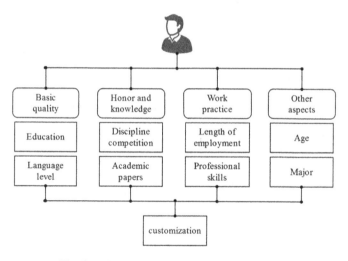

Fig. 2. The customization process of factor set

In the tree structure shown in Fig. 2, the root node represents a deterministic evaluation model. Factor set U is divided into four primary factors in the system: basic information, honor, work experience and other factors. Four primary factors constitute four child nodes under the root node. The new customization factor will be the next layer of child nodes connected in turn. Figure 2 shows the formation of U in the evaluation model.

The model system is based on J2EE platform and is developed with Spring MVC, Spring, MyBatis and other frameworks. The integrated development of framework makes good use of MVC architecture in software development. The process of customizing the evaluation model for enterprise users will be implemented by the view layer in the system, which is also responsible for displaying the evaluation factors for different positions to different participants. The system uses HTML DOM and JavaScript front-end technology to achieve this function. HTML DOM is the HTML

Document Object Model. HTML DOM is a document object model specially applicable to HTML/XHTML. In HTML DOM, everything is a node. DOM is HTML that is regarded as a node tree, and each node has attributes that contain some information about the node. It regards every element in the web page as an object, so that the elements in the web page can also be acquired or edited by computer language. For example, JavaScript can dynamically modify Web pages using HTML DOM.

For a certain added customized factor, the required information includes: name, rank number (i.e. dividing the factor into several ranks), corresponding to each rank of single factor evaluation vector r (r will constitute a row of matrix R in Sect. 2 (2), and secondary weight coefficients. In order to obtain the information input by enterprise users dynamically, the information collected by each user-defined factor can be regarded as a DOM object in the development process. JavaScript is used to write functions to control the increase and deletion of each factor. The number of factors and all factors under each sub-class should also be obtained when accessing page data, so as to facilitate the normalization of weight coefficients. Rationalize and determine the number of rows of the evaluation matrix R.

3.2   Implementation of Evaluation Module

The system will read the data in the database according to the corresponding job type and form different forms if the user starts to evaluate. The form can be filled out by the assessed user or partly by the assessed user and partly by the human resources department of the enterprise. The completed form data will be transferred from the view layer to the model layer under the control layer for calculation, and the results will be returned to the view layer after storing the data. For each evaluation factor, the process of data transmission transfers the marker 1, 2 or 3 which is used to distinguish the grade. The grade here is not relative to the evaluation grade V of the evaluation object, but different grades set by a certain evaluation factor. For example, for the education factor, it can be set as 1 below the undergraduate level, 2 below the undergraduate level, and 3 below the undergraduate level. For master's degree or above, it is 4, which makes it easy to record all data of an evaluation object in the system, and select different but factor evaluation vector r to form evaluation matrix R according to the identification of each factor. If nine factors are customized: age (F1), foreign language (F2), academic background (F3), honor (F4), competition (F5), thesis (F6), specialty (F7), skill (F8) and work experience (F9), then the intermediate data of some people in the system are shown in the Table 1 below. F1–F9 represents the nine different custom evaluation factors mentioned just now:

Table 1. Intermediate results transmitted in the system.

ID	NAME	F1	F2	F3	F4	F5	F6	F7	F8	F9
11	Hexinwei	2	1	2	1	1	2	3	2	1
32	Ronnannan	2	2	3	1	2	2	2	1	3
95	Wangdeshun	1	2	3	4	4	2	3	2	2
122	Liangyuntao	3	4	2	3	2	3	3	4	3
156	Jianghe	3	4	2	4	4	5	4	3	3

Among them, the single factor evaluation vector r and the full weights of the first and second levels can be obtained through Delphi method and Analytic Hierarchy Process (AHP) by a group of human resources management departments or other experts. The relevant evaluation data can be all written into the database, which can realize the systematization of the evaluation process in the future evaluation. At the same time, the system based on MVC is also convenient in updating data and expanding new functions.

The computing module of the evaluation model can be implemented in the Model layer. Spring MVC, as the implementer of the View layer, completes the user's request receiving function. Spring MVC Controller is used as the controller of the whole application to complete the forwarding of user requests and the response to users. MyBatis, as the implementer of DAO layer, completes the functions of adding, deleting, modifying and searching database. Spring will manage the entire application, and the life cycle behavior of all beans will be managed by Spring. That is to say, the creation, initialization, destruction of all objects and the maintenance of the relationship between objects in the whole application are managed by Spring. At the same time, the Model layer in the system will also be implemented through Spring.

The model layer receives the transferred intermediate data, chooses different single factor evaluation vectors r according to the identification of each factor to form the evaluation matrix R, calculates the matrix and stores the necessary results back to the View layer. The logic diagram of the system is as follows (Fig. 3):

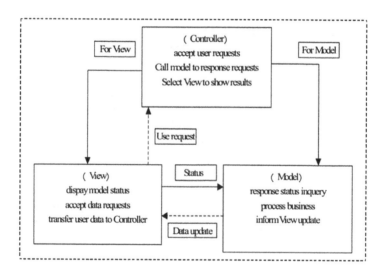

Fig. 3. Logical structure of the system

4 System Performance

Assuming that an enterprise needs to evaluate a job seeker who fills in resume information, specific data have been obtained through Delphi method and Analytic Hierarchy Process (AHP). In the system, the evaluation data can be written into the database in advance, which can realize the systematization of the evaluation process. For example, the data of job seekers can be obtained by filling out forms on the internet. After filling in the data needed for evaluation, the system can automatically evaluate the data. The evaluation and calculation process of the system is as follows:

(1) Delphi method and Analytic Hierarchy Process (AHP) are adopted by an evaluation team composed of human resources department or other experts to obtain relevant data, including single factor evaluation vector r, weight value W, etc., to serve as a reference value for enterprises when issuing new positions. Finally, enterprise users customize the evaluation model according to the type of position.

(2) The participants fill in the form online according to the type of position they choose, and complete the input of the initial data. The system transfers the initial data to the intermediate result data to the evaluation module.

(3) The evaluation matrix R is formed according to the intermediate data, and the final comprehensive evaluation vector B is obtained according to $B = W \cdot R$. Figure 4 is the result of system evaluation. The column chart shows the value of comprehensive evaluation vector B, the red represents the average value, and the black represents the current value.

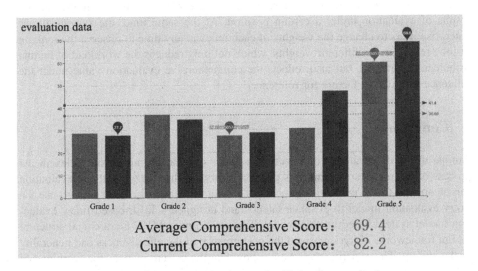

Fig. 4. Individual evaluation results (Color figure online)

B is the user's comprehensive evaluation vector at this time. The semantics of the five grades of the evaluation grade V are: very poor, poor, general, good and excellent. Each value in B represents the membership strength corresponding to different grades on V. The quantitative values of each element in the comment set are $V1 = 40$, $V2 = 55$, $V3 = 70$, $V4 = 85$, $V5 = 100$, and the final evaluation results are between 40 and 100. The closer to 100, the higher the score, and the closer to 40, the lower the score. The final evaluation result score is $N = B^T \cdot V = (B1 \cdot V1 + B2 \cdot V2 + B3 \cdot V3 + B4 \cdot V4 + B5 \cdot V5)$. In this case, the evaluation score is $N = 82.2$. The calculation results show that the job seeker is in the upper level in the evaluation of the position. The system evaluates 200 objects in a certain position. Some of the evaluation results will be fed back to users in the form of ranking, as shown in the following Fig. 5:

ID	NAME	TIME	SCORE
156	Jianghe	01/04/2019	92.6
32	Rongnannan	01/09/2019	91.0
11	Hexinwei	02/04/2019	90.5
122	Liangyuntao	12/04/2018	88.0
95	Wangdeshun	12/04/2018	87.6

Fig. 5. Sorted results in the system

Enterprise users can use this as a reference for screening after obtaining the ranking results of evaluation under a certain position. At the same time, the system allows enterprise users to change the weights of each index at any time to observe the ranking of job seekers under different weights, which not only reduces the workload of human resources department, but also reflects the comprehensive evaluation value under the influence of multiple factors for reference.

5   Conclusion

Aiming at the disadvantage of selecting resumes only according to one index in the process of Internet recruitment, this paper put forward that fuzzy synthetic evaluation can be applied to the evaluation process of recruitment, and discussed how to use the fuzzy evaluation model to evaluate talents, and designed a J2EE-based fuzzy evaluation model system based on this model. The system used MVC hierarchical structure design framework, which improved the performance of the effectiveness and generality of the system. The experimental results show that the system reduces the workload of enterprise human resources department, solves the problem that too many candidates can only be screened by a single factor, and enables enterprise users to customize the evaluation data. The model structure has good expansibility, and some complex fuzzy evaluation problems can be corrected properly. Other functions of the system, such as user rights management, can be further completed in the future work to make it a more practical system.

References

1. Smith, T.F., Waterman, M.S.: Identification of common molecular subsequences. J. Mol. Biol. **147**(1), 195–197 (1981)
2. Ruban, L.M.: Identification and assessment of gifted students with learning disabilities. Theory Pract. **44**(2), 115–124 (2005)
3. Kroner, S., Plass, J.L., Leutner, D.: Intelligence assessment with computer simulations. Intelligence **33**(4), 347–368 (2005)
4. Goodman, S.A., Svyantek, D.J.: Person–organization fit and contextual performance: do shared values matter. J. Vocat. Behav. **55**(2), 254–275 (1999)
5. Price, J.L.: Handbook of organizational measurement. Int. J. Manpower **18**(4/5/6), 305–558 (254) (1997)
6. Beynon, M., Curry, B., Morgan, P.: The Dempster–Shafer theory of evidence: an alternative approach to multicriteria decision modelling. Omega **28**(1), 37–50 (2000)
7. Hua, Z., Gong, B., Xu, X.: A DS–AHP approach for multi-attribute decision making problem with incomplete information. Expert Syst. Appl. **34**(3), 2221–2227 (2008)
8. Pang, J., Liang, J.: Evaluation of the results of multi-attribute group decision-making with linguistic information. Omega **40**(3), 294–301 (2012)
9. Wu, Y.H.: A study of applying fuzzy analytic hierarchy process on management talent evaluation model. In: IFSA World Congress & Nafips International Conference. IEEE Xplore (2001)
10. Jie, X.: Research on the realization of human resource management system. Adv. Mater. Res. **926-930**, 3930–3933 (2014)

Knowledge and Service Innovation

Understanding Consumers' Continuance Intention Toward Self-service Stores: An Integrated Model of the Theory of Planned Behavior and Push-Pull-Mooring Theory

Shan-Shan Chuang[1] and Hui-Min Lai[2(✉)]

[1] Fu Jen Catholic University Hospital, New Taipei City 24352, Taiwan, R.O.C.
[2] Chienkuo Technology University, Changhua City 50094, Taiwan, R.O.C.
hmin@ctu.edu.tw

Abstract. The development of self-service technologies (SSTs) has significantly changed the interactions between customers and enterprises. Similarly, traditional services are gradually being replaced. Self-service businesses are emerging one after the other, including self-service laundries, gas stations, car washes, ticketing machines, and even self-service stores. This is not merely a new trend, but a revolution in traditional consumption patterns and service models. Why do consumers continue to patronize self-service stores? Is the pushing force or the pulling force leading them to continue to switch from traditional shops to self-service stores? Or is this change the result of planned behavior or intention, determined by attitudes, subjective norms, and perceived behavioral control? This study integrates the theory of planned behavior and push-pull-mooring theory to determine the factors that influence consumers' continuance intention toward self-service stores. Data was collected and analyzed, using structural equation modelling, from 231 consumers who accessed self-service car washes. Results showed that attitude was the most important factor affecting consumers' continuance intention toward self-service stores. This was followed in order of relative importance by fun, habit, perceived behavioral control, and personal innovativeness. Subjective norms, low user satisfaction, perceived ease of use, and cost-savings did not affect consumers' continuance intention toward self-service stores. Implications for theory and practice are being derived from these findings.

Keywords: Theory of planned behavior · Push-pull-mooring theory · Self-service store · Self-service technology

1 Introduction

Enterprises are constantly looking to improve their competitiveness to survive in today's dynamic market environment, characterized by rapid advancements in technology and increase in labor costs. Many companies have responded to these challenges by integrating new technologies into their services, while others have replaced traditional manual services with self-service machines [1]. According to Meuter *et al.* [1], self-service technologies (SSTs) are 'technological interfaces that enable customers

© Springer Nature Switzerland AG 2019
L. Uden et al. (Eds.): KMO 2019, CCIS 1027, pp. 149–164, 2019.
https://doi.org/10.1007/978-3-030-21451-7_13

to produce a service independent of direct service employee involvement' (p. 50). An effective self-service system can help increase productivity, reduce labor costs, and provide more service opportunities [2]. SSTs have become a pillar of the service industries, which includes hotels, financial institutions, transportation and retail consumption environments [3]. Weijters, Rangarajan, Falk, and Schillewaert [4] note that a growing number of retailers are implementing SSTs because of the potential for improved productivity, enhanced quality of service, and reduced labor costs. One example of an SST in the retail sector within the United States is Amazon Go, which was launched in December 2016. This store changed the traditional consumption patterns of a physical supermarket by allowing consumers to purchase products automatically with mobile phones, eliminating the need for cashiers or checkout stations. Such a store not only allows consumers to save time, it also helps service providers to manage consumers' purchasing information accurately. Outside the United States, the largest retailers in Japan, AEON and Walmart, have also set up a number of self-checkout machines in their stores. In China, the Alibaba Group has launched unmanned Tao Cafe stores, and the parent company of RT-MART set up a 24-h checkout-free convenience store, Bingo Box, in 2016. These Chinese stores allowed consumers to scan their Alipay barcodes at the time of entry and pay for goods using self-checkout machines.

Self-service is different from the professional service in that consumers act differently without the assistance of employees and have different expectations when serving themselves [5]. Self-service not only enables consumers to better control the service process but also reduces the workload of service providers. Shorter service hours, fewer staff, and lower service costs have attracted many users to self-service businesses. In their study on selection of online financial services, Ding, Verma, and Iqbal [6] found that the potential for innovation in SST was far greater than that in traditional services. Furthermore, the development of SST has greatly changed the patterns of interaction between customers and enterprises [6–8], and traditional services have gradually been replaced by self-service patterns. Previous studies on SSTs have typically focused on factors affecting the service quality of SSTs [2], attitudes toward SSTs [9–13], consumers' intention to use an SST [2, 8–11, 14–17], actual use of SST [16, 18], and satisfaction with SSTs [1, 8, 14]. However, with the exception of Wang *et al.* [15], few scholars have explored the factors that can lead to the continued use of self-service stores. Bhattacherjee [19] indicates that consumers might not continue to use a new technology even after they have accepted it. A user's willingness to continue use is an important factor in measuring the success of self-service systems. Therefore, understanding the factors that affect consumers' continuance intention toward self-service stores is important for managing the customer–enterprise relationship. Thus, in this work, we address the following research questions: Why do people continue to use an innovative SST? Is continued use due to the influence of push and pull effects, leading customers to switch from traditional to self-service stores? Or is there a planned conversion that is governed by attitudes, subjective norms, and perceived behavioral control? This study integrates Moon's (1995) push-pull-mooring (PPM) theory and Ajzen's (1991) theory of planned behavior (TPB) to explore the factors that serve as the main motivations for consumers to continuously use self-service stores, as well as the relative importance of these motivations affecting consumers' continuance intention. In this way, this study has contributed to the management and administration of self-service stores.

2 Literature Review

2.1 Self-service Technologies

SSTs provide services to consumers through a technological interface, eliminating direct contact with service personnel [1]. The advantage of non-contact service technology is that users participate in the process of procuring a service, and thus, their satisfaction or dissatisfaction with the service becomes solely their responsibility. User participation in the process also makes self-service more enjoyable than traditional services [20]. Šavareikienė and Galinytė [20] suggest that self-service is innovative because it can provide consumers with more attractive features, increase an enterprise's competitiveness, create a new and basic SST, and ensure efficiency. Flexibility is another feature of self-service that influences consumers' satisfaction and enhances their motivation to use an SST. Whether it is Internet banking, online shopping, or package tracking, SSTs feature prominently in the interactions between customers and enterprises [6]. As a result, an increasing number of retailers have switched to SSTs to improve productivity and service quality while reducing costs [4, 6, 13]. According to Meuter *et al.* [1], patterns of SST interfaces include 'telephone-based technologies and various interactive voice response systems, direct online connections and Internet-based interfaces, interactive free-standing kiosks, and video or compact disc technologies' (p. 52). Listed below are the types of SSTs that have been implemented globally [1]: 1. Customer service technologies that provide services related to accounting, bill payments, frequently asked questions, and delivery tracking. 2. Direct transaction technologies that enable customers to order, buy, and exchange resources with companies without direct interaction with employees. 3. Self-help technologies that enable customers to learn, receive information, train themselves, and access self-services.

2.2 Theory of Planned Behavior and Push-Pull-Mooring Theory

The TPB comprises four core dimensions: attitude, subjective norms, perceived behavioral control, and behavioral intention. *Attitude* refers to the degree to which an individual likes or dislikes a particular behavior [21, 22]. If an individual has a more positive attitude toward an action, he or she has a strong intention to carry out such action; conversely, when an individual has a negative attitude toward an action, that individual has less of an intention to act in that way [22, 23]. *Subjective norms* refer to persons or groups (e.g., family, friends, and other persons of relative importance) who do or do not support a particular action and accordingly believe that others should or should not perform such action. In other words, whether an individual or a group supports an action can be affected by the social pressure acting on them when engaging in that action [21, 22, 24]. *Perceived behavioral control* refers to an individual's perception of the difficulty in performing a behavior, or the individual's perceived control over this behavior. This perception can also reflect the influence of past experiences and expected obstacles, and it is affected by the available resources and opportunities [22]. When an individual has more resources and opportunities, perceived behavioral control increases, and the behavioral intention becomes stronger. Therefore, perceived behavioral control can be used as an important factor in predicting individual behavior [21, 22]. *Behavioral intention* refers to the subjective probability that when an individual wants to engage in a certain behavior, the greater the individual's intention to act, the higher the likelihood that the individual will engage in the action [23]. Ajzen [22] reports a strong positive correlation between intention and behavior, adding that the intention can actually predict behavior.

The PPM theory can be traced back to Ravenstein's laws of migration from the nineteenth century [25]. These laws describe human migrations as influenced by push-pull effects. A push effect is a negative factor that forces people to leave their places of residence, such as lack of job opportunities and bad weather. A pull effect refers to the attraction of new places of residence, such as better job opportunities, higher incomes, and better schools. Some have used this model to describe the migration behaviors of human populations [26]. Longino [27] put forth the concept of a mooring force or a kind of situational constraint. This mooring force may be personal or social and can be either a positive or negative factor that directly or indirectly affects migration intentions and behaviors [28]. Moon [29] combined the concept of a mooring force with the push-pull model, to create the PPM theory. Mooring refers to the lifestyle that encourages or impedes immigrants in their decision making, with possible factors including all personal, social, and cultural differences as well as the possibility of changing the decision to relocate [30]. According to the PPM theory, human migration is affected by push, pull, and mooring forces [25, 27]. Bansal *et al.* [30] discussed the applicability of the migration model and found that the PPM theory was comprehensive. In addition to explaining a population's migration behaviors, the PPM theory can be used as a universal theoretical framework to further explore individuals' decisions to switch between different service providers. This model has been widely used in marketing to predict consumers' behaviors and intentions to switch providers, and other related social phenomena.

3 Research Model and Hypotheses

To develop a model of consumers' continuance intention to use an innovative SST (Fig. 1), we integrated the TPB and the PPM theories because they are appropriate frameworks for understanding human switching behavior. In this study, the pull force could be seen to come from self-service stores, and the push and mooring forces from traditional stores. The study hypotheses were discussed as below.

Ajzen and Fishbein [23] noted that attitudes have a strong and direct influence on intentions and that SST research had identified a direct and positive relationship between attitudes and intentions [9, 10]. The attitude has been deemed an important factor in determining behavioral intention: the more positive the attitudes, the stronger the intention to act [21–23]. Consumers' attitudes toward new technologies affect their usage behavior [2]. Thus, we hypothesized:

H1: Attitude positively affects consumers' continuance intention toward self-service stores.

Ajzen [21] explained subjective norm as the social pressure that an individual is expected to feel when taking part in a particular behavior. When individuals carry out

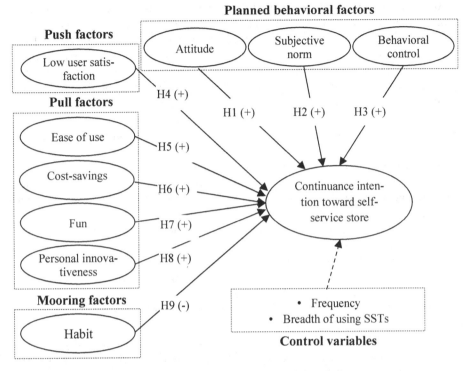

Fig. 1. The research model

an action, they are affected by whether important people or groups around them support such an action. Thus, subjective norms are expected to affect an individual's behavioral intention. In other words, the greater the subjective norm to carry out an action, the greater the behavioral intention [23]. Thus, as we predicted:

H2: Subjective norms positively affect customers' continuance intention toward self-service stores.

According to Ajzen [22], perceived behavioral control refers to people's perception of the level of ease or difficulty in performing a particular behavior. That is, the ease with which an action can be performed affects an individual's decision to engage in such behavior. Consumers choose self-services because they prefer more efficient selection and because self-service gives them a greater sense of control [31]. Thus, when users feel that self-service stores enhance their operational capabilities, the users' continuance intention is higher. Thus, we hypothesized:

H3: Perceived behavioral control positively affects consumers' continuance intention toward self-service stores.

Consumers' switching behavior can be examined using theories similar to those used in the study of human migration, as consumers' switching from one product, service, or service provider to another can be compared to human settlements moving from one geographical area to another. Keaveney and Parthasarathy [32] pointed out that consumers' migration is an important issue in today's rapidly changing market.

According to the traditional migration framework, push forces are the critical factors that cause people to be dissatisfied with their original place of residence and motivate them to leave it [30]. Furthermore, according to Dagger and David [33], satisfaction is an important factor influencing consumer switching behaviors. Previous studies have shown that satisfaction can be used as a predictor of repurchase intention [19, 34]. When satisfaction is high, consumers do not change their original behavioral intentions. However, when satisfaction is low, consumers easily change their behavioral intentions. When consumers receive low service quality and value, their feelings about the service provider are poor, and their trust in and commitment toward the service provider are low as well. This set of circumstances is more likely to produce the intention to switch [30]. In this study, the push factor was defined as a low level of satisfaction with traditional service stores. As a corollary, if consumers are less satisfied with traditional service stores, they are more likely to be attracted to switch to innovative self-service stores. Thus, we predicted:

H4: Low user satisfaction positively affects consumers' continuance intention toward self-service stores.

Another factor that motivates people to migrate is the hope of a better quality of life at the destination area [26]. The same concept can be applied to service switch research, where a company that provides higher quality customer service may attract more consumers [30, 35–37]. In this study, ease of use, cost-savings, fun, and personal innovativeness are being defined as the pull factors of self-service stores.

Perceived ease of use can affect consumers' acceptance of new information technology [10, 38]. Furthermore, studies on ATM use have shown that perceived ease of use is an important factor for customers [11]. Simple operation of an SST, with a clear description and a straightforward process, should lead to customer satisfaction [1] and confidence in the use [15]. Developing a user-friendly SST to increase perceived ease of use is key to SST acceptance [39, 40]. When users think that an SST is easy to use, they have more positive attitudes toward the technology [13]. This study suggests that the more ease consumers experience when using an SST, the more likely they are to continue using self-service stores. Thus, we hypothesized:

H5: Perceived ease of use positively affect consumers' continuance intention toward self-service stores.

Cost-savings is defined as the extent to which a person believes that using a particular system will save money spent on the service [6]. Previous studies have highlighted that SSTs enable users to save money [1]. Howard and Worboys [41] also suggested that cost-savings are one of the great advantages of SSTs. Thus, we hypothesized:

H6: Cost-savings positively affects consumers' continuance intention toward self-service stores.

Fun has also been identified as an important factor for consumers' use of SSTs [3, 31]. In a study of key factors influencing the selection of SSTs, Dabholkar [2] proposed that expected enjoyment is an important measure of the quality of SSTs. If customers believed that they were likely to find self-services interesting, this belief would positively impact their behavioral intention to use the SSTs. In their study of self-service food ordering systems in restaurants, Dabholkar and Bagozzi [10] showed that a sense of fun strongly affected consumers' behavioral intentions. Research on the use of SSTs among retailers had also shown that fun could affect consumers' attitudes toward the SST [4, 13] and their behavioral intentions [17]. Thus, as we predicted:

H7: Fun positively affects consumers' continuance intention toward self-service stores.

Agarwal and Prasad [42] showed that personal innovativeness is an important indicator of behavioral intentions toward new technology products. A high degree of personal innovativeness may increase the likelihood that a product or technology will be adopted early, and thus, the level of personal innovativeness can be used as an indicator for measuring the acceptance of innovative technologies. In a study of online shopping, Boyle and Ruppel [43] argued that if consumers feel a high level of personal innovativeness when using an SST, they were more likely to continue to use it. Thus, we hypothesized:

H8: Personal innovativeness positively affects consumers' continuance intention toward self-service stores.

In migration studies, mooring force variables are understood to alleviate the relationships between push-pull factors and the migration decision [30]. Habits reflect a person's past automatic behavioral tendencies [44, 45], and therefore, a habit is a decisive factor in predicting people's future behaviors [46]. When behavior becomes a habit, users tend to automatically reference a specific system when making decisions. This study defined habit as the custom of using traditional service stores. When consumers are more accustomed to traditional service stores, they are more likely to continue to use traditional service stores and less likely to switch behaviors and intentions. In other words, consumers will be less inclined to use self-service stores. Thus, we hypothesized:

H9: Habit negatively affects consumers' continuance intention toward self-service stores.

4 Research Methodology

4.1 Data Collection

Data was collected from individuals who had used both self-service car washes and traditional manual car washes in Changhua City, Taiwan. A paper-based questionnaire was distributed to users of self-service and traditional manual car washes, and the respondents who volunteered to participate were given a cleaning cloth (market price NT$50) as a thank-you present. An online survey, identical to the paper-based questionnaire, was also used to increase the response rate. A total of 140 paper surveys was delivered to customers on-site, and 117 valid questionnaires were returned. Furthermore, a total of 127 online surveys were collected, of which 114 were deemed valid. A total of 231 valid questionnaires (117 paper surveys and 114 online surveys) was obtained. Basic information about the population sample is given in Table 1. Men accounted for 91.8% of the total sample, and 92.7% of the responses came from individuals between the ages of 20 and 49 years. Before merging the two datasets, we used the chi-square (χ^2) test to compare the differences between the means of the dependent variable in the paper-based and online surveys. There were no statistically significant differences (p = 0.117) between the two datasets.

4.2 Measures

The questionnaire design was mainly based on previous literature, and preliminary interviews were conducted in self-service car wash shops to understand which factors might affect customers' continuance intention toward self-service car washing. The survey instrument was pre-tested by three experts to determine whether the semantics were suitable to self-service car washing contexts. Questions found to be inappropriate were removed. A pilot test was conducted among self-service car wash consumers, and a total of 40 surveys was recovered in the pilot. The questions with poor reliability and validity were revised. The survey items were measured using a five-point Likert scale (1 = strongly disagree to 5 = strongly agree).

Table 1. Demographic information of sample (N = 231)

Variables	Count	Variables	Count
Gender		**Experience in using SST**	
Female	19	Self-service car wash	231
Male	212	ATMs	182
Age		7-11 ibon machine	172
20 years old and younger	11	Self-service gas station	159
20–29 years old	61	Online banking	136
30–39 years old	96	Easy Card value-adding machines	131
40–49 years old	57	Self-service ticketing	129
50–59 years old	5	Self-service laundry	100
60 years old and older	1	Delivery tracking	100
Education level		Voicemail system	84
High school degree and below	69	Self-check-in at an airport	76
Bachelor's degree	128	Others	4
Master's degree	28	**The frequency of use of a self-service car wash**	
PhD degree	6	Less than once a month	33
		Once a month	39
		2–3 times per month	86
		More than 4 times per month	73

5 Results

5.1 Reliability and Validity

Reliability refers to the dependability of the data or the degree of consistency of repeated measurement results [47]. This study used Cronbach's alpha coefficient and composite reliability (CR) to perform the relevant measurements. The higher the reliability of the questionnaire, the higher the reliability of the scale. The coefficients for all the constructs ranged from 0.62 to 0.95, with all measures surpassing the acceptable Cronbach's alpha value of 0.6 [47]. The composite reliability test also produced similar results, with all measures ranging from 0.81 to 0.97, surpassing the recommended level of 0.7 for reliable constructs [48].

Convergent validity is a measure of the degree of convergence of each dimension or the degree to which the relevant factors are classified in the same dimension. Convergent validity exists when factor loadings are greater than the threshold value of 0.50 [47] and the average variance extracted (AVE) is at least 0.50 [49]. All factor loadings for the corresponding constructs were higher than the threshold value of 0.50, and the AVE values ranged from 0.684 to 0.934, confirming adequate convergent validity (Table 2). Discriminant validity was assessed using the Fornell and Larcker [49] criterion. The Fornell–Larcker criterion assessed whether the square roots of the AVE values were greater than the inter-construct correlations. In the Fornell–Larcker criterion calculations shown the bold values, along with the diagonal line, were the AVE square root of each variable, which were greater than the correlation coefficients of the other variables, indicating good discriminant validity.

5.2   Structural Model

We created a partial least squares (PLS) model—a component-based structural equation modeling technique—in SmartPLS 3.0 to test the research hypotheses [51]. We used PLS in this study because (a) PLS maximizes the variance explained in the dependent variables, (b) it is less demanding on the sample size, and (c) it does not assume multivariate normality [52]. Some variables were not normal, such as fun, ease of use, and continuance intention, and had high skewness or high kurtosis. We used the bootstrapping technique with 5,000 iterations to estimate the path coefficient, where the path coefficient indicated the strength between the variables. Figure 2 displays the path coefficients and the explained construct variances.

6   Discussion, Implications, and Limitations

6.1   Discussion

There are four main findings. *First*, the results showed that subjective norms did not have a statistically significant correlation with the continuance intention of self-service stores, possibly because self-service car washing is a personal preference for consumers in addition to a need. One respondent explained that car washing was sometimes a hobby through which he could provide good car maintenance and in addition to while away time. This might be why subjective norms do not seem to affect the choice and continuance intention. *Second*, in the theory of migration, the push effect refers to the negative factors that force people to leave their place of origin [26]. In this study, low user satisfaction with the traditional, manual car washing services was considered a push factor affecting the consumers' continuance intention toward self-service stores. The results of this study showed that low service satisfaction with traditional manual car washing did not significantly affect consumers' continuance intention toward self-service stores. In interviews, consumers explained that they did not choose self-service car washes because they were dissatisfied with the traditional manual car wash services.

Table 2. Convergent validity

Variables and items	Factor loading	AVE
Attitude [24]		0.685
1. Using a self-service car wash is a good idea	0.857	
2. Using a self-service car wash is a wise idea	0.845	
3. I like the idea of using a self-service car wash	0.850	
4. Using a self-service car washing is a pleasant experience	0.755	
Subjective norm [24]		0.727
1. People who influence my behavior would think that I should choose a self-service car wash	0.926	
2. People who are important to me would think that I should choose a self-service car wash	0.773	
Perceived behavioral control [24]		0.822
1. I am able to operate the self-service car wash equipment	0.910	
2. Using self-service car wash machinery is entirely within my control	0.917	
3. I have the resources, knowledge, and ability to help me use the self-service car wash equipment	0.893	
Low user satisfaction (adapted from Wang [50])		0.837
1. I'm not satisfied with traditional manual car washes	0.874	
2. I feel traditional manual car washes have no way of providing high-quality car washing services	0.932	
3. The traditional manual car wash cannot meet my expectations	0.936	
Ease of use [4]		0.718
1. I think the operation of self-service car wash equipment is effortless	0.855	
2. I think self-service car wash equipment is user-friendly	0.840	
Cost-savings (developed based on Meuter, Ostrom [1])		0.684
1. Compared to a traditional manual car wash, a self-service car wash is cheaper	0.967	
2. I choose self-service car washes because I want to save money	0.659	
Fun [10]		0.906
1. I feel it's very interesting to use a self-service car wash	0.948	
2. I think it's fun to use a self-service car wash	0.955	
3. I enjoy the process of using a self-service car wash	0.952	
Habit [45]		0.724
1. Compared to self-service car washes, the use of traditional manual car washes is automatic to me	0.875	
2. Compared to self-service car washes, the use of traditional manual car washes is natural to me	0.892	
3. Compared to self-service car washes, if there is demand, traditional manual car washes are an obvious choice for me	0.781	

(continued)

Table 2. (*continued*)

Variables and items	Factor loading	AVE
Personal innovativeness [42]		0.717
1. If I hear about a new self-service technology, I would look for ways to experiment with it	0.772	
2. Among my peers, I am usually the first person to try out new self-service technologies	0.871	
3. In general, I don't hesitate to try out new self-service technologies	0.827	
4. I like to experiment with new self-service technologies	0.911	
Continuance intention toward self-service store [45]		0.934
1. If possible, I would like to continue to use self-service car washes	0.967	
2. After considering all the circumstances, I will continue to use self-service car washes in the next two months	0.966	

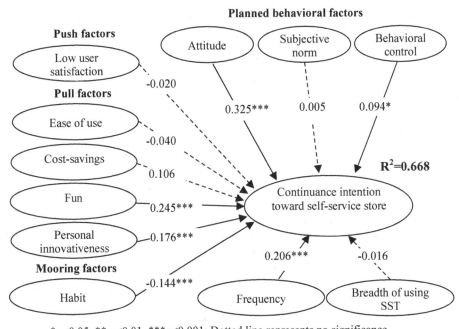

*p<0.05; ** p<0.01; ***p<0.001; Dotted line represents no significance.

Fig. 2. Research model results

Rather, their choice was influenced by the time factor, as they were sometimes too busy to park their cars in the traditional manual car washes for several hours. A 24-h self-service car wash is different from the traditional manual car wash service in that it is not limited by business hours; consumers have the flexibility to choose their period of consumption. Moreover, the self-service car wash provides a variety of self-help services, such as high-pressure flushing, foaming, water wax, air guns, vacuum cleaners, and pneumatic waxing machines. These car washes also have automatic cash machines, vending machines, and various car washing tools (e.g., all kinds of sponges, maintenance and waxing supplies, and absorbent cloths). Consumers can choose from all of these services, which makes the service highly convenient and a good alternative service choice. Apart from these reasons, personal preference also played an important role. Some consumers simply preferred a self-service car wash regardless of whether the car was old or new and even if they were busy, because they enjoy the process of a self-service car wash. This result was consistent with the that shared by Ganesh, Arnold [53], who found that users did not switch shops because of dissatisfaction but because of other factors. *Third*, with regard to pull factors, ease of use did not affect the consumer's continuance intention toward self-service stores, which was inconsistent with previous researches [4, 40]. Consumers explained that ease of use did not influence their choice of self-service car wash as it actually required considerable time and effort to use. There was no statistically significant relationship between cost-savings and continuance intention, which was also inconsistent with the results proposed by Howard and Worboys [41]. In interviews, consumers said that they chose the self-service car washing because of their love for and interest in cars. They wanted to spend more time taking care of their cars, and they typically spent elsewhere from 2–3 h to 6–8 h. *Finally*, a sense of fun was the most statistically significant pull factor vis-à-vis consumers' continuance intention. With technology that is substitutable, customers are more concerned with the enjoyment in using the service than with the service itself [40].

6.2 Implications

From a theoretical perspective, the present study made important contributions to the SST literature. Firstly, this study integrated the TPB and the PPM theory. In addition to approaching intention formation from the perspective of attitudes, subjective norms, and perceived behavioral control, this study combined factors from information system and SST literatures, such as user satisfaction, ease of use, cost-savings, fun, personal innovativeness, and habits. These factors are often cited in the study of acceptance, adoption, or use of an innovative technology. This integration not only enhanced the richness of this research stream but also improved the integrity of the research framework. Secondly, research on SST outcomes had mostly studied factors such as user motivation, intention to use, satisfaction, service quality, technology readiness, and customer loyalty. Few studies had approached the issue from the perspective of continuance intention. This study enhanced one's understanding of SST continuance intention by viewing the topic through a new lens: push-pull-mooring factors. This study provided empirical support for and insights into previous SST literature, which often emphasized the technological factors of SSTs (i.e., perceived ease of use, usefulness, and fun), but not factors related to traditional services. Thirdly, the example of self-service car wash, used in this study, presented a new, innovative SST that is currently in its initial stage of implementation. Thus, this study can be used as a behavioral model for understanding switching intentions toward early SSTs. Finally, the self-service car-wash shops studied in this work were environments requiring a high level of user involvement, and the results showed that in highly involved environments, fun was a statistically significant predictor of continuance intention. Such fun was very important to SST providers because it formed the basis for self-help in the long term.

The present study makes the following practical contributions. Firstly, it found that traditional shops and self-service shops might be business models that could coexist, as consumers chose SSTs not because of their dissatisfaction with traditional service technologies but because they sought more flexibility. Therefore, company managers must realized that consumers needed alternative solutions to meet their requirements. Secondly, fun was an important factor influencing consumers' continuance intention. Accordingly, we recommend firstly that SST providers focus on a practical strategy for designing a hedonic-oriented interaction. This can enhance the continuance intention toward the SST. Secondly, SST design should shift from a transaction-first approach to an experience-first approach to maintain customer loyalty. For instance, SST providers should offer an interactive and attractive interface to improve consumers' experience with the use process. Finally, this study showed that an individual's habit of using traditional stores tends to reduce his or her continuance intention toward self-service stores. Hence, the marketing strategies of SST providers should focus on the pull factors (e.g., perceived fun) so that customers are willing to switch from a satisfactory situation.

6.3 Limitations

This study has certain limitations. Firstly, the study might have regional limitations. The paper-based questionnaire was distributed at two self-help car wash shops in central Taiwan; therefore, the sample data might not be representative of the vast majority of consumer opinions across Taiwan. However, we tried to mitigate this limitation by collecting some of the data via an online questionnaire. The second limitation pertains to the case studied. This study explored only self-service car wash shops, and it is difficult to generalize the results to other types of self-service stores. However, it is important to add that self-service car wash shops are a gradually emerging SST in Taiwan, and these research results can be extended to other self-service stores to improve the understanding of switching intention among early technology users. Additionally, in view of the increasing popularity of self-service stores and the novelty of interactive interfaces for self-service, we believe that future researchers should conduct an empirical analysis of other types of self-service and provide a broader and more diversified reference for enterprises and operators planning their business models.

References

1. Meuter, M.L., et al.: Self-service technologies: understanding customer satisfaction with technology-based service encounters. J. Market. 6(3), 50–64 (2000)
2. Dabholkar, P.A.: Consumer evaluations of new technology-based self-service options: an investigation of alternative models of service quality. Int. J. Res. Market. 13(1), 29–51 (1996)

3. Rosenbaum, M.S., Wong, I.A.: If you install it, will they use it? understanding why hospitality customers take "technological pauses" from self-service technology. J. Bus. Res. **68**(9), 1862–1868 (2015)
4. Weijters, B., et al.: Determinants and outcomes of customers' use of self-service technology in a retail setting. J. Serv. Res. **10**(1), 3–21 (2007)
5. Globerson, S., Maggard, M.J.: A conceptual model of self-service. Int. J. Oper. Prod. Manag. **11**(4), 33–43 (1991)
6. Ding, X., Verma, R., Iqbal, Z.: Self-service technology and online financial service choice. Int. J. Serv. Ind. Manag. **18**(3), 246–268 (2007)
7. Rayport, J.F., Sviokla, J.J.: Exploiting the virtual value chain. Harv. Bus. Rev. **73**(6), 75–85 (1995)
8. Lin, J.-S.C., Hsieh, P.-L.: The influence of technology readiness on satisfaction and behavioral intentions toward self-service technologies. Comput. Hum. Behav. **23**(3), 1597–1615 (2007)
9. Curran, J.M., Meuter, M.L., Surprenant, C.F.: Intentions to use self-service technologies: a confluence of multiple attitudes. J. Serv. Res. **5**(3), 209–224 (2003)
10. Dabholkar, P.A., Bagozzi, R.P.: An attitudinal model of technology-based self-service: moderating effects of consumer traits and situational factors. J. Acad. Mark. Sci. **30**(3), 184–201 (2002)
11. Curran, J.M., Meuter, M.L.: Self-service technology adoption: comparing three technologies. J. Serv. Mark. **19**(2), 109–113 (2005)
12. Liu, S.-F., Huang, L.-S., Chiou, Y.-H.: An integrated attitude model of self-service technologies: evidence from online stock trading systems brokers. Serv. Ind. J. **32**(11), 1823–1835 (2012)
13. Elliott, K., Meng, G., Hall, M.: The influence of technology readiness on the evaluation of self-service technology attributes and resulting attitude toward technology usage. Serv. Mark. Q. **33**(4), 311–329 (2012)
14. Liu, S.: The impact of forced use on customer adoption of self-service technologies. Comput. Hum. Behav. **28**(4), 1194–1201 (2012)
15. Wang, C., Harris, J., Patterson, P.: The roles of habit, self-efficacy, and satisfaction in driving continued use of self-service technologies: a longitudinal study. J. Serv. Res. **16**(3), 400–414 (2013)
16. Demoulin, N.T.M., Djelassi, S.: An integrated model of self-service technology (SST) usage in a retail context. Int. J. Retail. Distrib. Manag. **44**(5), 540–559 (2016)
17. Elliott, K.M., Hall, M.C., Meng, J.G.: Consumers' intention to use self-scanning technology: the role of technology readiness and perceptions toward self-service technology. Acad. Mark. Stud. J. **17**(1), 129–143 (2013)
18. Gelderman, C.J., Ghijsen, P.W.T., Diemen, R.: Choosing self-service technologies or interpersonal services—the impact of situational factors and technology-related attitudes. J. Retail. Consum. Serv. **18**(5), 414–421 (2011)
19. Bhattacherjee, A.: Understanding information systems continuance: an expectation-confirmation model. MIS Q. **25**(3), 351–370 (2001)
20. Šavareikienė, D., Galinytė, R.: Self-Service as a Motivation to Choose Innovative Service. Socialiniai tyrimai/Soc. Res. **2**(27), 19–28 (2012)
21. Ajzen, I.: From intentions to actions: a theory of planned behavior. In: Kuhl, J., Beckmann, J. (eds.) Action Control. SSSSP, pp. 11–39. Springer, Heidelberg (1985). https://doi.org/10.1007/978-3-642-69746-3_2
22. Ajzen, I.: The theory of planned behavior. Organ. Behav. Hum. Decis. Process. **50**(2), 179–211 (1991)

23. Ajzen, I., Fishbein, M.: Belief, Attitude, Intention and Behavior: An Introduction to Theory and Research. Addison-Wesley, Reading (1975)
24. Taylor, S., Todd, P.A.: Understanding information technology usage: a test of competing models. Inf. Syst. Res. 6(2), 144–176 (1995)
25. Ravenstein, E.G.: The laws of migration. J. Stat. Soc. Lond. 48(2), 167–235 (1885)
26. Lee, E.S.: A theory of migration. Demography 3(1), 47–57 (1966)
27. Longino, C.F.: The Forest and the Trees: Micro-Level Considerations in the Study of Geographic Mobility in Old Age, in Elderly Migration and Population Redistribution, pp. 23–24. Belhaven Press, London (1992)
28. Nimako, S.G., Ntim, B.A.: Construct specification and misspecification within the application of push-pull-mooring theory of switching behaviour. J. Bus. Manag. Sci. 1(5), 83–95 (2013)
29. Moon, B.: Paradigms in migration research: exploring'moorings' as a schema. Prog. Hum. Geogr. 19(4), 504–524 (1995)
30. Bansal, H.S., Taylor, S.F., James, Y.: "Migrating" to new service providers: Toward a unifying framework of consumers' switching behaviors. J. Acad. Mark. Sci. 33(1), 96–115 (2005)
31. Langeard, E., et al.: Services Marketing: New Insights from Consumers and Managers. Marketing Science Institute, Cambridge (1981)
32. Keaveney, S.M., Parthasarathy, M.: Customer switching behavior in online services: an exploratory study of the role of selected attitudinal, behavioral, and demographic factors. J. Acad. Mark. Sci. 29(4), 374–390 (2001)
33. Dagger, T.S., David, M.E.: Uncovering the real effect of switching costs on the satisfaction-loyalty association: the critical role of involvement and relationship benefits. Eur. J. Mark. 46(3/4), 447–468 (2012)
34. Lam, S.Y., et al.: Customer value, satisfaction, loyalty, and switching costs: an illustration from a business-to-business service context. J. Acad. Mark. Sci. 32(3), 293–311 (2004)
35. Bansal, H.S., Taylor, S.F.: The service provider switching model (SPSM) a model of consumer switching behavior in the services industry. J. Serv. Res. 2(2), 200–218 (1999)
36. Jones, M.A., Mothersbaugh, D.L., Beatty, S.E.: Switching barriers and repurchase intentions in services. J. Retail. 76(2), 259–274 (2000)
37. Keaveney, S.M.: Customer switching behavior in service industries: an exploratory study. J. Mark. 59(2), 71–82 (1995)
38. Venkatesh, V., et al.: User acceptance of information technology: toward a unified view. MIS Q. 27(3), 425–478 (2003)
39. Wang, C.: Consumer acceptance of self-service technologies: an ability–willingness model. International Journal of Market Research 59(6), 787–802 (2017)
40. Xiaoren, Z., Xiangdong, C., Ling, D.: Comparative study of self-service technology adoption based on product function. Inf. Technol. J. 12(12), 2350–2357 (2013)
41. Howard, M., Worboys, C.: Self-service – a contradiction in terms or customer-led choice? J. Consum. Behav. 2(4), 382–392 (2003)
42. Agarwal, R., Prasad, J.: A conceptual and operational definition of personal innovativeness in the domain of information technology. Inf. Syst. Res. 9(2), 204–215 (1998)
43. Boyle, R.J., Ruppel, C.P.: The effects of personal innovativeness, perceived risk, and computer self-efficacy on online purchasing intent. J. Int. Technol. Inf. Manag. 15(2), 61–73 (2006)
44. Limayem, M., Hirt, S.G.: Force of habit and information systems usage: theory and initial validation. J. Assoc. Inf. Syst. 4, 65–97 (2003)
45. Limayem, M., Hirt, S.G., Cheung, C.M.K.: How habit limits the predictive power of intention: the case of information systems continuance. MIS Q. 31(4), 705–737 (2007)

46. Bamberg, S., Ajzen, I., Schmidt, P.: Choice of travel mode in the theory of planned behavior: the roles of past behavior, habit, and reasoned action. Basic Appl. Soc. Psychol. **25**(3), 175–187 (2003)
47. Hair, J., et al.: Multivariate Data Analysis, 6th edn. Pearson Education, New Jersey (2006)
48. Nunnally, J.C.: Psychometric Theory. McGraw Hill, New York (1978)
49. Fornell, C., Larcker, D.F.: Evaluating structural equation models with unobservable variables and measurement error. J. Mark. Res. **18**(1), 39–50 (1981)
50. Wang, Y.S.: Assessing ecommerce systems success: a respecification and validation of the DeLone and McLean model of IS success. Inf. Syst. J. **18**(5), 529–557 (2008)
51. Ringle, C.M., Wende, S., Becker, J.M.: SmartPLS 3. SmartPLS GmbH, Boenningstedt (2015). http://www.smartpls.com
52. Chin, W.W.: The partial least squares approach for structural equation modeling. In: Marcoulides, G.A. (ed.) Modern Methods for Business Research. Lawrence Erlbaum Associates, Mahwah (1998)
53. Ganesh, J., Arnold, M.J., Reynolds, K.E.: Understanding the customer base of service providers: an examination of the differences between switchers and stayers. J. Mark. **64**(3), 65–87 (2000)

Public Innovation: Concept and Future Research Agenda

Lizeth Fernanda Serrano Cárdenas[1,2](✉) (iD),
Yessika Lorena Vásquez González[1] (iD),
Flor Nancy Díaz-Piraquive[2] (iD),
and Javier Eloy Guillot Landecker[3] (iD)

[1] Universidad Jorge Tadeo Lozano, Bogotá, Colombia
{lizethf.serranoc,lorena.vasquezg}@utadeo.edu.co
[2] Universidad Católica de Colombia, Bogotá, Colombia
{lfserranoc,fndiaz}@ucatolica.edu.co
[3] Equipo de Innovación Pública (EiP), Dirección de Innovación y Desarrollo
Empresarial, Departamento Nacional de Planeación, Bogotá, Colombia
jguillot@dnp.gov.co

Abstract. The complexity and uncertainty that increasingly characterize public issues in contemporary societies indicate the relevance of public innovation, which designates a collection of approaches for exploring, testing and validating new ideas that create added value for society. Despite its relevance, studies are still needed to go further in analyzing the literature built on the subject, and to identify new research agendas that can generate inputs to translate theories into practice. Hence, the purpose of this article is to analyze the concept of public innovation and establish a future research agenda about the topic, on the basis of a systematic literature review of documents published between 2004 and 2018 in the Web of Science® multi-disciplinary database. For this purpose, the data mining software Vantage Point® and the qualitative analysis software MAXQDA® were used to study 148 documents. The results show the need to deepen the construction of public innovation theory from the perspective of the actors who interact in its dynamics. Finally, from the methodological perspective, it was found relevant to study the topic using a triangulation of methods, and through developing longitudinal and comparative studies, in order to understand the conditioning factors and results of the network collaboration exercises implicit in public innovation processes.

Keywords: Public innovation · Trends · Systematic literature review · Research agenda

1 Introduction

Social problems are frequently multi-dimensional and with low structuring, not sensitive to segmented treatments, and integrate complex cause-effect relationships. The implementation of public policies involves mobilizing interventions in response to issues which, in general, do not have shared definitions, involve a plurality of actors

© Springer Nature Switzerland AG 2019
L. Uden et al. (Eds.): KMO 2019, CCIS 1027, pp. 165–177, 2019.
https://doi.org/10.1007/978-3-030-21451-7_14

with particular perceptions and aspirations, and at the same time, imply the interaction of multiple and complex dynamics [1]. Public innovation becomes relevant in response to these challenges [2]. Innovation has been considered as a key factor for private businesses [3], understood as a dynamic process in which problems are defined, new ideas are developed, and solutions are selected and implemented [4]. Some studies have analyzed the differences between the private sector and the public sector in terms of their innovation capability, proposing that innovation capability is more developed in the private sector since it is driven by competition. In contrast, public organizations could be less innovative, because the nature of their work dynamics makes them reluctant to take risks [5, 6]. The challenges of public sector innovation can also be related with a limited understanding of the dynamics of innovation in public organizations [7]. Public innovation is tied with the diversity of objectives and results expected from the public sector: providing high-quality services to people, encouraging the innovation capabilities of the private sector, guaranteeing public values such as democracy, trust and safety [8], and responding to multiple and complex social challenges [9, 10]. Within these dynamics, public innovation becomes a possibility to break public policy deadlocks, reduce their costs and improve services for the benefit of citizens and other stakeholders [11–14]. In the literature, a growing interest in the measurement and evaluation of public innovation has arisen, to understand its contribution for improving the efficiency of the public sector and the quality of its services [15]. However, some authors argue that although there are gaps in the measurement of public innovation, first it is necessary to understand the concept [16, 17], achieve a deep comprehension of how it has been developed over time and what factors promote or hinder it [6, 18–20]. As Liddle [21] points out, the urgency of measurement has often left aside addressing the more fundamental question: What is public innovation? and perhaps more importantly, why should the public sector innovate? [22].

The field of public innovation still requires more research to deepen the conceptualization of the topic from an integrative vision [23–25] that articulates preceding research literature, to avoid considering it a "magical concept" or a mere trend [26]. For this reason, more studies are needed to both to understand public innovation and to generate critical stances to the public innovation strategies on which many governments have embarked [27, 28]. Accordingly, the purpose of this research is to analyze research trends about public innovation, to deepen the knowledge of the concept and establish an agenda for future research in this field. A systematic review of the literature published between 2004 and 2018 in the multi-disciplinary database Web of Science® was carried out to make a theoretical contribution to the comprehension of Public Innovation. It also pretends to make a methodological contribution through the rigorous documentation of a systematic literature review, integrating cutting-edge tools for the analysis of research trends over a field of study, in order to become a reference for future research. The paper starts with a description of the methodological structure of the research [29]. Subsequently, the results of the review process are synthesized in three sections: (1) an analysis of research trends on the topic; (2) the contributions of the reviewed literature about the topic in a timeline; and finally, (3) the definition of a research agenda on the basis of the gaps identified in the analyzed documents. Lastly, the implications of the findings are discussed.

2 Methodology

A literature review is defined by Onwuegbuzie, Bustamante and Nelson [30] as the interpretation of a selected set of documents published about a specific topic. Fink [31] considers a literature review to be a systematic and reproducible method to identify, evaluate and synthesize research work in a particular area. In this study, a systematic literature review was conducted with the aim of developing a conceptual consolidation in a fragmented field of study. The three-phase methodology proposed by Tranfield, Denyer and Smart [29] was followed:

2.1 Planning

In this phase, the research purpose was defined and the information sources were identified. The purpose was to identify research trends, analyze convergences and divergences about the concept of Public Innovation, and establish a research agenda. The search was limited to documents from peer-reviewed journals, considering the suggestion of some authors [32] regarding validity and potential greater impact in the field of study. Specifically, the Web of Science database was selected under the premise of being considered one of the most complete databases of peer-reviewed journals in the social sciences [33]. It includes over 20,000 multi-disciplinary, peer-reviewed, high-quality scholarly journals published worldwide [34]. Finally, a quality criterion in the filtering process was established: the inclusion of documents that contribute to explore how the concept of Public Innovation reflects in the practice.

2.2 Development

The second phase was structured in five stages. In the *first stage*, the search equation applied in the Web of Science database includes "public innovation" as a keyword in the "Topic" field. All available years were included (2004–2018/November) and all languages. With this search equation, a total of 148 documents were obtained. In the *second stage*, the 148 documents were analyzed using the data mining software VantagePoint®. In the *third stage*, the following aspects about the field of study were identified: publication dynamic by countries, publication dynamic by authors, and correlation between research topics related with public innovation. In the *fourth stage*, a reading of the titles and abstracts of the 148 resulting documents was done in order to verify compliance of the quality criterion described above; as a result, 62 documents were selected. In the *fifth stage*, a complete reading and coding of the 62 documents was done using the qualitative analysis software MAXQDA®. As a result, 58 documents were added to the sample by snowball, leaving as a result 120 documents that were analyzed (See Fig. 1).

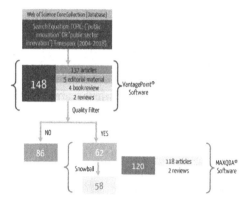

Fig. 1. Systematic literature review process. Source: Authors

2.3 Reporting Research Findings

During the reading process of the 120 articles resulting from the methodological stages described above, five analytical categories were designed to codify the information: (1) definition, (2) timeline, (3) concept relevance, (4) conceptual gaps and (5) methodological gaps.

3   Results

3.1 Descriptive Analysis of the Public Innovation Field

Since 2004, there has been an annual growing trend in publications about Public Innovation (See Fig. 2). The three most cited documents published in 2015 were focused on analysis from a theoretical perspective [35] and the practice of public innovation processes [36], from a collaborative perspective among networks [37]. The analysis of the publication dynamic by country (Fig. 3), found that Denmark is the country in which the highest number of documents during the studied period was

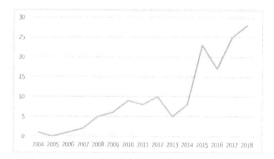

Fig. 2. Growth of articles about public innovation in the Web of Science database. *Value for 2018 was estimated based on data up to 14/11/2018.

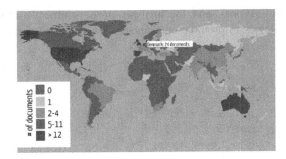

Fig. 3. Publication dynamic in the public innovation field -by country

published, followed by Australia, the United States and Spain. The most cited documents generated in Denmark were oriented towards the analysis of collaborative networks for public innovation [38, 39], and the study of sustainability strategies for innovation initiatives in the public sector [40].

The most outstanding author is Professor Eva Sørensen from Roskilde University, Denmark. Her publications have appeared almost uninterruptedly from 2011 to 2018. Her main topics of interest in the knowledge field are: collaborative governance with emphasis on multiple actors [39, 41], the analysis of the proliferation of governance networks and their relationship with the growing demand for public innovation [38, 42, 43], the study of key drivers for political innovation [38, 44], and the need for innovations in polity, politics and policy [45]. Another prominent author is professor Jacob Torfing, who has published books in the field of Public Innovation [46–48], and contributed to the study of the generation of public value through governance networks [49].

The journal with the greatest interest in the topic is *Public Management Review* of the United Kingdom (12 publications), with an emphasis on documents that explore the development of the public management field and that study the governance of intersectoral relationships. The next outstanding journal is *Research Policy* of the Netherlands (8 publications), with a focus on articles that examine, empirically and theoretically, the interaction between innovation and economic, social, political and organizational processes [51]. Last among the three most featured journals in the field is the *International Review of Administrative Science* of the United States (6 publications), which focuses on comparative analysis, seeking to shape the future agenda of public administration.

Finally, research topics associated with the study of Public Innovation were analyzed. Figure 4 shows the keywords repeated at least five times in the documents analyzed (established criterion for visibility effects). In this co-relation map, the number in parenthesis indicates the number of documents about this topic, and the blue bubbles show the relationships between topics. In synthesis, the study of public innovation has been focused on the analysis of drivers that make this concept a reality in practice (21 publications), the study of instruments such as public innovation laboratories (13 publications) which promote collaboration strategies between actors (13 publications), the understanding of governance in the implementation of innovation initiatives in the public sector (11 publications), emphasizing the implicit dynamics of network governance (11 publications), and the analysis of government's challenges in the development of strategies to promote open innovation (9 publications).

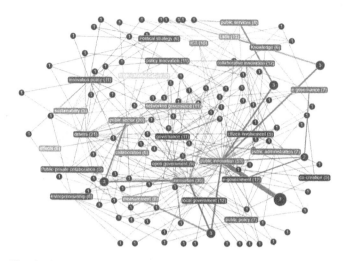

Fig. 4. Correlation between key topics in the public innovation field

3.2   Understanding the Concept of Public Innovation

In order to structure a definition of Public Innovation in a timeline, the three phases in which intellectual development about the topic is divided will be considered as a reference [38, 52], as well as the authors' analysis in the systematic literature review process: (1) *competitive innovation: the Schumpeterian period* [53]; (2) *innovation through systems: the autochthonous-theory period*; and finally, (3) *collaborative innovation*.

In the *first phase,* we find Schumpeter's contributions [3, 54], which studied the innovation of products and processes within private companies, defining innovation as the production of something new, or doing things in a different way. In 1977, Pierce and Delibes's [55] approaches consider that the concept of innovation is influenced by the context. Thompson points to the need for innovation capability to be developed from a business perspective as well as from a government perspective [56]. Although it is unclear when academic researchers began to systematically examine public sector innovation, for some authors Roessner's study *"Incentives to innovate in public and private organizations"* [57] could be regarded as the first study that directly examined the concept of innovation in the public sector. In 1984, Kingdon [58] proposes that innovation implies a deliberate attempt to change, understanding it as a mixture of intentional and non-intentional results [59]. In the following year, Porter's [60] study was published, arguing that innovation is a source of competitive advantage. Consistent with this approach, Damanpour [61] defines innovation as the implementation of an idea related to a device, system, process, policy, program or service, new to the context of implementation. In 1990, Cohen and Levinthal [62] argued that the main contribution of innovation to the organizational context is the improvement of the capability to recognize the value of new ideas, assimilate them and apply them [63]. However, according to Rodgers [64, 65], the fact that innovation implies novelty does not necessarily mean that it implies invention [66]. Some authors from the 1990 s [67, 68], as well as from the more recent literature [40, 69], agree in four criteria to differentiate public innovation from other change processes in the sector: (1) it must generate an impact in terms of social development; (2) it must be repeated, not just a point-like initiative [70, 71]; (3) it must represent significant or radical changes; and (4) it must be intentional [17]. For some authors [5, 72–74], in the 1990 s, with the growing attention to public management, literature about innovation in this sector expanded rapidly and the concept was integrated not only in research perspectives but as a rhetorical element of public life, as part of modernizing proposals in different parts of the world [75].

The emergence of monopoly capitalism shifted the focus from the individual businessman to the analysis of cooperative business initiatives. For this reason, in the *second phase*, the concept of public innovation was focused on inter-organizational collaboration between actors [76, 77]. In this phase, the importance of analyzing the innovation potential of regions and industrial groups was highlighted [78]. Likewise, literature on public innovation since 2000 moves away from a focus on the private sector, proposing new conceptualizations to respond to public sector realities [25, 79–84]. In this sense, some authors [85] have described public innovation as a "magical" concept. To point out the need for clarification, Cunningham and Kempling [86] add that public sector innovation is typically addressed to improved performance and public benefits, rather than the exclusive generation of competitive advantages. In conclusion, in this phase, public sector innovation was understood as the process of adopting ideas [87] and organizational practices that are new for a public organization [88] and add value to society [26, 89].

Finally, the *third phase* evidences a growing interest on how collaborative interaction can encourage public innovation [90]. According to this group of authors [38, 47], public innovation is the result of collaboration [5, 35, 41, 46], defining it as a "collective effort" to generate public value [39]. Public innovation is understood as the attempt to improve public administration in order to make it more efficient, equitable, receptive, integrated, innovative and democratic [91, 92]. For Bekkers, Edelenbos and Steijn [93], public innovation is defined as a learning or search process in which governments attempt to face social challenges. The term "attempt" [16] is important here, because it signals that innovation involves potential failure.

3.3   Future Research Agenda

There is agreement in the literature that innovation requires novelty and implementation, but there are divergences on the level of novelty required, and on the specific types of innovation found in the public sector [19]. This shows the need for the construction of typologies about the concept. A solid and shared comprehension of what innovation is in the public sector, and how this sector perceives it, is vital both for research on the characteristics of public sector innovation and for the development of measurement models [40]. Specifically, more analysis is needed to understand what is the relationship between public governance and public innovation? [94]. It is here where the need to deepen the analysis of new interactions between government and society becomes increasingly relevant [95], in order to respond to so-called *wicked problems*. It may be useful to understand these relationships by using the approaches generated under the vision of Network Governance. For Ojasalo and Kauppinen [96], carrying out scientific research is relevant, as well as developing pilot tests to analyze new governance schemes in the context of collaborative innovation. Under the above premises, more research is required to propose approaches and scenarios for the implementation of open innovation platforms and mechanisms that facilitate collaboration. Although there are previous studies developed with this aim [97], there is still not enough research that specifically refers to laboratories as intermediaries for open innovation [98].

In summary, the future research agenda on the topic should contribute to the analysis of drivers [99], values, barriers [100], results, impacts, mechanisms, types and phases [72] related with processes of public innovation [2], emphasizing a deep understanding of contextual elements that support these processes. The literature review carried out indicates that research efforts are still needed to contribute to the development of indicators and reference frameworks to measure innovation [16, 40]. From the methodological perspective, is necessary to go deeper in three dimensions: (1) greater variety in methods: moving from a qualitative domain to mixed methods [25]; (2) the development of theory by analyzing the relationship of interdependence between *polity, politics and policy* [45], generating empirical tests about theoretical constructions; and lastly, (3) more transnational studies. Finally, more evidence about the results of public innovation must be provided from an empirical perspective, integrating longitudinal approaches [6].

4   Discussion and Conclusions

The study of public innovation is a growing topic of interest, from the perspective of research as well as practice. However, as this systematic review has shown, research on the topic is fragmented, and there are still theoretical as well as methodological gaps. The main contribution of this research, from a theoretical perspective, is the consolidation of a great body of knowledge about public innovation from a parsimonious vision. This allows future researchers interested in the topic to devote themselves to the specific gaps identified in the literature and generate contributions relevant to the field of study. The second contribution is the application of a rigorous and transparent review methodology, in which the field of knowledge was analyzed descriptively.

In synthesis, regarding the concept of public innovation, it was found that contributions in the literature on the topic can be divided in three groups: authors interested in the analysis of innovation from a competitive perspective; authors who contribute to the analysis if innovation through a systems perspective, separating the scope of innovation in the private and public sectors; and finally, in the most recent literature, an open debate on the challenges for collaborative innovation among multiple actors. Finally, gaps in the literature that create opportunities for research can be highlighted, in three dimensions. (1) From the theoretical perspective, there is a need to better understand the concept, which implies contrasting the literature with the contributions of public sector actors and making a rigorous analysis of the drivers, values, barriers, results, impacts, mechanisms, types and phases of public innovation processes, as well as deepening the understanding of new structures for network governance that may be integrated in collaborative innovation processes. (2) From the methodological perspective, it is important to develop more multi-method research approaches that can combine empirical, longitudinal and cross-country comparative studies, in order to explore the validity of particular case studies and reveal deeper patterns in the field. (3) Finally, more efforts need to be carried out to understand the interface between research about public innovation and its practice in both local and global contexts, in order to identify feedback loops that may contribute to the future development of the field.

References

1. Martínez-Nogueira, R.: La coherencia y la coordinación de las políticas públicas. Aspectos conceptuales y experiencias. Documento Final del Proyecto" Modernización del Estado", en el marco del Préstamo BIRF (2008)
2. Agolla, J., Van, L., Burger, J.: An empirical investigation into innovation drivers and barriers in public sector organizations. Int. J. Innov. Sci. 8(4), 404–422 (2016)
3. Schumpeter, J.: The Theory of Economic Development. Harvard University Press, Cambridge (1934)
4. Sørensen, E., Torfing, J.: Collaborative innovation in the public sector. Innov. J. Public Sect. Innov. J. 17(1), 1–14 (2012)
5. Hartley, J.: Innovation in governance and public services: past and present. Public Money Manage. 25(1), 27–34 (2005)
6. Lewis, J.M., Ricard, L., Klijn, E.: How innovation drivers, networking and leadership shape public sector innovation capacity. Int. Rev. Adm. Sci. 84(2), 288–307 (2017)
7. Demircioglu, M., Audretsch, D.: Conditions for innovation in public sector organizations. Res. Pol. 46(9), 1681–1691 (2017)
8. Kelly, G., Mulgan, G. and Muers, S.: Creating Public Value: An Analytical Framework for Public Service Reform (Strategy Unit, Cabinet Office) (2002)
9. Mazzucato, M.: Financing innovation: creative destruction vs. destructive creation. Ind. Corp. Change 22(4), 851–867 (2013)
10. Cels, S., de Jong, J., Nauta, F.: Agents of Change: Strategies and Tactics for Social Innovation (2012)
11. Valdivia, V.A., Ramírez-Alujas, Á.V.: Innovación en el sector público chileno: la experiencia y aprendizajes del laboratorio de gobierno. Revista de Gestión Pública 6(1), 43–80 (2017)
12. Aschhoff, B., Sofka, W.: Innovation on demand—Can public procurement drive market success of innovations? Res. Policy 38(8), 1235–1247 (2009)
13. Edler, J., Georghiou, L.: Public procurement and innovation—resurrecting the demand side. Res. Policy 36(7), 949–963 (2007)
14. Damanpour, F., Schneider, M.: Characteristics of innovation and innovation adoption in public organizations: assessing the role of managers. J. public Adm. Res. Theory 19(3), 495–522 (2008)

15. Rolfstam, M.: Public procurement as an innovation policy tool: the role of institutions. Sci. Public Policy **36**(5), 349–360 (2009)
16. Arundel, A., Huber, D.: From too little to too much innovation? Issues in measuring innovation in the public sector. Struct. Change Econ. Dyn. **27**, 146–159 (2013)
17. Bugge, M., Bloch, C.: Between bricolage and breakthroughs—framing the many faces of public sector innovation. Publ. Money Manag. **36**(4), 281–288 (2016)
18. Bloch, C., Bugge, M.: Public sector innovation—from theory to measurement. Struct. Change Econ. Dyn. **27**, 133–145 (2013)
19. Torugsa, N., Arundel, A.: Complexity of innovation in the public sector: a workgroup-level analysis of related factors and outcomes. Public Manage. Rev. **18**(3), 392–416 (2016)
20. Dosi, G.: Sources, procedures, and microeconomic effects of innovation. J. Econ. Lit. **26**, 1120–1171 (1988)
21. Nelson, R., Winter, S.: The Schumpeterian tradeoff revisited. Am. Econ. Rev. **72**(1), 114–132 (1982)
22. Liddle, J.: Innovation in the public sector: linking capacity and leadership-edited by Victor Bekkers, Jurian Edelenbos and Bram Steijn. Public Adm. **91**(2), 511–513 (2013)
23. Stewart Weeks, M., Kastelle, T.: Innovation in the public sector. Aust. J. Public Adm. **74**(1), 63–72 (2015)
24. Mulgan, G., Albury, D.: Innovation in the Public Sector. Strategy Unit, Cabinet Office, vol. 1, p. 40 (2003)
25. De Vries, H., Bekkers, V.J.J.M., Tummers, L.: Innovation in the public sector: a systematic review and future research agenda. Public Adm. **94**(1), 146–166 (2016)
26. Agolla, J., Van, L., Burger, J.: Public sector innovation drivers: a process model. J. Social Sci. **34**(2), 165–176 (2013)
27. Pollitt, C.: Innovation in the public sector: an introductory overview. In: Bekkers, V., Edelenbos, J., Steijn, B. (eds.) Innovation in the public sector, pp. 35–43. Palgrave Macmillan, London (2011). https://doi.org/10.1057/9780230307520_2
28. De Vries, H., Tummers, L., Bekkers, V.: A stakeholder perspective on public sector innovation: why position matters. Int. Rev. Adm. Sci. **84**(2), 269–287 (2017)
29. Tranfield, D., Denyer, D., Smart, P.: Towards a methodology for developing evidence-informed management knowledge by means of systematic review. Br. J. Manag. **14**(3), 207–222 (2003)
30. Onwuegbuzie, A., Bustamante, R., Nelson, J.: Mixed research as a tool for developing quantitative instruments. J. Mixed Methods Res. **4**(1), 56–78 (2010)
31. Fink, A.: Conducting research literature reviews, 4th edn, p. 257p. Sage Publications Inc., California (2013)
32. Podsakoff, P., et al.: The influence of management journals in the 1980 s and 1990s. Strateg. Manage. J. **26**(5), 473–488 (2005)
33. Crossan, M., Apaydin, M.: A multi-dimensional framework of organizational innovation: a systematic review of the literature. J. Manage. Stud. **47**(6), 1154–1191 (2010)
34. Clarivate Analytics. Platform Web of Science: Introduction (2018). http://clarivate.libguides.com/webofscienceplatform. Accessed 14 Nov 2018
35. Voorberg, W., Bekkers, V., Tummers, L.: A systematic review of co-creation and co-production: embarking on the social innovation journey. Public Manage. Rev. **17**(9), 1333–1357 (2015)
36. Arundel, A., Casali, L., Hollanders, H.: How European public sector agencies innovate: the use of bottom-up, policy-dependent and knowledge-scanning innovation methods. Res. Policy **44**(7), 1271–1282 (2015)
37. Veeckman, C., Van Der Graaf, S.: The city as living laboratory: empowering citizens with the citadel toolkit. Technol. Innov. Manag. Rev. **5**(3), 6–17 (2015)

38. Sørensen, E., Torfing, J.: Enhancing collaborative innovation in the public sector. Adm. Society **43**(8), 842–868 (2011)
39. Hartley, J., Sørensen, E., Torfing, J.: Collaborative innovation: a viable alternative to market competition and organizational entrepreneurship. Public Adm. Rev. **73**(6), 821–830 (2013)
40. Fuglsang, L., Sørensen, F.: The balance between bricolage and innovation: management dilemmas in sustainable public innovation. Serv. Ind. J. **31**(4), 581–595 (2011)
41. Sørensen, E., Torfing, J.: Co-initiation of collaborative innovation in urban spaces. Urban Aff. Rev. **54**(2), 388–418 (2018)
42. Sørensen, E., Torfing, J.: Metagoverning collaborative innovation in governance networks. Am. Rev. Public Adm. **47**(7), 826–839 (2017)
43. Sørensen, E.: Enhancing policy innovation by redesigning representative democracy. Policy Polit. **44**(2), 155–170 (2016)
44. Agger, A., Sørensen, E.: Managing collaborative innovation in public bureaucracies. Plan. Theory **17**(1), 53–73 (2018)
45. Sørensen, E.: Political innovations: innovations in political institutions, processes and outputs. Publ. Manag. Rev. 1–19 (2017)
46. Torfing, J.: Collaborative Innovation in the Public Sector. Georgetown University Press, Washington (2016)
47. Hartley, J.: Innovation in governance and public service: past and present. Publ. Money Manag. **25**(1), 27–34 (2005)
48. Torfing, J., et al.: Interactive Governance: Advancing the Paradigm. Oxford University Press on Demand (2012)
49. Crosby, B.C., Thart, P., Torfing, J.: Public value creation through collaborative innovation. Public Manage. Rev. **19**(5), 655–669 (2017)
50. Elsevier (2018). https://www.journals.elsevier.com/research-policy/. Accessed 15 Nov 2018
51. SAGE Publishing (2018). https://us.sagepub.com/en-us/sam/journal/international-review-administrative-sciences#aims-and-scope. Accessed 15 Nov 2018
52. Kattel, R.: What would Max Weber say about public-sector innovation? J. Public Adm. Policy **8**(1), 9–19 (2015)
53. Schumpeter, J.A.: Th eorie der wirtschaft lichen Entwicklung. Duncker & Humblot, Berlin (1912)
54. Schumpeter, J.: Capitalism, Socialism and Democracy (UK 1943) 5th edn. (1976). George Allan and Unwin, London (1942)
55. Pierce, J., Delbecq, A.: Organization structure, individual attitudes and innovation. Acad. Manage. Rev. **2**(1), 27–37 (1977)
56. Thompson, V.: Bureaucracy and innovation. Adm. Sci. Q. **10**(1), 1–20 (1965). Special Issue on Professionals in Organizations
57. Roessner, J.D.: Incentives to innovate in public and private organizations. Adm. Soc. **9**(3), 341–365 (1977)
58. Kingdon, J.: Agendas, Alternatives, and Public Policies. Little, Brown, Boston (1984)
59. Fagerberg, J.: Innovation—a guide to the literature. In: Fagerberg, J., et al. (eds.) The Oxford Handbook of Innovation, Oxford University Press (2005)
60. Porter, M.: Competitive Advantage. Creating and Sustaining Superior Performance. The Free Press, New York (1985)
61. Damanpour, F.: The adoption of technological, administrative, and ancillary innovations: Impact of organizational factors. J. Manage. **13**(4), 675–688 (1987)
62. Cohen, W., Levinthal, D.: Absorptive capacity: a new perspective on learning and innovation. Adm. Sci. Q. **35**(1), 128–152 (1990)

63. Damanpour, F.: Organizational innovation: a meta-analysis of effects of determinants and moderators. Acad. Manage. J. **34**(3), 555–590 (1991)
64. Rogers, E.: The Diffusion of Innovation, 4th edn. The Free Press, New York (1995)
65. Rogers, E.: Diffusion of Innovations, 5th edn. Free Press, New York (2003)
66. Roberts, N., King, P.: Transforming Public Policy: Dynamics of Policy Entrepreneurship. Jossey-Bass, San Francisco (1996)
67. Amabile, T., Conti, R., Coon, H., Lazenby, J., Herron, M.: Assessing the work environment for creativity. Acad. Manage. J. **39**(5), 1154–1184 (1996)
68. Kanter, R.M.: The Change Masters. Corporate Entrepreneurs at Work. International Thompson Business Press, London; Boston (1996)
69. Mulgan, G., Albury, D.: Innovation in the Public Sector. Strategy Unit, Cabinet Office, London (2003)
70. Moore, H., Sparrow, M., Spelman, W.: Innovation in policing: from production lines to jobs shops. In: Altshuler, A.A., Behn, R.D. (eds.) Innovation in American Government. The Brookings Institution Press, Washington (1997). Chapter 12
71. Brown, K; Osborne, S.: Managing Change and Innovation in Public Service Organizations. Routledge (2012)
72. Meijer, A.: From hero-innovators to distributed heroism: an in-depth analysis of the role of individuals in public sector innovation. Public Manag. Rev. **16**(2), 199–216 (2014)
73. Altshuler, A., Behn, R. (eds.): Innovation in American Government. Brookings, Washington (1997)
74. Institution Bekkers, V., Edelenbos, J., Steijn, B. (eds.): Innovation in the Public Sector. Linking Capacity and Leadership. Palgrave MacMillan, Houndmills (2011)
75. Osborne, S., Brown, L. (eds.): Handbook of Innovation in Public Services. Edward Elgar Publishing (2013)
76. Teece, D.: Competition, cooperation, and innovation. J. Econ. Behav. Organ. **18**, 1–25 (1992)
77. Lundvall, B.: Product Innovation and User-Producer Interaction. Aalborg University Press, Aalborg, Denmark (1985)
78. Edquist, C., Hommen, L.: Systems of innovation: Theory and policy for the demand side. Technol. Soc. **21**, 63–79 (1999)
79. Katt el, R., Cepilovs, A., Drechsler, W., Kalvet, T., Lember, V., Tõnurist, P.: Can We Measure Public Sector Innovation? A Literature Review, LIPSE Project paper (2013)
80. Sahni, N., Wessel, M., Christensen, C.: Unleashing breakthrough innovation in government. Stanford Soc. Innov. Rev. **11**(3), 27–31 (2013)
81. Lagunes Marin, H., Rubalcaba Bermejo, L.: External sources for innovation in public organisations. Serv. Ind. J. **35**(13), 710–727 (2015)
82. Bugge, M., Bloch, C.: Between bricolage and breakthroughs—framing the many faces of public sector innovation. Public Money Manage. **36**(4), 281–288 (2016)
83. Demircioglu, M., Audretsch, D.: Conditions for innovation in public sector organizations. Res. Policy **46**(9), 1681–1691 (2017)
84. Light, P.: Sustaining Innovation: Creating Nonprofit and Government Organizations That Innovate Naturally. Jossey-Bass, San Francisco (1998)
85. Hood, C., Peter, H.: Talking about government. Public Manage. Rev. **13**(5), 641–658 (2011)
86. Cunningham, J., Kempling, J.: Implementing change in public sector organizations. Manage. Decis. **47**(2), 330–344 (2009)
87. Mulgan, G.: Ready or not?: taking innovation in the public sector seriously. Nesta (2007)
88. OECD: Achieving Public Sector Agility at Times of Fiscal Consolidation, OECD Public Governance Reviews. OECD Publishing, Paris (2015)

89. Bason, C.: Leading Public Sector Innovation: Co-creating for a Better Society. The Polity Press, London (2010)
90. Von Hippel, E.: Democratizing Innovation. MIT Press (2005)
91. Wagenaar, H., Wood, M.: The precarious politics of public innovation. Politics Gov. **6**(1), 150–160 (2018)
92. March, J.G., Olsen, J.P.: Rediscovering Institutions. Simon and Schuster, New York (2010)
93. Bekkers, V., Edelenbos, J., Steijn, B. (eds.): 'An Innovative Public Sector? Embarking in the Innovation Journey' in Innovation in the Public Sector. Linking Capacity and Leadership, pp. 197–221. Palgrave MacMillan, Houndmills (2011)
94. Scupola, A., Zanfei, A.: Governance and innovation in public sector services: the case of the digital library. Gov. Inf. Q. **33**(2), 237–249 (2016)
95. Bekkers, V., Tummers, L.: Innovation in the public sector: towards an open and collaborative approach. Int. Rev. Adm. Sci. **84**(2), 209–213 (2018)
96. Ojasalo, J., Kauppinen, H.: Collaborative innovation with external actors: an empirical study on open innovation platforms in smart cities. Technol. Innov. Manage. Rev. **6**(12), 12 (2016)
97. Gascó, M.: Living labs: implementing open innovation in the public sector. Gov. Inf. Q. **34**(1), 90–98 (2017)
98. Mcgann, M., Blomkamp, E., Lewis, J.M.: The rise of public sector innovation labs: experiments in design thinking for policy. Policy Sci. **51**, 1–19 (2018)
99. Andersen, S., Jakobsen, M.: Political pressure, conformity pressure, and performance information as drivers of public sector innovation adoption. Int. Public Manage. J. **21**(2), 213–242 (2018)
100. Van Acker, W., Bouckaert, G.: What makes public sector innovations survive? An exploratory study of the influence of feedback, accountability and learning. Int. Rev. Adm. Sci. **84**(2), 249–268 (2018)

Improvement on Subjective Weighing Method in Attribute Coordinate Comprehensive Evaluation Model

Xiaolin Xu[1(✉)], Yan Liu[1(✉)], and Jiali Feng[2]

[1] Shanghai Polytechnic University, Shanghai, China
xlxu2001@163.com, liuyan@sspu.edu.cn
[2] Shanghai Maritime University, Shanghai, China
jlfeng@shmtu.edu.cn

Abstract. Attribute coordinate comprehensive evaluation model provides an evaluation method for allowing the evaluator to subjectively weigh the indexes of the evaluated object. Specifically, the process of weighing is implemented by rating the given sample data to reflect the evaluator's psychological weight upon some indexes. However, if the evaluated object includes many indexes, it is difficult for the evaluator to intuitively judge and accurately rate the sample data, which causes the great possibilities of rating the samples randomly and further influencing the final evaluation results. To address the problem, the paper changes the quantitative rating mode into qualitative judgment, and then converts the qualitative judgment into psychological weight, and finally evaluates all objects by the attribute coordinate comprehensive evaluation method. The experiment result shows the effectiveness of the improved method.

Keywords: Subjective · Weighing ·
Attribute coordinate comprehensive evaluation · Barycentric coordinate ·
Local satisfactory solution · Satisfaction

1 Introduction

Comprehensive evaluation is used for evaluating the evaluated objects good or bad. When certain uniform-dimension attribute value is endowed to all the evaluated objects, the optimum evaluated object is A = (10, …, 10) with each index value full score (the full score is assumed as 10). However, the optimum principle is not usually adopted in comprehensive evaluation, instead the satisfaction principle is usually adopted. That is, in actual decision making, we usually obtain the satisfactory solution rather than the optimum solution. That also explains why comprehensive evaluation tends to explore the most satisfactory solution meeting some conditions of weight [1–5].

The attribute coordinate comprehensive model features allowing the evaluator to subjectively weigh the evaluated objects by scoring the given samples, which reflects

---

X. Lu and Y. Liu—The work was supported by the Key Disciplines of Computer Science and Technology of Shanghai Polytechnic University (No. XXKZD1604).

© Springer Nature Switzerland AG 2019
L. Uden et al. (Eds.): KMO 2019, CCIS 1027, pp. 178–186, 2019.
https://doi.org/10.1007/978-3-030-21451-7_15

the evaluator's preference upon some indexes (attributes), and then calculate the satisfactory value of each evaluation index [6–13]. However, the method has its disadvantage. If there are too many evaluation indexes and samples, it is usually difficult for the evaluator to accurately give the score to each sample, so such result may not well reflect the psychological weight of the evaluator, thus influence the subsequent process and accordingly the accuracy of the final evaluation. The paper improves the weighing method for the evaluator in the way that the evaluator is not required to give the specific scores to the samples but rank the given samples, and then the ranking values are converted into the evaluator's psychological weight. Thus it is much easier for the evaluator to rank the samples than rate them, and also more accurate to obtain the evaluator's psychological weight.

In the paper, firstly, the attribute coordinate comprehensive evaluation model is briefly introduced; then, the improved weighing method is described; finally, the evaluation results obtained by the two methods before and after improvement are compared through the simulation experiment.

2 Brief Introduction to Attribute Coordinate Comprehensive Evaluation Model

2.1 Local Satisfactory Solution

When evaluating the multi-attribute object, the evaluator usually thinks that some attributes are more important than others, and should be endowed with more weights. The importance of attributes can possibly change along with the advantageous or disadvantageous degree of the evaluated objects, and such change reflected in the evaluation model is the dynamic change of the weight of one attribute.

One of the main characteristics of the attribute coordinate comprehensive evaluation is to endow attributes with different weights according to the evaluator's preference. The specific method is to give ratings on the given samples. Suppose T_0 is the critical total scores, and T_{max} is the maximum total scores. In the interval $[T_0, T_{max}]$, several scores $T_1, T_2, \ldots, T_{n-1}$ are uniformly selected according to the requirement for curve fitting. For the total score $T_i (i = 1, 2, 3 \ldots n - 1)$, several samples are selected for the evaluator and rated according to the evaluator's psychological preference. Then, the barycentric coordinate with total score of $T_i (i = 1, 2, 3 \ldots n - 1)$ is calculated by Formula (1).

$$b(\{v^h(z)\}) = \left(\frac{\sum\limits_{h=1}^{t} v_1^h f_1^h}{\sum\limits_{h=1}^{t} v_1^h}, \cdots, \frac{\sum\limits_{h=1}^{t} v_m^h f_m^h}{\sum\limits_{h=1}^{t} v_m^h} \right) \tag{1}$$

Where, $b(\{vh(z)\})$ is the psychological barycentric coordinate of the evaluator z; $\{x_k, k = 1, \ldots, s\}$ is the set of all the samples with total score of T_i, and each sample has m indexes, with the values respectively of f_i, $i = 1 \ldots m$. The evaluator selects t sets of samples $\{f_h, h = 1, \ldots, t\}$ which are believed thereby to be satisfactory, and respectively rates as $v^h(f^h)$, which is taken as the evaluator's psychological weight; then, the weighted average method is adopted to find the psychological barycentric coordinate of the evaluator for the total score T_i, and also seen as the evaluator's local satisfactory solution. The process is called as the learning of the evaluator's psychological weight.

2.2 Satisfactory Solution Curve

Obviously, with plenty of training samples and training times, the barycenter $b(\{v^h(z)\})$ will be gradually approximate to the local most satisfactory solution $x*|T$ in total score T, namely: $\lim\limits_{h\to\infty} b(\{vh(z)\}) \to x*|T$. Through the learning of each total score $T_i(i = 1, 2, 3 \ldots n - 1)$, $b_i(\{vh(z)\})$ can be obtained. After T traverses the interval $[T_0, T_{max}]$, the set $\{b'(\{v^h(z)\})|T \in [T_0, T_{max}]\}$ for all local most satisfactory solutions can be obtained. Generally speaking, the psychological criteria of the evaluator z on different total score T_i are consistent with each other. In other words, $\{b'(\{v^h(z)\})|T \in [T_0, T_{max}]\}$ can form a continuous curve, recorded as $L(b'(\{v^h(z)\}))$, which is called as the local most satisfactory solution curve of the evaluator z. $L(b'(\{v^h(z)\}))$ can be obtained by polynomial curve fitting. For example, three local most satisfactory solutions are taken as the interpolation points and input into Lagrange interpolation Formula (2) to calculate and the most satisfactory solution curve:

$$g_i(T) = \frac{(T - x_1^*)(T - x_2^*)}{(x_0^* - x_1^*)(x_0^* - x_2^*)}a_{i0} + \frac{(T - x_0^*)(T - x_2^*)}{(x_1^* - x_0^*)(x_1^* - x_2^*)}a_{i1} + \frac{(T - x_0^*)(T - x_1^*)}{(x_2^* - x_0^*)(x_2^* - x_1^*)}a_{i2} \quad (2)$$

Normally, when T value is larger, the evaluator is better satisfied with the local most satisfactory solution $b'(\{v^h(z)\})$ corresponding to T in $L(b'(\{v^h(z)\}))$.

2.3 Calculate the Satisfaction Degree for Each Object

With many satisfactory solutions which construct satisfactory solution curve $L(b(\{f^h(z)\}))$, we can calculate the global satisfaction degree according to (3) for each object to reflect how satisfactory it is compared with the satisfactory solution of the total plane to which the object belongs.

$$sat(f, z) = \left(\frac{\sum\limits_{i=1}^{m} f_{ij}}{\sum\limits_{j=1}^{m} F_j}\right)^{\left(\frac{\sum\limits_{i=1}^{m} f_j}{3\left(\sum\limits_{j=1}^{m} f_{ij}\right)}\right)} * \exp\left(-\frac{\sum\limits_{j=1}^{m} w_j|f_j - b(f^h(z_j)|}{\sum\limits_{j=1}^{m} w_j\delta_j}\right) \quad (3)$$

Where, $sat(f, Z)$ is the satisfaction of evaluated object f, whose value is expected to be between 0 and 1. f_j is the value of each index. $|f_j - b(f^h(z_j)|$ is to measure the difference between each attribute value and the corresponding barycentric value (satisfactory solution). w_j and δ_j are used as the factor which can be adjusted to make the satisfaction comparable value in the case where the original results are not desirable. $\sum_{j=1}^{m} F_j$ is the sum of F_j with each index value full score. $\sum_{ij=1}^{m} f_{ij}$ is the sum of the values of all the indexes F_{ij} of F_i.

3 Improvement of Attribute Coordinate Comprehensive Evaluation Model

3.1 Improvement of Rating Mode on Samples

As mentioned in Sect. 2, the evaluator is required to rate the samples to reflect this psychological weight upon some indexes. The scores of 9 courses of 4 sample students with the total score of about 770 are shown in Table 1. Specifically, 9 courses include liberal-arts courses (Chinese, English, politics, history, geography) and science courses (maths, physics, chemistry, biology), and the evaluator needs to rate each student and give the psychological weight according to the scores in order to present his preference upon the students with good liberal-arts scores or science scores.

With so many indexes, if the 10-score system is adopted, it is difficult for the evaluator to provide the score which can accurately reflect his psychological weight according to the sample difference. Therefore, there exists the possibility of rating randomly in practice. Instead, if the evaluator only needs to qualitatively rank the evaluated object, it becomes much easier for the evaluator to do the judgement.

For example, if an evaluator prefers science, he or she may provide a reasonable ranking for the samples shown in the column "Ranking (Science Preference)" of Table 1.

Table 1. Sample data ranking

No.	Chinese	Maths	English	Physics	Chemistry	Biology	Politics	History	Geography	Total Score	Ranking (Science Preference)	Ranking (Liberal-arts Preference)
28	79	112	92.5	81	92	88	70	67	91	772.5	2	3
29	85	103	90.5	87	84	89	76	78	79	771.5	4	1
30	74	118	89.5	92	92	85	73	69	79	771.5	1	4
31	86	117	78.5	86	96	89	69	70	79	770.5	3	2

The evaluator preferring liberal-arts courses may provide the reasonable ranking as shown in the column "Ranking (Liberal-arts Preference)" of Table 1.

3.2 Conversion from Ranking Value into Weight Value

After obtaining the evaluator's qualitative evaluation upon the samples, it is necessary to convert the ranking value into weight value, namely qualitative evaluation (ranking) into quantitative value (weight), which is done by inverse qualitative mapping method [14]. Specifically, various conversion functions can be applied in the inverse qualitative mapping method. Here, we believe that the samples ranked in front are more important, so they should have larger weight when calculating barycentric coordinates. Therefore, we adopt $y = 1/(nx)$ function (as shown in Fig. 1) to calculate the evaluator's psychological weight. If n is the number of the samples and x is the ranking value of a certain sample, the weight y of the sample is shown in Table 2.

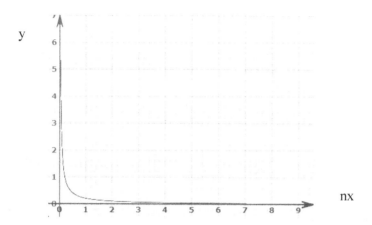

Fig. 1. Conversion function for converting ranking value into weight value

Table 2. Conversion from ranking value to weight value (Sample volume n = 4)

Ranking(x)	Weight(y)
1	0.25
2	0.125
3	0.083
4	0.0625
5	0.05

4 Simulation Experiment

In order to verify the reasonability of the improvement method, we have carried out the simulation experiment. We took the test scores of certain senior high school as the sample data, including 1,200 samples in total. We selected a small amount of samples to illustrate the local satisfactory solution, the local satisfactory solution curve and the satisfaction in order to find the difference in results before and after improvement.

4.1 Difference Between Local Satisfactory Solutions

Firstly, the original method is adopted by the evaluator to score the samples, as shown in Table 3. It is a little difficult for the evaluator to provide the exact score with so many indexes and samples to be looked through. It can be seen from the ratings that some same scores exist, and the scores are in 6 to 10 range. Such ratings are not plausible enough to present exactly the evaluator's psychological weight.

Whereas, it is much easier for the evaluator to rank the samples (as shown in the last column in Table 3), without duplicate scores.

Table 3. Sample ratings and rankings based on psychological weight

No.	Chinese	Maths	English	Physics	Chemistry	Biology	Politics	History	Geography	Rating	Ranking
11	88	111	96	90	91	87	79	70	84	7	7
12	85	118	100.5	75	79	88	79	81	90	8	6
13	89	117	85	91	84	91	74	76	88	8	4
14	85	120	97	83	78	82	81	83	83	10	8
15	84	116	99.5	92	92	88	64	75	81	8	2
16	84	105	97	96	83	95	74	79	78	6	10
17	81	120	92	98	88	92	72	67	78	10	1
18	77	120	82.5	94	78	89	89	83	73	9	3
19	89	119	95	88	78	91	72	69	84	9	5
20	91	111	94.5	87	84	90	84	73	70	7	9

Table 4 shows the local satisfactory solutions before and after improvement, obtained according to Formula (1). From the result, it is obvious to reflect that the evaluator has stronger preference for science courses after improvement than before improvement.

Table 4. Local satisfactory solutions before and after improvement (Total score plane 790)

	Maths	Physics	Chemistry
Before improvement	116.378	89.35366	83.2561
After improvement	117.5865	92.41553	85.4055

Figure 2 illustrates the two local satisfactory solutions. The upper point represents the local satisfactory solution after improvement, and the lower one represents the local satisfactory solution before improvement. Obviously, the former solution is superior to the latter solution.

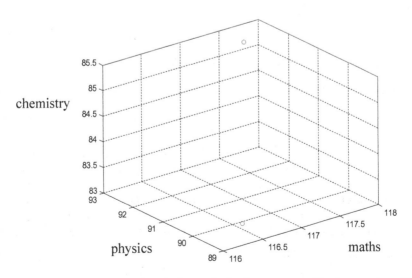

Fig. 2. Local satisfactory solutions before and after improvement (Total score plane 790)

Likewise, we respectively obtain the local satisfactory solutions of total score plane 736 as shown in Table 5 and Fig. 3. The improved local satisfactory solution can better represent the evaluator's psychological preference for science courses. In Fig. 3, the upper point is the local most satisfactory solution after improvement while the lower point is the local most satisfactory solution before improvement. Obviously, the former solution is superior to the latter solution.

Table 5. Local satisfactory solutions before and after Improvement (Total score plane 736)

	Maths	Physics	Chemistry
Before improvement	107.1728	70.81481	81.65432
After improvement	109.7243	71.90882	81.88755

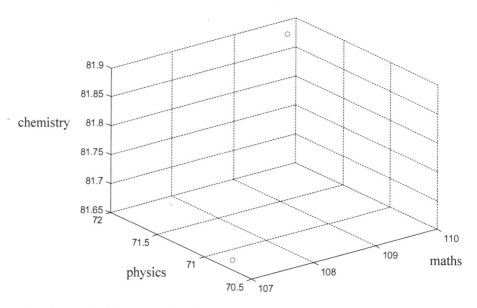

Fig. 3. Local satisfactory solutions before and after improvement (Total score plane 736)

4.2 Calculation of Most Satisfactory Solution Curve

The most satisfactory solutions before and after improvement are interpolated according to Interpolation Formula (2) to obtain the mathematically most satisfactory solution curve, as shown in Fig. 4. Specifically, the full curve represents the most satisfactory line obtained by the original algorithm, and the dashedcurve represents the most satisfactory line obtained by the improved algorithm. Graphically, the improved algorithm can better represent the evaluator's preference to science courses, so more weight is given to such courses as maths.

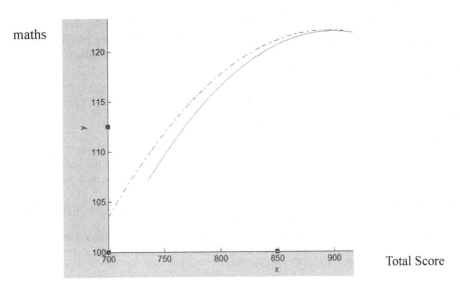

Fig. 4. Most satisfactory solution (Barycentric) curves before and after improvement

4.3 Satisfaction Comparison

Finally, the satisfaction degree for each object before and after the improvement is illustrated according to Formula (3). On the premise that the evaluator prefers to science score, No. 115 student and No. 116 student have the same total score, and we can see No. 116 student has better science scores, however if the original method is applied, it is unreasonable that No. 115 student obtains higher satisfaction than No. 116 student (showed in the column "Satisfaction (before)" Table 6). Whereas, if the improved algorithm is applied, higher satisfaction is given to No. 116 student rather than No. 115 student (showed in the last column in Table 6), thus indicating that the improved algorithm can better present the evaluation preference and is more effective.

Table 6. Satisfaction before and after improvement

No.	Chinese	Maths	English	Physics	Chemistry	Biology	Politics	History	Geography	Satisfaction (before)	Satisfaction (after)
115	79	115	75	80	84	90	66	75	65	0.7891	0.7653
116	83	114	88	81	88	75	65	73	62	0.7737	0.7884

5 Conclusion

The paper aims at researching how to simply and accurately weigh the indexes subjectively when the evaluated object has too many indexes in the attribute coordinate comprehensive evaluation method. Specifically, the quantitative rating on samples is converted into qualitative ranking, and then is converted into the evaluator's psychological weight. The most satisfactory solution and the most satisfactory solution curve obtained thereby are superior to those obtained by the original scoring method, so the evaluation result becomes more reasonable and can better reflect the evaluator's psychological preference and better present the advantages of the attribute coordinate comprehensive evaluation method.

References

1. Qian, G.: Research on the index weight of logistics integration in Beijing-Tianjin-Hebei region based on cloud models. J. Yunnan Univ. Fin. Econ. **34**(6), 96–104 (2018)
2. Ling, G.A.O., Li, J., Mu, H.: Stability evaluation method of surrounding rock based on cloud model and weight back analysis. Water Power **44**(9), 42–46 (2018)
3. Yang, T.-m., Li, J.-m., He, B.-f.: Drought evaluation model based on improved fuzzy comprehensive evaluation. J. Comput. Appl. **32**(z2), 41–44 (2012)
4. Tao, L., Shengyu, W.: Research on evaluation system of electricity market transaction in China based on gray relational grade analysis and fuzzy analytic hierarchy process. Ind. Technol. Econ. **37**(9), 130–137 (2018)
5. Zhang, S., Du, W.: Analysis on influence factors of train reentrant ability based on analytic hierarchy process. Railway Comput. Appl. **27**(9), 13–16 (2018)
6. Xu, X., Xu, G., Feng, J.: A kind of synthetic evaluation method based on the attribute computing network. In: IEEE International Conference on Granular Computing (GrC), pp. 644–647 (2009)
7. Xu, G., Min, S.: Research on multi-agent comprehensive evaluation model based on attribute coordinate. In: IEEE International Conference on Granular Computing (GrC), pp. 556–562 (2012)
8. Xu, G., Xu, X.: Study on evaluation model of attribute barycentric coordinates. Int. J. Grid Distrib. Comput. **9**(9), 115–128 (2016)
9. Xu, X., Xu, G., Feng, J.: Study on updating algorithm of attribute coordinate evaluation model. In: Huang, D.-S., Hussain, A., Han, K., Gromiha, M.M. (eds.) ICIC 2017. LNCS (LNAI), vol. 10363, pp. 653–662. Springer, Cham (2017). https://doi.org/10.1007/978-3-319-63315-2_57
10. Xu, X., Xu, G.: Research on ranking model based on multi-user attribute comprehensive evaluation method. Appl. Mech. Mater. **644**, 644–650 (2014)
11. Xu, X., Xu, G.: A recommendation ranking model based on credit. In: IEEE International Conference on Granular Computing (GrC), pp. 569–572 (2012)
12. Xu, G., Wang, L.: Evaluation of aberrant methylation gene forecasting tumor risk value in attribute theory. J. Basic Sci. Eng. **16**(2), 234 (2008)
13. Xu, X., Liu, Y., Feng, J.: Attribute coordinate comprehensive evaluation model combining principal component analysis. In: Shi, Z., Pennartz, C., Huang, T. (eds.) ICIS 2018. IAICT, vol. 539, pp. 60–69. Springer, Cham (2018). https://doi.org/10.1007/978-3-030-01313-4_7
14. Xu, X., Feng, J.: A quantification method of qualitative indices based on inverse conversion degree functions. In: Enterprise Systems Conference, pp. 261–264 (2014)

Conceptualization of Differences Between Entrepreneurs and Non-entrepreneurs of Undergraduate Emirati Students

Rasha Abou Samra[1]([✉]), Amal Al Ali[2], and Shaikha Al Naqbi[3]

[1] Business Department, Higher Colleges of Technology,
British University in Dubai, Academic City, Dubai, UAE
rabousamra@hct.ac.ae
[2] Faculty in Business Department, University of Sharjah, University City,
Sharjah, UAE
Amal_al_ali@sharjah.ac.ae
[3] Higher Colleges of Technology, University City, Sharjah, UAE
salnaqbi@hct.ac.ae

Abstract. Innovation is the transformation of the creative idea into real life project. This research is comparing between the perception of entrepreneurship between the creators of ideas who are still in the process of thinking and those who were able to transfer their ideas to real life projects. Before becoming an entrepreneur and during the first year of entrepreneurship are two critical stages that need further studies. This research is a focus group research which focuses on two groups; the first group is a group of undergraduate students who had creative ideas and worked on transferring those ideas into prototypes and tested those prototypes and the second group is a group of students who took further step to the real life market where they were able to open their business and start gaining returns on their investments. The conclusion of the study shows qualitative differences and the rationalization behind each one.

Keywords: Entrepreneurship · Innovation · Business sciences · Motivation · Experience · Resource capability

1 Introduction

This research is a qualitative research about the differences between entrepreneurs and non-entrepreneurs after receiving educational material about innovation and entrepreneurship and after preparing tested prototypes. The aim of this research is to come up with a conceptual framework about the main factors influencing the transformation of a creative idea into a real life business. Many researchers focused on entrepreneurship from marketing point of view or economic point of view, other researchers focused on organizational level of entrepreneurship versus individual level of entrepreneurship. In this research the researchers are focusing on the perceptual level of entrepreneurship among senior students and graduates in the UAE. This is because of the relatively high importance of conducting such research in this period of time where the UAE is diversifying its resources of economic income away from the oil

© Springer Nature Switzerland AG 2019
L. Uden et al. (Eds.): KMO 2019, CCIS 1027, pp. 187–198, 2019.
https://doi.org/10.1007/978-3-030-21451-7_16

economy. Alternative sources of energy make it difficult for UAE to depend on oil economy as a main source of income nowadays. Federal educational sectors are moving toward injecting the private sectors with higher percentages of local entrepreneurs to increase the economic surplus in the country [1]. After conducting this research it is clear that the theories and schools of thought that explain the motives to become an entrepreneur are not enough to explain the differences between entrepreneurs and non-entrepreneurs among emirate youth. Researchers found that they have to use more than one theory to explain the different motives for becoming an entrepreneur and that there are some motives that exist in the UAE context among youth. In the following part researchers explain the different theories that explained the motives to become an entrepreneur.

2 Literature Review

The total entrepreneurship activities in the UAE are equal to 13.25% in the year 2009/2010 [24]. The global entrepreneurship monitor reveals that there are two reported reasons of becoming an entrepreneur in the UAE; they are finding an opportunity in the market and lacking better job alternative [24]; however, these two reasons are related to the ages between 25 to 44 years old [24]. Researchers think that the study of the motives behind becoming entrepreneurs should start earlier to increase the ratio of TEA "total entrepreneurship activity". The reasons found in the global entrepreneurship monitor report are relatively occasional reasons that may interpret the tendency to become an entrepreneur for some youth but not for others. The research is about the different justifications of the motivation behind becoming an entrepreneur. The literature is full of different schools of thought about that. In the year 1949 and the early fifties, there was a mix between the concept of innovation and the concept of market novelty [12]. At that era Schumpeter looked at innovation as an invention and at the same time as a technical or an organizational novelty that could be introduced to the market. This shows interaction between novelty and marketing in defining the word entrepreneurship. The motive behind having an entrepreneurship is the ability to innovate something of value. At early sixties McClelland in his longitudinal study argued the idea of achievement and found that the need for achievement could represent a motive behind becoming an entrepreneur [10]. In a way or another there is intersection between the ability to innovate and the need to feel the achievement. This is was reinforced by a number of psychological theories of entrepreneurship. Group of researches attributed the positive attitude toward the tendency to become an entrepreneur to psychological traits [4]. Scientists were able to differentiate between entrepreneurs and non-entrepreneurs based on a group of attitudinal and psychological attributes [8]. Moreover that literature shows that scientists were able to classify entrepreneurs to successful versus unsuccessful entrepreneurs based on attitudes and psychological aspects of personality [11]. McClelland (1961) was one of the group of scientists who had this approach of psychological analysis. Rotter belonged to the same school of thought by introducing his theory of locus of control in 1966 [14]. Another theory in the same school of thought was introduced by Kets De Vries who talked about psychodynamic model [15]. Risk taking for example was one of the attributes that distinguish between entrepreneurs and non-entrepreneurs as found by Kets De Vries during sixties. Kets talked about tuff circumstances that plays a role in making an entrepreneur by affecting his or her psychological system. During the early stages of childhood the formulation of the motive to become an entrepreneur starts due to number of researched reasons like losing one or both parents, lack of security and feeling low level of self-esteem, and child abuse. During youth and teenagers stage there are other reasons behind the motive to become an entrepreneur like experiencing extreme poverty and refugees. During later stages persons may have negative psychological effects due to broken marriage. Due to such reasons entrepreneurs may felt that entrepreneurship was the only exit from this environment to become again well controlled and to get their psychological balance [5]. Researchers found that during childhood those children who had negative psychological effects tend to dislike structural environments. This led to the emergence of a new terminology which is "the innovative rebelliousness" [9]. It was found that rebellious children and youth are not fitting in any organization because they averse structures and orders and hate to be controlled by anybody. This category of people are not balanced and they are representing an extreme category of people. This was an observation that represented a criticism to this theory. Another criticism was hat the same circumstances may exist and do not correlate with the innovative rebelliousness behavior. Research revealed that the same negative psychological effect may lead to criminal behavior or to drugs addicts or alcoholics [11]. There is no evidence that the same negative psychological effects are existing in the United Arab Emirates [24] especially that the country is classified as a wealthy nation and poverty is not one of the childhood problems [24]. Another indicator is about the happiness indicators of living in the UAE. The country is caring about the happiness of its citizens and they have the Ministry of happiness and there are activities and social work initiatives to grow the citizenship development and loyalty rates. Belongingness and strength of the Emirati passport are perceived by UAE citizens and they are proud of being Emirati citizens. The question is does this belongingness play a role in the motivation of youth to become entrepreneurs or not? McClleland in 1961 presented a new model called the achievement model [21]. The model is explaining the theory of achievement where people would like to achieve something just because they want to experience the feeling of accomplishment; however this theory had limited evidence in applied research and results showed that in some cases the theory works well and in other cases it does not and without clear justification of the reasons of this difference. One of the critical issues in this theory is that it lacks a direction of causality [13]. The researchers found that the literature mentioned that this theory differs in western cultures than eastern ones. In western contexts the theory works and this was attributed to the relatively high level of appreciation of achievement compared to eastern contexts and cultures. The United Arab Emirates is one of the eastern cultures that lacks applied research about the role of the need of achievement as a motive behind becoming an entrepreneur [19]. The theory was focused on business people; however non-business people tend to have the same need and would like to experience achievement as well in their lives. The focus on the business people is in the scope of this research but the comparison between the eastern and western contexts in not one of the objectives of this research. Researches preferred to investigate the UAE youth motives behind their tendency to become entrepreneurs and this was more realistic in finding the main motives rather than applying previous theories and going for the deductive research approach. During sixties Harvey Leibenstein came up with his X-efficiency theory which was the first economic theory of entrepreneurship [20]. Both entrepreneurship and economy live in the business environment where there are some factors that reinforce the long term living of both entrepreneurship and economic efficiency [23]. Entrepreneurship may lead to higher economic surplus. According to Harris who was an advocate of this theory, the economic incentives feed the entrepreneurship activities in any country. The entrepreneurship activities in the UAE are classified into three categories [24]; the manufacturing, services, and trading and the highest percentage of getting access to fund is found in the trading sector and the least is found in the services sector [24]. This gives an economic motive due to inequality of acquiring sources of fund [23]. There are some enablers like for example the availability of bank credits to fund entrepreneurship projects, the availability of investment capitals and flow of savings among investors, lower rates of interests on bank loans, high levels of demand on consumer goods and services, availability of productive resources, supportive fiscal and monetary policies, and availability of communication and transportation means. All these economic efficiency factors were found to have significant effect in the free market conditions and motivates people to become entrepreneurs in such environments [18]. John Stewart Mill and Knight presented a new theory to explain entrepreneurship by risk bearing behavior [17]. They found that the ones who accept to take risks are the ones who are most likely are welling to become entrepreneurs; however they accept calculated risks. They also found that business people and entrepreneurs accept moderate levels of risk and not relatively high or low. Those business men and entrepreneurs significantly believe that not coming up with a new innovation or a new product is more risky. They discussed different types of risks beside financial risks like for example image risks, or relationship risks. This contribution to the body of knowledge interacts with the first school of thought that relates innovation to entrepreneurship. The researchers found that it is relatively more logic to depend on respondents who have knowledge about innovation and entrepreneurship [2]. The stage in which sampling units are performing is critical one in classifying them into entrepreneurs versus non-entrepreneurs bearing in mind that they have facilities and capabilities of free choice to become entrepreneurs or non-entrepreneurs [17]. The image of local citizens who contribute to their country's image and development is another factor that emerged from the literature review. One more factor of this research is about the scope of relationships, size, quality, and tendency to socialize and to make new relationships especially with experts and new stakeholders in the market. This factors emerged from the relationship risks observed in applied research about risk bearing theory. The study of innovation and entrepreneurship is enhanced by empirical research support and conclusions of literature review reveals that entrepreneurs who have education and occupational experience about the social and economic factors of their success are more objective in measuring this success [6]. This is a conclusion of the interaction between the entrepreneur and his or her society. In this school of thought we found empirical researches about the concepts of inter-generation inheritance of enterprise culture, social marginality and ethnicity [22]. In the social marginality model there is a significant positive relationship between the levels of strength of perception of incongruence of personal attributes and the motivation to change or reconstruct the social reality. This change may take the form of becoming entrepreneurs. A marginal person is the one who is less integrated with his or her society. They do not adhere to the value system of the society and they refuse to adopt with it. They develop their own unconventional patterns of behavior which enhances their tendency to become entrepreneurs; however this is found to be insufficient explanation of the tendency to become an entrepreneur. This intersects with the adherence to ethnic origins of entrepreneurs [1]. Research reveals that the entrepreneurship tendency is higher for certain ethnic origins than others. For example it is higher in Nigeria, Kenya, and Tanzania. Entrepreneurs in these countries are less integrated the values of their societies, ethnic groups, or by their hosts. Even those entrepreneurs who lived in their homelands were having higher tendency to become entrepreneurs [3]. Accordingly researchers concluded that becoming entrepreneurs is more affected by cultures than by ethnic groups. In the UAE parents paly relatively significant role in motivation their sons whether to become employees or to become entrepreneurs. The researchers thought of the effect of parents' cultural values about entrepreneurship and their experience as well as their support as relatively valuable effects on motivating their sons to become entrepreneurs. This proposition is reinforced by the inter-generational inheritance theory that states that if one or both parents are entrepreneurs, it is more likely that their sons become entrepreneurs like them compared to the sons of non-entrepreneurs. It is representing a driving force during early childhood stage to formulate the desires of future careers choice. Moreover that the support of business experience, networking, skills, fund, sources of advice, credit, and well established markets for the entrepreneurship business is caused by having one of both parents owning a business [3]. This is a main factor that researchers would like to study in the UAE where there are famous successful businessmen who have their sons studying the innovation and entrepreneurship courses in the educational sector of the country. This study of innovation and entrepreneurship became mandatory for all educational institutions all over the UAE and then all male students are the same in this aspect; however there are differences among those male students in having one or both parent's support in the field of business. The findings of empirical research provides evidence on having this happen to males more than females which enhances the applying this study on male students and graduates. It is more rational to have the study applied on the fresh graduates or the senior students because this is matching with the findings of the findings of previous researches. The literature shows that those who have educational background about entrepreneurship are more likely to become entrepreneurs [7]. Researchers also found that the previous experience in the field of entrepreneurship like they worked in small businesses and their work was close to the entrepreneurs of these business, they are more likely to understand quickly the whole system of the business they are working in and hence, they are more capable to become entrepreneurs [16]. Researches had an evidence that those who work as senior managers and in high level positions are less likely to become entrepreneurs. In this case applying the research on senior students or fresh graduates who had the education about entrepreneurship and are less likely with a bachelor degree to work in senior level management positions is more logic.

3   Methodology

The UAE economy is classified as a mixed economy where some sectors are controlled by the government and this includes prices of main products and certain service sectors in the country. Other sectors are representing a growing private sector and the country is trying to formulate policies to increase the private sector percentage that is managed and controlled by locals not foreigners. The UAE has three main universities which are representing the public sector of education that is funded by the federal authority of the country. They target having 5% of the total number of graduates as entrepreneurs. They also target having 50% of graduates working in the private sector and the remaining 45% to work in the governmental sector which is about to exaggerate. This explains the importance of focusing this research on studying the motives behind the tendency to become entrepreneurs. Researchers focused on the male students who are about to graduate and this is due to cultural believes in the Middle East that families depend highly on its males members to work. Females are introduced to the labor market and they are achieving relatively high rates of employment; however it is more accepted in the Arabic culture for females to set at home but it's not accepted for males to do so and wait for females to work and bring them what they need. The aim of the study is to describe the relationship between motivation, knowledge about business sciences, experience, and resource capabilities in one hand and the ability to transfer the creative idea into entrepreneurship project. The sample of this study consists of two types of students. Both groups are educated on innovation and entrepreneurship for one whole semester. Both groups have entered at least two competitions in the field of innovation challenges and are aware of competitive positioning, elevator pitching and opportunity analysis. Both were exposed to prototyping and testing their prototypes as well as having the evaluation from internal and external examiners to assure the neutral evaluation of their projects and to have better suggestion for improvement and transferring their ideas into real life projects.

At this stage they are the same but the question is why do students differ in their transformation stage?

To be able to answer this question the researcher proposed the following propositions:

1. Students who took the course have different motives to become entrepreneurs afterwards
2. Students who want to become entrepreneurs lack knowledge about business sciences that are needed to have marketable opportunities
3. Students who have experienced entrepreneurship before taking the course are more capable to try again after taking the course
4. There is a difference between the students who did not transfer their ideas into entrepreneurship projects and those who did in the resource capability.

Researchers formulated two focus groups of students. The first group has creative ideas and prototypes but does not have any real market entrepreneurship project. The second group has creative ideas and tested prototypes and moreover that they were able to have real market entrepreneurship projects. The age of students in both groups ranges between 20 and 25 years old. Specializations are Engineering, Business, and IT students. All of students were Emirati students. Number of members in each group is 10 students. Maintaining the Integrity of the Specifications. The following Table 1 shows some descriptive statistics of the two focus groups of the research sample:

Table 1. Descriptive statistics of the two focus groups of the study.

Criteria of comparison	Group of non-entrepreneurs	Group of entrepreneurs
No. of senior students	8	5
No. of fresh graduates	2	5
In general, With becoming an entrepreneur	6	10
In general, Against becoming an entrepreneur	4	0

In the table above it is observed that the sample contains the same number of senior entrepreneurs and the graduate entrepreneurs. This indicates that there is possibility to motivate both ages to become entrepreneurs and that studying is not a significant barrier at least for the sampling units of the research at hand. It is also obvious that most of non-entrepreneurs are still studying. This indicates that there could be some factors in the society that affects the seniors' perception and attitude toward entrepreneurship negatively. Occupational life may create better opportunities to motivate youth to become entrepreneurs than university academic life. It is also found that not all non-entrepreneurs have negative attitude toward becoming entrepreneurs, however; no one of entrepreneurs had a negative attitude toward becoming an entrepreneur. The following Table 2 shows the cross tabulation of the descriptive statistics of this study:

Table 2. Crosstabs of descriptive statistics of the focus groups of the study.

Non-entrepreneurs - 10				Entrepreneurs - 10			
Seniors - 8		Graduates - 2		Seniors - 5		Graduates - 5	
With	against	With	Against	With	Against	With	Against
4	4	2	0	5	0	5	0

Crosstabs show that senior students who are non-entrepreneurs are equally divided between positive attitude and negative attitude toward entrepreneurship, however graduates who are not working as entrepreneurs have positive attitudes toward entrepreneurship. This means that extra effort should be exerted by the country to transfer this positive attitude to a real action. All entrepreneurs have positive attitude toward entrepreneurship which means that their choice is not accompanied with thinking of changing to employees. The potential of increasing number of entrepreneurs among UAE youth who were sampled is relatively high. Another probability sample should follow to be able to generalizè these findings to the UAE youth.

4 Conceptual Framework

The research model shows that the demographics are not included as one of the variables that may influence the ability to transfer creative ideas to projects. The demographic factors of both focus groups are almost the same to neutralize their influence as possible (Fig. 1).

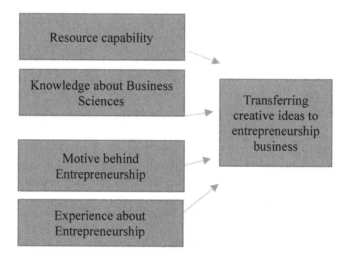

Fig. 1. The conceptual model of the research

4.1 Discussion to Results

The discussion revealed that resources and their capacity for most of the students who were not able to transfer their creative ideas into real market opportunities were relatively weak compared to the capabilities of the other group resources. They entrepreneurs where able to access more information about the market. They were able to receive supportive experiential guidance from other successful entrepreneurs some times. They were also able to get funds from their families in the first place.

The other group struggled with acquiring different resources like data resources, financial resources, and resources to supportive guidance in the market. One of the important resources is relationships where the group of entrepreneurs showed many social interactional capabilities compared to the other focus group.

Regarding the knowledge about business sciences it was found that highest number of entrepreneurs in the entrepreneurs group were engineering students not business or it ones; however; they showed tendency to study more about business and they realized that the study of business improves their strategic planning and running their entrepreneurship projects. For the other focus group the students were not interested in studying business and even business students were not interested knowing about the latest in the field of business which shows that the knowledge in the field of business is a critical difference between the two groups.

Talking about the motive behind becoming an entrepreneur both group were motivated by financial motives and becoming the owner of the business not just an employee. For the entrepreneurs group they had more motives than the other group. They were motivated by expanding their network of relationship and becoming famous as quickly as possible. Reaching the VIP more easily in the future after becoming famous entrepreneurs. This motive of fame was not that strong in the other group. Both groups were equal when thy spoke about the motive of representing their country locally and internationally. Safety has different definition for each group. For non-entrepreneurs safety means a regular stable financial resource which can be easily achieved by getting monthly salary or at least a temporarily secured source for funding the entrepreneurship business on the long run.

For the entrepreneurs they define safety as a long term view of survival in the market place. They look at future growth as a critical value and they can take risk for that reason. As a conclusion we can notice the different perceptual view and scopes of thinking about the future career. More intrinsic and long term motives will lead to creation of entrepreneurs and business owners more than employees.

One more thing is the experience. Students who had experienced entrepreneurship even before studying the innovation and entrepreneurship course were able to start a new entrepreneurship project faster than those who did not experience before graduation. Experience gives students ideas about challenges and possible reactions to those challenges so this increases their "immunity" and risk taking against real life market changes and competition. Especially if they have enough funds to repeat this again. One of the major differences between entrepreneurs and non-entrepreneurs is that entrepreneurs are accepting failure and it does not cause frustrations and quitting "higher immunity" but non-entrepreneurs are more vulnerable and sensitive to failure and it can easily affect their ability to get into an entrepreneurship business or even continue after starting it. This shapes their short term estimation of risks rather than a long term estimation as found in the entrepreneurs group.

5   Conclusion and Recommendations

Researchers believe that further research is needed in the area of classification of entrepreneurs into successful and non-successful ones as well as the differences between males and females in their motives to become entrepreneurs. It is possible the females struggle more or have different childhood circumstances that may have a sort of psychological effects that are not as the same as males' childhood circumstances. There are differences between entrepreneurs and non-entrepreneurs in that entrepreneurs have better knowledge or are welling to learn more about business sciences. This matches with the group of researchers who found that educational background has a significant effect on the motive to become an entrepreneur; however not all entrepreneurs believe that education is a main reason of success, especially when we compare this to the findings of psychological theories. In psychological theories of entrepreneurship child abuse and failure at school may motivate a person to become the boss of his or her own business. This is contradicting with the group of researchers who found an evidence that the education is a motive to become an entrepreneur. In the research at hand it is observed that UAE locals upon which the research is applied have got educational background and being in a relatively rich country decreases the probability of poverty for example as a psychological motive behind entrepreneurship. Entrepreneurs also have long-term scope of risk estimation. This is coping with the risk bearing theory and shows that entrepreneurs at UAE are sensitive to long-term risks. Entrepreneurs in the research sample have more connections and higher level of support than non-entrepreneurs. In one hand this finding contradicts with the social marginality model. Entrepreneurs in the UAE do not isolate themselves, and they do not seek avoiding the social value system of the country. They most likely have a motive of "become famous in a short period of time". They have higher capabilities of resources or they know how to use it in a better way compared to non-entrepreneurs. Resources include exposure to experts and information which matching with the literature in the area of considering experience of others like parents as a motive for youth to become entrepreneurs. If students have previous experience about risk taking and entrepreneurship they are more likely to repeat entrepreneurship again especially if their experience was positive. As a recommendation this conceptual model is effective to be used to measure the before and after status of undergraduates and entrepreneurs and non-entrepreneurs during the first year after studying innovation and entrepreneurship. Educational policies should stress on connectivity to the real markets and opening incubators or sponsoring tested prototypes to increase the safety of becoming entrepreneurs at least during the first year of its life. Researchers recommend engaging parents in the motivational process of their sons, especially is they have their own businesses. Even if they are employees and do not like to bear long-term risks, they can motivate their sons by providing financial support. On the other hand they may represent negative motivation to their sons if they transfer the idea of safety by becoming an employee as a long term philosophy of life. In this case sons will refuse to become entrepreneurs because of psychological effects of their parents; unless they choose to avoid the cultural value systems of their families and follow the social marginality model. In general the role of one or both parents is critical in motivating their sons to become entrepreneurs and the UAE may plays a role with parents about how to guide their sons and what benefits they can get and what support they may have from the country and hence, the effect of the educational sector with the senior students may become higher.

Teaching business sciences and how to transfer data to money are essential training or educational courses for students who want to become entrepreneurs. Learning and getting support from successful entrepreneurs is another motive for success in transferring non-entrepreneurs to entrepreneurs and this may replace the lack of experience with the real market challenges. Researchers suggest that this qualitative research is followed by a quantitative one about the effects of research variables on the transformation of creative ideas to entrepreneurship businesses. Researchers also suggest conducting the same research in other campuses of HCT and in the educational sector in general where students have got educational background about entrepreneurship. They also recommend to implement the same study on the female students to investigate in there are differences between males and females regarding the motives of becoming entrepreneurs. Besides the gender there may be other demographic differences that may have an effect on the motivation of fresh graduates and senior students to become entrepreneurs. The aim of the study is to describe the relationship between motivation, knowledge about business sciences, experience, and resource capabilities in one hand and the ability to transfer the creative idea into entrepreneurship project. The two focus groups of the research gave a qualitative evidence on the existence of these four factors and that they represent a difference between entrepreneurs and non-entrepreneurs in the researched sample. This conclusion is not generalized because this is a convenient sample. Researchers recommend conducting the same research on larger scale of respondents and may be to use stratified sample to represent different categories of respondents and to be able to generalize the research results and have significantly accepted contribution to the body of knowledge. The area of entrepreneurship studies in the UAE is still gray among youth because the first choice of fresh graduates is still to become an employee. The perception of the definition of safety is a critical difference between entrepreneurs and non-entrepreneurs. According to the research results Rampini, A. "Entrepreneurial activity, risk, and the business cycle" Journal of Monetary Economics 51 (2004): 555–573 .There are different motives for entrepreneurship, there are differences in the knowledge and experience about business, and there are difference in resource capability between entrepreneurs and non-entrepreneurs.

References

1. Amorós, J.E., Cristi, O., Minniti, M.: Driving forces behind entrepreneurship: differences in entrepreneurship rate level and its volatility across countries. Front. Entrepreneurship Res. **29**(16), 2 (2009)
2. Andreeva, T., Kianto, A.: Knowledge processes, knowledge-intensity and innovation: a moderated mediation analysis. J. Knowl. Manag. **15**(6), 1016–1034 (2011)
3. Autio, E., Pathak, S., Wennberg, K.: Consequences of cultural practices for entrepreneurial behaviors. J. Int. Bus. Stud. **44**(4), 334–362 (2013)
4. Aziz, N., et al.: Entrepreneurial motives and perceived problems: an empirical study of entrepreneurs in Kyrgyzstan. Int. J. Bus. Res. **18**(2), 163 (2013)
5. Black, E.L., Burton, F.G., Wood, D.A., Zimbelman, A.F.: Entrepreneurial success: differing perceptions of entrepreneurs and venture capitalists. Int. J. Entrepreneurship Innovation **11**(3), 189–198 (2010). https://doi.org/10.5367/000000010792217272. Accessed 28 July 2016
6. Bonaccorci, A., Daraio, C.: Universities and Strategic Knowledge Creation. Edward Elgar Publishing Limited, Aldershot (2007)
7. Brady, T., Söderlund, J.: Projects in innovation, innovation in projects selected papers from the IRNOP VIII conference. Int. J. Project Manag. **26**(5), 465–468 (2008)
8. Constant, A.F., Zimmermann, K.F.: Self-employment against employment or unemployment: Markov transitions across the business cycle. Eurasian Bus. Rev. **4**(1), 51–87 (2014)
9. Friedman, B.A., et al.: Predictors of students' desire to be an entrepreneur: Kyrgyzstan, Georgia, and the United States. Eurasian J. Bus. Econ. **5**(9), 129–140 (2012)
10. Giacomin, O., et al.: Entrepreneurial intentions, motivations and barriers: differences among American, Asian and European students. Int. Entrepreneurship Manag. J. **7**(2), 219–238 (2011)
11. Gorgievski, M., Ascalon, M.E., Stephan, U.: Small business owners'success criteria, a values approach to personal differences. J. Small Bus. Manag. **49**(2), 207–232 (2011)

12. Hagedoorn, J.: Innovation and entrepreneurship: Schumpeter revisited. Ind. Corp. Change **5**(3), 883–896 (1996)
13. Hirschi, A., Fischer, S.: Work values as predictors of entrepreneurial career intentions. Career Dev. Int. **18**(3), 216–231 (2013)
14. Jayawarna, D., Rouse, J., Kitching, J.: Entrepreneur motivations and life course. Int. Small Bus. J. **31**(1), 34–56 (2011)
15. Smith, M.: Why risk-taking is Important as an Entrepreneur. Best Business Books Blog (2017)
16. Parker, S.C., Congregado, E., Golpe, A.: Is entrepreneurship a leading or lagging indicator of the business cycle? Evidence from UK self-employment data. Int. Small Bus. J. **30**(7), 736–753 (2012)
17. Ramoglou, S.: Who is a 'non-entrepreneur'? Taking the 'others' of entrepreneurship seriously. Int. Small Bus. J. **31**(4), 432–453 (2013). https://doi.org/10.1177/0266242611425838
18. Rampini, A.: Entrepreneurial activity, risk, and the business cycle. J. Monetary Econ. **51**, 555–573 (2004)
19. Shane, S., Nicolaou, N.: The genetics of entrepreneurial performance. Int. Small Bus. J. **31**(5), 473–495 (2013). https://doi.org/10.1177/0266242613485767
20. Thurik, A.R., Audretsch, D.B., Stam, E.: The rise of the entrepreneurial economy and the future of dynamic capitalism. Technovation **33**(8–9), 302–310 (2013)
21. Verheul, I., et al.: Factors influencing the entrepreneurial engagement of opportunity and necessity entrepreneurs. EIM Research Reports, H201011, pp. 1–24 (2010)
22. Williams, N., Williams, C.C.: Evaluating the socio-spatial contingency of entrepreneurial motivations: a case study of English deprived urban neighbourhoods. Entrepreneurship Reg. Dev. **24**(7–8), 661–684 (2012)
23. Xavier-Oliveira, E., et al.: What motivates entrepreneurial entry under economic inequality? The role of human and financial capital. Hum. Relat. **68**(7), 1183–1207 (2015)
24. Bosma, N., Levie, J.: Global Entrepreneurship Monitor – 2009 Executive Report. Global Entrepreneurship Research Association (2010)

Knowledge and Organization

Knowledge Drivers of Japanese Foreign Direct Investment Location

Remy Magnier-Watanabe[1,2]([⊠])

[1] Graduate School of Business Sciences, University of Tsukuba, Tokyo, Japan
magnier-watanabe.gt@u.tsukuba.ac.jp
[2] Weatherhead Center for International Affairs, Program on US-Japan Relations,
Harvard University, Cambridge, MA, USA

Abstract. With rising globalization, several countries have been expanding outside their borders through not only trade, but also foreign direct investment. In doing so, they establish subsidiaries in little-known distant countries where they must overcome knowledge gaps to be successful.

This research examines some knowledge-related factors that affect the state location choices of Japanese investors when they established affiliates in the United States between 2003 and 2017. The results, constructed from an original database, showed that Japanese foreign direct investment favor states that are closer to Japan and with more direct flight access, which have higher industry concentration, and in which more Japanese firms are already located. These findings suggest that beyond economic considerations, Japanese firms select locations considered to be superior sources of knowledge, knowledge spillovers, and learning for foreign direct investment.

These results are specific to Japanese investments in the United States over the past 15 years which tend to be concentrated in manufacturing and IT industries.

Keywords: Foreign direct investment · Knowledge · Japan · United States

1 Introduction

Historically, Japan relied on exporting rather than investing abroad to finance its development (Murphy 2010). This export-led growth model was complemented later by a rise in outward foreign direct investment (FDI), itself facilitated by globalization. Globalization is understood as "the growing economic interdependence and integration between countries brought about through the increasing cross-border mobility of goods, services, capital and people facilitated by technological change, the rise of multinational enterprises and the liberalizing policies of nation states and international regulatory institutions" (Roberts and Fuller 2010, p. 902).

Indeed, economic growth, relative political stability, deregulation, and advances in communication technologies and transportation which marked the years after World War II created favorable conditions for Japanese companies to engage in FDI. Data from the Japan External Trade Organization (JETRO) indicates that Japan's outward investments have been increasing steadily over the past 20 years, with a year-on-year

© Springer Nature Switzerland AG 2019
L. Uden et al. (Eds.): KMO 2019, CCIS 1027, pp. 201–212, 2019.
https://doi.org/10.1007/978-3-030-21451-7_17

growth rate of about 9.1%, while its economy has contracted by 0.5% over the same period, as measured by GDP in real terms (Fig. 1) (JETRO 2018). The years 2016 and 2017 logged record outward FDI, USD 174 billion and USD 169 billion respectively, since comparable numbers were first documented in 1996.

Over almost the same period, between 1996 and 2016, Japan's exports of goods and services in constant 2010 US dollar, went from USD 438 billion to USD 981 billion, registering a year-on-year growth rate of about 3.9%, less than half than that of outward investment (World Bank 2018). It has therefore become clear that the growth of Japanese firms originates today more from outward investment than exports.

Japan has consistently ranked as the second largest foreign direct investors in the U. S. economy, after the United Kingdom (Cortez 2017). And Japan holds by far the largest stock of FDI, 68%, from firms headquartered in Asia-Pacific (BEA 2017). At the same time, the United States remains the largest investment destination for the country, attracting about 30% of total Japanese investment, or USD 491 billion out of the stock of USD 1.55 trillion as of 2017 (JETRO 2018).

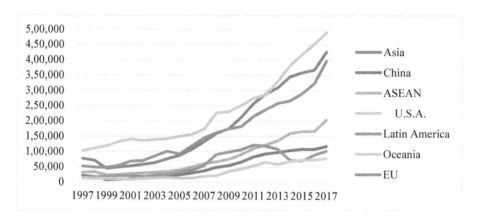

Fig. 1. Japan's outward foreign direct investment by country/region (Source: JETRO, 2018)

However, setting up a business in a distant foreign country is fraught with challenges. In order to lower the risks linked to uncertainty, firms try to access relevant knowledge through several channels and from diverse sources. When expanding abroad, knowledge is key (Kogut and Zander 1993) and firms need to learn about target locations (Johanson and Vahlne 1977).

This paper builds on previous research (Hernandez 2014) that has showed that firms make location decisions in order to maximize learning and knowledge acquisition opportunities, partly drawn from the concentration of immigrants, established co-national firms, and industry. Hernandez (2014) has investigated these effects among subsidiaries from 27 countries in the United States and he confirmed that states with higher immigrant concentration witnessed higher FDI by firms from the same countries, but that the concentration of co-national firms had no effect.

Given that Japanese immigration is low in the United States and that Japanese have the lowest share of foreign born among US Asians (López et al. 2017), I therefore ask how specific knowledge sources related to the concentration of co-national firms and industry affect the state location choices of Japanese affiliates in the United States. I decided to use a single source country and a single receiving country so as to better isolate the relationship between location characteristics and knowledge-related firm decision-making.

2 Literature Review

2.1 Classic Rationale for Location Decision

One of the longstanding views on location decision does not distinguish market entry from establishment modes, and it considers location and entry modes are selected on the basis of control, resource commitment and risk (Anderson and Gatignon 1986; Erramilli and Rao 1990). Another view separates these modes depending on whether they are contract- or equity-based; the former consists of licensing, franchising, distribution, supply agreements, technical assistance, and management contracts, while the latter include joint-ventures and wholly-owned subsidiaries (Hennart 1988, 1989, 2000). In this research, we do not focus on entry mode but rather on state selection.

The most commonly used theoretical perspectives to examine entry and location decision for FDI are transaction cost economics, the resource-based view, institutional theory, and Dunning's eclectic framework (Brouthers and Hennart 2007).

The goal for the firm is to minimize costs related to make-or-buy decisions, specifically those associated with asset specificity, uncertainty (internal and external), and frequency (Williamson 1985). The resource-based view (RBV) recognizes that firm-specific resources and capabilities are the basis for building competitive advantage on the basis of resources that are valuable, rare, costly to imitate and with no substitutes (Barney 1991). Institutional theory contends that a country's institutions, both at home and abroad, affect the firm and its activities because those institutions fix and enforce the play rules of business (North 1990). And last, Dunning (2000)'s eclectic approach, often referred to as the OLI framework, posits that firms will engage in FDI when ownership-, location-, and internalization-advantages exist together.

However, these frameworks are more concerned with economic rationale rather than knowledge acquisition constraints. Social network theory can bring a helpful perspective to account for knowledge sources.

2.2 Social Network Theory and Knowledge

Social networks stem largely from personal relationships, social ties, corporate connections, and inter-organizational bonds. They are defined alternatively based on the opportunities afforded by relationships (Burt 1997), knowledge exchanged for business purposes (Zhou et al. 2007), and patterns of connections (Scott 2017). Social networks are the foundation for social capital which describes the knowledge rooted and accessible through one's interpersonal network (Nahapiet and Ghoshal 1998).

Social networks have been found to enable knowledge exchange and resources in general within the organization (Wang et al. 2015) and between firms (Díez-Vial and Montoro-Sánchez 2014). Social networks have been used when looking at internationalization processes. (Jean et al. 2011)'s research showed that ethnic ties among top managers of Taiwanese firms facilitated location choice in FDI decisions.

I extend the concept of ethnic ties beyond individuals to include networks of corporations with the same national origin, headquarter language, or historic incorporation region. This extension is consistent with previous findings whereby the shared ethnicity of managers from different firms act as an important interorganizational tie (Luo and Chung 2005), which is the foundation of shared corporate ethnicity.

These networks can be conduits for knowledge and learning (Shaver et al. 1997). Beyond shared ethnicity, industry concentration can also be a powerful reason to locate an affiliate as it has been showed to create knowledge spillovers which can be sources of competitive advantage (Chung and Alcácer 2002). Firms engage in knowledge acquisition, defined as the process of gaining new knowledge, from either inside or outside the organization and in either tacit or explicit form (Massa and Testa 2009). Knowledge acquisition can be aimed at reducing risk and increasing the likelihood of success when evaluating locations for FDI.

It is argued here that Japanese firms may favor states which they perceive to be either better sources of valuable knowledge as a result of the higher concentration of Japanese firms and of same-industry firms, or more accessible from Japanese headquarters so as to facilitate control and knowledge transfer. Co-national firms share a language and culture, which lead to easier cooperation and support norms of reciprocity drawn from trust (Putnam 1993). Indeed, Japanese firms are known for giving preference to other Japanese firms in supplier-customer relations, sometimes beyond economic considerations (Magnier-Watanabe and Lemaire 2018). This homophily (McPherson et al. 2001) extends beyond culture to industry and geographical locations for Japanese firms, thus benefiting concentrated supplier-customer networks (Krichene et al. 2018). And proximity, co-location, or frequent contacts are often required when dealing with tacit knowledge, which by definition is hard to codify and therefore transfer (Polanyi 1966; Nonaka and Takeuchi 1995).

3 Method

3.1 Sample

I obtained a list of corporate affiliates in the United States owned by a Japanese parent, using the Directory of Corporate Affiliations published by LexisNexis. I selected new entries between 2003 and 2017 to allow a long enough period of observations and a sufficient number of cases. I identified 218 new entries made by 167 parent firms. However, these reflect the years when the companies were first established, not necessarily when they passed under Japanese control, as in the case of acquisitions. Furthermore, the database does not indicate the type of equity entry modes, such as greenfield investments, acquisitions, or joint-ventures. Therefore, checking each company's website, corporate directories, and Toyo Keizai's overseas Japanese companies' database, I manually confirmed the year each firm passed under Japanese control and the type of entry mode. I removed repeated investments in any given state so as to eliminate reverse causality, consistent with Hernandez (2014).

The final list of subsidiaries under Japanese control over the period 2003–2017 consists of 143 firms, of which 101 (71%) are greenfield investments, 33 (23%) are acquisitions, and 9 (6%) are joint-ventures.

Table 1. Industry distribution of new Japanese FDI (2003–2017)

	Frequency	Percent
Agriculture, forestry, fishing and hunting	1	.7
Mining, quarrying, and oil and gas extraction, utilities, and construction	5	3.7
Manufacturing	44	32.8
Trade and transportation	35	26.1
Information, financial activities, and professional and business services	45	33.6
Education and health services	1	.7
Leisure and hospitality	3	2.2
Total	134	100.0

Fig. 2. A figure caption is always placed below the illustration. Short captions are centered, while long ones are justified. The macro button chooses the correct format automatically.

Figure 2 shows new entries over the period by state, while Table 1 clearly indicates that the majority of Japanese FDI over the period was in Manufacturing, Trade and Transportation, and Information, Financial Activities, and Professional and Business Services. In the subsequent analysis, I have only retained greenfield investments and acquisitions as the number of joint-ventures is small, and some of these joint ventures were with US companies and some with other Japanese firms, thus complicating the understanding of such undertakings.

3.2   Variables

Firm data covers Japanese FDI over the years 2003 to 2017, while some variables use 2010 data as that year is centered over that period. Variables cover location choice, industry, population, state physical features, and Japanese concentration. Table 2 provides descriptive statistics of the main variables under study.

Table 2. Descriptive statistics of main variables under study

		N	Minimum	Maximum	Mean	Std. Deviation
Industry	3Y industry growth	134	−5.906%	6.199%	−0.938%	2.512%
	Industry concentration	134	.005	.163	.064	.041
Population	2010 census	134	1360301	37253956	19682083.22	13560734.030
	2010 real GDP per capita	134	31687	64901	49201.13	7142.769
	2010 employment	134	478838	12536402	6851307.96	4454630.673
	Spending per pupil 2010	134	7848.084	18618.240	10963.383	2739.647
State physical features	Area (Sq. Mi.)	134	5543	268596	97286.18	64802.715
	Distance to Tokyo (nautical miles)	134	3354.510	6132.710	5241.478	672.470
	Direct flight (TYO-State)	134	0	1	.82	.385
Japanese concentration	Number of Japanese affiliates 2010	134	36	509	306.04	159.546
	Employment of Japanese affiliates 2010	134	1.700	110.200	53.767	42.016
	Japanese school MEXT	134	0	1	.14	.350
	Japanese supplementary school	134	0	1	.90	.297

Location Choice. The dependent variable state entry is coded as 1 if an entry by the parent company occurred within a state and 0 otherwise. Industries are those of the subsidiaries, not the parent, as some parent companies are active in several industries.

Industry. Industry growth rates can act encourage firms to enter the market so as not to miss out. I calculated industry growth over the 3 years preceding state entry, for each industry based on the first digit code of the North American Industry Classification System (NAICS) (US Census Bureau 2017). Moreover, higher industry concentration can act as a learning environment, where active competitors and same industry players can offer a pool of qualified workers, potential partners, and take-over targets. I calculate industry concentration rates for each year of entry and each industry based on those same NAICS codes.

Population. Population size can be attractive to foreign direct investors as a terminal market (2010 census) in relation to their purchasing power (2010 real GDP per capita). At the same time, large states can also constitute sizeable reservoirs of potential workers (2010 employment). In order to reflect the quality of potential workers, the level of education of the population is assessed examining the state spending per student in 2010.

State Physical Features. The size of states can also be an attractive factor when evaluating investment locations, so the area in square miles in used. Considering the difficulty of managing a distant business, states physically closer to Japan and that can be accessed with direct flights from Japan could be at an advantage. So, I included the distance to Tokyo (nautical miles) and the number of direct flights between Tokyo and each state.

Japanese Concentration. For the same reasons industry concentration can be a powerful driver to locate investment, a high number of Japanese affiliates and a large number of employees of Japanese affiliates can act as a source of knowledge for new investors. Likewise, Japanese companies may be more likely to locate a subsidiary where Japanese educations services exist, catering to the Japanese expatriate population. Therefore, I included the presence of official Japanese schools of the Japanese Ministry of Education (MEXT), and of Japanese supplementary week-end schools.

4   Results and Discussion

Location choice is binary (0 for state non-entry and 1 for state entry) and therefore best analyzed using the t-test to evaluate whether statistically significant differences exist between the states entered by Japanese investors versus those that are not entered. Table 3 shows mean differences while Table 4 indicates statistical significance of the mean differences. Of all the variables under investigation, only the three-year industry growth, the 2010 real GDP per capita, and state spending per pupil in 2010 were found to not be significant for state entry by Japanese investors over 2003–2017.

4.1 Industry

Japanese investors entered states with a higher concentration in their respective industry; states they entered had an average industry concentration of 6%, versus 2% for those states they did not enter. Rather than shy away from competition which most likely strives in highly- industry concentrated states, Japanese investors prefer to enter states where their industry is very active. This could be partially explained by the fact that state entries over the period concern industries (Manufacturing, Trade and Transportation, and Information, Financial Activities, and Professional and Business Services), which by nature need to be integrated into long and complex value-chains of suppliers upstream and clients downstream.

Table 3. Comparison of means between state entry and non-entry

		State entry	N	Mean	Std. deviation	Std. error mean
Industry	3Y industry growth	0	9433	−1.15%	2.51%	0.03%
		1	134	−0.94%	2.51%	0.22%
	Industry concentration	0	9433	0.02	0.02	0.00
		1	134	0.06	0.04	0.00
Population	2010 census	0	9433	5423118.51	5731675.97	59014.23
		1	134	19682083.22	13560734.03	1171469.00
	2010 real GDP per capita	0	9433	48680.67	19353.373	199.265
		1	134	49201.13	7142.769	617.041
	2010 employment	0	9433	1978510.58	2034246.24	20944.92
		1	134	6851307.96	4454630.67	384821.48
	Spending per pupil 2010	0	9433	10932.63	2784.39	28.67
		1	134	10963.38	2739.65	236.67
State physical features	Area (Sq. Mi.)	0	9433	73714.51	97663.55	1005.56
		1	134	97286.18	64802.72	5598.10
	Distance to Tokyo (nautical miles)	0	9433	5389.03	649.79	6.69
		1	134	5241.48	672.47	58.09
	Direct flight (TYO-State)	0	9433	0.31	0.46	0.00
		1	134	0.82	0.38	0.03
Japanese concentration	Number of Japanese affiliates 2010	0	9433	104.98	79.06	0.81
		1	134	306.04	159.55	13.78
	Employment of Japanese affiliates 2010	0	9433	11.09	14.68	0.15
		1	134	53.77	42.02	3.63
	Japanese school MEXT	0	9433	0.05	0.23	0.00
		1	134	0.14	0.35	0.03
	Japanese supplementary school	0	9433	0.40	0.49	0.01
		1	134	0.90	0.30	0.03

From a knowledge perspective, Japanese firms prefer to locate their operations in states where their industry flourishes so as to access relevant knowledge from suppliers and/or customers, and potentially poach away potential employees. This is possible thanks to knowledge spillovers drawn from regular and reciprocal exchange predicated on positive social relationships and trust.

Table 4. Independent samples t-test (Levene's test for equality of variances)

		F	Sig.	t	df	Sig. (2-tailed)
Industry	3Y industry growth	.30	.58	−.98	9565.00	.325
	Industry concentration	440.79	.00	−27.85	9565.00	**.000**
Population	2010 census	529.96	.00	−27.72	9565.00	**.000**
	2010 real GDP per capita	7.930	.01	−.311	9565.00	.756
	2010 employment	432.26	.00	−26.83	9565.00	**.000**
	Spending per pupil 2010	1.40	.24	−.13	9565.00	.899
State physical features	Area (Sq. Mi.)	1.61	.20	−2.79	9565.00	**.005**
	Distance to Tokyo (nautical miles)	9.87	.00	2.61	9565.00	**.009**
	Direct flight (TYO-State)	70.51	.00	−12.85	9565.00	**.000**
Japanese concentration	Number of Japanese affiliates 2010	304.94	.00	−28.63	9565.00	**.000**
	Employment of Japanese affiliates 2010	976.88	.00	−31.85	9565.00	**.000**
	Japanese school MEXT	62.38	.00	−4.35	9565.00	**.000**
	Japanese supplementary school	1267.47	.00	−11.77	9565.00	**.000**

Statistically significant differences are indicated in bold.

4.2 Population

Japanese firms entered states with a larger population (19.7 million vs. 5.4 million on average) and employed workforce (6.8 million vs. 1.9 million on average). This is consistent with the industries in which Japanese investors are present (Manufacturing, Trade and Transportation, and Information, Financial Activities, and Professional and Business Services), since larger states act both as reserves for skilled personnel and large terminal markets.

4.3 State Physical Features

Japanese investors preferred entering states that are larger in size (97,286 vs. 73,714 sq. mi. on average), are slightly closer to Japan (5,241 vs. 5,389 miles on average), and accessible through direct flights (0.81 vs. 0.31 direct flights per day). Japanese subsidiaries rely on the use of expatriates who often go back and forth between the head office in Japan and the overseas subsidiary they manage (Wong 2001). Relatively closer distance and better accessibility support physical knowledge flows, which are especially fit for personal control relying on tacit knowledge exchange.

4.4   Japanese Concentration

Japanese firms selected states with a higher number of Japanese affiliates (306 vs. 105 firms on average), a larger workforce employed by Japanese affiliates (54 vs. 11 employees on average) and equipped for the offspring of Japanese expatriates in the form of official Japanese schools (0.14 vs. 0.05 per state) or supplementary schools (0.9 vs. 0.4 per state).

This is a strong sign that Japanese foreign direct investing corporations seek locations with a strong network of Japanese actors, who constitute a powerful source of knowledge about local opportunities and best practices. Moreover, consistent with homophily-based reasoning, locating their affiliate in an area with high ethnic corporate concentration allows to reduce uncertainty and increase the chances of learning through the use of a shared language and culture. Last, the existence of Japanese schools can convince reluctant Japanese employees to become expatriates and alleviate their families' anxieties about living abroad (Miyamoto and Kuhlman 2001).

5   Conclusion

Japanese foreign direct investment in the United States over the past 15 years have been located in states which can provide advantageous conditions for knowledge sourcing and learning, besides purely economic considerations. While this is consistent with previous findings, this research provides strong empirical evidence for recent FDI from Japan to the United States, which tends to be concentrated in manufacturing and IT industries in the state of California closer to Japan. Relative proximity and better access are valuable to share tacit knowledge which is a tenet of Japanese management in its use of expatriate managers and personal control when expanding abroad.

These Japanese affiliates, often in industries with long, complex and integrated value-chains, favor states with higher industry concentrations, likely taking advantage of knowledge spillovers. Moreover, Japanese subsidiaries select states with a higher concentration of Japanese firms and an existing structure of Japanese-language education geared towards the children of expatriates. These affiliates derive considerable knowledge from ethnic corporate networks because of Japanese preferences for homophily and uncertainty reduction through increased learning.

Future research should examine whether such location criteria affect the success and survival of Japanese affiliates.

References

Anderson, E., Gatignon, H.: Modes of foreign entry: a transaction cost analysis and propositions. J. Int. Bus. Stud. 17(3), 1–26 (1986)

Barney, J.: Firm resources and sustained competitive advantage. J. Manag. 17(1), 99–120 (1991)

BEA: Foreign Direct Investment in the US: Balance of Payments and Direct Investment Position Data. U.S. Bureau of Economic Analysis (2017). http://www.bea.gov/international/di1fdibal. htm

Brouthers, K.D., Hennart, J.F.: Boundaries of the firm: insights from international entry mode research. J. Manag. 33(3), 395–425 (2007)

Burt, R.S.: The contingent value of social capital. Adm. Sci. Q. 42(2), 339–365 (1997)

Chung, W., Alcácer, J.: Knowledge seeking and location choice of foreign direct investment in the United States. Manage. Sci. 48(12), 1534–1554 (2002)

Cortez, M.: Foreign Direct Investment in the United States: Update to 2017 Report, ESA Issue Brief #06-17, Office of The Chief Economist, Economics and Statistics Administration, U.S. Department of Commerce, 3 October 2017. http://www.esa.doc.gov/sites/default/files/ FDIUS2017update.pdf

Díez-Vial, I., Montoro-Sánchez, Á.: Social capital as a driver of local knowledge exchange: a social network analysis. Knowl. Manage. Res. Pract. 12(3), 276–288 (2014)

Dunning, J.H.: The eclectic paradigm as an envelope for economic and business theories of MNE activity. Int. Bus. Rev. 9(2), 163–190 (2000)

Erramilli, M.K., Rao, C.P.: Choice of foreign market entry modes by service firms: role of market knowledge. MIR Manag. Int. Rev. 30(2), 135–150 (1990)

Hennart, J.F.: A transaction costs theory of equity joint ventures. Strateg. Manag. J. 9(4), 361–374 (1988)

Hennart, J.F.: Can the "new forms of investment" substitute for the "old forms?" A transaction costs perspective. J. Int. Bus. Stud. 20(2), 211–234 (1989)

Hennart, J.F.: The transaction cost theory of the multinational enterprise. In: Pitelis, C., Sugden, R. (eds.) The Nature of the Transnational Firm, 2nd edn, pp. 81–116. Routledge, London (2000)

Hernandez, E.: Finding a home away from home: effects of immigrants on firms' foreign location choice and performance. Adm. Sci. Q. 59(1), 73–108 (2014)

Jean, R.J.B., Tan, D., Sinkovics, R.R.: Ethnic ties, location choice, and firm performance in foreign direct investment: a study of Taiwanese business groups FDI in China. Int. Bus. Rev. 20(6), 627–635 (2011)

JETRO: 1996–2017 FDI stock (Based on International Investment Position, net), Japanese Trade and Investment Statistics. JETRO (2018). https://www.jetro.go.jp/en/reports/statistics.html

Johanson, J., Vahlne, J.E.: The internationalization process of the firm—a model of knowledge development and increasing foreign market commitments. J. Int. Bus. Stud. 8(1), 23–32 (1977)

Kogut, B., Zander, U.: Knowledge of the firm and the evolutionary theory of the multinational corporation. J. Int. Bus. Stud. 24(4), 625–645 (1993)

Krichene, H., Arata, Y., Chakraborty, A., Fujiwara, Y., Inoue, H.: How Firms Choose their Partners in the Japanese Supplier-Customer Network? An Application of the Exponential Random Graph Model (No. 18011) (2018)

López, G., Ruiz, N.G., Patten, E.: Key Facts about Asian Americans, a Diverse and Growing Population. Pew Research Center, Washington, DC (2017)

Luo, X., Chung, C.N.: Keeping it all in the family: the role of particularistic relationships in business group performance during institutional transition. Adm. Sci. Q. 50(3), 404–439 (2005)

Magnier-Watanabe, R., Lemaire, J.P.: Inbound foreign direct investment in Japan: a typology. Int. Bus. Rev. 27(2), 431–442 (2018)

Massa, S., Testa, S.: A knowledge management approach to organizational competitive advantage: evidence from the food sector. Eur. Manag. J. 27(2), 129–141 (2009)

McPherson, M., Smith-Lovin, L., Cook, J.M.: Birds of a feather: homophily in social networks. Ann. Rev. Sociol. **27**(1), 415–444 (2001)

Miyamoto, Y., Kuhlman, N.: Ameliorating culture shock in Japanese expatriate children in the US. Int. J. Intercultural Relat. **25**(1), 21–40 (2001)

Murphy, R.T.: A loyal retainer? Japan, capitalism, and the perpetuation of American hegemony. Asia Pac. J. **41**(3), 1–10 (2010). http://www.japanfocus.org/-R_Taggart-Murphy/3425

Nahapiet, J., Ghoshal, S.: Social capital, intellectual capital, and the organizational advantage. Acad. Manag. Rev. **23**(2), 242–266 (1998)

Nonaka, I., Takeuchi, H.: The Knowledge-Creating Company: How Japanese Companies Create the Dynamics of Innovation. Oxford University Press, New York (1995)

North, D.C.: Institutions, Institutional Change, and Economic Performance. Cambridge University Press, Cambridge (1990)

Polanyi, M.: The Tacit Dimension. Peter Smith, Gloucester (1966)

Putnam, R.D.: The prosperous community. Am. Prospect **4**(13), 35–42 (1993)

Roberts, J., Fuller, T.: International business: past, present and futures. Futures **42**(9), 901–909 (2010)

Scott, J.: Social Network Analysis. Sage, London (2017)

Shaver, J.M., Mitchell, W., Yeung, B.: The effect of own-firm and other-firm experience on foreign direct investment survival in the United States, 1987–92. Strateg. Manag. J. **18**(10), 811–824 (1997)

US Census Bureau: North American industry classification system (2017)

Wang, X.H., Fang, Y., Qureshi, I., Janssen, O.: Understanding employee innovative behavior: integrating the social network and leader–member exchange perspectives. J. Organ. Behav. **36**(3), 403–420 (2015)

Williamson, O.E.: The Economic Institutions of Capitalism. Free Press, New York (1985)

Wong, M.M.: Internationalizing Japanese expatriate managers: organizational learning through international assignment. Manag. Learn. **32**(2), 237–251 (2001)

World Bank: Exports of Goods and Services (constant 2010 US$). The World Bank (2018). https://data.worldbank.org/indicator/NE.EXP.GNFS.KD?end=2016&locations=JP&start=1996

Zhou, L., Wu, W.P., Luo, X.: Internationalization and the performance of born-global SMEs: the mediating role of social networks. J. Int. Bus. Stud. **38**(4), 673–690 (2007)

Research on the Mode of Cultural Integration After M&A—Based on Boundary Penetration Theory

Yongmei Cui[(✉)], Xiangfei Fu[(✉)], and Ya Zhang

School of Economics and Management,
Beijing Jiaotong University, Beijing 100044, China
{ymcui,14113165}@bjtu.edu.cn, 875821517@qq.com

Abstract. Through the multi-case study of the cultural integration model after the M&As of three state-owned enterprises, this paper reveals how to carry out cultural integration under cultural differences after the merger of state-owned enterprises. Based on boundary permeability theory, we put forward three cultural integration mode: the absorption, promotion and separation. In conclusion, from the different types of state-owned enterprises' mergers and acquisitions, we propose a theoretical framework for cultural differences identification, cultural matching, cultural integration, and ultimately cultural synergy. This paper broadens the application situation of the cultural integration pattern and provides some references for the reform of mixed ownership of state-owned enterprises.

Keywords: Merger and acquisitions · Boundary permeability ·
Culture integration · State-owned enterprises

1 Introduction

The Third Plenary Session of the 18th Central Committee proposed to develop mixed ownership economy. In this context, mergers and acquisitions have become the way for state-owned enterprises to redeploy resources and promote the mixed-ownership reform. The value creation of M&A comes from the integration after M&A, and the prime reason why 60% of Chinese companies fail to achieve the expected value increase after M&A is the poor cultural integration. In general, the research on the mode of cultural integration of merger and acquisition is of great significance for China's current mixed-ownership reform.

This paper focuses on the core issue of how to carry out cultural integration in the M&A of state-owned enterprises, through the China National Machinery Industry (SINOMACH) M&A of YTO group (YTO), Shanghai Fila Sound (Fila sound) M&A of Beijing ShenAn Group (ShenAn) and China Minmetals Corporation (CMC) M&A of Australia OZ Minerals company (OZ). This paper puts forward that the key point of the M&A of the state-owned enterprises is to identify the cultural differences, identify the infiltration boundary and determine the integration mode. It comes to three conclusions. First, in the process of state-owned enterprise merger and acquisition of state-owned enterprises with small cultural difference, it takes strategic location to carry out

© Springer Nature Switzerland AG 2019
L. Uden et al. (Eds.): KMO 2019, CCIS 1027, pp. 213–224, 2019.
https://doi.org/10.1007/978-3-030-21451-7_18

mergers and acquisition. In addition, based on the shift of roles - the role of organizational culture, it is suitable to carry out fuzzy boundaries and adopt the absorption type cultural integration mode. Second, when it comes to the merger between state-owned enterprises and private enterprises with big cultural difference, it needs to absorb the positive culture of private enterprises. Based on the change of role-power organizational culture form, it is suitable to use the mode of promoting cultural integration and adopt the cross-border in technical. Thirdly, there are dual differences between national culture and corporate culture when state-owned enterprises merge foreign enterprises. It needs to have a deep understanding of the local system, environment and culture for Chinese enterprises. Based on the change of role-task organizational culture form, resource merger and acquisition is suitable to strengthen the boundary and adopt separate integration mode.

This article expands the application situation of cultural integration model from horizontal M&A, vertical M&A and diversification M&A integration model. Based on the theory of boundary permeability, this paper analyzes three kinds of modes through corporation merger and acquisition of state-owned enterprises, state-owned enterprises M&A of state-owned enterprises and state-owned enterprises M&A foreign company. It increases the explanatory power of the cultural integration model, in order to contribute to the theory of cultural integration.

2 Literature Review

2.1 Organizational Culture

Organizational culture can be approached from different directions. Martin [1] identified three theoretical perspectives in studies on organizational culture and named them integration, differentiation, and fragmentation. Harrison [2] defined four different organization ideologies and named them power orientation, role orientation, task orientation, and person orientation (Fig. 1).

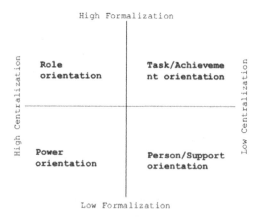

Fig. 1. Harrison's culture model (Based on Harrison 1972)

2.2 Boundary Infiltration

When integrating organizational business units, organizations can implement different border penetration strategies. Border infiltration strategy can be divided into different methods according to the content of infiltration. One view is that there are two border infiltration approaches. One is separation strategy. In this strategy, the organization can clearly identify the boundaries and identify the boundaries that need to be crossed among different organizations. The other is integration strategy. One business unit can flexibly infiltrate into another by means of fuzzy boundary. Another view divides the PMI into three types, which are absorption, symbiosis and protection. In absorption, one organization absorbs another directly and then merges into an integrated culture. Symbiosis is a strategy that is suitable for both highly dependent organizational culture and highly autonomous organization. The protective mode applies to low levels of interdependency and high levels of autonomy. When the degree of interdependence of business units is low, and business units adopt the same business model before integration, the protective mode becomes the most effective boundary penetration mode. The degree of interdependence between the business units determines the degree of requirement of boundary penetration [3].

2.3 Cultural Integration

Cultural integration refers to the activity or process that adjusts and re-combines various elements in the system to make them consistent and constitute a system, eventually maximizing the effectiveness of elements [4]. Berry [5] was the first to point out that cultural integration has three characteristics. First, it requires contact between two separate cultural groups. Secondly, it includes three typical stages, namely contact stage, conflict stage and adaptation stage. Thirdly, it takes place at both individual levels and collective levels. From the perspective of cultural conflict, Nahavandi and Malekzadel [6] argue that two enterprises with different corporate cultures will inevitably have cultural conflicts after merger and acquisition. After that, the process that constant adjustment and coordination will be made is called cultural integration.

Berry [7] firstly proposes the M&A cultural integration mode, believing that there are usually four cultural integration modes between the two sides of M&A. Cultural Integration refers to forming a mixed culture of the cultural elements of the two sides, the goal of which is to acquire the cultural advantages of the two parties. Cultural Assimilation refers to employees in the target enterprise are willing to give up their organizational operation system and their original organizational culture and assimilate into the culture of the merging enterprise. Cultural Separation refers to controlling the two parties' contact, maintaining the cultural independence of both sides and reducing their culture revolution. Cultural Deculturation refers to there is little cultural change in the merging enterprise, however the merged enterprise which is in a state of cultural confusion, gives up the original enterprise culture and is unwilling to accept the enterprise culture of the merging enterprise. Based on Berry's cultural integration model, Vaara [8] put forward "the newly created" mode that cultural integration can adopt four integration models in practice. They are separation (i.e., both sides of M&A keep the separation of cultures), blending (i.e., selecting the best elements from each culture), absorption (i.e., the absorption of one culture into the other), and the newly created (i.e., building new cultures to adapt to new organizations).

With the deepening of research, other researchers in China such as Zheng [9], Bao [10], begin to try to put forward their own cultural integration strategies and models. But whether cultural integration mode is fusion mode, substitution mode, promotion mode nor conquest mode, symbiosis mode, integration mode, robbing mode, etc. it is basically based on Berry's research framework.

3 Research Methodology

3.1 Method Selection

This paper adopts the horizontal multi-case study method and selects the post-merger cultural integration mode of three Chinese enterprises for analysis. First, this study aims to explore how enterprises conduct cultural integration after merger and acquisition, and studies the question of "How". The case study method matches the above research objectives [11]. Second, compared with single case study, multi-case study method has a more solid theoretical foundation and better effect in theoretical expansion, repeatability and exclusivity [12]. Third, this paper studies the mode of cultural integration under different M&A situations and forms the general model of cultural integration. Therefore, multi-case study method is more suitable (Table 1).

Table 1. Case description

The acquirer	The acquired party	Year	Transaction amount	Equity transfer ratio
SINOMACH	YTO	2007	Free of charge transfer	67%
Fila Sound	Shen An	2014	1.59 billion Yuan	100%
CMC	OZ Minerals	2009	1.386 billion dollars	100%

3.2 Data Analysis and Coding

When it comes to analyze and encode the data, we use the content analysis method of Strauss and Corbin [13]. The first-order concept, second-order concept, third-order concept and summarizing concept involved in this paper are shown in Fig. 2.

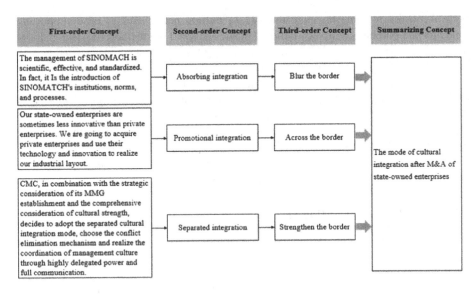

Fig. 2. Data structure coding

4 Case Description

4.1 SINOMACH Merged YTO

In December 2007, YTO Group Corporation (YTO) announced that Luoyang State-owned Assets Management Co. Ltd, the controlling shareholder of YTO (holding 52.48% of shares of YTO), signed an equity transfer agreement with China National Machinery Industry Corporation Ltd. (SINOMACH) on December 13, 2007, and the former transferred its 67% of equity of YTO to SINOMACH free of charge. Upon the completion of the equity transfer agreement, SINOMACH and Luoyang State-owned Assets Management Company held 67% and 17.63% of the equity of YTO respectively, and China Huarong Asset Management, China Orient Asset Management, and China Construction Bank Henan Branch hold other equity.

SINOMACH and YTO come from the tacit understanding that "Born in the Same Root". They share the same meme. Both SINOMACH and YTO are rooted in the original ministry of machinery industry. The two groups share the same root, similar culture and similar philosophy, and have a solid foundation for restructuring. The core values of "performance, rules and integrity" and the enterprise spirit of "coordination, innovation and excellence" all reflect the profound spiritual strength inherited from China's mechanical industry.

4.2 Feilo Acoustics Merged Shen An

On December 18, 2014, Shanghai Feilo Acoustics Co. Ltd. (Feilo Acoustics) announced that the CSRC approved Feilo Acoustics to issue 168 million shares to Beijing Shen An Group Co. Ltd (Shen An) to purchase related assets, and approved

Feilo Acoustics to issue no more than 77.71 million new shares to raise supporting funds for the purchase of assets. Feilo Acoustics adopted the method of issuing shares and paying cash to acquire 100% equity of Beijing Shen An, which was valued at 1.59 billion Yuan. Feilo Acoustics was unique in its way of reorganization through the acquisition of private enterprises rather than the introduction of strategic investors. It achieved mixed ownership reform while expanding and strengthening its businesses. After the reorganization, the Chairman of Feilo Acoustics unchanged, was still the representative of the state-owned investor. While at the insistence of the majority shareholder Yidian Group, the board of directors appointed the private entrepreneur as the new CEO, demonstrating its determination to build a mixed-ownership economy and stimulate the vitality of state-owned enterprises.

4.3   CMC Merged OZ Minerals

On June 11, 2009, China Minmetals Corporation (CMC) officially announced that China Minmetals Non-Ferrous Metals Co. Ltd acquired Australia OZ Minerals Corporation (OZ Minerals)'s main assets with a total consideration of $1.39 billion, including all the remaining assets apart from Prominent Hill Mines, Philippines branch, Indonesia branch and other branches. OZ Minerals was taken over by Minerals and Mining Group Limited (MMG), a wholly owned subsidiary of CMC in Australia.

In 2010, according to the strategic arrangement, Minmetals Resources Company, a subsidiary of Minmetals Corporation, acquired MMG and established a new Minmetals Resources Company (the English name follows MMG). The management teams of new Minmetals Resources are still held by former MMG personnel. The trust and the delegation of power of the board of directors and the professionalism and responsibility of the MMG management team make the cooperation between the two sides extremely harmonious and fruitful, which play an important role in CMC's overseas investment and operation. It can be said that the cultural integration of CMC and MMG is relatively successful. In this regard, Andrew Michelmore highly praised that CMC's success came from understanding and respect for two different cultures. The success of the cultural integration of CMC, fundamentally speaking, stems from the respect, understanding and tolerance towards the other party's corporate culture.

5   Case Discussion

Cultural integration refers to the active integration of internal and external resources of a company to achieve the assimilation of its members under the influence of multiple cultural environments. At the same time, the company has established a unique and active cultural management structure system that is capable of both development and hierarchy, to create an excellent cultural atmosphere and bring good social and economic benefits to the company. This article divides the cultural conformity pattern into the absorption pattern, the promotion pattern and the separation pattern [7]. This paper will make a summary and analysis of the three cases, and use the boundary penetration theory to build a model to discuss which mode of cultural integration is applicable in the process of state-owned enterprises' merger with state-owned enterprises, state-owned enterprises' merger with private enterprises and state-owned enterprises' merger with foreign enterprises.

5.1   Absorbing Integration

Also known as injection and unified cultural difference management mode, it refers to the mode of blurring the cultural infiltration boundary between the merger and acquisition parties. The merger and acquisition enterprise inputs a complete set of corporate culture into the enterprise of the acquired party, including core values, enterprise spirit, service concept, quality concept, talent concept, etc. It accepts the corporate culture of the acquired party completely, so that the acquired party can fully gain control of the enterprise and achieve cultural integration, as shown in Fig. 3 below. Applicable to the situation with strong and excellent culture of the acquiring company, this mode can win the unanimous recognition of the employees of the acquired company. At the same time, the original culture of the acquired company is weak or similar to the culture of the acquired company. Meanwhile, it is also applicable to the situation that the original culture of the acquired company is weak or similar to the culture of the acquired company.

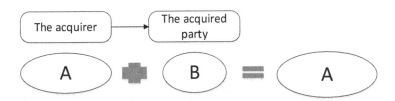

Fig. 3. Absorbing cultural integration model

Both SINAMACH and YTO are state-owned enterprises with the relatively obvious bureaucratic hierarchy. In the process of work implementation, formal procedures, written rules and systems, role requirements and power boundaries are clearly defined, so the transformation of organizational culture type belongs to role-role.

SINAMACH and YTO were subordinate units of the ministry of machinery industry, both of them were similar in system and culture, as Zhao Shan said in YTO, "SINAMACH and YTO group were congeneric". Therefore, in the process of cultural integration, the cultural boundary between SINAMACH and YTO can be blurred, and the management and culture of SINAMACH can be directly applied to the operation of YTO. The fuzzy cultural boundary between SINAMACH and YTO is mainly reflected in the following aspects.

First, the boundary of human resources. In order to make employees of YTO get the same treatment and status as the employees of SINAMACH, SINAMACH applies its own salary system and training system to YTO to blur the boundary of human resources of employees of both sides. For the staff of YTO, the most obvious feelings of joining the national machine personal are as below. Firstly, the salary level is improved. In 2016, the average annual income is above 50,000 yuan. Secondly, participating in the national pension plan, which is a good guarantee for the employee's welfare, is not only to increase the attractiveness of the enterprise, but also the second pillar of the endowment insurance. Thirdly, the employees of YTO can participate in the online training platform of SINAMACH.

Second, financial management boundary. Through a series of financial support, SINAMACH blurs the boundary of financial management with YTO. First of all, in 2009, SINAMACH injected 1.7 billion yuan into YTO, part of which was used to repay debts to reduce the asset-liability ratio and provide working capital for the development of YTO, so as to promote the development and growth of YTO.

Third, the boundary of governance structure. In terms of corporate governance, the controlling shareholder of YTO was Luo Yang municipal government before the joint reorganization of SINAMACH and YTO. Due to the imperfect structure of corporate governance, the board of directors of and management personnel in YTO are highly overlapping. Based on it, the duty of the board of directors changed from originally to hire and evaluate the management to self-assessment and self-evaluation, leading to the board of directors in name only. After the reorganization of the machine, with the opened boundary, it changed the situation on the height overlapping of the board of directors and management layer.

5.2   Promotional Integration

Also known as integrated cultural difference management mode, it refers to that in the post-merger integration, the two parties of merger and acquisition cross the cultural boundary and regard cultural difference as the favorable factor for integration in purpose to absorb the excellent cultural achievements or experience of the other party. The merger and acquisition parties should learn from each other, promote and assimilate mutually, to learn from each other and adjust different degrees. On the premise of not changing the respective cultural standards, the two different cultures will eventually merge into a better new corporate culture to achieve synergies, as shown in Fig. 3 below.

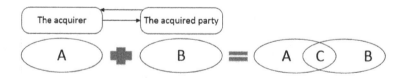

Fig. 4. Promotional cultural integration model

Fila sound, as a state-owned enterprise, has a relatively obvious bureaucratic hierarchy. In the process of work implementation, it emphasizes formal procedures, written rules and systems, and clearly defines role requirements and power boundaries. As a private enterprise, Shen-An group focuses on the role of individuals rather than groups when making decisions. So the organizational culture type of the M&A of Fila sound with Shen-An belongs to the transformation of role-power. As a private enterprise that has been in the market for many years, Shen-An has obvious advantages in resources, technology and overall service, and the two sides of the transaction are highly complementary. Through border penetration in culture integration, they finally draw the best composition between them. This process mainly includes the following aspects:

Firstly, the boundary of technological innovation. In order to achieve the industrial layout, crossing the boundaries of technology innovation, Fila sound actively absorb the technology and innovative resources of Shen An. In 2013, Fila sound achieved a total revenue of 2.142 billion yuan, of which 90.32% was the production and sales of light source appliances and lamps. The revenue from lighting equipment installation and contract energy management only accounted for 2.07%.

Secondly, the boundary of value identification. Merger and acquisition of the two sides across the boundary of each other's value identity with mutual coordination, in order to achieve complementary and win-win. As state-owned listed companies, Fila sound has advantages of capital, technology, talent, and management, while Shen-An as a well-known private enterprise in the industry, in terms of overall market development, has advantages of customer resources and services. There is a great complementarity between the two sides of the transaction, and there is a huge space for synergistic integration effect in the future.

Finally, the decision mechanism boundary. Due to the differences in the governance structure of state-owned enterprises and private enterprises, the two sides of the transaction will also form a governance mechanism of mixed ownership and equity diversification at the level of shareholders. It should not only give full play to the advantages of state-owned enterprises and private enterprises, but also avoid the monopoly of one share, and improve the decision-making and governance level. State-owned incentive mechanism should have decision-making procedures and be open, but the former private enterprises do not have a systematic incentive mechanism, and the operators pay more attention to realistic benefits. State-owned enterprises are responsible for the removal and paid attention to social responsibility. Private enterprises are not used to our management style. Therefore, this cultural integration is a big problem.

In this process, it emphasizes the importance of cultural infiltration in the process of post-merger integration rather than direct integration. With the acquirer's intention to infiltrate the culture, the continuous promotion of business integration, and the constant contact between the two acquirers' cultures, Fila sound only absorbs the high-quality culture of Shen-An, which may eventually form a culture different from the two enterprises before the merger, reflecting the progressive and continuous integration.

5.3   Separated Integration

Also called independent type or isolation type of management mode of the different cultural. It refers to the integration after enterprise in mergers and acquisitions, both sides have strong excellent enterprise culture with different cultural and different cultural background. Employees, in the enterprise, are reluctant to the change of cultural. At the same time, the contact of the two sides is not much, after the M&A. It will have not some big conflicts, due to cultural inconsistent. Both sides remain independent of integration patterns in cultural, within a certain period. The following is shown in

Fig. 4. After that, with the different development stages of cultural integration, it should act appropriately to separate the differentiated boundaries and further integrate the businesses and cultures of the two sides. There are many separated cultural integration modes in transnational mergers and acquisitions (Fig. 5).

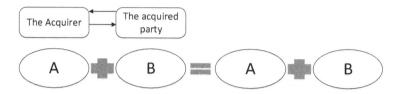

Fig. 5. Separated cultural integration model

Fully aware of the cultural differences between the two sides in the cultural integration after the acquisition, it adopts the principle of respect and non-interference in each other's cultural boundaries for integration. As a state-owned enterprise, the type of CMC belongs to role in organizational culture. OZ Minerals, as a foreign enterprise, has centralized power, and the way of organizing work is determined by the requirements of the task. It has a high degree of flexibility and worker freedom, so the organizational culture type is in line with the task. OZ Minerals, as a relatively mature foreign enterprise, has certain advantages in terms of its unique corporate culture, management team and system control, as well as market resources and strategic position. It brings a lot of internal resources and external resources to CMC, so the merger of the two is a resource merger.

First, the boundary of cultural environment. The psychological fluctuation caused by foreign employees' incomprehension of Chinese culture and CMC culture. This is a inevitable problem faced in overseas M&A. With its own unique corporate culture, management and control mode and system process, the original OZ Minerals has a completely international management team and a high degree of professional staff. CMC, as a Chinese state-owned enterprise, is in a period of rapid development and striving to achieve international strategic goals. At the beginning of the merger, some employees did not understand or complained. For example, employees in Laos misread the merger information at the beginning of the merger, showing anxiety and dissatisfaction about that CMC would send a batch of low-cost Chinese workers to replace them. The concept and perception of "Chinese enterprises are often subject to complete control" make western executives fear Chinese enterprises.

Second, the boundary of management style. CMC proposed that OZ Minerals would be managed by the Australian management team after the merger, and China would not interfere too much in its business activities. This kind of behavior fully authorized by the management also made OZ minerals' shareholders believe that CMC acquisition of OZ Minerals is not only for its rich resources of CMC, but also to create a win-win situation on the basis of common progress. It is from the strategic perspective that CMC considers the problem of the human resource management of the acquired enterprises and avoids the loss of key personnel of the acquired enterprises.

Since the early days of the acquisition, CMC has promised OZ Minerals and the Australian government to retain all the team members involved in the assets, including more than 4,000 people in exploration, production, management, operation and sales.

6 Conclusion

This paper focuses on the core issue of how to carry out cultural integration in the M&A of state-owned enterprises. Through the case study of three state-owned enterprise mergers and acquisitions, i.e., SINOMACH merger with YTO, Fila sound merger with ShenAn and CMC merger with OZ Minerals. This paper comes to the conclusion that: First, in the process of state-owned enterprise merger and acquisition of state-owned enterprises with small cultural difference, it takes strategic location to carry out mergers and acquisition. And based on the shift of roles - the role of organizational culture, it is suitable to carry out fuzzy boundaries and adopt the absorption type cultural integration mode; Second, when it comes to the merge between state-owned enterprises and private enterprises with big cultural difference, it needs to absorb the positive culture of private enterprises. Based on the change of role-power organizational culture form, it should merger and acquisition in technical. And it is suitable to use the mode of promoting cultural integration and adopt the cross-border; Third, there are dual differences between national culture and corporate culture when state-owned enterprises merge foreign enterprises. It needs to have a deep understanding of the local system, environment and culture for Chinese enterprises. Based on the change of role-task organizational culture form, resource merger and acquisition is suitable to strengthen the boundary and adopt separate integration mode (Fig. 6).

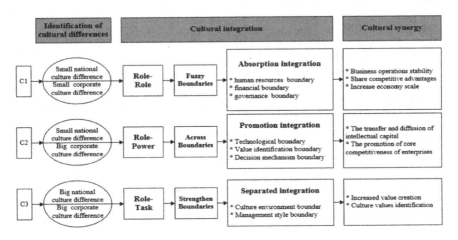

Fig. 6. Integration model

This paper mainly has the following three contributions. First, this paper extends the application of cultural integration model, analyze the consolidation pattern on the basis of corporation merger and acquisition of state-owned enterprises, state-owned enterprises M&A of state-owned enterprises and state-owned enterprises M&A of foreign company from horizontal M&A, vertical M&A and diversification M&A, and increase the explanatory power of cultural integration model. Second, based on the new perspective of boundary penetration theory, this paper explores the cultural integration mode of state-owned enterprises after M&A, analyzes the role of boundary penetration theory in the process of cultural integration, and provides a new theoretical perspective for the study of cultural integration mode. Thirdly, the analysis framework of the mode of cultural integration of M&A of state-owned enterprises constructed in this paper has practical significance to guide the reform of China's current mixed-ownership, then further exert the role of private economy and foreign economy, and enhance the vitality and innovation of state-owned economy.

References

1. Martin, J.: Organizational Culture: Mapping the Terrain. Sage Publications, Thousand Oaks (2001)
2. Harrison, R.: How to describe your organization. Harvard Bus. Rev. **50**(3), 119–128 (1972)
3. Haspeslagh, P.C., Jemison, D.B.: The challenge of renewal through acquisitions. Strategy Leadersh. **19**, 27–30 (1991)
4. Igor Ansoff, H., Cao, J.-D., Fan, Y.-H., et al.: New Company Strategy. Press of Southwestern University of Finance and Economics (2009)
5. Berry, J.W.: Human Assessment and Cultural Factors. NATO Conference Series. Springer, London (1983). https://doi.org/10.1007/978-1-4899-2151-2
6. Nahavandi, A., Malekzadeh, A.R.: Organizational Culture in the Management of Mergers. Quorum Books, London (1993)
7. Berry, J.W., Berry, J.W.: Handbook of cross-cultural psychology. Basic Process. Hum. Dev. **5**(4), 228–231 (1980)
8. Vaara, E.: On the discursive construction of success/failure in narratives of post-merger integration. Organ. Stud. **23**(2), 211–248 (2002)
9. Zheng, F.: The process, types and methods of cultural integration in M&A. China Soft Sci. **08**, 91–95 (2000)
10. Bao, S.: The cultural integration mode and path choice of Chinese enterprises' transnational merger and acquisition. Stat. Decis. **5**, 164–167 (2008)
11. Eisenhardt, K.M.: Agency theory: an assessment and review. Acad. Manag. Rev. **14**(1), 57–74 (1989)
12. Yiu, D., Makino, S.: The choice between joint venture and wholly owned subsidiary: an institutional perspective. Organ. Sci. **13**(6), 667–683 (2002)
13. Strauss, A., Corbin, J.: Basics of Qualitative Research Techniques. Sage publications, Thousand Oaks (1998)

Cryptocurrency and Its Digital Panorama in the Colombian Government

Alejandro Vásquez[⊠], Jhon F. Bernal[⊠], and Giovanni M. Tarazona[⊠]

Department of Engineering, Francisco José de Caldas District University,
Bogotá, Colombia
{alvasquezc, jfbernalv}@correo.udistrital.edu.co,
gtarazona@udistrital.edu.co

Abstract. Throughout recent years as well as in the use of cryptocurrencies factors that have been influenced by technologies such as Blockchain. This article investigates the current situation of the so-called cryptocurrencies in the international scene, as well as the acceptance, rejection or indifference position of different nations. Afterwards, the current situation of Colombia and its position with respect to the Cryptocurrencies is evaluated. Followed by this, a meet with a panel of experts is issued in order to provide a series of proposals that they evaluate and based on these a series of contributions regarding the concept of the cryptocurrency that is re-defined. Therefore, proceeding to characterize the actors involved in the transactions carried out with this medium. Finally, a brief recommendation is given to preserve the integrity of the Colombian users and a suggestion to form an interdisciplinary group under the concept of e-government that aims to investigate and observe the potential use of the applications of the technology that surrounds cryptocurrencies and their relationship with e-government.

Keywords: Cryptocurrencies · E-government · Digital currency · Regulation

1 Introduction

The global economy is adapting to new developments and computational innovations that have the potential to transform the way goods, assets and services are exchanged in the economy [1], for this reason, the incursions of cryptocurrencies into the virtual market have generated changes in the way transactions are conducted due to their attributes and technology that they use. The report on cryptocurrencies published in November 2015 by the Committee on Payments and Market Infrastructure identifies three characteristics of the cryptocurrency: electronic, does not constitute a passive of no one and lastly, allow the interchange between pairs (P2P) [2]. These characteristics become intrinsic attributes of the currency that generate diverse positions, in regards to their acceptance and their condition like average of payment. Colombia is not indifferent to this latent problem and it is clear that it must define its position regarding this situation. This is why it is vital to analyze the antecedents on the international level and then propose what your treatment should be in the country. Last off, the contribution of

© Springer Nature Switzerland AG 2019
L. Uden et al. (Eds.): KMO 2019, CCIS 1027, pp. 225–234, 2019.
https://doi.org/10.1007/978-3-030-21451-7_19

this document focuses on re-difined of the concept of cryptocurrency. Therefore, we proceed to characterize the actors involved in the transactions made with this medium. Finally, a brief recommendation is given to preserve the integrity of Colombian users and a suggestion to form an interdisciplinary group under the concept of electronic government that aims to investigate and observe the potential use of technology applications surrounding cryptocurrencies and their Relationship with electronic government.

2 Cryptocurrencies and Their Function

Cryptocurrencies, such as Bitcoin, are a decentralized electronic cash system, initially designed and developed by Satoshi Nakamoto. This was first seen in an article published under the name *A Peer to Peer Electronic Cash System* [3]. After this event, the concept of cryptocurrencies arose. Cryptocurrencies are means of digital exchange that, by their design and operation, fulfill the functions of traditional money allowing the exchange of goods and services [4] where users are the ones who generate the currency and verify that the transactions are carried out through a cryptographic process [5].

In order to carry out transactions with cryptocurrencies, the Blockchain technology or chains of blocks are used. This is a database that can be shared by a large number of users in a peer to peer [2, 3] manner and allows information to be stored in an immutable and orderly way [6], this chain of blocks must guarantee two fundamental properties:

A. *Availability*: ensures that an honest transaction that has been issued ends up being added to the chain of blocks, preventing a denial of service from nodes products.
B. *Persistence*: when a node gives a transaction as stable, the rest of the nodes, if they are honest, will validate this as stable, making it immutable and organized [7].

3 Blockchain Technology Connected to e-Government

Cryptocurrencies and the underlying Blockchain technology are an emerging platform for greater innovation, not only in financial systems but also in the public sector. Some of the most important characteristics of the Blockchain technology is its nature and global reach, its built-in transparency and its independence in the trust of third parties [8]. These characteristics are not of equal significance for all governments, but they will be of importance in countries vulnerable to corruption and lack of confidence in general, such as Colombia, which can benefit from the global reach and transparency offered by this technology and therefore implement tools that allow a development in e-government in countries like Colombia.

Tools, such as Smart contracts and proof of existence are born from the exploitation of Blockchain technology and can provide important solutions in corruption matters and at the same time increase the little confidence currently existing between governments and their respective citizens. The following is a brief description of the meaning of the previously mentioned tools:

3.1 *Smart contracts:* intelligent contracts represent the implementation of a contractual agreement whose legal provisions are formalized in a programming code and are verified through a network of pairs [2, 3], these contracts are executed by the code without the need for a trusted third party [33].

3.2 *Proof of existence*: is a web-based service that is used to show the authorship of things like software or documents. This tool demonstrates ownership of the document without revealing the information it contains [33].

4   Problems Related with Cryptocurrencies

Some sectors, both public and private, have generated a scrutiny and have concluded that there are questionable characteristics that impede the international acceptance of this virtual currency. Some of the problems and risks which the governments may face, in economic facets and public security wise, are tax frauds, cybercrimes related with software (fake antivirus), or entry of platforms that provide illegal services in exchange of cryptocurrencies [9].

The cryptocurrencies are in a stage of development that has several risks involved. First of all, it is still not widely accepted as a method of payment by merchants, since changes or refunds are normally not accepted due to the price volatility [10] of these virtual currencies and the changes that can be presented in its value from one day to the next [11]. The destabilization of the centralized financial system is another of the problems facing virtual currencies [12] due to the use acquired by cryptocurrencies over time, this could affect the use of traditional currencies of different governments obtaining as a consequence the devaluation in its price and subsequently the loss of purchasing power in the different industries in which governments and financial entities interact. The anonymity as property present in cryptocurrencies contributes to the increase in the generation of criminal operations by some of the users [13, 14].

5   Regulation of Cryptocurrencies in the World, Antecedents and Repercussions

Several governments have already given the task of moving some jurisdictions with the objective of regulating cryptocurrencies, countries like China have banned the Yuan as a means of deposit for the exchange of cryptocurrencies. Other countries such as Germany, Korea and Thailand have also indicated a repudiation with respect to cryptocurrencies as a means of legal payment. However, the generation of some forms of regulation of cryptocurrencies implemented by other nations, will be of great importance to solve the negative aspects they generate, that is why it is not really necessary to prohibit their use as private currency due to the possibility of weakening monetary control [15]. The regulation, acceptance or prohibition on the part of the

Table 1. Cryptocurrencies at the international level, own calculations

Country	Acceptance	Regulation	Description
Ecuador	No	Yes	The national assembly banned the use of Bitcoin and any decentralized virtual currency [4]
United States	Yes	Yes	In the guide FIN-2013-G001 on March 18, 2013 the applicability of the rules that are implemented to the Banking Secrecy Act (BSA) to the people who create, obtain, distribute, exchange, accept or transmit virtual currencies is clarified [4, 7]
Brasil	Yes	Yes	Law 12,865 of October 9, 2013 created the possibility of standardization of mobile payment systems and the creation of virtual currencies [4]
Bolivia	No	Yes	Board Resolution 044/2014 prohibits the use of coins not issued or regulated by the state [4]
Argentina	Yes	Yes	The Financial Information Unit (FIU) requires financial entities operating in the country to report monthly on all transactions made with virtual currencies [4, 16]
Spain	Yes	No	No type of regulation, although there are already cases in which the use of cryptocurrencies as a means of payment is [4, 17]
France	Yes	Yes	The government limited the anonymity in the purchase of Bitcoin and proposes a maximum amount in the payment with virtual currencies [4, 18]
China	Yes	No	Prohibited banks from trading with Bitcoin but users can buy and sell them [4, 19]
Singapur	Yes	Yes	It is not seen as a currency but as a commodity that is bought and sold and therefore taxes must be paid [4]
Japan	No	No	It is not a currency, but they consider taxing it as a value. They do not intend to legislate on bitcoin [4, 19]

countries in the world and their central banks have direct and indirect repercussions on the economic ecosystem they govern. Table 1 shows the repercussions of the actions taken by the governments of different countries with respect to cryptocurrencies can be observed.

6   Colombia Faced with Cryptocurrencies

On March 26, 2014, the Financial Superintendence of Colombia (SFC) issued letter 029 of 2014 entitled: Risks of transactions carried out with virtual currencies, directed both to entities supervised by the Superintendency and to the general public [20, 21]. One of the arguments the entity explains in its document is supported by the Law 31 of 1992. It establishes that the peso is the only means of payment of legal means with unlimited liberating power, consequently, Bitcoin "is not an asset that has equivalence to the currency of legal tender in Colombia since it has not been recognized as a currency in the country [20, 22], also, the Law 964 of 2005 does not constitute cryptocurrencies as a concept of value [24].

The Bank of the Republic of Colombia supported the SFC and its circular issued on the subject, made a press release where it reported three considerations on the use of Bitcoin, these are:

A. The only monetary and account unit in Colombia is the peso, consisting of bills and coins issued by the Bank of the Republic.
B. Bitcoin is not considered a legal currency in Colombia.
C. Bitcoin cannot be considered a currency because it does not have the endorsement of the central banks of other countries [1, 23].

The intermediaries of the exchange market have not been authorized by the Bank of the Republic to issue or sell cryptocurrencies according to the External Regulatory Circular DCIN 83 (Chapter 10) and External Resolution 8 of 2000 [1] that limits them to transactions exclusively with the legal currency in Colombia and with the currencies allowed by the central banks of the other countries in the international scope.

Asobancaria, which is the Association representing the Financial Sector in Colombia, through an email expressed that cryptocurrencies do not have an obvious benefit against fiduciary money and instead they carry a series of advantages and disadvantages [4]. In April 2018 the entity released a publication expressing its concern about the volatility of the value of cryptocurrencies in the market and the reasons for the risks they entail [25]. Finally, it should be noted that the Bank of the Republic of Colombia and the Superintendency of Finance in the second semester of 2018 have already started the work of researching studies regarding cryptoactives, but at the moment no pronouncement or contribution has been attributed to this topic.

7 Fieldwork

As a fieldwork, a panel of experts is carried out, in which a series of proposals are exposed and subjected to an evaluation through a questionnaire using the Likert scale as a measuring instrument [26]. For the validation of the instrument the Cronbach Coefficient [27] that will be used which will be obtained using the following formulas:

$$\propto = \left(\frac{k}{k-1}\right)\left(1 - \frac{\sum_{i=1}^{k} s_i^2}{s_t^2}\right) \tag{1}$$

Where s_i^2 is the variable of item i; s_t^2 is the variable of the total values obtained and k is the number of questions or items. To obtain the average of the values obtained by question, the following formula is used:

$$M_j = \frac{\sum_{i=1}^{n} x_{ij}}{n} \forall j \tag{2}$$

Where M_j is the average of the question j; x_{ij} are the points of the expert i in the question j and n are the number of experts (Table 2):

Table 2. Characterization of the experts, own elaboration

Profession	Years of experience
Industrial Engineer, Specialists in Occupational Health and Hygiene, Masters Web Design and Direction, Phd. Computation, Economist, Phd. Economy	10
Economist, PhD Economy	10
Lawyer, PhD Sociology, Legal and Political Institutions	18
Electrical Engineer, MA in Computer and Communication Sciences	7
System Engineering, Msc in Computer Systems Engineering	5
Public Accountant, Specialist in International Audits, Statutory Auditor and International Standards of Financial Information	20

Table 3 briefly summarizes the initial proposals suggested by the working group:

Table 3. Proposals for the treatment of cryptocurrencies in Colombia, own calculations.

Proposals
The government should regulate crypto actives in Colombia
The definition described in the proposal is coherent
The government can accept and ratify the definition proposed by the working group
Do you agree with the proposed actors and their characterization?
Income taxes should be applied to operations carried out of an occasional rent to operations done with crypto active agents
Is it feasible to use tools that arise from the exploitation of Blockchain technology as a complement to the development of e-government in Colombia?
Do you agree with the likelihood of generating smart contracts, which allow for greater control over the movements of Cryptocurrencies in the country?

Table 4 presents the results obtained on the proposals, taking into account each of the experts consulted.

Table 4. Results of the questionnaire, own elaboration.

Survey	P1	P2	P3	P4	P5	P6	P7	Total
1	3	4	2	2	4	4	3	22
2	4	4	3	4	4	4	4	27
3	3	2	1	2	1	1	1	11
4	3	2	2	3	4	3	3	20
5	3	1	1	1	1	3	1	11
6	4	1	2	4	3	4	3	21

The result of the cronbach coefficient is:

$$\alpha = 0,9053 \tag{3}$$

Therefore, the measuring instrument is considered excellent. Then the average of the obtained values is calculated and the results are shown in Table 5:

Table 5. Average of the results by proposal, own elaboration

Variable	P1	P2	P3	P4	P5	P6	P7
Mean	3,33	2,33	1,83	2,67	2,83	3,17	2,5

With the calculated mean it is allowed to prioritize the proposals according to the values obtained, Table 6 shows the results obtained.

Table 6. Prioritization of proposals, own preparation

Affirmation	Mean	Priority
P1	3	1
P2	2,1428	6
P3	1,71428	7
P4	2,42857	4
P5	2,57142	3
P6	2,85714	2
P7	2,28571	5

Based on the results obtained, a series of contributions is proposed that are described in the following chapter.

7.1 Limitations

Currently, Colombia government is investigating everything about to cryptocurrencies and how they work, for this reason, today, it cannot issue a clear position or communicate with other institutions that intend to collaborate in future research based on cryptocurrency technology such as Blockchain. This generates a limitation for the creation of communication and research channels to develop new tools that allow creating improvement policies for e-government from Colombia. The short number of individuals specialized in this topic and filters to communicate with them generate a restriction in the research and reduce the sources to consultation about this topic.

8 Future Contributions and Research

In Colombia, only a public warning has been generated about the risks involved in its use. The logical procedure is that, if this virtual currency is allowed, a regulation or protection protocol should be developed for individuals who wish to use them. As a first step, the concept of the cryptocurrency should be fully described in order to identify its object of use. Next, we propose the definition of cryptocurrency that is built based on the concept presented in the article "Necesaria regulación legal del Bitcoin en España" [17] and financial considerations disclosed by public entities:

Cryptoactive: it is an asset of digital nature, as well as of private property, characterized by its non-fungible asset status and is part of the non-tangible assets of the owner [17, 22, 27].

In this concept, the crypto active is associated as an asset because "it is a resource controlled by an entity as a result of past events, from which the entity expects to obtain, in the future, future economic [29] and is not taken as an effective equivalent (highly liquid short-term investments that are easily convertible to known amounts of cash and that are subject to an insignificant risk of changes in value [30] because the only currency of legal course in Colombia is the Colombian Peso, according to the Law 31 of 1992 [22] and in this way the conflict of the Crypto active for the Bank of the Republic is eliminated as a virtual currency. The crypto active is considered non-tangible heritage because in the course of its transaction [29] or exploitation generates a susceptible income for those actors involved and therefore modify their occasional earnings, which must be reported in their respective income declarations, this being an effect of a tax nature associated with the cryptoactive [28]. The concept applies to all virtual currencies and not only for Bitcoin, because although this is the most widely used crypto active nowadays, an error that can be committed by not covering all virtual currencies under the concept of cryptoactive is that to intervene exclusively Bitcoin, can promote its users to use other cryptoactives and therefore evade any imposed restriction.

Once the definition has been proposed, the actors involved in a transaction with crypto actives continue to be described in Table 7, thus establishing a necessary pattern that aims to generate specific roles in the transaction process of the crypto actives in the Colombia´s foreign exchange market, with the objective that each entity, whether natural or legal, can observe which role fits the activities carried out in the transaction process, therefore, it can establish basic criteria for carrying out commercial activities with crypto active in the national market.

Table 7. Actors involved in a transaction process with crypto actives, own elaboration

Actor	Description
Administrator	Legal entity contracted as a company to issue (put into circulation) a Crypto active and that also has the power to exchange (withdraw from circulation) the Crypto active [34]
User	Who gets a Crypto active to buy goods or services [34]
Exchanger	Legal entity contracted as a company for the exchange of Crypto actives, funds or other real currencies [34]

Because of the evidence of an upward trend and companies such as Athena Bitcoin reporting their plans regarding the entry of more than 200 ATMs to the Latin American region, more specifically to the countries of Argentina, Mexico and Colombia [32] it is proposed develop a regulation to the percentages of commission obtained by private sector companies for the provision of services through ATMs to carry out transactions, whether bidirectional or unidirectional with the crypto active. This is proposed in order to prevent excessive limitation to which users may be subjected by private companies.

Altogether, based on the contributions of the experts it is concluded that it is convenient to form an interdisciplinary group with the purpose of investigating and observing the potential use of the applications of the technology surrounding Cryptocurrencies and their relationship with e-government due to that this technology seems to be evolving towards a support infrastructure for the safe handling of documents that cannot be corrupted through the help of tools such as Smart contract, Proof of Existence [33] and the protection for voting suffrage, underlying Blockchain technology.

References

1. Arango, C., Bernal, J.: Criptomonedas, Banco de la Republica – Colombia (27), pp. 1–27 (2016)
2. Bech, M., Garratt, R.: Criptomonedas de bancos centrales. Informe Trimestral Del BPI 2017, pp. 1–20. BIS Quarterly Review, Switzerland (2017)
3. Barber, S., Boyen, X., Shi, E., Uzun, E.: Bitter to Better — How to Make Bitcoin a Better Currency. Palo Alto Research Center. University of California, pp. 399–414 (2012)
4. Sarmiento, J., Luis, J., Bautista, G.: Criptodivisas en el entorno global y su incidencia en Colombia. Revista Lebret **8**, 1–11 (2016)
5. Palacios Cárdenas, Z., Vela Avellaneda, M., Tarazona Bermudez, G.: Bitcoin Como Alternativa Transversal De Intercambio Monetario En La Economía Digital. Redes de Ingeniería **6**(1), 106–128 (2015)
6. Dolader Retamal, C., Bel Roig, J., Muñoz Tapia, J.: La blockchain: fundamentos, aplicaciones y relación con otras tecnologías disruptivas. Economía Industrial **405**, 33–40 (2017). ISSN 0422-2784
7. Garay, J., Kiayias, A., Leonardos, N.: The bitcoin backbone protocol: analysis and applications. In: Oswald, E., Fischlin, M. (eds.) EUROCRYPT 2015. LNCS, vol. 9057, pp. 281–310. Springer, Heidelberg (2015). https://doi.org/10.1007/978-3-662-46803-6_10
8. Ølnes, S., Jansen, A.: Blockchain technology as s support infrastructure in e-government. In: Janssen, M., et al. (eds.) EGOV 2017. LNCS, vol. 10428, pp. 215–227. Springer, Cham (2017). https://doi.org/10.1007/978-3-319-64677-0_18
9. Nakamoto, S.: Bitcoin: A Peer-to-Peer Electronic Cash System. Www.Bitcoin.Org. https://doi.org/10.1007/s10838-008-9062-0. Accessed 4 Apr 2018
10. European Banking Authority. EBA Opinion on virtual currencies. European Banking Authority, In: EBA (eds) EBA Op 2014, pp. 1–46 (2014)
11. Alberto, E., Garcia, M.: Monedas Virtuales Se Suman Al Comercio Electronico. Universidad Militar Nueva Granada, pp. 1–34. Universidad Militar Nueva Granada, Bogota (2016)
12. Gómez Rodríguez, C.: Bitcoin: Problemas Reales, Universidad Nacional Autonoma de Mexico, pp. 266–297. Infotec, Mexico (2016)
13. ACPR - Bancque de France: Position de l'ACPR relative aux opérations sur Bitcoins en France, Position 2014-P-01, pp. 0–1. ACPR - Bancque de France, France (2014)

14. Gandal, N., Moore, T.: Price manipulation in the Bitcoin ecosystem, VOX CEPR Policy Portal. http://voxeu.org/article/price-manipulation-bitcoin-ecosystem. Accessed 10 Apr 2018
15. Blundell Wignall, A.: The bitcoin question: currency versus trust-less transfer technology. In: OECD Working Papers on Finance, Insurance and Private Pensions 2014, vol. 37, pp. 1–19. OECDiLibrary (2014)
16. OroyFinanzas.com. Regulación de Bitcoin en Argentina. https://www.oroyfinanzas.com/2015/02/regulacion-bitcoin-argentina/. Accessed 01 Apr 2018
17. Salmerón Maldonado, E.: Necesaria regulación del Bitcon en España. Revista de Derecho Civil **4**, 293–297 (2017)
18. OroyFinanzas.com. Bitcoin: Nuevas regulaciones en Argentina, Francia, Italia y Japón. Oro y Finanzas. https://www.oroyfinanzas.com/2014/07/bitcoin-nuevas-regulaciones-argentina-francia-italia-japon/. Accessed 04 Apr 2018
19. Gómez Jiménez, L: ¿Qué tan legítimo es invertir en bitcoins? Revista Semana. https://www.semana.com/tecnologia/novedades/articulo/que-tan-legitimo-es-invertir-en-bitcoins/381503-3. Accessed 10 Apr 2018
20. Superintendencia Financiera de Colombia: Riesgos de las operaciones realizadas con "Monedas Virtuales". https://www.superfinanciera.gov.co/jsp/loader.jsf?lServicio=Publicaciones&lTipo=publicaciones&lFuncion=loadContenidoPublicacion&id=10082781. Accessed 10 Apr 2018
21. López, A.: Implicaciones jurídicas del uso del bitcoin en Colombia. Validez del contrato de compraventa comercial con bitcoins, pp. 1–106 (2015)
22. BANCO DE LA REPÚBLICA: LEY 31 DE 1992. Ley Del Banco De La República, pp. 1–26 (1992)
23. Banco de la Republica de Colombia. COMUNICADO BITCOIN. http://www.banrep.gov.co/es/comunicado-01-04-2014. Accessed 11 Apr 2018
24. El Congreso de Colombia: Ley 964 de 2005, No. 45.963 (2005)
25. Castro, S., Malag, P.J., Econ, M.: Bitcoin: el antes y el durante, ¿habrá un después?, ASOBANCARIA, ed. 1132, pp. 1–11 (2018)
26. Fernández de Pinedo, I: NTP 15: Construcción de una escala de actitudes tipo Likert. Instituto Nacional de Seguridad e Higiene En El Trabajo, pp. 1–8 (2006)
27. González Alonso, J., Pazmiño Santacruz, M.: Cálculo e interpretación del Alfa de Cronbach para el caso de validación de la consistencia interna de un cuestionario, con dos posibles escalas tipo Likert. Revista Publicando **2**, 62–67 (2015)
28. Fernández, F.: Colombia busca gravar transacciones en Bitcoin sin tener marco legal. https://es.panampost.com/felipe-fernandez/2017/06/27/colombia-gravar-bitcoin/?cn-reloaded=1. Accessed 15 Apr 2018
29. Consejo Técnico de la Contaduría Publica: Criptomonedas o monedas virtuales (2018)
30. Dolader Retamal, C., Bel Roig, J., Muñoz Tapia, J.L.: La blockchain: fundamentos, aplicaciones y relación con otras tecnologías disruptivas. Economía Industrial **405**, 33–40 (2017). ISSN 0422-2784
31. Estrella Morales, A.: Valor – Razonable. Argumentos a Favor y en Contra dentro de las Burbujas Financieras. NIIF 13, pp. 1–5 (2015)
32. González, C.: En 2018 habrá 200 cajeros de bitcoin en toda la región, director de Athena Bitcoin. La Republica. https://www.larepublica.co/finanzas/en-2018-habra-200-cajeros-de-bitcoin-en-toda-la-region-2577749. Accessed 15 Apr 2018
33. Forte, P., Romano, D., Schmid, G.: Beyond Bitcoin – Part I : A critical look at blockchain-based systems, pp. 1–34 (2015)
34. Department of the Treasure, Financial Crimes Enforcement Network: Application of FinCEN's Regulations to Persons Administering, Exchanging, or Using Virtual Currencies, pp. 1–6 (2013)

The SECI Model in Moroccan Context: A Case Study of Payment Solution Software Sector

Meriem Talaskou$^{(\boxtimes)}$ and Lhacen Belhcen

Hassan II University, Casablanca, Morocco
meriemtalaskou@gmail.com, lbelhcen@gmail.com

Abstract. Von Krogh [33] has emphasized that knowledge management community claimed the universality of some models in application and conception, Nonaka's SECI model is one of them. Organizational knowledge creation theory has revolutionized knowledge management discipline through visualizing the conversion of individual tacit knowledge to organizational tacit dissemination. Few voices stated that contextual elements influence the applicability of this model. Consequently, the paradigm of universality is called into question. This article explores, to what extent the four modes of SECI Model exist in the Arab context, particularly in Morocco. For that purpose we used a single case research design, we collected and analyzed rich information from semi-structured interviews, documentation, and taking notes during non-participant observation in a multinational Moroccan company (payment solution software sector), the findings related to the four modes namely socialization, externalization, combination and internalization were very pivotal, explained in details in the rest of the article.

Keywords: SECI model · Culture · Universality ·
Organizational knowledge creation

1 Introduction

In the broadest context, Knowledge is considered as a number one resource followed by human capital and land [3], to achieve a strong competitive advantage in an unpredictable environment and turbulent economy, organizations invest more in knowledge management practices to deal with such challenges, many scholars, academics, practitioners stated that knowledge management is surrounded by a titanic complex cultural context. For example, few authors stated that "Knowledge cannot be understood outside of the cultural parameters" [34, p. 89]. Besides, Easa [8] agrees with Weir and Hutchings [34] about the importance to emphasize the roots of the organizational knowledge management theory anchored in Japanese culture. For this reason, the SECI model cannot be applicable across different cultures. The aim of this article is to answer this following question: are the four modes of the SECI model exist in the Moroccan context? We adopted a single case study research design to verify the trace of SECI modes in Moroccan context, we used multiple sources of evidence namely, interviews, observation and documents conducted in Multinational Moroccan company, HPS company (High tech Payment Systems), we had arrived at some interesting

© Springer Nature Switzerland AG 2019
L. Uden et al. (Eds.): KMO 2019, CCIS 1027, pp. 235–246, 2019.
https://doi.org/10.1007/978-3-030-21451-7_20

results. To some level, the four modes of this KM model are available in individual and organizational practices, this finding disconfirms an important part of literature [1, 8, 34], however, it confirms the SECI founder's claims about the universality.

2 What Is Knowledge?

In his famous article "A dynamic theory of organizational knowledge creation" Nonaka [20] considered that knowledge concept is multifaceted with multilayered meaning, the efforts in the definition are rooted in the ancient contribution of classical Greek philosophers like Plato and other philosophers like Descartes, Locke, Hume, Kant. Till now the concept of knowledge is not clearly defined. The huge work of Plato the "Theaetetus" which is a Platonic dialogue examined the nature of knowledge and delivered three definitions. "Knowledge is a Perception", "Knowledge is a True Judgment" and "Knowledge Judgment With an Account". No one can deny that it is the greatest work on epistemology, however, the dialogue had ended with no satisfying results (impasse) [5] and it was not discovered what the knowledge is but what the knowledge is not.

In the literature, defining the concept of knowledge is cryptic, however, many authors yielded a good understanding and some convincing description. In the article "Working Knowledge: how organization manage what they know" Davenport et al. [7] suggested a "working definition" of knowledge. They considered that it is "A fluid mix of framed experience, values, contextual information, and expert insight that provides a framework for evaluating and incorporating new experiences and information. It originates and is applied in the minds of knowers. In organizations, it often becomes embedded not only in documents or repositories but also in organizational routines, processes, practices, and norms" (p. 5). In the same year, the same author [7] considered that knowledge is information mixed with experience, context, interpretation, and reflection were inspired from the traditional epistemology and he considered that knowledge as a dynamic human process of justifying personal beliefs as part of an aspiration for the "truth" [7, p. 15]. Bennet and Bennet [2] considered that "knowledge is the capacity (potential or actual) to take effective action in varied and uncertain situations" (p. 73). They had distinguished between two parts of knowledge the "informing" and "proceeding", the first one is concerned with insights, meaning, understanding, expectations, and the second represents the "process and the action part of knowledge" [2, p. 74].

For Nonaka et al. [21] information and knowledge are two terms often used interchangeably, however, there is a distinction between them. For some authors "Data is simply raw facts without context, whereas information is data that comes with context. For example, the number 5,551,687 would be considered data. However, adding the context of a phone number turns the data into information. The continued use and understanding of this information will turn it into knowledge" [15, p. 28].

3 The Organizational Knowledge Creation Theory

Organizational knowledge creation theory of [25] was a result of a sophisticated study on Japanese companies concerning creativity and innovation [6]. This theory has revolutionized the knowledge management discipline, most cited as a major international reference and received wide commendation [34]. Organizational Knowledge creation was defined as "a process of amplifying individual knowledge and making it organizational, it means taking individual knowledge and connected to the organization knowledge system" [26, p. 1179]. The model of Nonaka is based on two different types of knowledge, namely tacit and explicit knowledge, they are considered as the cornerstone of their epistemology [22]. Nonaka [20] highlighted a distinction between an epistemological and ontological dimension, the former is related to the difference between tacit and explicit as two distinct types of knowledge and the latter is more concerned with "the extent of social interaction between individuals that share and develop knowledge" [21, p. 15]. In his book "The Tacit Dimension" [27] was the first to point out the concept of tacit knowledge, as the hidden part of knowledge dissimilated in intuition, people's mind and experiences.

Tacit comparing to explicit one is more related to individuals, as previously mentioned, it is concealed in people's brain. However, explicit knowledge is kept in repositories, it is accessible and easy to exploit compering to tacit one, the continual dialogue between tacit and explicit helped the emergence of new knowledge [21] that's why researchers and practitioners had suggested different models highlight the importance of knowledge creation. Such as Nonaka's model [25], Boisot's information space model (1998), Nissen's Knowledge flow model (2005), and other models built on the earlier contribution [22]. The model of Nonaka [25] is composed of four modes consecutively, socialization, externalization, combination and internalization, every mode required certain practices (see the table below) and the interaction between the four modes leads to organizational knowledge creation, to move knowledge from individual to the organizational level.

Table 1. Practices of different modes of SECI model.

Mode	Practices
Socialization	- Informal meeting (like coffees, social activities) [23] - Preparing for social activities outside the workplace [18] - Informal activities (outside the workplace) [23] - Activities related to mentoring [23, 26] - Make a team of interaction to share members' experience and perspectives [20] - "The extent to which managers gather information from sales and production sites, share experience within suppliers and customers and engage in dialogue with competitors" [21, p. 344] - "The extent to which managers create a work environment that allows peers to understand the craftsmanship and expertise through practice and demonstration by the master" [21, p. 344]

(*continued*)

Table 1. (*continued*)

Mode	Practices
Externalization	- The manifestation of the corporate, mission vision, values, organizational history through documents, [23, 31] - Organizational routines expressed in Schemes, organizational charts, flowcharts, etc. [16] - Metaphors analogies and models to clarify concepts and ideas [19, 24] - Translating the tacit knowledge of customers or experts into a readily understandable form [9] - Participation of internal collaborators and experts to set the training and seminars [17, 18, 20]
Combination	- Information restored in files, databases, intranets, corporate networks, company software (classified and no problem of accessibility.) [23] - Add, combine and classify already available information, to develop written reports [18] - Repositories of information [9] - Free access to corporate information [8] - "The extent to which managers build and create manuals, documents and databases on products and services build by material by gathering management figures and or technical information from all over the company" [21, p. 344]
Internalization	- Prepare meetings to explain the content of documents through flow charts schemes [4, 16, 20, 30] - Proposing for collaborators to make a postgraduate course e.g. Diploma, Master, or PhD [17, 29, 32] Learning by doing [20] - Training programs [8]

4   The Universality of Organizational Knowledge Creation and Its Application in the Arab Context

For Hofstede [11], management discipline was considered as universal, especially, between 1950 and 1970. However, context became an important feature to take into consideration while studying managerial practices in the organization. Authors and practitioners claimed the responsibility of context in the success and the failure of certain management models. Knowledge management has witnessed the same debate when the discussion surrounded the organizational knowledge creation. In his book, Holden claimed that "diversity in terms of language, cultural and ethnic background, gender and professional affiliation are compressed into one giant independent variable, which is, in any case, pushed to the side" [12, p. 81]. In the article "Contextual Constraints in Knowledge Management Theory: The Cultural Embeddedness of Nonaka's Knowledge-creating Company" Glisby and Holden [10] considered that the universal validity of Nonaka and Takeuchi's model was admitted by the knowledge management community but some of SECI processes have a limited application in other contexts since the model emerged in a Japanese specific environment, they stated that "the socialization mode is heavily dependent on Japanese personal commitment to the organization (…). The externalization mode is strongly influenced by Japanese communitarianism (…). The combination mode fundamentally requires a holistic, open and participatory management style, which is often associated with Japanese management; and the internalization mode is largely facilitated by the Japanese acceptance of job-rotation schemes" [10, p. 36]. Moreover, Weir and Hutchings [34] refused the universal applicability of the SECI model and they listed the characteristics and specifications in the Arab world and China compared to Japan. They argued that socialization worked effectively compared to the rest of organizational knowledge. Furthermore, in the Russian context, the four modes of SECI model are limited, because of multiple reason, like the unwillingness to share knowledge in the internal and external knowledge limited the existence of the socialization mode, the individualistic character of Russians influence the externalization, the lack of accessibility to corporate information hampered the combination process and the fear of mistakes constrain the internalization phase [1].

Morocco is well known about his political, economic, environmental particularities, and especially his cultural context, its national culture is widely different than other countries, it has a high power distance, high uncertainty avoidance, high score of masculinity and collectivistic society and this might impact the existence of organizational knowledge creation modes in Moroccan context [28]. The aim of this article is to verify the existence of the four modes of organizational creation in Moroccan firms and confirm its universal or non-universal applicability in this context.

5   Research Methodology

We chose qualitative methodology demonstrated in the single case study research method, this choice is justified by the exploratory nature of our study, and because of the substantial and the significant feature given to the context, the case study is very prominent and sensible to contextual elements in given research. Yin [35] considered that the case study, is "an empirical inquiry that investigates a contemporary phenomenon within its real-life context; when the boundaries between phenomenon and context are not clearly evident; and in which multiple sources of evidence are used" [35, p. 23]. The empirical research was conducted in a multinational Moroccan small and medium enterprise (SME), operating in payment solutions software sector, HPS is very competitive, it provides innovative payment solutions with over 400 clients in 90 countries in the five continents, it is considered as one of the strongest payments technology providers in the industry. We have chosen this organization for several reason, mainly because it is a Moroccan company managed typically in a Moroccan way, which has the potential to have "knowledge creation initiatives" demonstrated in the detention of several data centres, documentation, IT services and a department in charge of training for collaborators and clients named "HPS Academy" department. Without these elements, it will be unfair to investigate the existence of organizational knowledge modes in the Moroccan context.

6   Data Selection Method

Because of the exploratory nature and contextual elements of our research, qualitative methodology is more appropriate to extract prominent results. Therefore, I acted as a non-participant observer, in an open space office. I had started making brief meetings and taking notes as a part of the observation process in order to select the right department and profile to make the interviews. So, the data were collected through semi-structured interviews, and the interview session was in a closed office to ensure the right climate for the interviewee, 5 collaborators (with different profiles (account manager, in Sales department, training assistant, in Human Resources department, senior trainer and consultant in HPS Academy department, intern auditor, and project engineer, respectively in Audit and Documentation or Data Processing department.)) were asked to answer 17 questions classified in four themes. We stopped at the fifth interviewee because we noticed the redundancy at the level of answers. Furthermore, we had used different sources of evidence making an observation and taking notes during my research internship in the company for the period of 3 months, moreover, we had used reports and documentation from the company website plus the posters available in the organization. The interviews took between 36 min to 1 h and 18 min, all interviews were recorded and transcribed for further analyses.

7   Findings

In this part of the article, we foreground the results obtained from interviews concerning the four modes of organizational knowledge creation in a Moroccan company, the Table 2 below highlight the existence of the four modes, through the different practices expressed in interviews citations.

Table 2. Interviews' findings

Mode	Practices/citations
Socialisation	- "We made a team building this year, it was in April (…) effectively, we have some moments, we are out of the professional area, we made some extra professional activities as a part of the team building" - "I had a mentoring from my superior, he teaches me everything about the metier" - "Normally, there is mentoring from the department, when there is a new employee, he is surrounded by former colleagues" - "From time to time, they organize a technical seminar, to share experiences, results and new projects" - "(…) the clients are invited to the Users' meeting event, just people from the field are invited"

(*continued*)

Table 2. (*continued*)

Mode	Practices/citations
Externalisation	- «Nearby the printer, there is a board, you will find the list of values and company mission» - «Next to the door, there is the history of the company from the creation to the present» - "Sometimes when you talk about a concept, it is not sufficiently clear for them, at that time we should use schemes, and explain the concept by metaphors and analogies" - "Through an email or meeting, the project manager, express the need of the client in term of training, (....) after that we prepare an agenda, we validate with the project manager and clients to prepare the training"
Combination	- "Generally, documents are listed in «Market Leader CRM Solution» software, when people from the marketing or sales department prepare a very interesting presentation, it could be shared in this software, and when there is a need for it we use it, the accessibility for "Market Leader CRM Solution" is for marketing, pre-sale, the account managers, General manager" - "We have the SharePoint, it is a specific place for the HPS Academy department, we organize and archive presentations (…) the access is just for the academy" - "As an account manager, I have the right to get access to the server, however, when I was an engineer in the company, I was not able to use it, the company manage the accessibility depending on the users' role" - "I consult the "business solution description", (…) to prepare the users' guide, the "Product Functional Flow" and the table description" - "they send «Connect'in» once in three months, it is an internal newsletter (…) shared in emails, it shares the news and achievements of the collaborators in the company"
Internalisation	- "When we schematize, we have a global vision, and generally, people privilege images, they have more impact, for this reason, we schematize, we have models we use them" - "I took advantage from a lot of training this year" - "We ensure training for everybody, collaborators and clients (..) when the human resources department ask for training concerning a product we are the first interlocutor" - "We make workshops, (…) we ask participants to set up a product (..) and the objective is to carry out what we have explained in the presentation, and through this workshop, we make sure that everything is clear"

8   Discussion

Through this section, we exploited three sources of evidence, and related them to literature concerning organizational knowledge creation [21, 24], we highlighted the existence of the four modes of SECI model in Arab context, particularly in Morocco, so as to answer the question raised by scholars concerning the universality of SECI Nonaka's model.

8.1   Socialization

Socialization focused on creating knowledge through sharing experiences [20], different practices reflect socialization existence within this organization, and collaborators exchange their experiences in informal activities and meetings through team buildings at the national and international level [18, 23]. Furthermore, the company reserve a football field every Friday after work to play football as an extra professional activity. During my internship, I noticed that when the collaborator is confused, the more experienced colleague or manager try to monitor him for more than 30 min until he understands, which was the case of engineers with developers and senior trainer with a junior trainer. All interviewees claimed that there is informal monitoring especially when a new employee ask for help in a given situation [23, 26]. To make a team of interaction and share members' experience, the company prepare every year a technical seminar to encourage departments to present their projects, share their experiences, exchange with each other and take advantage from the different feedbacks [20]. The organization makes a huge investment every 2 years to prepare a successful event named users' meeting to highlight their new products, new strategies, their position in the market and honoured clients by preparing the event on their behalf [21]. The results confirm the existence of socialization in this company which confirms the theoretical contribution of some authors [34] considering networking as a disseminated practice in the Arab context.

8.2   Externalization

This second mode of knowledge conversion consists on converting tacit to explicit form and this is considered as very critical because of the complex nature of tacit knowledge. In HPS, values, mission, and company history is clearly manifested and expressed in documents, [23, 31]. For example, communication departments has mentioned in the annual report of (2017) [13, 14] that values are "excellence, responsibility, solidarity, passion for innovation, and integrity, we create optimal conditions for our employees to drive forward our strategy on a daily basis" [14, p. 34] and their mission "is to offer innovative products and services within the payment and associated technology industry, transforming (…) into a world-class company" [14, p. 20]. Furthermore, in the organization, there are boards explaining the different values, mission and texts describing the history printed in the wall in the open space offices.

Generally, the organizational routines are not expressed in schemes and flow charts, [16], however, the Internal Audit and Quality departments develop the conversion of tacit knowledge to explicit through making workshops to exchange with engineer and describe the process of their daily work and make it more explicit through the software "Outil mega" that helps to translate this process to organized flowcharts. Moreover, the trainers in HPS Academy department use the "side by side" technic, they stayed next product engineer so as to ask questions and take notes to transform the technical information to functional one, demonstrated in schemes and flows, exploited later in training programs. Further, the most important part of externalization process namely metaphors and analogies are not used by everyone in the organization but trainers use them continually in training sections to visualize the different concepts and make them more understandable, [19, 24]. Another practice witness the existence of externalization is the translation of customers and experts' tacit knowledge to understandable forms [9]. Which is done through the collaboration between project managers (PM) and account managers to make adapted presentations, and the synergy between (PM) and organization's trainers to prepare tailored training programs, because (PM) remained the first to communicate and deal with customers. The externalization mode is surprisingly anchored in collaborators practices in HPS company, efforts are made at the individual and organizational level to encourage the move from tacit to explicit unlike the arguments of the literature related to the struggle of these modes in Arab context explained by the preference of Arabs tend to "keep their powder dry' in business situations, and to sit on winning hands until there is an absolute need for disclosure" [34, p. 94].

8.3 Combination

All combination citations in Table 2 confirm the strong availability of combination mode on this organization, which correspond adequately to combination practices indicated by authors and mentioned in Table 1. Software, graphics interfaces like "SharePoint", "Outilmega", "Market Leader CRM Solution", "Data model" serve as repositories where information is restored carefully [9, 23]. The organization manage the accessibility of the information constantly to make it accessible for all collaborators in their daily needs, [9]. Interviewees confirm the accessibility to this repositories and to information in general, with respecting confidentiality boundaries, like any given organization. In addition to this, the IT department invites all collaborators worldwide to send their information to the virtual space of storage, (clouds). In order to protect any data available within the organization, not to mention the several data centres established by the company to ensure large protections of information. This time, empirical results concurred with the claims of authors the literature, especially, of Weir and Hutchings, [34] they arrived at the conclusion that combination can work effectively in Arab context unlike the limited application in the Chinese context.

8.4 Internalization

Internalisation is the last mode of the SECI model, it is characterized by moving from explicit to tacit knowledge [20]. This feature is embodied fundamentally in Learning by doing [20], training programs [8] and preparing meeting to explain the content of documents through flow charts schemes [14, 16, 23, 30]. These three characteristics are clearly spread in the organization. For instance, there are sufficient workshops held by the company, these workshops reflect the practice of "learning by doing", which is centralized, especially in training sessions. The trainer makes sure that the content of the presentation is well grasped by clients or collaborators, through experimentation and application under the observation of the trainer. Beside this, 14000 h of training were ensured in 2017 and the number of hours is developing according to the training assistant. The distribution of training in 2017 was 67% for technical Training 22% in soft skills and 11% in management and the rate of this training has intensified in 2018 compared to 2017. For the third time, the result of our research contradict [10] claims concerning the non-universality of internalization as described in the SECI model.

Moreover, as Weir and Hutchings stated [34] knowledge internalization is affected by confidence, however, when the organization make a program like training and adopt practices such as "learning by doing" and ensure the conversion of explicit to tacit through this practices, confidence remain without big power to alter internalization modes. The same case was for this company, and even in the interviews, an important element was repeated "our collaborators don't hesitate to share knowledge" so the confidence matter doesn't hamper the explicit-tacit conversion.

9 Conclusion

The SECI is a very influential model in knowledge management discipline, and the knowledge management community agreed its universality primarily by the founder, some authors, like [1, 10, 34] agreed that there is a shortage of applicability out of Japanese cultural framework.

In one hand, our findings contradict authors initiated the debate, concerning the potential impact of the contextual elements on the universality of organizational knowledge management model, on the other hand, our results confirm the other extreme part of belief which defend the universal paradigm of knowledge management [20]. Our empirical work is considered as a prelude in the applicability of the SECI model in the Arab context, we invite researches in the field to give more attention to this area of research because there is a huge gap in studying the relationship between culture and knowledge management in general and organizational knowledge creation in particular.

References

1. Andreeva, T., Ikhilchik, I.: Applicability of the SECI model of knowledge creation in Russian cultural context: theoretical analysis. Knowl. Process. Manag. 18(1), 56–66 (2011)
2. Bennet, D., Bennet, A.: Engaging tacit knowledge in support of organizational learning. Vine 38(1), 72–94 (2008)
3. Bray, D.A.: Literature Review - Knowledge Management Research at the Organizational Level, pp. 1–18. SSRN (2007). https://ssrn.com/abstract=991169
4. Brown, J.S., Duguid, P.: Organizing knowledge. Calif. Manag. Rev. 40(3), 90–111 (1998)
5. Chappell, S.G.: Plato on Knowledge in the Theaetetus. The Stanford Encyclopedia of Philosophy (2005)
6. Dalkir, K.: Knowledge Management in Theory and Practice. Elsevier Butterworth-Heinemann, Jordan Hill (2013)
7. Davenport, T.H., Prusak, L.: Working Knowledge: How Organizations Manage What They Know. Harvard Business School Press, Brighton (1998)
8. Easa, N.F.: Knowledge management and the SECI model: a study of innovation in the Egyptian banking sector, thesis, pp. 1–341 (2012)
9. Fernandez, I., Sabherwal, R.: Organizational knowledge management: a contingency perspective. J. Manag. Inf. Syst. 18(1), 23–55 (2001)

10. Glisby, M., Holden, N.: 1 management theory: the cultural embeddedness of Nonaka's knowledge-creating company. Knowl. Process. Manag. 10(1), 29–36 (2003)
11. Hofstede, G.: The cultural relativity of organizational practices and theories. J. Int. Bus. Stud. 14(2), 75–89 (1983)
12. Holden, N.: Cross-Cultural Management: A Knowledge Management Perspective. Pearson Education, Canada (2002)
13. HPS Homepage. https://www.hps-worldwide.com/about-hps. Accessed 14 Jan 2019
14. HPS's annual report. https://www.hps-worldwide.com/investor-relations/annual-reports. Accessed 14 Jan 2019
15. Jones, K., Leonard, L.N.: From tacit knowledge to organizational knowledge for successful KM. In: King, W. (ed.) Knowledge Management and Organizational Learning, pp. 27–39. Springer, Heidelberg (2009). https://doi.org/10.1007/978-1-4419-0011-1_3
16. Kogut, B., Zander, U.: What firms do? Coordination, identity, and learning. Organ. Sci. 7(5), 502–518 (1996)
17. Li, Y.-H., Huang, J.-W., Tsai, M.-T.: Entrepreneurial orientation and firm performance: the role of knowledge creation process. Ind. Mark. Manag. 38(4), 440–449 (2009)
18. Martin-de-Castro, G., López-Sáez, P., Navas-López, J.E.: Processes of knowledge creation in knowledge-intensive firms: empirical evidence from Boston's Route 128 and Spain. Technovation 28(4), 222–230 (2008)
19. Nonaka, I.: The Knowledge-Creating Company. Harvard Business Review. November–December. Google Scholar (1991)
20. Nonaka, I.: A dynamic theory of organizational knowledge creation. Organ. Sci. 5(1), 14–37 (1994)
21. Nonaka, I., Byosiere, P., Borucki, C.C., Konno, N.: Organizational knowledge creation theory: a first comprehensive test. Int. Bus. Rev. 3(4), 337–351 (1994)
22. Nonaka, I., Takeuchi, H.: The knowledge-creating company: how Japanese companies create the dynamics of innovation. Long Range Plan. 4(29), 592 (1996)
23. Nonaka, I., Toyama, R., Byosiere, P.A: Theory of organizational knowledge creation: understanding the dynamic process of creating knowledge. In: Dierkes, M., Antal, A., Child, J., Nonaka, I. (eds.) Handbook of Organizational Learning and Knowledge, Oxford University Press, Oxford (2001)
24. Nonaka, L., Takeuchi, H.: The Knowledge-Creating Company. Oxford University Press, New York (1995)
25. Nonaka, I., von Krogh, G., Voelpel, S.: Organizational knowledge creation theory: evolutionary paths and future advances. Organ. Stud. 27(8), 1179–1208 (2006)
26. Payne, S.C., Huffman, A.H.: A longitudinal examination of the influence of mentoring on organizational commitment and turnover. Acad. Manag. J. 48(1), 158–168 (2005)
27. Polanyi, M.: The Tacit Dimension. The University of Chicago Press, Chicago (1966)
28. Results of Hofstede about Morocco. https://www.hofstede-insights.com/country/morocco/
29. Rice, J.L., Rice, B.S.: The applicability of the SECI model to multi-organisational endeavours: an integrative review. Int. J. Organ. Behav. 9(8), 671–682 (2005)
30. Sanchez, R.: Knowledge Management and Organizational Competence. Oxford University Press, New York (2001)
31. Schulz, M.: The uncertain relevance of newness: organizational learning and knowledge flows. Acad. Manag. J. 44(4), 661–681 (2001)
32. Tsai, M.-T., Li, Y.-H.: Knowledge creation process in new venture strategy and performance. J. Bus. Res. 60(4), 371–381 (2007)

33. Von Krogh, G., Ichijo, K., Nonaka, I.: Enabling Knowledge Creation. Oxford University Press, New York (2000)
34. Weir, D., Hutchings, K.: Cultural embeddedness and contextual constraints: knowledge sharing in Chinese and Arab cultures. Knowl. Process. Manag. **12**(2), 89–98 (2005)
35. Yin, R.K.: Case Study Research: Design and Methods. Sage Publications, Beverly Hills (1984)

Data Mining and Intelligent Science/Big Data and IOT

Webpages Classification with Phishing Content Using Naive Bayes Algorithm

Jorge Enrique Rodríguez Rodríguez[✉],
Víctor Hugo Medina García[✉], and Nelson Pérez Castillo[✉]

District University "Francisco José de Caldas", Bogotá, Colombia
{jerodriguezr, vmedina, nelsonp}@udistrital.edu.co

Abstract. Phishing attacks cause people to be scammed and cheated because of the impossibility to visually detect fraudulent websites. As is known, the attack occurs from emails sent to collect or update information supposedly from an entity, there are also cases of phone calls or instant messages. There is ignorance of such attacks by people in general, which means that the user is not alerted, which means that he is not attentive to the digital certificates present on the page that authenticate the content of the same. For this reason, the web pages designed have required tools that counteract and alert the user of the "phished" webpages, which commit the theft of money from the account from which information has been provided.

Keywords: Webpage · Suspicious · Legitimate · Phishing · Naive Bayes · Machine learning · Data mining

1 Introduction

The new era of Phishing that comes from the English word phishing (fishing) [1], such meaning and metaphorically speaking, makes reference to the "hunt" that hackers perform in media as widely used by society as the Internet, stealing information from the netizens of their private accounts, and as not from their bank accounts. Phishing people are known as phishers [2]. These individuals have the main function of sending emails to different people in order to get them to believe that the email they receive is from a reliable sender and generate the private data of the people there in order to later carry out the thefts [3].

There are two major segments of phishing: First, a potential victim receiving a phishing email and the second, where the victim is driving to the spoofed website via a fake email. There could be a chance of including an attachment too to install malware or replying with sensitive information [4].

The above shows that the traditional phishing class is a form that despite being something primitive, is considered dangerous and of utmost importance for the safety of netizens. However, at present there are no real figures of losses due to phishing or the number of people affected by this modality. Currently, email fraud has become a problem that affects security and the global economy, whose detection through The use of filters for traditional mail has been recognized as not very effective [5].

© Springer Nature Switzerland AG 2019
L. Uden et al. (Eds.): KMO 2019, CCIS 1027, pp. 249–258, 2019.
https://doi.org/10.1007/978-3-030-21451-7_21

The aim is to obtain relationships between the parameters found in this data set so that, based on this study, specific filters for this type of online theft can be developed [6].

In this paper we show the process to make the classification phishing using machine learning algorithms, such as Naive Bayes; in the same way, we describe the whole process to find new knowledge from the collection and integration to the knowledge patterns attainment. In addition, we use some algorithms to detect outliers and features selection Finally, naive bayes machine learning algorithm applied to phishing is used.

2 Problem

Phishing is a specialized attack whereby the attacker intelligently uses spoofed emails or websites to trick the victims into sharing their confidential and sensitive information, or by installing malware into the victims' computer. It clearly circumvents the security measures adopted by both individuals as well as business organizations at large. However, there are a number of issues that concern the gap between academic literature and practical evidence [4].

The banking entities and in general the web pages that offer electronic payment services, have been exposed during the last years to the malicious attacks, of false pages that are in charge of stealing the private information of the users that use their services.

The people who access the web pages' trust in the authenticity of these; since the false page has in general a style very similar to the main one, it is for this reason that the user is deceived and his information is stolen. The attack occurs from emails sent to collect or update information allegedly from the financial institution, there are also cases of phone calls or instant messages.

Any impersonation of web pages with attempted theft of information is known as phishing, this can have negative effects for the personal or financial life of any person or entity, the different ways of trying to deceive the cybernauts are becoming more complex, that arises the need to provide some guidelines on how these fraudulent web pages can be detected where this famous way of digital theft is used.

Phishers always take the benefit of human factors that generally ignore the critical warning messages. Lack of awareness about phishing attacks in society is the main reason, due to which phishing attacks have become so much successful. According to the fact that phishing is mainly used for financial gains, there are other factors such as social gains, motivate phishers to commit the crime [7].

The effect of being scammed by a phishing email depends on exactly what the scammer wants to take from you. There are plenty of different types of phishing attacks, but they all rely on the same basic mechanism: exploiting human trust, ignorance, or apathy in order to get us to do something we really should not be doing.

According to the 2012 UK Cards Association report, a significant increase of phishing attacks in online transaction caused £21.6 million loss in 2012, which was a growth of 28% from the previous year. Such attacks had created a risk for many e-commerce websites and industries too. Phishing can be referred to as an automated identity theft, which takes the advantage of human nature and the Internet to trick millions of people and take a large amount of money [8].

A study conducted to evaluate the impact of anti-phishing software, where 400 users participated with a high precision tool (90%) or a low precision software (60%) to make a decision about a legitimate or phishing website, It showed that users who use high-precision software outperformed others in their ability to: distinguish legitimate websites from suspects, avoid visiting phishing websites and avoid transactions on phishing websites, but these users They often ignored the software's correct recommendations, which resulted in 15% lower phishing detection rates compared to the anti-phishing software used [9].

3 Methodology

The type of scientific research applied in this paper is descriptive-exploratory with an experimental approach [10]. According to the formal research process, a hypothetical - deductive method was used in which a hypothesis was formulated, which through empirical validation was validated through deductive reasoning. It was established, based on the experimentation, a mechanism for weighting the algorithm evaluation indicators in such a way that it was possible to evaluate said mechanism when changing the dataset.

The methodology called KDD (knowledge Discovery in databases) was applied, which arises as a need to analyze large volumes of information stored in databases [11]. KDD provides the ability to discover new and meaningful information using existing data and data mining, emerging as a technology that attempts to help understand the content of a database. KDD includes five stages:

(1) Problem definition
(2) Data Collection and integration
(3) Data preprocessing.
(4) Estimation and data mining model construction
(5) Validation model

4 Naive Bayes Classification Algorithm

Machine learning has become one of the most important topics within development organizations that are looking for innovative ways to leverage data assets to help the business gain a new level of understanding. Why add machine learning into the mix? With the appropriate machine learning models, organizations have the ability to continually predict changes in the business so that they are best able to predict what's next. As data is constantly added, the machine learning models ensure that the solution is constantly updated. The value is straightforward: If you use the most appropriate and constantly changing data sources in the context of machine learning, you have the opportunity to predict the future [12].

Bayesian methods provide a way to incorporate external information into the data analysis process, that is, completely change the vision of the data analysis process with respect to the classical approach [13].

One ways to classify information is using Bayesian methods; which are based on subjective interpretation of probability and its central point, "Bayes Theorem". Among the applications of probability theory, it applies to state the Bayes theorem as an expression of conditional probability that demonstrates the benefits obtained from estimates based on intrinsic knowledge. Bayesian methods specify a probability model containing any previous knowledge about a research setting, thus the probability model is conditioned to adjust the assumptions [14–16]. The probabilistic Thomas Bayes theorem (ec. 1) is useful when we know the outcome of an experiment, but we do not know any of the intermediate steps in which you are interested.

$$P(H|O) = \frac{P(O|H)P(H)}{P(O)} \tag{1}$$

Where:

$P(H)$, $P(O)$: Unconditional probabilities

$P(O|H)$: Conditional probability

The concept of conditional probability is introduced in Elementary Statistics. We used $P(O|H)$ to denote the conditional probability of event O occurring, given that event H has already occurred [17].

Naive Bayes has proven effective in many practical applications, including text classification, medical diagnosis, and systems performance management [18, 19]. The success of Naive Bayes in the presence of feature dependencies can be explained as follows: optimality in terms of zero-one loss (classification error) is not necessarily related to the quality of the fit to a probability. The key problem in Naive Bayes method is the class conditional density estimation. Traditionally the class conditional density is estimated based on data points. For classification problems, however, we should learn the class conditional density from data represented by probability distributions functions.

Naive Bayes is attractive as it has an explicit and sound theoretical basis which guarantees optimal induction given a set of explicit assumptions. There is a drawback in which the independency assumptions of features with respect to the class are violated in some real world problems. However, it has been shown that Naive Bayes is remarkably robust in the face of such violations; is fast, easy to implement with the simple structure, and effective. It is also useful for high dimensional data as the probability of each feature is estimated independently [20].

A Naive Bayes classifier assumes that the value of a particular feature of a class is unrelated to the value of any other feature, so that:

$$P(C_k|A_i) = P(C_k) \prod_{i=1}^{n} P(A_i|C_k) \tag{2}$$

Where:

A_i is the *i-th* feature

n is number of features

C_k is the *k-th* class

For qualitative (descriptive) features, the rule of Laplace can be used [21]; that is:

$$P(x_i|Pa(x_i)) = \frac{n(x_i, Pa(x_i)) + 1}{n(Pa(x_i)) + |\Omega x_i|} \tag{3}$$

Where:

$n(x_i, Pa(x_i))$ Is favorable sample

$n(Pa(x_i))$ Is total sample

Ω_{x_i} Is possible samples

For numerical features, we used normal probability distribution function.

$$f(x) = \frac{1}{\sqrt{(2\pi)}\sigma} \exp\left[-\frac{(x-\mu)^2}{2\sigma^2}\right] \tag{4}$$

5   Results

Different features related to legitimate websites and sites used for phishing have been identified; a dataset was used (Website Phishing Dataset) that was taken from UCI Machine Learning Repository which consists of the response of websites of 1353 and 10 features to evaluate the reliability of the sites (Table 1). The legitimate websites were collected from Yahoo and starting point directories using a web script developed in PHP. The PHP script was plugged with a browser and we collected 548 legitimate websites out of 1353 websites. There is 702 phishing URLs, and 103 suspicious URLs.

Table 1. Data description

Feature	Description
SFH	SFHs (Server Form Handler) that contain an empty string or "about: blank" are considered doubtful because an action should be taken upon the submitted information
popUpWindow	This feature has been used in some legitimate websites and its main goal is to warn users about fraudulent activities or broadcast a welcome announcement
SSLfinal_State	is an industry standard and is used by millions of websites in the protection of their online transactions with their customers
Request_URL	Examines whether the external objects contained within a webpage such as images, videos and sounds are loaded from another domain. In legitimate webpages, the webpage address and most of objects embedded within the webpage are sharing the same domain
URL_of_Anchor	An anchor is an element defined by the <a> tag. This feature is treated exactly as "Request URL"

(*continued*)

Table 1. (*continued*)

Feature	Description
web_traffic	This feature measures the popularity of the website by determining the number of visitors and the number of pages they visit
URL_Length	Phishers can use long URL to hide the doubtful part in the address bar
age_of_domain	This feature can be extracted from WHOIS database (Whois 2005). Most phishing websites live for a short period of time
having_IP_Address	An IP address is a number that identifies, logically and hierarchically, a network interface of a device that uses the IP protocol, which corresponds to the network level of the TCP/IP model
Result (class)	When a website is considered SUSPICIOUS that means it can be either phishy or legitimate, meaning the website held some legit and phishy features

Next, we applied feature selection as a data preprocessing stage to data mining, proves to be valuable in that it eliminates the irrelevant features that make algorithms ineffective. Sometimes the percentage of instances correctly classified is higher if a previous feature selection is applied, since the data to be mined will be noise-free [22].

We used WEKA tool for features selection, this is divided into two parts: Attribute Evaluator and Search Method [23]. The attribute evaluator is the technique by which each attribute in your dataset is evaluated in the context of the output variable (e.g. the class). The search method is the technique by which to try or navigate different combinations of attributes in the dataset in order to arrive on a short list of chosen features.

We employ CfsSubsetEval evaluator (evaluates the worth of a subset of attributes by considering the individual predictive ability of each feature along with the degree of redundancy between them) and BestFirst search method (searches the space of attribute subsets by greedy hill climbing augmented with a backtracking facility). The BestFirst selection method, is a supervised features filter that can be used to select features and allows various search and evaluation methods to be combined.

The relevant features selected, are: SFH, popUpWindow, SSLfinal_State, web_traffic, and URL Length; the remaining 4 attributes are not relevant and therefore we are removed from the dataset. Figure 1 shows the Naive Bayes network, after relevant features select. This network indicates that each feature has dependency on the class (Result), but among these features there is no dependency.

To determine if there are outliers, we apply DBSCAN algorithm (Density Based Spatial Clustering of Applications with Noise) which is considered a pioneer of density based clustering technique. This algorithm grows regions with sufficiently high density into clusters and discovers clusters of arbitrary shape in spatial databases with noise [24]. After applying this algorithm no outliers were detected. We applied by defect parameters used in WEKA tool.

Since the dataset is free of noise, we proceed to apply the Naive Bayes algorithm to evaluate reliability of the websites. Dataset is composed of 5 features (SFH, popUpWindow, SSLfinal_State, web_traffic, URL Length) and the class (result), after making a features selection process.

Numeric estimator precision values are chosen based on analysis of the training data. For this reason, the classifier is not an UpdateableClassifier (which in typical usage are initialized with zero training instances) if you need the UpdateableClassifier functionality, use the NaiveBayesUpdateable classifier. The NaiveBayesUpdateable classifier will use a default precision of 0, 1 for numeric features when buildClassifier is called with zero training instances [25].

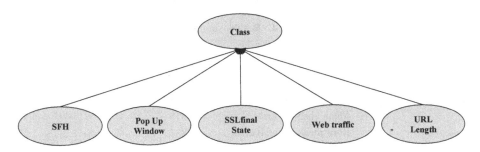

Fig. 1. Naive Bayes network

Table 2, shows the configured parameters of the Naive Bayes.

Table 2. Naive Bayes parameters

Parameter	Description
useKernelEstimator	Use a normal distribution
batchSize	The preferred number of instances to process if batch prediction is being performed
displayModelInOldFormat	Use old format for model output
useSupervisedDiscretization	Convert numeric attributes to nominal ones

The confusion matrix, show the degree of effectiveness of the Naive Bayes to classify reliability of the websites (Suspicious, Legitimate and Phishing), as shown in the Table 3.

Table 3. Effectiveness of the Naive Bayes algorithm

	Suspicious	Legitimate	Phishing	Correctly classified
Suspicious	5	49	49	4.85%
Legitimate	6	490	52	89.4%
Phishing	1	61	640	91.16%

The classification effectiveness for the "Suspicious" class is low (4.85%), while the effectiveness for the "Phishing" class is the highest (91.16%) of the three classes, instances only 103 belong to "Suspicious" and 702 to the class "Phishing"; one reason for the great difference in effectiveness is that machine learning algorithms tend to learn better those data that are more representative, that is, the greater the number of instances, the greater the effectiveness in the classification.

In training the Naive Bayes learned correctly classified 1135 instances (83.8877%); similarly, algorithm learn that 218 instances (16.1123%) incorrectly Classified (Table 4).

Table 4. Results summary

Parameter	Naive Bayes
Correctly classified samples	83.8877%
Incorrectly classified samples	16.1123%
Kappa statistic	0.6991
Mean absolute error	0.1519
Root mean squared error	0.283
Relative absolute error	40.5987%
Root relative squared error	65.4374%
Total number of samples	1353

6   Conclusions

One way to restrict phishing webpages is to analyze the structural content, for which an original page and a suspicious page are required to be "phished". The database servers contained with the original webpages and "phished", allow to minimize the processing time and facilitate the structural comparison of the html content. From developing data mining models with their respective architecture, we could benefit the people that navigates daily in the largest network on the planet, detecting with the subsequent development of software for web pages where data theft is presented through the modality phishing.

Machine learning algorithms allow the discovery of knowledge patterns from historical data sets that reflect a behavior of problem. In this article we use and show the Naive Bayes algorithm in order to determine the risk of fraud in webpages; supporting in this way the networks administrator in the detection of Internet fraud.

Data preprocessing is fundamental for the subsequent obtaining of the best knowledge patterns; in this case we use an algorithm to features selection, which allowed us to discard non relevant information, selected in total five relevant features. Likewise, an algorithm was used to detect outliers, concluding the non-existence of these.

Naive Bayes is a simple algorithm to use and in spite of not contemplating the dependency between features (predictor variables), it has a good performance in classification problems, as shown in this paper; where this algorithm obtained an effectiveness in the classification close to 84%. However, a disadvantage of this algorithm is that the more instances a class contains, the greater its effectiveness in the classification, and the less the instances the lower the classification. This problem can be resolved by selecting a number of similar instances.

As future work, we recommend using TAN Bayesian network (Tree Augmented Naive Bayes), which includes the option of dependencies between the predictor variables; this can improve the effectiveness in classifying webpages with phishing content.

References

1. Baykara, M., Grürel, Z.: Detection of phishing attacks. In: 6th International Symposium on Digital Forensic and Security (ISDFS), Antalya (2018)
2. Karabatak, M., Mustafa, T.: Performance comparation of classifiers on reduced phishing website dataset. In: 6th International Symposium on Digital Forensic and Security (ISDFS), Antalya (2018)
3. Fadheel, W., Abusharkh, M., Abdel-Qader, I.: On Feature selection for the prediction of phishing websites. In: 15th International Conference on Dependable, Autonomic and Secure Computing, 15th International Conference on Pervasive Intelligence and Computing, Orlando (2017)
4. Shaikh, A., Shabut, A., Hossain, M.: A literature review on phishing crime, prevention review and investigation of gaps. In: 10th International Conference on Software, Knowledge, Information Management and Applications, Chengdu (2016)
5. Gaonkar, M.N., Sawant, K.: AutoEpsDBSCAN: DBSCAN with Eps automatic for large dataset. Int. J. Adv. Comput. Theor. Eng. 2319–2526 (2013)
6. Ester, M.: A density-based algorithm for discovering clusters in large spatial databases with noise. In: Proceedings of the 2nd International Conference on Knowledge Discovery and Data Mining, Oregon (1996)
7. Gupta, B., Nalin, A., Psannis, K.: Defending against phishing attacks: taxonomy of methods, current issues and future directions. Telecommun. Syst. Model. Anal. Des. Manag. **67**, 247–267 (2018)
8. Gupta, B., Tewari, A., Jain, A., Agrawal, D.: Fighting against phishing attacks: state of the art and future challenges. Nat. Comput. Appl. Forum 1–26 (2016)
9. Abbasi, A., Zahedi, F.M., Chen, Y.: Impact of anti-phishing tool performance on attack success rates. In: 10th IEEE International Conference on Intelligence and Security Informatics (ISI), Washington (2012)
10. Mockford, A.: An exploratory descriptive study of the needs of parents after their young child is discharged from hospital following an admission with an acute illness, Victoria University of Wellington, Wellington (2008)
11. Rogalewicz, M., Sika, R.: Methodologies of knowledge discovery from data and data mining methods in mechanical engineering. Manag. Prod. Eng. Rev. **7**(4), 97–108 (2016)
12. Hurwitz, J., Kirsch, D.: Machine Learning for Dummies. Wiley, New York (2018)
13. Berthold, M., Hand, D.: Intelligence Data Analysis - An Introduction. Springer, New York (2002)
14. Mesa, O. Rivera, M., Romero, J.: Descripción general de la Inferencia Bayesiana y sus aplicaciones en los procesos de gestión, La simulación al servicio de la academia, vol. 2, pp. 1–3 (2011)
15. Mitchell, T.: Machine Learning. McGraw-Hill, United States of America (1997)
16. Chai, K., Hn, H.T., Chieu, H.L.: Bayesian online classifiers for text classification and filtering. In: 25th Annual International ACM SIGIR Conference on Research and Development in Information Retrieval, Tampere (2002)
17. Witten, I., Eibe, F.: Data Mining: Practical Machine Learning Tools and Techniques with Java Impletations. Morgan Kaufmann, San Diego (2000)

18. Hellerstein, J., Thathachar, J., Rish, I.: Recognizing end-user transactions in performance menagement. In: Proceedings of AAAI-2000, pp. 596–602 (2000)
19. González O, F.A.: Diplomado en Inteligencia de Necogios - módulo minería de datos, Universidad Nacional de Colombia. http://dis.unal.edu.co/~fgonza/courses/2007-II/mineria/bayesianos.pdf
20. Taheri, S., Mammadov, M.: Learning The Naive Bayes Classifier With Optimization Models. Int. J. Appl. Math. Comput. Sci. (2013)
21. Hernández Orallo, J., Ramírez Quintana, M., Ferri Ramírez, C.: Introducción a la minería de datos, Pearson (2004)
22. Guyon, I., Elissee, A.: An introduction to variable and feature selection. J. Mach. Learn. Res. **3**, 1157–1182 (2003)
23. Rodriguez, J.E., Medina, V.H., Ospina, M.A.: Corporate networks traffic analysis for knowledge management based on random interactions clustering algorithm. J. Commun. Comput. Inf. Sci. **877**(1), 523–536 (2018)
24. Shah, G.: An improved DBSCAN, a density based clustering algorithm with parameter selection for high dimensional datasets. In: Nirma University International Conference on Engineering, Gujarat (2012)
25. John, G., Langley, P.: Estimating continuous distributions in Bayesian classifiers. In: Eleventh Conference on Uncertainty in Artificial Intelligence, pp. 338–345. Morgan Kaufmann Publisher (1995)

Artificial Intelligence Tool Penetration in Business: Adoption, Challenges and Fears

Stephan Schlögl[✉], Claudia Postulka, Reinhard Bernsteiner,
and Christian Ploder

Department Management, Communication and IT,
MCI Management Center Innsbruck,
Universitätsstraße 15, 6020 Innsbruck, Austria
stephan.schloegl@mci.edu

Abstract. Artificial Intelligence (AI) and its promise to improve the efficiency of entire business value chains has been headlining newspapers for the last years. However, it seems that many companies struggle in finding the right tools and use cases for their distinct fields of application. Thus, the aim of the presented study was to evaluate the current state of machine learning and co in various European companies. Talking to 19 employees from various different industry sectors, we explored applicability of AI tools as well as human attitudes towards these technologies. Results show that AI implementations are still in their early stages, with a rather small number of viable use cases. Tools are predominantly bespoke and internally built, while off-the-shelf solutions suffer from a lack of trust in third party service providers. Although companies claim to have no intention of reducing the workforce in favor of AI technology, employees fear job loss and thus often reject adoption. Another important challenge concerns data privacy and ethics, which has grown in relevance with respect to recent changes in European legislation. In summary, we found that companies recognize the competitive advantage AI may attribute to their value chains, in particular when it comes to automation and increased process efficiency. Yet they are also aware of the rather social challenges, which currently inhibit the proliferation of AI-driven solutions.

Keywords: Artificial intelligence · Technology adoption ·
Implementation challenges · Interview study

1 Introduction

Buzzwords such as machine learning, digital assistants, chatbots, or the more general term natural language processing, dominate day-to-day tech news and media, with the increased use of these artificial intelligence (AI) technologies being rather controversially discussed. Products whose AI underpinnings are less obvious, such as Amazon's product recommendations, Spotify's song suggestions, or simply Google's search engine results, have been well established in everyday life. While some users are not aware of their use of AI technology, nor might they know what AI actually means, enterprises have long recognized the power of said technology, and thus shown an increased interest in integrating different types of 'smartness' into their business

© Springer Nature Switzerland AG 2019
L. Uden et al. (Eds.): KMO 2019, CCIS 1027, pp. 259–270, 2019.
https://doi.org/10.1007/978-3-030-21451-7_22

applications. To this end AI integration has become a main indicator for business innovation, in spite of its often misunderstood and consequently overrated capabilities. This, in turn, increases anxiety with the work force, as employees see their value dropping. In particular statements such as *"AI systems are already better than all but a very few people and also much more reliable. They're not going to get drunk and fail to show up at work. They're not going to embezzle money. They're not going to quit and go work for someone else"* (Ben Goertzel, chief scientist, Aidyia), seem to paint a slightly de-motivating picture of reality. Yet, the real use of AI technology and how it affects employee's work has barely been explored. While there is an overwhelming number of tools available, it seems that many companies struggle (1) in choosing the right solutions for their specific use, and (2) in effectively integrating them, so that productivity is raised. Thus, our goal was to conduct a reality check by asking "how companies currently use artificial intelligence technology to boost productivity in their work environments, and how such is perceived by employees?"

2   Related Work

There is no doubt that AI technology increasingly influences the way companies act and re-act [30], which sometimes may even cause changes in existing business models [15]. Areas, such as finance [34], social commerce [58], predictive analytics [21], as well as business intelligence and analytics [13] have already been affected by AI. Estimates also show that implementing AI may trigger competitive advantages, as it increases productivity and degrees of innovation [30]. To this end, enterprises propagate their application of AI and big data so as to explore new business territories [28] and establish marketing mix frameworks [18]. Yet the abundant number of AI solutions renders it difficult to identify the right types of technology for given contexts [30]. Small organizations in particular, lack the necessary resources (financial as well as staff wise) to sufficiently screen the market and eventually implement the right tool [46].

2.1   Business Applications

There are multiple fields of application through which AI may foster business value chains. Some of them are described below:

Decision Support. Given its high level of responsibility, decision-making is still considered an inherently human task. Yet, a constant increase in complexity and the consequent fluctuation in decision quality have led to a boost in the facilitation of technology [41]. Here AI provides decision aid with recurring, repetitive tasks found in finance, marketing, commerce, cybersecurity [50] or project management [59].

Predictive Maintenance. Huge amounts of money are not only spent in the acquisition of new technology but also in its maintenance. Depending on the industry, those can amount to 60% of a product's total production costs [33]. Respective inefficiencies may trigger both financial losses as well as decreased equipment lifecycles [47], which highlights the need for modern, data-driven support tools [56]. Predictive Maintenance (PM) describes the process of *"predict[ing] machine failures in advance based on* *historical data [...]*" [47]. In doing this, PM for example helps predict and consequently avoid HDD failures in which large amounts of customer and business data may otherwise be lost [47].

Customer Support and Relationship Management. Customer satisfaction and loyalty count as important drivers for a company's success [17, 27, 44, 53, 57]. AI and data mining tools can be used to support the customer relationship management (CRM) process [5, 25, 39]. Mukherjee and Bala [35] for example applied algorithms for detecting sarcasm in customer tweets to better trace and analyze customer opinions. This type of sentiment analysis helps understand customers and consequently improve product recommendations. Another AI-driven CRM tool may be found in chatbots, which increasingly handle customer support and foster direct user engagement [8, 55].

Process Acceleration. A key objective of using AI in business concerns the efficiency of daily work practices. Simple and repetitive tasks, for example, may be automated so that employees can focus on the type of work machines cannot (yet) perform. Those tasks include information pre-processing to support decision making, email-management through better spam-detection [23], or automated information retrieval in knowledge databases [37], whereby the use of intelligent algorithms ensures that tool support is not static but rather improves autonomously through the intake of new data [51]. Also, the proliferation of smart objects and Internet of Things technology adds to this boost in the implementation of artificial intelligence solutions [60].

Knowledge Management. It has been shown that data-driven companies often hold a competitive advantage over their competitors [9, 10]. Here it is in particular Knowledge Management (KM) processes, such as knowledge acquisition and data processing, which require tool support [24]. To this end, expert and decision support systems help with knowledge acquisition, e.g. the transformation from tacit into explicit knowledge, and data mining techniques can deliver key words, related concepts, or clusters of similar ideas [38].

2.2 Organizational Challenges

Countering the above highlighted advantages of using AI, the literature has also identified a number of social and technical challenges that hinder successful implementations. For example, while companies may be criticized if their decision-making process lacks AI support, they will be equally lambasted if decisions are too dependent on the technological input [1, 4, 48], in particular if AI suggestions are preferred over human judgement [26].

Discussions about transparency and data security are also of paramount importance [16]. A major issue is, for example, that the AI algorithms often behave like 'black boxes', masking the overall reasoning process [32]. Furthermore, the data, which is fed to the algorithms, is often rather sensitive and thus must not be disclosed. To this end the introduction of the European General Data Protection Regulation (GDPR), in May 2019, poses new challenges, as companies now have to provide information as to what the data is used for and explain the logic behind tools that work with the it[1]. Furthermore, as by the GDPR, companies have to delete personal data upon request, which does not only concern the used databases but also the AI tools which use the data.

Another often-discussed challenge concerning the use of AI in the workplace is its threat to replace jobs currently performed by human employees [7, 11]. This might go as far as that entire business sectors could be taken over by 'machines'. Especially tasks that concern specific aspects of natural language processing, such as translation or call-center activities, are likely to be soon performed by AI. Even a retail salesperson may be replaced by an artificial counterpart. Various researchers and studies, such as Frey and Osborne [20], Nam [36] and Prisecaru [43], confirm this development, in which AI or other technologies, pose a threat to employment.

Even if technologies do not replace certain human tasks, it seems certain that the requirements for jobs will change and that inherently human competencies, such as creativity and innovation, will become more important [30]. Besides, there will be an even bigger impact on developing countries, as it is mainly the repetitive mundane tasks usually performed by unskilled workers, which will be substituted by AI [30]. Companies that have outsourced their production facilities might thus increasingly relocate back [19].

A final challenge may be seen in the impact the use of AI tools and technologies has on customers and the consequent attitude changes it may trigger if, for example, a chatbot is used instead of a human customer care agent [3]. Such is of growing relevance, as the relationship between companies and consumers is *"[...] gradually evolving to become technology dominant (i.e. Intelligent Assistants acting as a service interface) rather than human-driven"* [29]. Thus, companies do not only face the technical challenge of implanting a tool but also the rather social challenge of adequately informing both employees and customers about the resulting effects [3].

3   Empirical Analysis

Building upon the above outlined theoretical basis, the goal of our empirical study was to provide a cross-sector analysis focusing on the use of AI in companies. As we were not only interested in the type of tools that are used but also in existing challenges and fears, a semi-structured interview analysis was chosen as a research method.

3.1   Selection of Participants

Potential study participants were recruited via social media and relevant events (such as the "Rise of AI" fair taking place on May 17th in Berlin, Germany).

There were no strict selection criteria, as characteristics such as age, gender, social background or religion were not thought to affect the study outcome. A total of 19 people agreed to participate. They came from 18 different companies representing various industry sectors (cf. Table 1). Four of these companies may be classified as

---

[1] http://fortune.com/2018/05/25/ai-machine-learning-privacy-gdpr/ [Retrieved: August 31st 2018].

Table 1. Interview participants.

Pseudonym	Position	Industry sector
P01	Data scientist	Information technology
P02	Managing director	Consumer discretionary (media)
P03	Vice president purchase	Industrials
P04	Digital transformation	Industrials (aerospace & defense)
P05	Chief digital officer	Health care
P06	Project manager	Telecommunication services
P07	Managing director	Consumer discretionary, real estate
P08	Managing director	Consumer discretionary (media)
P09	Business developer	Telecommunication services
P10	Project manager	Non-profit
P11	Business developer	Consumer discretionary (automobiles)
P12	Digital purchase	Financials
P13	Manager	Information technologies
P14	Manager	Industrials (aerospace & defense)
P15	Managing director	Industrials (professional services),
P16	Managing director	Industrials (professional services)
P17	Product manager	Consumer discretionary
P18	Unit manager	Consumer staples
P19	Director	Consumer discretionary (retail)

small, with less than 50 employees, and 14 companies as mid-size or large with more than 250 employees (note: seven of the companies had more than 20.000 employees at the time of the study).

3.2 Study Procedure and Environment

Interviews were semi-structured and lasted between 7 and 42 min (M = 24 min.). They were recorded, transcribed and subsequently analyzed using the MaxQDA software package[2] and Mayring's Qualitative Content Analysis method [31]. The applied category system consisted of 20 categories of which five were used for in-depth analysis. The categorization of the entire material was performed twice by the same person so as to assure intra-coder reliability.

4 Discussion of Study Results

In the following, we present the insights gained from the analysis of those 19 interviews (i.e. P01 – P19). The discussion is structured along the emerging key categories and compared with the findings presented in the literature.

---

[2] https://www.maxqda.com/.

4.1 Reasons for AI Implementation

Interviewees presented several reasons for implementing AI in their company. Those include for example the need for increased productivity (P16, P18, P19) and process optimization (P04, P13, P14), the required 24/7 availability of tools (P01, P11) or a lack of human resources (i.e. time or money wise) (P10, P12, P17). Yet, the decisive factor, which often led to the selection of an AI driven technology over a more traditional one, was usually found in the technology's ability to learn and consequently adapt to a company's peculiarities [12, 30, 42]. That is, interviewees mentioned that they did not have to adapt to the technology. Rather the technology would adapt to their day-to-day business (e.g. P04, P16). Results also showed that sometimes companies instead of having a concrete reason for 'jumping on the AI bandwagon', they were simply curious about what benefits AI may deliver. To this end, it was also highlighted that the technology does often not live up to its hyped expectations (e.g. P02) – although such may be related to the still rather young age of most implementations, with the majority of them being productive for only one year or even less.

4.2 Areas of Use

Most interviewees (12 out of 19) named the general optimization of internal services as the main task supported by AI technology. Other mentioned areas such as customer service (4x), sales (2x), marketing (2x), planning and forecast (2x), finance (1x) and procurement (1x). With respect to customer service the technology mainly applies filters and uses semantic analyses to categorize user comments. Only one interviewee mentioned the use of a chatbot system the way it is sometimes described in the literature (e.g. [8, 55]).

Regarding sales, one interviewee highlighted the company's efforts in automating negotiations with their suppliers (P03). So far, their employees had to call suppliers to negotiated discounts. Now, a chatbot makes these calls. Another interviewee spoke of plans to integrate a chatbot into their app, in order to simulate sales processes and consequently train their personnel.

As for marketing, the literature highlights a number of possible application fields for AI, including market segmentation [6], customer response modelling [40], or the use of artificial neural networks for marketing data mining and acceptance research [52]. Yet, our interviews show that businesses seem to not be aware of this potential, as the only marketing relevant use of AI was found in a platform aimed at automatically sending advertisements to customers (P05). Similarly, its use for forecasting and planning dose not fulfill the expectations. Although literature has been describing potential uses cases for decades (e.g. [14, 49, 54]), only two interviewees mentioned their company's use of intelligent algorithms to generate forecasts (P19) or predict behavioral patterns based on previous data (P08). The use of AI for different financial applications was also barely discussed, although this may be caused by a lack of participating companies working in finance.

Finally, one of the interviewees highlighted their use of AI technology in procurement. That is, they use software to automatically process more than 120.000 documents and generate contracts (P04). In parallel, an algorithm extracts contract clauses and stores them in a database, which on the one hand lets the software learn and on the other hand creates the basis for a knowledge management system for various contractual questions. In general, knowledge management (KM) seems to have finally proven a viable area for AI applications. One involved company for example uses IBM's Watson to structure and analyze error logs produced by their medical devices and consequently support maintenance. Another one uses a Chabot on top of their document management and guideline system to optimize internal processes.

4.3   Tools and Technologies

Interviewees were also asked about the company's tool usage, i.e. to what extent off-the-shelf and to what extend bespoke AI solutions were in use. A surprisingly high number of involved companies (i.e. 10 of the 18) rely either entirely or at least partly on tools specifically built for them. Particularly the sensibility of the used data and the particularity of the given use cases impede external solutions (P02, P12). It also felt as if on the one hand companies would not trust AI tool suppliers, and on the other hand that they would take a lot of pride in their 'self-made' tool landscape (note: such is the interviewer's personal impression based on the slightly pejorative language used by the interviewees when talking about AI tool suppliers). Only one interviewee justified the company's choice of an external solution provider by admitting that developing their own tool was beyond their scope of competencies (P14).

4.4   Organizational Challenges

Regarding the organizational challenges companies face when implementing AI solutions, interview participants focused little on technical difficulties and more on general problems affecting employees. Participants from both small and large companies mentioned struggles originating in human resistance to AI or technology. P19, for example, stated that a great challenge for employees were process changes associated with the introduction of the AI technology. That is, in the past sales forecasts were always done manually using Excel tables, for which employees built up years of experience in this task. With the introduction of the AI tool and the accompanying automation, this task was reduced to either accepting or adapting a proposal. Yet, fearing the loss of importance, tool proposals were almost always changed so that they were in accordance with the initial Excel table predictions, which diminished the benefits of the AI solution. In line with this example of social fear and consequent rejection, P08 highlights *"Problems are in fact only human resistance. Technology is controllable"*. Surprisingly, interviewees hardly mentioned that AI could become a threat to employment, as it is often discussed in the literature (e.g. [7, 11]). This may be rooted in the fact that companies currently do not seem to aim for such a reduction in employees but rather see AI as a complementary tool to increase productivity and consequently gain a competitive advantage.

Another challenge of AI is, however, seen it its data security and privacy issues (mentioned by P07, P06, P12, P15), in particular with respect to the implementation of Europe's General Data Protection Regulation (GDPR). Consequently, tools, which use features provided by US service providers such as Apple or Amazon pose an increasing challenge for the AI penetration in European companies (P06). Those legal regulations are of even greater importance to firms that operate in the health care sector, as data is significantly more sensitive (P05) and thus makes AI's 'black box' characteristics a particularly tricky problem [7, 11].

Finally, interviewees stated that their companies have often collected sufficient data (which is an important prerequisite for AI algorithms), yet they do not know what to do with it (P06, P10, P16). On the one hand there seems to be a lack of knowledge about available tools, on the other hand those tools that are known to companies are deemed difficult to integrate and complex to use (highlighted by half of the interviewees).

4.5 Employee Fears

Employees are afraid of significant changes in work processes triggered by the implementation of AI tools and technologies (mentioned by 14 of our 19 interviewees). In particular, they fear a loss of their job when mundane, repetitive tasks are increasingly performed by machines, described also in the literature [20, 30, 36, 43]. Discomfort is further induced by a certain lack of knowledge about the functioning of AI and how such may be best used so that it does not lead to cutbacks on personnel.

Companies try to counter these fears by selling their AI initiatives as a way to alleviate staff bottlenecks (P05, P16) or to free up employee time so that it can be used for more creative tasks (P05, P08, P10). Also, they often promote the opinions of Acemoglu [2], Goos et al. [22] or Rodrik [45] who state that certain jobs might be eliminated, but others will be created instead. Job loss may thus not be the result of increased digitalization, but rather attributed to general changes in society.

5   Conclusion and Future Work

We conducted 19 interviews to investigate the current use of AI tools and technologies in European companies. Results show that the majority of companies are still at the very starting point when it comes to the implementation of respective solutions. Missing information on potential uses cases and the consequent lack of relevant skills lead to a situation where solutions are mainly used to optimize the efficiency of internal processes or occasionally for customer relationship management (e.g. social media data mining tasks) and support. With those who managed to get their foot into the AI application field, we found a dominance of in-house AI implementations caused by the predominant lack of trust in third party service providers – an issue, which seems of particular importance with respect to recent changes in European data privacy regulations. As for challenges dedicated to the implementation of AI tools, it is mainly social hurdles that need to be overcome. Lack of employee acceptance is particularly rooted in a predominate fear of job loss as well as missing transparency with respect to how this type of technology may improve work efficiency without replacing significant parts of the human workforce.

Our study does not paint a complete picture of activities and challenges found in European companies – for this, the sample size of 19 interviewees is simply too small. However, we accumulated views from various industry sectors and had representatives from both small and large companies, so that it may at least serve as a starting point for further research. In particular, the fears of employees and their consequent lack of tool acceptance is an area that requires more in-depth investigation so as to better tackle social concerns. Another future field of study concerns the analysis of the existing tool landscape. Our goal is to lower the entry barrier for companies by offering them advice on application areas and respective solutions. Finally, legal and ethical regulations require additional reflection on the use of data and tools.

References

1. Abdolmohammadi, M., Usoff, C.: A longitudinal study of applicable decision aids for detailed tasks in a financial audit. Intell. Syst. Acc. Financ. Manag. **10**(3), 139–154 (2001). https://doi.org/10.1002/isaf.204
2. Acemoglu, D.: Technical change, inequality, and the labor market (working paper no. 7800). National Bureau of Economic Research (2000). https://doi.org/10.3386/w7800
3. Araujo, T.: Living up to the chatbot hype: the influence of anthropomorphic design cues and communicative agency framing on conversational agent and company perceptions. Comput. Hum. Behav. **85**, 183–189 (2018). https://doi.org/10.1016/j.chb.2018.03.051
4. Ashton, R.H.: Pressure and performance in accounting decision settings: paradoxical effects of incentives, feedback, and justification. J. Acc. Res. **28**, 148–180 (1990). https://doi.org/10.2307/2491253
5. Bahari, T.F., Elayidom, M.S.: An efficient CRM-data mining framework for the prediction of customer behaviour. Proc. Comput. Sci. **46**, 725–731 (2015). https://doi.org/10.1016/j.procs.2015.02.136
6. Bloom, J.Z.: Market segmentation: a neural network application. Ann. Tour. Res. **32**(1), 93–111 (2005). https://doi.org/10.1016/j.annals.2004.05.001
7. Bostrom, N., Cirkovic, M.M.: Global Catastrophic Risks. OUP, Oxford (2011)
8. Braun, A.: Chatbots in der Kundenkommunikation. Springer-Verlag, Heidelberg (2014)
9. Brynjolfsson, E., Hitt, L.M., Kim, H.H.: Strength in numbers: how does data-driven decision making affect firm performance? (SSRN Scholarly Paper No. ID 1819486). Social Science Research Network, Rochester (2011)
10. Brynjolfsson, E., McAfee, A., Cummings, J.: The Second Machine Age: Work, Progress, and Prosperity in a Time of Brilliant Technologies. WW Norton & Company, New York (2014)
11. Brynjolfsson, E., Mitchell, T.: What can machine learning do? Workforce implications. Science **358**(6370), 1530–1534 (2017)
12. Čerka, P., Grigienė, J., Sirbikytė, G.: Liability for damages caused by artificial intelligence. Comput. Law Secur. Rev. **31**(3), 376–389 (2015). https://doi.org/10.1016/j.clsr.2015.03.008
13. Chen, H., Chiang, R., Storey, V.: Business intelligence and analytics: from big data to big impact. MIS Q. **36**, 1165–1188 (2012)
14. Coakes, E., Merchant, K.: Expert systems: a survey of their use in UK business. Inf. Manag. **30**(5), 223–230 (1996). https://doi.org/10.1016/S0378-7206(96)01054-3
15. Corea, F.: Artificial Intelligence and Exponential Technologies: Business Models Evolution and New Investment Opportunities. Springer, Heidelberg (2017). https://doi.org/10.1007/978-3-319-51550-2
16. Dirican, C.: The impacts of robotics, artificial intelligence on business and economics. Proc. - Soc. Behav. Sci. **195**, 564–573 (2015). https://doi.org/10.1016/j.sbspro.2015.06.134

17. Dunphy, S., Herbig, P.A.: Acceptance of innovations: the customer is the key! J. High Technol. Manag. Res. **6**(2), 193–209 (1995). https://doi.org/10.1016/1047-8310(95)90014-4
18. Fan, S., Lau, R.Y.K., Zhao, J.L.: Demystifying big data analytics for business intelligence through the lens of marketing mix. Big Data Res. **2**(1), 28–32 (2015). https://doi.org/10.1016/j.bdr.2015.02.006
19. Ford, M.: Rise of the Robots - Technology and the Threat of a Jobless Future. Basic Books, New York (2016)
20. Frey, C.B., Osborne, M.A.: The future of employment: how susceptible are jobs to computerisation? Technol. Forecast. Soc. Change **114**(C), 254–280 (2017)
21. Gandomi, A., Haider, M.: Beyond the hype: big data concepts, methods, and analytics. Int. J. Inf. Manage. **35**(2), 137–144 (2015). https://doi.org/10.1016/j.ijinfomgt.2014.10.007
22. Goos, M., Manning, A., Salomons, A.: Explaining job polarization: routine-biased technological change and offshoring. Am. Econ. Rev. **104**(8), 2509–2526 (2014). https://doi.org/10.1257/aer.104.8.2509
23. Guzella, T.S., Caminhas, W.M.: A review of machine learning approaches to Spam filtering. Expert Syst. Appl. **36**(7), 10206–10222 (2009). https://doi.org/10.1016/j.eswa.2009.02.037
24. Hoeschl, H.C., Barcellos, V.: Artificial intelligence and knowledge management. In: Bramer, M. (ed.) Artificial Intelligence in Theory and Practice, vol. 217, pp. 11–19. Springer, Heidelberg (2006). https://doi.org/10.1007/978-0-387-34747-9_2
25. Hui, S.C., Jha, G.: Data mining for customer service support. Inf. Manag. **38**(1), 1–13 (2000). https://doi.org/10.1016/S0378-7206(00)00051-3
26. Jarrahi, M.H.: Artificial intelligence and the future of work: human-AI symbiosis in organizational decision making. Bus. Horiz. **61**(4), 577–586 (2018). https://doi.org/10.1016/j.bushor.2018.03.007
27. Kadam, R., Hokama, L., Feinberg, R.A., Kim, I.: The state of electronic customer relationship management in retailing. Int. J. Retail Distrib. Manag. **30**(10), 470–481 (2002). https://doi.org/10.1108/09590550210445344
28. Kwon, O., Lee, N., Shin, B.: Data quality management, data usage experience and acquisition intention of big data analytics. Int. J. Inf. Manage. **34**(3), 387–394 (2014). https://doi.org/10.1016/j.ijinfomgt.2014.02.002
29. Larivière, B., et al.: Service Encounter 2.0: an investigation into the roles of technology, employees and customers. J. Bus. Res. **79**, 238–246 (2017). https://doi.org/10.1016/j.jbusres.2017.03.008
30. Makridakis, S.: The forthcoming artificial intelligence (AI) revolution: its impact on society and firms. Futures **90**, 46–60 (2017). https://doi.org/10.1016/j.futures.2017.03.006
31. Mayring, P.: Qualitative content analysis: theoretical foundation, basic procedures and software solution, Klagenfurt (2014)
32. Mehta, N., Devarakonda, M.V.: Machine learning, natural language programming, and electronic health records: the next step in the artificial intelligence journey? J. Allergy Clin. Immunol. **141**(6), 2019–2021 (2018). https://doi.org/10.1016/j.jaci.2018.02.025
33. Mobley, R.K.: An Introduction to Predictive Maintenance. Elsevier, Amsterdam (2002)
34. Moro, S., Cortez, P., Rita, P.: Business intelligence in banking: a literature analysis from 2002 to 2013 using text mining and latent Dirichlet allocation. Expert Syst. Appl. **42**(3), 1314–1324 (2015). https://doi.org/10.1016/j.eswa.2014.09.024
35. Mukherjee, S., Bala, P.K.: Detecting sarcasm in customer tweets: an NLP based approach. Ind. Manag. Data Syst. **117**(6), 1109–1126 (2017). https://doi.org/10.1108/IMDS-06-2016-0207
36. Nam, T.: Technology usage, expected job sustainability, and perceived job insecurity. Technol. Forecast. Soc. Change (2018). https://doi.org/10.1016/j.techfore.2018.08.017

37. Nassiri-Mofakham, F.: How does an intelligent agent infer and translate? Comput. Hum. Behav. **38**, 196–200 (2014). https://doi.org/10.1016/j.chb.2014.05.019
38. Nemati, H.R., Steiger, D.M., Iyer, L.S., Herschel, R.T.: Knowledge warehouse: an architectural integration of knowledge management, decision support, artificial intelligence and data warehousing. Decis. Support Syst. **33**(2), 143–161 (2002). https://doi.org/10.1016/S0167-9236(01)00141-5
39. Ngai, E.W.T., Xiu, L., Chau, D.C.K.: Application of data mining techniques in customer relationship management: a literature review and classification. Expert Syst. Appl. **36**(2, Part 2), 2592–2602 (2009). https://doi.org/10.1016/j.eswa.2008.02.021
40. Olson, D.L., Chae, B.: Direct marketing decision support through predictive customer response modeling. Decis. Support Syst. **54**(1), 443–451 (2012). https://doi.org/10.1016/j.dss.2012.06.005
41. Phillips-Wren, G.: AI tools in decision making support systems: a review. Int. J. Artif. Intell. Tools **21**, 1240005 (2012). https://doi.org/10.1142/S0218213012400052
42. Poole, D.L., Mackworth, A.K.: Artificial Intelligence: Foundations of Computational Agents, 2nd edn. Cambridge University Press, Cambridge (2017)
43. Prisecaru, P.: Challenges of the fourth industrial revolution. Knowl. Horiz. – Econ. **8**(1), 57–62 (2016)
44. Ranaweera, C., Prabhu, J.: On the relative importance of customer satisfaction and trust as determinants of customer retention and positive word of mouth. J. Target. Measure. Anal. Mark. **12**(1), 82–90 (2003). https://doi.org/10.1057/palgrave.jt.5740100
45. Rodrik, D.: Premature deindustrialization (working paper no. 20935). National Bureau of Economic Research (2015). https://doi.org/10.3386/w20935
46. Ruiz-Mezcua, B., Garcia-Crespo, A., Lopez-Cuadrado, J.L., Gonzalez-Carrasco, I.: An expert system development tool for non AI experts. Expert Syst. Appl. **38**(1), 597–609 (2011). https://doi.org/10.1016/j.eswa.2010.07.009
47. Su, C.-J., Huang, S.-F.: Real-time big data analytics for hard disk drive predictive maintenance. Comput. Electr. Eng. **71**, 93–101 (2018). https://doi.org/10.1016/j.compeleceng.2018.07.025
48. Sutton, S.G., Young, R., McKenzie, P.: An analysis of potential legal liability incurred through audit expert systems. Intell. Syst. Acc. Financ. Manag. **4**(3), 191–204 (1995). https://doi.org/10.1002/j.1099-1174.1995.tb00091.x
49. Torkzadeh, G., Rao, S.S.: Expert systems for small businesses. Inf. Manag. **15**(4), 229–235 (1988). https://doi.org/10.1016/0378-7206(88)90048-1
50. Turban, E.: Information Technology for Management, 5th edn. Wiley, New York (2008)
51. Turchi, M., Bie, T.D., Cristianini, N.: An intelligent agent that autonomously learns how to translate. In: Proceedings of the 2009 IEEE/WIC/ACM International Joint Conference on Web Intelligence and Intelligent Agent Technology, vol. 02, pp. 12–19. IEEE Computer Society, Washington (2009). https://doi.org/10.1109/WI-IAT.2009.120
52. Vellido, A., Lisboa, P.J.G., Vaughan, J.: Neural networks in business: a survey of applications (1992–1998). Expert Syst. Appl. **17**(1), 51–70 (1999). https://doi.org/10.1016/S0957-4174(99)00016-0
53. Wikhamn, W.: Innovation, sustainable HRM and customer satisfaction. Int. J. Hospit. Manag. **76**, 102–110 (2019). https://doi.org/10.1016/j.ijhm.2018.04.009
54. Wong, B.K., Monaco, J.A.: Expert system applications in business: a review and analysis of the literature (1977–1993). Inf. Manag. **29**(3), 141–152 (1995). https://doi.org/10.1016/0378-7206(95)00023-P

55. Xu, A., Liu, Z., Guo, Y., Sinha, V., Akkiraju, R.: A new chatbot for customer service on social media. In: Proceedings of the 2017 CHI Conference on Human Factors in Computing Systems, pp. 3506–3510. ACM, New York (2017). https://doi.org/10.1145/3025453.3025496

56. Yam, R.C.M., Tse, P.W., Tu, P.: Intelligent predictive decision support system for condition-based maintenance. Int. J. Adv. Manuf. Technol. **17**, 383–391 (2001)

57. Zairi, M.: Managing customer dissatisfaction through effective complaints management systems. TQM Mag. **12**(5), 331–337 (2000). https://doi.org/10.1108/09544780010341932

58. Zhou, L., Zhang, P., Zimmermann, H.-D.: Social commerce research: an integrated view. Electron. Commer. Res. Appl. **12**(2), 61–68 (2013). https://doi.org/10.1016/j.elerap.2013.02.003

59. Martínez, D.M., Fernández-Rodríguez, J.C.: Artificial intelligence applied to project success: a literature review. IJIMAI **3**(5), 77–84 (2015). https://doi.org/10.9781/ijimai.2015.3510

60. García, C.G., Meana-Llorián, D., Lovelle, J.M.C.: A review about smart objects, sensors, and actuators. Int. J. Interact. Multimed. Artif. Intell. **4**(3), 7–10 (2017). https://doi.org/10.9781/ijimai.2017.431

Digital Twins Approach and Future Knowledge Management Challenges: Where We Shall Need System Integration, Synergy Analyses and Synergy Measurements?

Jari Kaivo-oja[1,2]([✉]), Osmo Kuusi[1]([✉]), Mikkel Stein Knudsen[1], and Theresa Lauraeus[1,2]

[1] Finland Futures Research Centre, Turku School of Economics, University of Turku, 20014 Turku, Finland
{Jari.kaivo-oja,mikkel.knudsen, theresa.lauraeus}@utu.fi, osmo.kuusi@aalto.fi
[2] Kazimieras Simonavicius University, 02189 Vilnius, Lithuania

Abstract. We're in the midst of a significant transformation regarding the way we produce products and deliver services thanks to the digitization of manufacturing and new connected supply-chains and co-creation systems. This article elaborates Digital Twins Approach to the current challenges of knowledge management when Industry 4.0 is emerging in industries and manufacturing. Industry 4.0 approach underlines the importance of Internet of Things and interactions between social and physical systems. Internet of Things (and also Internet of Services and Internet of Data) are new Internet infrastructure that marries advanced manufacturing techniques and service architectures with the I-o-T, I-o-S and I-o-D to create manufacturing systems that are not only interconnected, but communicate, analyze, and use information to drive further intelligent action back in the physical world. This paper identifies four critical domains of synergy challenge: (1) Man-to-Man interaction, (2) Man-to-Machine interaction, (3) Machine-to-Man interaction and finally (4) Machine-to-Machine interaction. Key conclusion is that new knowledge management challenges are closely linked to the challenges of synergic interactions between these four key interactions and accurate measurements of synergic interaction.

Keywords: Digital Twins Approach · Human-machine interaction · Synergy challenges · Synergy measurements · Industry 4.0

1 Introduction

The Fourth Industrial Revolution, commonly known as Industry 4.0 transformation, is changing the way business models and platforms function and, by extension, the stakes by which they are forced to compete. We know that Industry 4.0 is a global concept, but it can take many different forms and transition paths, and names, around the world. In the United States, the Industry 4.0 focus tends to be more on a more holistic digital evolution, and many use the term digital supply network or digital supply-chain.

© Springer Nature Switzerland AG 2019
L. Uden et al. (Eds.): KMO 2019, CCIS 1027, pp. 271–281, 2019.
https://doi.org/10.1007/978-3-030-21451-7_23

Within Europe and in Germany, where the Industry 4.0-concept originated, the phenomenon tends to be more factory-based or manufacturing. While the Industry 4.0 terminology may differ, the overall concept remains largely the same and encompasses the same technologies and applications. Organizations today must decide how and where to invest in these new technologies and identify which ones might best meet their business needs and business model.

There are many digital technologies, which are relevant for Industry 4.0 approach. Without a full understanding of the changes and opportunities Industry 4.0 brings, companies risk losing ground of their operations. This is one key scientific motivation for this article and its conceptualization – to help organizations and firms to focus on key issues and systems.

In this article we first discuss about key technical drivers of Industry 4.0 (Sect. 2). In Sect. 3 we elaborate Digital Twins Approach with key ides of Digital Twin Thinking. We suggest a wider operationalization of this concept than commonly use d to date. In Sect. 4 we present key interactions between man and machine which are affected by this new Digital Twin-ideas. Section 5 is integrative chapter which identifies key needs of synergy measurements and system integration in knowledge management in organizations, when Digital Twin and Industry 4.0 approaches will be applied in real system development process. In Sect. 6 final conclusions are drawn.

2   Technological Drivers of Industry 4.0 Era

Dating back to around 1760, the First Industrial Revolution (Industry 1.0) was the transition to new manufacturing processes using water and steam. Steam power was a key driving force of Industry 1.0. It was hugely beneficial in terms of manufacturing a larger number of various goods and creating a better standard of living for some. The textile industry, in particular, was transformed by industrialization, as was transportation systems. The era of Industry 1.0 represented the period between the 1760s and around 1840 [1].

Around 1840 is the time-period, where the second industrial revolution (Industry 2.0) picked up. Historians sometimes refer to this as "The Technological Revolution" occurring mainly in Britain, Germany and America. During this period, new industrial technological systems were introduced, most notably superior electrical technology, which allowed for even greater production and more sophisticated machines. It began with the first computer era (Industry 3.0) [1].

Around 1970 the Third Industrial Revolution (Industry 3.0) involved the use of electronics and Information Technology (IT) to further automation in production. Manufacturing and automation advanced considerably thanks to Internet access, connectivity and renewable energy. Industry 3.0 introduced more automated systems onto the assembly line to perform human tasks. The use of Programmable Logic Controllers (PLC) was introduced. Although automated systems were in place, they still relied on human input and intervention [1, 2]. Some authors have noted that Industry 1–4 phases were: pre-electricity age, mid-electricity age, post-electricity age, pre-computer age, mid-computer age, post-computer age, pre-digital age, mid-digital age and post-digital age [3].

New Industry 4.0 era is expected to be founded on Cyber-Physical Systems (CPS) and the Internet of Things (IOT). Other key technologies are Cloud computing, Big Data analytics and Extended ICT. The expected changes will lead to new integrated systems, where sensors, actuators, machines, robots, conveyors, etc. are connected to and exchange information automatically. Factories are expected to become conscious and intelligent enough to predict and maintain the machines and control the production process. Business models of Industry 4.0 imply complete communication network(s) between various companies, factories, suppliers, logistics, resources and customers (Fig. 1).

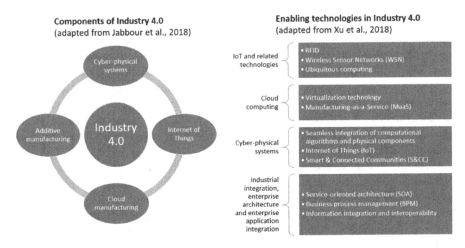

Fig. 1. 'Components' and 'enabling technologies' in Industry 4.0. [6].

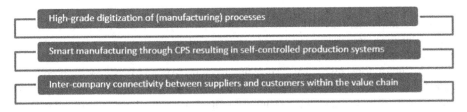

Fig. 2. 3 dimensions of Industry 4.0 (adapted from [7]).

For business leaders and KMO managers accustomed to traditional linear data and communications, the strategic shift to real-time access to data and intelligence enabled by Industry 4.0 would fundamentally transform the way they conduct business and manage their business model. The integration of digital information from many different sources and locations (Big Data) can drive the physical act of doing business, in an ongoing cycle. Throughout this cycle, real-time access to data and intelligence is driven by the continuous and cyclical flow of information and actions between the physical and digital worlds. After Industry 4.0 we can expect that there will be Industry 5.0, when you begin to allow customers to customize what they actually want in real-time (Fig. 2).

3   The Digital Twins Approach

An emerging key idea within Industry 4.0 is the concept of digital twins. We believe that understanding this concept will be paramount for the future tasks of knowledge management. The concept of a digital twin has been used around since 2002. The digital twin has been defined as the virtual model of a process, product or service. Almost all hitherto considerations of Digital Twin-technology has been related to manufacturing or 'shopfloor digital twin' (e.g. [8–10]). We will suggest in this paper wider interpretations of the concept. It allows the possibility of creating a digital twin of an organization and also for human beings to have digital twins. After looking at the concept of the digital twin as a virtual model we will discuss the digital twin of a person.

As a virtual model, a digital twin functions as a bridge between the physical and digital world. The digital twin is composed of three components, which is physical entities in the physical world, virtual models in the virtual world, and the connected data between these two worlds [11]. This pairing of the virtual and physical worlds allows analysis of data and monitoring of systems to eliminate problems before they even occur, prevent downtime, develop new opportunities and even plan for the future by using simulations [12].

According to Panetta (2018, Trend 4) in Gartner report: "A digital twin is a digital representation that mirrors a real-life object, process or system. Digital twins can also be linked to create twins of larger systems, such as a power plant or city. The idea of a digital twin is not new.", but "today's digital twins are different in four ways: (1) The robustness of the models, with a focus on how they support specific business outcomes, (2) The link to the real world, potentially in real time for monitoring and control, (3) The application of advanced big data analytics and AI to drive new business opportunities, (4) The ability to interact with them and evaluate "what if" scenarios" [13].

With the spread of IoT the virtual models and digital twins have become cost-effective to implement in industries and services. Digital twins are now becoming almost a business imperative, covering the entire lifecycle of an asset or process and forming the foundation for connected products and services. We can claim that digital twins lead ubiquitous revolution. The Digital Twins Approach is based on complex cyclical flows. A complex flow occurs through an iterative series of three steps, collectively known as the physical-to-digital-to-physical (PDP) loop (see Fig. 3). There are

- Step 1: Physical to digital: Capture information from the physical world and create a digital record from physical data.
- Step 2: Digital to digital: Share information and uncover meaningful insights using advanced analytics, scenario analysis, and artificial intelligence, and
- Step 3: Digital to physical: Apply algorithms to translate digital-world decisions to effective data, to spur action and change in the physical world.

To achieve this PDP process various technological tools are available. Industry 4.0 combines relevant physical and digital technologies, including data analytics, additive manufacturing (Manufacturing 4.0), industrial and service robotics, high-performance computing, natural language processing, artificial intelligence (AI), cognitive technologies, advanced materials, and virtual or augmented reality (V/AR).

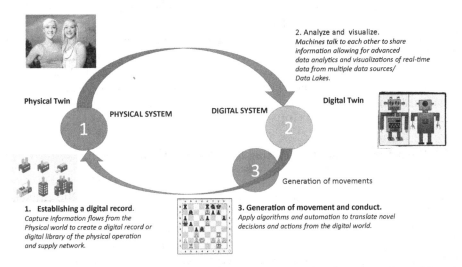

Fig. 3. The physical-to-digital-to-physical (PDP) loop and Digital Twins Approach, modificated (see also [14, p. 3).

Many platforms include various PDP loops and have potential to create well-functioning Digital Twins, which operate in specific contexts of production and consumption. Understanding specific contexts of PDP loops is critical success factor of well-functioning platforms [15]. Platforms businesses are claiming a large growing share of the economy in every region of the world. A platform is a business based on enabling value-creating interactions between external producers and consumers [16].

3.1 Applying the Digital Twin-Approach Beyond Manufacturing

In manufacturing Digital Twin offers opportunity to simulate and optimize production systems, including logistical aspects, and enables detailed visualization of processes from single components to the entire assembly process [17]. Within manufacturing industries, the approach has already become a key element in Product Lifecycle Management [10] and frontrunner organizations are integrating the approach into the entire lifecycle from product design, assembly to usage monitoring [11].

The new era for the Digital Twin-approach in knowledge management is applications beyond manufacturing contexts. The immediate challenge will be for organizations to manage the 'Physical to digital'-step, and capture different types of data into a digital record.

We can use an office building as example. Today people are employed at the premises to transport physical objects around the complex, for example mail, stationery, or IT equipment, In the near future all this might be transported faster and more cost-efficient by autonomous drones or robots, also reducing the need for decentralized storage and office space. However, for this to work effectively, digital records of the premises – effectively capturing four dimensions, including both the air and time – needs to be established in order to capture what humans today can capture immediately with their bare eyes. Those organizations succeeding in adapting digital twins will be those skilled at Semantic Data Management [18].

Similarly, we expect the challenge of capturing human and tacit knowledge into digital twins will be a dominant issue for the future of knowledge management in organizations. This connects to the rising term "Digital Twin of an Organization" (DTO) which enables the dynamic virtual representation of an organization in its full operational context, and which is considered by Gartner as one of the top 10 Strategic Technology Trends for 2019 [19].

3.2 From Individualized Marketing to Personal Digital Twins

Already for long time, marketers have successfully used rule-based personalization (e.g. "If a person falls into Segment A, then show him Experience X") [20]. Artificial Intelligence has made possible to proceed from this segment based personalization towards the marketing practice that deserves the name "individualization". From the point of view of the marketer of a product, the ideal individualization means that a person as a unique individual gets experience that in the most effective way promotes the buying of the product. Using machine-learning-based algorithms and predictive analytics there are much better opportunities to produce this kind of experience than before.

The problem of the above kind of individualization is that there is no guarantee that the experience of an individual is also the best or even good from the point of view of the individual. We suggest Personal Digital Twins (PDT) as a smart tool or an algorithm that regularly provides from the available Big Data or other information sources the best experience from the point of view of a person.

In their Internet of People (IoP) manifesto Miranda et al. [21] suggested four guidelines for how the human interaction with machines should work. These principles with modifications are used in the definition of targeted features of a Personal Digital Twin:

(1) Be Social. Interactions between a person, his or her Personal Digital Twin (PDT), other human beings and other machines should be social. A person and his or her PDT should have a platform of common learning in which they through continuously interacting develop mutual understanding. For example, when the PDT communicates with the person using human language it should use the concepts of the language in similar meanings as the person. Based on mutual understanding, the PDT is able to be the trusted representative of the person in social interaction with other persons or machines.

(2) Be Individualized. The Personal Digital Twin should promote genuine interests[1] of the person. Interactions between the PDT and other people or machines must

---

[1] The concept "genuine interest" is discussed e.g. in [22].

represent the person's individual interests and not just the average interests of a group into which the person belongs.

(3) Be Proactive. The interactions between the person and other people or machines should proactively take place so that also the PDT can proactively initiate interactions. The person should, however, decide what kinds of interactions are acceptable and when these interactions are allowed.

(4) Be Predictable. The content of interactions with other persons and machines started by the PDT must be predictable or they must follow before agreed principles between the person and his or her PDT. Especially important is that the person and the PDT agree how to share the information about the person and how to deliver the information/knowledge resources owned by the person.

Using the concepts introduced by Miranda et al. [21] Personal Digital Twin belongs to Companion devices of persons like recent smartphones or smart tools that use human language in the communication with their owners (e.g. Apple's Siri or Amazon's Alexa). Recent companion devices maintain contextual and sociological information concerning their owners and share that information to other Companion or non-Companion devices according to rules that are poorly controlled by the owners of the Companion devices. A recent companion device may also start its own or its owner's interaction with some other device or even independently give orders to a non-Companion device e.g. to open a television.

A basic difference between a true Personal Digital Twin and recent Companion devices of persons is that a true PDT should be a trusted promoter of interests of an individual. This is no way confirmed concerning Companion devices that are used for marketing though in some connections they might function like a true PDT. An example is presented in the illustrating scenario of Miranda et al. [21]. In the scenario story, the smartphone of a driver starts to speak to the driver telling about a traffic accident and ways to handle the problem. The smartphone is also social sending informing messages to smartphones of other drivers.

4 Man-Machine-Interactions

4.1 Man-Machine Synergy Puzzle

In Fig. 4 we have presented key Man-Machine interactions. In the ubiquitous technology environment it is important to understand that directions of influence in interaction are relevant issues. There are four critical interactions: (1) Man-Man interactions, (2) Man-Machine interactions, (3) Machine-Man interaction and (4) Machine-to-Machine interactions (Fig. 4).

When we measure the nature of interactions, it is always good to find right variables to perform measurements. Expected explaining and explained variables must be carefully selected, when we measure synergies between human beings and machines. This aspect is going to be more critical issue in the field of organizational knowledge management. It is also good to understand that human beings are simultaneously influenced by other human beings and other machines. This imply that we need to measure synergy with combined synergy measurements. Final outcome of synergy is a

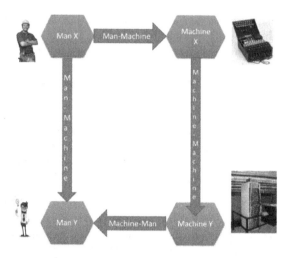

Fig. 4. Four key interactions between ManX-MachineY-MachineY-ManY.

combination of various Man-Machine interactions. This kind of perspective is highly relevant issue, if want to create positive welfare synergy between human beings and machines.

4.2   Learning Process Synergy Puzzle

In Fig. 5 we present key learning processes. We can observe that in ubiquitous society there four key learning processes: (1) a process where human being teach each other (X-Y process), (2) a process where AI/Robot apps teach human beings (X-X process, (3) a process where human beings teach AI/Robot apps (Y-Y-process) and finally (4) where AI/Robot apps teach other AI/Robot apps (Y-X process). This kind of complex interaction of learning processes will challenge knowledge management processes in organizations of digital networks. If want to create positive learning loops in modern organizations, we must start to analyze these four learning processes.

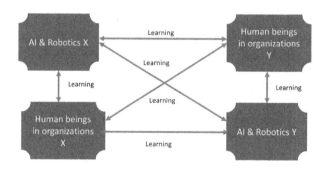

Fig. 5. Four key learning processes in the ubiquitous society [23].

5 Integrative Elements of New Knowledge Management in the Industry 4.0 Era

5.1 Industry 4.0 Era and Management Challenges

As presented above there are many needs for system integration between physical systems and non-physical digitalized systems. In the field of organizational management there are own management systems of (1) Leadership [24], (2) Human Resource Managements [25], and (3) Digital data, web-engineering and information management systems (especially pervasive Internet of Things, see [26]). To see viable Industry 4.0 systems, Internet of Things and also Internet of Services and Internet of Data must be linked to leadership and HRM functions.

System integration is needed, because Internet of Things embodies a vision of merging heterogeneous objects to establish seamless interaction among physical and virtual entities (see e.g. [26]. Seamless interaction is not possible without system integration. If we want be successful in new era of system integration in Industry 4.0 systems, we must somehow integrate these three critical systems, which combine human resources, leaders and digital infrastructures and platforms.

In Fig. 6 we have visualized obvious system integration challenge between these three elements of knowledge management in Industry 4.0 era. If we want to analyze relevant synergies between physical and digitalized systems (key technologies of Industry 4.0) we must create more integrative systems between leadership function, HRM systems and Information, Data and Web-engineering systems and focus our synergy analyses on these critical Man-Machine interactions.

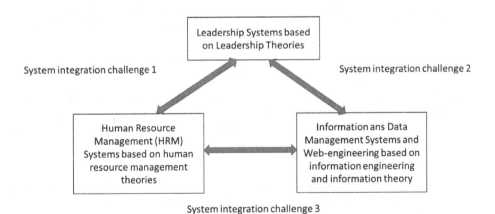

Fig. 6. System integration challenges of Industry 4.0 era.

In the era of Industry 4.0 there are more or less challenging system integration challenges. As we have noted before, Man-machine integration and learning process integration require special attention in organizations.

6 Conclusions

In the era of Industry 4.0 and Internet of Things, IoT devices and solutions are capable of sensing, processing, communicating and storing the data acquired from physical world. New way of thinking is Digital Twin Approach, which is based on the physical-to-digital-to-physical (PDP) process. This approach is already a business imperative in the manufacturing industry sector, but in the future the approach can be highly powerful beyond manufacturing as well. System integration enables Industrial Internet of Things, Industry 4.0 platforms.

In this article we have discussed key needs of system integration and concludes that system integrations must be based on (1) the understanding on Human-Machines interactions, (2) on the understanding of learning processes in organizations and finally (3) on the understanding of leadership, Human Resource Management Systems and (3) Information and Data Management Systems and Web-engineering.

If we want to understand critical synergies of leadership functions, HRM and data and information flows, we must focus on critical interactions in the whole knowledge management system. Knowledge management in Industry 1.0, Industry 2.0 and Industry 3.0 was different compared to Industry 4.0. Many challenges are linked to system integration questions of learning and knowing human beings. Key system integration will be needed in the systems of leadership, HRM and digital systems, when we discuss about knowledge management in organizations.

References

1. Schwab, K.: The Fourth Industrial Revolution. World Economic Forum, New York (2017)
2. Liffler, M., Tschiesner, A.: The internet of things and the future of manufacturing. McKinsey & Company (2013). https://www.mckinsey.com/business-functions/digital-mckinsey/our-insights/the-internet-of-things-and-the-future-of-manufacturing
3. Goodwin, T.: Digital Darwinism. Survival of the Fittest in the Age of Business Disruption. Kogan Page Limited. London (2018)
4. de Sousa Jabbour, A.B.L., Jabbour, C.J.C., Foropon, C., Godinho Filho, M.: When titans meet – can industry 4.0 revolutionise the environmentally-sustainable manufacturing wave? The role of critical success factors. Technol. Forecast. Soc. Change **132**, 18–25 (2018)
5. Xu, L.D., Xu, E.L., Li, L.: Industry 4.0: state of the art and future trends. Int. J. Prod. Res. **56**(8), 2941–2962 (2018)
6. Knudsen, M.S., Kaivo-oja, J.: Are we in the midst of a fourth industrial revolution? New Industry 4.0 insights from future technology analysis professionals. FFRC-blog, 20 August 2018. https://ffrc.wordpress.com/2018/08/20/are-we-in-the-midst-of-a-fourth-industrial-revolution/
7. Müller, J.M., Buliga, O., Voight, K.-I.: Fortune favors the prepared: how SMEs approach business model innovations in Industry 4.0. Technol. Forecast. Soc. Change **132**, 2–17 (2018)
8. Rosen, R., von Wichert, G., Lo, G., Bettenhausen, K.D.: About the importance of autonomy and digital twins for the future of manufacturing. IFAC-PapersOnLine **48**(3), 567–572 (2015)

9. Tao, F., Zhang, M.: Digital twin shop-floor: a new shop-floor paradigm towards smart manufacturing. IEEE Access **5**, 20418–20427 (2017)
10. Tao, F., Cheng, J., Qi, Q., Zhang, M., Zhang, H., Sui, F.: Digital twin-driven product design, manufacturing and service with big data. Int. J. Adv. Manuf. Technol. **94**(9–12), 3563–3576 (2018)
11. Qi, Q., Tao, F.: Digital twin and big data towards smart manufacturing and industry 4.0: 360 degree comparison. IEEE Access **6**, 3585–3593 (2018)
12. Marr, B.: What is digital twin technology - and why is it so important? Forbes, 6 March 2017. https://www.forbes.com/sites/bernardmarr/2017/03/06/what-is-digital-twin-technology-and-why-is-it-so-important/#1f5e9eb32e2a
13. Panetta, K.: Gartner top 10 strategic technology trends for 2019. Gartner Top 10 Strategic Technology Trends for 2019, 15 October 2018. Gartner. https://www.gartner.com/smarterwithgartner/gartner-top-10-strategic-technology-trends-for-2019/
14. Deloitte: Forces of Change: Industry 4.0. A Deloitte series in Industry 4.0 (2017). https://www2.deloitte.com/content/dam/insights/us/articles/4323_Forces-of-change/4323_Forces-of-change_Ind4-0.pdf
15. Scoble, R., Israel, S.: Age of Context. Mobile, Sensors, Data and the Future of Privacy, 1st edn. Patrick Brewster Press (2014)
16. Parker, G.G., van Alstyre, M.W., Choudary, S.P.: Platform Revolution. How Networked Markets Are Transforming the Economy and How to Make Them Work For You. W.W. Norton Company. New York and London (2016)
17. Kritzinger, W., Karner, M., Traar, G., Henjes, J., Sihn, W.: Digital twin in manufacturing: a categorical literature review and classification. IFAC-PapersOnLine **51**(11), 1016–1022 (2018)
18. Abraovici, M., Göbel, J.C., Dang, H.B.: Semantic data management for the development and continuous reconfiguration of smart products and systems. CIRP Ann. **65**(1), 185–188 (2016)
19. Cearney, D.: The Top 10 Strategic Technology Trends for 2019, 29 November 2018. https://www.slideshare.net/ratinecas/the-top-10-strategic-technology-trends-for-2019. Accessed 10 Mar 2019
20. Digital Growth Unleashed: The Future of Personalization with AI and Machine Learning, 09 April 2018. https://digitalgrowthunleashed.com/the-future-of-personalization-with-ai-and-machine-learning/. Accessed 10 Mar 2019
21. Miranda, J., et al.: From the internet of things to the internet of people. IEEE Internet Comput. **19**(2), 40–47 (2015)
22. Kuusi, O.: Expertise in the Future Use of Generic Technologies. Government Institute for Economic Interest, Helsinki (1999)
23. Kaivo-oja, J.: The future of education – new methods and skills demanded by future professions. In: ThinkBDPST Conference, Budabest, Hungary, 30 Mar 2017, 14:20–15:30 @ Panel III (2017)
24. Asrar-ul-Hag, M., Anwar, S.: The many faces of leadership: Proposing research agenda through a review of literature. Future Bus. J. **4**, 179–188 (2018)
25. HMRR: Managing people in organizations: integrating the study of HRM and leadership. Hum. Res. Manag. Rev. **28**, 249–257 (2018)
26. Zahoor, S., Mir, R.N.: Resource management in pervasive internet of things: a survey. J. Kind Saud University – Comput. Inf. Sci. (2018, in press). https://doi.org/10.1016/j.jksuci.2018.08.014

Performances of OLAP Operations in Graph and Relational Databases

Antonia Azzini[1]([✉]), Paolo Ceravolo[2], and Matteo Colella[2]

[1] Consortium for the Technology Transfer-C2T, Milan, Italy
antonia.azzini@consorzioc2t.it
[2] Universita' degli Studi di Milano, Milan, Italy
{paolo.ceravolo,matteo.colella}@unimi.it
http://www.consorzioc2t.it/en/
http://sesar.di.unimi.it

Abstract. The increasing volume of data created and exchanged in distributed architectures has made databases a critical asset to ensure availability and reliability of business operations. For this reason, a new family of databases, called NoSQL, has been proposed. To better understand the impact this evolution can have on organizations it is useful to focus on the notion of Online Analytical Processing (OLAP). This approach identifies techniques to interactively analyze multidimensional data from multiple perspectives and is today essential for supporting Business Intelligence.

The objective of this paper is to benchmark OLAP queries on relational and graph databases containing the same sample of data. In particular, the relational model has been implemented by using MySQL while the graph model has been realized thanks to the Neo4j graph database. Our results, confirm previous experiments that registered better performances for graph databases when re-aggregation of data is required.

Keywords: Graph models · Relational models · OLAP Systems

1 Introduction

The increasing adoption of the Internet has allowed many companies to expand their catchment area by bringing online a huge amount of content and services so that, data management is nowadays a prominent task for any organization. Since Codd introduced the relational model [8]. Databases represent the primary technology for storing data, as they simplify management and coordinates their use.

In recent years, the increasing volume and distribution of data have made database even more crucial to ensure availability and reliability of services while integrating continuously evolving data flows [2,7]. For this reason, a new family of databases, called NoSQL, an acronym for "Not only SQL", has been proposed. This approach moves away from the relational model as it does not require a

© Springer Nature Switzerland AG 2019
L. Uden et al. (Eds.): KMO 2019, CCIS 1027, pp. 282–293, 2019.
https://doi.org/10.1007/978-3-030-21451-7_24

schema to model data. Non-relational databases aim, in fact, to flexibility for supporting unstructured data originating from multiple sources. Nevertheless, flexibility comes at a cost as a distributed databases cannot guarantee data consistency, availability and partition tolerance at the same time, as stated by the so-called CAP Theorem [4].

To better understand the impact a NoSQL database can have on organizations it is useful to focus on the notion of Online transaction processing (OLTP), where, by transaction, we refer to a unit of work performed by a database. In fact, any organization is required to efficiently process and store business transactions and make them immediately available to client applications in a consistent manner.

For example, Data Analytics, which is based on aggregated calculations of millions of individual transactions, requires the usage of a lot of resources for an OLTP system and the execution of calculations can be long-lasting, causing slowdowns that could block other transactions in the database.

On-Line Analytical Processing (OLAP) have then been developed to facilitate the extraction of information from databases. The goal is performing complex queries without adversely affecting the transactional system, aimed at storing and updating fluent data.

The objective of this paper is to benchmark OLAP queries on relational and graph databases containing the same data. For both databases, the execution time of the OLAP queries will be measured with increasing numbers of data stored. The relational database has been implemented using MySQL while the NoSQL database has been realized thanks to the Neo4j graph database.

The remaining of this paper is organized as follows: after a brief summary of the related works in Sect. 2, an overview of the main concepts of Graph and Relational Models is presented in Sect. 3. Their main properties, as well as their main differences, are detailed into Sect. 3.1. In Sect. 4 the reference Scenario and the OLAP implemented operations used in the experimental analysis are presented. Finally, after discussion on performances, concluding remarks are reported into Sect. 5.

2   Related Work

Several studies have been presented in the literature highlighting the main application areas of relational and graph databases, as well as their most important features and their main critical aspects. Graph Database applications have been described into [14]. The authors show that graph databases work well with highly connected data and compare relational database systems (Oracle, MySQL) with graph databases (Neo4J) focusing on aspects as data structures, data model features, and query facilities.

An interesting review about Neo4j graph database as a practical alternative to Relational Database Management Systems (RdatabaseMS) has been presented in [13], while a framework for building OLAP cubes on graphs has been reported in [9] and a case study on OLAP over the graph data has been presented in [10]. Have et al. [11] presented other advantages of Neo4j, showing its use to find the shortest path traversing the graph and to obtain, this way, fast query execution. Cattuto et al. [6] considered Neo4j to increase the execution performance on simultaneous queries, by combining a set of chosen data models; interesting results were obtained in performing exploratory data analysis. Pacaci confirms in [15] that Neo4j is the faster query engine. Another research work on architecture and query performance based on distributed graph database has been presented in [12]. The authors showed that performance changes according to the kind of query performed. They also evaluated such query performance from several dimensions, as data size, query complexity, and query number.

An interesting comparative analysis of relational and graph databases has been described by Batra and colleagues [17]. Such work pointed out that graph databases obtain better results than relational databases in query execution and that graph database is more flexible as new relations can be added to the graph without the need of re-defining the schema structure. Another interesting similar comparison has been carried out by Vicknair and colleagues [18] aimed at benchmarking database systems for social network applications. Also Angles et al. [1], confirm that graph databases have better performance than the relational ones. The results showed that the graph database is able to obtain better results with structural type queries. Better performances have been measured also by considering full-text character searches.

Different considerations about the performances of graph databases have been discussed by Peinl and colleagues [16]. They deeply analyzed the use of different query languages as well as several options for data transfer, such as different compression options, multiple WebSocket connections, as well as multithreading on client and server side, for achieving the highest possible throughput. The result shows that Neo4j is usually faster than MySQL, even if cases exist where the order is inverted.

Despite this variety of works that confirm the relevance of the graph model for distributed databases and analyze the conditions that impact on performances, to the best of our knowledge, a benchmark on OLAP operations is missing. For this reason, we designed a set of experiments in order to verify the behavior of MySQL and Neo4J in handling an increasing flow of data stored in their physical memory.

3   Graph and Relational Models

Generally speaking, a *Graph Model* [13,14] is defined as a set of interlinked nodes and arcs. Nodes represent the entities of the graph, they are identified using labels and can contain a number of attributes called properties that can be specified by values, such as numeric data or strings. Arcs also referred as relations, provide direct and named connections between two nodes, they have a direction, a type, a starting and an ending node (that may be coincident in case of reflexive relations). Similarly to nodes, relations may have properties. In most cases, they have quantitative properties, such as weights, costs, distances, evaluations, time intervals, and so on. Since relations are efficiently archived, two nodes can share any number or type of relations without sacrificing performance. Because a relation has a starting and ending nodes, it's not possible to delete a node without first deleting the associated relations. A graph database management system is a management system that allows a user to create, read, update and delete graph databases. The Graph's Theory has algorithms that allow you to find the minimum path to connect two nodes or the path traversing a node or a cluster of nodes. For the analysis of graph databases two aspects have to be considered:

- the underlying storage, as some graph databases use native graph storage, optimized and built to store and manage graphs. Other graph databases can serialize graph data into a relational database, an object database, or other database models;
- the processing engine, as some graph databases require the use of index-free adjacency, in which each node has an explicit reference to adjacent nodes and does not require additional indexes. Other databases, instead, although they look like a graph database, do not use the native processing engine, but, for example, relational processing engines.

On the other hand, the *Relational Model* [8,18] is based on two fundamental concepts: relation and table. Relation is a mathematical concept, coming from the set theory, while table is a simple and intuitive notion exploited for aggregating data records following the same schema, also referred as tuples. The relational model responds to the requirement of data independence, i.e. allowing application programs that use a database to interact at a high level of abstraction, regardless of the details with which the database was built. In particular, the physical independence allows the modification of the physical structures without affecting the descriptions of the data at a high level and the logical independence allows keeping the external structures unchanged while changing the logical level. The structures of the relational model allow organizing useful information by means of homogeneous data tuples.

3.1 Properties of Graph and Relational Models

Over the years, relational databases have been one of the most successful solutions in Information Systems. Through the definition of entities connected by relations. SQL databases use the Structured Query Language (SQL) [5] to define and manipulate data. This is extremely powerful and versatile, as well as widely used. Nevertheless, it could be restrictive because it requires the use of predefined schemes to determine the structure of the data before using it and, subsequently, all data must follow the same structure. This involves a priori design on which all subsequent database operations will depend following a set of rules and constraints in data storage, which do not allow the easily adapt the model to situations not foreseeable at the design stage. The most widely used conceptual model is the Entity/Relational (ER) schema, which aims to graphically represent the data and their relations within a certain situation. In today's scenario, with the emergence of new network services, such as Cloud and Big Data technologies, more agility, more speed and, above all, more connections between increasingly heterogeneous information are required. Therefore, it is necessary to have a database model capable of representing situations that cannot be predicted a priori. Relational databases they are a source of data consistency and integrity. This lead to the birth of NoSQL databases, the new database models on which to store more and more types of information and link them together in different ways. NoSQL databases cannot escape an appropriate design procedure. In particular, for the creation of a graph database, it is necessary to identify how the data will have to be aggregated to meet the queries and identify the entities that will make up the graph and their relations. However, in this case, the focus is not on the structure of the model but on the queries that must be executed by the users. This is because graphs are naturally expandable, meaning that new types of relations, nodes, labels, and sub-graphs can be added to an existing structure without modifying the existing queries and, consequently, the application functionality. It is, however, important to remark that the relational model has been designed by focusing on reliability and consistency of managed data, by guaranteeing the ACID properties, that, instead, cannot be guaranteed by the NoSQL databases. This could appear as a critical aspect for NoSQL, by generating strong data inconsistencies. In fact, what that could be useful in some situations, could not be relevant in other ones. Nevertheless, Neo4j, unlike most NoSQL databases, is able to support transactional operations and ensure ACID properties as well, while maintaining the usage of a dynamic structure.

3.2   Standardization and Denormalization

Data normalization is a well-established technique for relational databases aimed to avoid data redundancy on multiple tables and make faster writing operations. At the same time, however, there is a dispersion of the information contained on several tables that must be linked together, burdening the complexity of data recovery (execution of multiple joins) and consequently on the execution time for this operation. In NoSQL databases instead, the data is not normalized but "de-normalized", since the information is repeated between the various entities without worrying about data redundancy, in order to speed up the reading operations and provide a piece of complete information in the shortest possible time. It is clear that the writing operations involve more processing than those carried out on a relational database (for example, the modification of information must occur on all the entities on which it is present).

4   Comparative Experiments and Discussion

In order to compare the performances of relational and graph databases on OLAP operations, a set of experiments has been conducted. Two databases implementing respectively the Relational and the Graph Model have been considered: MySQL for the former and Neo4j for the latter. OLAP operations have been realized by using queries defined in SQL for MySQL and in Cypher for

Neo4j. By incrementally loading data, in the databases, we also compared the performance of the two databases. Three dimensions were considered for the assessment of the results. The *Fact* dimension verifies if the operation can be realized, the *Initialization* reports about the performances in loading data into the memory, the *Size* reports about the scalability of the system when data size increase.

The results obtained are shown in diagrams by demonstrating that for OLAP operations Neo4j performs in a shorter time w.r.t. to MySQL. In addition, while for MySQL the execution time increases proportionally as the data grows, Neo4j is able to "stabilize" the execution, avoiding a perceptive increment of the execution time w.r.t. the data increasing.

4.1   Reference Scenario and Data Modeling

To ensure a correct comparison between the two databases we designed a conceptual model from the same scenario that was then translated into the logical models of the two databases. Moreover, we decided to identify a scenario making possible to automatically feed these models by using data provided by an API. After a careful analysis the scenario selected involved the forum discussions on *StackOverflow*[1]. A graphical representation of the models is proposed in Figs. 1 and 2, respectively, for the relational and the graph examples.

In particular, the API methods *Questions* and *Answers* were exploited to feed and entity labeled *Question_Answer*, central in both the logical models of the two databases. The *Questions* method made possible to create flexible queries, as parameters such as *date, type of tag*, and others can filter the posts listed in the body of an API response. The *Answer* method returns all the answers given to the various questions listed in the dataset, with a classification based on keywords. Each entity "question" or "answer" is also associated with an "owner" who in turn owns certain attributes.

4.2   OLAP Operations

A set of queries have been defined to realize primary OLAP operations. The implemented OLAP operation are briefly summarized as follows.

Roll-up (drill-up): summarize data by climbing up the hierarchy or by dimension reduction. Roll up consists of an aggregation of the data of a cube in which an aggregation function is applied, typically the sum. Aggregation can take place along the levels of one or more dimensions of the cube, going up into the respective hierarchies. It is also possible to eliminate one dimension of the cube by applying an aggregation function. Examples of such operations are reported into Figs. 3a and b.

Drill down (roll down): reverse of roll-up from higher level summary to lower level summary or detailed data, or by introducing new dimensions since it allows

---

[1] defined on the website https://api.stackexchange.com/.

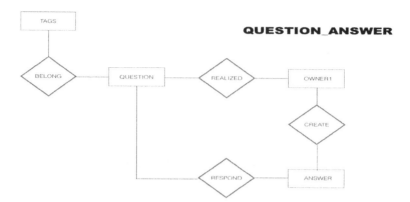

Fig. 1. Example of the implemented Relational Model.

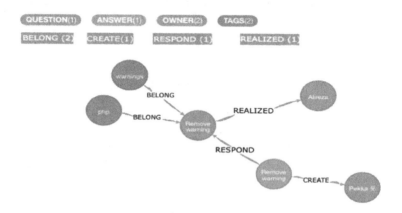

Fig. 2. Example of the implemented Graph Model.

to analyze a cube with greater precision by dis-aggregating it over one or more dimensions, and by providing more detail of the information. Unlike roll-up, drill down requires data to be available at an appropriate level of detail. In the opposite case, the result would be null. Examples of Drill down operations are showed into Figs. 4a, b, and 5a.

Slice and Dice: project and select: is the operation of selecting a subset of cells of a cube. In particular, the Slice operation selects one particular dimension from a given cube and provides a new sub-cube; Dice selects two or more dimensions from a given cube and provides a new sub-cube. Figures 5b, 6a, and b show the results of the Slice and Dice operations carried out in the experimental phase.

4.3   Performance Results

The execution times measured for each query can be observed in the following diagrams.

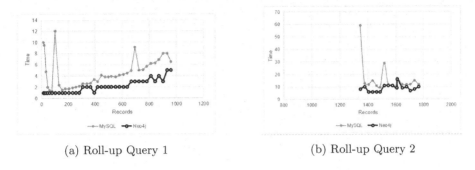

(a) Roll-up Query 1   (b) Roll-up Query 2

Fig. 3. Roll-up execution time comparison

Figures 3a and b show the execution times for two different $Roll-up$ operations. The sum is used as an aggregation function. The execution time increases proportionally to the number of data, for both databases.

In the $Roll-up$ operation reported into Fig. 3a an empty database is defined at the first iteration; the execution time is calculated over the data incrementally stored into the database. Different parameters have been used in the queries realizing the same operation. This choice has been made to have a broader investigation of the performances obtained, by expanding the research database.

Figures 4a and 4b are show the results obtained from the execution of the $DrillDown$ operation. The first one reported in Fig. 4a starts from an empty database.; the execution time is measured at each increase of the data stored in the database. A different $DrillDown$ operation is shown in Fig. 4b. In this case, the database the analysis starts with a non-empty database.; the execution time is measured at each increase of the data added into the database.

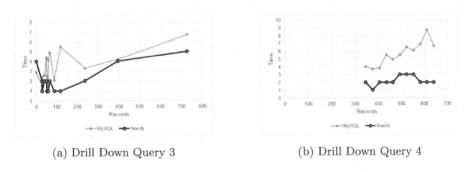

(a) Drill Down Query 3   (b) Drill Down Query 4

Fig. 4. Drill down execution time comparison

Also, Fig. 5a shows the execution times resulting from a $DrillDown$ operation, while Fig. 5b shows those resulting from a $SliceandDice$ operation: also in this last case, it has been considered an empty database at the starting phase.

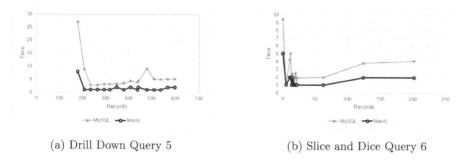

(a) Drill Down Query 5   (b) Slice and Dice Query 6

Fig. 5. Drill down vs slice and dice execution time comparison

Finally, the last two *SliceandDice* operations are illustrated in Figs. 6a and b. Also in these cases, new insertions have been carried out by increasing the data that are stored in the database.

A common factor for all the operations we considered is that the query execution time is lower in Neo4j than in MySQL. Another common element is that we observe relatively high performances with a low number of records/nodes, for both types of databases. This is related to the in-memory load time of the databases. In MySQL, the query manager is a crucial module of the architecture, since it is responsible for the efficient execution of operations specified at a higher level. When a query is executed the first time, it is initially analyzed to determine any lexical, syntactic or semantic errors, which are properly reported. During this phase, the system accesses the data dictionary to read the information, execute the controls and read statistical information relating to the size of the tables from the data dictionary. Once accepted, the query is translated into an algebraic and optimized form. At this point, if the query is compiled once and executed multiple times, the resulting code is stored into the database, ready for a possible re-usage. If the database changes significantly, e.g. because an index is added, then the query is invalidated and optimized again. The source code of the implemented queries is available online [3].

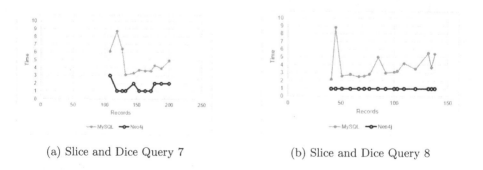

(a) Slice and Dice Query 7   (b) Slice and Dice Query 8

Fig. 6. Slice and dice execution time comparison

Even for Neo4j, the initialization stage is relevant. During this stage, execution plans are created and the query optimizer. The task of executing a query is divided into operators, where each of them implements a specific job. Operators are combined into a tree structure organizing the execution plan. Each operator in such an execution plan is represented as a node in the tree. This way, if the query is executed multiple times, the execution plan is reused.

Finally, the results obtained show that the response times of Neo4j scale better than those of MySQL: by increasing the data, the execution times increase for MySQL while remaining quite stable for Neo4j. This is due to the fact that relational databases search for data, having the features required by the queries, always on the entire database, while graph database search is carried out on adjacent nodes. This way, the overall database nodes are not always visited. The search time of relational databases is proportional to the dataset. Table 1 summarizes our results. We remark that all OLAP operations can be implemented in both the databases. The values reported in the *fact* column of Table 1 are computed taking the average of all query executions and matching to 1 the best recorder results, values greater than 1 express a distance from the best value. In other words, Neo4J obtains better performances, this is confirmed also considering *load time* and *scalability*. Load time is assessed as the average time required for the first query execution when data are loaded in memory for the first time. Scalability is assessed by the average time and the standard deviation of all the other executions, with increasing data load.

Table 1. Comparison of the execution time resulting from the experimental phase.

Operation	My SQL				Neo4J			
	Fact	Load time	Scalability AVG	Scalability STD	Fact	Load time	Scalability AVG	Scalability STD
Roll Up	1.30	9.75	8.06	8.78	1.00	1.00	4.11	3.63
Drill Down	1.40	2.25	4.86	3.92	1.00	3.00	1.91	1.33
Slice and Dice	1.20	5.30	3.65	1.95	1.00	3.00	1.34	0.75

5   Conclusion

In this paper, the performances in handling OLAP operations of a relational and graph database have been compared. In fact, such operations allow an organization to interactively analyze multidimensional data from multiple perspectives, by appearing today essential for supporting Business Intelligence. In particular, the relational model has been implemented by using MySQL while the graph model has been realized thanks to the Neo4j graph database. The comparison between the two models has considered three dimensions: the fact, the load time, and the scalability. The fact dimension verifies if the operation can be realized in the model, the load time reports about the performances during loading data into the memory, the scalability reports about the performances of the system when data size increase. The results confirm that all OLAP operations can be implemented in both the databases but Neo4j get better performances on both load time and scalability.

References

1. Angles, R., Prat-Pérez, A., Dominguez-Sal, D., Larriba-Pey, J.L.: Benchmarking database systems for social network applications. In: First International Workshop on Graph Data Management Experiences and Systems, GRADES 2013, pp. 15:1– 15:7. ACM, New York (2013)
2. Ardagna, C.A., Ceravolo, P., Damiani, E.: Big data analytics as-a-service: issues and challenges. In: 2016 IEEE International Conference on Big Data (Big Data), pp. 3638–3644, December 2016. https://doi.org/10.1109/BigData.2016.7841029
3. Azzini, A., Ceravolo, P., Colella, M.: Source code of the implemented queries. https://github.com/matteocol/Performances-of-OLAP-Operations-in-Graph-and-Relational-Databases/tree/master. Accessed 15 Mar 2019
4. Brewer, E.: A certain freedom: thoughts on the cap theorem. In: Proceedings of the 29th ACM SIGACT-SIGOPS Symposium on Principles of Distributed Computing, p. 335. ACM (2010)
5. Cattell, R.: Scalable SQL and NoSQL data stores. ACM SIGMOD Rec. **39**(4), 12–27 (2011)
6. Cattuto, C., Quaggiotto, M., Panisson, A., Averbuch, A.: Time-varying social networks in a graph database: a Neo4j use case. In: First International Workshop on Graph Data Management Experiences and Systems, GRADES 2013, pp. 11:1–11:6. ACM, New York (2013)
7. Ceravolo, P., et al.: Big data semantics. J. Data Semant. **7**(2), 65–85 (2018). https://doi.org/10.1007/s13740-018-0086-2
8. Codd, E.: A relational model of data for large shared data banks. Commun. ACM **13**(6), 377–387 (1970)
9. Ghrab, A., Romero, O., Skhiri, S., Vaisman, A., Zimányi, E.: A framework for building OLAP cubes on graphs. In: Morzy, T., Valduriez, P., Bellatreche, L. (eds.) ADBIS 2015. LNCS, vol. 9282, pp. 92–105. Springer, Cham (2015). https://doi.org/10.1007/978-3-319-23135-8_7
10. Gómez, L., Kuijpers, B., Vaisman, A.: Performing OLAP over graph data: query language, implementation, and a case study. In: Proceedings of the International Workshop on Real-Time Business Intelligence and Analytics, BIRTE 2017, pp. 6:1–6:8. ACM, New York (2017)
11. Have, C.T., Jensen, L.J.: Are graph databases ready for bioinformatics? Bioinformatics **29**(24), 3107–3108 (2013)
12. Huang, H., Dong, Z.: Research on architecture and query performance based on distributed graph database Neo4j. In: 2013 3rd International Conference on Consumer Electronics, Communications and Networks, pp. 533–536, November 2013
13. Melchor Santos Lopez, F., De La Cruz, E.G.S.: Literature review about Neo4j graph database as a feasible alternative for replacing RDBMS. Int. J. Ind. Data **18**, 135 (2015)
14. Miller, J.J.: Graph database applications and concepts with Neo4j. In: Association for Information Systems AIS Electronic Library (AISeL) (2013)

15. Pacaci, A., Zhou, A., Lin, J., Özsu, M.T.: Do we need specialized graph databases? Benchmarking real-time social networking applications. In: Proceedings of the Fifth International Workshop on Graph Data-management Experiences & Systems, GRADES 2017, pp. 12:1–12:7. ACM, New York (2017)
16. Peinl, R., Holzschuher, F.: Querying a graph database - language selection and performance considerations. J. Comput. Syst. Sci. **81** (2015, forthcoming)
17. Shalini, B., Charu, T.: Comparative analysis of relational and graph databases, May 2012
18. Vicknair, C., Macias, M., Zhao, Z., Nan, X., Chen, Y., Wilkins, D.: A comparison of a graph database and a relational database: a data provenance perspective. In: Proceedings of the 48th Annual Southeast Regional Conference, ACM SE 2010, pp. 42:1–42:6. ACM, New York (2010)

Knowledge and Organization/Social Network and Social Aspect of KM

Quality Measurement in Sterilization Processes at Healthcare Organization in Colombia Using Six Sigma Metrics

Ivanhoe Rozo-Rojas[1]([⊠]) (iD), Flor Nancy Díaz-Piraquive[1]([⊠]) (iD),
Mayra Samara Ordoñez-Díaz[2] (iD),
and Yasser de Jesús Muriel-Perea[1] (iD)

[1] Universidad Catolica de Colombia, Bogotá, Colombia
{irozo, fndiaz, yjmuriel}@ucatolica.edu.co
[2] Fundación Universitaria de Ciencias de la Salud, Bogotá, Colombia
msordonez@fucsalud.edu.co

Abstract. The article's aim is to focus on the application of Six Sigma to measure defects and identify improvement opportunities as part of knowledge management in the sterilization department in a Colombian private hospital. The methodology was established in three stages: Recognize, Define and Measure as an exploratory study using data from all instrument sterilized (N = n = 12.846).

Quality Management System's information was considered to recognize the context because work team had not hired in the organization directly. Sigma level was calculated in three sterilization processes: autoclave, ethylene oxide and hydrogen peroxide using data from 2017 and 2018.

Outcomes of this study provides information about behavior of sterilization processes to establish a baseline based on the historical data. Furthermore, employees require improve their skills and competences in statistics and data processing.

Future works are related to reducing waste evidenced in excessive time of processing or storing, instrumental availability and knowledge management using lesson-learned in the processes as a result of Analyze and Control Stages of DMAIC cycle implementation.

Keywords: Six Sigma · Sterilization Department · Quality · Improvement · DMAIC

1 Introduction

According to the World Health Organization (WHO), Healthcare-Associated Infections (HCAI) cause 16 million extra-days of hospital stay, 37,000 attributable deaths and contribute to an additional 110,000 deaths every year. At the same time, annual financial losses are estimated at approximately USD 9 million including direct cost only [1].

The cost of health care in developed countries is around 10% of gross domestic product and is expected to increase [2]. The sterilization process incurs significant expenses within health care, in this area microorganisms present in the necessary

© Springer Nature Switzerland AG 2019
L. Uden et al. (Eds.): KMO 2019, CCIS 1027, pp. 297–306, 2019.
https://doi.org/10.1007/978-3-030-21451-7_25

supplies are eliminated to perform the procedures on patients, therefore it requires the use of high-cost technologies and resources. In fact, sterile processes also incur a high opportunity cost and it impacts affects profitability in hospitals [3].

Sterilization Departments (SD) has an important role in the supply chain in healthcare organizations because it provides material and other inputs for medical processes and it allows to ensure the patient's safety policy. Disinfection is the process that eliminates micro-organisms or inanimate objects except for the bacterial endospore using chemicals or wet pasteurization [4].

Worldwide healthcare organizations have implemented advanced methodologies to improve their processes and it has been reported in literature analyzed in Rozo et al. [5]. Cases studies are related on missional processes, but other processes as sterilization were not found in databases. In specific, descriptive and economic studies explain current status of logistic activities to characterize processes oriented to the productivity [6].

This article presents a case study about Six Sigma (SS) application in a Sterilization Departments (SD) in a Colombian healthcare organization, using Z-score metric to analyze issues in three processes: autoclave, hydrogen peroxide and ethylene oxide. SD had not implemented SS methodology before to this study.

1.1 Six Sigma

Six sigma (SS) is a methodology that has been applied in several sectors, including manufacturing and transactional processes, and its deployment for improvement Is based on a methodology following steps Define, Measure, Analyze, Improve and Control established in DMAIC cycle. It was established as a process improvement initiative designed by manufacturing companies and extended for service organizations.

This methodology is a systematic data-driven approach to minimize defects and errors focusing on organizational outcomes and the most critical requirements of customers, implying the application of statistical tools and techniques in processes to obtain 3.4 or fewer defects per million opportunities [7]. Migita et al. explain sigma values and corresponding defects and defects per million opportunities DPMO [8]: (see Table 1).

Table 1. Sigma values and corresponding defect rates and Defects Per Million Opportunities (DPMO). Source: Authors

σ level	Defect rate (%)	DPMO (n)
1	69.76120%	697612
2	30.87700%	308770
3	6.68100%	66810
4	0.62090%	6209
5	0.00034%	3.4

Hence, health care error rates are estimated to be between 2700 and 45500 errors per million opportunities.(between 2 and 3 sigma) [8] representing a social problem for nations and it had been included into development plans.

1.2 DMAIC Cycle

DMAIC is the acronym of Define-Measure-Analyze-Improve-Control. It is the improvement cycle of Six Sigma methodology and it has a several cases of implementation, including production and transactional processes [9]. In addition, DMAIC was conceived from Plan-Do-Check-Act or PHVA that is supported by statistical and non-statistical tools focusing efforts to improving business processes [10] and integrating with international standards for operational excellence [11].

DMAIC is a framework that many studies found solutions for improving baseline and get benefits in medium and long term [12]. The steps of DMAIC cycle are [13, 14]:

- Define: to clarify the problem and analyze the benefits;
- Measure: to assess the current situation and translate the problem into a measurable parameter (CTQ);
- Analyze: to determine the effect of factors and causes that affect the CTQ's behavior;
- Improve: to improve the CTQs performance by designing and implementing the adjustments to the process; and
- Control: to control the system and adjustment of the process management for sustainable improvements.

In fact, SS allows the empowerment of employees on their activities having benefits reflected by some financial bottom line with DMAIC implementation. This improvement cycle admits knowledge is being acquire, created, packaged, applied and disseminated, and the relevance of Six Sigma to generate knowledge is a topic very discussed in the literature [15].

1.3 Six Sigma and Knowledge Management

Quality improvement, learning and knowledge-based activity emphasizes in knowledge creation [16]. Hence, knowledge creation and SS are related to business strategy, innovation and competitive advantage highlighting productivity, process improvement and competitive position of the organization [17]. In Six Sigma projects, teams generate knowledge across functional boundaries considering discussions, seeking information, critical observation and other methods [18].

Six Sigma and knowledge management in healthcare organizations have not implemented in large scale because the majority of case studies are descriptive [19] and empirical research [15]. Likewise, some cases report healthcare organizations that have not utilized potential of SS to generate and manage the knowledge in processes, including to establish base-line and improve the performance.

On the other hand, statistics tools allow to reduce variability and manage processes in the organizations oriented to the improvement in terms of efficiency and efficacy [20–22].

2 Methodology

2.1 Methodology Design

Six Sigma projects use an improvement cycle called DMAIC for problem-solving and its deployment depends on the complexity of the organization and the aim of the research. Its phases are Define, Measure, Analyze, Improve and Control, similar to PDCA cycle -plan, do, check, act- established by Deming in 1994. The approach presented in this case study takes into account the Six Sigma breakthrough methodology to deploys. The methodology was structured in the follow steps based on four phases as follow: (see Table 2).

Table 2. Methodology design. Source: Authors

Phase	Activities
Recognize	0. Characteristics of the case study
Define	1. Identify internal processes at SD
	2. Describe sterilization processes using sigma tool SIPOC (Supplier, Input, Process, Output, Customer)
	3. Identify Critical to Quality (CTQ)
Measure	4. DPMO calculation
	5. Sigma level calculation

The approach of the study is exploratory as an innovative methodology to establish the baseline and improve the process performance.

3 Results

3.1 Recognize

Characteristics of the Case Study. The case study was realized in a healthcare organization located in Bogota (Colombia) whose medical services cover all complexity levels defined by regulations: outpatient and inpatient care, diagnosis and surgical treatment. This organization has implemented ISO 9001 and other accreditation guidelines in their medical processes as result of several attempts to improve and control the activities.

More than 500 employees (including doctors, nurses, technicians, training doctors and medical interns) are high-qualified in medical areas, even getting specialization and master's degrees in recognized universities. Processes are managed using specialized software and patient traceability provides confident information to facilitate the decision-making process.

Sterilization Departments (SD) is a large area in the healthcare organization located near to surgical area to reduce probability of contamination before instrumental use. SD has three sterilization processes to reduce microbial charge according to the material: autoclave, hydrogen peroxide and ethylene oxide.

The healthcare organization implemented a Quality Management System based on ISO 9001 in 2017 as a consequence of improvement plans to obtain the national accreditation by Health Ministry of Colombia. However, quantitative approach had not been implemented before in any medical and transactional processes, generating a non-conformity in internal audits' reports.

3.2   Define

Identify Internal Processes at SD. Sterilization Departments (SD) had not structured its internal processes before Six Sigma implementation, but it had defined its areas using labels and activities were documented. Thus, based on the literature review and using SIPOC the internal processes were identified and documented in 23 procedures and more than 50 record formats (see Table 3. Internal processes SD).

Describing Sterilization Processes Using SIPOC. To understand the sterilization cycle in the SD was necessary to describe the process using a SIPOC (Supplier, Input, Process, Output, Customer). This tool allows identify key aspects from the process to understand the interrelation with other processes and activities. The SIPOC diagram of sterilization process at the case study is shown in Table 4:

Table 3. Internal processes at Sterilization Departments (SD). Source: Authors

Level	Name of the internal process
Strategic	Management Quality assessment
Value chain	Disinfection Drying Packing Sterilization Storing Delivering
Support	Purchasing Human talent

Table 4. SIPOC – Sterilization Department. Source: Authors

Supplier	Input	Process	Output	Customer
Medical processes Trading houses Internal processes at hospital	Own instrumental External instrumental Raw material	Production programming Disinfection Drying Packing Sterilization Storing Delivering	Sterilized instrumental	Medical processes Patients

SIPOC represents the interactions that Sterilization Department (SD) has in the hospital based on the information to establish a correct programming in order to obtain suitable and sterilized instrumental.

Identifying Critical to Quality (CTQ). Sterilization process requirements are important and meaningful to improve the service perceived by the internal processes. To describe drivers and indicators to establish the quality level of sterilization processes it was necessary use CTQ diagram [23–26] (see Fig. 1).

CTQ diagram explain that drivers to enhancement customer satisfaction are related with "sterilization cycle" and "packaging". In addition, five key indicators were identified as fundamental part of the sterilization processes but considered suggestions found in the literature review the study only includes DPMO and sigma level.

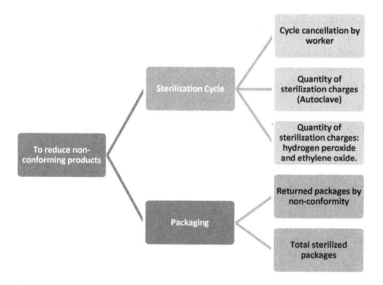

Fig. 1. Critical to quality in SD. Source: Authors

DMPO Calculation. DPMO is an indicator that represents a ratio of the number of defects in one million opportunities when an item can contain more than one defect. To calculate DPMO is necessary use the equation:

$$DPMO = \frac{total\ number\ of\ defects\ found\ in\ a\ sample}{total\ number\ of\ defect\ opportunities\ in\ the\ sample} \quad (1)$$

$$DPMO = \frac{total\ number\ of\ defects\ found\ in\ a\ sample}{sample\ size\ x\ number\ of\ defect\ oppotunities\ per\ unit\ in\ the\ sample} \quad (2)$$

Number of defects (D), total units (U) and defect opportunities (O) were considered to calculate DPMO index. To identify defect opportunities packages were observed and employees were interviewed in the SD. Defect opportunities identified were:

- Presence of water on the instrumental.
- Packages poor sealed.
- Manipulation by the operator.
- Machine programming.

Tables 5 and 6 provide information about sterilized packages and defective products that were processed in 2017 and 2018. This data was collected manually because system information was not integrated to visualizing it.

Table 5. Sterilized packages in 2017

Month	Sterilized packages	Defective product
January	420	5
February	338	7
March	457	8
April	320	8
May	431	7
June	467	6
July	878	5
August	393	6
September	403	10
October	605	9
November	659	8
December	740	9
Total	**6111**	**88**

Table 6. Sterilized packages in 2018

Month	Sterilized packages	Defective product
January	420	4
February	338	9
March	457	8
April	320	5
May	431	7
June	658	6
July	878	8
August	742	7
September	486	6
October	606	5
November	659	4
December	740	3
Total	**6735**	**72**

According to the information shown in the Table 7 processes present a sigma level equivalent to 4. This rate is 2 times higher than data reported in the literature review and it represents an accurate decision about Quality System Management implementation in the healthcare organization at the end of 2017. From the identification of the factors that contribute to reprocessing and the presence of errors, a specific improvement plan is organized for the sterilization center that aims to generate awareness and empowerment of the worker in the process.

Table 7. Calculation of Six Sigma metrics in the case study. Source: Authors

Metric	Period	
	2017	2018
Defects	88	72
Opportunities	4	4
Units	6111	6735
DPO	0.00360	0.00267
DPMO	3.600	2.673
DPU	0.01440	0.01069
YIELD	0.99640	0.99733
SIGMA	4.19	4.29

4   Conclusions

Data analysis of cycle cancellation presents a variation at the beginning of the year, but it increases for rising medical attention. All medical services require instrumental sterilized and it is possible that ensure the delivery and assess the Safety Patient Policy using the correct procedures in all activities at sterilization processes.

SD has increased its sigma level from 4.19 to 4.29 from 2017 to 2018, highlighting the effects of QMS implementation in the processes. The SS business goal is therefore to reduce the probability of defects to 3.4 (three and four tenths) per million occasions. However, this measurement has not comparison with a previous period, making it difficult to evidence the improvement and its actions. The systematization of sterilization processes is a tool that is being adapted for the case study, this tool allows to make more effective the traceability of the process and sigma calculation to improve the decision-making process.

Authors explain that SS implementation in SD is not reported in literature and making comparison between other cases studies is not possible because sigma level calculation in sterilization processes is not reported in literature. This is an opportunity to establish a baseline as background of SS implementation in SD.

Future works should consider analyzing the root causes, identify improvement actions and control plans to generate competition in the implementation of DMAIC cycle because our approach was intended to establish the baseline in this area. On the other hand, information systems must include tools to process the information and generate informs automatically. These results suggest including other indicators related with Lean Management recommended by authors in order to minimize waste [25]. Limitations were time for information processing, availability of employees and data acquiring process because data was not systematized by SD for fast processing. Finally, training plans are key factor to achieve business goals and reduce risk in the processes [26, 27]. The study suggest design and implement a training plan that includes project management and quality management with SS approach. This proposal should be articulated with Higher Education Institutions as a strategy for improvement skills of SD's employees [28, 29].

References

1. Schiffers, H., Zaatreh, S., Mittelmeier, W., Bader, R.: Potential infection control risks associated with roaming healthcare industry representatives. J. Infect. Prevent. **17**(1), 22–28 (2016)
2. Carter, M.: Diagnosis: mismanagement of resources. OR/MS Today **29**(2), 26–33 (2002)
3. Van Klundert, J., Muls, P., Schadd, M.: Optimizing sterilization logistics in hospitals. Health Care Manage. Sci. **11**, 23–33 (2008)
4. Rutala, W., Weber, D.: Infection control: the role of disinfection and sterilization. J. Hosp. Infect. **43**, S43–S55 (1999)
5. Rozo, I., Díaz-Piraquive, F.N., Serrano, L.: Revisión de literatura de prácticas para evaluar la calidad del servicio en instituciones de salud: Hacia un enfoque de Lean Healthcare. Instituto Antioqueño de Investigación. 2nd edn., Medellín (2018)
6. Velasco, N., Barrera, D., Amaya, C.: Logística Hospitalaria: Lecciones y retos para Colombia. La salud en Colombia: Logros, retos y recomendaciones. Bogotá, Ediciones Uniandes (2012)
7. Gowen, C., Stock, G., Mcfadden, K.: Simultaneous implementation of Six Sigma and knowledge management in hospitals. Int. J. Prod. Res. **46**(23), 6781–6795 (2008)
8. Migita, R., Yoshida, H., Rutman, L., Woodward, G.: Quality improvement methodologies: principles and applications in the pediatric emergency department. Pediatr. Clin. North Am. **65**(6), 1283–1296 (2018)
9. Hakimi, S., et al.: Application of Six-Sigma DMAIC methodology in plain yogurt production process. Int. J. Six Sigma **9**, 562–578 (2018)
10. Rozo, I., Díaz-Piraquive, F.N., Cárdenas, L.: Revisión de literatura de prácticas para evaluar la calidad del servicio en instituciones de salud: Hacia un enfoque de Lean Healthcare. Desarrollo e Innovación en Ingeniería. Instituto Antioqueño de Investigación, pp. 270–277 (2018)
11. Rozo, I., Serrano, L., Díaz-Piraquive, F.N., Coronel, J.: Integración de herramientas de la metodología Lean Six Sigma y Sistemas de Gestión Normalizados para la eficiencia energética. Desafíos en Ingeniería: Investigación, Innovación y Desarrollo. Fundación Tecnológica Antonio Arévalo, pp. 187–205 (2018)
12. Godley, M., Jenkins, J.B.: Decreasing Wait Times and Increasing Patient Satis-faction. J. Nurs. Care Qual. (1) (2018). https://doi.org/10.1097/ncq.0000000000000332
13. Srinivasan, K., Muthu, S., Prasad, N., Satheesh, G.: Reduction of paint line defects in shock absorber through Six Sigma DMAIC phases. Procedia Eng. **97**, 1755–1764 (2014)
14. Antony, J., Gijo, E., Childe, S.: Case study in Six Sigma methodology: man-ufacturing quality improvement and guidance for managers. Prod. Planning Control **23**(8), 624–640 (2012)

15. Barry, R., Murcko, A., Brubaker, C.: The Six Sigma Book for Healthcare. Health Administration Press, Chicago (2002)
16. Choo, A., et al.: Method and context perspectives on learning and knowledge creation in quality management. J. Oper. Manage. **25**, 918–931 (2007)
17. Anand, G., Ward, P., Tatikonda, M.: Role of explicit and tacit knowledge in Six Sigma projects: an empirical examination of differential project success. J. Oper. Manage. **28**, 303–315 (2010)
18. Arumugam, V., Antony, J., Kumar, M.: Linking learning and knowledge creation to project success in Six Sigma projects: an empirical investigation. Int. J. Prod. Econ. **141**, 388–402 (2013)
19. Goh, T.: A strategic assessment of Six Sigma. Qual. Reliab. Eng. Int. **18**, 403–410 (2002)
20. Lee, K., Choi, B.: Six sigma management activities and their influence on corporate competitiveness. Total Qual. Manage. Bus. Excellence **17**, 893–911 (2006)
21. Markarian, J.: Six Sigma: quality processing through statistical analysis. Plast. Add. Compd. **6**, 28–31 (2004)
22. Bertolaccini, L., Viti, A., Terzi, A.: The statistical point of view of quality: the Lean Six Sigma methodology. J. Thorac. Dis. **7**, E66–E68 (2015)
23. Goh, T., Xie, M.: Statistical control of a Six Sigma Process. Qual. Eng. **15**, 587–592 (2003)
24. He, Y., Tang, X., Chang, W.: Technical decomposition approach of critical to quality characteristics for product design for Six Sigma. Qual. Reliab. Eng. Int. **26**, 325–339 (2010)
25. Fischman, D.: Applying lean Six Sigma methodologies to improve efficiency, timeliness of care, and quality control in an internal medicine residency clinic. Qual. Manage. Health Care **19**, 201–210 (2010)
26. Serrano, L.F., Rozo, I., Díaz-Piraquive, F.N., Bravo, E., González, R.: Design thinking application methodology for pediatric service innovation. Commun. Comput. Inf. Sci. **877**, 215–222 (2018)
27. Rozo, I., Díaz-Piraquive, F.N., Ordoñez-Díaz, M., Ospina, L., Muriel, Y.J.: Risk management framework as technovigilance support at sterilization unit in the San Jose Hospital. Commun. Comput. Inf. Sci. **877**, 437–451 (2018)
28. Muriel, Y.J., Díaz-Piraquive, F.N., González-Crespo, R., Rozo, I.: Non profit institutions IT governance: private high education institutions in Bogota case. Commun. Comput. Inf. Sci. **731**, 254–269 (2017)
29. Vega, M., Muriel-Perea, Y., Díaz-Piraquive, F.N., Rodríguez, L.: Análisis del entorno para la creación de una empresa de asesoría en el sistema de gestión de seguridad y salud en el trabajo. Desafíos en Ingeniería: Investigación, Innovación y Desarrollo. Fundación Tecnológica Antonio Arévalo, pp. 54–67 (2018)

Customer Knowledge Management: Micro, Small and Medium - Sized Enterprises in Bogotá - Colombia

Yasser de Jesús Muriel-Perea[1]([⊠]) [iD],
Flor Nancy Díaz-Piraquive[1]([⊠]) [iD], Rubén González-Crespo[2] [iD],
and Trinidad Cortés Puya[2] [iD]

[1] Universidad Catolica de Colombia, Bogotá, Colombia
{yjmuriel,fndiaz}@ucatolica.edu.co
[2] Universidad Internacional de la Rioja, Madrid, Spain
{ruben.gonzalez,trinidad.cortes}@unir.net

Abstract. The idea of Customer Knowledge Management (CKM) is quite new, especially linked to operations within an organization. In this context, it is required to recall 80's worldwide concepts as Customer Relation Ship (CRM) or Customer Lifetime Value (CLV). CRMs were complex and focused on large companies in the 90's. At the beginning, CRMs worked through connections in infrastructures; nonetheless, from 2010 it was normal to use Cloud Computing versions. CRMs arose in Colombia firstly in large companies, now it is available for micro, small and medium enterprises (MSME). There are approximately 2.5 million MSME operating in a competitive environment, pursuing their market share. Besides, customer loyalty appears to be a difficult issue as well. Hence, the present paper aims to identify the Customer Knowledge Management Strategies developed by Colombian MSME. The methodology incorporates primary data, through a validated instrument by experts. Research results confirm that MSME work on customer loyalty strategies without systematization or measurement technology. Thus, an opportunity emerges for MSME regarding the use of cloud computing or CKM.

Keywords: Customer Knowledge Management - CKM ·
Customer Relationship Management - CRM · Cloud computing ·
Customer retention · Customer satisfaction

1 Introduction

Colombian MSMEs are basic for the economy of the country. According to the Ministry of Commerce, Industry and Tourism (MINCIT), there are 2.518.120 MSMEs, representing nearly 98% of total Colombian enterprises and 80.8% of national employment [1]. Despite of its significance, there is a lack of resources to access to technology and innovation. Therefore, MSMEs currently compete through two main factors: customer service and quality [2]. Large companies play acceptable in this scenario, while MSMEs in Bogota do not. According to the Chamber of Commerce

© Springer Nature Switzerland AG 2019
L. Uden et al. (Eds.): KMO 2019, CCIS 1027, pp. 307–316, 2019.
https://doi.org/10.1007/978-3-030-21451-7_26

Network (CONFECAMARAS), 90.000 enterprises failed in 2016 [3] and the Business Survival Rate was just around 30%.

In November 2017, MINCIT launched the "Productive Colombia" Program, aim to help MSMEs to boost their competitiveness, efficiency and export capacity. The strategy has five key ideas to reduce energy consumption, row material waste, delivery timing, customer claims, staff turnover and unsatisfied customers or defective products [4]. Most of these matters, without a doubt, favour customer loss.

The formulated hypothesis stands that MSMEs are not developing CKM strategies to foster customer loyalty; consequently, they are risking their profits and the opportunity to survive. The main objective of this research is to identify the Customer Knowledge Strategies used by the MSMEs in Bogota, representing 30% of total Colombian MSMEs.

The article structure is as follows: Sects. 2 and 3 describe the CKM concept (nature, characteristics and typology) and Micro, Small and Medium – Sized enterprises in Colombia; Sect. 4 defines the research methodology and the instrument design; Sect. 5 displays and studies the results of research; Sect. 6 include discussion about research; Sect. 7 define an adaptation roadmap for MSMEs; Finally, Sect. 8 disclosures conclusions and future research proposals.

2   Customer Knowledge Management

In 1990, authors as Karl Erik Sveiby and Leif Edvinson were interested in defining processes in order to describe how companies transfer, share and appropriate knowledge for continuous improvement. The CKM concept is quite recent, for that reason, it is mandatory to define the previous concepts, in order to set an appropriate context as a research basis.

Customer Relationship Management: CRM is a business strategy aim to create and sustain profitable customer relationships, in the long term. These initiatives rise on the company's strategy and philosophy and should be customer focus [5].

Collaborative CRM: Its objective is to optimize the customer contact, meaning e-mail, conferences or websites. Besides, Customer Lifetime Value establishes a relationship with society [6–8].

Operational CRM: It gives access to relevant customer data to Sales and After-Sales Departments.

Customer Knowledge: Integrates the customer and customer knowledge within the organization processes. This concept develops 3 key elements: knowledge about customer, specifically information linked to sales, payment behaviour, demand habits [9]; knowledge from customer, meaning customer experience about products, services and processes and expectations [10]; and knowledge for customer, which identifies customer knowledge gaps [11].

Co-creation: It is de key strategic element of CKM. It is a strategy to create value from the customer. It recalls a new customer role in innovation which creates value for the company and it self [12]. Without doubt, the innovation needs ideas from customers who are engaged with the products or services. They use products or services, hence, they probably can give ideas about improvement of products or service more easily than the employees or company o product research department.

Bigdata: It is management and analysis of big amount of data of different kind in order to make decisions. This is an important tool for identifying expectations of customers [12].

3   Micro, Small and Medium – Sized Enterprises in Colombia

In Colombia, according to Law 905/2004, Colombian Enterprises Typology is based on two criteria: number of employees and assets [13] (See Table 1).

Table 1. Enterprise classification

Size	Work unit or total assets $COP
Micro	Work <= 10 employees, or total assets, excluding house <= $368.858.500
Small	Work >= 11 and <= 50 employees, or total assets > $368.858.500 and <= $3.688.585.000
Medium	Work >= 51 and <= 200 employees, or total assets > $3.688.585.000 <= $22.131.510.000
Large	Work > 200 employees, or total assets > $22.131.510.000

Source [13]

Micro-Companies generate 50.3% of employment, while Small and Medium create 30.5% of it. MSMEs are mostly concentrated in Bogota, Antioquia, Valle del Cauca, Atlántico and Santander regions. Exports grew up to $1.437 million in 2016, experienced a contraction, by 5.7% since 2015. United States of America and Ecuador are the most relevant Colombian products importers. Indeed, industrialists represent about 90.6% of exports. Regarding legal aspects, 40% of businesses establish as companies' society and 60% operates under legal natural person.

Furthermore, "Productive Colombia" Program refers to current situation for MSMEs, aiming efficiency. According to MINCIT, MSMEs require double employees to generate the average value of a large company. Because of this situation, MINCIT objectives for 2032 remain in competitiveness. Data confirm that MSMEs are key to achieve this goal [14].

3.1   MSMEs Weaknesses

Colombian MSMEs weaknesses are similar to other countries: poor use of technology (see Fig. 1), lack of experience in technology of information and communication and unawareness of real opportunities given by the State or market. As a result of this, MSMEs are operating under low efficiency and competitiveness rates [15].

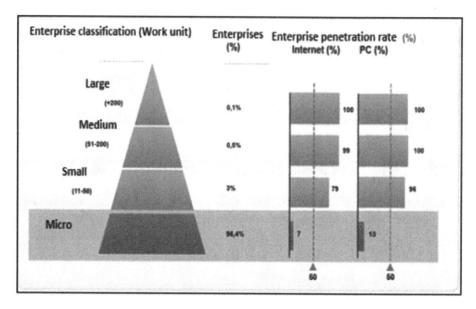

Fig. 1. Internet penetration rate for enterprises. Source [15]

3.2 MSMEs Strength

Access to credit is one of the most relevant advantages for Colombian MSMEs. According to the World Bank "Doing Business, 2017" Report, Colombia scores second at this dimension, overpassed by New Zealand [16]. In addition, MSMEs size favour flexibility and quick change.

4 Study

The study aims to identify strategies and mechanisms used by Colombian MSMEs, in Bogota, in order to reach customer loyalty. To define universe of study, it was taking into account criteria from Law 905/2004. Since, the Study incorporates 102 MSMEs. This sample integrates different economic sectors.

4.1 Research Methodology

This Study uses the quantitative methodology to achieve the research objective, through a validated instrument (on-line survey) by experts. The goal is to confirm the research assumption. For the calculation of the sample, the probabilistic sampling, simple random technique was used. For this purpose and in order to make the sample representative, in the universe of the one hundred and two companies, it was taken into account that they were heterogeneous in terms of economic sectors: manufacturing, services, commercial.

4.2   Research Design

The on-line survey integrates 14 questions. The questions of survey come from, mainly, concepts about CKM and CRM. It was sent to general managers and sales managers, bearing in mind these are profiles aware of the importance of customer loyalty for company's results. Each participant received a unique username and password, valid for just one attempt. This reinforces the research reliability.

The on-line survey was structured as follows: three questions about general aspects (Economic sector, Time, Number of employees); then, eleven questions regarding CKM (see Table 2).

Table 2. Survey

No.	Question	Answer options
1	What is the economic sector of the company?	Manufacturing, Services, Commercial, Extractive, Farming
2	How long was the company established?	4–5, 6–10, 11–15, 16–20, 21–30, 31–100 years
3	What is the numbers of employees of the Enterprise?	1–10, 11–50, 51–200 employees
4	Does the company have frequency and loyalty programs?	Yes, No
5	Does the company have reward programs?	Yes, No
6	Does the company offer customized products?	Yes, No
7	Does the company offer products for different market segments?	Yes, No
8	Does the company measure the customer retention?	Yes, No
9	Does the company publicize its products or services?	Yes, No
10	What is the means used to advertise your products or services?	This question is multiple choice. Radio, TV, Press, Home visits, Leaflet, voice to voice, Phone, Coupons, E-mail, Poster, Telemarketing, none
11	Does the Enterprise use some technological tool for customer knowledge management with the aim of monitoring them, to retain them or to learn of them?	Yes, No
12	Does the Enterprise ask about customer needs?	Yes, No
13	Does the company carry out satisfaction studies?	Yes, No
14	Does the company analyse the studies results?	Yes, No

4.3 Research Question

The question that conduct this research is: what strategies of Customer Knowledge Management are developed by Colombian MSME?

5 Survey Results

The next table shows the result of survey applied to the 102 enterprises (See Table 3).

Table 3. Obtained responses

Question	Responses
1	Regarding the company's economic sector, 52% of companies belong to commercial sector, 35% to manufacturing, 13% to services sector
2	Regarding the company's age, 54% of survivor companies are 4–5 years old, 39% are 6–10, 7% are 1 a 15. All enterprise are considered mature enterprises
3	Regarding the number of employees of the companies, the result shows that the majority of survivor companies correspond to micro (81%) and small (10%) and medium–sized (9%) companies
4	Regarding the question of whether the company has frequency and loyalty programs, 90% of the surveyed companies states that they do not use incentive programs for the frequency and loyalty of clients. Only, 10% reports to have this programs
5	When inquiring about reward programs, 57% of companies reports that they have reward programs for purchases. The remaining 43% indicate that they do not
6	34% of survivor companies reports that they develop customized products according to the needs of the clients. 66% of companies reports that they do not develop customized products
7	77% of survivor companies state that they do not develop products for different customer segments, that is, they are specialized in a single market segment. The remaining 23% indicate that they do
8	82% of companies indicate that they do not measure the customer retention
9	95% of survivor companies state that they publicize its products or services. The remaining, 5% report that they do not
10	When inquiring about means used to advertise your products or services, the leaflet is used by 60% of survivor companies. Poster by 53% of companies, 41% voice to voice, 7% phone, 6% e – mail, 5% none, 1% home visit, and 1% of companies use telemarketing
11	77% of survivor companies report that they do not use of technological tools (widely interpreted) to Customer Knowledge Management
12	77% of survivor companies report that they do not ask about customer needs
13	85% of survivor companies indicate that they do not carry out satisfaction studies
14	85% of survivor companies report that they do not analyse studies results

As can be seen, most of the companies studied belong to commercial economic sector, have less than 5 years of established, and belong to micro enterprises sector, that is to say, equal or less than 10 employees. Most of them, do not use incentive programs for the frequency and loyalty of clients, neither develop customized products, neither measure customer retention. Regarding the use of technological tools, most of them report that they do not use of technological tools to Customer Knowledge Management. In addition, most of them use informal means to advertise its products or services.

This scenario is very coincides with the characteristics of companies throughout the country in general. Moreover, is a risky scenario in terms of survival. Obviously, there is no CKM. It only recognizes some CRM initiatives, such as reward programs, which are very common in Colombian culture.

6 Discussion

Despite the opportunities that MSMEs have in the Colombian economy, represented in financial leverage, availability of technological tools and support in productive processes, these are not taken advantage of to deploy aspects such as customer loyalty strategies, client linkage in processes of innovation and anticipation of the client's needs, which, without a doubt, would strengthen them to reduce the gap with the large company, making them more efficient, effective and competitive. The misuse of opportunities is due to ignorance on the part of MSMEs, in which there is a shortage of qualified personnel [17].

The study shows that MSMES in Bogotá do not formally apply the concept of CKM, which includes three topics associated with the client (knowledge about the client, from the client and for the client); the analysis shows that the companies surveyed only manage information about the client -CRM-, but do not consider the other two elements that are necessary to identify and comprehensively address the client's needs, that is, they do not use CKM, but CRM.

Therefore, in order to move from customer relationship management to customer knowledge management in MSMES, it is necessary to aggressively enter into permanent training programs, process socialization and monitoring of the use and appropriation of technologies.

Although at this time MSMEs partially manage the CKM, they are considered to be in the correct sequence and can capitalize on the strategies developed to strengthen their knowledge management of the client, adding knowledge management programs where the client is linked and identifying deficiencies that the client does not know, integrating the elements that make up the CKM.

7 Adaptation Roadmap

Based on the current study and theoretical framework – mainly PDCA of Demming - we propose this step in order to incorporate customer knowledge management in organization MSMEs in Bogotá (see Fig. 2).

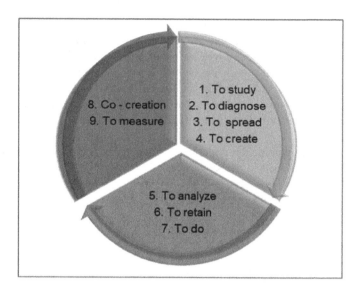

Fig. 2. Adaptation Roadmap. Source: Author

The details of the step of roadmap for MSMEs are:

- Step 1: To study about Customer knowledge management.
- Step 2: To diagnose current situation of enterprise related to CKM.
- Step 3: To spread results within company.
- Step 4: To create database with information about customers.
- Step 5: To analyze database in order to segment customers.
- Step 6: To retain customer through frequency, loyalty, reward, and customization programs.
- Step 7: To do satisfaction survey.
- Step 8: to engage customers in creation of new products or services.
- Step 9: To measure the CKM Strategy.

The proposal of new knowledge to strengthen the management of clients in the organizations under study, can be described in the development of a systemic procedure to support the proposal in the construction and appropriation of new knowledge, which is developed from the identification of the entry of triggers related to the detailed and relevant information of the clients, which in one way or another, are taken into account to increase their benefits and, as a consequence, the productivity of the organization, these are: products, services, preferences, integration and others (see Fig. 3) [18, 19].

With these triggers and their management process to meet expectations, it is expected to strengthen the management of customer knowledge, loyalty to the organization, as well as the design of personalization strategies in the service.

The analysis of the knowledge management of the client supports the decision making process that strengthens the productivity of the organizations, generating greater benefits for the organization, but above all and especially for the clients.

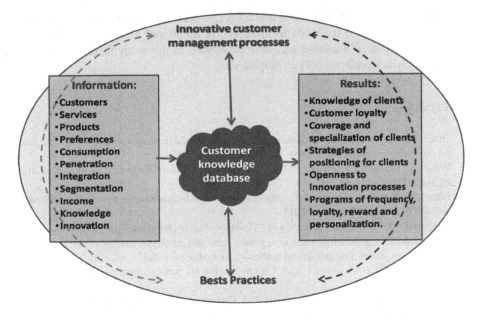

Fig. 3. Procedures to strengthen customer management. Source: Author

8   Conclusions and Future Works

Nowadays, the rules of the game have changed, the customer – enterprise relationship goes in double way. Customer can be both, user of products or service or supplier of ideas. if companies do not engage their customers in their value chain, is most difficult to satisfy them.

The research carried out allows us to reach the following conclusions:

- Most companies use Customer Knowledge Management strategies regarding information about the CRM customer, nor systematically or using the use of significant technology.
- Most Colombian MSMEs have never implemented a CRM project within their organization.
- In most cases, the implementation is five years or less, this is most likely associated with the emergence of versions of CRM, open source and cloud computing technologies.
- CRM projects have been successfully implemented; therefore, the experience can be replicated by other MSMEs.
- The study shows that the tools used are free or low cost. This allows lower that there is sensitivity to the price. To the extent that MSMEs know the benefits and affordable cost of some CRM tools, they will most likely opt for its implementation.
- The studied companies seek to have information about the client, but not from and for the client. Companies do more Customer Relationship Management than Customer Knowledge Management. Evolution is not yet mature.

- Future work needed to confirm and reinforce project conclusions. In the future, it is necessary to expand the study to more Micro, Small and Medium - Sized Enterprises in Bogota and another region in Colombia. In this study it was a limitation due to it was developed only in Bogotá city.

References

1. Dinero. http://www.dinero.com/edicion-impresa/caratula/articulo/porcentaje-y-contribucion-de-las-pymes-en-colombia/231854. Accessed 30 Nov 2017
2. Wilde, S.: Customer Knowledge Management. Springer, Heidelberg (2011). https://doi.org/10.1007/978-3-642-16475-0
3. Portafolio. http://www.portafolio.co/negocios/empresas/cerca-90-mil-empresas-han-cerrado-ano-49120. Accessed 30 Nov 2017
4. Ministerio de Comercio Industria y Turismo. http://www.mincit.gov.co/publicaciones/39492/colombia_productiva_para_que_pymes_sean_tan_eficientes_competitivas_y_exportadoras_como_las_grandes_empresas. Accessed 1 Nov 2017
5. Greenberg, P.: Las claves de CRM: Customer relations management, p. 39. McGraw Hill, Madrid (2002)
6. Corredor, A.: Technology Adaptation CRM, Open Source, in the Microenterprise Easysoft of Colombia, p. 22. Pontifical Javeriana University. Faculty of Engineering. Degree Work Mode, Bogotá (2007)
7. Winer, R.: A Framework for Customer Relationship Management, p. 17. Stern School of Business New York University, California (2001)
8. Langford, N.: Aprender las claves del CRM, p. 48. Gestión 2000, Barcelona (2006)
9. Cristofolini, M.: Wissenstransfer im Marketing, Lern- und Austauschprozesse des kundenbezogenen Wissens von Kundenkontaktmitarbeitern, diss. St. Gallen (2005)
10. Gibbert, M., Leibold, M., Probst, J.: Five styles of customer knowledge management, and how smart companies use them to create value. Eur. Manag. J. **20**(5), 459–469 (2002)
11. Kindcaid, J.W.: Customer Relationship Management: Getting It Right! Hewletpackard Company. Prentice Hall (2003)
12. Prahalad, C.K., Ramaswamy, V.: The Future of Competition: Co-Creating Unique Value. Harvard Business School Press, Bostos (2004)
13. Congreso de la República de Colombia. Ley 905 de 2004. Capítulo 1
14. Productive transformation program. https://www.ptp.com.co/categoria/Colombia_Productiva.aspx. Accessed 1 Dec 2017
15. DANE: Departamento Administrativo Nacional de Estadísticas. Informe estadístico (2015)
16. World Bank: Doing Business 2017: Equal Opportunity for All. World Bank, Washington, DC. License: Creative Commons Attribution CC BY 3.0 IGO (2017). https://doi.org/10.1596/978-1-4648-0948-4
17. Dinero. http://www.dinero.com/edicion-impresa/pais/articulo/escasez-de-mano-de-obra-en-calificada-en-colombia-2017/242020. Accessed 4 Dec 2017
18. Expotecnología: Análisis del entorno para la creación de una empresa de asesoría en el sistema de gestión. Desafíos en ingenieria: investigacion, innovacion y desarrollo. Ediciones TECNAR, pp. 54–67. Cartagena, Bolívar. Colombia (2018). ISBN: 978-958-59242-7-7
19. Díaz-Piraquive, F.N., Medina-García, V.H., Tarazona-Bermúdez, G.M.: Modelo de Gestión de Conocimiento como apoyo a la Gestión de Proyectos. Editorial, Universidad Distrital Francisco José de Caldas (2019). ISBN 978-958-787-097-8

Leveraging Knowledge Management to Promote Higher Education Programs Using Paid Social Media

Rebeca Cordero-Gutiérrez[1,2] and Eva Lahuerta-Otero[3,4(✉)]

[1] Faculty of Computer Science, Pontifical University of Salamanca,
Salamanca, Spain
rcorderogu@upsa.es
[2] School of Languages and Education, Nebrija University, Madrid, Spain
[3] Business Administration, University of Salamanca, Salamanca, Spain
eva.lahuerta@usal.es
[4] IME/University of Salamanca, Salamanca, Spain

Abstract. Information and communication technologies have become the center of many aspects of our daily life, including education as we live in the era of digital revolution. The use of social network sites is well disseminated across businesses and organizations, but the adoption of paid social media to promote higher education institutions and to create awareness is scarce. This research is unique as it examines the results of Facebook ads campaigns promoting higher institutions' teaching programs using the data envelopment analysis technique to assess their efficiency. We also used a Multidimensional Scaling technique (MDS) to graphically represent the analyzed ads to determine the variables affecting efficiency. The results show that investments on social paid advertising are an effective way to promote higher education centers.

Keywords: Higher education programs · Social media advertising · Efficiency

1 Introduction

Social media users reached 2.62b worldwide in 2018, and with 4.57 b mobile phone users across the globe, the use of web 2.0 technologies shows no sign of stopping [30, 31]. Students arriving to higher education institutions have grown up in a generation dominated by Internet and digital technologies. Adopting social network sites and integrating them into the promotional strategies of higher education institutions is nowadays a real possibility than can overcome isolation or lack of community problems [17].

Internet and social network sites are participatory communities where users and brands interact. Therefore, 75% of Spaniards click on interesting ads and 40% of them agree on sharing personal information to get personalized offers and promotions [8, 9]. The more customers use, engage and interact with social media, the more companies can know them better and provide personalized advertising to suit their needs more efficiently. The use of this commercial tools enables for cost and time savings [20] as paid social advertising (i.e. Facebook Ads) offers strong personalization power that can

© Springer Nature Switzerland AG 2019
L. Uden et al. (Eds.): KMO 2019, CCIS 1027, pp. 317–323, 2019.
https://doi.org/10.1007/978-3-030-21451-7_27

attract customers attention leading to efficiency. Consequently, digital marketing expenditures represent 43.5% of total media ad spending worldwide and they will reach 53.9% of the total advertising expenditures by 2020 [7].

Although researchers have widely investigated the impact of personalized ads in traditional media [35], website [8], or mobile [14], little has been made to examine the effects of personalized ads on Facebook [13, 33] and its impact on students attraction. Furthermore, there are still questions regarding the use of social media technologies in teaching and professional practices of higher educational institutions [21]. This research aims to fill in this gap by analyzing the efficiency results of different Facebook advertising campaigns in the higher education sector.

2 Theoretical Framework

2.1 Social Network Sites and Advertising Acceptance

The use of paid social advertising in horizontal networks such as Facebook fits perfectly with the principles of personalized marketing as prospective students engage on them looking for entertainment, but also updated information.

Companies and institutions throughout the world claim that the use of social media and paid social advertising brings measurable benefits such as improved customer satisfaction, increased sales, better customer support, reduced marketing expenses and higher customer reach [2, 15, 16]. Moreover, there is a growing body of research that is examining the use of various social media applications within the context of higher education, as thousands of higher education centers have successfully used this technique to socially promote their programs [4, 32].

Regarding academic theory and following the uses and gratifications theory [12], users are willing to expose themselves to social media to get benefits. These benefits generate positive aspects that will directly influence the attitude towards this medium. On the other hand, we must not forget that users on social networks are integrated into a community, which in the case of Facebook is enormous. These relationships with peers, makes users have an influence on other users' opinions or behaviors, taking a major role in what in literature is called the subjective norm. The relationship between the benefits of using a medium, the attitude towards it and the subjective norm affect the different behaviors in that medium. These relationships have been extensively tested in literature in different fields, including of social networks [5, 15, 22].

According to these theories, users will become fans of a Facebook page to get updates, promotions and relevant information from the community. They can interact with information by liking. commenting, tagging others or sharing it, contributing to e-wom and expanding the reach of the original content, serving as one of the most powerful and trustworthy sources of information [4]. As a result, paid social advertising can become an excellent and affordable way to create and maintain interaction between universities and former, current and prospective students.

Based on the roots of perceived utility (benefits or rewards) of advertising, personalized advertising can match customer needs based on demographic characteristics, interests, behaviors and so on. When an ad is interesting for students, it provides useful information (benefits) and it affects the way viewers respond when they are exposed to it, usually leading to acceptance. On the contrary, some users may not be interested in ads, so they will try to prevent their exposure, resulting in ad avoidance [29].

2.2 Social Network Sites and Advertising Efficiency

Although there are many elements to consider when launching an advertising campaign in terms of duration, budget, buying personas, segmentation criteria, objectives, expected outcomes. Facebook is one of the most cost-effective advertising platforms available [27]. The growth of the Facebook community (Facebook, Instagram, Facebook Messenger or WhatsApp) turns this paid platform into the best place to get leads for a business in 2017 [1]. Although the cost of Facebook advertising has increased in recent years, the average cost-per-click (CPC) in this platform is $1.72, an exceptionally low number considering its efficiency [27]. Note, for example, that the average CPC across all industries in Google Ads in 2017 was $2.32 [10, 11].

As the role of paid social is to find the optimal user to show the ad to, there is an increasing pressure to justify expenditures and become more precise and effective. Academic research in Internet advertising has grown accordingly and early research in assessing its performance focused on ROI [6], cost/sales ratio [28] or its effects on sales [3]. However, scholars across the world have recently recognized that marketers also need to take into account environment and competition when measuring the productivity of digital advertising [26, 34].

These metrics are important to measure ads performance, but a campaign success cannot be based on them alone. The reason is that a Facebook ads campaign usually have one definite goal different from clicks, and it is usually a specific action such as driving traffic to the website. Therefore, the main purpose of the study is to assess Facebook ads efficiency in the promotion of higher education postgraduate and masters' programs. Hence, our research questions are:

- Are Facebook ads efficient when promoting higher education institutions' programs?
- How do we identify efficient ads when the only variables the institution can control are campaign budget and duration?
- What effect do efficient ads have on social engagement in the context of higher education?

3 Methodology

3.1 Sample

In order to assess empirically the efficiency of social advertising on higher education, a total of 45 valid advertisements were analyzed on Facebook by an organization which, among other activities, manages training programmes and master degrees from different disciplines over the last three years from 2015 to 2018 (from postgraduate courses to master degrees) and which only uses Facebook for the social paid promotion. Ads are divided into four quartiles in order to reflect different levels of efficiency and inefficiency. In this way, the analysis will offer more interesting and richer results in relation to the research questions proposed in this study. Hence, quartile 1 represents ads ranking from 0 to 25% of efficiency, quartile 2 represents inefficient ads ranking from 25–50% efficiency and quartiles 3 and 4 represent efficiency, from 50–75% and over 75% respectively.

The sample of ads used in this research represents a total investment of 11,395.06 euros with more than fifty million impressions that have almost reached 10 million Facebook users (total reach = 9,694,366 people) and has generated more than one million clicks in the ads. Therefore, we are working with a sample that although a priori is small in relation to the number of ads, is important both for the volume of expenditures and the results obtained by such campaigns.

3.2   Procedure

To test the effect of social networks efficiency in the higher education context, we followed a two-stage research approach. In the first stage, we calculated efficiency scores for the ads of our sample using the Data Envelopment Analysis (DEA) technique.

Data Envelopment Analysis (DEA)

Among the multitude of statistical techniques for estimating efficiency is Data Envelopment Analysis (DEA). DEA is a non-parametric, linear programming based technique designed to measure the relative performance of decision making units (DMUs) where the presence of multiple inputs and outputs poses difficulties for comparisons. In this case, the units will be the different advertisements on Facebook.

This technique has been recurrent in the literature since its estimates are based on ordinary least squares and is consistent with the definition of the production function [24]. The use of DEA techniques when different outputs exist offers several advantages: (1) it allows the global analysis of each unit of analysis but does not require a prior definition of a production function that requires creating a unit to make a comparison with [25], (2) to provide information on best practices for each inefficient unit, (3) to allow the inclusion of exogenous variables as uncontrollable inputs, and (4) not to require the assumption of normality and absence of heteroskedasticity.

The efficiency of a DMU is measured as the maximum ratio of the linear combination of inputs and outputs. The maximum is obtained by selecting the optimal weights associated with these inputs and outputs. The highest possible efficiency reaches the value of 1, indicating a point at the frontier and therefore a technically efficient DMU. Non-efficient DMUs will be presented with values lower than 1, which will indicate their level of efficiency taking into account the analyzed data set.

For this study, we opted for an input-oriented model of the DEA technique, looking for efficiency by proportionally reducing inputs. This is a recurrent option in the context of advertising efficiency since the budgets and duration of the advertisements are fixed a priori and the objective is usually the maximization of results according to the budget and time available [19, 23]. In addition, we propose in this study variable returns to scale (VRS) in order to control for potential economies of scale given by the size effect of the ad.

DEA requires a positive correlation between input and output variables [18], which was previously tested. To perform the efficiency analyses of our work, we used the EMS 1.3 software. Thanks to this software, not only can we determine the efficient and inefficient units in the database of our study, but we can also determine how an inefficient unit (a Facebook advert in this case) could become efficient by combining characteristics of other DMUs.

We used the following variables as inputs and outputs to calculate the DEA index of the advertisements' sample:

- Duration (input): shows the duration of the ad in days
- Amount spent (input): includes the total amount spent in euros during
- Reach (output): Number of people who have seen the ad at least once.
- Impressions (output): Number of times the ad has been shown on the screen.
- Clicks (output): Number of clicks on the ad.
- Reactions to the publication (output): Number of reactions in the ad. The reaction buttons in an ad allow people to share different feelings about the content with six different animated emoticons: love, haha (funny), wow (amazing), sad, angry and like.

4   Discussion and Conclusions

4.1   Findings

In this section, we are going to analyze the results obtained by means of PROXSCAL routine in IBM SPSS 25 statistical package. After the efficiency analysis, a total of 9 efficient ads were obtained from those analyzed in the sample, which represents 20% of the cases. Additionally, 5 cases obtained a high efficiency with values higher than 80%. On the other hand, 44.44% of the ads analyzed did not achieve an efficiency of 50%, with the lowest value of the sample being an efficiency of 3.41%.

After the analysis of the paid advertising actions carried out on the advertising platform of the world's largest social network (Facebook Ads) by a training management organization in the higher education sector between 2015 and 2018, we found that efficient ads in the context analyzed obtain a greater volume of clicks, impressions and reach of their content. This means that the contents of the ads considered to be efficient have a greater diffusion, which exponentially increases the potential for attracting students for the different training plans promoted through Facebook. In addition, they are characterized by promoting interaction with the content which results in greater involvement of the prospective student with the ad. This will indirectly increase the organic positioning of this organization's fan page on Facebook and, therefore, of the website it owns and which is the final destination of the ads.

Another interesting aspect that should be highlighted is the amount spent on the execution of the ads. While it is true that those ads that are more efficient have had a higher amount of expenditure in absolute terms, it should be noted that they have been the ads with a lower cost in relative terms. Thus, they are capable of generating much greater results both in terms of visualization and diffusion as well as in actions taken by the prospective students that imply a greater involvement with the organization.

This fact is fundamental because it allows us to affirm that organizations in the context of higher education that do not make at least a minimal investment in advertising do not manage to exploit the full potential offered by social network advertising platforms such as Facebook Ads.

Therefore, an adequate investment in this type of platform reinforces the advertising and promotion results, improving the results of the training programmes in terms of visibility and increasing the possibilities of attracting new students to the higher education sector.

Future research will try to overcome limitations such as the small sample used and will also include additional variables to the models that can yield more robust results for a better understanding of the potential of paid social for promoting higher education studies.

References

1. Andrews, M.: Why Facebook ads will make you successful in 2017 and beyond (2017). https://blog.hubspot.com/marketing/facebook-ads-successful-2017. Accessed 1 Nov 2018
2. Angel, R., Sexsmith, J.: Social networking: the corporate value proposition (2011). http://iveybusinessjournal.com/topics/leadership/social-networking-the-corporate-value-proposition#.VL90JUeG840. Accessed 5 Oct 2018
3. Assmus, G., Farley, J.U., Lehmann, D.R.: How advertising affects sales: meta analysis of econometric results. J. Mark. Res. **21**, 65–74 (1984)
4. Chu, S.C., Kim, Y.: Determinants of consumer engagement in electronic word-of-mouth (eWOM) in social networking sites. Int. J. Advert. **30**(1), 47–75 (2011)
5. Cordero Gutiérrez, R.: Redes sociales horizontales y su impacto empresarial y social. Tesis doctoral. University of Salamanca, Spain (2018)
6. Dhalla, N.K.: Assessing the long term value of advertising. Harvard Bus. Rev. **54**(1), 87–95 (1978)
7. eMarketer: eMarketer releases new global media ad spending estimates (2018). https://www.emarketer.com/content/emarketer-total-media-ad-spending-worldwide-will-rise-7-4-in-2018. Accessed 1 Nov 2018
8. Ho, S.Y., Bodoff, D.: The effects of web personalization on user attitude and behavior: an integration of the elaboration likelihood model and consumer search theory. MIS Q. **38**(2), 497–510 (2014)
9. IAB Spain: Estudio Anual de Redes Sociales 2018 (2018). https://iabspain.es/wp-content/uploads/estudio-redes-sociales-2018_vreducida.pdf. Accessed 1 Nov 2018
10. Irvine, M.: Facebook Ad Benchmarks for YOUR Industry [New Data] (2018a). https://www.wordstream.com/blog/ws/2017/02/28/facebook-advertising-benchmarks. Accessed 15 Oct 2018
11. Irvine, M.: Google Ads Benchmarks for YOUR Industry [Updated!] (2018b). https://www.wordstream.com/blog/ws/2016/02/29/google-adwords-industry-benchmarks. Accessed 15 Oct 2018
12. Katz, E., Foulkes, D.: On the Use of the mass media as "escape": clarification of a concept. Public Opin. Q. **26**(3), 377–388 (1962)
13. Keyzer, F.D., Dens, N., Pelsmacker, P.D.: Is this for me? How consumers respond to personalized advertising on social network sites. J. Interact. Advert. **15**(2), 124–134 (2015)

14. Kim, Y.J., Han, J.: Why smartphone advertising attracts customers: a model of web advertising, flow, and personalization. Comput. Hum. Behav. **33**, 256–269 (2014)
15. Lahuerta-Otero, E., Cordero-Gutiérrez, R.: How to promote teaching centers by using online advertising. a case study. In: Encyclopedia of E-Commerce Development, Implementation, and Management. Western Illinois University, USA (2016)
16. Otero, E.L., Gutiérrez, R.C.: Using social media advertising to increase the awareness, promotion and diffusion of public and private entities. In: Omatu, S., et al. (eds.) Distributed Computing and Artificial Intelligence, 12th International Conference. AISC, vol. 373, pp. 377–384. Springer, Cham (2015). https://doi.org/10.1007/978-3-319-19638-1_43
17. Lam, T., Cho, V., Qu, H.: A study of hotel employee behavioral intentions towards adoption of information technology. Int. J. Hospit. Manag. **26**, 49–65 (2007)
18. Lou, X., Donthu, N.: Assessing advertising media spending inefficiencies in generating sales. J. Bus. Res. **58**(1), 28–36 (2005)
19. Low, G.S., Jakki, J.M.: Setting advertising and promotion budgets in multi-brand companies. J. Advert. Res. **39**(1), 67–78 (1999)
20. Malhotra, N.K., Peterson, M.: Marketing research in the new millennium: emerging issues and trends. Mark. Intell. Plan. **19**(4), 216–235 (2001)
21. Manca, S., Ranieri, M.: Yes for sharing, no for teaching!: social media in academic practices. Internet High. Educ. **29**, 63–74 (2016)
22. Peslak, A., Ceccucci, W., Sendall, P.: An empirical study of social networking behavior using theory of reasoned action. J. Inf. Syst. Appl. Res. **5**(3), 12 (2012)
23. Piercy, N.F.: The marketing budgeting process: marketing management implications. J. Mark. **51**, 45–59 (1987)
24. Russell, R.R.: Measures of technical efficiency. J. Econ. Theory **25**, 109–126 (1985)
25. Shang, J., Sueyoshi, T.: A unified framework for the selection of a flexible manufacturing system. Eur. J. Oper. Res. **85**, 295–315 (1995)
26. Sheth, J.N., Sisodia, R.S.: Marketing productivity: issues and analysis. J. Bus. Res. **55**(5), 349–362 (2002)
27. Shewan, D.: Does Facebook advertising work? (2017). https://www.wordstream.com/blog/ws/2016/01/25/does-facebook-advertising-work. Accessed 30 Sept 2018
28. Smith, D.C., Park, W.: The effect of brand extensions on market share and advertising efficiency. J. Mark. Res. **29**, 296–313 (1992)
29. Speck, P., Elliott, M.: Predictors of advertising avoidance in print and broadcast media. J. Advert. **26**(3), 61 (1997)
30. Statista: Number of social media users worldwide from 2010 to 2021 (in billions) (2018a). https://www.statista.com/statistics/278414/number-of-worldwide-social-network-users/. Accessed 1 Nov 2018
31. Statista: Number of mobile phone users worldwide from 2015 to 2020 (in billions) (2018b). https://www.statista.com/statistics/274774/forecast-of-mobile-phone-users-worldwide/. Accessed 1 Nov 2018
32. Tess, P.A.: The role of social media in higher education classes (real and virtual)–a literature review. Comput. Hum. Behav. **29**(5), A60–A68 (2013)
33. Tucker, C.E.: Social networks, personalized advertising, and privacy controls. J. Mark. Res. **51**(5), 546–562 (2014)
34. Vakratsas, D., Ambler, T.: How advertising works: what do we really know? J. Mark. **63**(1), 26–43 (1999)
35. Yu, J., Cude, B.J.: Possible disparities in consumers' perceptions toward personalized advertising caused by cultural differences: U.S. and Korea. J. Int. Consum. Mark. **21**(4), 251–269 (2009)

The Topics Dynamics in Knowledge Management Research

Yuri Zelenkov$^{(\boxtimes)}$ [ID]

National Research University Higher School of Economics, Moscow, Russia
yuri.zelenkov@gmail.com

Abstract. The intellectual structure of an academic discipline can be viewed as a set of interacting topics evolving over time. Dynamics of those topics i.e. changes in their popularity and impact is the subject of special attention because it reflects a shift in actual researchers' interest. This paper analyzes topics of knowledge management (KM) on the base of the topic modeling technique (namely Latent Dirichlet Allocation). Studying the flow of academic publications in 7 leading journals in 2010–2018, we identified 8 topics that concern different aspects of knowledge management science. Three topics, what focus on the social aspects of knowledge management (namely the context supporting knowledge transfer, the employees' incentives to share knowledge, and innovation), grow in terms of popularity and impact. Opposite, popularity and impact of topics, which focus on the practice of the knowledge management and organizational learning also as on the impact of intellectual capital on performance, decline. It is consistent with the opinion of other researchers that in the contemporary flow of scientific publication role of KM is identified more as a social process than a management engineering method.

Keywords: Knowledge management · Bibliometrics · Topic modeling · LDA

1   Introduction

Empirical evaluations of science and technology research play a crucial role in creating effective science policies. The results of the analysis can shed light on the intellectual structure of an academic discipline and evaluate the impact of scientific journals, papers, and researchers thereby guide scholars towards producing impactful studies [1].

Knowledge management (KM) is a field of research that has gained wide acceptance in the scientific community and management literature [2] since the role of knowledge in the development of economics and productivity was acknowledged [3]. Bibliometrics is widely used in research in the field of knowledge management [1, 2, 4].

There are two main directions of bibliometric analysis: performance analysis and science mapping. The first one based on quantitative metrics such as the number of citations and helps to identify most influenced journals, papers, and authors. The second one deals with the spatial representation of how different scientific actors are related to one on another. In particular, this flow pays special attention to the identification of topics of research, their dynamics, and relation. The main drawback is that most of the bibliometric research use more or less subjective and informal approaches

© Springer Nature Switzerland AG 2019
L. Uden et al. (Eds.): KMO 2019, CCIS 1027, pp. 324–335, 2019.
https://doi.org/10.1007/978-3-030-21451-7_28

to topic identification. However, there is a number of formal methods allowing identify topics in the corpus of documents based on words frequencies. These are topic analysis techniques developed as a part of the wider discipline - machine learning.

The goal of the presented paper is to identify main topics of KM research since 2010 on the base of topic analysis and study their dynamics.

2 Related Works

2.1 The Knowledge Management Scientometrics

Gaviria-Marin et al. [2] identify four generations in the development of KM as an academic discipline. On the first stage (1960–1980) concept of knowledge as a tool that impact economic performance has emerged. On the second stage (1990's decade) knowledge was acknowledged as a process. The third generation of research (2000's decade) had linked knowledge management to the success of organizations. In the current generation (2010's decade) KM role is identified more as a social process than a management engineering method [5].

It should be noted that since 1980 three relatively independent areas of research on the role of knowledge have emerged. The first is related to the study of such a phenomenon as the intellectual capital of an organization [6], the second to the operationalization of knowledge management [7] and third studies the organizational learning [8].

There is a number of scientific journals devoted to knowledge management exclusively. For example, Serenko and Bontis [9] list 27 journals publishing now, which meet the requirements of academic quality. In addition, journals devoted to other disciplines, such as computer science, innovation, general management publish research related to KM [1, 4]. This is since knowledge management is a broad area that connects to many applied disciplines. Among the recent studies analyzing this flow of publications are the following.

Akhavan et al. [1] identified 62 different keywords that had frequently appeared in the title of papers in Web of Science Core Collection (WoS CC) between 1980 and 2014 and were directly related to KM stream. According to this set of keywords, authors selected 3,198 articles. To avoid the bias that related to the time elapsed since publication, they designed and calculated a citation index for each study as the average number of citations per year. Then, they ranked the studies in the sample based on this index to identify the top 500 articles with the highest citation index. This sub-sample was used for analyses.

In fact, scholars from various backgrounds have attempted to apply KM related concepts in their research domains. According to the analysis of [1], main research streams in KM are business & economics, information science & library science, computer science, organizational research & management science, engineering, and psychology. Research flow linked with computer science prevailed before 2009, in 2009–2012 the largest number of publications was related to business & economics, and in 2012 publications regarding to KM and engineering moved in the focus of researchers.

Authors of work [1] do not single out research topics explicitly. In addition, they analyze only the articles titles; this can be a source of bias.

Gaviria-Marin et al. [2] also based their research on papers selected by keywords from WoS CC. They considered documents published between 1961 and 2015 (total 23,494 studies). Authors identified 20 areas related to KM (business & economics, computer science, etc.), which are consistent with [1] and found that the KM literature most significantly grew in the areas of business and management.

Most interesting in the context of our paper part of this research dedicates to science mapping. To map the KM research, authors of [2] used two techniques: a co-citation analysis (separately by authors and journals) and co-occurrence of keywords. The networks formed by the co-occurrence of keywords are evolving in time. In the first decade of analysis (1985–1995), keywords cluster by different topics of interest, among which knowledge acquisition and expert systems stand out, these topics connect to concepts in the area of information systems. In the following decades, it is observed that 'knowledge management' is the most frequently used keyword and it links strongly to the rest of the keywords. In the last decade of analysis (2006–2015), authors identify five subnets of keywords co-occurrence, that can be described as

- knowledge management (including organizational learning, knowledge sharing, and information systems),
- knowledge transfer (including strategic alliances and tacit and explicit knowledge),
- innovation (including knowledge creation, organizational knowledge, entrepreneurship, and knowledge spillovers),
- the subnet of general concepts (knowledge, learning, epistemology), and
- the small subnet that joins such issues as knowledge acquisition, knowledge-based systems, and artificial intelligence.

These results provide an insight into the structure of KM as an academic discipline, but the absence of bias remains unproven since only keywords are used as data.

Wang et al. [4] acquired the data by searching for papers with the term "knowledge management" in titles, abstracts, or indexing terms in the WoS CC database. After filtering out the less representative records, the dataset reduced to 7628 original research articles. For bibliometric analysis, authors used popular software packages such as Citespase [10], VOSviewer [11] and other. In particular, they used Citespace to divide co-citation network into clusters of co-cited references. These references are tightly connected within the same cluster but loosely connected between different clusters, hence, these clusters can be viewed as research topics. Authors of [4] identified 15 main clusters. Ranked by cited frequency, the core members of the largest cluster represent major milestones in relation to knowledge management in or across organizations, including knowledge performance, competency, knowledge for innovation, and knowledge sharing. The core members of the next largest clusters represent topics in relation to knowledge value and knowledge management from the psychological perspective. It is a mature approach that helps to identify more or less divided research areas. But it does not take into consideration the distribution of key terms inside the topic and cannot identify a mixture of topics presented in the document.

Table 1 lists the results of works cited here also a few earlier publications. As we can see the results of various authors are inconsistent, they identify research topics differently, because of using different methods of data collection and analysis.

Table 1. Topics of knowledge management research identified in recent publications.

Paper	Source of analyzed data	Time period and number of analyzed works	Identified KM research topics
Dwivedi et al. [12]	Titles of papers (WoS)	1974–2008 (1,043)	KM systems, environment, KM processes, KM: planning, policy, evaluation, strategy, KM research and education, KM others
Lee and Chen [13]	Keywords (MAS)	1995–2010 (10,974)	software engineering, organizational memory, KM systems, knowledge creation, ontology
Akhavan et al. [1]	Titles of papers (WoS)	1980–2014 (3,198)	No topics identified
Wang et al. [4]	Titles, abstracts, indexed terms (WoS)	1974–2017 (7,628)	knowledge management in or across organizations, knowledge value, KM research from the psychological perspective (see cited work for information about other topics)
Gaviria-Marin et al. [2]	Keywords (WoS)	1961–2015 (23,128)	knowledge management, knowledge transfer, innovation, general concepts, knowledge-based systems and AI

MAS – Microsoft Academic Search
WoS – Web of Science

2.2   Topic Modeling

A topic is a special terminology of the subject area, i.e. a set of words often co-occur in texts related to a given subject area. It is assumed that there is a finite set of topics T, and each use of the term w in each document d is associated with some topic $t \in T$, which is not known. A collection of documents is considered as a set of triples (d, w, t) selected randomly and independently from the discrete distribution $p(d, w, t)$ defined on a finite set $D \times W \times T$. Documents $d \in D$ and the terms $w \in W$ are observable variables, the topics $t \in T$ are latent variables. So, probabilistic topic modeling is based upon the idea that documents are mixtures of topics, where a topic is a probability distribution over words [14]. It can be presented as a conditional distribution of a set of words $p(w|t)$, that is the probability (frequency) of the word w in the topic t. The topic of the document is the conditional distribution, i.e. the probability (frequency) $p(t|d)$ of the topic t in document d.

The topic model automatically detects latent topics by the observed frequencies of words in the documents $p(w|d) = \sum_{t \in T} p(t|d)p(w|t)$. We will use Latent Dirichlet Allocation (LDA) that is based on additional assumption that the distribution Θ of documents θ_d and distribution Φ of topics φ_t are spawn by a Dirichlet distributions [15]. It is an unsupervised learning model, so LDA does not require any prior labeling of the documents. All the topics emerge naturally from the statistical structure of document-word data itself.

To build the model one should define number of T topics, distributions Θ and Φ are computed by LDA algorithm. As a result, each topic is presented by the weighted list of words, weight of word corresponds to its importance in topic definition. Each document is presented by the weighted list of topics, the weight of the topic corresponds to its significance in the document.

Representation of scientific papers as a mixture of topics opens a lot of new capabilities of analysis, but this approach is still used relatively rarely.

Mann et al. [16] used a combination of topic modeling and citation analysis to estimate the impact factor of the topic over time and topical diversity of documents in computer science. Gatti et al. [17] applied topic modeling technique to the field of operations research and management science. They also studied the topics dynamics but in addition, a composite probabilistic representation of documents allowed them to investigate diversity and uniqueness of journals and identify clusters of journals. Dam and Ghose [18] used topic modeling to analyze the content of the Proceedings of the International Conference on Principles and Practices of Multi-Agent Systems (PRIMA). They identified most popular topics and papers that are most representative for each topic. Sun and Yun [19] applied this approach to transportation research. Authors introduced few metrics for the journal diversity, identified topics that popularity grows or reduces over time and presented the structure of the word co-occurrence across topics.

3 Research Method

3.1 Data Collection and Preprocessing

Most researchers for the selection of publications for analysis use a search on terms that in their opinion define the area under study. We use another approach. In order to focus exclusively on publications in the field of knowledge management, we use the rating of KM journals presented Serenko and Bontis [9]. The authors identified seven most influential journals presented in Table 2. We limit the time frame for research 2010–2018 because according to [2, 5] it was in 2010 that a new stage of research in the field of KM began. Table 2 lists the titles of journals selected, number of publications and the abbreviations that will be used to reference on sources.

Table 2. KM journal list.

Rank[a]	Title	Number of pubs in 2010–2018[b]	Abbr
1	Journal of Knowledge Management	640	JKM
2	Journal of Intellectual Capital	322	JIC
3	The Learning Organization	258	TLO
4	Knowledge Management Research & Practice	342	KRP
5	Knowledge and Process Management: The Journal of Corporate Transformation	216	KPM
6	VINE: The Journal of Information and Knowledge Management Systems	88	VIN
7	International Journal of Knowledge Management	168	IJK
	Total	2058	

[a]According to Serenko and Bontis [9]
[b]According to Scopus database

Bibliographic data for each article, including the title, authors, time of publication, keywords, abstract and citation index was downloaded from the Scopus database. In total, we received 2058 publications. Figure 1 presents the number of articles in each journal from 2010 to 2018.

According to the empirical study [20], differences between abstract and full-text data are more apparent within small document collections. Unfortunately, there is no widely-accepted metric, that measures the size of the collection. From another hand, the computational time is an obvious constraint of research. Therefore, we have selected abstracts as an object of analysis.

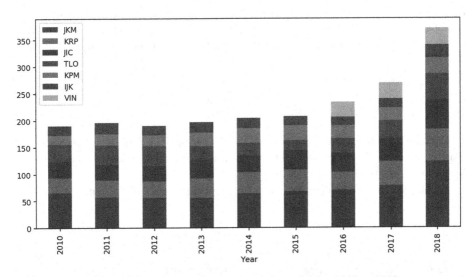

Fig. 1. The number of articles of each journal from 2010 to 2018.

Abstract data were tokenized, and single- and two-character words, numbers, and punctuation marks were removed. We also removed words that occurred less than 10 times in all documents, and words that belong to a standard English stop word list. We also created bigrams to join terms often co-occurred beside. Next, the normalization method was applied, namely, lemmatization that converts word to its standard form. In total, we received 9005 words in the vocabulary.

Finally, a matrix $D \times W$ of word frequencies was created, which cells n_{dw} contain counts of the word w in document d.

3.2   Definition of the Number of Topics

One of the most important issues of the topic modeling is the determination of the number of topics in the corpus under study. Very often, a researcher sets this number a priori. However, it is desirable to have an independent metric that would allow evaluating the quality of the model based on the Φ and Θ matrices that it has built. For this, we use perplexity $P(D) = \exp\left[\frac{1}{2}\sum_{d \in D}\sum_{w \in d} n_{dw} \ln p(w|d)\right]$.

The perplexity of collection D is a measure of the language quality and often used in computational linguistics. In our case, language is the distribution of words in documents $p(w|d)$. The less perplexity, then more uneven the distribution of words in the corpus. Perplexity is closely related to the likelihood, in fact, it is the reciprocal of the likelihood logarithm.

To avoid overfitting, we used the hold-out procedure. The dataset was divided into two samples in proportion 60/40, the model was trained on first of them, the second was used to evaluate perplexity.

3.3   Further Analysis

The first issue that we should study after the topic amount definition is the dynamics of the topics over time. Denote θ_{dt} the proportion of topic t in document d (noting that $0 \leq \theta_{dt} \leq 1$). So, the overall popularity of topic across all documents can be defined as [17, 18]

$$\widehat{\theta}_t = \frac{1}{D}\sum_{d \in D} \theta_{dt} \tag{1}$$

Equation (1) defines popularity over whole period under study, to measure the relative proportion of papers in a certain year y, it is enough to change D on D_y, where D_y is the set of all papers in year y.

By analogy, we introduce a measure to assess the impact of the topic

$$\widehat{i}_t = \frac{1}{C}\sum_{d \in D} \theta_{dt} C_d \tag{2}$$

where C_d is the number of citations of document d and $C = \sum_{d \in D} C_d$.

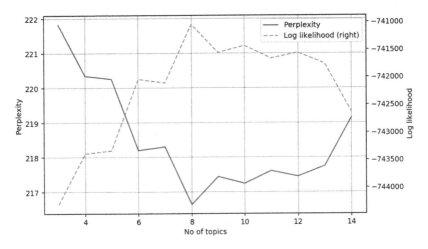

Fig. 2. Perplexity and log-likelihood for various numbers of topics.

4 Results and Discussion

Figure 2 shows the dependence of perplexity and loglikelihood on the number of topics during the LDA analysis. As it follows from data presented, the optimal number of topics is 8. To confirm the quality of the topics selected, two recent visualization techniques were applied. The Fig. 3(a) presents a global view of the topic model [21]. The topics are plotted as circles whose centers are determined by computing the distance between topics and then these distances are projected into two dimensions by using multidimensional scaling. The areas of circles correspond to topics prevalence. To draw Fig. 3(b), we used another multidimensional scaling technique. The documents described by their topical distributions were projected into two dimensions by using the UMAP method [22]. Each document is presented by point, which color corresponds to the dominant topic of the document. As we can see from the data presented, selected topics are not overlapping that confirms the quality of model.

Figure 4 presents word clouds that built on a base of ten most important words describing topics, the size of the word corresponds to its weight in distribution φ_t. More detailed information on the topics is presented in Table 3. The most representative paper in each topic satisfies two conditions: the greatest weight of the topic among all the works under consideration and the maximum number of citations.

Table 3 lists also overall topics popularity and impact computed by Eqs. (1) and (2), Fig. 5 presents dynamics by years. In order to quantify the dynamics of topics, for each of them a trend line was calculated as a regression $trend = \alpha + \beta * y$, where y a certain year. The coefficients β allow us to estimate the slope of the trend line, a positive value corresponds to an increase in the trend, a negative one - to its decrease. These values are presented in Table 3. Note that the absolute values of β's are not interpretable, only their relative values have meaning because they allow comparing trends of various topics.

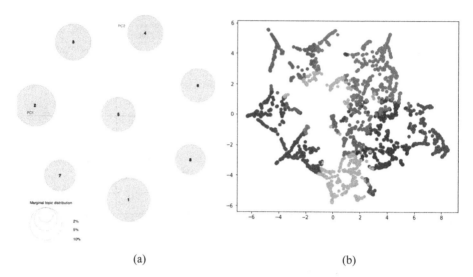

(a)   (b)

Fig. 3. Global view of the topic model.

Fig. 4. Word clouds for topic.

As it follows from data presented, the most popular and influential topics for the entire period under study are topic 4 and topic 6. A deeper study shows that topic 4 is more concerns about the practical implementation of knowledge management processes. This topic is dominant in 470 articles in the corpus studied. However, it should be noted that this area of research shows a significant downward trend both in popularity and influence, values of β's are -0.0072 and -0.0055 respectively. In the publications of 2018, it only on the 3rd place, behind topics 5 and 6 both in popularity and impact.

A similar dynamic is demonstrated by Topic 2, which focuses on organizational learning (OL) processes, and Topic 7 that concerns the impact of intellectual capital (IC) on firm performance.

Table 3. Topics popularity and impact.

Topic	Description	Most representative paper	Popularity		Impact	
			Overall	Trend	Overall	Trend
0	Capabilities based on IC	[23]	0.083	0.0015	0.101	–0.0020
1	General issues of KM	[24]	0.085	–0.0005	0.094	0.0009
2	OL processes	[25]	0.135	–0.0059	0.101	–0.003
3	Incentives to share knowledge	[26]	0.109	0.0063	0.121	0.0022
4	KM processes	[27]	0.195	–0.0072	0.163	–0.0055
5	Innovation	[28]	0.109	0.0074	0.091	0.0052
6	Knowledge transfer	[29]	0.164	0.0019	0.167	0.0110
7	Impact of IC	[30]	0.111	–0.0033	0.153	–0.0087

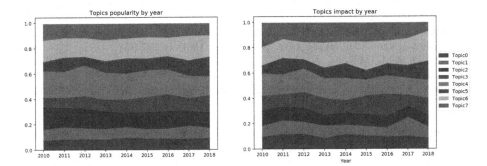

Fig. 5. Topics popularity and impact by year

Studies related to Topic 6 concern on the managerial issues that are fairly close to Topic 4 but focus more on context that supports the transfer of knowledge. This is the most popular and influential topic in 2018 (values of $\widehat{\theta}_6$ and $\widehat{i}_6$ in 2018 are 0.168 and 0.233, respectively).

Topic 5 that focus on innovation and Topic 3, which deals with incentives of employees to share knowledge, also significantly grow.

Topic 0 (capabilities based on intellectual capital) and Topic 1 (general issues of knowledge management, in particular, tacit knowledge) attract enough stable interest of researchers.

These results are consistent with papers [2, 5] which noted that the current stage of KM research more focuses on social aspects that support knowledge sharing, than the engineering of managerial systems. Results presented here confirm this shift in researchers' interests, especially it is perceptible over the past three years.

5   Conclusion and Future Research

The data presented show that the topic modeling technique provides useful bibliometric results. The presentation of themes as the distributions of words and documents as the distributions of topics also allows us to explore many aspects that remain beyond the margins of this work. In particular, this is a study of the uniqueness of the thematic orientation of academic journals, a study of the connections between topics based on the intersection of a set of words defining them. Such analysis of KM as an academic discipline is the goal of our future works.

References

1. Akhavan, P., Ebrahim, N.A., Fetrati, M.A., Pezeshkan, A.: Major trends in knowledge management research: a bibliometric study. Scientometrics 107(3), 1249–1264 (2016)
2. Gaviria-Marin, M., Merigó, J.M., Baier-Fuentes, H.: Knowledge management: a global examination based on bibliometric analysis. Technol. Forecast. Soc. Change 140, 194–220 (2019)
3. Lambe, P.: The unacknowledged parentage of knowledge management. J. Knowl. Manage. 15(2), 175–197 (2011)
4. Wang, P., Zhu, F.W., Song, H.Y., Hou, J.H., Zhang, J.L.: Visualizing the academic discipline of knowledge management. Sustainability 10(3), 682 (2018)
5. Tzortzaki, A.M., Mihiotis, A.: A review of knowledge management theory and future directions. Knowl. Process Manage. 21(1), 29–41 (2014)
6. Inkinen, H.: Review of empirical research on intellectual capital and firm performance. J. Intellect. Capital 16(3), 518–565 (2015)
7. Heisig, P., Suraj, O.A., Kianto, A., Kemboi, C., Perez Arrau, G., Fathi Easa, N.: Knowledge management and business performance: global experts' views on future research needs. J. Knowl. Manage. 20(6), 1169–1198 (2016)
8. Argote, L., Miron-Spector, E.: Organizational learning: from experience to knowledge. Organ. Sci. 22(5), 1123–1137 (2011)
9. Serenko, A., Bontis, N.: Global ranking of knowledge management and intellectual capital academic journals: 2017 update. J. Knowl. Manage. 21(3), 675–692 (2017)
10. Chen, C.: CiteSpace II: detecting and visualizing emerging trends and transient patterns in scientific literature. J. Am. Soc. Inf. Sci. Technol. 57(3), 359–377 (2006)
11. van Eck, N., Waltman, L.: Software survey: VOSviewer, a computer program for bibliometric mapping. Scientometrics 84(2), 523–538 (2009)
12. Dwivedi, Y.K., Venkitachalam, K., Sharif, A.M., Al-Karaghouli, W., Weerakkody, V.: Research trends in knowledge management: analyzing the past and predicting the future. Inf. Syst. Manage. 28(1), 43–56 (2011)
13. Lee, M.R., Chen, T.T.: Revealing research themes and trends in knowledge management: from 1995 to 2010. Knowl. Based Syst. 28, 47–58 (2012)
14. Steyvers, M., Griffiths, T.: Probabilistic topic models. In: Landauer, T., McNamara, D., Dennis, S., Kintsch, W. (eds.) Latent Semantic Analysis: A Road to Meaning, pp. 424–440. Laurence Erlbaum, Hillsdale (2007)
15. Blei, D.M., Ng, A.Y., Jordan, M.I.: Latent Dirichlet allocation. J. Mach. Learn. Res. 3, 993–1022 (2003)

16. Mann, G.S., Mimno, D., McCallum, A.: Bibliometric impact measures leveraging topic analysis. In: Proceedings of the 6th ACM/IEEE-CS Joint Conference on Digital Libraries, pp. 65–74. ACM (2006)
17. Gatti, C.J., Brooks, J.D., Nurre, S.G.: A historical analysis of the field of OR/MS using topic models. arXiv preprint arXiv:1510.05154 (2015)
18. Dam, H.K., Ghose, A.: Analyzing topics and trends in the PRIMA literature. In: Baldoni, M., Chopra, A.K., Son, T.C., Hirayama, K., Torroni, P. (eds.) PRIMA 2016. LNCS (LNAI), vol. 9862, pp. 216–229. Springer, Cham (2016). https://doi.org/10.1007/978-3-319-44832-9_13
19. Sun, L., Yin, Y.: Discovering themes and trends in transportation research using topic modeling. Transp. Res. Part C: Emerg. Technol. **77**, 49–66 (2017)
20. Syed, S., Spruit, M.: Full-text or abstract? examining topic coherence scores using latent Dirichlet allocation. In: 2017 IEEE International Conference on Data Science and Advanced Analytics (DSAA), pp. 165–174. IEEE (2017)
21. Sievert, C., Shirley, K.: LDAvis: a method for visualizing and interpreting topics. In: Proceedings of the Workshop on Interactive Language Learning, Visualization, and Interfaces, pp. 63–70. Association for Computational Linguistics (2014)
22. McInnes, L, Healy, J.: UMAP: Uniform Manifold Approximation and Projection for Dimension Reduction, ArXiv e-prints arXiv:1802.03426 (2018)
23. Kamukama, N., Ahiauzu, A., Ntayi, J.M.: Competitive advantage: mediator of intellectual capital and performance. J. Intellect. Capital **12**(1), 152–164 (2011)
24. Nobre, F.S., Walker, D.S.: A dynamic ability-based view of the organization. Int. J. Knowl. Manage. **7**(2), 86–101 (2011)
25. Cauwelier, P., Ribière, V.M., Bennet, A.: Team psychological safety and team learning: a cultural perspective. Learn. Organ. **23**(6), 458–468 (2016)
26. Rutten, W., Blaas-Franken, J., Martin, H.: The impact of (low) trust on knowledge sharing. J. Knowl. Manage. **20**(2), 199–214 (2016)
27. Minonne, C., Turner, G.: Business process management—are you ready for the future? Knowl. Process Manage. **19**(3), 111–120 (2012)
28. Wang, C., Han, Y.: Linking properties of knowledge with innovation performance: the moderate role of absorptive capacity. J. Knowl. Manage. **15**(5), 802–819 (2011)
29. Massaro, M., Dumay, J., Garlatti, A.: Public sector knowledge management: a structured literature review. J. Knowl. Manage. **19**(3), 530–558 (2015)
30. Zeghal, D., Maaloul, A.: Analysing value added as an indicator of intellectual capital and its consequences on company performance. J. Intellect. Capital **11**(1), 39–60 (2010)

Big Data and IOT

Extending the UTAUT2 Model to Understand the Entrepreneur Acceptance and Adopting Internet of Things (IoT)

Ahmad Abushakra[✉] and Davoud Nikbin

Faculty of Business, Sohar University, Sohar, Oman
{ashakra, dnikbin}@soharuni.edu.om

Abstract. The aim of this empirical study is to explore and discuss the factors that affect entrepreneurs acceptance and adoption of the Internet of Things (IoT) using UTAUT2 model. The study data was collected using a survey that was distributed among Omani entrepreneurs in six months period. The results showed that the relationship between information technology knowledge and entrepreneurs acceptance and adoption of the IoT was supported, like most other hypothesized relationships in the study.

Keywords: Internet of Things (IoT) · UTAUT2 · IT knowledge ·
Entrepreneurs · Oman

1 Introduction

1.1 Internet of Things (IoT)

The Internet of Things (IoT) also known as 'future internet' is a unique pattern with a simple idea of linking all things in the globe through the internet [1]. Defining schemes of physical objects that are independently connected together is one of IoT uses. IOT allows users to have limitless connection and linkage of physical objects to the internet in order provide better services. These linked or connected physical objects should have computation and communication abilities, such as mobile and social networks, in addition to smart elements and devices [2]. With recent developments and progresses in the internet technologies, internet of things (IoT) technology impact on our lives is increasing, and beginning to propose interesting and useful new services. The attention towards IoT technologies have been remarkably rising and with large number of applications in many different fields [3, 4]. The growing development of IoT has quickly increased in the world including Asian countries. In Oman the uses and applications of IoT can be described as primitive and still tyro, as the IoT industry is still a newfangled in the world. In addition that the individual users of IoT technologies may have some concerns related to privacy, security and data accessibility, specially collected by governments and companies [5, 6].

Modern and recent research nowadays tend to emphasis on the IoT design, architecture and implementation from the technical and practical perspective [7–10]. For example, [11] demonstrated the structure of IoT and talked about some essential

© Springer Nature Switzerland AG 2019
L. Uden et al. (Eds.): KMO 2019, CCIS 1027, pp. 339–347, 2019.
https://doi.org/10.1007/978-3-030-21451-7_29

topics and subjects of the IoT, such as its architecture and the interoperability, etc. [12] illustrated main technical topics, including internet scalability, heterogeneity, identification and addressing. Most of modern existing IoT studies have examined the application of IoT business model from the firm and government viewpoints [6, 12–14]. The research into the IoT acceptance from consumer perspective (e.g. entrepreneurs) is still in its early stages [15]. Furthermore, studies and research into the user acceptance of information technology (IT) has always been an important matter in information management [16–20].

Previous research comprehended poor insufficient fundamentals about consumer reception and acceptance of the new IT technology (i.e. IoT technology). The necessity of engaging more IoT users and maintaining them, casts the lights on identifying the influential factors of consumer acceptance of IoT applications, products and services. An overall inclusive study focusing on these factors can develop essential managerial modulations, on better, effective IoT products and services marketing to gain more consumer acceptance.

1.2   The Unified Theory of Acceptance and Use of Technology (UTAUT)

UTAUT was developed by Venkatesh in 2003 after he studied all different models that were suggested by other researchers aiming to understand users acceptance and adoption of technologies and innovation. Such models are TAM, TPB, TRA and in 2003. UTAUT was developed - which is the base model for this research, surpassed all other models- and later came UTAUT2. [21] Initially, [21] UTAUT involved four core constructs (performance expectancy, effort expectancy, social influence, and facilitating conditions), [19] reviewed and improved the model by adding more variables such as (price value, hedonic motivation and habit) in order to increase its descriptive power and named it UTAUT2. Therefore, in this study UTAUT2 was used as the base for this research for its validity and strength compared to other models.

UTAUT was criticized by different researchers such as [22] and [23] for not being tested on non-western countries such as Arab countries, which considered to show bias results through countries and contexts [24–27] testing UTAUT in this culture and situation is considered to be significant, as it can make it more strong and applicable model. [28] Reviewed the literature discussing UTAUT, and emphasized that researchers from other regions can start on original UTAUT studies related to context, since most of the studies were conducted in the USA. [28] focused on opportunities in the field for researchers to involve more and assist in improving UTAUT model, even though it has been previously developed, tested and improved by researchers, using the existing models, combining them with UTAUT, and addition of variables.

This research aims to extend the UTAUT2 model, by adding a new variable namely "IT Knowledge" in the field of technology, acceptance and adoption. This is an important consideration for a country such as Oman, in which several previous studies have clearly emphasized its significant role. For example, it has been clearly highlighted in past literature that people's lack of IT knowledge is a strong barrier to new technologies adoption in Oman [29]. The same issue has also been highlighted in other GCC countries such as Kuwait and Saudi Arabia [30, 31] making it an important variable to consider while adopting UTAUT2 in such countries.

2 Literature Review

The internet of things (IoT) is an interactive process that uses three internet layers in order to connect people with networks, smart objects and active intelligence [32, 33].

First and lowest part in the IoT structure is the device [34] it uses technologies such as RFID, NFC to collect data from substantial network and smart objects. [32, 35] and WSN [15, 34, 36] the availability of IoT services for users plays a great role in measuring how useful and valuable it's perceived.

Gateway and the main network are considered to be the second layer which is called the connection [34], the different devices and technologies at the device layer are evenly connected through the gateway, while the network provides the IP connection, which is supported by a range of different telecommunication infrastructure. using mobile devices and through cloud computing, data stored at the connection layer can be used, activated and observed by users. Services and applications used by the end user are considered to be the third layer, it can be situated at home, transportation and broader community such as retail, environment, factories and etc. [34]. The IoT concept have been described by different terms such as widespread or prevailing computing, machine to machine (M2 M), and sensor networks. [32, 34, 37].

The IoT applications are in various fields such as Health [35] logistics, [38], public services, transportations, retailing, agriculture and construction [38], manufacturing, supply chain management [34]. In order to improve operations and make them more effective, some of the applications allows gathering data on site and real-time [36, 38]. Numerous theories and models that were used to simplify and explain the relation between user acceptance and the use of technology such as the model of perceived credibility (PC), behavioral intentions (BI), theory of planned behavior (TPB), theory of reasoned action (TRA), innovation diffusion theory (IDT), technology acceptance models (TAM) [39], a hybrid model merging concepts from TAM and TPB and more, only few of them that have lead the path in investigations and results [19, 21].

Unified theory of acceptance and use of technology (UTAUT) was a result of studying and investigating different models and theories that discuss the user acceptance and its relation to the use of technology [15, 19, 35, 39, 40].

There are four main fundamentals for UTAUT that influence the behavioral intention to use technology, its performance expectancy (PE), effort expectancy (EE), social influence (SI), and facilitating conditions (FC) [19, 21, 41]. And in 2012 UTAUT was extend to UTAUT 2 including three new fundamentals hedonic motivation (HM), price value (PV), and Experience and Habit (EH) by Venkatesh named UTAUT2 [19].

3 IT Knowledge

The way people interact with the internet and its applications including IoT services is called IT knowledge [42]. According to [43] IT knowledge includes employees' knowledge of systems analysis and design, internet security knowledge, programming, web site design and skills in developing technologies. The customers' awareness of the current used technology and how it's being used and operates is important for the adoption of new technology and decreases their anxiety [44]. By examining the adoption of a third party apps in the US [45] concluded that technology awareness is a very significant factor for the adoption.

IT knowledge showed that it is an essential variable that influences the adoption of new technologies in Arab countries. For example, a research in Jordan was conducted on the intention to adopt electronic government services concluded that there are difficulties related to the computer knowledge and it plays a major role in the adoption of the technology by Jordanian [46]. Similarly, another study on innovation adoption in Saudi Arabia highlighted that organizations' technological willingness and employees' IT knowledge are amongst the main organizational characteristics influencing innovation adoption in Saudi Arabia [31]. Moreover, additional similar studies such as [47] and [43] emphasized that e-commerce adoption is influenced by the organizational IT readiness which denotes the technology infrastructure and employees' IT knowledge. Additionally, [48] pointed that organizational knowledge (training availability, technical expertise, and the level of knowledge) are connected to the level of e-business systems adoption (Fig. 1).

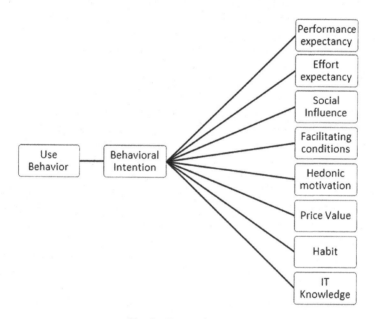

Fig. 1. Research model.

4 Methodology

This empirical study used a self-administered questionnaire for data gathering that was distributed to Omani entrepreneurs. The questionnaire was translated from English to Arabic for more effectiveness; some alterations were done for finalization after the reliability of measurement was confirmed through pilot test. Data collection period from February until June with a total of 110 collected questionnaires, by excluding incomplete and outlier cases, 93 questionnaires could be used. The respondents were mostly male with 56% compared to female who were 44%. In terms of marital status, most of the respondents were married (56%), followed by single (42%) and others (2.2%). With regards to education most of the respondents were educated with having bachelors (71%) and diploma (25%). All the items used in this research were adopted from previous literature.

5 Results

In order to test the significant path coefficients (relationship between variables in the model) bootstrapping with 500 sample cases was used. To find out whether the relationship is significant, we have looked at t-values derived from bootstrapping and all t-values above 1.65 were considered as significant relationships. This is based on [49] recommendation. In summary, out of 8 relationships in the model, 6 of them were supported. More specifically, the relationships between Performance Expectancy (PE), Social Influence (SI), and Facilitating Conditions (FC), Hedonic Motivation (HM), Habit (HT) and IT Knowledge (ITK) with Behavioral Intention (BI) were significant while the relationship between Effort Expectancy (EE) and Price Value (PV) with BI were not supported. Among all these significant relationships the effects of PE on BI was the strongest, implying that performance expectancy has the highest effect among all variables in UTAUT2 on intention to adopt Internet of Things (Table 1).

Table 1. Summary of relationship tests.

Relationship	t-values	Decision
PE => BI	2.420	Supported
EE => BI	0.101	Not Supported
SI => BI	1.959	Supported
FC => BI	1.865	Supported
HM => BI	1.775	Supported
HT =>BI	1.759	Supported
PV => BI	0.395	Not Supported
ITK => BI	1.648	Supported

6 Discussion and Conclusion

The aim of this study was to find the factors that influence entrepreneurs' adoption of IoT in Oman, through the use of UTAUT2 and extend the model after applying it to the study by adding a new variables. The additional variable was IT knowledge which hasn't been tested in the framework of IoT. The study results were harmonious with previous studies that applied such a model [50]. It indicated that performance expectancy is significant and powerful variable that influence the IoT adoption by entrepreneurs. Results showed entrepreneurs will not adopt IoT unless it's beneficial of their processes and operations. Furthermore, the results of this study did not confirm the relationship between effort expectancy and behavioral intentions which contradicts previous studies such as [51]. The social influence had a major and positive influence on IoT adoption as well. Another result that corresponded with pervious study for [52] was that entrepreneurs will go toward adopting IoT if they find that their competitors are using it. Moreover, it was found through the study that the simpler and easier the conditions were the greater the intention is to adopt to IoT by entrepreneurs, this is consistent with results of [53].

The hypothesized effect of hedonic motivation, which concentrates that entrepreneurs' motivation to adopt IoT is caused by the fun and pleasure of using the technology was confirmed and is consistent with previous literature [19, 54]. The study hypothesized that there is a relationship between price value and IoT adoption, but the results showed no relationship between them, which contradicts with the result from a study by [19]. Previous studies highlighted that effort expectancy is probably has no significant effect on IoT adoption. Comparing the influences of social and individual factors on entrepreneurs' perception on using IoT with the influence of its information technology knowledge will show a main factor, as they don't see that it's expensive. On the other hand the results showed a definite strong relationship between habit and IoT adoption. It shows that entrepreneurs are more likely to adopt the technology, if using the IoT services becomes a habit, this compound with the result of [19].

Lastly, the results of studying IT knowledge and its relation to IoT adoption, found that they have a strong relationship with each other. It shows that people motivation to adopt new technologies such as IoT is related to their knowledge and awareness of information technology, which agrees with the study by [55] in the field of technology adoption.

References

1. Tsai, C.-W., Lai, C.-F., Chiang, M.-C., Yang, L.T.: Data mining for Internet of Things: a survey. IEEE Commun. Surv. Tutorials **16**, 77–97 (2014)
2. Bekara, C.: Security issues and challenges for the IoT-based smart grid. Procedia Comput. Sci. **34**, 532–537 (2014)
3. Fantana, N., et al.: IoT applications—value creation for industry. In: Internet of Things: Converging Technologies for Smart Environments and Integrated Ecosystems, p. 153 (2013)
4. Schlick, J., Ferber, S., Hupp, J.: IoT applications–value creation for industry. River Publisher, Aalborg (2013)
5. Medaglia, C.M., Serbanati, A.: An overview of privacy and security issues in the Internet of Things. The Internet of Things, pp. 389–395. Springer, New York (2010). https://doi.org/10.1007/978-1-4419-1674-7_38
6. Weber, R.H.: Internet of Things-new security and privacy challenges. Comput. Law Secur. Rev. **26**, 23–30 (2010)
7. Khan, R., Khan, S.U., Zaheer, R., Khan, S.: Future internet: the internet of things architecture, possible applications and key challenges. In: 2012 10th International Conference on Frontiers of Information Technology (FIT), pp. 257–260. IEEE (2012)

8. Gubbi, J., Buyya, R., Marusic, S., Palaniswami, M.: Internet of Things (IoT): a vision, architectural elements, and future directions. Future Gener. Comput. Syst. **29**, 1645–1660 (2013)

9. Sundmaeker, H., Guillemin, P., Friess, P., Woelfflé, S.: Vision and challenges for realising the Internet of Things. Cluster Eur. Res. Projects Internet Things Eur. Commision **3**, 34–36 (2010)

10. Uckelmann, D., Harrison, M., Michahelles, F.: An architectural approach towards the future internet of things. In: Uckelmann, D., Harrison, M., Michahelles, F. (eds.) Architecting the Internet of Things, pp. 1–24. Springer, Heidelberg (2011). https://doi.org/10.1007/978-3-642-19157-2_1

11. Tan, L., Wang, N.: Future internet: the Internet of Things. In: 2010 3rd International Conference on Advanced Computer Theory and Engineering (ICACTE), pp. V5-376–V375-380. IEEE (2010)

12. Haller, S., Karnouskos, S., Schroth, C.: The Internet of Things in an Enterprise Context. In: Domingue, J., Fensel, D., Traverso, P. (eds.) FIS 2008. LNCS, vol. 5468, pp. 14–28. Springer, Heidelberg (2009). https://doi.org/10.1007/978-3-642-00985-3_2

13. Peoples, C., Parr, G., McClean, S., Scotney, B., Morrow, P.: Performance evaluation of green data centre management supporting sustainable growth of the internet of things. Simul. Model. Pract. Theory **34**, 221–242 (2013)

14. Zhao, J., Zheng, X., Dong, R., Shao, G.: The planning, construction, and management toward sustainable cities in China needs the Environmental Internet of Things. Int. J. Sustain. Dev. World Ecol. **20**, 195–198 (2013)

15. Gao, L., Bai, X.: A unified perspective on the factors influencing consumer acceptance of internet of things technology. Asia Pac. J. Market. Logistics **26**, 211–231 (2014)

16. Bandyopadhyay, K., Bandyopadhyay, S.: User acceptance of information technology across cultures. Int. J. Intercultural Inf. Manage. **2**, 218–231 (2010)

17. Luarn, P., Lin, H.-H.: Toward an understanding of the behavioral intention to use mobile banking. Comput. Hum. Behav. **21**, 873–891 (2005)

18. Mathieson, K.: Predicting user intentions: comparing the technology acceptance model with the theory of planned behavior. Inf. Syst. Res. **2**, 173–191 (1991)

19. Venkatesh, V., Thong, J.Y., Xu, X.: Consumer acceptance and use of information technology: extending the unified theory of acceptance and use of technology. MIS Q. **36**, 157–178 (2012)

20. Said Al Shibli, S., Abushakra, A., Khan, D., Rahman, F.: Perception of Academic Staff Over Their Career Due to Technology Implementation at Sohar University (2018)

21. Venkatesh, V., Morris, M.G., Davis, G.B., Davis, F.D.: User acceptance of information technology: toward a unified view. MIS Q. **27**, 425–478 (2003)

22. Teo, A.-C., Tan, G.W.-H., Ooi, K.-B., Hew, T.-S., Yew, K.-T.: The effects of convenience and speed in m-payment. Ind. Manage. Data Syst. **115**, 311–331 (2015)

23. Dwivedi, Yogesh K., Rana, Nripendra P., Chen, H., Williams, Michael D.: A meta-analysis of the Unified Theory of Acceptance and Use of Technology (UTAUT). In: Nüttgens, M., Gadatsch, A., Kautz, K., Schirmer, I., Blinn, N. (eds.) TDIT 2011. IAICT, vol. 366, pp. 155–170. Springer, Heidelberg (2011). https://doi.org/10.1007/978-3-642-24148-2_10

24. El-Masri, M., Tarhini, A.: Factors affecting the adoption of e-learning systems in Qatar and USA: extending the Unified Theory of Acceptance and Use of Technology 2 (UTAUT2). Educ. Technol. Res. Dev. **65**, 743–763 (2017)

25. Kamoun, F., Basel Almourad, M.: Accessibility as an integral factor in e-government web site evaluation: the case of Dubai e-government. Inf. Technol. People **27**, 208–228 (2014)

26. Alalwan, A.A., Dwivedi, Y.K., Rana, N.P., Lal, B., Williams, M.D.: Consumer adoption of Internet banking in Jordan: examining the role of hedonic motivation, habit, self-efficacy and trust. J. Financ. Serv. Market. **20**, 145–157 (2015)
27. Zhao, F., José Scavarda, A., Waxin, M.-F.: Key issues and challenges in e-government development: an integrative case study of the number one eCity in the Arab world. Inf. Technol. People **25**, 395–422 (2012)
28. Williams, M.D., Rana, N.P., Dwivedi, Y.K.: The unified theory of acceptance and use of technology (UTAUT): a literature review. J. Enterp. Inf. Manage. **28**, 443–488 (2015)
29. AlShihi, H.: E-government development and adoption dilemma: Oman case study. In: 6th International We-B (Working for e-Business) Conference (2005)
30. AlAwadhi, S., Morris, A.: The use of the UTAUT model in the adoption of e-government services in Kuwait. In: Hawaii International Conference on System Sciences, Proceedings of the 41st Annual, p. 219. IEEE (2008)
31. Al-Somali, S.A., Gholami, R., Clegg, B.: A stage-oriented model (SOM) for e-commerce adoption: a study of Saudi Arabian organisations. J. Manuf. Technol. Manage. **26**, 2–35 (2015)
32. HWA, L.J.: Antedecents and Outcome of Internet of Things Adoption: A Perspective of Public Listed Companies on Main Market Board of Bursa Malaysia (2015)
33. Luthra, S., Garg, D., Mangla, S.K., Berwal, Y.P.S.: Analyzing challenges to Internet of Things (IoT) adoption and diffusion: an Indian context. Procedia Comput. Sci. **125**, 733–739 (2018)
34. Hsu, C.-L., Lin, J.C.-C.: An empirical examination of consumer adoption of Internet of Things services: network externalities and concern for information privacy perspectives. Comput. Hum. Behav. **62**, 516–527 (2016)
35. Karahoca, A., Karahoca, D., Aksöz, M.: Examining intention to adopt to internet of things in healthcare technology products. Kybernetes **47**, 742–770 (2018)
36. Tu, M.: An exploratory study of Internet of Things (IoT) adoption intention in logistics and supply chain management-a mixed research approach. Int. J. Logistics Manage. **12**, 131–151 (2018)
37. Valmohammadi, C.: Examining the perception of Iranian organizations on Internet of Things solutions and applications. Ind. Commercial Training **48**, 104–108 (2016)
38. Dong, X., Chang, Y., Wang, Y., Yan, J.: Understanding usage of Internet of Things (IOT) systems in China: cognitive experience and affect experience as moderator. Inf. Technol. People **30**, 117–138 (2017)
39. Tarhini, A., El-Masri, M., Ali, M., Serrano, A.: Extending the UTAUT model to understand the customers' acceptance and use of internet banking in Lebanon: a structural equation modeling approach. Inf. Technol. People **29**, 830–849 (2016)
40. Oh, J.-C., Yoon, S.-J.: Predicting the use of online information services based on a modified UTAUT model. Behav. Inf. Technol. **33**, 716–729 (2014)
41. Brown, S.A., Venkatesh, V.: A model of adoption of technology in the household: a baseline model test and extension incorporating household life cycle. Manage. Inf. Syst. Q. **29**, 4 (2005)
42. Al-Momani, A.M., Mahmoud, M.A., Sharifuddin, M.: Modeling the adoption of internet of things services: a conceptual framework. Int. J. Appl. Res. **2**, 361–367 (2016)
43. Zhu, K., Kraemer, K., Xu, S.: Electronic business adoption by European firms: a cross-country assessment of the facilitators and inhibitors. Eur. J. Inf. Syst. **12**, 251–268 (2003)
44. Dimitrova, D.V., Chen, Y.-C.: Profiling the adopters of e-government information and services: the influence of psychological characteristics, civic mindedness, and information channels. Soc. Sci. Comput. Rev. **24**, 172–188 (2006)

45. Han, B., Wu, Y.A., Windsor, J.: User's adoption of free third-party security apps. J. Comput. Inf. Syst. **54**, 77–86 (2014)
46. Khasawneh, S., Jalghoum, Y., Harfoushi, O., Obiedat, R.: E-government program in Jordan: from inception to future plans. Int. J. Comput. Sci. Issues (IJCSI) **8**, 568 (2011)
47. Doolin, B., McQueen, B., Watton, M.: Internet strategies for established retailers: five case studies from New Zealand (2003)
48. Lin, H.-F., Lee, G.-G.: Impact of organizational learning and knowledge management factors on e-business adoption. Manage. Decis. **43**, 171–188 (2005)
49. Hair, J.F., Ringle, C.M., Sarstedt, M.: Partial least squares structural equation modeling: rigorous applications, better results and higher acceptance. Long Range Plann. **46**, 1–12 (2013)
50. Merhi, M.I.: Factors influencing higher education students to adopt podcast: an empirical study. Comput. Educ. **83**, 32–43 (2015)
51. Venkatesh, V., Zhang, X.: Unified theory of acceptance and use of technology: US vs. China. J. Glob. Inf. technology Manage. **13**, 5–27 (2010)
52. Chu, T.-H., Chen, Y.-Y.: With good we become good: understanding e-learning adoption by theory of planned behavior and group influences. Comput. Educ. **92**, 37–52 (2016)
53. Sawang, S., Sun, Y., Salim, S.A.: It's not only what I think but what they think! The moderating effect of social norms. Comput. Educ. **76**, 182–189 (2014)
54. Chen, Z., Xia, F., Huang, T., Bu, F., Wang, H.: A localization method for the Internet of Things. J. Supercomputing **63**, 657–674 (2013)
55. Thong, J.Y.: An integrated model of information systems adoption in small businesses. J. Manage. Inf. Syst. **15**, 187–214 (1999)

Internet of Things Adoption: Empirical Evidence from an Emerging Country

Davoud Nikbin[(⊠)] and Ahmad Abushakra

Faculty of Business, Sohar University, Sohar, Oman
{dnikbin, ashakra}@soharuni.edu.om

Abstract. The purpose of this study was to investigate factors affecting entrepreneurs' intention to adopt Internet of Things (IoT) in Oman using UTAUT2 theory. Data for this study were collected from Omani entrepreneurs in a time period of five months. Results indicated that all hypothesized relationships are supported except for the effects of price value and effort expectancy on intention to adopt IoT.

Keywords: Internet of Things (IoT) · UTAUT · Entrepreneurs · Oman

1 Introduction

Internet of things (IoT) is a process which is all about connecting people with networks smart objects, and active intelligence, through internet using three layers [1]. The very first layer is the device which is the lowest part of the IoT structure [2]. Second layer is the connection that consists of the gateway and the main network [2]. Third layer is the application layer which is the services and applications used by the end user [2]. With recent advances in internet technologies, IoT's impact on our lives has increased as it provides several advantages and new services. Due to that, IoT's development has increased rapidly not only in the world but also in Asian countries. However, it can be said that IoT is still an unexperienced industry worldwide, and this technology's application in Oman is still primitive and limited. From the individual users' perspective, such as entrepreneurs the IoT technologies is associated with certain concerns such as security and privacy [3, 4].

Different models have been used to understand users' acceptance and adoption of technologies and innovation. For examples, models such as TAM, TPB, TRA, UTAUT, and UTAUT2 were all popular for this purpose. [5] did his study by comparing the models and found that UTAUT is the best model for the purpose of understand technology acceptance and adoption. Researchers such as [6] and [7] have criticized UTAUT for showing bias across countries and contexts, since it has not been tested in non-western countries much, such as Arab countries [8–10]. Due to that, it is worthwhile to test the model in Arab countries which can increase the applicability and robustness of the model. In addition to above, [11] highlighted that although UTAUT has evolved and been tested and augmented by researchers making use of existing models in conjunction with UTAUT, but there are still ample and clear opportunities

© Springer Nature Switzerland AG 2019
L. Uden et al. (Eds.): KMO 2019, CCIS 1027, pp. 348–352, 2019.
https://doi.org/10.1007/978-3-030-21451-7_30

for researchers to engage with and further shape and develop the field. This research has extended the model by introducing personal innovativeness.

2 Literature Review

UTAUT was developed by [5] including four key constructs namely performance expectancy (PI), effort expectancy (EE), social influence (SI), and facilitating conditions (FC) that affect behavioral intention to use a technology [5, 12, 13]. Then [12] extended the UTAUT by adding three more constructs namely, hedonic motivation (HM), price value (PV), and Experience and Habit (EH) and was renamed as UTAUT2.

Performance expectancy (PE) has been defined as "the degree to which an individual believes that using the system will help him or her to attain gains in job performance" [5]. In both UTAUT and UTAUT2 performance expectancy has been considered as a predictor of behavioral intentions. Second variable is effort expectancy (EE) which has been defined as "the degree of ease associated with the use of the system" [5]. Similar to performance expectancy, effort expectancy has been a predictor of behavioral intentions in UTAUT. Third variable in the model is social influence (SI) which refers to "the degree to which an individual perceives that important others believe he or she should use the new system" [5]. Social influence is all about social pressure which comes from the external environment of the individual person and may affect his perception and behavior towards an action [5]. Social influence effect on behavioral intentions has been documented in past literature as well. Fourth variable in the model is facilitating conditions (FC) which is all about "the degree to which an individual believes that an organizational and technical infrastructure exists to support use of the system" [5]. In other words, and based on [14], it is all about providing external resources needed for the purpose of facilitating the performance of a behavior.

Besides all those UTAUT variables mentioned above, UTAUT2 includes few more variables. The first one is hedonic motivation (HM) which refers to the enjoyment which derives by using a technology [12]. in information system research it has been found that hedonic motivation positively and significantly affects intention to adopt a new technology [10, 12, 13]. The second additional variable in UTAUT2 is price value (PV) which refers to an "individuals' cognitive trade-off between the perceived benefits of the applications and the monetary cost for using them" [12]. [15] found that price value has a significant effect on behavioral intentions. The third additional variable is habit (HB) which is the extent to which people tend to perform behaviors automatically because of learning accumulated from their experience in using certain technology [12]. [16] have evidenced the role of habit as a determinant of technology usage and adoption.

This study has contributed to UTAUT2 theory by adding personal innovativeness. Personal innovativeness refers to the development or adoption of new behaviors or ideas that may relate to a technology, service, product, system, or practice [17]. It has also been defined as "the degree to which an individual is relatively earlier in adopting new ideas than the other members of a system" [18]. It clearly highlights that when a person is open to new ideas and intends to explore new things, that person is high in personal innovativeness. This suggest that being open to new ideas and frequently exploring new products determine the level of personal innovativeness. [19] found that personal innovativeness of the CEO is positively and significantly related to the information systems adoption in businesses.

3 Methodology

Data for this study were collected using a self-administered questionnaire. All items used in the survey (UTAUT2 factors and personal innovativeness) were borrowed and adapted from existing literature to ensure content validity. Omani entrepreneurs were respondents of this study and for that purpose the original items were translated into Arabic. Back translation approach was used to validate the finalized survey. Further to that, we conducted a pilot to test the reliability of measurement items which resulted in few minor modifications. The data collection was carried out from February to June for five months. Out of 110 received responses, only 93 items could be used as there were incomplete responses.

4 Results

SmartPLS 2.0 was used for data analysis as it is appropriate for small samples. A two-step approach recommended by [20] was utilized for analysis of data. The first step testing the validity and reliability of measures was the measurement model, while the second steps testing the relationships between main constructs was structural model. The analysis in the measurement model confirmed the discriminant and convergent validity thus allowing for further analysis.

Bootstrapping with 500 samples was utilized to test relationships among main constructs. To check the significance of the relationships among variables, recommendation from [20] was considered. Based on [20], relationships with t-values of 1.65 and above derived from bootstrapping are considered as significant relationships. In summary, out of 7 relationships stated in UTAUT2 model, 5 were supported. Additionally, the contributing factor to UTAUT2 which was personal innovativeness had a significant relationship with intention to adopt IoT (t-value = 1.77). Results did not find a significant relationship between price value (t-value = 0.329) as well as effort expectancy (t-value = 0.190) and intention to adopt IoT. Among all factors in UTAUT2 and personal innovativeness, performance expectancy had the strongest effect on entrepreneurs' intention to adopt IoT (t-value = 2.271).

5 Discussion and Conclusion

This study intended to find out factors that affect the adoption of IoT by entrepreneurs in a developing country. It intended to extend UTAUT2 by introducing a new variable. to do that, this study adopted all the variables in the model and extended the model by personal innovativeness which has not been tested before and especially in the context of IoT.

Practically, our results indicated that performance expectancy is an important and influential variable affecting adopting of IoT by entrepreneurs. This result is consistent with previous studies which adopted this model (e.g. [21, 22]). This result implies that entrepreneurs will adopt IoT if they find it useful in their operation. Our results however, highlighted that effort expectancy does not affect IoT adoption which contradicts with previous literature [e.g. 23]. Additionally, it was found that social influence affects IoT adoption positively and significantly. It implies that when entrepreneurs find that others or their competitors are using IoT, they will have higher intention to use this technology which is consistent with the results of [22]. Furthermore, our results found that facilitating conditions is significantly related to IoT adoption. It implies that when all facilitation conditions are there, entrepreneurs have a higher intention to adopt IoT which is consistent with the findings of [24].

Our results also confirmed the hypothesized effect of hedonic motivation on IoT adoption which is consistent with past literature [12, 25]. It highlights that fun and pleasure of using the technology motivates entrepreneurs to adopt this technology. Regarding the hypothesized relationship between price value and IoT adoption, our study did not find a significant relationship between them which contradicts with the findings of [12]. The possible reason could be that price value is more influential in other applications (e.g. e-commerce, e-ticketing and e-services) which is also highlighted in past studies. In fact, users feel that IoT services may not be expensive, and hence, it is not a major factor when compared to other social and individual factors in influencing entrepreneurs' perceptions towards using IoT. Moreover, our results confirmed the positive relationship between habit and IoT adoption supporting the results of [12]. It is clear that when using IoT services become a habit, entrepreneurs are most likely to adopt and use this technology.

Finally, as hypothesized our results found that personal innovativeness is significantly related to IoT adoption. It implies that a person's openness to try new things motivates a person to adopt the new technologies such as IoT. This is consistent with past studies in the area of technology adoption such as the study conducted by [19].

References

1. Luthra, S., Garg, D., Mangla, S.K., Berwal, Y.P.S.: Analyzing challenges to Internet of Things (IoT) adoption and diffusion: an Indian context. Procedia Computer Sci. **125**, 733–739 (2018)
2. Hsu, C.-L., Lin, J.C.-C.: An empirical examination of consumer adoption of Internet of Things services: Network externalities and concern for information privacy perspectives. Comput. Hum. Behav. **62**, 516–527 (2016)
3. Medaglia, Carlo Maria, Serbanati, Alexandru: An overview of privacy and security issues in the Internet of Things. The Internet of Things, pp. 389–395. Springer, New York (2010). https://doi.org/10.1007/978-1-4419-1674-7_38
4. Weber, R.H.: Internet of Things-new security and privacy challenges. Computer Law Secur. Rev. **26**, 23–30 (2010)
5. Venkatesh, V., Morris, M.G., Davis, G.B., Davis, F.D.: User acceptance of information technology: toward a unified view. MIS Q. **27**, 425–478 (2003)

6. Teo, A.-C., Tan, G.W.-H., Ooi, K.-B., Hew, T.-S., Yew, K.-T.: The effects of convenience and speed in m-payment. Ind. Manage. Data Syst. **115**, 311–331 (2015)
7. Dwivedi, Yogesh K., Rana, Nripendra P., Chen, Hsin, Williams, Michael D.: A Meta-analysis of the Unified Theory of Acceptance and Use of Technology (UTAUT). In: Nüttgens, Markus, Gadatsch, Andreas, Kautz, Karlheinz, Schirmer, Ingrid, Blinn, Nadine (eds.) TDIT 2011. IAICT, vol. 366, pp. 155–170. Springer, Heidelberg (2011). https://doi.org/10.1007/978-3-642-24148-2_10
8. El-Masri, M., Tarhini, A.: Factors affecting the adoption of e-learning systems in Qatar and USA: extending the Unified Theory of Acceptance and Use of Technology 2 (UTAUT2). Educ. Technol. Res. Dev. **65**, 743–763 (2017)
9. Kamoun, F., Basel Almourad, M.: Accessibility as an integral factor in e-government web site evaluation: the case of Dubai e-government. Inf. Technol. People **27**, 208–228 (2014)
10. Alalwan, A.A., Dwivedi, Y.K., Rana, N.P., Lal, B., Williams, M.D.: Consumer adoption of Internet banking in Jordan: examining the role of hedonic motivation, habit, self-efficacy and trust. J. Financ. Serv. Mark. **20**, 145–157 (2015)
11. Williams, M.D., Rana, N.P., Dwivedi, Y.K.: The unified theory of acceptance and use of technology (UTAUT): a literature review. J. Enterp. Inf. Manage. **28**, 443–488 (2015)
12. Venkatesh, V., Thong, J.Y., Xu, X.: Consumer acceptance and use of information technology: extending the unified theory of acceptance and use of technology. MIS Q. **36**, 157–178 (2012)
13. Brown, S.A., Venkatesh, V.: A model of adoption of technology in the household: A baseline model test and extension incorporating household life cycle. Manage. Inf. Syst. Q. **29**, 4 (2005)
14. Ajzen, I.: The Theory of Planned Behavior. Organizational Behavior and Decision Processes. University of Massachusetts at Amhers, Academic Press. Inc. (1991)
15. Tarhini, A., El-Masri, M., Ali, M., Serrano, A.: Extending the UTAUT model to understand the customers' acceptance and use of internet banking in Lebanon: a structural equation modeling approach. Inf. Technol. People **29**, 830–849 (2016)
16. Davis, F.D., Venkatesh, V.: Toward preprototype user acceptance testing of new information systems: implications for software project management. IEEE Trans. Eng. Manage. **51**, 31–46 (2004)
17. Damanpour, F., Wischnevsky, J.D.: Research on innovation in organizations: distinguishing innovation-generating from innovation-adopting organizations. J. Eng. Technol. Manage. **23**, 269–291 (2006)
18. Rogers, E.M.: Diffusion of innovations. Simon and Schuster (2010)
19. Thong, J.Y.: An integrated model of information systems adoption in small businesses. J. Manage. Inf. Syst. **15**, 187–214 (1999)
20. Hair, J.F., Ringle, C.M., Sarstedt, M.: Partial least squares structural equation modeling: Rigorous applications, better results and higher acceptance. Long Range Plan. **46**, 1–12 (2013)
21. Merhi, M.I.: Factors influencing higher education students to adopt podcast: an empirical study. Comput. Educ. **83**, 32–43 (2015)
22. Chu, T.-H., Chen, Y.-Y.: With good we become good: understanding e-learning adoption by theory of planned behavior and group influences. Comput. Educ. **92**, 37–52 (2016)
23. Venkatesh, V., Zhang, X.: Unified theory of acceptance and use of technology: US vs. China. J. Glob. Inf. technology Manage. **13**, 5–27 (2010)
24. Sawang, S., Sun, Y., Salim, S.A.: It's not only what I think but what they think! The moderating effect of social norms. Comput. Educ. **76**, 182–189 (2014)
25. Chen, Z., Xia, F., Huang, T., Bu, F., Wang, H.: A localization method for the Internet of Things. J. Supercomputing **63**, 657–674 (2013)

Design of an Identification System for Crop Monitoring as First Step to Implementing Precision Agriculture Technology: The Case of African Palm

Jose Cruzado Jimenez[1] and Katherine Andrea Cuartas Castro[2(✉)]

[1] Department of Engineering, District University Francisco Jose de Caldas,
Bogota, Colombia
[2] Department of Master on Business Administration,
National University of Kaohsiung, Kaohsiung City, Taiwan
kathecc91@gmail.com

Abstract. The use of emerging technologies brings multiple benefits to the agricultural sector, not only at an economic level, but also in reference to sustainability and the use of natural resources. Some technological systems make it possible to, among others things, improve the monitoring process of crops through (1) the identification of pests and diseases in plants to implement corrective and preventive measures, (2) the planning of different activities and crop rotation times such as planting, collection, pollination, etc. having a direct impact on the product quality, the crop useful life, its productivity and the producer income. In Colombia, the monitoring of extensive crops such as African palm (465,985 ha) is still manually done, therefore this work proposes a prototype identification system, designed and validates to provide data to an information system for the monitoring of each plants in African palm crops as a starting point (data collection) to implement precision agriculture in this agro sector.

Keywords: Precision agriculture · African palm · Crop productivity ·
Near field communication

1 Introduction

African palm has the highest yield in oil metric tons per hectare. In Colombia, the African palm farming contributes approximately 70% of the total production of vegetable oil. Colombia is currently the leading producer of palm oil in America and the fourth in the world [1], only in 2017 the production of crude palm oil was 1,632,667 tons, with an estimated value of 3.3 billion COP, its crops are present in more than 160 municipalities in 21 different departments, rallying more than 6000 producers and generating more than 170 thousand direct and indirect jobs [2], being a key sector in agriculture and national economy, however, agricultural activity is technologically lagging behind.

© Springer Nature Switzerland AG 2019
L. Uden et al. (Eds.): KMO 2019, CCIS 1027, pp. 353–363, 2019.
https://doi.org/10.1007/978-3-030-21451-7_31

Activities such as the monitoring of pests and diseases, and the planning of the different crop cycles are done manually increasing the error probability in the recognition, treatment and eradication of contaminated plants, as well as in the planning of planting activities, pollination, harvest, etc. which directly affects crop production, causing economic losses for farmers. The African palm crops are extensive, that is, its cover a vast territory, consequently the constant monitoring of the state and progress of the crop is a hard work, the workforce involve must supervise the cultivation lines and write down the information of each plant, when a diseased or contaminated palm is found, it is marked to be identified, which is why many of the palms are often overlooked and some of them are not treated, In addition, is cumbersome to walk a whole field again to find all sick plants marked, the workers responsible feel tedious and sometimes tend to get confused between crop lines [3–5].

Therefore, it is necessary to improve the techniques used for the oil palm production, to facilitate the farmers work and real-time monitoring of the variables that influence the growth of crops in order to increase their production. This work proposes the creation of an identification and monitoring system in place to get the individual data of each palm, to identify pests and diseases in a timely manner, and to facilitate the planning of different activities such as harvesting of fruits or pollination for the case of the hybrid plants, as well as supervising if the workers do their work properly. This work includes the first part of the project to implement precision agriculture in this sector, developing the first step concerning to data collection.

2 Precision Agriculture (PA) or Site Specific Crop Management (SSCM)

Precision agriculture corresponds to a management strategy that uses information and communications technology to collect data in order to support decisions associated with crop production [6]. Precision agriculture provides the ability to collect, interpret and apply specific information by transforming data and information into knowledge and profitability. These systems not only allow a more efficient agronomic management, but also allow to increase the precision of the tasks and the efficiency of the equipment (See Fig. 1).

Three stages are required to the PA [8, 9]:

1. **Data collection.** It is carried out with specialized equipment such as satellites or remote sensors.
2. **Data analysis.** An expert analyzes the data and issues suggestions to properly handle the detected spatio-temporal variation.
3. **Implementation.** The producer cultivates the land according to the recommendations.

Precision Agriculture, therefore groups systems used to analyze and control the spatio-temporal variation of land and crops, defined as (see Table 1).

PA manages the variables to use raw materials efficiently (e.g. water or fertilizers) [10]. It achieves greater sustainability by minimizing both the resources invested, as well as the environmental impact and agrifood risks, while maximizing production

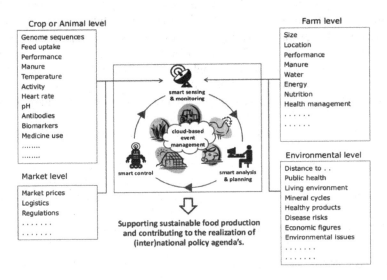

Fig. 1. Precision agriculture – Smart farming (Monitoring, Planning, Control [7])

Table 1. Spatio-temporal variation in crops

Set of variation	Variation factor	Description
Spatial	Soil fertility	• Physicochemical conditions (The acidity-alkalinity or pH, the content of nitrogen or metals, etc.) • Moisture content, organic matter and pollutants • Electrical and hydraulic conductivity • Texture, mechanical strength and depth • Salinity • The relief or topography of the land • Microbiota and fauna of the soil
	Vegetal growth and development	• Scrub • Pests (insects, viruses and microorganisms) • Genetic characteristics of the crop (such as resistance to drought and speed of development)
Temporal	Harvest	• Productive variation between different sowing periods • Weather conditions between different seasons

[11]. It also reduces up to 90% the use of agricultural inputs that are released to the environment (e.g. pesticides) [12]. Its use depends on information technologies, where communication between devices is one of the most important tools [13].

The technologies associated with precision agriculture can be grouped into five:

(a) **GPS:** The Global Positioning System is a space-based radio navigation system that provides reliable positioning, navigation, and timing services. GPS consists of three elements: satellites in orbit around the Earth, ground stations for tracking and control, and GPS receivers owned by users. In the PA, GPS has allowed registering the spatio-temporal variability and - controlling with geographical accuracy the agricultural machinery [14]. This is used in performance monitors, satellite banderilleros, autopilots or in variable application equipment [8]

(b) **Geographic information systems:** GIS are computer systems used to store, visualize and analyze geographically referred data In the PA, they allow the analysis of the information get through the different receptors (e.g. remote sensors), to make decisions about the management of the space-time variability [8]

(c) **Remote sensors:** Remote sensors are systems (satellite or portable) that get information about the crop, without having a physical contact with it. They are used in the data collection on the management of irrigation water, content of organic matter, vigor of plants (e.g. their content of chlorophyll), plant diseases, pests, mapping of scrubs, drought and floods [15]

(d) **Performance and application monitors:** are used to get information about the quantity and quality crop. Another type of monitors, those of variable application, are used to dose the amount of inputs for each section of the land (e.g. the dose of seeds or agrochemicals). Both types of monitors depend on the GPS. With the information gathered, productivity and soil characteristics maps are created, as well as models of plant growth. With these maps, the samples (as herbicides) are applied, covering the needs of each area of the crop [16]

(e) **Smart machines:** Some products harvest like fruits, requires intensive manual labor by temporary workers, which increases production costs. Smart harvesters capable to differentiating mature and immature fruits have been developed [17]. There are also flower detection systems in fruit trees that allow estimating production, the variable application of agrochemicals and automated fruit harvesting. In addition, there are automatic pilot systems that control agricultural machinery via GPS [18]

3 Methodology

The identification and monitoring system for African palms is an integrated system conformed by 3 operating subsystems: (1) identification system, (2) storage system and (3) WEB platform visualization system. The subsystems development is presented below.

3.1 Identification System

When the mobile device is close enough to the NFC label, it can read the data and redirect immediately to the location within the web page containing database. NFC technology is used due to its low operating cost in terms of response times (milliseconds) and power consumption (the reading of the identifiers is instantly).

The identification system is made up of:

(a) **NFC tags** (RFID 13.56 MHz/NFC KEYRING): key-type passive devices resistant to humidity, shock, constant handling and adverse weather conditions. They do not need electrical power and are activated only when the active device makes contact. The label contains a 1S50 chip (which can store up to 8 Kbits of memory, in 16 partitions, where each partition handles up to two group cryptography passwords, these partitions can be rewritten up to one hundred thousand times), and has an antenna that is powered passive of the reading and writing device when the latter approaches the label. The reading and writing distance respect to the active device is approximately 2.5 cm with a response time of maximum 2 ms.

(b) **The active -reader device** is a Samsung Galaxy S5 Smartphone because it is a reading device compatible with the selected labels.

For NFC writing, the "NFC tools" is used, it is a specialized and open software allows reading and writing in different types of data such as texts, applications links, e-mails, contacts, telephone numbers, messages, GPS location, WEB addresses, etc. of NFC tags and some RFID chips.

For the present project the system consists of an integrated application within the Smartphone and is migrated to a local server within it, the application NFCTools writes on the labels the URL to the palm of which is necessary to get information to consult or modify the data. The labels are written, with the corresponding URL in the network where the WEB page with local server is located, in addition to the individual identification code of each palm. In this way the reading device (Smartphone) does not need to be connected to the WIFI network, except when is necessary to visualize the location of the palms because the location reference is brought from Google maps. In addition to this the Smartphone must have enabled the use of the NFC system.

3.2   Storage System

It is the database system, for its construction first a model is made in tables, and then it is modeled in the MySQL WorkbenchS software.

3.2.1   Model in Tables

In this case, the database is formed by the following tables:

(a) **General crop characteristics**, it includes:

- The identification of each palm (corresponds to an 8-character code JCCJ00XX)
- Planting date (age)
- The classification of the palm that is given by its origin (Oleifera, Guineensis, hybrid) color of fruit (Nigrescens, Virescens, Albescens) and thickness of the shell (hard, piscifera, tenera). Including the possible combinations that these three parameters can generate.

- The state of the fruit (indicates if it is mature or immature)
- The density (indicate the space between a palm and the next one)
- The location into the crop that is determined by rows (furrow), columns (Palm) and lot.
- The geographical location refers to the coordinate on a satellite map.

(b) **Pests:** It stores information about the eight most significant pests affecting African palm crops. These pests can damage the foliage of crops, their stem, roots, etc. But as in other types of crops, it is possible to treat them to control or exterminate them. Each pest is identified with a name, the area of the affected palm and the treatment must be applied. There is also the "no-pest" field for plants that are not contaminated.

(c) **Diseases:** It stores information about the eight most significant diseases affecting African palm crops. The disease is identified with code, name, the palm area affected and its corresponding treatment.

(d) **Pollination**: This table apply only for Hybrid palms. In this case, it is necessary to know if the palm was pollinated or not and keep a pollination record. This table has the following fields: Palm code, pollination status, pollination date, census, Number of pollinations, user.

(e) **Productivity:** In this table is the number of bunches on which one normally works in fruit production and a relationship with the production level according to the number of bunches. The fields are: palm code, number of bunches, evaluation date, census and user.

(f) **Users:** The access records are stored per user. The parameters of the main user table correspond to an identification, user name, password and the user type. A user can be an Administrator, Supervisor or Evaluator, depending of it can have visualization, access, and permission to edit certain information.

3.2.2 Design of the Database Using MySQL Workbench

After specifying the design by tables, it is necessary to make a schema with a relationship entity model using the MySQL Workbench tool.

The relationship between all the tables results in a general database scheme that is shown below (see Fig. 2).

3.3 Visualization System

The web platform visualization system is created based on the principle of WAMP SERVER, a web development environment manages an Apache server, PHP and MySQL database. In the first instance, the graphic interface is developed using Artisteer. This interface consists of a series of tabs. These tabs are modified in PHP code using Notepad ++ text editor so that, each button and each integral part of the web page correctly execute the actions of both consultation and modification.

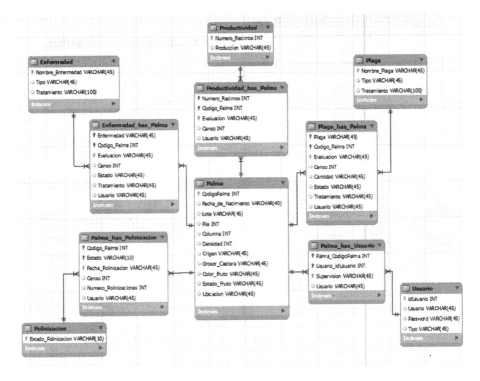

Fig. 2. General database scheme

After it works correctly, the system is migrated to the mobile device through the AndroPHP application. In the same way, the database is imported into PHPMyAdmin inside the device and then the server is restarted. This way, security is guaranteed in the system and its use without an internet connection, integrating the identification system, with the storage system inside the reading device, thus it is not necessary to consume external resources.

4   Results

The prototype identification and monitoring system is implemented by entering 100 records corresponding to 100 palms listed from 0 to 99 into the database. It is verified:

- When using the mobile device and reading the labels, it instantly redirects to the authentication platform where the access can be in three ways, as an administrator, an evaluator and a supervisor. In the three profiles, modifications and consultations are made.

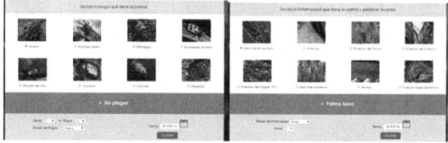

Fig. 3. Some System Visualizations when modifying and consulting

- The different viewing and access restrictions depending on the profile, which work correctly, checking the aesthetic and functional performance of the interface and the database.

Below are some visualizations of system tabs when modifying and consulting (See Fig. 3):

- Data is entered and modifications are made in some information about users and palms generating new records.
- Consultants of the modified and existing data are made, making random consults in the different tabs.
- The location of the palms is checked in a latitudinal way using the Google maps tool (See Fig. 4)
- Finally, the Update tab generates a file in SQL format, which will allow not only to have a backup copy of the modified database but also the possibility of uploading this data to a platform with WEB hosting. Then, files are generated and verified. In the spreadsheet of each of the previous cases, these spreadsheets are in a format that can be read Microsoft Excel (See Fig. 5)

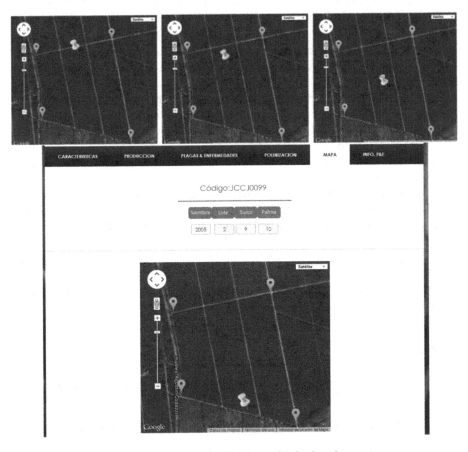

Fig. 4. System visualizations of Palm location

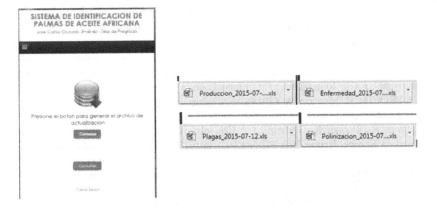

Fig. 5. Update tab and file generated

5 Conclusions

The identification system based on NFC tags allows to characterize individual traits of each of the palms within a crop quickly and conveniently, making use of two devices (mobile device + label) of low consumption and high communication speed. The consultations and records are made instantly, which represents an advantage in the supervision of the staff because it is necessary to be close to the Tag to make the readings and in this way it is guaranteed that the worker who makes the evaluation of the crop really comes to the plants to review it.

The storage system built on a MySQL database allows keeping a record of each palm in the crop as well as generating automatic records of evaluation and consultation of each worker responsible to supervise the crop. Generating a history for each one of the palms and workers involved, allowing a control of their work. A platform assembled on a web scheme using PHP allows the users involved in the process to visualize a friendly interface to manage a database, generating records in a simple way. In addition, it allows the identification and location of the palms within the crop while allowing to identify factors that affect the plant, such as diseases and pests.

In general, this project allows users to manage, recognize and control the parameters within the crop due to the information that the operation system provides.

References

1. Eric, J., Owen, B.: Fertilización de palma africana (Elaeis Guineensis Jacq.) Colombia (1992)
2. Fedepalma: The African palm indicators in Colombia (2018)
3. Leventin, E., McMahon, K.: Plants and Society, 5th Ed., pp. 177–86. McGrowHill, Chicago (2008)
4. Laura, C.N.: Informe Near Field Communication (NFC) (2012)
5. Junsuft, Tecnología NFC Near field communication [En línea], Noviembre del 2012
6. Best, S., León, L. Méndez, A., Flores, F., Aguilera, H.: Adopción y Desarrollo de tecnologías en Agricultura de Precisión. Boletín Digital N° 3, Progap-INIA, 100 p. Progap-INIA, Instituto de Investigaciones Agropecuarias, Chillán, Chile (2014)
7. Locker, R., Sander, J.: SC2 Workshop 1: Big Data challenges and solutions in agricultural and environmental research (2015)
8. Bongiovanni, R., Mantovani, E.C., Best, S., Roel, Á.: PROCISUR. Montevideo (2006)
9. Mantovani, E.C., Magdalena, C.: Manual de agricultura de precisión, pp. 1–178. IICA/PROCISUR, Montevideo (2014)
10. Plant RE. Comput Electron Agric. (2001)
11. Schrijver, R., Poppe, K., Daheim, C.: Brussels. Precision agriculture and the future of farming in Europe. Report No.: PE 581.892 (2016)
12. Aubert, B.A., Schroeder, A., Grimaudo, J.: IT as enabler of sustainable farming: An empirical analysis of farmers' adoption decision of precision agriculture technology. Decis. Support Syst. **54**(1), 510–520 (2012)
13. Nash, E., Korduan, P., Bill, R.: Precis. Agric. **10**, 546–60 (2013)
14. Neményi, M., Mesterházi, P.Á., Pecze, Z., Stépán, Z.: Comput. Electron. Agric. **40**, 45–55. (2012)

15. Lamb, D.W., Brown, R.B.: J. Agric. Eng. Res. **78**(2), 117–25 (2016)
16. Tellaeche, A., Burgos-Artizzu, X.P., Pajares, G., et al.: Comput. Electron. Agric. **6**, 144–55 (2016)
17. Nguyen, T.T., Vandevoorde, K., Wouters, N., et al.: Biosyst. Eng. **1**(46), 33–44 (2016)
18. Wouters, N., De Ketelaere, B., Deckers, T., De Baerdemaeker, J., Saeys, W.: Comput. Electron. Agric. **113**, 93–103 (2015)

Construing Microservice Architectures: State-of-the-Art Algorithms and Research Issues

Amit V. Nene[(⊠)], Christina Terese Joseph, and K. Chandrasekaran

Department of Computer Science and Engineering,
National Institute of Technology, Surathkal, Karnataka, India
amitnene1995@gmail.com

Abstract. Cloud Computing is one of the leading paradigms in the IT industry. Earlier, cloud applications used to be built as single monolithic applications, and are now built using the Microservices Architectural Style. Along with several advantages, the microservices architecture also introduce challenges at the infrastructural level. Five such concerns are identified and analysed in this paper. The paper presents the state-of-art in different infrastructural concerns of microservices, namely, load balancing, scheduling, energy efficiency, security and resource management of microservices. The paper also suggests some future trends and research domains in the field of microservices.

Keywords: Microservices · Scheduling · Load balancing ·
Energy efficiency · Security · Resource provisioning

1 Introduction

Cloud Computing is one of the key distributed paradigms driving the IT industry. It provides users the ability to avail cloud services without concerns about the scalability, availability and integrity. Earlier, the cloud services were built along the lines of monolithic architecture which meant that the entire service will be built as a single entity. This is currently being replaced by the Microservices architectural style. The Microservice Architecture fragments applications into independent, autonomous components called microservices. These microservices can be deployed across multiple Cloud datacenters which enables the Cloud Service Providers (CSPs) to cater to geographically wide spread users as well. The difference between Monolithic and Microservice architectural style is diagramatically illustrated in Figs. 1 and 2.

The use of microservices offers several benefits over the monolithic architecture. Along with these benefits, there are some issues in implementing microservices which need to be addressed.

© Springer Nature Switzerland AG 2019
L. Uden et al. (Eds.): KMO 2019, CCIS 1027, pp. 364–376, 2019.
https://doi.org/10.1007/978-3-030-21451-7_32

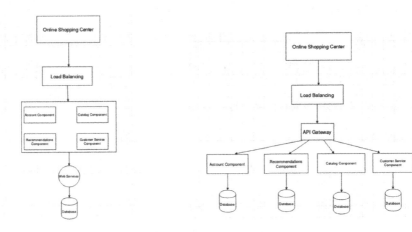

Fig. 1. Web Application (Monolithic) for online shopping application

Fig. 2. Microservice Application for online shopping application

The microservices run on multiple virtual entities. When a service request is received, it may have to be processed by one or more microservices. Thus, it may happen that some of the virtualized entities are overloaded others may be underloaded or even idle. Load Balancing needs to be done here to ensure proper distribution of the workload.

The Microservices are inter-connected with each other and communicate with each other through APIs. While designing microservices, it is believed that microservices trust each other. Thus, security attack on any of the microservice is a plausible threat to the entire application. This necessitates the need to implement stringent security policies.

The paper presents a critical review of the relevant works done in the 5 different concerns of microservices, namely load balancing for microservices, scheduling of microservices, security, energy efficiency and resource management for microservice applications as shown in Fig. 3 and presents some of the important findings with respect to these algorithms.

The remainder of the paper is organised as follows: In Sect. 2 state-of-art approaches for load balancing are presented, Sect. 3 presents approaches for scheduling of microservices, Sect. 5 presents security-related approaches, Sect. 6 discusses resource management approaches for microservices. Future research directions are presented in Sect. 7 and the paper is concluded in Sect. 8.

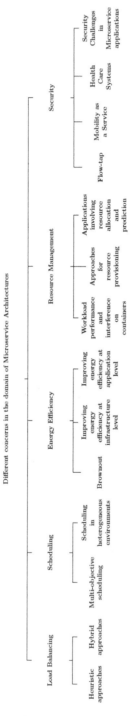

Fig. 3. Organization of this Survey

2   Load Balancing

The incoming requests are processed through various microservices. The arriving workload in the form of requests to microservices must be uniformly distributed across the various microservice instances. This is performed by load balancing algorithms. In this Section, heuristic and hybrid approaches for load balancing in microservice applications have been discussed.

2.1   Heuristic Approaches for Load Balancing

Benchara et al. proposed a heuristic algorithm for load balancing [1]. The tasks to be executed are submitted to a proxy microservice. This proxy microservice is responsible for deciding which microservice is most suitable for doing the job and assigns the job to that microservice. The microservice which is assigned the job executes it. The team leader microservice is assigned the job of co-ordinating among the team members and return the results to the proxy microservice, which in turn, returns the result to the requesting application.

2.2   Hybrid Strategies for Load Balancing

The hybrid algorithm proposed by Yin et al. [2] considers the following setup: Any task submitted to cloud environment for processing is first tried to be processed on edge devices, which if not possible, is sent to the cloud.

Various approaches designed for load balancing are as follows:

Single edge nodes: Single edge node is assigned the job of performing all the tasks.

Multi edge nodes: Each module of the given job is assigned to the most optimal edge node.

Edge node and cloud part: Some part of job is assigned to the edge nodes and the rest of the job is uploaded to the cloud to be executed on the cloud platform.

Entire cloud part: Entire job is uploaded to the cloud to be processed onto the cloud.

This algorithm considers network bandwidth, load of the task and available capacity of edge nodes.

2.3   Scenarios Where Load Balancing Can Be Applied

This section discusses about the application of load balancing in microservices based serverless computing scenario.

Serverless Computing. Serverless platforms [3] run RESTful web applications which are small in size and often termed as microservices.

For Load Balancing, either round robin policy is implemented, or the load balancing is done as per CPU load and incoming requests.

For experimentation purposes, Amazon Web Services (AWS) lambda has been used. The behavioural patterns are monitored for both containers and VMs. The standard deviation (SD) of number of service requests to different containers is calculated. Higher SD denotes unbalanced loads. During experimentation, it has been found out that SD for containers becomes almost zero as service requests increases while that for VMs remains same. Thus, it has been concluded that containers balance the load better than VMs.

A consolidated review of the different research works on load balancing is provided in Table 1.

Table 1. Summarisation of Load Balancing approaches for Microservices Applications

Paper	Parameters	Findings
[1]	Computation Time, Latency Time, Execution Time	This algorithm runs for every request
[2]	Send Time, Propagation Time, Processing Time, Bandwidth, Load of Task, Available Capacity of edge nodes	Reduces latency by assigning tasks to edge nodes instead of uploading to cloud
[3]	Average Service Execution Time, Number of operands, Array Size, Function Calls	Containers balance load better than VMs

3   Scheduling

The cloud providers receive high amount of service requests and they need to be executed within the constrained resources. This necessitates designing optimal scheduling algorithms. In this section, the different approaches for scheduling microservices like, Multi-objective Scheduling, Scheduling in heterogeneous environments have been analysed.

3.1   Multi-objective Scheduling

In the approach proposed by Bhamare et al. [4], it is assumed that there are N number of microservices to be scheduled on M machines. Each of the microservice has defined finish times. A weight is assigned to every microservice which is dependent on *number of dependent services in that chain* & *Time Spent in waiting queue*. The limitation of this algorithm is that it does not consider propagation latencies.

3.2 Microservices Scheduling in Heterogeneous Environments

Filip et al. proposed a scheduling algorithm for microservices across the Cloud and Edge environments [5]. This approach considers various parameters such as: *Submission Time* which is the time when the job is submitted. *Data in* which is the size of input data to the microservice. *Data out* which is the size of result data which the microservice outputs. *Deadline* which is the time before which the microservice has to be executed. *Bandwidth* which is the bandwidth offered by the network for transfer of data across the network. *Latency* is time required to send the data from one processing element to other. Execution time (i,j) is time to execute microservice i on processing element j. *Waiting time* is the time for which the processing element waits for new job.

The microservice request is executed on processing element which takes least processing time and would remain idle for least amount of time.

A summary of the comparison between various works on scheduling is provided in Table 2.

Table 2. Summarisation of Scheduling approaches for Microservices Applications

Paper	Parameters	Findings
[4]	Dependent jobs in chain, time spent by jobs in waiting queue	This approach does not consider propagation latencies
[5]	Submission Time, Data in, Data out, Deadline, Bandwidth, Latency, Execution Time, Waiting Time	Finding time for which processing element (PEs) has to wait cannot be found in advance

4 Energy Efficiency

Microservices execute on VMs or containers. As the amount of requests increase, CSPs may have to spawn new VMs to cater to those requests. But when the amount of requests decrease, CSPs may opt to de-spawn excess VMs to save energy. Also, it is observed that data-centers operate at only 30% efficiency. Thus, lots of energy gets consumed unnecessarily, which in turn increases operating costs. Thus, designing energy efficient solutions has become necessary. This section analyses different techniques to achieve energy efficiency like brownout, and energy efficiency techniques that can be adopted at infrastructure and application levels.

4.1 Brownout

The techniques like *Dynamic Voltage Frequency Scaling* and *VM consolidation* were used to save energy. But they cannot be effected when holistic data centers are heavily overloaded. To overcome these problems, a new solution of brownout [6] has been introduced wherein, the unnecessary components are shut down in emergency situations. This helps in power saving which in turn, helps to cater more consumers.

The algorithm finds out the mandatory microservices and optional microservices, as well as the connections between them. In this, the optional microservices are not shut down if a mandatory microservice is dependent on it or connected to it.

In *Least Discount* (LD) (to be paid to consumer on deactivating component) approach, components where least discounted needs to be offered are deactivated. In *Highest Utilisation, Lowest Discount* (HULD) approach, components with highest utilisation to discount ratio are deactivated. In *Least Utilisation* (LU) approach, components with lowest utilisation are deactivated.

4.2   Improving Energy Efficiency at Infrastructure Level

The algorithm proposed by Ruiu et al. [7] simply finds out the cost associated with SLA violation, degradation of QoS, and excessive usage of resource. It finds out which servers are idle or underloaded and simply shut them down. This algorithm simply shuts down the idle or underloaded VMs.

4.3   Improving Efficiency at Application Level

The algorithm [7] focusses on data intensive and latency sensitive applications. This algorithm tries to place application at proper locations for improving server utilization. For this, it uses the difference between latencies and Service Level Objectives. With this, it decides the application location for improving server utilization without compromising Quality of Service parameters. A consolidated view of the different works on energy efficiency is provided in Table 3.

Table 3. Summarisation of Energy Efficiency approaches in Microservice Applications

Paper	Parameters	Findings
[6]	Energy Saving Discount	LD approach is not dependable. HULD approach gives best results. LU approach does not give results as good as HULD
[7]	Underloaded or idle VMs	This approach does not find if some tasks of overloaded VMs can be migrated to underloaded or idle VMs
[7]	SLA constraints, Application latency	Approach designed under wrong assumption that latency increases only due to overload which may not always be true

5   Security

The services which get executed on microservices may tend to trust each other. Thus, compromise of any of the microservice may lead to security breach and breakdown of entire application. Thus, CSPs have to adopt security policies for cloud application. Detailed analysis of some of the solution follows.

5.1 Solutions to Provide Security to Microservice Based Applications

In this section, some of the solutions to provide security to microservice based applications like Flow-tap, Software defined membrane have been discussed and analysed.

Flow-Tap. Flow-tap [8] provides a mechanism of monitoring of network traffic. For this, it makes use of Software Defined Networking (SDNs). The Flow-tap creates a security VM which is responsible of analysing network traffic, anticipating possible threat and preventing attack. The issue with Flow-tap is that if source, destination are on same node while security is on other node, latency is increased due to tunnelling (sending messages to security VM).

5.2 Security Policies in Various Applications Based on Microservices

In this section, some of the applications like mobility applications, healthcare applications designed using microservices. These applications have been analysed for their various security requirements and the security measures which have currently been deployed.

Mobility as a Service. Callegati et al. [9] presented a case study about Mobility as a Service. The application provides for authentication of user profiles which provides that only the right user is going to access the required information and encryption which helps to maintain the integrity of the data. In this paper, author talks about security issues like *Data Provenness*, which means that the source of data is verifiable, *Data Trustworthiness*, which means that data should be cross-verifiable and should be good for error correction, *Maliciousness*, which means the ability of attacking the system from inside the system, and *External Threats*, which are caused because the microservices are exposed to public.

Health Care Systems. This case study [10] deals with Health Care Data Management systems. The different security concerns in such systems are as follows:

Break the Glass access facility is provided for emergency access to the system. To avoid possible threat, limited access to system can be provided in case of Break the Glass access.

Semantic Access Control also has to be done. This provides controlled privileges to different actors who would be accessing the system.

Privacy Protection has to be done in order to make sure that the sensitive data is protected from unauthorised access of the data. Data needs to be encrypted to avoid malicious use of sensitive data.

Protection Breach is responsible for notifying the events of privacy breaching. This is helpful in diagnosis of system in case of security breach of application.

5.3   Security Challenges in Microservices Based Application

This section briefs about various levels of microservice architecture which are directly under the threat of security attacks. Also, some of the principles, which can be adopted for security of microservice applications have been analysed.

In the paper [11], Yarygina et al. presented the different levels of microservices architecture where possible attacks can be done, which are (1) *Hardware*, which is vendor designed and can easily be compromised.

(2) *Virtualization* - Since, OS processes are tightly coupled to each other compromising one of them makes the job of taking entire system under control. Some of the possible attacks can be hypervisor compromise, shared memory attacks.

(3) *Services*, which include possible attacks like SQL injection, disruption on authentication, exposing of sensitive data possibly leading to data theft.

(4) *Cloud*, which is entirely under control of provider highly makes it possible for the provider to encroach the system or disrupting the normal behaviour of the system.

(5) *Network* level attacks which include sniffing, Man in the Middle (MiTM) attack, Denial of the Service (DoS).

and (6) *Orchestration* which means making proper arrangements of the system so that the system renders required results. At this level, normal scheduling of microservices can be disrupted, network routing may be disrupted, malicious nodes may be inserted in the system leading to possible loss of the data.

As opposed to the popular assumption of mutual trust among all the microservices, the author proposes a law of *Trust No One* to avoid Daisy Chaining in case of compromise of any of the microservices.

The author suggests use of 2 techniques namely (1). Mutual Transport Layer Security (MTLS) with self-hosted Public Key Infrastructure (PKI) & (2). Token based local authentication.

The various works on security for microservices are listed and compared in Table 4.

6   Resource Management

CSPs receive enormous number of microservice requests which they need to process within limited resource constraints meeting the SLA constraints and without any loss of performance. Resource management is the allocation of limited resources for execution of incoming requests, so that all the requests can be processed optimally. Discussion of some of such algorithms follows.

6.1   Workload Performance and Interference on Containers

In the research conducted by Kant et al. [12], the usage of CPU, memory, disk and network on containerised docker platform has been studied. The authors have calculated the execution time when the containers were placed on n different cores, same cores with and without equal shares to resources. The author

Table 4. Summarisation of Security approaches for Microservice Applications

Paper	Parameters	Findings
[8]	Monitoring Network Traffic, Network latency	Redirection of necessary flows reduces Network Traffic
[9]	Data Provenness, Trustworthiness, Maliciousness, External Threats	Provenness of originator on the basis of reputation is not dependable Function call tracing is a good measure to prevent internal attacks
[10]	Access Control, Privacy Protection, Breach notification	Limited access to system can be done to avoid losses in Breaking Glass access Logging network events can prevent future damages
[11]	Security Tokens, Mutual Transport Layer Security	Clock synchronisation between Sender and Receiver is necessary Confidentiality of private key is necessary Period for update of CA certificate is very crucial

also calculated the bandwidth requirements for operations like copy, add, scale, triad for different number of containers. Containers incur high network latencies when network usage increases. Performance on containers becomes worse as compared to native hosts when workload increases since CPU cannot process NIC interrupts. I/O processing speed remains same even on increase in number of containers.

6.2 Approaches for Resource Provisioning

This section focusses mainly on analysis of application which provides service to multiple users while maintaining mutual exclusion of resources, privacy of users constrained to maintained performance of application for every user, within the limited amount of resources.

Multi-tenancy. The cloud provider would like to provide cloud services to multiple number of consumers. The services of different consumers running on containers have to be isolated from each other. The containers expose management functionality through APIs. Nikol et al. [13] aims to isolate service of different tenants, removing unused software from the containers.

The solution proposes memory saving techniques by keeping only the essential parts in the container and removing the needless parts. The externalised parts can be achieved outside the container using APIs.

6.3   Applications Involving Resource Allocation and Prediction

This section mainly analyses a video surveillance application which involves prediction of resources for different video applications and allocation of resources to those applications depending upon their availability.

In the resource prediction approach [14] suggested by the Zhang et al., they consider CPU usage, memory, uplink bandwidth, and downlink bandwidth. The resource prediction process occurs after every p time intervals. The resources are rescheduled as predicted by the model.

This algorithm implements best fit policy so that most of the services can be satisfied. Initial resource prediction used to be based on past experiences which is not so dependable. Initial prediction of resources is based on similar task. Finding similar task may be time consuming. While Resource allocation, if none of the physical machines meet resource requirements of the task, task is randomly assigned to the host.

Various works on resource management for microservices are summarized and analysed in Table 5.

Table 5. Summarisation of approaches for Resource Provisioning in Microservice Applications

Paper	Parameters	Findings
[12]	CPU Usage, Disk Performance, Memory Performance, Network Performance	High Network usage causes High latency on containers I/O speed remain unaffected by increase in containers Increase in requests increase the latency irrespective of number of containers Increase in containers causes High Disk contention Resource sharing Increases latency Latency remains constant when containers are pinned to separate or same cores CPU resources are shared equally among all the containers Increase in Containers decrease memory bandwidth Pinning containers to separate sockets provides high bandwidth
[13]	Hard Disk, RAM, Time for first response (TFFR)	Separate runtime for each service. Increased service overhead 3 resource freeing choices Reduction in usage 37% in Hard Disk, 50% in RAM, 28% in TFFR
[14]	Resource Allocation, Resource Prediction	Initial Resource Prediction is done with respect to similar tasks in the past Containers support more requests than VMs

7   Research Opportunities in Microservices

This Section presents few research directions in the domain of microservices.

(1) The topic of Scheduling of microservices has not been explored by the researchers. This topic has a wide scope of research and improvements. Also, deciding the optimal node on which the microservice request is to be processed, so that the resource can be utilised to the fullest, minimising idle time of nodes, has not been researched upon.

(2) On the other hand, the domain of security of microservice applications have been quite a bit explored. But, solutions to prevent internal attacks (the attacks launched by users with privileged permissions to the system) have still a great scope to explore. Some of the papers suggest a solution of loging of events and analysis of such logs. But, such solutions cannot prevent damages.

(3) Some of the service requests require some specific execution environments for their execution. For example, some requests require some heavy packages to be pre-loaded in the environment before it can get executed. Loading these packages in the execution environment requires time which increases execution latency of the requests. This domain is wide open for future research.

(4) Most of the approaches have considered that total computational latency of any microservice request is necessarily equal to execution latency plus the fixed propagation latency. The propagation latencies are assumed to be fixed which may not always be true due to changing network conditions.

(5) Rescheduling policies for microservices, for improving utilisation of resources, is not explored. It has a very wide scope of research.

(6) Tools for performance evaluation of microservices at server is widely explored. But, tools for monitoring end to end performance of microservices like execution latency, is not explored much and has a great potential for research.

(7) Optimal algorithms to predict execution time of a service request on the basis of similar requests served in the past need to be devised.

8   Conclusion

In this paper, we have discussed various algorithms related to microservices from different aspects like Load Balancing, Scheduling, Energy Efficiency, Security and Resource Provisioning. A wide range of approaches regarding these aspects along with few case studies have been summarised, analysed to synthesize some important results which have been listed in this paper. The interested reader can take this work further to include the state-of-the-art algorithms, use the results to carry out research work which may include some good approaches and find methods to overcome some of the flaws in the existent algorithms. Future trends and research domains in microservices have also been included in this paper.

References

1. Benchara, F.Z., Youssfi, M., Bouattane, O., Ouajji, H.: A New Efficient Distributed Computing Middleware based on Cloud Micro-Services for HPC 978-1-5090-5146-5/16/$31.00©2016 IEEE (2016)
2. Yin, J., Ali, R., Li, L., Ma, W., Ali, A.: Edge Network Model Based on Double Dimension 978-1-5386-4649-6/18/$31.00©2018 IEEE (2018)
3. Lloyd, W., Ramesh, S., Chinthalapati, S., Ly, L., Pallickara, S.: Serverless computing: an investigation of factors influencing microservice performance. In: 2018 IEEE International Conference on Cloud Engineering (2018)
4. Bhamare, D., Samaka, M., Erbad, A., Jain, R., Gupta, L., Chan, H.A.: Multi-objective scheduling of micro-services for optimal service function chains. In: IEEE ICC 2017 SAC Symposium Cloud Communications and Networking Track (2017)
5. Filip, I.-D., Pop, F., Serbanescu, C., Choi, C.: Microservices scheduling model over heterogeneous cloud-edge environments as support for IoT applications. IEEE Internet Things J. https://doi.org/10.1109/JIOT.2018.2792940
6. Xu, M., Dastjerdi, A.V., Buyya, R.: Energy efficient scheduling of cloud application components with brownout. IEEE Trans. Sustain. Comput. 1(2), 40–53 (2016)
7. Ruiu, P., Scionti, A., Nider, J., Rapoport, M.: Workload management for power efficiency in heterogeneous data centers. In: 2016 10th International Conference on Complex, Intelligent, and Software Intensive Systems (2016)
8. Sun, Y., Nanda, S., Jaeger, T.: Security-as-a-service for microservices-based cloud applications. In: 2015 IEEE 7th International Conference on Cloud Computing Technology and Science (2015)
9. Callegati, F., Giallorenzo, S., Melis, A., Prandini, M.: Data security issues in MaaS-enabling platforms. In: 2016 IEEE 2nd International Forum on Research and Technologies for Society and Industry Leveraging a better tomorrow (RTSI) (2016)
10. Esposito, C., Castiglione, A., Tudorica, C.-A., Pop, F.: Security and privacy for cloud-based data management in the health network service chain: a microservice approach. IEEE Commun. Mag. 55(9), 102–108 (2017)
11. Yarygina, T., Bagge, A.H.: Overcoming security challenges in microservice architectures. In: 2018 IEEE Symposium on Service-Oriented System Engineering (2018)
12. Garg, S.K., Lakshmi, J.: Workload Performance and Interference on Containers 978-1-5386-0435-9/17/$31.00©2017 IEEE (2017)
13. Nikol, G., Träger, M., Harrer, S., Wirtz, G.: Service-oriented Multi-tenancy (SO-MT): enabling multi-tenancy for existing service composition engines with docker. In: 2016 IEEE Symposium on Service-Oriented System Engineering (2016)
14. Zhang, H., Ma, H., Fu, G., Yang, X., Jiang, Z., Gao, Y.: Container based video surveillance cloud service with fine-grained resource provisioning. In: 2016 IEEE 9th International Conference on Cloud Computing (2016)

Knowledge Transfer and Learning

Knowledge Governance Helps Minimizing the Risks of External Knowledge Transfer

Reinhard Bernsteiner[(⊠)], Johannes Strasser, Christian Ploder,
Stephan Schlögl, and Thomas Dilger

Department Management, Communication and IT,
Management Center Innsbruck, Innsbruck, Austria
reinhard.bernsteiner@mci.edu

Abstract. Initiatives to cooperate with external stakeholders are set up by more and more companies. The intention of those initiatives is to get a better understanding of market developments and new technologies very quickly. This should improve innovation processes which should lead a competitive advantage.

Transferring knowledge from the company to external stakeholders is required in order to enable them to contribute in the innovation project effectively. This knowledge transfer incorporates risks in terms of knowledge leakage, which can easily harm an organization.

This paper focusses on the risks of external knowledge transfer and potential countermeasures. Based on a literature review an empirical survey was conducted. A qualitative research approach was used to gain diversified opinions and insights on the research domain.

The results show that the experts are highly aware of the potential risks that go in line with knowledge transfer initiatives for example in the context of open innovation settings. Countermeasures are proposed in literature and by the participants of the survey.

Consequently, the study reveals that knowledge governance processes, that are part of a comprehensive knowledge management system, have to be implemented. They are intended to avoid unintentional knowledge leakage and guide knowledge transfer processes.

Keywords: Knowledge governance · Knowledge leakage ·
Knowledge transfer · Open innovation

1 Introduction

Over the past decade, more and more enterprises reach out beyond their company borders in order to improve their innovation processes and guarantee their competitive advantage by cooperating with external stakeholders [1–3]. Their primary aim is to understand new technological as well as market developments outside the company in a more effective way [4]. Open innovation applies "the use of purposive inflows and outflows of knowledge to accelerate internal innovation, and expand the markets for external use of innovation, respectively" [5]. Typical examples of open innovation concepts are crowdsourcing, co-creation, user innovation or design thinking [6–10].

© Springer Nature Switzerland AG 2019
L. Uden et al. (Eds.): KMO 2019, CCIS 1027, pp. 379–391, 2019.
https://doi.org/10.1007/978-3-030-21451-7_33

These concepts are "active, dynamic, and social process based on interactions and relationships between firms and external stakeholders, oriented toward the generation of new products (i.e., goods and/or services)" [11].

All these initiatives require knowledge transfers to external stakeholders. External knowledge transfer in a systematic way is indispensable for companies to fully benefit from the value of knowledge provided by their stakeholders [12]. However, transferring information to the wrong external parties may lead to knowledge leakage and can therefore easily harm an organization [13].

The central aim of this work is to identify the risks of external knowledge transfer initiatives and their potential countermeasures as part of a knowledge governance system.

2 Knowledge Management and Knowledge Transfer

Knowledge is a key-driver within the modern economy [14]. Within the fast moving and globalized world, knowledge can be acquired and transferred rapidly across large geographical areas by using the internet [12]. "A firm's competitive advantage depends more than anything on its knowledge, or to be slightly more specific, on what it knows – how it uses what it knows – and how fast it can know something new" [15].

Constant innovation, the free flow of knowledge and the ability to manage intangible assets require a solid Knowledge Management (KM).

One of the most influencing models on knowledge management is the work of Nonaka and Takeuchi. Their SECI-model defines a knowledge creation and conversion process, from implicit knowledge to explicit knowledge [16]. Polanyi plays a crucial role in the Nonaka's theories because Nonaka often refers to Polanyi [17].

It is not only about generating the right knowledge. The concept of KM also aims to provide organizations with the knowledge that will actually create benefit for them. Successful KM assumes that the right knowledge is provided at the right place at the right time [18]. The management of knowledge is consequently becoming increasingly important in order to stay competitive as well as to gain sustainable and effective benefits related to profitability and organizational survival [19]. Literature describes KM therefore as a "mainstream organizational necessity" [20].

The terms "knowledge transfer" and "knowledge sharing" are sometimes used synonymously. Paulin and Suneson discuss different definitions of these terms in a broad way [21]. In this work the term knowledge transfer is used, based on the definition of [22] who defines knowledge transfer as "The focused, unidirectional communication of knowledge between individuals, groups or organizations such that the recipient of knowledge (a) has a cognitive understanding, (b) has the ability to apply the knowledge, or (c) applies the knowledge."

This definition is appropriate with respect to the research endeavour, because enterprises first have to transfer knowledge to external parties in order to enable them to contribute to the open innovation initiative.

3   Knowledge Leakage

Knowledge leakage in general is defined as "the loss of knowledge intended to stay within a firm's boundaries" [23]. In other words, it is described as "the extent to which the focal firm's private knowledge is intentionally appropriated by or unintentionally transferred to partners" [24]. Hence, literature differs between intentional and unintentional leakage of knowledge [25]. Intentional knowledge leakage occurs through voluntary knowledge transfer to external parties by integrating them into business activities [26]. Unintentional or accidental knowledge leakage emerges when the focal organization is not aware of the knowledge transfer to a third party [27]. In this paper the term knowledge leakage explicitly represents both forms, more precisely, knowledge leakage in form of knowledge exposure [28]. Knowledge exposure is hard to avoid, especially if a firm develops an innovative new product [29]. It primarily arises through interactions and collaborations with people [26].

Within the operating environment, there is on the one hand the organizational environment which represents the innovative company. On the other hand, it also considers external parties within the knowledge transfer initiatives. Externals brainstorm ideas and knowledge either through offline or online initiatives in order to solve a certain problematic for the innovative firm [30]. The activity of knowledge exploration then represents the outbound knowledge inflow towards the organizational environment which further aims to maintain this knowledge [31]. This knowledge retention combined with the knowledge transfer can already encourage a reduction of the risks related to knowledge leakage [32].

Dedicated KM finally leads to new organizational knowledge which potentially can be commercialized on the market (Gould, 2012). Knowledge leakage emerges due to the dynamic interactions between the innovative company and its customers, competitors, suppliers or other external stakeholders [33]. As soon as a firm opens-up to the outside, e.g. through collaborating within an Open innovation network, the risk of knowledge seepage appears [28]. Innovation initiators may transmit important information or knowledge to external participants within the Open innovation environment [26, 34]. Organizations may lose their competitive advantage and industry position due to this knowledge leakage [23].

The risk of knowledge exposure may increase due to different factors. It increases with the external partner's disposability of adequate absorptive capability [28]. Absorptive capacity is "the ability to recognize the value of new information, assimilate it, and apply it to commercial ends" [35]. Also the absorptive capability embraces knowledge leakage. It describes the external partner's feasibility, e.g. to implement the knowledge he or she gained from the other partner [36].

In order to prevent from knowledge leakage, companies require sophisticated knowledge protection mechanisms.

4   Knowledge Guarding

Ensuring knowledge security is among the top issues in KM [37, 38]. However, studies show that organizations lack comprehensive and systematic mechanisms in order to guarantee knowledge security [39]. This enhances knowledge leakage and implicates negative productivity consequences [40]. In general, research argues that less participants in open innovation initiatives decrease the risk of knowledge leakage. Small compositions of teams ensure a better information control [28, 41]. Moreover, the type of the external partner has a significant impact on potential knowledge disclosure. For instance, competitors have a higher tendency to expose and misuse knowledge rather than non-competitors. A reduction of the scope of cooperation decrease the risk of knowledge leakage as well [38]. Retaining a safe distance in the participants' engagement as well as a limitation of communication confine knowledge transfer. All these measures may contribute to a "myopia of protectiveness" [42]. This anxiety for knowledge leakage motivate organizations to not participate in collaboration initiatives at all [43]. The result may be a reduction of collaborations which then leads to less innovative ideas. Fear of knowledge loss therefore harms the competitiveness of a firm. It requires therefore a well-developed balance between openness and closeness [30].

Four different measures to foster knowledge protection within an organization can be identified: stakeholder engagement, strategic-level management initiatives, operational-level management initiatives, and legal measures. Literature suggests to combine these protective mechanisms in order to maximize knowledge security [39].

4.1   Stakeholder Engagement

Knowledge leakage is mostly the result of collaborations and knowledge exchanges with different internal as well as external stakeholders. The key-stakeholders in open innovation are customers, competitors, suppliers, innovation networks and universities [40]. However, it is fundamental to mention that knowledge leakage can occur everywhere as soon as there are interactions between people and organizations [28]. Examples could be universities or public services. Therefore, a solid stakeholder management is indispensable to cope with knowledge leakage [44].

Researchers argue that authentic stakeholder engagement helps to prevent fraudulent use of knowledge [30]. As a result, it is vital to consider not only organizational, but also ethical and social benefits related to relationship building with innovation partners [45]. Effective engagement represents a dialogue of the involved parties, not a one-way communication. Stakeholder engagement and knowledge transfer need to be based on trust and loyalty. The reason behind is the fact that "a culture of loyalty is likely to reduce leakage of knowledge" [32]. The meaning of trust assumes that an organization may expect its innovation partners to behave in a positive way. There are two different types of trust, goodwill and competence trust [24]. Goodwill trust is based on good faith, emotions, integrity and aims to care about another partner's wellbeing. Competence trust on the contrary is more rational and represents the partner's capability of fulfilling obligations and tasks based on past behaviors, dependability as well as predictability. In this paper, the term trust represents both forms.

Attentive stakeholder engagement strengthens the performance as well as the accountability among the participants [46]. The resulting relationship development leads to a social value creation. Organizations may now put the potential threat of knowledge leakage into relation with all the benefits gained from the valuable stakeholder relationships [30].

4.2   Strategic-Level Management Initiatives

Companies need to exactly figure out what kind of knowledge needs to be guarded and different confidential levels have to be defined. Literature recommends organizations to develop, implement and resource relevant policies, processes and guidelines concerning knowledge guarding. These measures focus on knowledge transfer, intellectual property rights, screening of participants before assigning them in the firm and refer to an appropriate usage of communication technologies like social media collaboration [39]. Resulting, the identification of key roles within the firm is required. A key role may for instance be a gatekeeper who monitor and control the potential knowledge leakage threat. Another role may involve a management role which oversees the entire efforts related to knowledge guarding [47]. Apart from creating role positions, literature also suggest to establish a whole knowledge management department [48]. Furthermore, knowledge protection procedures shall monitor knowledge exchange among people. Creating a security culture including regular trainings concerning knowledge guarding measures embrace the awareness of the participants and reduces the risk of knowledge leakage [39].

4.3   Operational-Level Management Initiatives

It is fundamental to develop and implement protective processes in order to guarantee the security of sensitive knowledge. Such procedures impact on the one hand the frequency of knowledge flows. Limiting knowledge flows decreases the risk of knowledge leakage. On the other hand, protective processes also impact the direction of knowledge flows. They affect collaboration activities related to knowledge sharing within the organization [39]. Knowledge guarding activities also include knowledge interactions with external parties like customers or partners [49]. Knowledge processes can be supported by information systems. These systems guarantee knowledge capturing before it leaks. Information systems also consider social factors and support businesses to be aware of the knowledge leakage procedure. As a consequence, organizations may take suitable actions like succession planning or risk management in order to ensure an effective and beneficial knowledge flow.

4.4   Operational-Level Management Initiatives

Non-disclosure agreements (NDAs), confidentiality agreements and contracts represent common legal frameworks to safeguard critical knowledge. Companies may protect their sensitive knowledge with copyrights [50]. Newly developed products can be protected with patents.

5 Empirical Survey

An empirical survey was conducted in order to get further insights from industry experts in order to get closer to the central aim of this project which is to identify the risks of external knowledge transfer and their potential countermeasures.

A qualitative research approach was selected to gain diversified opinions and insights on the research domain. Hence, the outcome of these conversations with the experts should be experience-centred. In order to assure a particular flexibility and openness, a problem-centric interview was used.

Based on the literature review a system of categories was derived deductively which represents the basis for the interview guideline.

Overall, ten interviews with experts, mainly in leading positions, in the field were conducted. The duration of the interviews was between 40 and 70 min. Every expert comes from a different country, nine from Europe and one from the United States. The interviews were recorded and transcribed verbatim. The material was analysed following Mayring's Qualitative Content Analysis procedure [51].

The following sections present the results of the interviews and reflects them against scientific literature.

5.1 Risks for Large Firms Applying External Knowledge Transfer

Literature identifies various risks related to the collaboration with different parties that require knowledge transfers [13]. Based on the analysis of the empirical data two sub-categories can be identified, (a) risks regarding the internal environment and (b) risks regarding the company's confidentiality.

Risks Related to the Internal Environment: The interviewed experts stress the importance of aligning the people and firm's culture with the objectives and purpose of the knowledge transfer initiative in order to gain the required internal support and attraction. Literature confirms that open innovation needs to become a part of the organization's culture in order to guarantee a high commitment of the involved parties [52]. Otherwise, internal R&D members may not be willing to accept external ideas and can even ignore the entire input from outside the company [42]. According to the interview partners, this so-called NIH-syndrome (Not-Invented-Here) emerges from the disruption of the internal culture. It leads to the fact that external innovations may get rejected by internal teams. Also the effective management of the enormous knowledge inflow is highly challenging [52]. Some participants consider coordination problems, communication problems, network management as well as project management as serious challenges when applying open innovation.

Risks Related to the Firm's Confidentiality: There are serious risks for large firms in regards to the protection and confidentiality of the generated ideas [53]. As reported by the interview partners, knowledge leakage and the resulting knowledge loss may emerge from the collaboration and knowledge transfer to external parties. Giving too much insights to external partners related to the organization's core knowledge and market opportunities can provoke the contamination of intellectual property. The experts underline that knowledge transfer initiatives enable partners to access critical knowledge and information. These external partners could generate valuable market benefits from leaked ideas and consequently might harm the competitiveness of initiator. Literature confirms that unauthorized knowledge leakage can have a negative impact on the confidentiality of an organization [54]. Moreover, the discussions with the interview participants reveal that unintentional knowledge outflow may further lead to lost investments and a damaged reputation of the leaked organization.

Intentional Knowledge Leakage: Intentional exposure of knowledge emerges from the voluntary transfer of knowledge with external partners by involving them into innovation activities [26]. The experts characterize intentional knowledge leakage as a voluntary transfer of knowledge to partners. This type of knowledge leakage arises from planned interactions with individuals within the innovation network. The experts point out that intentional knowledge leakage does not always need to be harmful for the focal firm. Research shows that positive knowledge leakage may result for instance from the knowledge spill over among collaboration partners [55]. One expert even stressed that "otherwise you don't have the necessary knowledge". Additionally, the participants point out that deliberate knowledge leakage in open innovation is easier to manage rather than unintentional knowledge exposure, since the focal organization may set up structured processes in order to tackle the leakage.

Unintentional Knowledge Leakage: Unintentional or so-called accidental leakage of knowledge occurs when the initiator is unaware of transferring the knowledge to external parties [56]. Involuntary or unplanned knowledge leakage is perceived by the interview experts as much more problematic compared to intentional knowledge leakage. As reported by the participants, accidentally communicated knowledge might lead to a misuse by a third party, for instance a critical competitor, and consequently provoke negative consequences for the open innovation initiator.

5.2   Implications of Knowledge Leakage for Large Firms

The central aim of this research project is to identify risks and related countermeasures of knowledge transfer. Nevertheless, knowledge leakage may also have positive effects on the organization. This is also confirmed by most participants of the empirical survey. Therefore, the beneficial effects are presented as well.

Positive Implications of Knowledge Leakage: Positive effects of knowledge exposure occur when the focal firm is actually taking advantage of the collaborations and interactions with innovation partners. The resulting knowledge inflows through external parties guarantee sustainable innovations as well as constant improvements [57]. A large portion of the experts underlined this fact. According to them, the positive effects result from knowledge spill over situations. Through knowledge transfer initiatives with interdisciplinary teams consisting of internal and external actors, the organization may generate valuable new ideas for product development as well as enhance its capacity of skills. Research approves that positive implications primarily emerge from intentional knowledge leakage.

Negative Implications of Knowledge Leakage: Negative effects of knowledge exposure may result from the usage of the generated ideas by a competitor [58]. As reported by the interview partners, this misuse can harm the competitiveness of the leaked organization. Other firms may benefit from the knowledge gained by the knowledge transfer initiatives. Besides, they might make use of the innovation before the focal firm can benefit from. The discussions with the experts reveal that the external partner's absorptive capability negatively influences the risk of knowledge leakage. When the partner actually possesses the capacity to successfully implement the leaked ideas on the market as well as to commercialize the resulting innovation, then the focal firm may lose its market position. As mentioned previously, research confirms that the negative implications of knowledge leakage increase with the partner's absorptive capability [28]. The experts further highlight that knowledge leakage may cause lost opportunities, lost investments and reputational damage for the leaked company. Literature shows that organizations may indeed lose their competitive advantage and industry position due to the negative implications of knowledge leakage [23].

5.3   Protective Mechanisms to Prevent Large Firms from Knowledge Leakage

Literature recommends to combine several protective mechanisms in order to reduce the risk of knowledge exposure [39]. A large portion of the interviewed experts also stresses that there are many combinable tactics for large firms to prevent knowledge leakage. Based on the literature review, the potential safeguard measures can be divided into four major categories. They are (a) stakeholder engagement, (b) strategic initiatives, (c) operational initiatives and (d) legal initiatives.

Stakeholder Engagement: It is proven that stakeholder engagement and knowledge transfer need to be based on trust and loyalty in order to lower the threat of knowledge leakage [33]. This goes in line with the statements from the experts, almost every expert confirmed that building and maintaining trust is among the top issues when preventing large firms from knowledge leakage. Research reveals that dedicated stakeholder engagement helps to mitigate the risk of knowledge exposure [59]. According to the participants, knowledge transfer initiatives have to include elements that are able to establish a trustworthy relationship. There is a necessity of a notion of trust and confidence among the stakeholders. Consequently, the experts recommend large firms to build dedicated partner relationships as well as to explicitly focus on relational and social capital. Additionally, creating social value with innovation partners may put the potential risk of knowledge leakage into relation with all the benefits gained from the valuable stakeholder relationships [30].

Strategic Initiatives: Companies exact need to figure out what knowledge needs to be guarded and how it has to be protected [39]. A large portion of the participants also suggests enterprises to clearly understand what their core knowledge is. Core knowledge is highly linked with the innovation or business. According to the experts, this critical knowledge should be protected very well and should not be part of knowledge transfer initiatives. Creating a security culture including regular trainings concerning knowledge guarding measures embrace the awareness of the parties and consequently reduces the threat of knowledge exposure. The interview partners underlined these findings: it is fundamental for large firms to sensualize and ensure that their employees exactly know what the core knowledge is and what cannot be transferred to other parties. Regular trainings and workshops motivate the staff to not leak the core knowledge in order to mitigate and prevent the leakage of knowledge [39].

Operational Initiatives: It is vital for large firms to develop and implement protective processes in order to assure the security of sensitive knowledge. Such procedures impact the frequency of knowledge flows. Therefore, the experts recommend to instruct and educate the internal staff about what they can release to externals and what they cannot transfer to others. Most interview partners advise enterprises to only share the necessary knowledge that is useful for the innovation partner to solve a problem, but not more. A possible method derived from the expert interviews is decontextualizing the problem. According to the experts' opinions, it is vital for the focal company to take the problem out of context when conducting knowledge transfer initiatives. The initiator defines a statement of the problem in a very generic way. Then the organization addresses components of this problem one by one at the time to the collaboration partner. This incremental delivery of a generic problem to external parties may hinder competitors to steal innovative ideas, since dozens of other firms could have the same generic problem.

Legal Initiatives: NDAs (Non-Disclosure-Agreements), confidentiality agreements and contracts are common legal frameworks to ensure the protection of critical knowledge [39]. In addition to that, most interview partners stated that NDAs, legal contracts or cooperation agreements may prevent the contamination of intellectual property and avoid inadvertent knowledge leakage. Nevertheless, studies show that trust among the innovation partners is still more effective against knowledge leakage rather than formal contracts [24]. Some experts explained that one single agreement cannot prevent firms from knowledge leakage and consequently recommend a combination of several protective tactics.

6   Conclusion and Limitations

External knowledge transfers concepts are applied by more and more organizations to reach out and integrate external stakeholders in their innovation processes. Those initiatives however, introduce also significant risks especially with respect to confidentiality and the misuse of sensitive information related to intellectual property.

When it comes to more confidential knowledge transfer with external parties, protective measures in order to reduce risks regarding knowledge leakage have to be implemented. The research clearly reveals knowledge leakage as a central strategic issue when knowledge is transferred to external stakeholders, e.g. in the context of open innovation settings.

In literature some measures to avoid knowledge leakage can be found, which were mainly supported by the experts from the field. In addition to that, they proposed new measures or refined measures based on their experiences. In a more general way, those measures have to be integrated in a comprehensive knowledge governance system, that (a) supports all internal and external knowledge transfer activities and (b) enables the organizations to select and adjust the suitable mechanisms to a specific project.

Knowledge governance involves choosing mechanisms to advance the process of creating, using, sharing, and integrating knowledge. The goal of knowledge governance is to implement "organizational structures and mechanisms that can influence the process of using, sharing, integrating, and creating knowledge in preferred directions and toward preferred levels" [60].

A main focus of the knowledge governance literature is consequently the mechanisms that facilitate and steer the development and transfer of knowledge.

In general, the qualitative research approach was suitable to reach the central aim of this research project, because the insights gained from the experts were very valuable. Due to the limited number of experts the results cannot be generalized. The risks and potential countermeasures have been identified.

7 Further Research

Further research is required to get a better and more comprehensive understanding of the risk and countermeasures in different industries and company sizes. The same is true for companies in different countries or regions with different cultural backgrounds.

The research also restricted in terms of the aspects how to create a knowledge sharing culture including the presentation of relevant reward systems or incentives in order to increase individuals' participation in open innovation initiatives.

After having implemented knowledge governance processes on different levels [61] in a company further research would be interesting to explore the risks with those processes applied. Differences in terms of risks between transfer process guided by knowledge governance processes and unguided knowledge transfer initiatives can be identified and analyzed.

References

1. Kazadi, K., Lievens, A., Mahr, D.: J. Bus. Res. (2016). https://doi.org/10.1016/j.jbusres.2015.05.009
2. Piller, F.T., Vossen, A., Ihl, C.: From social media to social product development: the impact of social media on co-creation of innovation. Die Unternehmung **65**(1), 7–27 (2012). SSRN: https://ssrn.com/abstract=1975523
3. Brunswicker, S., Chesbrough, H.: Res. Technol. Manag. (2018). https://doi.org/10.1080/08956308.2018.1399022
4. Vanhaverbeke, W., Cheng, J., Chesbrough, H.: A Profile of Open Innovation Managers in Multinational Companies (2017)
5. Chesbrough, H.: Open innovation: researching a new paradigm (2006)
6. Papa, A., Dezi, L., Gregori, G.L., Mueller, J., Miglietta, N.: J. Knowl. Manage. (2018). https://doi.org/10.1108/jkm-09-2017-0391
7. Della Peruta, M.R., Del Giudice, M., Lombardi, R., Soto-Acosta, P.: J. Knowl. Econ. (2018). https://doi.org/10.1007/s13132-016-0356-x
8. Heim, I., Han, T., Ghobadian, A.: J. East-West Bus. (2018). https://doi.org/10.1080/10669868.2018.1467841

9. Wilhelm, M., Dolfsma, W.: Int. J. Oper. Prod. Manage. (2018). https://doi.org/10.1108/ijopm-06-2015-0337
10. Howe, J.: Crowdsourcing: Why the Power of the Crowd is Driving the Future of Business. Three Rivers Press, New York (2008)
11. Ind, N., Iglesias, O., Schultz, M.: Building brands together: emergence and outcomes of co-creation. Calif. Manage. Rev. **55**(3), 5–26 (2013)
12. Omotayo, F.O.: University of Nebraska - Lincoln, vol. 1 (2015)
13. Coras, E.L., Tantau, A.D.: Open innovation–the good, the bad, the uncertainties. USV Ann. Econ. Publ. Adm. **14**(1), 38–47 (2014)
14. Chivu, L., Popescu, D.: Human resources management in the knowledge management. Rev. Informatica Economica **48**, 54 (2008)
15. Bhatia, K., Mittal, S.: Manpower Development for Technological Change. Excel Books, New Delhi (2009)
16. Nonaka, I., Takeuchi, H.: The Knowledge-Creating Company: How Japanese Companies Create the Dynamics of Innovation. Oxford University Press, New York (1995)
17. Polanyi, M.: The Tacit Dimension. Doubleday, Garden City (1966)
18. Dzunic, M., Boljanovic, J.D., Subotic, J.: The importance of concepts of knowledge management and learning organization in managing the knowledge - flow in organizations. In: Management, Knowledge and Learning, International Conference (2012)
19. Ruhi, U., Al-Mohsen, D.: J. Organ. Knowl. Manage. **1** (2015). https://doi.org/10.5171/2015.789394, https://ibimapublishing.com/articles/JOKM/2015/789394/789394.pdf
20. Girard, J., Girard, J.: Defining knowledge management: toward an applied compendium. Online J. Appl. Knowl. Manage. **3**(1), 1–20 (2015)
21. Paulin, D., Suneson, K.: Knowledge transfer, knowledge sharing and knowledge barriers–three blurry terms in KM. Electron. J. Knowl. Manage. **10**, 82 (2012)
22. Schwartz, D.G.: Encyclopedia of Knowledge Management. IGI Global, Hershey (2006). (701 E. Chocolate Avenue Hershey Pennsylvania 17033 USA)
23. Frishammar, J., Ericsson, K., Patel, P.C.: The dark side of knowledge transfer: Exploring knowledge leakage in joint R&D projects. Technovation **41**(42), 75 (2015)
24. Jiang, X., Li, M., Gao, S., Bao, Y., Jiang, F.: Ind. Mark. Manage. (2013). https://doi.org/10.1016/j.indmarman.2013.03.013
25. Kale, P., Singh, H., Perlmutter, H.: Learning and protection of proprietary assets in strategic alliances: building relational capital. Strateg. Manage. J. **21**, 217 (2000)
26. Mohamed, S., Mynors, D., Grantham, A., Walsh, K., Chan, P.: Understanding one of the knowledge leakage concept: people. In: European and Mediterranean Conference on Information Systems (EMCIS) (2006)
27. Mohr, J.J., Sengupta, S.: J. Bus. Ind. Mark. (2002). https://doi.org/10.1108/08858620210431688
28. Durst, S., Ferenhof, H.A.: Knowledge risk management in turbulent times. In: North, K., Varvakis, G. (eds.) Competitive Strategies for Small and Medium Enterprises, pp. 195–209. Springer, Cham (2016). https://doi.org/10.1007/978-3-319-27303-7_13
29. Lau, A.K., Yam, R.C., Tang, E.P., Sun, H.: Factors influencing the relationship between product modularity and supply chain integration. Int. J. Oper. Prod. Manage. **30**, 951 (2010)
30. Gould, R.W.: **7**(1) (2012). https://doi.org/10.4067/S0718-27242012000300001, https://www.jotmi.org/index.php/GT/article/view/925
31. Lichtenthaler, U., Lichtenthaler, E.: A capability-based framework for open innovation: complementing absorptive capacity. J. Manage. Stud. **46**, 1315 (2009)
32. Andersén, J.: Protective capacity and absorptive capacity: managing the balance between retention and creation of knowledge-based resources. Learn. Organ. **19**, 440 (2012)

33. Inkpen, A., Minbaeva, D., Tsang, E.W.K.: J. Int. Bus. Stud. (2018). https://doi.org/10.1057/s41267-018-0164-6
34. Alexy, O., George, G., Salter, A.J.: Acad. Manage. Rev. (2013). https://doi.org/10.5465/amr.2011.0193
35. Cohen, W.M., Levinthal, D.A.: Adm. Sci. Q. **35**, 128 (1990). https://doi.org/10.2307/2393553, https://www.jstor.org/stable/2393553?seq=1#page_scan_tab_contents
36. Oxley, J.E., Sampson, R.C.: The scope and governance of international R&D alliances. Strateg. Manage. J. **25**, 723 (2004)
37. Zieba, M., Durst, S.: Knowledge risks in the sharing economy. In: Vătămănescu, E.-M., Pînzaru, F.M. (eds.) Knowledge Management in the Sharing Economy. KMOL, vol. 6, pp. 253–270. Springer, Cham (2018). https://doi.org/10.1007/978-3-319-66890-1_13
38. Tsang, H.W.C., Lee, R.W.B.: Open innovation and knowledge management in small and medium enterprises. Durst, S., Temel, S., Ferenhof, H.A. (ed.), p. 183. World Scientific (2018)
39. Ahmad, A., Bosua, R., Scheepers, R.: Protecting organizational competitive advantage: a knowledge leakage perspective. Comput. Secur. **42**, 27 (2014)
40. Chan, P.W., et al.: A taxonomy of knowledge leakage: some early developments. In: Boyd, D. (Ed.) Proceedings of 22nd Annual ARCOM Conference (2006)
41. Coyte, R., Ricceri, F., Guthrie, J.: The management of knowledge resources in SMEs: an Australian case study. J. Knowl. Manage. **16**, 789 (2012)
42. Laursen, K., Salter, A.: Strateg. Manage. J. (2006). https://doi.org/10.1002/smj.507
43. Myers, M.B., Cheung, M.S.: Sharing global supply chain knowledge. MIT Sloan Manage. Rev. **49**, 66 (2008)
44. Freeman, R.E., Harrison, J.S., Wicks, A.C.: Managing for Stakeholders: Survival, Reputation, and Success. Yale University Pres, New Haven (2007)
45. Noland, J., Phillips, R.: Stakeholder engagement, discourse ethics and strategic management. Int. J. Manage. Rev. **12**, 39 (2010)
46. Gao, S.S., Zhang, J.J.: Stakeholder engagement, social auditing and corporate sustainability. Bus. Process Manage. J. **12**, 722 (2006)
47. Gold, A.H., Malhotra, A., Segars, A.H.: Knowledge management: an organizational capabilities perspective. J. Manage. Inf. Syst. **18**, 185 (2001)
48. Aiman-Smith, L., Bergey, P., Cantwell, A.R., Doran, M.: The coming knowledge and capability shortage. Res. Technol. Manage. **49**, 15 (2006)
49. Desouza, K.C., Paquette, S.: Knowledge Management: An Introduction. Neal-Schuman Publishers, New York (2011)
50. Núñez, R.G.A.: Intellectual property and the protection of traditional knowledge, genetic resources and folklore: the peruvian experience. Max Planck Yearb. United Nations Law Online **12**, 485 (2008)
51. Mayring, P.: Qualitative Content Analysis. Theoretical Foundation, Basic Procedures and Software Solution (Beltz 2014)
52. Sloane, P., (ed.): A Guide to Open Innovation and Crowdsourcing: Expert Tips and Advice, 1st edn. Kogan Page, London (2011)
53. Bogers, M.: European Journal of Innovation Management **14**, 93 (2011)
54. Harmancioglu, N.: The open innovation paradox: knowledge sharing and protection in R&D collaborations. Ind. Mark. Manage. **38**, 394 (2009)
55. Ferenhof, H.A.: Int. J. Knowl. Syst. Sci. (2016). https://doi.org/10.4018/ijkss.2016070104
56. Durst, S., Aggestam, L., Ferenhof, H.A.: Constantin Bratianu. Vine (2015). https://doi.org/10.1108/vine-01-2015-0009. ssoc. Prof. Et, Professor

57. Markovic, S., Bagherzadeh, M.: How does breadth of external stakeholder co-creation influence innovation performance? analyzing the mediating roles of knowledge sharing and product innovation. J. Bus. Res. **88**, 173–186 (2018)
58. Islam, A.M.: Int. J. e-Educ., e-Bus., e-Manage. e-Learn. (2012). https://doi.org/10.7763/ijeeee.2012.v2.130
59. Wehn, U., Montalvo, C.: J. Cleaner Prod. (2018). https://doi.org/10.1016/j.jclepro.2016.09.198
60. Foss, N.J., Husted, K., Michailova, S.: Governing knowledge sharing in organizations: levels of analysis, governance mechanisms, and research directions. J. Manag. Stud. **47**(3), 455–482 (2010)
61. Pemsel, S., Söderlund, J., Wiewiora, A.: Technol. Anal. Strateg. Manage. (2018). https://doi.org/10.1080/09537325.2018.1459538

Study of Entrepreneurial Students' Perceptions of the Impact of Digital Literacy Skills on Their Future Career: Evidence from Tunisian Higher Education

Souad Kamoun-Chouk[(✉)]

Ecole Supérieure de Commerce de Tunis, LIGUE Research Laboratory,
Campus Universitaire de La Manouba, Manouba, Tunisie
Souad.kamoun@esct.uma.tn

Abstract. Entrepreneurs need early access to information to seize the opportunities offered by the economic environment and avoid threats that could undermine their businesses. In the age of the internet economy, speed of access to information is dependent on the young entrepreneurs' mastery of technological tools that promote access to the right information at the right time. The skills in digital literacy in terms of selection, interpretation and knowledge construction and also in terms of communication and insertion in the digital culture are essential to face the competition and to be competitive. The role of education is important here to prepare literate entrepreneurs.

By conducting a qualitative study using a focus group technique with entrepreneurship students at the Tunisian University level, we aimed to deeply explore: (1) the familiarity of the students with Digital Literacy, (2) students' perception of the knowledge acquired through their education programs and if it seemed to them sufficient compared to the competences that they perceived as necessary for their future job as entrepreneurs. The results show that the concept and the skills it contains were a discovery for the students. The focus group was also an opportunity for students to collectively reflect on their training and their ability to launch themselves as future entrepreneurs.

Keywords: Digital literacy · Information literacy · Competence · Entrepreneurship · Education

1 Introduction

The Information age, Computer Age, Digital Age, or New Media Age is the age of digital revolution. This era is characterized by problems related to information access, overload, and quality. Educational institutions are nowadays more and more challenged to review their teaching strategies and methods of access to knowledge. Schools are perceived as the provider of meaningful learning opportunities. Schumpeter's theory (1911; 1942) predicts that an increase in the number of entrepreneurs leads to an increase in economic growth. Even though there is a dearth of evidence based on empirical data about the role of entrepreneurs in deriving innovation and contributing

© Springer Nature Switzerland AG 2019
L. Uden et al. (Eds.): KMO 2019, CCIS 1027, pp. 392–402, 2019.
https://doi.org/10.1007/978-3-030-21451-7_34

to economic growth, a copious theoretical and descriptive literature exists on how entrepreneurship affects the economy. (Porter 1990; Baumol 1993; Lumpkin and Dess 1996), Wong et al. (2005).

Many developing countries, and Tunisia for instance, are using entrepreneurship as a lever of economic growth. According to the Human Development Index, Tunisia has a high level of human development. This index takes into account factors such as education and life expectancy. Tunisia, with its high level of human development and relatively good ranking in ICT development and infrastructure, should be expected to have a strong basis for entrepreneurship. Information Literacy (IL), and more precisely Digital Literacy (DL), could be a core competency for emerging startups who want to benefit from this enabling on-going entrepreneurship environment.

Information Literacy (IL) is the ability to identify the information needed, to know where to obtain the information, and how to evaluate the information obtained to be used to solve problems effectively and Digital Literacy (DL) is the ensemble of skills required for accomplishing these tasks and the ability to apply them. These had been advocated by Kamoun Chouk (2018, 2005) to remedy the lack of such skills in the SMEs and the university workplace. This study conducted under my supervision, within the context of a master degree thesis (Zammouri 2018), attempts to provide a beginning answer to the next question:

How do entrepreneurship students perceive skills in digital literacy? Which skills are perceived as the most important for them?

The paper is structured in four parts. First, the conceptual framework of Digital Literacy is outlined to identify the competencies needed by entrepreneurs when starting their business. Secondly, the research methodology is specified and the themes to be used in the investigation are discussed. In the third part, the results of the empirical study are presented and discussed. The paper concludes with a summary of the findings and considers some implications for policy-makers.

2 The Conceptual Framework

2.1 The Role of Information in the Entrepreneurial Context

Digital Literacy (DL) requirements in the entrepreneurial context are related to opportunities for discovering or creating needs, the basis for future investment, employment, and profit. Entrepreneurs are constantly looking for and using information as part of their daily lives. Information about work, money, and a host of other topics is sought from a wide range of digital sources. The ability to identify potential business opportunities is an important entrepreneurial feature identified by Wheelen and Hunger (2000). From the point of view of entrepreneurship, the systematic search for information from a limited number of areas most clearly related to entrepreneurs' previous knowledge should increase the chances of identifying business opportunities (Patel and Fiet 2009). A high degree of diverse information should be linked to new and original ideas, even if this information goes beyond the realm of the entrepreneur's current expertise and knowledge. However, diverse information should help generate a set of original ideas that contribute to later stages of evaluation and refinement (Santanen et al. 2004). Information provided by the environment triggers and directs the thought process that leads to the accumulation of ideas (Amabile 1983). The important role of information is also recognized by entrepreneurship researchers. Fiet and Patel (2009) have argued that it is difficult to understand the identification of opportunities without including information. To develop the entrepreneurial capacity and accompany evolving digital information technology, authors think that the universities have to build high-impact entrepreneurship programs (Morris et al. 2015).

2.2   The Concept of Information Literacy (IL)

Zurkowski (1974), President of the "Information Industry Association, coined the term "Information literacy". He suggested the following definition: "Learned techniques and skills for utilizing the wide range of information tools as well as primary sources in molding information solutions to [one's] problems". According to Zukowski, the degree of informational literacy is represented as proportional to the perceived value of the information. Being literate means being able to find what we know about any subject by focusing on the value of the information and the framework in which it is operated. It is a problem-solving approach. The field of information continues to evolve rapidly as digital technology changes the nature of information and the way people interact and learn from/with information from the Web (Stevenson 1989).

2.3   Digital Literacy Versus Information Literacy

The term of "digital literacy" has become popular thanks to by Paul Gilster in 1997. The term "digital literacy" is now used to describe our engagement with digital technologies as they mediate most of our interactions (Lankshear and Knobel 2003). Pawinun and Kemparaju (2004) proposed a new definition of IL, which they called "literacy in information technology." The authors argued that this definition includes basic technological knowledge that deals with computer skills and skills focused on Internet literacy. More precisely, Eshet-Alkali and Amichai-Hamburger (2004) highlighted specific skills in the field of digital literacy, including: visual photo literacy skills, reading and reproduction skills, information literacy skills, branched literacy, and social literacy-affective. For Bawden (2008), the concept of DL is considered as broader than ICT literacy since it involves the acquisition and use of knowledge, skills, attitudes, and personal qualities and includes the ability to plan, execute and evaluate digital information. The interaction between information literacy and digital literacy is according to Cordell (2013) a catalyst of skills to seize good opportunities and hence the generation of value and improvement of the performance of entrepreneurs in the workplace. Information Literacy and Digital Literacy are not competing concepts; these are complementary areas.

2.4   The Digital Literacy Competencies

The literature review allowed us to identify references relevant for establishing a list of skills in digital literacy. For Gilster (1997), Digital Literacy requiring technical skills, is the ability to use information and communication technologies to: (1) Find;

(2) Evaluate; (3) Create; (4) Communicate information. Bawden (2008), and Martin (2006) add more precisely (1) The assembly and construction of knowledge; (2) Internet search and analysis and synthesis of digital resources; (3) Hyper-textual navigation; (4) Evaluation of digital content; and (5) Knowledge of oneself as a person with a digital culture and communication to enable constructive social action. ALA Digital Literacy Task Force (2011) defines a numerically literate person as someone who: (1) Has the technical and cognitive skills allowing him to: (2) Locate, assess, evaluate, create and communicate digital information in different formats; (3) Mobilizes available technologies appropriately and effectively to extract information, interpret results and judge the quality of this information and also to communicate and collaborate with peers, colleagues, family and possibly larger communities; (4) capture what connects technology, lifelong learning, confidentiality and information management and become an active citizen in civil society. More recently UNESCO (2018) proposed five competence areas of DL. The three first eras (Information and data literacy, Communication and collaboration, Digital content creation), seem to fit with what we found in the literature about Digital literacy competencies. The areas 4 and 5 (safety and Problem solving) seem to represent further steps of the learning and reflection process. While safety is concerned with protecting devices, personal data and privacy, health and well-being and the environment, the problem solving era is about technical problems, identifying needs and technological responses, identifying digital competence gaps and creatively using digital technologies. In the map below, we tried to put together the skills belonging to the same category by trying to eliminate the redundancies and by regrouping those that look consistent with the entrepreneurs' informational needs (Fig. 1).

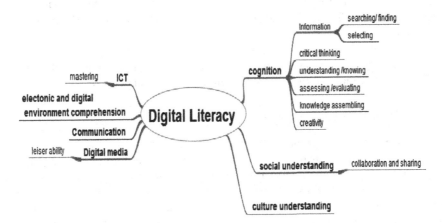

Fig. 1. Conceptual map of Digital literacy eras and competences

3 Design of the Research

In this study, we adopt an interpretative epistemological stance. Our goal is to understand the perceptions of the DL concept by students in entrepreneurship and "the subjective meanings that underlie the behavior of the individuals it studies" (Perret and Seville 2007). To answer our research question, we have adopted a qualitative approach because, according to Charrerie and Durieux (2007), it is generally used when "the studied phenomenon is recent or little known or when the processes are complex and difficult to measure".

3.1 Data Collection

The purpose of this analysis is to study the perception of entrepreneurship master's degree students and emphasize the importance of digital literacy as necessary skills. So in this context, a qualitative exploratory study seems to be appropriate. The main objective of this study is to identify, from student focus group collective interviews, elements that could highlight the actual situation of Digital literacy learning among future entrepreneurs and the competencies perceived as necessary to reinforce the training programs.

3.2 Participants

The participants in the focus group were 25 students in entrepreneurship masters programs divided into two groups of 12 and 13 participants. The ideal number of participants in a focus group is between six people minimum and twelve maximum (Tynan and Drayton 1988). The chosen group is fairly homogeneous, with a little diversity to ensure different points of view and stimulate discussion (Peterson 1975). For a group to develop a relaxed, comfortable and natural discussion, its members must have a "community of interest," (Goldman 1962, p. 61), which is true for our population. Tynan and Drayton (1988) recommend having a sufficient number of groups to achieve content saturation. In our case two groups were enough to reach this saturation.

3.3 The Focus Group Technique

The focus group is a qualitative technique whose purpose is to gather discussions centered on particular concrete situations on topics relevant to the research (Steward et al. 2007). It is always oriented towards the collection of information thanks to a semi-directive or non-directive stimulus or interview guide, which helps to stimulate a debate of opinions. Most authors agree that the main benefit of focus group is the deliberate use of the interaction to generate data (Morgan 1996). Participants can thus make associations of idea, bounce back and react to what the previous person said, and bring new elements for the qualitative study (Morgan and Smircich 1980). Interactions lasted 45 min at each meeting. They have been fully recorded and transcribed. They were then analyzed and interpreted through a semantic analysis structured by a free software tool: TROPES.

3.4 Semi-structured Interview

Data collection was conducted in two group meetings using a semi-structured interview guide. The choice of this method of data collection is justified on the one hand by the nature of the information sought and on the other hand by the wealth of information potentially to be collected (enumeration of important elements probably omitted by the literature). In fact, semi-structured interviews are an open and framed way of dealing with specific themes in depth (Evrard et al. 2003).

3.5 Conduct of the Investigation

The interviews were conducted on two different dates, with two groups. The first group consisted of 12 students and the second group consisted of 13 students. The sessions were moderated by two moderators/researchers. The first researcher explained and presented the purpose of the research and facilitated the conversation by facilitating and managing the exchanges between the participants. The second researcher took note of all the exchanges and recorded them. Participants were prepared for this experiment in three stages:

- **Step 1**: We brought together all the contributors to whom we explained our objectives concerning our research on digital literacy. We distributed to them notes containing definitions of the notions of information literacy and digital literacy.
- **Step 2**: We have, whenever we thought necessary, clarified the concepts in order to stimulate the interactions and to minimize the shadows which could slow down and/or prevent the progress of the investigation.
- **Step 3**: We then followed our interview guide with the objectives: (1) to collect the student's perceptions about DL, mastering ICT and the role of digital culture in acquiring this global competence, (2) to identify the skills in digital literacy needed for a future entrepreneur and the areas of Digital Literacy training that could be identified as priorities by entrepreneurship students.

4 Analysis of the Results

4.1 Knowledge of the Concepts of Information Literacy and Digital Literacy

The analysis of students' speeches and their exchanges revealed that the latter were completely ignorant of both concepts. The definitions we offered them allowed to put into words and make sense of what they perceived to be important. Finally, they set priorities for what steps towards access to useful information was most important for them to undertake. The analysis of the results shows that focus group participants often mentioned ICT literacy as a determinant of digital literacy. They see this skill as a key resource for knowledge generation within the company and for innovation. They see ICT literacy as a concept as important as DL's. But, they are far from realizing that DL is a broader concept than ICT, since it includes not only the mastery of technology but also other skills. The use of knowledge and the ability to plan and evaluate digital technology are part of that.

4.2   Role of Digital Culture in Mastering the Information Process

This dimension did not appear during the first part of our investigation. The participants did not discuss the subject and we did not find it useful to guide them, especially to avoid biasing our results. Moreover, in view of the progress of the exchanges during the focus group sessions we felt that it was premature to talk about culture. This relatively complex concept encompasses the core competencies of digital culture that we address in the second theme of our interview guide. In our conceptual framework, we can say that entrepreneurship of our focus group has a superficial knowledge on the concepts of IL and DL. Their perception is related to 3 dimensions: (1) Cognition (information, searching, finding but not selecting). Critical thinking, understanding and knowing, assessing/evaluating, creativity are not evoked. It is a deeper level of cognition to which students have not yet accessed. (2) ICT as a tool to master the access to information, (3) communication associated with ICT (Fig. 2).

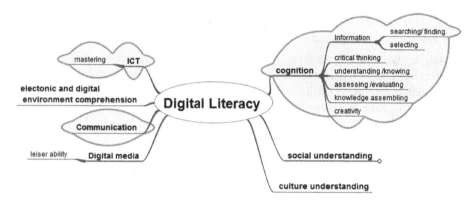

Fig. 2. The emerging dimensions of the students perceptions

4.3   The Competences Considered as Priorities

According to the participants, Digital Literacy as a concept wider than Information Literacy is an essential skill to possess as future entrepreneurs. They consider that the acquisition of skills that constitute it is a guarantee of success.

They classify these competences in this descending order:

- Technological competencies: As future entrepreneurs they see that they are forced to master navigation on the Internet and to use computer technologies skillfully.
- Competence in seeking information through digital tools: It is considered a priority, and should begin to be taught at the secondary school level. This is where, according to them, the institutionalization of digital culture should begin.
- Competence in interpretation and understanding of information: It requires early training in critical-thinking. This skill is perceived as part of a lifelong learning process. Participants think that this skill should start very early in the life learning cycle (i.e. at the primary school level) and continue in the workplace.

- The institutionalization of a digital culture: The students think that it is a national policy choice that consists in creating an enabling environment allowing the creation of structural conditions favoring access to education and learning in DL. It is considered crucial to create an environment conducive to entrepreneurship. Participants are calling for more active learning pedagogies based on the use of digital technology.

5   Discussion

Our study confirmed the strong awareness among the entrepreneurship students of the determining role of Digital literacy in their profession. They perceive systematic search for information as a critical success factor which is consistent with authors arguing that these practices should increase the chances of identifying business opportunities (Patel and Fiet 2009). In accordance with Pawinun and Kemparaju (2004), the focus group participants see DL as a capsule including computer literacy and information and communication technology (ICT) skills. However, the entrepreneurship students in our study, do not relate the information search to creativity and discovering of new ideas as advocated by Amabile (1983). Their perception of DL and IL seems to be rather utilitarian. They seem to have a short-term vision that does not fit into a profound cultural approach aimed at perpetuating a process of learning with the aim of creativity and continuous innovation. This short-term vision is in contradiction with Gibbons (1998), and the perception that informational abilities should be developed as skills for lifelong learning. The limitations in their perceptions about this phenomenon can be attributed (1) to their insufficient knowledge of IL and DL concepts and (2) to their lack of practice in this area. The part of the survey on the skills required and those judged to be a priority brought out results rather in agreement with the literature. The first part of the investigation on the students' perceptions allowed the participants to familiarize themselves with the concepts and progressively discover their meaning with the help of the facilitator and through the social interactions. Students of our focus group, see themselves lacking the Digital Literacy (DL) skills required to become a good entrepreneur. Their perception of DL skills is rather consistent with Gilster (1997) early proposition of cognitive abilities. Deeper use of information suggested by Bawden (2008) does not seem close to their perception. They are also far from Martin (2006) who described abilities of construction of new knowledge and creation of expression in the media. ICT mastering is perceived as the key to access to information and entrepreneurial opportunities. They seem to have a limited understanding of the meaning of Digital Literacy, denoting a restriction of the concept to the effective use of ICT exclusively as deplored by Bawden (2008). To gain knowledge and technological skills in search and retrieval, students are aware that by using computers, browsers, software and databases they can improve their ability to achieve quick and relevant access to information as advocated for students by Sharkey and Brandt (2008). Their prioritization of those skills to acquire first reflects an immediate concern for technological and cognitive skills, which they perceive as intimately linked. To have access to entrepreneurial opportunities, they are aware of the importance of such cognitive skills as understanding, knowing, selecting, and evaluating that are common to all the references of our conceptual framework. They also perceive communication and insertion within social networks as keys of entrepreneurial success in the digital era. A strong fear of failure in the entrepreneurial adventure is perceptible among the future entrepreneurs. This lack of competence noted by Kamoun Chouk (2005) was at the origin of the failure to set up a monitoring system in a panel of Tunisian PMI, as an external information system to help decision and strategic action. This concern of university students is also echoed in the work of Kamoun Chouk (2018), confirming the existence in the academic world of a real need for access to information and mastering ICT, in other words, of Digital Literacy skills.

6 Conclusion

Our study aimed to answer the following research question:

How do entrepreneurship students perceive skills in Digital Literacy? Which skills are perceived as the most important for them?

The results allowed us to discover that students perceive the education system as dominated by enrollees that do not always recognize the need to upgrade their digital literacy level. Computer and Internet Certification (CIC) course, as a common core subject in all university curricula, is perceived as insufficient to provide the competences needed to become a digital literate entrepreneur. Tangible Evidence of Positive Outcomes of Digital Literacy Programs [These caps do not belong!] is necessary to convince users and authorities such as policy makers and education strategists of the complex and disconcerting Information gaps in an Information-Driven Digital Society. Further research should be interested in the content of training programs for access, processing and use of information to be able to identify and evaluate what are the most important shortcomings in relation to what the entrepreneurs' jobs require, then comparing them to the inadequacies as perceived by students. Identifying any mismatch could help spur solutions to the obstacles students may be creating in failing to understand the importance and value to their future of acquiring higher level Digital Literacy skills. Another track of research could experiment, on a larger scale, with the application of a digital literacy program, and conduct a longitudinal study allowing researchers to go further than the limited subjective perceptions of the future entrepreneurs observed in this study. Following this group of students through a DL training cycle using participant observation technique could be a useful research perspective allowing verifying the validity of the students' perceptions of the competencies most urgently needed for entrepreneurship.

For practitioners and particularly decision-makers in the educational sector, this research is challenging. It draws attention to the need to adapt entrepreneurial training programs to the reality of the internet economy and the digital world: one does not become an entrepreneur by necessity but one needs to acquire a digital education from an early age to participate successfully in a digital world.

References

Amabile, T.M.: Social psychology of creativity: a componential conceptualization. J. Pers. Soc. Psychol. **45**, 997–1013 (1983)

Association of Colleges and Research Libraries, American Library Association. Information literacy defined (2011). http://www.ala.org/ala/mgrps/divs/acrl/standards/informationliteracy competency.cfm

Baumol, W.: Entrepreneurship, Management, and the Structure of Payoffs. MIT Press, Cambridge (1993)

Bawden, D.: Origins and concepts of digital literacy. In: Lankshear, C., Knobel, M. (eds.) Digital Literacies: Concepts, Policies and Practices, pp. 17–32. Peter Lang, New York (2008)

Charreire Petit, S., Durieux, F.: Explorer et tester: les deux voies de la recherche. In: dans R.-A. Thiétart, Méthodes de recherche en management, (3ème éd.), Dunod, Paris, pp. 59–83 (2007)

Cordell, R.M.: Information literacy and digital literacy: competing or complementary? Commun. Inf. Lit. **7**(2), 177–183 (2013)

Eshet-Alkali, Y., Amichai-Hamburger, Y.: Experiments in digital literacy. CyberPsychology Behav. **7**(4), 421–429 (2004)

Evrard, Y., Pras, B., Roux, E.: Market, Études et recherches en marketing, 3ème édition. Dunod, Paris (2003)

Gibbons, M.: Higher Education Relevance in the 21st Century. World Bank, Washington http://www.worldbank.org/html/extdr/educ/edu-pb/giboeng3.pdf. Accessed 17 Jan 2019

Gilster, P.: Alphabétisation numérique. Wiley, New York (1997)

Goldman, A.E.: La profondeur d'entretien du groupe. Journal du Marketing, vol. 26, no. 3, pp. 61–68 (1962) (réimprimé dans Seibert, J., Wills, G. (eds.) Recherche en marketing: Lectures choisies, Penguin, Harmondsworth, Middlesex, pp. 266–271 (1970))

Kamoun Chouk, S.: Veille anticipative stratégique: processus d'attention à l'environnement: application à des PMI tunisiennes. Thèse Grenoble 2 (2005)

Kamoun Chouk, S.: Knowledge Management in Organizations. In: Proceedings of 13th International Conference, KMO 2018, Žilina, Slovakia, 6–10 August 2018 (2018)

Lankshear, C., Knobel, M.: New Literacies: Changing Knowledge in the Classroom. Open University Press, Buckingham (2003)

Lumpkin, G.T., Dess, G.G.: Clarifying the entrepreneurial orientation construct and linking it to performance. Acad. Manag. Rev. 21(1) (1996). ABI/INFORM Global p. 135

Martin, A.: Literacies for the digital age. In: Martin, A., Madigan, D. (eds.) Digital Literacies for Learning, pp. 3–25. Facet, London (2006)

Morgan, D.L.: Focus groups. Ann. Rev. Sociol. **22**, 129–152 (1996). https://doi.org/10.1146/annurev.soc.22.1.129

Morgan, G., Smircich, L.: The case for qualitative research. Acad. Manag. Rev. **5**, 491–500 (1980). Gareth Morgan; Linda Smircich Academy of Management, ABI/INFORM Global

Morris, M.H., Neumeyer, X., Kuratko, D.F.: A portfolio perspective on entrepreneurship and economic development. Small Bus. Econ. **45**(4) (2015). https://ssrn.com/abstract=2720603. Kelley School of Business Research Paper No. 16–9. SSRN

Pawinun, P., Kemparaju, T.D.: The information literacy program: a case of digital libraries SRELS. J. Inf. Manage. 41(1), 67–78 (2004)

Patel, P.C., Fiet, J.O.: Systematic search and its relationship to firm founding. Entrep. Theory Pract. **33**(2), 501–526 (2009)

Perret, V., et Seville, M.: Fondements épistémologiques de la recherche. In: Thietart, R.A. (ed.) Recherche en Management, Dunod, pp. 13–33 (2007)

Peterson, K.I.: L'influence du chercheur et sa procédure sur la validité des séances de groupe. à Mazze, E.M., Procédions groupés, l'association américaine de marketing, Chicago, pp. 146–8 (1975)

Porter, M.E.: The Competitive Advantage of Nations. Free Press, New York (1990)

Santanen, E.L., Briggs, R.O., de Vreede, G. J.: Causal relationships in creative problem solving: comparing facilitation interventions for ideation. J. Manag. Inf. Syst. 20(4), 167–197 (2004)

Schumpeter, J.A.: The Theory of Economic Development. Cambridge University Press, Cambridge (1911)

Schumpeter, J.A.: Capitalism, Socialism and Democracy, vol. 36, pp. 132–145. Harper & Row, New York (1942)

Sharkey, J., Brandt, D.S.: Integrating technology literacy and information literacy. In: Rivoltella, P.C. (ed.) Digital Literacy: Tools and Methodologies for Information Society, pp. 85–97. IGI Global, Hershey (2008)

Stevenson, R.J. Hashim, S.: Variation in Diatom community structure among habitation sandy streams (1989). https://doi.org/10.1111/j.0022-3646.1989.00678.x

Stewart, D.W., Shamdasani, P.N., Rook, D.W.: Focus Groups: Theory and Practice, vol. 20, 2nd edn. (2007)

Tynan, C., Drayton, J.L.: conduire d'entretien des groupes - un guide pour les utilisateurs de la première fois. Mark. Intell. Plan. 6(1), 5–9 (1988)

UNESCO: A Global Framework of Reference on Digital Literacy Skills for Indicator 4.4.2, Information Paper No. 51 June 2018 UIS/2018/ICT/IP/51 (2018). http://uis.unesco.org/sites/default/files/documents/ip51-global-framework-reference-digital-literacy-skills-2018-en.pdf

Wheelen, T.L., Hunger, D.L.: Strategic Management and Business Policy. Addison-Wesley Publishing, New York (2000)

Wong, P.K., Ho, Y.P., Autio, E.: Entrepreneurship, innovation and economic growth: evidence from GEM data. Small Bus. Econ. **24**, 335–350 (2005). https://doi.org/10.1007/s11187-005-2000-1

Zammouri. Etude des perceptions des compétences en littératie informationnelle et littératie digitale pour la promotion de l'entrepreneuriat: cas des étudiants de mastère entrepreneuriat en Tunisie, mémoire de fin d'études en mastère de recherche en Sciences de Gestion, spécialité: Entrepreneuriat, supervisé par Kamoun Chouk Souad (2018)

Zurkowski, P.G.: The Information Service Environment Relationships and Priorities, Related Paper No. 5., National Commission on Libraries and Information Science, Washington, DC., National Program for Library and Information Services (1974). http://eric.ed.gov/PDFS/ED100391.pdf. Accessed Jan 2019

Relationship Between Context-Social and Academic Performance: First Notes

Ortega C. Juan[1]($\boxtimes$), Gómez A. Héctor[2]($\boxtimes$),
Villavicencio Alvarez Victor Emilio[3]($\boxtimes$),
Lozada T. Edwin Fabricio[4]($\boxtimes$), and Francisco R. Naranjo C[5]($\boxtimes$)

[1] Subdirección de Posgrados,
Universidad Católica de Cuenca, Cuenca 010107, Ecuador
jcortegac@ucacue.edu.ec
[2] Universidad Tecnica de Ambato, Ambato, Ecuador
hf.gomez@uta.edu.ec
[3] Departamento de Ciencias Humanas y Sociales, ESPE, Sangolqui, Ecuador
vevillavicencio@espe.edu.ec
[4] Carrera de Software, Universidad Autónoma de los Andes-UNIANDES,
Ambato, Ecuador
ua.edwinlozada@uniandes.edu.ec
[5] Facultad de Ingeniería en Ciencias Aplicadas, Universidad Técnica del Norte,
Ibarra, Ecuador
frnaranjo@utn.edu.ec

Abstract. Context: Student performance based on interaction with virtual learning environments and traditional classroom.

Problem: In the academy it is not clear what variables can influence the academic score, since there are different conclusions according to the context in analysis.

Objective: To find academic and social variables that influence academic performance in virtual environments of learning and traditional classroom.

Methodological Proposal: Apply data mining and correlation of variables as a first step to the identification of variables that influence academic score.

Experiment: We worked with two datasets according to the context under study. The results of the first experiment showed 83% of effectiveness that the level of education and the number of previous credits of the student directly influence their performance, while the interaction with the virtual learning environment does not directly influence the score. The high ratings in this data set is difficult to classify. In the second experiment, we worked on a traditional classroom. The results showed that academic performance is not linked to alcohol consumption at the end or midweek. Free days have no relation to performance. For the case of gender it seems to be better that women have a university preparation to achieve a better score. In relation to health, women are more affected with absences. Finally, if there is a relationship between internet access and performance. The results of this work are not conclusive, they are only the first notes to determine and corroborate the influence of academic and social variables in the academic score.

Keywords: Score · Variables · Influence

© Springer Nature Switzerland AG 2019
L. Uden et al. (Eds.): KMO 2019, CCIS 1027, pp. 403–415, 2019.
https://doi.org/10.1007/978-3-030-21451-7_35

1 Introduction

In the educational field, finding variables that are related to academic performance is very important, these variables can be followed directly to the improvement of academic score and thus avoid student disappointment and desertion. And the issue is not only to investigate the fields that are in view of the educational field but also to observe those external variables that correlate directly with the academic environment. The problem is to identify what those variables are and how they affect a score. The proposal of this research has also been analyzed by some authors, for example; working while studying a university career is considered as detrimental to the academic score, especially in the first year of study [1]. The abandonment of the university studies in the level of degree, is a global phenomenon in the university system, that comports the need to develop politics of student retention. These politics require the identification of the possible causes of desertion and temporally withdrawals that on time are not of academic exclusivity, existing also an influence of social type [2]. The effectiveness of the actions developed by the university to address the problem of desertion will depend on the quality of the identification, the causality, the problem that can be identified, the process of analyzing the facilities, the discovery of desertion patterns and temporary withdrawals. Understanding by desertion as the abandonment by a student of the formal studies of a certain career, there are many factors that affect this type of decision, from the sociological point of view there are two theories that have a lot of force: The Integration Model of the student and model of student's wear, patterns that address different dimensions of the analysis: psychological, economic, sociological, organizational and interaction. According to [3], temporary withdrawals, in the academic year, in the presence of rigid academic structures in IES that do not allow the continuity of studies and that are alien to the flexibility and changes that affect society in their different activities, showing an attitude of disinterest and consolidation of their inbreeding practice, which has an impact on the students' scores. Parental involvement and family income are vitally important in student achievement, including part-time work by parents having direct influence on the final average [4]. The acculturation and alcohol problems reflect affectation in the educational field, especially in Latin teenagers [5]. The use of free time and inter-family relationships have a direct relationship in student achievement, rather than home rules or verbal interventions. Hence, the participation of parents in the free time of children is of vital importance in student motivation [6]. Health directly interferes with the performance and educational success of university students, so it is necessary to intervene with prevention programs in education field [7]. The student motivation is of vital importance for the improvement of the score, as the positive emotional work results in the improvement of the level of student attention. It does not occur the same with student's previous, since the motivational approach can suspend the affectation of knowing or not a specific topic [8–10]. Interaction with the virtual environments and the handle of internet especially in the last decades can turn into student allies for the academic improvement [11]. In fact, you can track the way students interact in the virtual learning environment in order to try to predict their behavior online [12]. In this work we emphasize the variables studied in the works described in the previous paragraph, but we also discover others that affect positively or negatively academic performance. Hence, this work focuses on identifying the academic and social variables prior knowledge of the student, previously approved modules, access to material in the virtual learning environment, alcohol consumption, days off, level of education, gender, state of health, absence from classes and access to the internet, whose motive is to trace a follow-up mechanism so that it can be applied in other educational studies. Datamining and statistical algorithms are applied to obtain the conclusions and recommendations of this investigation. In the first experimental phase the Multilayer Perceptron algorithm since its operation has been successfully tested in [13], and in the second base the correlation of variables was applied based on [14]. The clustering also observes conclusive results in this work for what was applied based on [15]. The dataset used in the first phase can be downloaded from Open University Learning Analytics. It is a set of data about courses, students and their interaction with the virtual learning environment. The results showed that 83% of correct answers allow us to conclude that the level of education and the number of previous credits of the student, if they directly influence their performance. For the following experiment we changed the dataset based on the structure proposed by UCI Machine Learning Laboratory. [16]. The data was collected anonymously from a research methodology course. The records have no interaction with the virtual learning environment. The results showed that academic performance is not linked to alcohol consumption at the end or midweek, although in fact alcohol consumption is considered very dangerous for concentration and student tasks. Also, days off have no relation to performance. For the case of gender, it seems to be better that women have a university preparation to achieve a better score. In relation to health, women are more affected in absences. Finally, if there is a relationship between internet access and performance, which corroborates our research described in [11, 16]. In order to adequately describe this work, the following section explains the methodology applied in the two experimental phases. The results of the experiment generate conclusions and recommendations described in the corresponding section, which are affirmative only for the contexts analyzed in this work.

2 Methodology

The objective of this work is to find academic and social variables that influence academic performance. Being an initial work, it is proposed to find datasets that allow to perform experiments to find these variables and then analyze them with data mining and statistical correlation. The following algorithm describes the methodological steps of this work:

1. Research of datasets in virtual surroundings of learning and in traditional classroom.
2. Surroundings of virtual Learning:
   a Analyze the correlation of variables
   b Apply Multilayer Perceptron
   c Apply clustering (K-Means)
3. Traditional class: Analyze the correlation of variables
4. Interpret the results of the virtual and traditional learning context

Initially, the methodology can be basic in this work. However, the application of the same based on previous studies, shows that the simplicity of the steps can generate easily comparable conclusions in two different learning environments. To corroborate this statement in the following section we describe the experiments carried out and the results obtained in this research work.

3 Experimentation

The dataset used can be downloaded from Open University Learning Analytics [17]. It is a set of data about courses, students and their interaction with the virtual learning environment. The database diagram (Fig. 1) shows a description of the tables and their relationships.

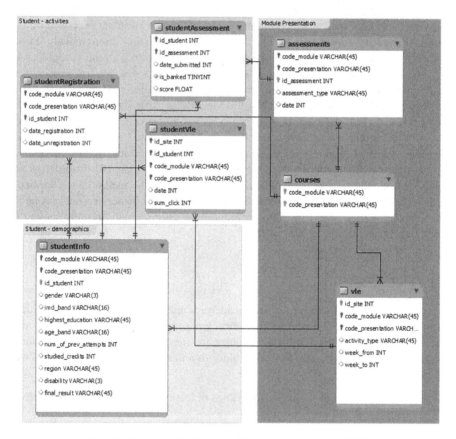

Fig. 1. Diagram of relations of the database. Source [17]

Figure 1 shows the tables and the relationships that allow registering the interaction of the students. Data mining was done with the Weka 3.8 software. The first experiment works with the fields in Fig. 2.

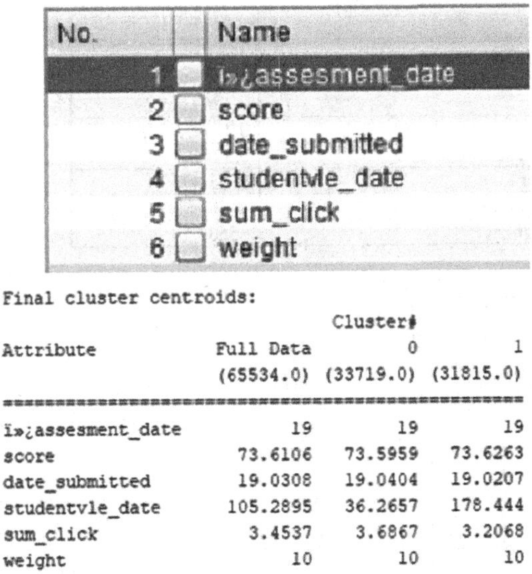

No.		Name
1	☐	ï»¿assesment_date
2	☐	score
3	☐	date_submitted
4	☐	studentvle_date
5	☐	sum_click
6	☐	weight

```
Final cluster centroids:
                                Cluster#
Attribute             Full Data        0           1
                     (65534.0)   (33719.0)   (31815.0)
================================================================
i»¿assesment_date           19          19          19
score                  73.6106     73.5959     73.6263
date_submitted         19.0308     19.0404     19.0207
studentvle_date       105.2895     36.2657    178.444
sum_click               3.4537      3.6867      3.2068
weight                      10          10          10
```

Fig. 2. Analysis by dates

Figure 2 shows a similar score and sum_click in the obtained clusters. Access to the virtual environment occurs on different dates (studentvle_date). One of the aspects that is important to analyze is the interaction with the virtual environment material (sum_click):

Table 1. Interaction with the virtual surroundings material

Final cluster centroids:	Cluster#		
Attribute	Full data	0	1
	(1043575.0)	(400052.0)	(648523.0)
i»¿score	76.6412	62.1141	85.6025
sum_click	3.2992	3.1754	3.3553

Table 1 shows that the number of interactions with the material is independent of academic performance. With the fields of Fig. 1 we proceeded to classify student performance by module:

Table 2 shows that it is possible to classify the performance of students except Distinction. With a different data set and applying the Multilayer Perceptron algorithm.

Table 2. Student performance

Correctly Classified Instances	46737	71.3172 %
Incorrectly Classified Instances	18797	28.6828 %
Kappa statistic	0,1767	
Mean absolute error	0,2072	
Root mean squared error	0,3246	
Relative absolute error	8833,47	
Root relative squared error	947845%	
Total Number of Instances	65534	

=== Detailed Accuracy By Class ===

	TP Rate	FP Rate	Precision	Recall	F-Measure	MCC	ROC Area	PRC Area	Class
	0,9470	0,8040	0,7370	0,9470	0,8290	0,2220	0,6940	0,8450	Pass
	0,2600	0,0560	0,4670	0,2600	0,3340	0,2620	0,7160	0,3470	Fail
	0,0000	0,0000	?	0,0000	?	?	0,8240	0,1940	Distinction
	0,0900	0,0020	0,7670	0,0900	0,1620	0,2520	0,6660	0,2040	Withdrawn
Weighted Avg.	0,7130	0,5750	?	0,7130	?	?	0,7060	0,6780	

=== Confusion Matrix ===

a	b	c	d	<—	classified as
43699	2347	0	97		a = Pass
7744	2719	0	0		b = Fail
5396	0	0	0		c = Distinction
2458	755	0	319		d = Withdrawn

Table 3 shows that it is possible to classify students by education, credits and interaction with the virtual environment, however; The disadvantage of not being able to classify Distinction type students follows.

Table 3. Classification of students: level of education, credits and interaction with the virtual surroundings

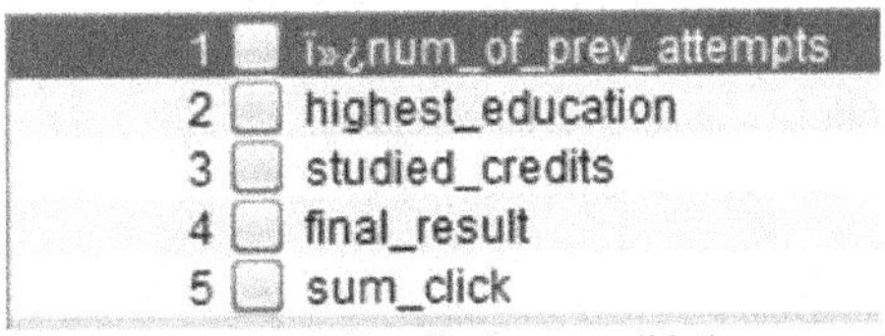

1	ï»¿num_of_prev_attempts
2	highest_education
3	studied_credits
4	final_result
5	sum_click

=== Stratified cross-validation ===
=== Summary ===

Correctly Classified Instances	18475	83,217%
Incorrectly Classified Instances	3726	16,783%
Kappa statistic	0,6594	
Kean absolute error	0,1803	
Root mean squared error	0,2994	
Relative absolute error	51,5287%	
Root relative squared error	71,5706%	
Total Number of Instances	22201	

=== Detailed Accuracy By Class ===

	TP Rate	FP Rate	Precision	Recall	F-Keasure	MCC	ROC Area	PRC Area
	0,000	0,000	?	0,000	?	?	0,780	0,209
	1,000	0,087	0,810	1,000	0,895	0,860	0,961	0,851
	0,899	0,280	0,843	0,899	0,870	0,636	0,851	0,897
Weighted Avg.	0,832	0,198	?	0,832			0,87	0,812

= Confusion Matrix ===

a	b	c	<—	classified as
0	0	2323	|	a = Distinction
0	5987	0	|	b = Fail
0	1403	12488	|	c = Pass

On next experiment we changed the dataset based on the structure proposed by UCI Machine Learning Laboratory [18]. The data was collected anonymously from a research methodology course. The records have no interaction with the virtual learning environment. A preview of the data is shown in Fig. 3.

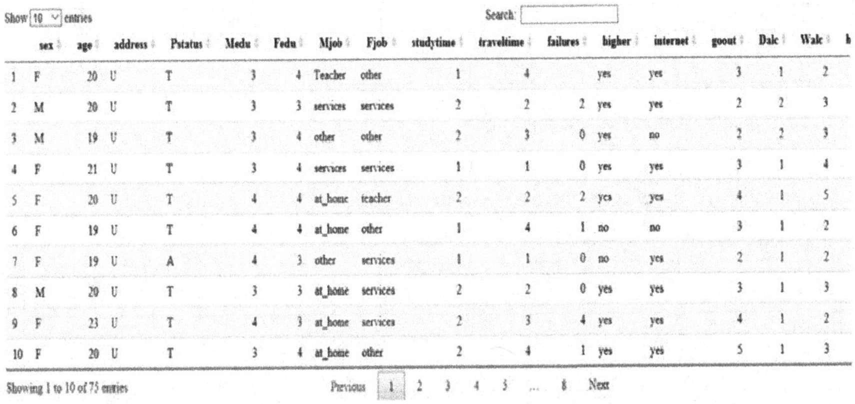

	sex	age	address	Pstatus	Medu	Fedu	Mjob	Fjob	studytime	traveltime	failures	higher	internet	goout	Dalc	Walc	h
1	F	20	U	T	3	4	Teacher	other	1	4		yes	yes	3	1	2	
2	M	20	U	T	3	3	services	services	2	2	2	yes	yes	2	2	3	
3	M	19	U	T	3	4	other	other	2	3	0	yes	no	2	2	3	
4	F	21	U	T	3	4	services	services	1	1	0	yes	yes	3	1	4	
5	F	20	U	T	4	4	at_home	teacher	2	2	2	yes	yes	4	1	5	
6	F	19	U	T	4	4	at_home	other	1	4	1	no	no	3	1	2	
7	F	19	U	A	4	3	other	services	1	1	0	no	yes	2	1	2	
8	M	20	U	T	3	3	at_home	services	2	2	0	yes	yes	3	1	3	
9	F	23	U	T	4	3	at_home	services	2	3	4	yes	yes	4	1	2	
10	F	20	U	T	3	4	at_home	other	2	4	1	yes	yes	5	1	3	

Showing 1 to 10 of 75 entries   Previous 1 2 3 4 5 … 8 Next

Fig. 3. Anonymous data of students of Methodology of investigation

Figure 3 shows the anonymous data of research methodology; the objective is to identify which fields (variables) are sufficient to predict academic performance. The analysis was carried out with the statistical software R (Table 4).

Table 4. Consumption of alcohol vs academic performance

```
> data%>%
+ group_by(Walc)%>%
+ aggregate(G3~Walc, data=., mean)%>%
+ arrarnge (desc (G3) )
```

	Walc	G3
1	1	17.61111
2	5	17.14286
3	4	17.13333
4	2	17.08333
5	3	16.95652

```
> data%>%
+ group_by(Dale)%>%
+ aggregate(G3~Dalc, data=., mean)%>%
=+ arrarnge (desc (G3) )
```

	Dale	G3
1	1	17.25412
2	3	17.25000
3	4	17.00000
4	5	17.00000
5	2	16.88885

Table 4 shows that there is no difference in academic performance if the consumption of alcohol is the weekend and during the same. The students' days off and their relationship with the final average is shown in Table 5:

Table 5. Free days vs student performance

```
+ group by(Dalc)%>%
+ aggregate(G3~Dalc, data=., mean)%>%
+ arrange(desc(G3))
```

	Dale	G3
1	1	17.29412
2	3	17.25000
3	4	17.00000
4	5	17.00000
5	2	16.88889

```
> data$goout <- as.factor(data$goout)
> data%>%
+ group by(goout)%>%
+ summarise (AverageScore= mean (G3, na. rm=TRUE) ) %>%
+ arrange(desc(AverageScore))
# A tibble: 5x2
```

	goout	AverageScore
	<fct>	<dbl>
1	1	17.4
2	3	17.3
3	4	17.2
4	2	17.1
5	5	17

Table 5 shows that days off have no relation to student performance. In relation to the preparation of higher level of students for their academic performance is observed that there is a difference in gender:

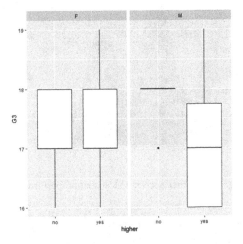

Fig. 4. Higher education level and gender

Figure 4 shows that in the case of women if having university knowledge influences to achieve improvements in their final academic performance, not so in the case of men who in fact generate a lower final score. In relation to the health field:

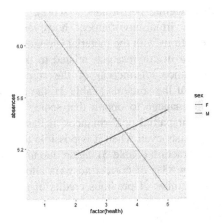

Fig. 5. Health and absence in classes

Figure 5 shows that women are more affected in absences due to their state of health. Access to the Internet can also influence academic performance:

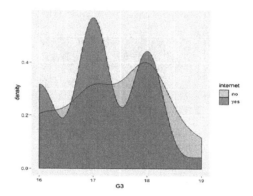

Fig. 6. Internet access and academic performance

Figure 6 shows that access to the Internet does have an influence on the academic performance of students. The results obtained with the analysis of data mining and correlation between variables allow conclusions and recommendations to be obtained, which are described in the following section.

4   Conclusions and Future Works

Figure 2 shows that there is no relationship between the dates of interaction in the virtual environment with academic performance (score). Teachers generate material that must be uploaded to the virtual environment, however; It is shown that not necessarily the number of interactions with the material is related to academic performance (Table 1), this is even shown in our research related to the number of tasks sent to students [19]. The performance Distinction of the students does not generate a mechanism of classification of the students (Table 2), the reason of this result is that few students of the sample manage to obtain that score. However, it is possible to classify students through their partial performances in Pass, Fail and Withdraw. The Distinction classification persists even when it is possible to classify students by level of education, credits and interaction (Table 3), again due to the low number of records with this label. But, obtaining 83% of correct answers allows us to conclude that the level of education and the number of previous credits of the student, if they directly influence their performance. These two fields must be taken into account at the time of student selection in order to propose improvements in their academic performance. The ROC curve shows that it is possible to classify students who failed in the course (Fail) with a high degree of accuracy:

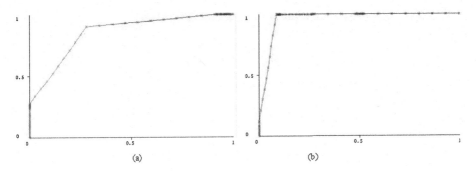

(a)   (b)

Fig. 7. (a) Fail ROC, (b) Pass ROC

Figure 7 shows that the accuracy to classify Fail and Pass students increases when it is related to students' prior knowledge. This implies that you can track the students' score from these two variables (fields):

Table 6. Cluster by level of education and credits

Final cluster centroids:		Cluster#	
Attribute	Full Data	0	1
	(22201.0)	(10150.0)	(12051.0)
i » ¿num_of_prev_attempts	0.2117	0.2672	0.165
highest_education	16.284	0	3
studied_credits	850.259	1.088.631	64.949
sum_click	1	1	1

Table 6 shows that it is possible to group students by the variables level of education and number of credits. It is again evident that the interaction with the virtual environment has no relevance, so to establish an adequate follow-up of a student's score, their prior knowledge is very important. Table 6 also shows the field of modules that previously the student took; however, as can be seen, it does not show a clear difference for the grouping, unlike the two variables discussed in this paragraph.

The social variables begin their analysis in Table 4, where it is observed that the academic performance is not linked to the consumption of alcohol at the end or midweek, although in fact the consumption of alcohol is considered very dangerous for concentration and student tasks:

Figure 8 shows a similar performance between alcohol consumption during the week and the weekend, confirming once again that there is no difference between the consumption of alcohol during and weekend for the final score. However, the precautions of the case must be taken in order to reduce consumption and this does not end in a social-academic problem. Table 5 shows that days off have no relation to student performance. This must be taken into account when generating tasks for the student to do during their vacation or rest days [20]. For the case of gender, it seems to be better

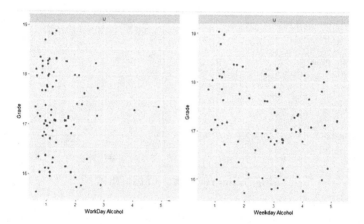

Fig. 8. Average vs alcohol consumption

that women have a university preparation to achieve a better score. This result may be due to the fact that the university career that was analyzed corresponded to being more of a female selection than a male one. In relation to health, women are more affected in absences and maybe that corroborates the fact that they need to have and improve their university knowledge (Fig. 5), in order to recover their grades and that their absences for health does not affect their performance academic. Figure 6 shows that, if there is a relationship between Internet access and performance, which corroborates our research described in [11].

References

1. Bartolj, T., Polanec, S.: Does work harm academic performance of students? Evidence using propensity score matching. Res. High. Educ. **59**, 401–429 (2018). https://doi.org/10.1007/s11162-017-9472-0
2. Lelli, R., García, R., Charczuk, N., et al.: Identificación de causales de deserción y desgranamiento de los estudiantes de la licenciatura en sistemas utilizando ingeniería de explotación de información. In: XVII Workshop de Investigadores en Ciencias de la Computación, Salta (2015)
3. García, J.C., Manuel, G., Zafrillo, A.I.: Desgranamiento university: student perspective in engineering, comunicaicón. In: International Colloquium on Gestao University na America do Sul, Florianopolis (2011)
4. Muller, C.: Parent involvement and academic achievement: an analysis of family resources available to the child. In: Parents, Their Children, And Schools. Taylor & Francis, New York, pp. 77–114 (2018)
5. Nair, R., Roche, K., White, R.: Acculturation gap distress among latino youth: prospective links to family processes and youth depressive symptoms, alcohol use, and academic performance. J. Youth Adolesc. **47**(1), 105–120 (2017)
6. Zuzanek, J., Hilbrecht, M.: Do parents matter? Teens' time use, academic performance and well-being. [En línea], 15 Mayo 2018. http://journals.openedition.org/efg/1888. Acceso 10 Noviembre 2018

7. Brewer, N., Thomas, K., Higdon, J.: Intimate partner violence, health, sexuality, and academic performance among a national sample of undergraduates. J. Am. Coll. Health **66** (7), 683–692 (2018)

8. Gomez, H.F.A., et al.: Emotional strategy in the classroom based on the application of new technologies: an initial contribution. In: Satapathy, S.C., Joshi, A. (eds.) Information and Communication Technology for Intelligent Systems. SIST, vol. 106, pp. 251–261. Springer, Singapore (2019). https://doi.org/10.1007/978-981-13-1742-2_25

9. Fong, W., Villa, A., Curiel, R.: Intrinsic motivation and its association with cognitive, actitudinal and previous knowledge processes in engineering student. Contemp. Eng. Sci. **11** (3), 129–138 (2018)

10. Gómez, H., Arias, S., Torres, P., et al.: Emotions analysis techniques: their application in the identification of criteria for selecting suitable Open Educational Resources (OERs). In: 2015 International Conference on Interactive Collaborative and Blended Learning (ICBL), Mexico (2015)

11. Torres, C., Duart, J., Goméz, H., et al.: Internet use and academic success in university students. Comunicar **14**(48), 61–70 (2016). Revista Científica de Comunicación y Educación

12. Gomez A, H.F., Arias T, S.A., Martinez, C.E., Martínez V, M.A., Sanchez, N.B., Sanchez-Cevallos, E.: Categorization of types of internautes based on their navigation preferences within educational environments. In: Rocha, Á., Serrhini, M. (eds.) EMENA-ISTL 2018. SIST, vol. 111, pp. 1–9. Springer, Cham (2019). https://doi.org/10.1007/978-3-030-03577-8_1

13. Iyanda, A., Ninan, O., et al.: Predicting student academic performance in computer science courses: a comparition of neural network models. Int. J. Mod. Educ. Comput. Sci. **6**, 1–9 (2018)

14. Marsh, H., Pekrun, R., Murayma, K., et al.: An integrated model of academic selfconcept development: academic selfconcept, grades, test scores, and tracking over six years. Dev. Psychol. **54**(2), 263–280 (2018)

15. Chen, C., Liu, K., Ma, K.: Research on evaluation of college students' professional ability based on k-means clustering. In: SMIMA (2018)

16. Torres, J.C., Gomez, H., Arias, S.: Social learning environments. In: 2015 International Conference on Interactive Collaborative Learning, Firence (2015)

17. Kuzilek, J., Hlosta, M., Zdrahal, Z.: Open university learning analytics dataset. Knowledge Media Institute, The Open University (2017). https://analyse.kmi.open.ac.uk/open_dataset. Acceso diciembre 2018

18. Cortez, P.: Student performance data set, April 2008. https://archive.ics.uci.edu/ml/datasets/student+performance. Acceso diciembre 2018

19. Gomez, H., Arias, S., Martinez, E., et al.: A methodology for identifying attributes of academic excellence based on a 20/80 Pareto distribution. In: 2016 IEEE Global Engineering Education Conference (EDUCON), Abu Dhabi (2016)

20. Cecilia, C., Pomerantz, E.: Does adolescents' disclosure to their parents matter for their academic adjustment? Child Dev. **84**(2), 693–710 (2013)

Knowledge Representation and Management for Precision Agriculture: A Case Study

Maryam Khalid, Habiba Saim, Zoha Qamar, Fahad Akhtar,
and Mian M. Awais$^{(\boxtimes)}$

Department of Computer Science, SBA-SSE, LUMS, Lahore, Pakistan
{maryam.khalid, habiba.saim, zoha.qamar, fahad.akhtar,
awais}@lums.edu.pk

Abstract. Precision Agriculture (PA) means the use of information technology for the management of crop growing procedures in such a way that farming methods implementation is accurate, controlled and done on time so that maximum yield can be obtained while reducing the losses, eliminating health hazards and cutting down the input costs. Despite the significance of PA, its practical implementation is yet scarce in Pakistan. The successful implementation of PA depends on gathering, storing, and sharing knowledge being generated at various levels. The knowledge that is needed to be shared includes best practices at farming level, results of various crop monitoring mechanisms, and the latest research findings at research institutes. An efficient knowledge storing and sharing system ultimately results in better crop plans, high yields and cost reduction. Due to slow knowledge sharing processes, stakeholders especially the farmers get delayed information. Also, the process level integration, that is responsible for calculating agricultural indices, crop health monitoring parameters, and parameter estimation techniques require coupling of different Knowledge Management (KM) technologies. Common KM systems lack such capabilities thus result in overall reduced benefits. This paper proposes a KM framework through which knowledge can be readily stored and shared with all the stakeholders through process automation. The system being proposed has three layered architecture with organizational layer at the top, connected to process layer and resources through a conceptual layer. This fully integrated KM framework has been applied to Rice Research Institute (RRI) at KalaShah Kaku, Lahore. Automation of manual processes done at RRI has been achieved through the application of proposed KM framework and is one of the main contributions of this paper. The RRI study shows that real time analysis can be shared promptly with the stakeholders through efficient knowledge management. The proposed KM model is generic and can be customized for any other organization related to agriculture or otherwise.

Keywords: Wireless rechargeable sensor network · Network planning ·
Meta-heuristic algorithm

© Springer Nature Switzerland AG 2019
L. Uden et al. (Eds.): KMO 2019, CCIS 1027, pp. 416–430, 2019.
https://doi.org/10.1007/978-3-030-21451-7_36

1 Introduction

Knowledge Management is a process through which knowledge can be created, captured, stored, and distributed effectively among stakeholders in order to generate a knowledge base of best practices, experiences and procedures adopted for efficient organizational working [1]. A high-quality knowledge management system (KMS) helps in providing shareable information to relevant people at right time and in right format. Instead of recreating the knowledge, a KMS can help in reusing the knowledge and making timely critical decisions. Not only explicit but also tacit knowledge sharing is required for the completion of a knowledge management system. Capturing, storing, sharing and analyzing the explicit knowledge is common and comparatively easier. While tacit knowledge is the most difficult type of knowledge to capture and write down, it is generated from the personal experience [2] and skills. It is hard to codify and can be revealed when it is being practiced in a particular context. A close personal contact through a common network or community of practice, helps to observe the tacit knowledge of different people of same school of thought.

The existing KM systems and approaches being adopted include categorization, analyses, and synthesis of the organizational knowledge being generated [3–7]. Lately systems have been developed that describe components, design aspects or technical architectures and their interdependencies [8–10], common understanding of the domain [8, 11, 12] structure approaches and practices [13] and research gaps [13, 14]. Other available KM frameworks include work presented in [15–17]. Most of aforementioned KM systems and others that are not listed here, do not provide a comprehensive view of the domain that combines organizational view with the organizational processes. These systems are simply frameworks of theoretical nature and also fall short of defining appropriate knowledge representation methods required for organizational view and processes integration. Further they address a partial knowledge management domain without giving a holistic view point. The Global KM Framework presented in [18] provides, to some extent, a global theoretical framework for KM, but the framework is still limited in terms of technology usage and lacks in presenting a view that enables technology-wide process integration.

In order to realize the benefits of PA, an integrated KM viewpoint is essential, as PA entails the use of different types of technologies in farming to obtain maximum possible crop yield and increased productivity. This is done by using new data (obtained through various sensors, drones and cameras), farmer's best practices, and previously stored data, to capture and manage inter and intra field variability like climatic conditions, soil condition, diseases, cropping practices etc. It involves the use of diverse data that is used by certain processes.

Most of the existing KM frameworks tackle partial aspects of the precision agriculture knowledge management dimensions mentioned above without an integrated viewpoint. The qualitative and quantitative KM technology integration across various agricultural aspects are not addressed in a way such that different process related ICTs can work together in a single framework. The existing systems also have limited ability to continuously change and obtain new understanding of the KM technologies [19–21].

Such limitations of KM systems reduce the use of these systems for fields like agriculture and specifically for precision agriculture.

The present study introduces a Knowledge Management Framework with following distinct advantages:

1. Defines comprehensive knowledge representation that ensures organizational structure and process integration
2. Integrates diverse perspectives of researchers and practitioners at the process level with the help of concept maps – thus helps the organization to store, manage and reuse its explicit as well as tacit knowledge
3. Bridges the gap between theory and practice
4. Combines different ICTs and knowledge management technologies in a single tool
5. Provides an easy to use framework for process creation and automatic speedy sharing
6. Integrates an explanation system that defines and explains concepts at the level of understanding of primary stakeholders

The remaining paper is organized as follows: Sect. 2 discusses the previous work done in the field of knowledge management for different organizations. Section 3 describes the proposed knowledge management framework, KMAT. Section 4 explains the application of the KMAT to Rice Research Institute (RRI). Section 5 concludes the paper with future research directions.

2   Literature Review

Gaviria-Marin et al. [22] have conducted a comprehensive study on KM research through bibliometric analysis specifically in the area of business and management. This study has shown that KM plays a vital role in improving the productivity of businesses resulting in a spectacular growth in KM related research in the last ten years. The most influential articles in KM, however, were published between 1991 and 2006.

Kang [23] has introduced Process Oriented Knowledge Management System (PKMS), which combines KM and Business Process Management (BPM). This study suggests that 75% of the Critical Success Factors (CSF) are positively associated with PKMS. Thus proving that PKMS based approach for KM is a successful intervention for organizations.

Soulignac et al. [24] have introduced methodological tools that are based on theoretical approaches for transforming explicit and tacit knowledge that are present within an organization. The study uses two tools; the CFK tool manages critical knowledge and TRACO, a decision support system, identifies the most relevant knowledge transfer methods. The middle-up-down knowledge management approach proposed in [25] has resulted in good communication among stakeholders and has eventually assisted in managing tacit knowledge.

Handzic [26] has mentioned that Small and Medium Enterprises (SMEs) lose their key personnel more often compare to larger organizations, thus are more dynamic and agile. SMEs therefore, need good knowledge management implementations that could save the company from losing best practices. The paper has identified critical steps, key factors, and possible alternative paths to knowledge management so that KM can be practiced in SMEs and does not remain only a theory.

Alavi et al. [14] have described knowledge management as complex and multi-faceted task, therefore highlighting the criticality of KM. The paper suggests to use an IT based KMS that could target all the KM requirements of an organization, which could in turn help in creating, storing, retrieving, sharing, and transferring knowledge.

Arshad et al. [27] have proposed an integrated IT based KM system that could be used by different stakeholders for making critical decisions based on the previously generated knowledge and knowledge that has been generated more recently. The paper has shown the application of the proposed IT based KM system to healthcare sector.

Muthuveloo et al. [28] have done research on the impact of tacit knowledge management by using Socialization, Externalization, Combination and Internalization (SECI) based dimensions on organizational performance. Their research has shown that socialization and internalization are comparatively important than externalization and combination in improving organizational performance. The reason identified for this difference mostly organization do not have the understanding of knowledge management and workforce quality importance, they rather focus on skills and hardware.

The existing literature suggests that not much work has been done in the area of agriculture regarding KM, especially that integrates agri-workflows, farmer and decision makers related processes and knowledge preservation with respect to processes. The present paper is an attempt to integrate the aforementioned aspects of KM into a single tool – KMAT. The proposed IT based tool has been designed in a way that it could be used easily for other than agriculture domains. The effectiveness of KMAT has been shown through its application to an Agriculture related research institute.

3 Proposed Knowledge Management Tool

KM in an organization is employed to identify, capture, and analyze the knowledge to help the organization work more effectively and efficiently through better communication, sharing best practices, avoiding repetition of mistakes and better decision making. This is necessary as most companies suffer when key staff members leave the company, and as a result best practices are lost. Most of the organizations practicing KM believe that it leads to enhanced productivity, creating new opportunities, sharing best practices, reducing costs, and causing staff attraction and retention.

The proposed knowledge representation and management tool, Knowledge Management for All Tool (KMAT), is a generic solution that incorporates interactions between an organization and end users. The objectives for the development of this system are achieved by incorporating different knowledge representation models: composition ladders, process ladders and concept maps along with the facility of linking users, resources and tools with each of these ladders and maps. It focuses on integrating and linking different users, departments and processes along with the resources required by each and the tools used in certain processes. Figure 1 shows the KMAT system architecture. KMAT provides an easy to use graphical user interface for creating and linking different modules that collectively represent the whole project and its past and ongoing activities in a graphical manner. The brief description of important modules in KMAT are described in the following section.

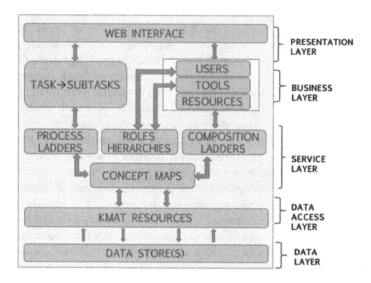

Fig. 1. KMAT architecture with various modules

3.1   Composition Ladder

A composition ladder illustrates the organizational hierarchy. This is the top layer in the KMAT architecture. This layer defines the stakeholders, internal to the organization, in a hierarchical fashion. These stakeholders are the primary owners of all the knowledge generating modules present within the organization.

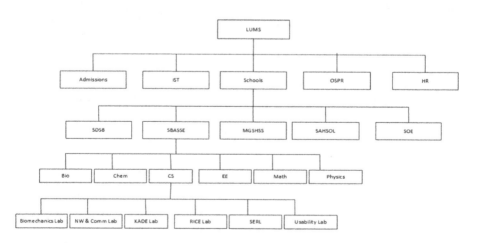

Fig. 2. Compositional ladder for an educational institute (LUMS)

The levels of hierarchical composition represent the levels of knowledge ownership. The stakeholders can directly interact with the process ladders (processes being followed in the organization and-or by the stakeholders). The stakeholders in the compositional ladder can design, and share processes through this module. They can also share the knowledge being generated stakeholders external to the organization. For example, an agronomist may initiate a process of estimating crop yields and could share the results with the director of the organization and also with the selected farmers of the crops. An example compositional ladder is shown in Fig. 2.

3.2 Process Ladder

A process is a set of interrelated activities that interact to achieve a result and is simply known as "program in excitation". It is a data structure that can be used to model a complete process such as student's course enrollment, point-of-sale transaction, forest preservation/management, crops disease diagnosis process etc.

The second most important layer within KMAT is the process ladder that is responsible for major internal knowledge generation. The process ladder in KMAT defines and implements processes present in the organization. For example, estimating crop yields is a process defined in an agriculture research organization. The user can define crop yield estimation as a process in KMAT as a connected graph and may also attach a third-party tool to any node on this graph. The graph defines the process sequence and enables implementation of various KM technologies. The authentic users can execute this process and share the results with others. An example process ladder depicting admission process in an educational institute is given in Fig. 3.

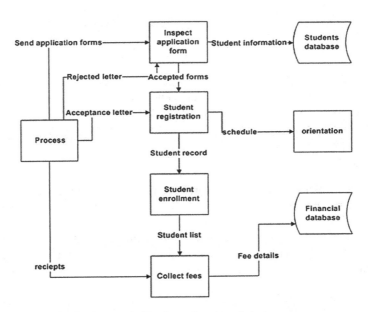

Fig. 3. Process ladder for university admission process

3.3 Resource Repositories

Every process in an organization has some resource repositories associated with it. These resources could be of different types. Currently, four types of data resources are being catered in the KMAT system. These are documents, audio/video files, images and web-links. KMAT user can open, edit/save and share each type of resource according to access privileges assigned to them. Figure 4 shows each type of resource, with the available format file that can be stored in KMAT data-store. All resources added in the system can be linked with processes and concept maps (to be discussed later). Each of these resources can contain different aspects of an entity and hold different information accordingly. For example, a basic resource for a tool can be its user guide which will be in the form of a text document. It can also be a web link. Since different types of resources require different tools for execution (e.g. a. docx resource needs MS Word), KMAT handles linking of resources, uploading and downloading them and opening them in their respective application on the end user's system.

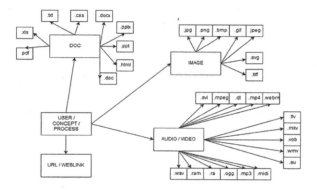

Fig. 4. KMAT - resource list

When a resource is added, it is uploaded on the server. A copy of the resource is also placed on the user's system where it is accessible to KMAT so that it does not have to be located every time. Deleting the local resource removes only its local copy.

3.4 Tools

Tools are applications or softwares that are used to assist in accomplishing some tasks. They mainly relate to processes. System allows to establish a link between the process node and the tool(s) that is associated to it, if any. This module is responsible for adding different tools to the system, and to link them with nodes of processes, compositions and concept maps. Tools are installed on the server, so that the high-speed server can execute the required processes and communicate the results to the relevant users.

3.5 Users

User module is required to register a user in the KMAT system. Each user has varying access rights according to the type of organization, the users' role in the organization (specifically the department that user is working in) and the duties that the person has to perform. Some important user type are given below:

Knowledge Engineer. Knowledge Engineer (KE) has access to all functions and features available within KMAT. KE can configure user access level, edit and maintain knowledge databases etc. KE can also add, edit and delete ladders, maps and their nodes and links. KE has complete access to the tools and resources and is responsible for setting up the environment for other users by formulating the knowledge of organization within the composition ladders, process ladders and concept maps.

Organization Stakeholders. *Admin.* An admin has access to all features and functions available within this product except knowledge-engineer's interface. He can add new users to the system, manage their access and handle different tools and resources. He also has complete access of editing ladders, maps and their nodes and links. A knowledge engineer can also be an admin.

Other Users. A user can perform tasks based on access privileges he has. Typically, any user can view nodes or ladders and concept maps that are shared with him. A user can be given ownership of a node or ladder or concept map. This allows the user to share the structure with other people, add details and attach more tools and resources, that are in the system, to the structure. There is the provision of addition of external users. These are typically people collaborating on projects or services but are not employees of the organization. Upon request, they can be given access to view particular components but not the complete system.

3.6 Concept Map

The link between composition and process layer (ladders) is realized through the implementation of a conceptual layer that has multiple uses. It provides an explanation system and resources in the form of documents, videos, and audio files associated with the given process. It defines the integration mechanism between layers and ladders and is part of the service layer of the tool. The concept map is very similar to a semantic network used in cognitive psychology. Concept map visually links together users, processes, compositions and all types of resources in a graphical network of nodes and edges. Nodes represent processes, compositions or resources, and edges represent the relationship between two nodes. Additionally, this network also consists of another type of node: 'Notes', which holds any other type of textual information needed by the concept map. If a farmer, an external stakeholder to an organization, wants to know as to how crop yield estimates are generated, what are the inputs, and outputs to this process; farmer could refer to the concept map layer, understand the process and could also know about the people responsible within the organization for this task. The stakeholder through this layer may access various resource modules.

3.7   Roles

Roles are the hierarchies that define roles and their relations. Roles are a special type of composition ladder called 'Roles Hierarchy'. The roles hierarchy interface allows a specific user to be linked with a role node.

4   Case Study – KMAT for Rice Research Institute (RRI)

Rice Research Institute, Kala Shah Kaku, Lahore is responsible to carry out research and development of rice crop in the Province of The Punjab in Pakistan. The main research disciplines under this institute are: Plant Breeding, Agronomy, Soil Chemistry, Entomology, Plant Pathology, Agricultural Engineering, Rice Technology and Economics & Statistics.

Some of the main services provided by RRI are:

- Provision of quality seed to the growers and seed companies
- Development of high yielding and early maturing rice varieties
- Development of optimum cultural and agronomic practices for rice growing
- Development of weeds, insects, and diseases control strategies
- Determination of macro and micro nutrients requirements for rice varieties under different soil conditions
- Advisory services to stakeholders

4.1   The Organizational Structure of 'Rice Research Institute' Includes

The Director, the top most role in the organizational hierarchy, is responsible for managing a team of Botanists, Pathologists, Entomologists, Agronomists, Statistical officers, Technologists, Agriculture Engineers. These experts are responsible for various functions. These functions are spread over the life cycle of the rice crop. The life-cycle of rice crop consists of three main phases i.e. vegetation, reproduction and ripening. Since these are sub-processes of the life-cycle process, they are represented in KMAT as process ladders. Among these phases, the vegetation phase can be customized. Thus, information sharing is at its maximum level in this phase. The process of monitoring is most important during the reproduction and ripening phases.

Based on the information gathered from RRI, following processes are undertaken during a crop life cycle and are assigned to different people in RRI: (i) soil analysis (ii) fertilizer requirement (iii) water plan (iv) weather plan (v) crops diseases (vi) pesticides requirements (vii) crop monitoring. Most of these processes are carried out manually at present. The present study has implemented all these processes through ICTs to achieve process automation for speedy information sharing and storage, except the weather and water plan implementation.

The customization of KMAT for RRI carried out during this study is discussed below.

4.2 RRI Composition Ladder

The director is the main role in the institute. The plant pathologist is the expert on plant diseases and studies their effects on plant growth, yield and quality. The plant pathologist is assigned an assistant. The botanist studies plants to enhance crop yield. The botanist studies various plant related problems and defines the processes accordingly. Botanist is assigned three assistants. The entomologist studies pests in order to prevent the crops while making sure that useful insects, like bees are not harmed. Two assistants are assigned to entomologist. The agronomist is responsible for modelling and planning of whole rice crop life-cycle and is assigned two assistants. Statistical officer analyzes data gathered from research being carried out at RRI. The assistant technologist's job involves taking field samples and conducting lab tests. The technologist also assists in studying diseases and improving methods related to managing weeds, pests and diseases. The agricultural engineer is responsible for machinery maintenance (Fig. 5).

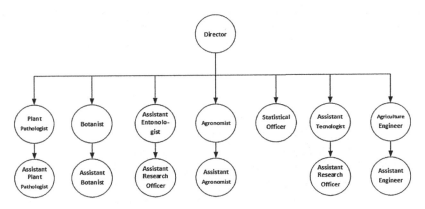

Fig. 5. RRI composition ladder for RRI

4.3 RRI Process Ladder

There are different processes being conducted at different levels at RRI. The present study focuses on the processes related to soil analysis, fertilizer requirements, disease prevention and crop health monitoring. The overview of the process ladder developed for RRI is shown in Fig. 6. The details of all the above processes are discussed below.

Soil Process. The purpose of soil process is to determine deficiency of different soil components present in the field. Soil contains multiple components which are categorized as major and minor components. The core components in soil include pH, electrical conductivity (EC), organic matter (OM), phosphorus (P), potassium (K), zinc, and soil texture. Some of these parameters can inform about the fertilizers' requirement i.e., nitrogen, potassium, phosphorous, sulphur, calcium and magnesium etc. Other parameters have other utilities i.e., EC value gives information about suitability of cultivating different crops. The soil analysis is conducted through a lab test. In KMAT

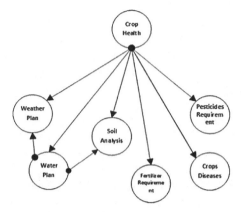

Fig. 6. RRI process ladder

the values of this lab test are entered manually for a particular farm. This process shares information with other processes such as fertilizer process (Fig. 7).

Fig. 7. Fertilizer requirement manual by RRI

Fertilizer Process. The purpose of this process is to determine fertilizer type and the quantity requirement for a particular field. There are multiple fertilizer types and each type fulfills different soil components requirement i.e., if phosphorus quantity is low then DAP fertilizer is used and if it is medium then Nitrophos fertilizer is preferred and so on. RRI has developed manuals for determining the fertilizer requirements. These quantities are determined manually. This process is implemented as fuzzy rule-based system. The inputs to fuzzy rule-based system are soil parameters and the crop type with fertilizer type and quantity as output. Figure 7 shows a typical manual developed by RRI.

Disease Process. The purpose of this module is to identify disease based on observed symptoms and suggests suitable sprays for encountering respective disease. For rice crop 18 different symptoms have been used as inputs. The user picks observed symptoms and the process in return predicts respective disease(s). The process also suggests different pesticides according to respective disease with their complete usage method. Case Based Reasoning has been used for disease process implementation.

Rice Crop Health Monitoring Process. The purpose of this process is to get the coverage, overall growth, health of rice crop related indices. Presently RRI carries out this manually through field inspection. The implementation of KMAT automated this process through integrating aerial (or otherwise) image capturing, image processing and indices calculations. The automated process has been implemented as part of a process ladder. The Inputs to this process include image acquisition through any device i.e., mobile phones, aerial images from drones and/or satellite images from google earth. Images of crop growth captured and monitoring is done at regular intervals i.e., say every 15 days. Any information related to the complete process is stored in the associated concept map. The first step involves data acquisition. Data can be in image form or video. The second is the pre-processing phase, where noise is removed using different filters. In case of a drone/ground image the green index is calculated. In case of a satellite image some further filtering is applied before calculating indices. Indices include greenness index, Biomass index, and Normalized Vegetation Index (NDVI). Sample output of this process is shown in Figs. 8 and 9.

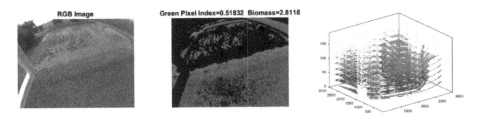

Fig. 8. Drone image, filtered image and intensity distribution for green index of the field

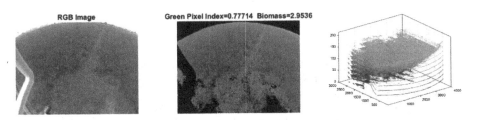

Fig. 9. Drone image, filtered image and intensity distribution for green index of the field

5   Conclusion

This paper presents a KM framework that integrates organizational structure, various processes within organizations, and the concept map that interlinks hierarchies, processes and resources. KMAT architecture is composed of compositional ladder, process ladder, and concept maps. KMAT provides easy integration of information and knowledge from different sources including images, forms, hand-written data, videos, websites and so on. The proposed system is adaptable with complete KM control. The proposed system has been applied to a local research institute, RRI which tries to implement diverse precision agriculture related features. The study has shown that using KMAT, ICTs can be easily integrated in management of farms, by handling inter and intra-field variability in crops. This would maximize food production, minimize environmental damage, reduce cost and knowledge sharing. The future work includes incorporating weather, water plans, crop plans, and rotations. An appropriate yield estimation along with a costing processes will be integrated with the KMAT implementation for RRI (Fig. 10).

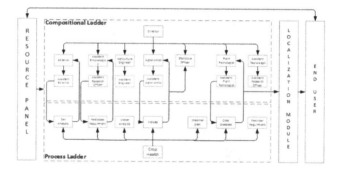

Fig. 10. RRI study - KMAT integrated view

Acknowledgements.   Our special thanks to Dr. Sabir at RRI for providing technical assistance for Rice crop, and to Higher Education Commission of Pakistan for funding the KMAT project.

References

1. KPMG, KPMG Management Consulting, Issue: Knowledge Management, p. 1 (1998)
2. Tacit, Explicit, and Implicit Knowledge: Definitions and Examples. https://bloomfire.com/blog/implicit-tacit-explicit-knowledge/
3. Arthur Andersen and The American Productivity and Quality Center: The American Productivity and Quality Center. The Knowledge Management Assessment Tool: External Benchmarking Version (1996)
4. Fahey, L., Prusak, L.: The eleven deadliest sins of knowledge managements. Calif. Manag. Rev. **40**, 265–276 (1998)

5. Leonard-Barton, D.: Wellsprings of Knowledge. Harvard Business School Press, Boston (1995)
6. van der Spek, R., Spijkervet, A.: Knowledge Management: Dealing Intelligently with Knowledge. Knowledge Management and Its Integrative Elements, Liebowitz, J., Wilcox, L. (eds.) CRC Press, New York (1997)
7. Wiig, K.: Knowledge Management Foundations. Schema Press, Arlington (1993)
8. CEN CWA 14924 European Guide to good Practice in Knowledge Management Brussels, 1–5 (2004)
9. Hahn, J., Subramani, M.R.: A framework of knowledge management systems: issues and challenges for theory and practice. In: Proceedings of the Twenty-First International Conference on Information Systems, Brisbane, Australia, pp. 302–312 (2000)
10. Heisig, P.: Harmonisation of knowledge management – comparing 160 KM frameworks around the globe. J. Knowl. Manage. **13**, 4–31 (2009)
11. Bhagat, R.S., Kedia, B.L., Harveston, P.D., Triandis, H.C.: Cultural variations in the cross-border transfer of organizational knowledge: an integrative framework. Acad. Manage. Rev. **27**, 204–221 (2002)
12. Maier, R.: Knowledge Management Systems: Information and Communication Technologies for Knowledge Management, 3rd edn. Springer, Heidelberg (2007). https://doi.org/10.1007/978-3-540-71408-8
13. Grover, V., Davenport, T.H.: General perspectives on knowledge management: fostering a research agenda. J. Manage. Inf. Syst. **18**, 5–21 (2001)
14. Alavi, M., Leidner, D.E.: Knowledge management and knowledge management systems: conceptual foundations and research issues. MISQ **25**, 107–136 (2001)
15. Snowden, D.: Complex acts of knowing: paradox and descriptive self-awareness. In: Proceedings of the European Conference on Knowledge Management (ECKM 2002), Dublin, September 2002 (2002)
16. Handzic, M., Hasan, H.: The search for an integrated KM framework. In: Australian Studies in Knowledge Management, Chapter 1, pp. 3–34. UOW Press (2003)
17. Liebowitz, J.: Putting more rigor into knowledge management. In: Proceedings of the Knowledge Management Aston Conference (2003)
18. Pawlowski, J., Bick, M.: The global knowledge management framework: towards a theory for knowledge management in globally distributed settings. Electron. J. Knowl. Manage. **10**, 92–108 (2012)
19. Liao, S.: Knowledge management technologies and applications—literature review from 1995 to 2002. Expert Syst. Appl. **25**, 155–164 (2003)
20. Ramsden, S.: Facilitating Sustainable Agriculture: Participatory Learning and Adaptive Management in Times of Environmental Uncertainty, Roling, N.G., Wagemakers, M.A.E. (eds.) Cambridge University Press, Cambridge (1998). ISBN: 0 521 58174 5. The Journal of Agricultural Science. 131, 245–249 (1998)
21. Stirling, G.R.: Soil Ecosystem Management in Sustainable Agriculture. Biological Control of Plant-parasitic Nematodes (2014)
22. Gaviria-Marin, M., Merigó, J., Baier-Fuentes, H.: Knowledge management: a global examination based on bibliometric analysis. Technol. Forecast. Soc. Change **140**, 194–220 (2019). ISSN 0040-1625
23. Kang, H.: Critical success factors in implementing process-oriented knowledge management systems (PKMS) in the public sector in Korea. Graduate Theses and Dissertations, Iowa State University (2011)

24. Soulignac, V., Pinet, F., Vallas, M., Ermine, J.: Experiments on the use of knowledge management tools for agriculture. In: 12th European International Farming Systems Association (IFSA) Symposium, Social and Technological Transformation of Farming Systems: Diverging and Converging Pathways (2016)

25. Nagel, U.: Knowledge flows in agriculture; Linking Research, Extension and the farmer. Zeitschrift fürAusländische Landwirtschaft 18.Jg., Heft2: pp. 135–150 (1979)

26. Handzic, M.: Knowledge management in SMEs practical guidelines. J. Commer. Ind. **1**, 1–11 (2006)

27. Arshad, A., Noordin, M., Othman, R.: A Comprehensive Knowledge Management Process Framework for Healthcare Information Systems in Healthcare Industry of Pakistan, pp. 30–35 (2016)

28. Muthuveloo, R., Shanmugam, N., Ping Teoh, A.: The impact of tacit knowledge management on organizational performance: evidence from Malaysia. Asia Pac. Manage. Rev. **22**, 192–201 (2017)

Information Systems and Information Science

Case Studies on ISD Agility

Yi-Te Chiu[1], Houn-Gee Chen[2(✉)], and Yu-Qian Zhu[3]

[1] School of Information Management, Victoria Business School,
Victoria University of Wellington, Wellington, New Zealand
yi-te.chiu@vuw.ac.nz
[2] Department of Business Administration,
National Taiwan University, Taipei, Taiwan, R.O.C.
hgchen@ntu.edu.tw
[3] Department of Information Management, National Taiwan University
of Science and Technology, Taipei, Taiwan, R.O.C.
yzhu@mail.ntust.edu.tw

Abstract. Much attention is paid to information systems development (ISD) agility, which has positive consequences for ISD projects, teams, and their organizations. ISD agility enables organizations to react to ISD-related change with speed and flexibility while constantly contributing to the delivery of value via IS. This article investigates how IS departments maintain their continual readiness for ISD agility. **Drawing** on a dynamic capability perspective, we suggest that routines underlie ISD agility. The analysis of three high-performing IS departments identifies six aspects of routines conducive to ISD agility: continuous discovery and validation of customer needs, continuous evolution of IT-enabled products and services, resource optimization, continuous integration and deployment, continuous management of risk, and continuous learning. In light of microfoundations, individual competence and mindset, constructive dialogue, and structural arrangements are essential components of routines and ISD agility. Theoretical and practical insights are discussed.

Keywords: ISD agility · Dynamic capabilities · Routines · Microfoundations

1 Introduction

In a rapidly changing digital business world, information systems development (ISD) must be agile to address challenges caused by customer needs, emergent technologies, and disruptive markets. ISD methods, agile methods mainly, are in the spotlight concerning ISD agility as they are comprised of recommended means to engage stakeholders, increase delivery speed, respond to change, and add business value (Conboy 2009). Despite the promised benefits of agile methods, the majority of firms has not reaped the full benefits. In the State of Agile Survey with almost 1,500 practitioners across the world, 84% of respondents stated that their organization was at or below a "still maturing level of agility". After decades of agile movements, people still hold a fragmented understanding of ISD agility let alone achieving agility. For example,

© Springer Nature Switzerland AG 2019
L. Uden et al. (Eds.): KMO 2019, CCIS 1027, pp. 433–444, 2019.
https://doi.org/10.1007/978-3-030-21451-7_37

some equate agility with the velocity of delivery and overlook the development of capabilities to cope with ISD-related changes and generate value via IS. More recently, scaling agility exacerbates the challenges in the development of agility. The existing agile methods mostly provide recommendations at the project level and do not always achieve organization-wide impacts. The project-level methods disregard the interdependencies of projects, systems, and stakeholders and endanger delivering the value of IS (Jiang et al. 2018). A couple of nascent agile frameworks, such as the Scaled Agile Framework (SAFe) and Large-Scale Scrum (LeSS), tackle the scaling issues and touch upon management principles at the organizational level. However, the prescribed practices are not systematically validated, and the claimed benefits are experienced-based. It remains elusive what makes ISD agile and how ISD agility is attained.

Therefore, this study aims to clarify the underlying meaning of ISD agility and unveil mechanisms to develop ISD agility. Since ISD agility comes within the purview of the IS department (or any equivalent unit responsible for ISD), we suggest shifting the central focus away from selecting and adopting agile methods and looking into the development of organizational capabilities. Organizations can concentrate on resource configurations (e.g., people, processes, products, and technology) and formulate a holistic approach to achieve ISD agility. Drawing on a dynamic capabilities perspective, which concerns the capability development toward changing environmental dynamics, we apply the theoretical underpinnings of dynamic capabilities – routines and their microfoundations – to understand the development of ISD agility. Organizational routines build organizational capabilities as a result of "complicated, detailed, analytic processes that rely extensively on existing knowledge and linear execution to produce predictable outcomes". Consistency in complex problem-solving through routines shapes organizational capabilities. Such routines persist as they prove to be effective, but some of them have to evolve for change. The evolution of routines represents dynamism of capabilities. Recent research further delves into the sources of dynamism and study people, their interactions, and the context where individuals and routines are situated – so-called "microfoundations" (Barney and Felin 2013). We contend that the theory of routines advances our understanding of ISD agility by elucidating ISD routines for change. Microfoundations explain how routines evolve and in turn enhance ISD agility. In essence, routines and microfoundations expand the focus of ISD agility from an ISD method to the nature and origin of the dynamism of ISD agility and the context where ISD agility breeds. We illustrate the development of ISD agility based on data from three IS departments with high ISD agility. We do not move the level of analysis to the firm level because it requires capabilities more than ISD agility, that is, IT-dependent organizational agility – "the ability to respond operationally and strategically to changes in the external environment through IT". Besides ISD agility, IT-dependent organizational agility requires IT-dependent information agility as well as IT-dependent strategic agility. It contains far more elements and offers more robust outcomes for firms than ISD agility alone.

2   The Concept of ISD Agility

Considerable research has contributed to an understanding of ISD agility. Nevertheless, there is still no consistent definition (Abrahamsson et al. 2009; Conboy 2009; Gregory et al. 2016). An exhaustive review of the debate around ISD agility is beyond the scope of this article. Instead, we select seminal works that inform our understanding of ISD agility. Following MacKenzie et al. (2011), we analyze the conceptual domain (e.g., feeling, behavior) to which the construct refers (i.e., property), the entity of the property (e.g., individual, team), and the necessary and sufficient attributes to represent the conceptual theme of ISD agility. ISD agility has been referred to as a capability of an ISD method, a team, and a firm. Different entities in various definitions stem from researchers' propositions about whether ISD methods, teams, or firms account for ISD agility. As discussed in the introduction, we shift the entity from ISD methods to the IS department. Consistent with previous definitions, ISD agility is conceptualized as a capability in response to change. The common attributes of responses consist of flexibility (i.e., adapt without change or with minimum efforts) and speed (e.g., "quickly," "swiftly," "rapidly"). We side with Conboy that, besides reactive response, agility connotes proactive nature and should encompass continual improvement that adds value. To sum up, we define ISD agility as *IS department (or any equivalent unit responsible for ISD)'s capability to reacting to ISD-related change with speed and flexibility while constantly contributing to the delivery of value* via *IS*.

3   Achieving ISD Agility

Dynamic capability and ISD agility share a commonality as both are organizational capabilities that enable organizations to adapt to change in a complex business environment. The objective of dynamic capabilities is grander – not only adding value to customers but also sustaining competitive advantages. The goal of ISD agility, although it should contribute to business outcomes ultimately, is closely related to IS-enabled business. ISD agility can be considered as a subset of the broad area of dynamic capabilities. A dynamic capability perspective offers an insight into how organizational capabilities evolve and, therefore, should inform the development of ISD agility. Notably, we concentrate on two essential areas in dynamic capabilities: routines, which entail reliable and systematic performance while being adaptable to change, and microfoundations, which investigates how micro-level elements interact and emerge forming the collective phenomenon (i.e., routines and ISD agility). In the following section we introduce key theoretical ideas underpinning dynamic capabilities: routines, routine dynamics, and microfoundations.

3.1   Routines, Capabilities, and ISD Agility

It should first be noted that routines underlie capability (Winter 2000). Routines as "repetitive, recognizable patterns of interdependent actions, carried out by multiple actors" ensure organizations reliably provide services and products. Routines can be either rigid or fluid, and have benefits of stability and flexibility. An integration of routines supporting stability and flexibility is vital to ISD agility because a portfolio of routines allows response to change while maintaining productivity and quality. For instance, a time box defines a period for a team to achieve specified goals. If a 2-week sprint routine is adopted, a team needs to get agreed-upon deliverables done by then. Such a rigid routine assures steady delivery. Meanwhile, a team can implement another agile practice to generate flexibility. Instead of assigning tasks to a developer, in daily standup meetings team members share impediments they are facing and support each other. Task allocation can be fluid, in which available and capable team members work on tasks in need of resources to move the project forward.

3.2   Routine Dynamics and ISD Agility

Uncertainty demands changes of routines. Although cognitive and behavioral regularities rooted in routines imply inertia, routines can be livelier than they appear. Routines evolve and adapt when firms implement meta-routines (Adler et al. 1999). Put differently, firms need to leverage routines to change other routines that are no longer suitable for new environmental conditions. Zollo and Winter (2002) propose to enhance dynamic capabilities by engaging in experiential learning, articulating new knowledge for changes, and codifying knowledge. Deliberate learning is a type of meta-routines and can generate new routines and modify existing routines. A transformation of Ericsson, a Swedish telecommunications company, from a plan-driven to an agile method organization illustrates how deliberate trial-and-error processes help members in the ISD unit to learn and undertake changes in ISD routines. Besides a trial-and-error learning approach, various meta-routines embedded in agile methods support deliberate learning (Annosi et al. in press; Bjørnson and Dingsøyr 2008). For example, collaborative spaces, including physical and virtual ones, allow team members to learn from each other and share knowledge. Moreover, sprint and project retrospective meetings are designated to improve routines.

3.3   On Microfoundations of Routines and ISD Agility

Microfoundations explain the collective phenomenon by systematically looking at its origins and nature (Barney and Felin 2013). Multiple microfoundational elements form and explain routines and capabilities. Individuals serve as microfoundation because they operate routines and can make a change to routines. Routines mature over time as individuals learn and develop habits, supporting the reliable operations of organizations. Since individuals are not situated in a vacuum, other microfoundational constituents, such as interpersonal interactions and the context where individuals are embedded, can enable or hinder individual behaviors. We explain their role in ISD agility as follows.

(1) Individuals and their interactions
In the early literature of dynamic capability, the role of managers is emphasized. Their competence, such as dynamic managerial capabilities (Adner and Helfat 2003), influences the strategic choices and actions when facing change. Extending this line of work,

the literature on microfoundations of dynamic capabilities suggests that individuals, regardless of ranks, should all be considered (Abell et al. 2008). A dilemma lies in the diversity. Even though diverse expertise enables agility (Lee and Xia 2010) and improves routines, differences among individuals pose a risk. Some people have a propensity of overlooking opportunities and threats, resisting to change their behaviors, and holding negative emotion amid adaptation. The predicament calls for the investigation of ways to better manage diverse individual members. First, firms can nurture the talent by shaping their cognitive capability and attitudes, such as openness to change and learning (Balijepally et al. 2015) and tolerance for ambiguity. People possessing such attributes are more likely to improve routines and react swiftly when routines cannot operate. Although ISD personnel's competence for organizational capability is widely studied, limited empirical research has been done on what competence for ISD agility should be based on. Second, the recent research looks at the interactions among individuals, specifically, how diverse expertises collaborate to generate dynamic capabilities. The theoretical mechanisms of constructive dialogue reinforce the idea of communication and collaboration in agile methods. Cooperation, collective learning, and cohesion signal that people are "being agile" beyond "doing agile".

(2) Structure

Structure concerns "specialization of tasks, hierarchical arrangements, as well as formalization of objectives and procedures" (Bresman and Zellmer-Bruhn 2013, p. 1120). When adapting to change, organizations need to be organic, characterized by fluid roles and responsibilities, decentralized authority, and fewer rules and procedures. The flat organizational structure allows units to be responsive and nimble to change. However, the coordination cost can be heightened, leading to fragmentation. More recently, the matrix organizational structure encourages cross-unit collaboration. On the extreme is the so-called Spotify model where, to meet 70 million subscribers' needs, Spotify leverages tightly bonded small core units called squads. Squads with different development foci, when combined, bring new ideas and spark innovation. Squad members belong to other larger formal and informal teams, such as Chapters, Tribes, and Guilds, to build a shared understanding of tasks and teams.

4 Research Method

Our research question is to answer what fundamental elements prescribed the ISD agility In particular, to explore how routines and microfoundations constitute ISD agility, we adopted a qualitative research method using a positivist multiple-case study design. The multiple-case study approach is suitable for the less explored phenomenon that requires contextualized understanding. Multiple cases enable comparisons among sites and help demonstrate the influence of variability in context. We selected firms that have received wide recognition for their ISD agility. We sought firms which considered ISD a core competence where the continual evolution of IS applications and IS-enabled services are necessary to sustain competitive advantages. Per our working definition of ISD agility, we focus on the IS department (or any equivalent unit responsible for ISD).

We included IS departments from both the in-house and vendor setting to maximize variation in our sample and enhance the external validity. The cases involve one worldwide leading IS security software company (hereafter SoftCo), one regional bank (hereafter BankCo) famed for its digitization services and recognized by several awards in the Asia/Pacific region, and one leading system integration company in Asia (hereafter SysCo). All three firms, more than 30 years old, received IT innovation awards in 2017. We use multiple data collection methods, including semi-structured interviews and secondary data, to triangulate our findings. The sources and nature of data is described in Table 1. The content of the interviews were coded by applying triangulation approach including one of the authors and two other experts from the fields. The overview of cases is summarized in Table 2.

Table 1. Sources and nature of data

Sources of data	Description
Interviews	• Participants: managers who oversee ISD and understand the detailed operation of ISD as they possess comprehensive knowledge of the IS department; Senior engineers who possess good knowledge of routines as well as the interaction among colleagues • When and how: a total of eight semi-structured interviews lasting 90 min on average were conducted between May 2017 and October 2018 (three interviews in BankCo, three interviews in SoftCo, and two interviews in SysCo). Interviewees were asked to described ISD-related challenges their department/team face and how they cope with them with speed and flexibility • Trustworthiness: the interviews were recorded and transcribed. To strengthen content-validity from empirical induction, we discussed and clarified our research with our informants with condensed transcripts and summary writings within 2 weeks after each interview session
Secondary data	• Company documents and media coverage to understand their IT strategy, achievements, vision, and industry context • Publicly available interviews between 2017 and 2018 • Employee presentations in well-known practitioner-oriented conferences in 2018 (e.g., Agile Summit, Agile Tour). We include those presentations based on the speaker's position in the firm (e.g., seniority, team lead). The detailedness of the presentation or slides is another good indicator of the speakers' knowledge on ISD operations

Analysis of data began during data collection. We applied a thematic analysis approach starting with the deductive coding approach (Fereday and Muir-Cochrane 2006). The results of the analysis are presented in the next section.

Table 2. Overview of cases and collected data

	SoftCo	BankCo	SysCo
Business context	IT security software	Commercial banking	System integration and solution provider
Core values	Change, Customer, Collaboration, Innovations, Trustworthiness	Governance, Talent management, and IT innovation	Excellent personnel, Customer satisfaction, and Sustainable operation
The need for agility	Constant evolving cyber threats and risks, rapidly changing hardware and software that IT security software works upon and with, and ever-shifting customer demand	The unprecedented pace of technological disruptions along with big data, P2P lending, mobile payment, and deep learning, demands innovation in IS to meet customers' needs, desires, and expectations; the adaptation of IS for evolving cyber risks and the regulatory requirements	Intensified competition and changing market demand
Informants	VP of product development (interview), senior product manager (interview), VP of MIS (interview), VP of R&D (secondary data), project manager of R&D (secondary data), senior engineer and team lead (interview + secondary data), principal engineer (secondary data)	VP of MIS (interview - twice), Chief Digital Officer (interview), Chief Information Officer (secondary data)	CEO (interview – twice)
Outcomes of agility	Short release, high customer retention, highly responsive to customer needs, innovative services and products	Reduced operation cost, reduced operation risks, highly automated process, deeper customer insights, innovative services and products	On-time delivery, high client satisfaction, efficient use of resources, adaptation to risks and uncertainties

5 Findings

We group codes under routines into six clusters and illustrate how individuals, interactions, structure support ISD-related routines as follows.

1. Continuous discovery and validation of customer needs (Table 3): To enhance customer experience and rapidly respond to customer needs, all companies proactively detect needs of customers either through data analytics (BankCo and SoftCo) or

frequent interaction with customers (SysCo and BankCo). For example, BankCo creates the data science team to understand customers' preferences and behaviors. The specialized taskforce contributes to the development of chatbots that offers financial advice. SoftCo sets up the business intelligence system to capture customer profiles and usage behaviors. Alternatively, the discovery of customer needs can be done by interacting with customers. Senior managers in SysCo build their understanding of customer insights by site visits. The long-term relationships with customers support constructive dialogue. After sensing the environment, gathering feedback to validate customer needs is essential. BankCo and SoftCo engage customers via routines, such as applications of persona and user story mapping during the opportunity identification and solution development. In the development process, experiments through workshops and usability lab studies are conducted to validate the ideas (SoftCo). All three companies emphasized the importance of soft skills to engage customers. BankCo and SysCo explicitly state that they crave and nurture the specialized generalists, so-called T-shaped or π-shaped professionals. That is, the professionals possess expertise in one (i.e., the one leg of T) or a couple (i.e., the two legs of π) of domain area(s) and, more importantly, they should be able to span the boundaries within and between disciplines by holding communication skills and a broad understanding of multiple disciplines. Said differently, boundary spanners know how to work in the diverse and complex environment, integrate knowledge held by different people, engender trust and respect, and dedicate themselves to knowledge search and dissemination. The characteristics are conducive to constructive dialogue, which accordingly can lead to better coordination, learning, and cohesion required in the adaptation.

Table 3. Routines under continuous discovery and validation of customer needs

SoftCo	BankCo	SysCo
(1) Sensing customer needs: data analytics routine to discover customer insights (2) Validating customer needs via routines, such as user story mapping, paper prototyping, customer validation workshops, and usability test, *Supported by Individuals (collaboration mindset) and Interaction (constructive dialogue based on engaged relationships)	(1) Sensing customer needs: data analytics routine to discover customer insights *Supported by Structure - the data science team (2) Validating customer needs via routines, such as persona, prototyping, and on-site customers *Supported by Individuals (T-shaped professionals) and Interaction (constructive dialogue based on engaged relationships)	(1) Sensing customer needs: market research via site visits *Supported by Individuals (T-shaped professionals) Interaction (constructive dialogue based on engaged relationships)

2. Continuous evolution of IT-enabled products and services (Table 4): For firms that need to transform their IT-enabled products and services the routines related to design thinking, such as problem analysis (BankCo), product drawing games, design sprints, the creation of minimum viable products (SoftCo), are used to transform their

products. The idea of exploring problems and use design to solve them is the spirit of the routines. It also acknowledges that there is no perfect design. Instead, a design viable for business and feasible based on firms' resources should be pursued. Routines allow teams to experiment ideas across problems, solutions, customer segment, marketing, finance, etc. In other words, the notion of "fail fast and learn fast" is manifested in these routines. Both SoftCo and BankCo configures cross-functional teams to generate creative solutions. The teams are diverse, purpose-driven, and empowered so that they are not bounded by the silo-view of the problems and solutions as well as the authority. Furthermore, the effectiveness of these routines depends upon a few conditions. Team members are open to divergent ideas. When disagreement emerges, they dare to speak up and engage in the conversation. They put the collective benefits ahead of their own. The constructive dialogue is built upon cohesive relationships in these teams. The conflict remains in the meetings and rarely escalate to relationship issues. Besides collaborative mindset and solidarity in teams, the structure commonly prescribed by design-thinking routines, such as idea generation, ideas matching, idea presentation using visual-aid, idea discussion, and consensus building, facilitate the collaboration processes. SoftCo has launched several successful products within a short period originating from these routines. BankCo rolled out a new mobile banking app that differentiates itself from others, and 90% of customers adopted the new app.

Table 4. Routines under continuous evolution of IT-enabled products and services

SoftCo	BankCo	SysCo
(1) Problem identification and solution formulation using design thinking. e.g., customer journey maps, design spirits, brainstorming, product drawing games, and impact mapping *Supported by Structure – empowered, cross-functional team *Supported by Individuals (collaboration mindset) and Interaction (constructive dialogue based on team cohesion)	Problem identification and solution formulation using design thinking. e.g., problem identification process using business analysis techniques, brainstorming, prototyping *Supported by Structure – empowered, cross-functional team *Supported by Individuals (collaboration mindset) and Interaction (constructive dialogue based on team cohesion)	Not observed

The findings suggest six ISD-related routines conducive to ISD agility. Microfoundations, including individuals, interactions, and structure support ISD-related routines. Figure 1 illustrates a framework for ISD agility.

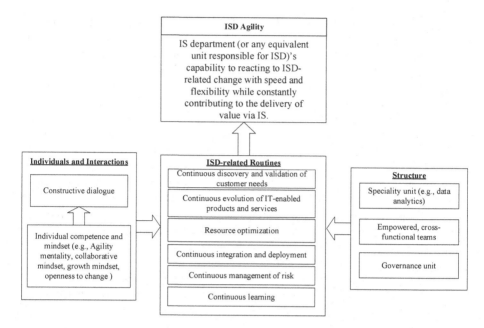

Fig. 1. A framework of the development of ISD agility

6   Discussion and Conclusion

Our study aims to understand how IS departments maintain its continual readiness for ISD agility. Our analysis of IS departments in three top performing firms reveals that, consistent with the literature of dynamic capabilities, routines underpin ISD agility. Extending research in ISD routines, we discover that routines for ISD agility can be established in six different aspects. We argue that the strategic orientation of the firm should determine which aspects of routines will receive more investment. In the adaptation context, firms can increase ISD agility by making the best use of what they have (i.e., exploitation). Routines under "resource optimization," "continuous integration and deployment," and "continuous management of risks" all conduce to discover what can be improved to adapt to changes. On the other hand, firms can be oriented to explore new opportunities through search, discovery, experimentation, and innovations (i.e., exploration). Routines related to "continuous discovery and validation of customer needs" and "continuous evolution of IT-enabled products and services" prepare IS departments to attain the exploration purpose. As shown in Table 5, BankCo and SoftCo devote efforts to exploration-related routines whereas SysCo mainly invests in exploitation-related routines. The business environment where a firm is situated can account for different strategic choices. BankCO and SoftCo are in hyper-competitive environments and thus their ISD agility should cover exploration. SysCo is a system integration vendor who needs to fulfill contractual obligations. Enhancing ISD agility by exploiting their human resources and ISD processes is the priority. BankCo and SoftCo both develop exploitation-related routines as these routines are the operational backbone (Ross et al., 2017). To what extent IS departments should invest in exploration or exploitation is beyond the scope of this research. The ambidexterity literature on whether the simultaneous pursuit of exploration and exploitation is desirable (Cao and Ramesh 2008) can shed lights on this challenge.

Table 5. The Relationship between Strategic Orientations and Routines

	Exploration	Exploitation
Continuous discovery and validation of customer needs	BankCo (high), SoftCo (medium), and SysCo (low)	
Continuous evolution of IT-enabled products and services	SoftCo	
Resource allocation optimization		BankCo, SoftCo, and SysCo
Continuous integration and deployment		SoftCo
Continuous management of risk		BankCo, SoftCo, and SysCo
Continuous learning	BankCo, SoftCo, and SysCo	BankCo, SoftCo, and SysCo

We also find that individual competence and mindset, constructive dialogue, and structural arrangements compose microfoundation of routines and ISD agility. Individuals should possess agility mindset and competence to operate routines. Since, over time, the routine may no longer serve the purpose, it is important to empower individuals to modify or decommission routines for the sake of ISD agility. The structural arrangements, such as the inclusion of the data analytics group for sensing, a governance unit for monitoring, a cross-functional team for knowledge creation and integration, further complement what individuals can accomplish. Finally, ISD agility lies in constructive dialogue as it indicates that stakeholders interact and make sure ISD is evolving.

References

Abell, P., Felin, T., Foss, N.: Building micro-foundations for the routines, capabilities, and performance links. Manag. Decis. Econ. **29**(6), 489–502 (2008)

Abrahamsson, P., Conboy, K., Wang, X.: 'Lots done, more to do': the current state of agile systems development research. Eur. J. Inf. Syst. **18**(4), 281–284 (2009)

Adler, P.S., Goldoftas, B., Levine, D.I.: Flexibility versus efficiency? A case study of model changeovers in the toyota production system. Organ. Sci. **10**(1), 43–68 (1999)

Adner, R., Helfat, C.E.: Corporate effects and dynamic managerial capabilities. Strate. Manage. J. **24**(10), 1011–1025 (2003)

Annosi, M.C., Martini, A., Brunetta, F., Marchegiani, L.: Learning in an agile setting: a multilevel research study on the evolution of organizational routines. J. Bus. Res. (in press)

Balijepally, V., Nerur, S.P., Mahapatra, R.: Task mental model and software developers' performance: an experimental investigation. Commun. Assoc. Inf. Syst. **36**(4), 53–76 (2015)

Barney, J.A.Y., Felin, T.: What are microfoundations? Acad. Manage. Persp. **27**(2), 138–155 (2013)

Bjørnson, F.O., Dingsøyr, T.: Knowledge management in software engineering: a systematic review of studied concepts, findings and research methods used. Inf. Softw. Technol. **50**(11), 1055–1068 (2008)

Bresman, H., Zellmer-Bruhn, M.: The structural context of team learning: effects of organizational and team structure on internal and external learning. Organ. Sci. **24**(4), 1120–1139 (2013)

Cao, L., Ramesh, B.: Agile requirements engineering practices: an empirical study. IEEE Softw. **25**(1), 60–67 (2008)

Conboy, K.: Agility from first principles: reconstructing the concept of agility in information systems development. Inf. Syst. Res. **20**(3), 329–354 (2009)

MacKenzie, S.B., Podsakoff, P.M., Podsakoff, N.P.: Construct measurement and validation procedures in mis and behavioral research. MIS Q. **35**(2), 293–334 (2011)

Zollo, M., Winter, S.G.: Deliberate learning and the evolution of dynamic capabilities. Organ. Sci. **13**(3), 339–351 (2002)

The Future Use of LowCode/NoCode Platforms by Knowledge Workers – An Acceptance Study

Christian Ploder[✉], Reinhard Bernsteiner, Stephan Schlögl, and Christoph Gschliesser

Management Center Innsbruck, Management, Communication & IT, Innsbruck, Austria
{christian.ploder, reinhard.bernsteiner, stephan.schloegl, christoph.gschliesser}@mci.edu

Abstract. Knowledge Workers have to deal with lots of different information systems to support daily work. This assumption leads to massive gaps in companies based on the complexity of legacy systems on one hand side and the development of the business processes on the other hand side. Many knowledge workers build their own shadow IT to get efficient process support without thinking about compliance, security, and scalability. One possible solution to deactivate this situation might be the idea of LowCode/NoCode platforms. The question is: Will knowledge workers be using this technology or are they not accepting the new trend? Therefore, the authors conducted a quantitative study based on an online questionnaire (N = 106) to check the acceptance of this upcoming technology for companies in the DACH region. The result of the study is a statement about the future willingness to use.

Keywords: Knowledge workers · LowCode/NoCode Platform · Process support · Shadow IT

1 Introduction

Most of the current knowledge workers [1] are using information systems especially database systems for lots of their daily tasks to extract information [2]. In the context of this paper knowledge workers are defined by their emphasis on "non-routine" problem-solving tasks that require a combination of convergent and divergent thinking [18] – this is not the case for all IS users in a company. Rarely the governed IT infrastructure can provide all the necessary tools for every preference of the individual working space. Current developments as cloud computing build the technological base for new initiatives like LCNC platforms as a widely opened platform to develop solutions for knowledge workers challenges on their own. - "on their own" means without any development skills.

Current IT landscapes in large companies have restricted budgets to pay for Hard-/Software but also to pay consultancy services in order to design and implement systems [3]. The so-called legacy systems (most of them are of high priority to run the company's

© Springer Nature Switzerland AG 2019
L. Uden et al. (Eds.): KMO 2019, CCIS 1027, pp. 445–454, 2019.
https://doi.org/10.1007/978-3-030-21451-7_38

business like ERP or MES systems) had very long development times, and their modification is very tricky after their initial implementation. While legacy systems expand beyond the original purpose in order to maintain new or changing business requirements, the implementation of new features is very cost intensive. Professional developers need to develop the new code and implement it to a very complex system. Apart from professional IT department lots of employees and entire departments, use their solutions based on MS Excel or MS Access in order to close the gap between existing information systems and their daily business processes. This behavior is called "shadow IT" and bears several risks on security, manageability, and compliance. The good thing about self-developed systems is that they are very task-oriented and focus on the support of the dedicated business process knowledge workers have to deal with.

The emergence of cloud-computing played an essential role in changing the IT-landscape situation from on-premise systems to affordable cloud solutions. As one benefit of cloud systems, their business models can be named: pay-per-use subscription models can help companies of every size to use powerful systems by only paying what they are using. Cloud platforms like MS Azure, or Amazon Web Services offer whole ecosystems for companies to use integrated database services, virtual machines, web services, BA/BI Tools or AI services.

One of these cloud-based concepts is the idea of LowCode/NoCode Platforms (further LCNC platforms), which enable the development of cloud-based solutions without traditional coding in a text-based editor. LCNC platforms rely on graphical interfaces to increase the speed of software development and loosen up the connection to the IT developers. In contrast to standard toolkits, the range of possibilities for the end-user is much more extensive than in toolkits usually provided for a dedicated case.

By trying to keep a balance between being easy enough for a knowledge worker to develop a simple solution and is sturdy enough for professional developers, LCNC platforms attempt to serve both target groups [4]. Another benefit of LCNC platforms besides saving time and costs in professional software development is the integration of other departments in a manageable way to improve the business process support level of information systems. As a future result, shadow IT would be able to produce manageable, scalable and compliant applications, which can be integrated into other systems too.

While LCNC platforms sound like a promising idea, it is also very disruptive and thus can encounter resistance from within organizations. IT-departments, for example, might fear for their jobs or loss of credibility. After years of telling stakeholders inside their company that it takes large budgets and long implementation times to establish enterprise software, similar results can now be produced with a fraction of people, time and money when using LCNC platforms. Additionally, professional developers (i.e., coders) might prefer to code instead of working with graphical interfaces – whether it makes sense or not [4]. Resistance might also come from the unwillingness of IT departments to explicitly give away software creation responsibilities to other departments.

The authors of the paper are convinced of LCNC platforms as a chance for companies to effectively support knowledge workers in their daily work and keep the system developments monitored and controlled. The first indicator if the new technology will be used can be acceptance testing. Therefore the study deals with the acceptance of LCNC platforms and elaborates the factors which influence the acceptance most to get at least some practical advice for implementations.

2 Theoretical Foundations

To get an idea of the acceptance of new technology, first of all, the authors had to focus on a geographical limitation to get experts on the side of providers and the side of users/future users for LCNC platforms. The second limitation the authors had to deal with was the decision about which LCNC platform to go with. Based on the assumption and own experience of the dissemination the authors will focus on Microsoft products to give participants a tangible example of LCNC platforms before taking part in the survey. The alignment on knowledge workers leads to the use of a user-centric technology acceptance model. Based on the given restrictions, the following research question will be answered: What is the current acceptance for LCNC platforms in companies located in German-speaking countries?

There are lots of different models out there with often discussed pros and cons, but for this study, the authors decided to go for a modified version of the TAM2 model developed by Opitz, Langkau, Schmidt, and Kolbe [5]. Their model was used to answer questions about the acceptance of cloud computing in Germany and should lead to representative results of the conducted study on the acceptance of LCNC Platforms. In TAM related literature, the line between acceptance and adoption is slightly blurred. This might originate from the fact that TAM has been proposed initially to examine user acceptance and subsequently determine whether users would adopt technology for personal use [6, 7]. For this first study on the acceptance of LCNC platforms for knowledge workers, the authors decided not to take the organizational aspects into consideration and therefore do not go for an enhanced model like the I-TOE by Rosli et al. [8].

The basis of the research design encompasses the hypotheses dealing with the core variables of the TAM2 [9] which has also been proposed for the original TAM [7]. Perceived Usefulness of the TAM2, as well as comparable constructs from other

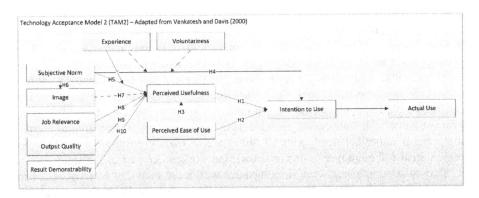

Fig. 1. TAM Model with the suggested correlations based on H1–H10

models like Job-Fit [10], Relative Advantage [11], and Outcome Expectations [12], has shown to be the strongest predictor of Intention to Use and remained significant in both voluntary and mandatory settings [13].

For measuring the theoretical constructs, validated items have been adopted from prior research to fit the context of this study. The same items as in the original TAM2 model [9] have been used. Items for all three original TAM constructs Perceived Usefulness, Perceived Ease of Use, and Intention to Use originate from Davis, Bagozzi, and Warshaw [14] and Davis [9]. Items for Image and Result Demonstrability originally have been proposed by Moore and Benbasat [11]. Items for Subjective Norm originate from Taylor and Todd [15]. Items for Job Relevance and Output Quality originate from Davis et al. [16]. Items for Voluntariness have been taken from Venkatesh and Davis [9].

Besides the constructs and items that have been adopted from the declared and given models, further items have been added to raise demographical data about the participants and the companies they are working in:

- gender (male, female, not specified),
- age (years),
- experience with LCNC platforms (yes, no),
- development of "shadow IT" (often, sometimes, rarely, never),
- position working in (head of a department, team leader, employee, assistant)
- company size based on the Austrian law (<10, 10–50, 51–250 and >250).

To investigate the given research question with the proposed research model, an online questionnaire has been set up with two different parts: (1) questions regarding the based TAM model and (2) questions regarding the demographic situation of every participant. There was a wide range of employees taken for participation based on the variety of use of LCNC platforms. After a pre-test with five participants, the questionnaire was sent out to more than 2000 relevant business experts, and the return rate was at 6%.

3   Results

From the survey, after data clearance, 106 accurate records have been retrieved (N = 106). The gender among participants is relatively unbalanced with 80 (75.5%) being male and 26 (24.5%) being female. Age among participants reaches from 22 to 57 years (mean = 38.94%, standard deviation = 8.908). Twenty participants (18.9%) stated to never make their solutions using tools like Excel or Access while 37 participants (34.9%) said rarely, 30 participants (28.3%) said sometimes, and 19 participants (17.9%) said often. Thirty-eight participants (35.8%) claimed to have already used LCNC platforms before, 66 (62.3%) did not, and two participants (1.9%) chose "I do not know." The number of participants in leading positions compared to normal employees is rather balanced, with 52 (49%) are in leading positions and 54 (51%) being normal full employees – many knowledge workers are part of the study.

Sixty-nine participants work in companies with more than 250 employees, 24 in companies with 51 to 250 employees, 7 in companies with 10 to 50 employees and 5 in companies with less than ten employees.

In the original TAM2 study by Venkatesh and Davis [9], the influence of Voluntariness on the effect of Subjective Norm on Intention to Use and the influence of Experience on the effects of Subjective Norm on Perceived Usefulness and Intention to Use has been examined by splitting the participants into respective voluntary/mandatory settings and experience groups. Due to the total sample size of 106, splitting participants into experienced/inexperienced as well as voluntary/mandatory would have led to groups which are too small for meaningful analysis. Hence, Experience and Voluntariness as moderating factors have been omitted from further analysis. Consequently, the hypotheses, which were concerned with these now oppressed variable constructs, were dropped/changed. H4a and H4b were merged into one single hypothesis H4 that reads "Subjective Norm will have a positive effect on Intention to Use." Hypothesis H5b was dropped after that hypothesis H5a was renamed to H5. All dedicated hypotheses are given in the appendix.

As a first step, the reliability of TAM2 constructs has been analyzed by calculating Cronbach's alphas with SPSS Statistics. Cronbach's alpha values reached from questionable to excellent with Output Quality having the lowest value at .656 and Perceived Usefulness having the highest value at .944. Due to the low Cronbach's alpha value, the construct of Output Quality was omitted together with hypothesis H9. Additionally, the item RD4 has been omitted in order to reach a better Cronbach's alpha value for Result Demonstrability. Afterward, factor analysis has been conducted with the remaining items. Since the model has already been validated before and its constructs and hypotheses are profoundly grounded in theory, confirmatory factor analysis has been conducted with SPSS Amos instead of exploratory factor analysis.

The factor loadings from the confirmatory factor analysis have been used to calculate the construct values from the respective items. Subsequently, three regression analyses have been conducted to test the hypotheses H1 to H10, exploring the effects of the various independent variables on the dependent variables Image, Perceived Usefulness and Intention to Use. Preliminary to the regression analyses, a correlation matrix (Table 1) has been created. Considering the hypotheses, it can be seen that Job Relevance has a moderate positive correlation with Image. All influencing factors of Perceived Usefulness except Perceived Ease of Use exhibit a significant correlation with it whereby the correlation between Result Demonstrability and Perceived Usefulness has to be considered as rather low. Both Subjective Norm and Perceived

Table 1. Pearson correlations between TAM2 constructs

	IU	PU	PEU	SN	RD	IMG	JR
IU							
PU	791***						
PEU	.119	.023					
SN	.458***	.569***	.083				
RD	.326***	.302**	.582***	.278**			
IMG	.634***	.645***	-.045	.513***	.156		
JR	718***	.711***	.026	.486***	.311**	.550***	

*p < .05 **p < .01 ***p < .001

Usefulness significantly positively correlated with the Intention to Use. Again, the correlation with Perceived Usefulness is insignificant. Furthermore, it can be seen that there are moderate correlations between constructs, which will be used together as independent variables in the regression analyses, which could lead to multicollinearity problems within the individual regression analyses.

First, simple regression analysis has been conducted to examine the influence of Subjective Norm on Image. The ANOVA shows that the model as a whole is significant (F (1, 104) = 37.187, p < .001). The adjusted R square value of .256 shows that Subjective Norm can explain 25,6% of the variance in Image.

Second, a multiple regression analysis examining Perceived Usefulness has been conducted. The ANOVA shows that the model as a whole is significant (F (5, 100) = 33.991, p < .001). An analysis shows that the independent variables with an adjusted R square value of .611 can explain 61,1% of the variance in Perceived Usefulness. Data additionally show that Job Relevance has the strongest significant positive effect on Perceived Usefulness with β = .403 (p < .001), followed by Image with β = .371 (p < .001), and Subjective Norm with β = .205 (p < .05), wherefore $H5_0$, $H7_0$, and $H8_0$ can be rejected. $H3_0$ and $H10_0$ cannot be rejected since Perceived Ease of Use, and Result Demonstrability show no significant effect on Perceived Usefulness. With all collinearity tolerance values > .2 and all VIFs < 3 it can be assumed that there are no multicollinearity issues.

Lastly, third multiple regression analysis has been conducted to examine the Intention to Use. The ANOVA shows that the model as a whole is significant (F (3, 102) = 59.506, p < .001). An analysis shows that the independent variables with an adjusted R square value of .626 can explain 62,6% of the variance in Intention to Use. Data additionally show that Perceived Usefulness is the only independent variable having a significant effect on Intention to Use with p < .001. The effect of furthermore is very high with β = .700. Both Subjective Norm and Perceived Ease of Use do not exert a significant effect on Intention to Use. Therefore, $H1_0$ can be rejected whereby $H2_0$ and $H4_0$ cannot be rejected. That the effect of Subjective Norm on Intention to Use is insignificant corresponds with assumptions of the TAM2 since settings were predominantly voluntary. With all collinearity tolerance values > .2 and all VIFs < 3 it can be assumed that there are no multi-collinearity issues.

Figure 2 shows the results of all regression analyses within the TAM2 including significance levels.

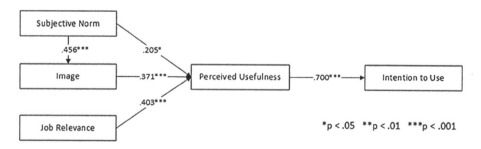

Fig. 2. Regression Results TAM2

4 Discussion of Results

The TAM2 was able to explain 62.6% of the variance in Intention to Use (adjusted R square). The data from this study, however, only supports the direct influence of Perceived Usefulness on Intention to Use. The strength of the effect is similar to the one which was found by Opitz et al. [5] when examining the adoption of cloud computing in companies. The effects of Perceived Ease of Use and Subjective Norm on Intention to Use are insignificant. While the effect of Perceived Ease of Use, in general, is considered a rather weak one compared to the other two constructs, it might have turned insignificant due to the nature of LCNC platforms. LCNC platforms are toolsets which can be used very flexible for various applications rather than one application or system, which is designed to serve a specific purpose. Since the difficulty of usage naturally scales with the complexity of the application, which is to be realized within the platform, there is no clearly defined goal (like completing a task in a clearly defined system/interface) where Ease of Use can be assessed upon. However, the same applies to cloud computing in which Perceived Ease of Use has previously been found to have a significant effect on the Intention to Use [5]. Another reason for the insignificance of Perceived Ease of Use could be that the majority of the participants presumably did not have much practical experience in working with LCNC platforms by themselves. Therefore, they might only have made assumptions about how easy they think it would be to work with LCNC platforms, based on the information they had received.

Next, the TAM2 proposes that the direct effect of Subjective Norm on Intention to Use is only significant in mandatory but not voluntary settings [9]. Subjective Norm did not exert a significant direct effect on Intention to Use which is coinciding with this proposal. It has to be assumed that most participants were prospects or interested parties (IT representatives, key users, decision makers), which did not have real pressure to either implement or use LCNC platforms. The TAM2 furthermore proposes social influences on Perceived Usefulness via both internalization and identification. In the direct influence due to internalization, people incorporate social influences into their usefulness perceptions while this effect is assumed to decrease with increased experience [9, 17]. Although the direct effect of Subjective Norm on Perceived Usefulness was supported, the effect was not very strong when considering again that participants, in general, were not very experienced. Due to the limited sample size, a comparison between an experienced and an inexperienced group of participants could not have been made in this study.

In the indirect influence due to the identification, people are assumed to use a system in order to gain status or influence within a group [17]. This assumption is supported by the data and the significant effect of Subjective Norm on Image. Lastly, the TAM2 proposes effects of cognitive instrumental processes on Perceived Usefulness. It is implied that Job Relevance is affecting judgments about how useful a system is because individuals match their job goals with the consequences of using the system [9]. With Job Relevance having the strongest effect on Perceived Usefulness, compared to Image and Subjective Norm, this implication is supported by the results of this study. Job Relevance furthermore strongly positively correlates with Intention to Use with $r = .718$ ($p < .001$).

With finding the negative impact of the factor *Complexity*, one practical implication can be the necessity of ease to deploy and implement into IT infrastructure as well as into the work practice for all knowledge workers. Suppliers of LCNC platforms can additionally offer a comprehensive toolset within the platform based on streamlined interfaces and new functionalities. It is essential to take the positive impact from the factor *Compatibility* into consideration and focus on internal and external systems without causing too much disruption. If companies want to go for LCNC platforms to support knowledge workers, it is essential to illustrate potential benefits to future users and future system administrators. Knowledge workers are willing to learn and use this new technology.

5   Limitations and Future Work

As shown in the methodology chapter, the selection of the region and the selection of Microsoft Business Application Platform for explanations are two strict limitations of the study. Currently, there is no extensive use of LCNC platforms in companies in the elaborated region, and therefore participants had to be informed about the topic before filling out the questionnaire in order to produce valid answers - an explanatory video did this. Combined with the lack of own experience, it is implied that participants' attitudes might have been shaped by the inputs that came from the video when answering the questionnaires.

This study solely aimed at companies including Austria, Germany, and Switzerland, which have a similar cultural background. To validate the outcomes of this study, similar studies could be conducted in other regions of the world with different cultural backgrounds. Because LCNC platforms target several groups within a company – reaching from different departments to different positions and job profiles – it would be fascinating to investigate how acceptance varies within those different groups. Unfortunately, this study failed in making the comparison between the groups by not gathering enough responses to split the sample into meaningful groups.

Appendix

Given are the H1–H10 used for the model shown in Fig. 1:

Hypothesis 1: Perceived Usefulness will have a positive effect on the Intention to Use.

Hypothesis 2: Perceived Ease of Use will have a positive effect on the Intention to Use.

Hypothesis 3: Perceived Ease of Use will have a positive effect on Perceived Usefulness.

Hypothesis 4a: Subjective Norm will have no significant effect on the Intention to Use when usage is perceived to be voluntary.

Hypothesis 4b: Subjective Norm will have a positive direct effect on Intention to Use when usage is perceived to be mandatory.

Hypothesis 5a: Subjective Norm will have a positive effect on Perceived Usefulness.

Hypothesis 5b: The positive effect of Subjective Norm on Perceived Usefulness will attenuate with increased experience.

Hypothesis 6: Subjective Norm will have a positive effect on Image.

Hypothesis 7: Image will have a positive effect on Perceived Usefulness.

Hypothesis 8: Job Relevance will have a positive effect on Perceived Usefulness.

Hypothesis 9: Output Quality will have a positive effect on Perceived Usefulness.

Hypothesis 10: Results Demonstrability will have a positive effect on Perceived Usefulness.

References

1. Maier, R., Hädrich, T., Peinl, R.: Enterprise Knowledge Infrastructures, 2nd edn. Springer, Heidelberg (2009). https://doi.org/10.1007/978-3-540-89768-2
2. Maier, R.: Knowledge Management Systems: Information and Communication Technologies for Knowledge Management, 3rd edn. Springer, Heidelberg (2007). https://doi.org/10.1007/978-3-540-71408-8
3. Satell, G.: The Future of Software is No-Code (2018). https://www.inc.com/greg-satell/how-no-code-platforms-are-disrupting-software.html. Accessed 15 Dec 2018
4. Bloomberg, J.: The Low-Code/No-Code Movement: More Disruptive Than You Realize (2017). https://www.forbes.com/sites/jasonbloomberg/2017/07/20/the-low-codeno-code-movement-more-disruptive-than-you-realize/#16c5e355722a. Accessed 15 Dec 2018
5. Opitz, N., Langkau, T.F., Schmidt, N.H., Kolbe, L.M.: Technology acceptance of cloud computing: empirical evidence from German IT departments. In: Sprague, R.H. (ed.) 2012 45th Hawaii International Conference on System Science: (HICSS); USA, 4–7 January 2012, pp. 1593–1602. IEEE, Piscataway (2012). https://doi.org/10.1109/HICSS.2012.557
6. Davis, F.D.: A technology acceptance model for empirically testing new end-user information systems: theory and results. Massachusetts Institute of Technology (1985)
7. Davis, F.D.: Perceived usefulness, perceived ease of use, and user acceptance of information technology. MIS Q. 13(3), 319 (1989). https://doi.org/10.2307/249008
8. Rosli, K., Yeow, P., Siew, E.-G.: Factors influencing audit technology acceptance by audit firms: a new I-TOE adoption framework. J. Acc. Auditing Res. Pract. 1–11 (2012). https://doi.org/10.5171/2012.876814
9. Venkatesh, V., Davis, F.D.: A theoretical extension of the technology acceptance model: four longitudinal field studies. Manage. Sci. 46(2), 186–204 (2000). https://doi.org/10.1287/mnsc.46.2.186.11926
10. Thompson, R.L., Higgins, C.A., Howell, J.M.: Personal computing: toward a conceptual model of utilization. MIS Q. 15(1), 125 (1991). https://doi.org/10.2307/249443
11. Moore, G.C., Benbasat, I.: Development of an instrument to measure the perceptions of adopting an information technology innovation. Inf. Syst. Res. 2(3), 192–222 (1991). https://doi.org/10.1287/isre.2.3.192
12. Compeau, D.R., Higgins, C.A.: Computer self-efficacy: development of a measure and initial test. MIS Q. 19, 189–211 (1995)

13. Venkatesh, V., Morris, M.G., Davis, G.B., Davis, F.D.: User acceptance of information technology: toward a unified view. MIS Q. **27**(3), 425 (2003). https://doi.org/10.2307/30036540
14. Davis, F.D., Bagozzi, R.P., Warshaw, P.R.: User acceptance of computer technology: a comparison of two theoretical models. Manage. Sci. **35**(8), 982–1003 (1989). https://doi.org/10.1287/mnsc.35.8.982
15. Taylor, S., Todd, P.A.: Understanding information technology usage: a test of competing models. Inf. Syst. Res. **6**(2), 144–176 (1995). https://doi.org/10.1287/isre.6.2.144
16. Davis, F.D., Bagozzi, R.P., Warshaw, P.R.: Extrinsic and intrinsic motivation to use computers in the workplace1. J. Appl. Soc. Psychol. **22**(14), 1111–1132 (1992). https://doi.org/10.1111/j.1559-1816.1992.tb00945.x
17. Kelman, H.C.: Compliance, identification, and internalization three processes of attitude change. J. Conflict Resolut. **2**(1), 51–60 (1958)
18. Reinhardt, W., Schmidt, B., Sloep, P., Drachsler, H.: Knowledge worker roles and actions – results of two empirical studies. Knowl. Process Manage. **18**(3), 150–174 (2011). https://doi.org/10.1002/kpm.378

Neuro-Symbolic Hybrid Systems for Industry 4.0: A Systematic Mapping Study

Inés Sittón$^{(\boxtimes)}$, Ricardo S. Alonso, Elena Hernández-Nieves,
Sara Rodríguez-Gonzalez, and Alberto Rivas

IoT Digital Innovation Hub, University of Salamanca,
Calle Espejo s/n, 37007 Salamanca, Spain
{isittonc, ralorin, elenahn, srg, rivis}@usal.es

Abstract. Neuro-symbolic hybrid systems (NSHS) have been used in several research areas to obtain powerful intelligent systems. A systematic mapping study was conducted, searching studies published from January 2011 to May 2018 in three author databases defining four research questions and three search strings. With the results a literature review was made to generate a map with main trends and contributions about the use of NSHS in Industry 4.0. An evaluation rubric based on the work of Petersen et al. (2015) was applied too. In a first exploratory search 544 papers was found, but only 330 had relation with research theme. After this first classification a second filter was applied to identify repeated articles or which had not relevance for solve the research questions, obtaining 118. Finally, 50 primary studies was selected. This paper is a guide aimed at researching and obtaining evidence on the shortage of publications and contributions about the use of neuro symbolic hybrid systems applied in Industry 4.0 environment.

Keywords: Neuro-symbolic hybrid system (NSHS) · Industry 4.0 ·
Artificial intelligence · Systematic mapping study

1 Introduction

A hybrid system of artificial intelligence is defined as several intelligent subsystems integrated and that collaborate and influence among them. A particular class of these systems are the *neuro-symbolic hybrid systems* (NSHS) defined in [1] as systems based primarily on artificial neural networks that allow a symbolic interpretation or an interaction with symbolic components. The main properties of NSHS are as follows: efficiency of global system, components with a strong fusion, global learning and complementarity between symbolic and numeric knowledge [2]. Sahin et al. (2012) offer an important literature review about hybrid systems and their trends, algorithms and areas where these systems are gaining interest [3]. The authors mention in their research the important number of new industrial applications developed using hybrid systems. In an exploratory search only one systematic mapping study about Industry 4.0 was found, but it had not any relationship with neuro-symbolic hybrid systems.

According to Wortmann et al. (2017) a systematic mapping study is the search and classifies of primary studies about an investigation area [4]. For this systematic

© Springer Nature Switzerland AG 2019

L. Uden et al. (Eds.): KMO 2019, CCIS 1027, pp. 455–465, 2019.
https://doi.org/10.1007/978-3-030-21451-7_39

mapping study, authors apply the guidelines, useful practices and suggestions established by Kitchenham, Petersen and others [4–10]. Therefore, the advantages described by the previously authors about systematic mapping studies have motivated the development of this with the aim of identifying trends in the application of hybrid systems in Industry 4.0. In computer sciences the first mapping studies developed were focused on software engineering and their authors recommended it for research areas with a few important and relevant primary studies [5, 6]. After the introduction, Sect. 2 presents a background about Neuro-Symbolic Hybrid Systems. The rest of the paper is structured as follows: the research method is described in Sect. 3; the results are summarized in Sect. 4 and finally conclusions are presented in Sect. 5.

2 Background

In this section an overview about the Neuro - symbolic hybrid systems and Industry 4.0 are making as previous point in the developing of our mapping study. Hybrid systems arise from the symbiosis of various artificial intelligence (AI) techniques such as: agents, neural computing, automatic learning, fuzzy logic, evolutionary algorithms [2, 11]. During the nineties a boom began in the implementation of hybrid systems for their ability to solve complex problems of a real environment [12]. To date, hybrid artificial intelligence systems, also identified as HAIS, are a multidisciplinary field of research that continues to expand [13]. Before introduce the Neuro-Symbolic Hybrid System's concept is necessary to talk about two approaches: (i) the connectionist (artificial neural networks) and (ii) the symbolic (rules, trees and others), both has been used by independent form with the aim to demonstrate which is the best to solve the problems. After the researches find that weaknesses of some of them can be integrated with the strengths of the other; such as: the difficulty of artificial neural networks to explain the results and the difficulty of symbolic approach to generalize knowledge, are integrated and complement each other in a single approach, as a consequence the Neuro-Symbolic Hybrid System emerges. Neuro- Symbolic Hybrid System uses the artificial neural networks algorithms as the principal option to solve the problems [14–16].

Industry 4.0 is a new term using to define an emerging organization concept in which there is a technological control over the life cycle of production and the entire value chain [17]. Industry 4.0 is an emerging structure established by the German Federal Government in which manufacturing and logistics systems make a match between a great volume of data, information, production and business processes by means of Cyber Physical Systems [17–21]. For Lee et al. [19] the principal objective of Industry 4.0 is the need to convert regular machines to self-aware-learning machines in order to improve their overall performance and maintenance process.

3 Research Method

A systematic mapping study is a secondary study based on the search for existing scientific evidences on a topic and then provide indication of the quantity of them. The benefits of a systematic mapping study are indicated as follows [22]:

- Identify groups of papers based on a specific theme through a systematic and objective procedure.
- Systematic mapping study helps to propose new researches in the analyzed field.
- A previous Mapping study facilitates futures systematic literature reviews (SLR) which aim resolve specific research issues.

In computer science, the guidelines, procedures and rubrics to develop a systematic mapping studies has been making in general by the software engineering community and are defined in [5, 6, 23, 24]. Therefore, the research method is organized in three stages: (1) Protocol definition and establishment of research questions; (2) Definition of search strategies and description of inclusion and exclusion criteria; (3) Selection of relevant publications.

3.1   Research Questions

With the aim to identify important researches about Neuro-Symbolic Hybrid Systems for Industry 4.0, the following research questions are proposed:

- **Q1**: What researches and contributions have been made regarding neuro-symbolic hybrid systems (NSHS) for Industry 4.0?
- **Q2:** What challenges in the Industry 4.0 context can be addressed through the application of NSHS?
- **Q3:** What predictive models with sensor network data have been designed from the integration of NSHS?
- **Q4:** In which environments have the found prediction models been applied?

3.2   Search Strategy

Finding relevant publications that possibly respond to the research questions we have asked requires designing appropriate search clauses and selecting the most relevant scientific libraries. For this research, the following repositories will be used: Web of Science, Scopus and IEEE Digital Library. In a scientific systematic mapping study a good practice is construct the search strings using a defined approach. In this case, authors use the PICO approach, suggested by [6, 9] in which: **P** is the Population that applied to this study which corresponds to Neuro Symbolic Hybrid Systems; **I** is the Interventions authors paper Intervention; **C** is the Comparison of found studies and finally **O** is the Outcome or study results. PICO helps authors to define the keywords and search strings and determine if it is necessary to use synonyms.

The search strings were defined to perform searches using exact words to avoid articles that not contain relevant information about the neuro-symbolic hybrid systems applied to industry or industry 4.0. For this reason, the search strings are enclosed in quotes (e.g., "Industry 4.0") to extend the obtained results. In Table 1, the search strings used in searches are described and identified with an ID. For example, the first search string is identified with B1 and next search strings also use an ID.

This research contemplates establishing criteria for the inclusion or exclusion of valid articles for the development of a systematic mapping study of the literature. In the following section the applied criteria are described.

Table 1. Search strings.

ID	Description
B1	"Industry 4.0" AND "systematic literature review" OR "literature review" OR "overview" OR "survey" OR "systematic mapping study"
B2	Neuro-symbolic hybrid system OR hybrid neuro-symbolic system OR hybrid expert system AND Industry
B3	Neuro-symbolic hybrid system OR hybrid neuro-symbolic system OR hybrid expert system AND Industry 4.0

3.3 Inclusion and Exclusion Criteria

Inclusion/Exclusion criteria are used to obtain only relevant papers to answer the research questions [5, 6]. Therefore, to select studies, the authors established inclusion/exclusion criteria as follows:

- Inclusion criteria:
  - Studies published in journals, conferences and workshops with peer revision whose title, abstract and keywords correspond with the search strings defined in Table 1.
- Exclusion criteria:
  - Papers that only mention the terms but they do not have an important contribution to the research theme.
  - Authors decide exclusion of all papers published in journals or conferences which do not have peer revision.
  - Papers duplicated in the repositories mentioned previously in this document and used to make the search.

3.4 Classification and Evaluation

To obtain the final publications with which the map was designed, a systematic classification process is defined by means of a stepwise scheme. Firstly, an exploratory search is carried out. In the second stage the authors identify the duplicated articles in the repositories and they will be eliminated to begin with the third stage, which is the revision of each one in search of relevant concepts for the research. In first exploratory search 544 papers was found but only 330 had relation with research theme. After this first classification a second filter was applied to identify repeated articles or which had not relevance for solve the research questions. A total of 330 relevant documents were found during the search, from which 118 were selected and 212 were excluded.

In this paper the Petersen's rubric presented in [6] was used. The rubric describes 26 actions to evaluate the quality of a systematic mapping study (SMS). One of the advantages of this rubric is that it can be used by readers to quickly evaluate the action applied in an SMS. In this sense, to determine the quality of an SMS, Petersen establishes an average of 33%. Therefore, the higher the percentage of actions taken, the better the quality of the study [22]. Figure 1 shows a total of 26 actions from the list defined by [6, 22], from which 15 were taken, which means a 57.69% of average and quality of mapping study presented in this paper.

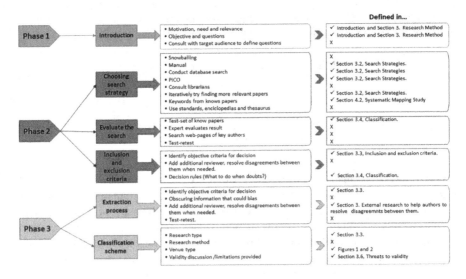

Fig. 1. Action conducted in this study: (✔) taken and not taken (×)

4 Results

In this section, after reading and analyzing each article in order to find the meaningful terms, the authors present: (i) clouds with the relevant keywords found in articles; (ii) tables with selected journals and conference papers and (iii) the answer to the initial research questions described in Sect. 3.1 of this document. Figure 2 shows the result obtained with the word cloud technique to extract the most representative terms from the articles by search string (B1, B2, and B3): (a) journal and (b) conference. Table 2 summarizes journal and conference papers that were selected papers by each search string. All of them are included in the reference section.

4.1 Answers to Research Questions

- **Q1: What research and contributions have been made in relation to neuro-symbolic hybrid systems for Industry 4.0?** After the mapping study, authors identify some papers related with neuro-symbolic approach, but principally with hybrid expert systems. Using Industry 4.0 in the search string, only one relevant paper was found: *"A hybrid expert decision support system based on artificial neural networks in process control of plaster production - An Industry 4.0 perspective"* in which their authors present a Hybrid Expert Decision Support System (EDSS) model, which integrates Neural Network (NN) and Expert System (ES) to detect unnatural CCPs and to estimate the corresponding parameters and starting point for the detected CCP [1]. The other papers propose the use of the following approaches:
  - Hybrid expert systems or expert systems: [40, 48, 73, 74]
  - Hybrid intelligent systems [49, 75]
  - Neuro-rules and neuro-symbolic approach [54–56]

The Question 1 (Q1) is important because authors found only a few relevant papers that used "neuro-symbolic hybrid systems applying to Industry 4.0".

Table 2. Selected journal and conferences papers

ID	Journal	Conference
B1	[25–39]	[4, 61–71]
B2	[40–53]	[1]
B3	[3, 54–60]	[72]

- **Q2: What challenges in the Industry 4.0 context can be addressed through the application of NSHS?** Fault diagnosis, prediction, detect unnatural behaviors are some of the principal challenges in Industry that researchers are working during last years to solve through neuro-symbolic approaches, neural rules, neural networks or hybrid systems. Some of their results are described in [1, 40, 48, 49, 54–56, 59, 73–75].
- **Q3: What predictive models with sensor network data have been designed from the integration of NSHS?** In this research, authors have identified some relevant papers with predictive model but using hybrid systems such as:
  - Karelovic et al. (2015) present a framework for modeling and representation of hybrid systems, and the design and development of hybrid predictive controllers [48].
  - Kim et al. (2017) develop a hybrid expert system to failure diagnosis and prediction for an automatic preventive maintenance system [74].
- **Q4: To which environments have the prediction models found been applied?** The prediction models found have been applied on: (i) mineral processing [48] (ii) steelworks industry [74]; and (iii) plaster production industry [1]. This means that the design of prediction models through the use of hybrid systems is an optimal area for the development of future research.

Fig. 2. (a) Cloud of the keywords found in articles classified by search ID B1. (b) Cloud of the keywords found in articles classified by search ID B2–B3.

5   Conclusions

Neuro-symbolic hybrid system are not a new concept, since 90's decade, the researches in this field began with the objective to develop systems and build mechanisms more powerful with less efforts, necessary to generate an only intelligent system. Hybrid systems with artificial intelligence techniques such as Genetic Algorithm (GA) and Artificial Neural Networks (ANN) have been used by researchers to find solutions to complex problems. The mapping study presented in this paper had the aim to demonstrate the hybrid systems advantages to achieve important solutions in predictive models for fault diagnosis and other Industry 4.0 challenges.

From the synergy in the application of artificial intelligence approaches, symbolic systems that are based on the conjunction of fuzzy systems, neural networks, expert knowledge, genetic algorithms or automatic learning arise. These new approaches of neuro-symbolic hybrid systems have a remarkable theoretical growth and potential to solve complex industrial problems. Using neural networks, genetic programming or machine learning algorithms it is possible to generate solutions or design models with good generalist capacity in a real industrial environment. The neuro-symbolic hybrid approach has progressively taken strength and being used for the development of large and complex systems. Therefore, authors propose as future work the application and use of neuro-symbolic hybrid systems in Industry 4.0.

Acknowledgments. This work has been supported by project IOTEC: "Development of Technological Capacities around the Industrial Application of Internet of Things (IoT)". 0123-IOTEC-3-E. Project financed with FEDER funds, Interreg Spain-Portugal (PocTep). Inés Sittón-Candanedo has been supported by IFARHU – SENACYT scholarship program (Government of Panama).

References

1. Ramezani, J., Jassbi, J.: A hybrid expert decision support system based on artificial neural networks in process control of plaster production – an industry 4.0 perspective. In: Camarinha-Matos, Luis M., Parreira-Rocha, M., Ramezani, J. (eds.) DoCEIS 2017. IAICT, vol. 499, pp. 55–71. Springer, Cham (2017). https://doi.org/10.1007/978-3-319-56077-9_5
2. Fdez-Riverola, F., Corchado, J.M.: Sistemas híbridos neuro-simbólicos: una revisión. Rev. Iberoam. Intel. Artif. **4**, 12–26 (2000)
3. Sahin, S., Tolun, M.R., Hassanpour, R.: Hybrid expert systems: a survey of current approaches and applications. Expert Syst. Appl. **39**, 4609–4617 (2012)
4. Wortmann, A., Combemale, B., Barais, O.: A systematic mapping study on modeling for industry 4.0. In: 2017 ACM/IEEE 20th International Conference on Model Driven Engineering Languages and Systems, pp. 281–291 (2017)
5. Petersen, K., Feldt, R., Mujtaba, S., Mattsson, M.: Systematic mapping studies in software engineering. In: 12th International Conference on Evaluation and Assessment in Software Engineering, vol. 17, p. 10 (2008)
6. Petersen, K., Vakkalanka, S., Kuzniarz, L.: Guidelines for conducting systematic mapping studies in software engineering: an update. Inf. Softw. Technol. **64**, 1–18 (2015)

7. Salehi, S., Selamat, A., Fujita, H.: Systematic mapping study on granular computing. Knowl. Based Syst. **80**, 78–97 (2015)
8. Kosar, T., Bohra, S., Mernik, M.: Domain-specific languages: a systematic mapping study. Inf. Softw. Technol. **71**, 77–91 (2015)
9. Kitchenham, B.A., Budgen, D., Pearl Brereton, O.: Using mapping studies as the basis for further research - a participant-observer case study. Inf. Softw. Technol. **53**, 638–651 (2011)
10. Macchi, D., Solari, M.: Mapeo Sistemático de la Literatura sobre la Adopción de Inspecciones de Software. In: Conf. Latinoam. Informática (CLEI 2012), pp. 1–8 (2012)
11. Fdez-Riverola, F., Corchado, J.M.: Forecasting red tides using an hybrid neuro-symbolic system. AI Commun. **16**, 221–233 (2003)
12. Osório, F.S., Amy, B.: INSS: a hybrid system for constructive machine learning. Neurocomputing **28**, 191–205 (1999)
13. Medsker, L.R.: Hybrid Intelligent Systems. Springer, Boston (2012). https://doi.org/10.1007/978-1-4615-2353-6
14. Hatzilygeroudis, I., Prentzas, J.: Symbolic-neural rule based reasoning and explanation. Expert Syst. Appl. **42**, 4595–4609 (2015)
15. Fdez-Riverola, F., Corchado, J.M.: CBR based system for forecasting red tides. Knowl. Based Syst. **16**, 321–328 (2003)
16. González-Briones, A., Chamoso, P., Yoe, H., Corchado, J.M.: GreenVMAS: virtual organization based platform for heating greenhouses using waste energy from power plants. Sensors **18**(3), 861 (2018)
17. Vaidya, S., Ambad, P., Bhosle, S.: Industry 4.0 - a glimpse. Procedia Manuf. **20**, 233–238 (2018)
18. Bahrin, M.A.K., Othman, M.F., Azli, N.H.N., Talib, M.F.: Industry 4.0: a review on industrial automation and robotic. J. Teknol. **78**, 137–143 (2016)
19. Chamoso, P., González-Briones, A., Rodríguez, S., Corchado, J.M.: Tendencies of technologies and platforms in smart cities: a state-of-the-art review. Wireless Commun. Mob. Comput. **2018**, 17 (2018)
20. Gonzalez-Briones, A., Prieto, J., De La Prieta, F., Herrera-Viedma, E., Corchado, J.M.: Energy optimization using a case-based reasoning strategy. Sensors (Basel) **18**(3), 865 (2018). https://doi.org/10.3390/s18030865
21. Lorenz, M., Rüßmann, M., Strack, R., Lueth, K.L., Bolle, M.: Man and Machine in Industry 4.0 (2015)
22. Montalvillo, L., Díaz, O.: Requirement-driven evolution in software product lines: a systematic mapping study. J. Syst. Softw. **122**, 110–143 (2016)
23. Budgen, D., Turner, M., Brereton, O.P., Kitchenham, B.A.: Using mapping studies in software engineering. In: XX Annual Meeting of the Psychology of Programming Interest Group (PPIG 2008), pp. 195–204 (2008)
24. Tofan, D., Galster, M., Avgeriou, P., Schuitema, W.: Past and future of software architectural decisions – a systematic mapping study. Inf. Softw. Technol. **56**, 850–872 (2014)
25. Dallasega, P., Rauch, E., Linder, C.: Industry 4.0 as an enabler of proximity for construction supply chains: a systematic literature review (2018). https://www.sciencedirect.com/science/article/pii/S0166361517305043?via%3Dihub
26. Liao, Y., Deschamps, F., de Loures, E.F.R., Ramos, L.F.P.: Past, present and future of Industry 4.0-a systematic literature review and research agenda proposal. Int. J. Prod. Res. **55**, 3609–3629 (2017)

27. Sittón, I., Rodríguez, S.: Pattern extraction for the design of predictive models in industry 4.0. In: De la Prieta, F., Vale, Z., Antunes, L., Pinto, T., Campbell, Andrew T., Julián, V., Neves, Antonio J.R., Moreno, María N. (eds.) PAAMS 2017. AISC, vol. 619, pp. 258–261. Springer, Cham (2018). https://doi.org/10.1007/978-3-319-61578-3_31

28. Kang, H.S., et al.: Do: smart manufacturing: past research, present findings, and future directions. Int. J. Precis. Eng. Manuf. Technol. **3**, 111–128 (2016)

29. Rojko, A.: Industry 4.0 concept: background and overview. Int. J. Interact. Mob. Technol. **11**, 77 (2017)

30. Zhong, R.Y., Xu, X., Klotz, E., Newman, S.T.: Intelligent manufacturing in the context of industry 4.0: a review. Engineering **3**, 616–630 (2017)

31. Hozdić, E.: Smart factory for industry 4.0: a review. Int. J. Mod. Manuf. Technol. **7**, 28–35 (2015)

32. Strozzi, F., Colicchia, C., Creazza, A., Noè, C.: Literature review on the 'Smart Factory' concept using bibliometric tools. Int. J. Prod. Res. **55**, 6572–6591 (2017)

33. Buer, S.-V., Strandhagen, J.O., Chan, F.T.S.: The link between Industry 4.0 and lean manufacturing: mapping current research and establishing a research agenda. Int. J. Prod. Res. **56**, 2924–2940 (2018)

34. Zheng, P., et al.: Smart manufacturing systems for Industry 4.0: conceptual framework, scenarios, and future perspectives. Front. Mech. Eng. **13**(2), 137–150 (2018)

35. Bullón, J., Arrieta, A.G., Encinas, A.H., Dios, A.Q.: Manufacturing processes in the textile industry. Expert systems for fabrics production. Adv. Distrib. Comput. Artif. Intell. J. **6**(1), 41–50 (2017). (ISSN: 2255-2863), Salamanca

36. Thames, L., Schaefer, D.: Industry 4.0: an overview of key benefits, technologies, and challenges. In: Thames, L., Schaefer, D. (eds.) Cybersecurity for Industry 4.0. SSAM, pp. 1–33. Springer, Cham (2017). https://doi.org/10.1007/978-3-319-50660-9_1

37. Oesterreich, T.D., Teuteberg, F.: Understanding the implications of digitisation and automation in the context of Industry 4.0: a triangulation approach and elements of a research agenda for the construction industry. Comput. Ind. **83**, 121–139 (2016)

38. Lu, Y.: Industry 4.0: a survey on technologies, applications and open research issues (2017). https://ac.els-cdn.com/S2452414X17300043/1-s2.0-S2452414X17300043-main.pdf?_tid=b8739e67-e22b-4158-a461-b5d97792ef90&acdnat=1525088363_5dcfb9a52f3e0e3732e67a69a27458ef

39. Liu, Y., Xu, X.: Industry 4.0 and cloud manufacturing: a comparative analysis. J. Manuf. Sci. Eng. **139**, 34701 (2017)

40. Yang, S., Bian, C., Li, X., Tan, L., Tang, D.: Optimized fault diagnosis based on FMEA-style CBR and BN for embedded software system. Int. J. Adv. Manuf. Technol. **94**, 3441–3453 (2018)

41. Kim, D., et al.: A hybrid failure diagnosis and prediction using natural language-based process map and rule-based expert system. Int. J. Comput. Commun. Control **5**, 1841–9836 (2017)

42. Chang, P.-C., Lin, J.-J., Dzan, W.-Y., Chang, P.-C., Lin, J.-J., Dzan, W.-Y.: Forecasting of manufacturing cost in mobile phone products by case-based reasoning and artificial neural network models. J Intell. Manuf. **23**, 517–531 (2012)

43. Piltan, M., Mehmanchi, E., Ghaderi, S.F.: Proposing a decision-making model using analytical hierarchy process and fuzzy expert system for prioritizing industries in installation of combined heat and power systems. Expert Syst. Appl. **39**, 1124–1133 (2012)

44. Zarandi, M.H.F., Mansour, S., Hosseinijou, S.A., Avazbeigi, M.: A material selection methodology and expert system for sustainable product design. Int. J. Adv. Manuf. Technol. **57**, 885–903 (2011)

45. Bahrammirzaee, A., et al.: Hybrid credit ranking intelligent system using expert system and artificial neural networks. Appl. Intell. **34**, 28–46 (2011)
46. Yazdi, M.: Hybrid probabilistic risk assessment using Fuzzy FTA and Fuzzy AHP in a process industry. J. Fail. Anal. Prev. **17**, 756–764 (2017)
47. Pask, F., Lake, P., Yang, A., Tokos, H., Sadhukhan, J.: Sustainability indicators for industrial ovens and assessment using Fuzzy set theory and Monte Carlo simulation. J. Clean. Prod. **140**, 1217–1225 (2017)
48. Karelovic, P., Putz, E., Cipriano, A.: A framework for hybrid model predictive control in mineral processing. Control Eng. Pract. **40**, 1–12 (2015)
49. Sáiz-Bárcena, L., Herrero, A., Del Campo, M.A.M., Del Olmo Martínez, R.: Easing knowledge management in the power sector by means of a neuro-genetic system. Int. J. Bio-Inspired Comput. **7**, 170–175 (2015)
50. Fazel Zarandi, M.H., Gamasaee, R., Turksen, I.B.: A type-2 fuzzy expert system based on a hybrid inference method for steel industry. Int. J. Adv. Manuf. Technol. **71**(5–8), 857–885 (2013)
51. Van Pham, H., Tran, K.D., Kamei, K.: Applications using hybrid intelligent decision support systems for selection of alternatives under uncertainty and risk. Int. J. Innov. Comput. Inf. Control **10**, 39–56 (2014)
52. Shahrabi, J., Hadavandi, E., Asadi, S.: Developing a hybrid intelligent model for forecasting problems: case study of tourism demand time series. Knowl. Based Syst. **43**, 112–122 (2013)
53. Vogel-Heuser, B., Legat, C., Folmer, J., Schütz, D.: An assessment of the potentials and challenges in future approaches for automation software. In: Leitao, P., Karsnouskos, S. (eds.) Industrial Agents: Emerging Applications of Software Agents in Industry. p. 476. Elsevier Inc. (2015). https://doi.org/10.1016/C2013-0-15269-5
54. Prentzas, J., Hatzilygeroudis, I.: Assessment of life insurance applications: an approach integrating neuro-symbolic rule-based with case-based reasoning. Expert Syst. **33**, 145–160 (2016)
55. Prentzas, J., Hatzilygeroudis, I.: Using clustering algorithms to improve the production of symbolic-neural rule bases from empirical data. Int. J. Artif. Intell. Tools **27**, 1850002 (2018)
56. Hatzilygeroudis, I., Prentzas, J.: Symbolic-neural rule based reasoning and explanation. Expert Syst. Appl. Int. J. **42**, 4595–4609 (2015)
57. Kasabov, N.K.: Evolving connectionist systems for adaptive learning and knowledge discovery: trends and directions. Knowl. Based Syst. **80**, 24–33 (2015)
58. Prentzas, J., Hatzilygeroudis, I.: Improving efficiency of merging symbolic rules into integrated rules: splitting methods and mergability criteria. Expert Syst. Appl. **32**, 244–260 (2015)
59. Elhoseny, M., Abdelaziz, A., Salama, A.S., Riad, A.M., Muhammad, K., Sangaiah, A.K.: A hybrid model of Internet of Things and cloud computing to manage big data in health services applications. Future Gener. Comput. Syst. **86**, 1383–1394 (2018)
60. Shihabudheen, K.V., Pillai, G.N.: Recent advances in neuro-fuzzy system: a survey. Knowl. Based Syst. **152**, 136–162 (2018)
61. Liao, Y., Felipe Pierin Ramos, L., Saturno, M., Deschamps, F., de Freitas Rocha Loures, E., Luis Szejka, A.: The role of interoperability in the fourth industrial revolution era. IFAC PapersOnline **50**, 12434–12439 (2017)
62. Hermann, M., Pentek, T., Otto, B.: Design principles for industrie 4.0 scenarios (2016)
63. Trotta, D., Garengo, P.: Industry 4.0 key research topics: a bibliometric review. In: 2018 7th International Conference on Industrial Technology and Management (ICITM), pp. 113–117 (2018)

64. Simas, O., Rodrigues, J.C.: The implementation of industry 4.0: a literature review. In: Proceedings of International Conference on Computers and Industrial Engineering, CIE (2017)
65. Pereira, A.C., Romero, F.: A review of the meanings and the implications of the Industry 4.0 concept. Procedia Manuf. **13**, 1206–1214 (2017)
66. Martín, A.M., Marcos, M., Aguayo, F., Lama, J.R.: Smart industrial metabolism: a literature review and future directions. Procedia Manuf. **13**, 1223–1228 (2017)
67. Dequeant, K., Vialletelle, P., Lemaire, P., Espinouse, M.-L.: A literature review on variability in semiconductor manufacturing: the next forward leap to Industry 4.0. In: Proceedings of the 2016 Winter Simulation Conference, pp. 2598–2609 (2016)
68. Santos, C., Mehrsai, A., Barros, A.C., Araújo, M., Ares, E.: Towards industry 4.0: an overview of European strategic roadmaps. Procedia Manuf. **13**, 972–979 (2017)
69. Barreto, L., Amaral, A., Pereira, T.: Industry 4.0 implications in logistics: an overview. Procedia Manuf. **13**, 1245–1252 (2017)
70. Casado-Vara, R., Novais, P., Gil, A.B., Prieto, J., Corchado, J.M.: Distributed continuous-time fault estimation control for multiple devices in IoT networks. IEEE Access **7**, 11972–11984 (2019). https://doi.org/10.1109/ACCESS.2019.2892905
71. Bassi, L.: Industry 4.0: Hope, hype or revolution? In: 2017 IEEE 3rd International Forum on Research and Technologies for Society and Industry (RTSI), pp. 1–6 (2017)
72. Ben Said, A., Shahzad, M.K., Zamai, E., Hubac, S., Tollenaere, M.: Towards proactive maintenance actions scheduling in the Semiconductor Industry (SI) using Bayesian approach. IFAC-PapersOnLine **49**, 544–549 (2016)
73. Morente-Molinera, J.A., Kou, G., González-Crespo, R., Corchado, J.M., Herrera-Viedma, E.: Solving multi-criteria group decision making problems under environments with a high number of alternatives using fuzzy ontologies and multi-granular linguistic modelling methods. Knowl. Based Syst. **137**, 54–64 (2017)
74. Casado-Vara, R., Chamoso, P., De la Prieta, F., Prieto, J., Corchado, J.M.: Non-linear adaptive closed-loop control system for improved efficiency in IoT-blockchain management. Inf. Fusion **49**, 227–239 (2019)
75. Pham, H.V., Tran, K.D., Kamei, K.: Applications using hybrid intelligent decision support systems for selection of alternatives under uncertainty and risk. Int. J. Innov. Comput. Inf. Control ICIC **10**, 39–56 (2014)

Method for Identification of Waste in the Process of Software Development in Agile Teams Using Lean and Scrum

Márcio Trovão Bufon$^{(\boxtimes)}$ and Adriano Galindo Leal$^{(\boxtimes)}$

Institute of Technological Research - IPT, São Paulo, Brazil
mubuffon@gmail.com, leal@ipt.br

Abstract. Waste in software development projects is defined as anything that consumes resources such as time, effort, room, and money without adding value to the customer. Methods and techniques to identify waste indicators, which are specific for each project, are applied to part of total interactions and the development phases; and spend analysts and developers' time and effort. Therefore, this paper aims to define a method to identify waste within the software development process in Scrum teams, from data based on JIRA tool, which supports software development planning, management and controlling activities. According to the bibliographic review are defined: (i) indicators for types of waste according to Lean software development principles; (ii) JIRA's attributes, mathematical operators, keywords, functions and reports related to such indicators. In the proposed method are defined requirements that establish a semantic relation between each indicator variables and formulas to the set of JIRA'S attributes, functions and keywords and, based on them, queries in JIRA Query Language are implemented to quantify the indicators. The method validation is performed using graphics that show queries results classified and grouped by project, indicator and type of waste, acquired from a software project base for a company in the Brazilian financial market. Through the quantitative analysis of results, it is possible to suggest a hypothesis for the occurrence of the types of observed wastes.

Keywords: Waste · Scrum · Lean · JIRA

1 Introduction

In software development processes, waste is defined as any action that interferes with delivering to the customers what they value at the time and place where this value is applicable. Doing what adds no value or what is not immediately necessary, generating delays, delivering a defective feature and consuming time, effort, room and financial resources without adding value to the customer are some examples of waste [1].

One way to eliminate waste in software development processes in dynamic teams that employ the Scrum method is to apply Lean Software Development (LSD) [2] principles and practices. Adapted from the Lean Manufacturing Thinking and the Toyota Production System, LSD defines as waste in software development projects partially finished or unfinished work, delivery of non-requested features or extra

© Springer Nature Switzerland AG 2019
L. Uden et al. (Eds.): KMO 2019, CCIS 1027, pp. 466–476, 2019.
https://doi.org/10.1007/978-3-030-21451-7_40

functionalities, relearning, control transfer, task switching, delays and delivery of defective software [3].

Aiming to measure such waste, indicators are defined to assess the software development flow continually [4]. These indicators allow to identify bottlenecks, to follow the ongoing development of requirements and to draw up a costs template that represents the perspectives related to investment; work performed and waste, separately. In software development projects that use Kanban it is possible to identify waste by mapping the sequence of activities [5]. For Scrum projects, waste is identified and eliminated during the planning phases by recognising unnecessary features or functionalities whose cost or deadline for development are higher or longer than the expected for the project. In [6], authors propose the identification and elimination of defects and the resulting reduction of waste in Scrum software projects using monitoring the development phase as well as the evolution of the system architecture quality. Furthermore, the identification of metrics and waste indicators are more effectual when combined with software tools to plan, manage and control the development process [2]. Also, the use of LSD analytical tools allows the application of Lean concepts and principles to software engineering processes [4]. Finally, in [7] authors recommend the development of applications aiming to evaluate the application of LSD concepts interactively.

Based on these statements and the growing application of such tools by dynamic teams [8]; in order to waste identification be an efficient process, it must be performed by, and integrated into, the same tools that provide support for the software development process planning, managing and control activities.

Therefore, the objective of this work is to propose a method to evidence indicators of waste from the data, graphs and reports available in the agile planning tool JIRA itself. The main contribution of the proposed method is to reduce considerably the effort required to identify the waste in software development projects, thus avoiding that the effort necessary to carry out such activities can be considered wasteful.

2   Lean Software Development – LSD

2.1   Principles

Lean Software Development expands the agile development foundations since it applies Lean principles to software development, and its crucial principle: **to eliminate waste** [1, 3, 9]. This principle involves total elimination of waste by identifying in a timeline the period from the customer's request to the actual delivery of value to the customer. Every activity that adds no value must be removed from the timeline.

The timeline starts when the development team, comprised of requirement and system analysts, developers, architects, software engineers, testers and so forth, receives a request to solve a set of the customer's need and finishes when the software is implemented in the production environment.

2.2 Identify and Eliminate Waste

There are two steps required to eliminate waste in the software development process. The first step involves visualising the types of waste and identifying their sources. The second step is the elimination of significant waste sources identified in the first step. These steps are repeated until all sources and wastes caused by them are removed [3]. These authors have adapted, for software development, the seven types of waste identified in the Toyota Production System. Table 1 shows these types of waste according to the Lean Software Development (LSD).

Table 1. Comparison between types of waste according Manufacturing and Lean Software Development.

The seven wastes of manufacturing	The seven wastes of software development
Inventory	Partially done work
Extra processing	Extra processes
Overproduction	Extra features
Transportation	Task switching
Waiting	Waiting
Motion	Motion
Defects	Defects

Each type of waste can be defined as [1, 9]:

- **Partially Done Work:** Refers to unfinished or partially finished software, that becomes obsolete, that hides quality problems or is subject to constant requests for changes. The stock of requirements to be solved represents the unfinished work.
- **Extra Processes:** Loss of knowledge and of processes created and executed between the development cycles, generating rework or the definition of other work processes to those mapped in the value chain.
- **Extra Features:** Inclusion of extra features to the system that was not initially mapped in the requirements, providing for a future need. These features add some technical capacity that will not be observed or that is not required for the work to be performed by the final user.
- **Task Switching:** Software development requires in-depth analysis, focusing on the complexity of what needs to be developed. When a software developer changes constantly between two different tasks, distraction can occur, adversely affecting the results of both tasks.
- **Waiting:** Waiting for documents to be signed, meetings to be held, machines to be cleared, for the availability of development environments, for tests to be performed or the approval of software versions, as well as waiting for people who are working on other areas or for the approval of changes, cause delays in the beginning of the software development process, increasing the inventory items to be developed and not delivering value to the final user.

- **Motion:** When software collaborators alternate between different projects, effort and time are required to understand the workflow and the context of the new project. At each transfer of control, there is a loss of knowledge or knowledge is limited to the person who creates it.
- **Defects:** Defects not identified in the first test cycles of software cost more to be corrected when already delivered in controlled environments for integration tests and production. The delivery of versions that repeatedly show defects is being produced by a defective software development process.

The specific software development process used in agile teams can cause waste for being excessively complex or for having characteristics of traditional development methods, such as the delivery of a large set of software functionalities after long periods of development without performing intermediary deliveries, developers with no autonomy to decide on technical questions associated to the requirements or to software quality attributes, adoption of new technologies, frameworks or processes without proper scientific analysis [1].

Additionally, development teams that not working the architecture or the refactoring the code during interactions aiming to eliminate or reduce technical debt before the end of the software project can cause wastes of defects and extra processes.

2.3   Value and Value Stream Mapping

Complying with the Lean fundamental principle of eliminating waste is only possible with the identification of what value is and with the mapping of work process flow to generate this value, referred to as value flow [3].

Value, under Lean context, is delivering to the customer what they effectively requested, within the minimum time possible, with quality and at the price they are willing to pay, while the value flow is comprised of all processes required to generate value, from the design to the delivery and utilization by the customer [10].

In [11], authors state that mapping of value flow identifies as types of waste only delays, task switching between collaborators and relearning, while [12] authors suggest that, to identify these and other types of waste, it is necessary an approach based on two different steps. The first step is the application of indicators to the existing value flow, and the second step is a detailed mapping of flows that show the worst results per indicator. In this way, it is possible to avoid the thorough mapping of flows that have no meaningful impact on value generation.

2.4   Waste Indicators

Petersen and Wohlin (2011), suggested waste indicators such as the identification of a number of bottlenecks (NB) considering the delivery time of a requirement and the number of accumulated items (NAI) of requirements for each collaborator in each development phase.

The volume of work in progress (WIP), has been used as a waste indicator regarding definitions, revisions or architecture refactoring [6]. Based on the WIP, it was proposed and applied corrections to the development flow reducing the waiting time to start the development of stories that depended on the architectural definition and on the amount of rework required to correct defects caused by architecture faults.

3   Method

The method suggested in this study relates, in four phases, waste indicators to charts and reports in the agile planning tool of JIRA.

The first phase in this method is the specification of requirements of queries in natural language, considering the definition and breakdown of each indicator into variables and mathematical operators. It was created the requirements in natural language (RNL) board for each indicator and type of waste. In each RNL board, containing one or more requirements, it was selected the keywords used in the second phase of the method.

In the second phase, it is established the semantic relation between RNL and JIRA elements. Columns A and B are filled out respectively with the indicator variables and mathematical operators and, subsequently, with JIRA sets of attributes, keywords, JQL functions, reports and graphics, whose meanings are related to the indicator according to the model defined in Table 2.

Table 2. Example of the board of requirements in natural language.

RNL_NB_PROJECT_01	**REQUIREMENT** **Number of bottlenecks**
RNL1.1 – When using the Control Flow Diagram (CFD), the start and end dates of each Sprint must be specified as the period, excluding from the analysis issues that are already in the Done phase (status Resolved, Closed). **Keywords for semantic relations:** • period; • *Sprint*; • issues; • phase; • status;	

The third phase is the Structured Query Specification in JQL (SQSJQL), considering the items produced in phases 1 (RNL) and 2 (TSR) (Table 3).

In the 4th phase, the JQL query code defined in each SQSJQL is saved as a filter in order to be reused in control panels created in JIRA, which may contain different gadgets, such as graphics and JQL queries results, data on version builds and code coverage. For the validation of this method, it is used only for graphics and report gadgets (Fig. 1 and Table 4).

Table 3. Example of table of semantic relation.

Table of semantic relation – (TSR)	
Column A – Indicator N	Column B - *JIRA*
Variables	**Set of attributes or keywords**
• variable1	• attribute1
• variable2	• attribute2
• variableN	• attributeN
	• keyword1
	• keyword2
	• keywordN
Mathematical Operators	**Set of functions JQL**
• operator1	• function1
• operator2	• function2
• operatorN	• functionN
	JIRA **Graphics**
	• graphic1
	• graphic2
	• graphicN

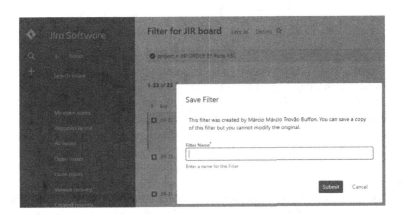

Fig. 1. Persistent filters from a JQL query

4   Method Validation and Analysis of Results

In order to validate the method, it was considered JIRA data, version v7.6.0, of a software development project, referred to in this study as PROJECT_01, for a financial market company in Brazil. The PROJECT_01 was created in JIRA as Scrum type, creating Kanban boards for control and follow-up of project activities regarding specification, implementation, tests and deployment of requirements in each Sprint.

Scrum is an agile development method designed by Jeff Sutherland in the early 1990s and later updated by Cohn (2009), Schwaber (2004) and Beedle (2001). In it, the software development process comprises the activities of requirements, analysis,

Table 4. Board **2.** Example of Structured Query Specification.

SQSJQL(VE_TI) • **RNL1.1** • **RNL1.2**	STRUCTURED QUERY SPECIFICATION JQL QUERY Value of Efficiency for Unfinished Work
Description	Returns by project, phase and period, the number of ISSUES.
Inputs	project identifier, identification of the phase, start date and end date or period (day, month or year), ISSUE status.
Outputs	List in Table format with the number of ISSUES, containing the Created columns, ISSUE_Key, Status, Summary, Assignee.
Constraints	The output of the query must be compatible with the expected input of the types of graphics or reports defined in step 2.
JQL code	project in ("<id_project>") and status in (Open, "On-Hold") and *Created*Date <= <data_final>
Filter Name	LSD - WASTE – VE_TI
Sort	Ascending Query Records by CreatedDate

design, evolution and delivery. These activities occur within a process pattern called Sprint, and prioritized requirements that generate customer value are added to a list called Backlog. Daily meetings of up to 15 min (stand-up meetings) allow Scrum teams to reveal problems or impediments in the development process that are reported to a team leader, called the Scrum Master. The Scrum Master is also responsible for defining with the project owner the list of requirements prioritized in the Backlog (requirements inventory) [13].

The data gathering period was restricted between SPRINT 02 (06/22/2018) starting date and the end of the third week of SPRINT 04 (09/06/2018). During the analysis period, the total of collaborators and their profiles were distributed into nine collaborators, more specifically, 01 Manager, 01 Scrum Master, 03 requirement analysts and 04 developers.

4.1 Number of Accumulated Items (NAI)

NAI allows you to identify whether there is a continuous workflow between Sprints or software versions. Over time, it is expected that its value will decrease, resulting in a reduction in the number of backlog requirements. Figure 2 represents the control panel created for this indicator in JIRA.

In PROJECT_01, dividing the number of delivered requirements by the number of weeks in each Sprint results in an average of 4.2 requirements delivered per week. Similarly, but this time dividing the number of open requirements by the number of

LEAN - NAI - PROJECT_01

Fig. 2. Persistent filters from a JQL query.

weeks in each Sprint, results in an average of 3.5 requirements added to the stock per week. Considering that the difference between these average values is approximately 1 REQUIREMENT delivered per week and if there is no change in this difference towards the requirements delivered in the period, it will be necessary 277 weeks or 69 Sprints so that the stock of requirements is settled.

4.2   Work in Progress (WIP)

Under the context of PROJECT_01, the WIP has been adjusted to quantify all requirements that deviate from the value flow, checking the number of transitions between the phases and the status that, for each REQUIREMENT, deviate from the value flow mapping described in Fig. 3.

Considering the values of each SQSJQL, it is possible to calculate the WIP percentage that deviates from the requirements and the defects grouped by Sprint according to Table 5.

According to the result of Table 5, it is possible to observe that the work in progress deviation for requirement tasks tends to double at each new Sprint, while the percentage of defects after a drop between SPRINT 02 and SPRINT 03, remains stable. Based only on the percentages presented it is not possible to state how much the deviations to the value flow affect the developers and analysts' efforts.

However, after categorizing the WIP deviation in requirements and defects and grouping them by Sprints, it was possible to identify the wastes related to unfinished work - it happened in tasks moved from Sprints Sprint 07/05 -18/05 and Sprint 11/06 - 22/06 to the Sprints within the analysis period; extra features – occurred when there were several types of requirements tasks and defects – categorized as Bugs and Defects.

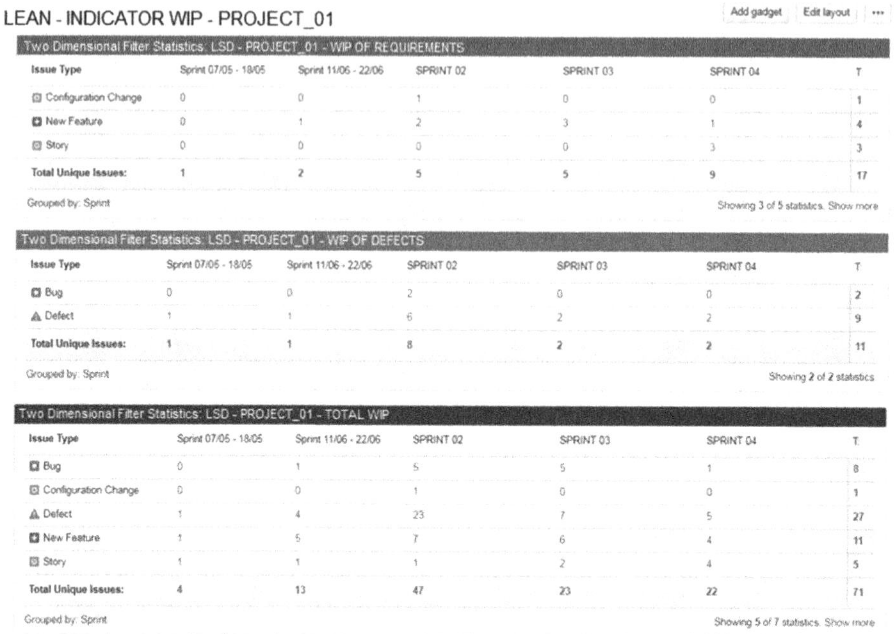

LEAN - INDICATOR WIP - PROJECT_01   Add gadget   Edit layout   ···

Two Dimensional Filter Statistics: LSD - PROJECT_01 - WIP OF REQUIREMENTS

Issue Type	Sprint 07/05 - 18/05	Sprint 11/06 - 22/06	SPRINT 02	SPRINT 03	SPRINT 04	T
Configuration Change	0	0	1	0	0	1
New Feature	0	1	2	3	1	4
Story	0	0	0	0	3	3
Total Unique Issues:	1	2	5	5	9	17

Grouped by: Sprint   Showing 3 of 5 statistics. Show more

Two Dimensional Filter Statistics: LSD - PROJECT_01 - WIP OF DEFECTS

Issue Type	Sprint 07/05 - 18/05	Sprint 11/06 - 22/06	SPRINT 02	SPRINT 03	SPRINT 04	T
Bug	0	0	2	0	0	2
Defect	1	1	6	2	2	9
Total Unique Issues:	1	1	8	2	2	11

Grouped by: Sprint   Showing 2 of 2 statistics

Two Dimensional Filter Statistics: LSD - PROJECT_01 - TOTAL WIP

Issue Type	Sprint 07/05 - 18/05	Sprint 11/06 - 22/06	SPRINT 02	SPRINT 03	SPRINT 04	T
Bug	0	1	5	5	1	8
Configuration Change	0	0	1	0	0	1
Defect	1	4	23	7	5	27
New Feature	1	5	7	6	4	11
Story	1	1	1	2	4	5
Total Unique Issues:	4	13	47	23	22	71

Grouped by: Sprint   Showing 5 of 7 statistics. Show more

Fig. 3. LEAN Control Panel – INDICATOR (WIP) – PROJECT_01.

Table 5. Result of the percentage of WIP deviations per type of task and *Sprint*.

Sprint	Issue type	
	Requirements	Defects
SPRINT 02 – 07/20/2018	11%	17%
SPRINT 03 – 08/17/2018	22%	9%
SPRINT 04 – 09/14/2018	41%	9%

4.3   Number of Bottlenecks (NB)

It was not possible to add the NB indicator to a control panel, as performed with the other indicators, since JIRA has a set of Sprints follow-up reports and, among the reports available, there is the CFD – Control Flow Diagram.

The CFD allows to analyse the number of requirements in each column of Kanban value flow, based on the premises that the requirements to the left of the board are those under the "To Do" status, and those to the right are the ones under the "Resolved" or "Closed" status. The CFD meets the NB calculation specification by demonstrating the occurrence of work overload in a specific phase of development interaction.

In the CFD description [14] it is expected that the number of requirements in each phase is graphically represented by a homogeneous surface, demonstrating the lack of bottlenecks and proper distribution of requirements in each phase.

Figure 4 shows that among the three Sprints there is a bottleneck when starting the "to do" requirements specification, implementation, tests and deployment activities, highlighted in orange in the graphics and SPRINT 04.

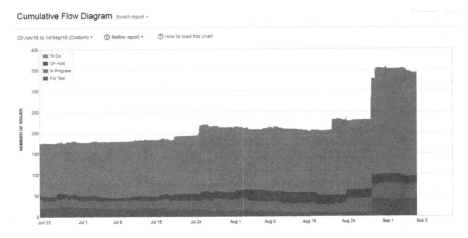

Fig. 4. Persistent filters from a JQL query.

Finally, a possible hypothesis for the bottlenecks previously mentioned is the distribution of PROJECT_01 team collaborators into 03 requirement analysts and 04 developers. It seems that this distribution is insufficient to fulfil a continuous flow of requirements over time.

5   Conclusion

The first three phases of the method have produced items that associate JIRA tool to waste indicators. These items are requirements in natural language (RNL); Tables of Semantic Relation (TSR) and; structured JQL query (SQSJQL) specifications. All these three items can be adapted to be applied to other projects.

The fourth phase of the method, which is the elaboration of reports and graphics per indicator, proved to be efficient when showing waste data in JIRA with a total effort time shorter than four week-period defined in the Sprints analysed, representing the most significant contribution of this study. The proposed method was able to identify in NAI and NB indicators the occurrence of waste in the form of delays, while the WIP indicator identified waste in the form of defects, extra features and unfinished work.

Additionally, only after performing qualitative analysis based on the indicators identified was it possible to accurately define the causes for the types of waste observed, through the identification of scenarios that directly affect the value flow transitions and the volume of requirements in stock or in each phase.

Further studies may, by adapting the semantic relation model, be extended to other agile planning tools (Monday.com, Wrike, Pipedrive, Glip etc.) or to other indicators, making it possible to identify the impact of waste reduction when effort is estimated in story points or in hours to delivery of a requirement. These studies can implement the 4th phase of the proposed method with the use of BI tools such as Alteryx Desktop, Tableau, Microsoft Power BI.

Acknowledgement. The second author gratefully acknowledges the financial support from grants #2019/01664-6 and #2017/50343-2, São Paulo Research Foundation (FAPESP).

References

1. Poppendieck, M.P.T.: Leading Lean Software Development: Results Are not the Point, 1st edn. Pearson, Upper Saddle River (2009)
2. Ikonen, M., et al.: Exploring the sources of waste in Kanban software development projects. In: Proceedings - 36th EUROMICRO Conference on Software Engineering and Advanced Applications, SEAA 2010, pp. 376–381 (2010)
3. Poppendieck, M.P.T.: Lean Software Development: An Agile Toolkit. Addison-Wesley Longman Publishing Co., Inc., Boston (2003)
4. Petersen, K., Wohlin, C.: Measuring the flow in lean software development BT - focus on agile software development. Softw. Pract. Exp. **41**(9), 975–996 (2011)
5. Behroozi, N., Kamandi, A.: Waste elimination of agile methodologies in web engineering. In: 2016 2nd International Conference on Web Research, ICWR 2016, pp. 102–107 (2016)
6. Nord, R.L., Ozkaya, I., Sangwan, R.S.: Making architecture visible to improve flow management in lean software development. IEEE Softw. **29**(5), 33–39 (2012)
7. Jonsson, H., Larsson, S., Punnekkat, S.: Synthesizing a comprehensive framework for lean software development. In: Proceedings - 39th Euromicro Conference Series on Software Engineering and Advanced Applications, SEAA 2013, pp. 1–8 (2013)
8. Murphy, T.E., West, M., Mann, K.J.: Gartner https://www.gartner.com/doc/reprints?id=1-3YWBN1Q&ct=170427&st=sb%255Bgartner.com. Accessed 11 Nov 2017
9. Poppendieck e Poppendieck (2011)
10. Bell, S.C., Orzen, M.A.: Lean IT: Enabling and Sustaining Your Lean Transformation. CRC Press, Boca Raton (2016)
11. Sedano, T., Ralph, P., Peraire, C.: Software development waste. In: 2017 IEEE/ACM 39th International Conference on Software Engineering (ICSE), pp. 130–140 (2017)
12. Petersen, K., Wohlin, C.: Software process improvement through the lean measurement (SPI-LEAM) method. J. Syst. Softw. **83**(7), 1275–1287 (2010)
13. Pressman, Roger S.: Software Engineering - A professional Approach, pp. 77–79. McGraw-Hill Science, New York (2016)
14. Atlassian: JIRA Software. https://br.atlassian.com/software/jira. Accessed 6 May 2018

Routing Protocols in Vehicular Ad-Hoc Networks: A Performance Evaluation

Raúl Lozada-Yánez[1]($\boxtimes$), Washington Luna-Encalada[1],
Danni Tierra-Quispillo[1], Fernando Molina-Granja[2],
and Jonny Guaiña-Yungan[1]

[1] Escuela Superior Politécnica de Chimborazo - Facultad de Informática
y Electrónica, Panamericana Sur Km 1 1/2, Riobamba, Ecuador
{raul.lozada, wluna, jguaina}@espoch.edu.ec,
dannytierra@outlook.com
[2] Universidad Nacional de Chimborazo - Facultad de Ingeniería,
Avda. Antonio José de Sucre, Km 1.5 Vía a Guano, Riobamba, Ecuador
fmolina@unach.edu.ec

Abstract. The presented article evaluates the routing protocols in connected Vehicular Ad-Hoc Networks (VANET) through 802.11p considering synthetic mobility models and vehicular traffic generators, Manhattan and Intelligent Driver Mobility (IDM) models were selected respectively. The following programs were installed on a Linux-based system to simulate the scenarios: SUMO for the traffic management, NS-2 for simulating the data network and MOVE for exporting the information from SUMO to NS-2. Proactive and reactive routing protocols classification was considered, to subsequently apply the DSDV and AOMDV protocols that proved to have better performance. In the simulated scenarios, a low, medium and high number of connections were used with two communication types: Vehicle to vehicle (V2V) and Vehicle to infrastructure (V2I) for VANET networks. The indicators that were analyzed to determine the performance of the protocols were Throughput, Packet delivery ratio relationship (PDR), Average End to End Delay and Normalized routing load (NRL). The study was found that for V2V communications, regardless of the connections or the mobility model, AOMDV or DSDV can be used since the difference in performance is minimal. The results indicate that the best protocol is AOMDV with a superiority to DSDV in most cases. It is concluded that the model closest to reality is IDM since it is based on a traffic generator while the Manhattan model, based on mathematical formulas offers ambiguous results.

Keywords: Vanet · Routing · Mobility model · Vehicular traffic · Linux

1 Introduction

For several years, wireless networks have evolved to offer various services to users, satisfying their needs in different fields of application. The improvements in the existing technologies allow the operation of new types of wireless networks that work in different frequency ranges that are not congested, allowing a better performance in

© Springer Nature Switzerland AG 2019
L. Uden et al. (Eds.): KMO 2019, CCIS 1027, pp. 477–488, 2019.
https://doi.org/10.1007/978-3-030-21451-7_41

the sending of data, fact that also makes that the transmission speed is optimized and reduce implementation costs due to the offer that exists in the market.

The communication between vehicles has aroused interest among researchers and developers around the world [1], one of these technological improvements is being applied to transport field to organize the transit and save human lives through implementation of a Vehicular Ad-hoc Network (VANET), a special class of Mobile Ad Hoc Networks (MANETs) [2]. A VANET is an emerging technology where inter-vehicle communication occurs in a highly dynamic environment, in this wireless networks, vehicles moving at various speeds communicate with the help of a suitable data-forwarding strategy in VANET [3]. This task is possible thanks in part to routing protocols, which must have a fast and efficient adaptive capacity in the face of topological changes that they arise within the network, having at the same time, to use the minimum amount of memory, bandwidth (which can be a bottleneck [2]) and transmission's power.

In Valencia, Spain the research entitled "Optimal Configuration of the OLSR Routing Protocol for VANETs Through Differential Evolution", indicates that the routing in a VANET network must be efficient to guarantee the quality of service, in this context, that work seeks an efficient configuration of the Optimized Link State Routing protocol (OLSR) for VANET based on the packet sending rate, routing management load and point-to-point delay [4].

A similar work, carried out in South America, is the study conducted in [5], which is entitled "Simulation and performance analysis of unicast protocols for VANET Networks". In this publication, emphasis is placed on the technological challenges represented by routing in VANET networks, since routing protocols, and mobility models are required to offer solutions to the inconveniences that arise in this type of network infrastructures, in which, unlike the static network infrastructures, the nodes are in constant movement, which causes the constant change of the network topology [5].

In Ecuador, one of the latest researches published about VANET networks was conducted by students of the Escuela Superior Politécnica de Chimborazo with the title "Study of the VANET for the Control of Vehicles on Roads in Ecuador". This work presents a description and comparison of some reactive and proactive routing algorithms used in VANET networks, in addition, that work makes use of a mobility model based on traffic simulator [6].

The present work pretends to determine which of the routing protocols analyzed for VANET networks has a better and more efficient adaptive capacity against topological changes in a data network, analyzing parameters such as: Throughput, PDR, Average end to end Delay, and NRL for each protocol considering the synthetic mobility models and based on traffic simulators. To do this, computational simulations are used to obtain metrics to compare the performance of the most widely used routing protocols for VANET.

For the simulations, a representation of an urban environment will be used, specifically for an area of the downtown sector of the city of Riobamba, Ecuador, since it has an influx of considerable vehicular traffic. The analysis of the obtained values for each protocol and for each mobility model will allow determining which of the analyzed protocols present the best performance.

2 Methodology

The present work has simulated and analyzed the data of three VANET networks scenarios in vehicle-to-vehicle mode (V2V) and three scenarios in vehicle mode to infrastructure (V2I), with the aim of evaluating the routing protocols in VANET networks connected through 802.11p, The reason for the analysis of both types of communication is that in a full VANET infrastructure, vehicles need to communicate with each other (V2V, vehicle to vehicle, communication) and with road-side infrastructure (V2I, vehicle to infrastructure, communication) [2]. Researchers considered the synthetic mobility models Intelligent Driver Mobility (IDM) and Manhattan and vehicular traffic generators. To this end, the SUMO tools for vehicular traffic, NS-2 for the data network and MOVE for exporting information have been installed in an Ubuntu distribution. Figure 1 shows a diagram with the methodology applied to perform the simulation of the different scenarios.

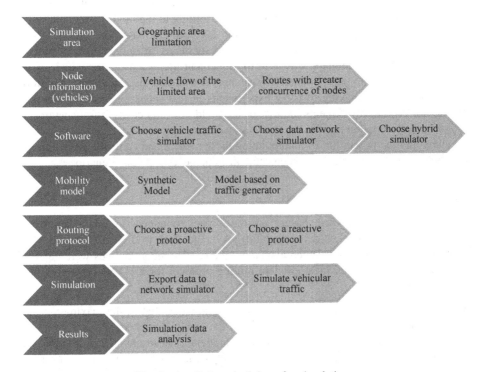

Fig. 1. Applied methodology for simulation

Table 1 details the specifications of the simulated scenarios for data collection that allowed the evaluation of routing protocols in connected VANET networks using 802.11p considering the synthetic mobility models and vehicle traffic generators.

Table 1. Simulated scenarios detail.

Scenario	Simulation time	Cars	Connections	Mobility model	Protocol
1 - V2V	500 s	10	5	IDM/Manhattan	AOMDV/DSDV
2 - V2V	500 s	50	30	IDM Manhattan	AOMDV/DSDV
3 - V2V	500 s	120	60	IDM Manhattan	AOMDV/DSDV
4 - V2I	500 s	10	5	IDM Manhattan	AOMDV/DSDV
5 - V2I	500 s	60	30	IDM Manhattan	AOMDV/DSDV
6 - V2I	500 s	120	60	IDM Manhattan	AOMDV/DSDV

3 Results

In this section, the results obtained in the different scenarios are analyzed, after executing the simulations and filtering the results to determine which routing protocol (AOMDV or DSDV) has a better performance according to the mobility model used in the scenario: Manhattan (synthetic model) and IDM (model based on a traffic generator). The presented study is the result of an experience in university education in which a computer's simulator was used to implement the test scenarios which generated the analyzed data was obtained. Researchers considered that the ability to perform simulations, without having to carry experiments in real scenarios, provide solutions that do not involve investments blindly, or the build new and costly infrastructures. In addition, the simulation used in the study allowed the capture of the interest metrics for the study and the possibility of manipulating these metrics and controlling the external variables. This fact would have been difficult to achieve in a real scenario.

3.1 Simulation Results Analysis

The results were analyzed based on the values obtained for the parameters: Throughput, PDR (Packet delivery ratio), Average End to End Delay and NRL (standardized routing load). When evaluating the results, the guidelines were obtained to determine which is the most efficient routing protocol for a VANET network simulation environment.

- *Throughput:* It refers to the efficient use of bandwidth, that is, the maximum speed at which a device does not discard any of the received packets [7].
- *PDR:* The packet delivery ratio is the quotient that results when dividing the number of packets sent for the received packets, it allows to know the packet loss rate.
- *Average end to end Delay:* Delay time that it takes the packages to arrive from their origin to their destination.
- *NRL:* The standardized routing load is equal to the relationship between the number of packets sent from the routing layer with respect to the packets received at the application layer.

Analysis of V2V Communication. In this subsection, the obtained values from the simulations of V2V communication are compared with different numbers of connections and simulation times.

Scenario 1. Scenario 1 consists of 5 V2V connections and 10 vehicles that interact for 500 s, using AOMDV reactive protocol and DSDV proactive protocol. The following results were obtained from the scenario simulations.

Table 2. Scenario 1 data.

V2V communication				
Simulation time	500 s			
Vehicles number	10			
Connections number	5			
Mobility model	IDM		MANHATTAN	
Protocol	AOMDV	DSDV	AOMDV	DSDV
PDR [%]	99,43	99,34	99,62	99,41
Throughput [Kbps]	1797,59	1728,54	1972,38	1925,83
NRL	0,06	0,09	0,06	0,08
Delay End to End [ms]	53	24,37	18,04	9,31

Data shown in Table 2, indicate that regardless of the use of the IDM or Manhattan model, the protocol with the best throughput is AOMDV, which exceeds the DSDV protocol in both cases.

Scenario 2. Scenario 2 consists of 30 V2V connections and 60 vehicles that interact for 500 s, using AOMDV reactive protocol and DSDV proactive protocol. The following results were obtained from the scenario simulations.

Table 3. Scenario 2 data.

V2V communication				
Simulation time	500 s			
Vehicles number	60			
Connections number	30			
Mobility model	IDM		MANHATTAN	
Protocol	AOMDV	DSDV	AOMDV	DSDV
PDR [%]	99,21	98,56	99,31	99,23
Throughput [Kbps]	1865,48	1686,55	2103,07	2002,54
NRL	0,4	2,77	0,38	2,46
Delay End to End [ms]	12,14	9,44	60,85	100,75

Data shown in Table 3, indicate that regardless of the use of the IDM or Manhattan model, the protocol with the best throughput is AOMDV, which exceeds the DSDV protocol in both cases.

Scenario 3. Scenario 3 consists of 60 V2V connections and 120 vehicles that interact for 500 s, using AOMDV reactive protocol and DSDV proactive protocol. The following results were obtained from the scenario simulations.

Table 4. Scenario 3 data.

V2V communication				
Simulation time	500 s			
Vehicles number	120			
Connections number	60			
Mobility model	IDM		MANHATTAN	
Protocol	AOMDV	DSDV	AOMDV	DSDV
PDR [%]	99,37	99,07	99,33	99,16
Throughput [Kbps]	1687,47	1560,89	1813,68	1701,49
NRL	0,87	16,25	0,79	16,58
Delay End to End [ms]	82,74	85,54	3,77	5,82

Data shown in Table 4, indicate that regardless of the use of the IDM or Manhattan model, the protocol with the best throughput is AOMDV, which exceeds the DSDV protocol in both cases.

Analysis of V2I Communication. In this subsection, the obtained values from the simulations of V2I communication are compared with different numbers of connections and simulation times (equal to the values used in the V2V communication).

Scenario 4. Scenario 4 consists of 5 V2I connections and 10 vehicles that interact for 500 s, using AOMDV reactive protocol and DSDV proactive protocol. The following results were obtained from the scenario simulations.

Table 5. Scenario 4 data.

V2V communication				
Simulation time	500 s			
Vehicles number	10			
Connections number	5			
Mobility model	IDM		MANHATTAN	
Protocol	AOMDV	DSDV	AOMDV	DSDV
PDR [%]	95,03	94,15	99,69	99,8
Throughput [Kbps]	632,96	534,07	1594,75	1557,31
NRL	0,27	0,34	0,1	0,11
Delay End to End [ms]	113,98	86,23	81,12	104,81

Data shown in Table 5, indicate that regardless of the use of the IDM or Manhattan model, the protocol with the best throughput is AOMDV, which exceeds the DSDV protocol in both cases.

Scenario 5. Scenario 5 consists of 30 V2I connections and 60 vehicles that interact for 500 s, using AOMDV reactive protocol and DSDV proactive protocol. The following results were obtained from the scenario simulations.

Table 6. Scenario 5 data.

V2V communication				
Simulation time	500 s			
Vehicles number	60			
Connections number	30			
Mobility model	IDM		MANHATTAN	
Protocol	AOMDV	DSDV	AOMDV	DSDV
PDR [%]	98,98	99,26	97,74	98,47
Throughput [Kbps]	1288,39	1199,77	321,42	388,34
NRL	0,69	3,98	2,79	14,91
Delay End to End [ms]	67,22	8,79	343,98	34,66

Data shown in Table 6, indicate that the protocol with the best throughput is AOMDV in relation to the DSDV protocol when using the IDM model. When applying the Manhattan model, the protocol with the best throughput is DSDV respect to AOMDV.

Scenario 6. Scenario 6 consists of 60 V2I connections and 120 vehicles that interact for 500 s, using AOMDV reactive protocol and DSDV proactive protocol. The following results were obtained from the scenario simulations.

Table 7. Scenario 6 data.

V2V communication				
Simulation time	500 s			
Vehicles number	120			
Connections number	60			
Mobility model	IDM		MANHATTAN	
Protocol	AOMDV	DSDV	AOMDV	DSDV
PDR [%]	98,06	98,79	99	99,02
Throughput [Kbps]	739,71	807,12	1065,73	1010,56
NRL	2,4	46	1,67	34,17
Delay End to End [ms]	10,37	107,94	113,92	125,97

Data shown in Table 7, indicate that the protocol with the best throughput is DSDV in relation to the AOMDV protocol when using the IDM model. When applying the Manhattan model, the protocol with the best throughput is AOMDV respect to DSDV.

3.2   Results Comparison

After collecting the data of the simulations under the established conditions, the values of the parameters mentioned in Sect. 3 are compared to determine the mobility model with the best performance in the simulated scenarios.

Communication V2V Comparison

PDR (Packet Delivery Ratio). Figure 2 shows the PDR values obtained from the simulations, with a value higher than 95% for both mobility models, independently of the routing protocol and the connections number. This high level of successful Packet delivery is due to the application of IEEE 802.11p technology in our scenarios.

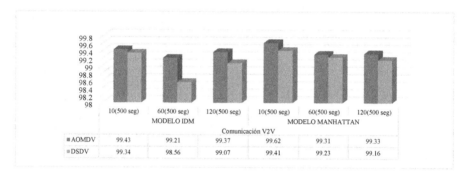

Fig. 2.   PDR parameter (5, 10 and 30 V2V connections).

Throughput. Figure 3 presents the obtained results in the simulations corresponding to the Throughput metric, it is evident that the use of the bandwidth of the AOMDV protocol is better in all cases in comparison with the DSDV protocol, independently of the mobility model that was used. The speed of sending information with AOMDV in all cases is higher than DSDV.

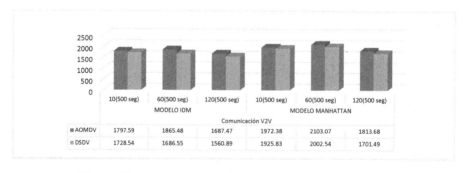

Fig. 3.   Throughput parameter (5, 10 and 30 V2V connections).

NRL (Normalized Routing Load). Figure 4 shows the results for the Normalized Routing Load parameter, in this figure can observe that for this metric the AOMDV protocol generates a lower routing overhead, for that reason, this protocol is faster and more efficient than the DSVD protocol regardless of the mobility model used in the simulation scenario.

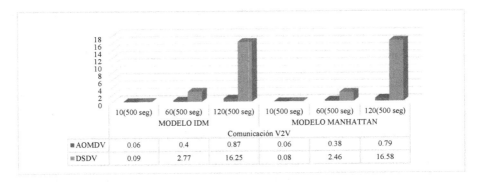

Fig. 4. NRL parameter (5, 10 and 30 V2V connections).

Average End to End Delay. Figure 5 shows the results for the Delay End to End parameter, it is observed that, with a small number of connections and long working times, the AOMDV protocol present greater delays than DSDV. However, for a high number of connections, the AOMDV protocol present lower delays than DSDV.

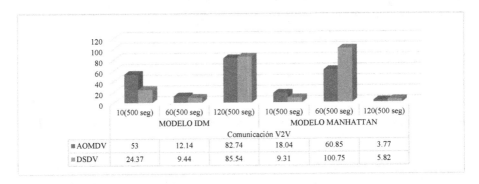

Fig. 5. Delay End to End parameter (5, 10 and 30 V2V connections).

Communication V2I Comparison

PDR (Packet Delivery Ratio). Figure 6 shows the values obtained in the simulations for the PDR parameter, a value greater than 99% is observed for both the IDM model and the Manhattan model independently of the routing protocol and the number of connections. This high level of successful Packet delivery is due to the application of IEEE 802.11p technology in the scenarios.

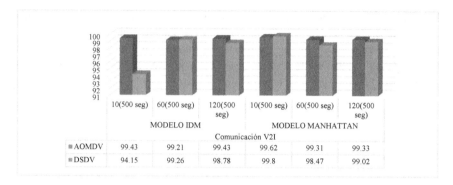

Fig. 6. PDR parameter (5, 10 and 30 V2I connections).

Throughput. Figure 7 shows the data for the Throughput parameter, in this is observed that for a small number of connections and long work times, the AOMDV protocol present better throughput than DSDV, independently of the mobility model used. With a value high of connections under the IDM model, The Throughput of the DSDV protocol is higher than the AOMDV protocol. When using the Manhattan model, the protocol with the best Throughput is AOMDV compared with DSDV protocol.

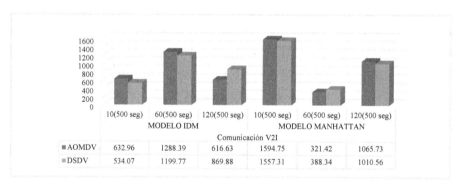

Fig. 7. Throughput parameter (5, 10 and 30 V2I connections).

NRL (Normalized Routing Load). Figure 8 shows the results for the Normalized Routing Load (NRL) parameter, it is observed that the AOMDV protocol generates a lower routing overhead for all cases, in cases with a high number of connections it is seen that the NRL generated by AOMDV is lower than that of DSDV with a high margin of difference.

Average End to End Delay. Figure 9 shows the results for the Delay End to End parameter, the AOMDV protocol registers greater delays than DSDV with the IDM mobility model. In contrast, for the Manhattan model, the AOMDV protocol presents minor delays than DSDV in most cases.

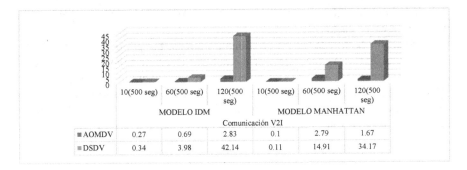

Fig. 8. NRL Parameter (5, 10 and 30 V2I connections).

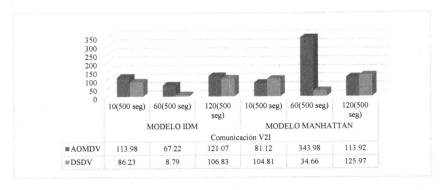

Fig. 9. Delay End to End parameter (5, 10 and 30 V2I connections).

4 Conclusions

- The most used protocols in VANET networks are reactive and proactive the most used in recent research are the DSDV and AODV protocols. Regarding the mobility models, the synthetic ones are the least reliable because they do not offer data close to reality, this is the case with models based on traffic generators.
- Manhattan synthetic mobility model was used since it is coupled to the topology of the simulated scenarios, while IDM was used as a traffic generating model since, in it, mobility not only depends on the predecessor car, it depends too on himself and the cars in the environment.
- When comparing the values of Throughput, PDR, Average End to End Delay and NRL, a better routing performance of the AOMDV protocol was observed compared to DSDV, but with a minimum difference, so it is concluded that for a V2V communication regardless of the model of Mobility and the number of connections can be used both the AOMDV reactive protocol and the proactive DSDV.
- For V2I communications the margin of difference between AOMDV and DSDV is more evident, in most cases the AOMDV protocol is more efficient, so it is

concluded that in V2I communication scenarios, AOMDV has a better performance in the routing of packages.

- In general, for both V2V and V2I communications, the protocol with the highest efficiency is AOMDV, regardless of the number of connections. Emphasizing that in V2V connections, AOMDV is superior with a relatively low margin while in a V2I communication the superiority of AOMDV over DSDV is more evident. This fact is since AOMDV, in addition to calculating routes at the request of the nodes, also offers backup routes to guarantee even more the delivery of packets to their destination.

References

1. Guevara, D., Chávez, I., Calderón, O.: Impacto del enrutamiento en el desempeño de la comunicación de datos en una red VANET. Puente **9**(1), 23–30 (2017)
2. Das, A., Roychoudhury, D.: Authentication schemes for VANETs: a survey. Int. J. Veh. Inf. Commun. Syst. **3**(1), 1–27 (2013)
3. Bhatt, R., Sharma, I.: Prediction based next-hop forwarding strategy in vehicular ad hoc networks. Int. J. Veh. Inf. Commun. Syst. **4**(1), 1–19 (2019)
4. Toutouh, J., García-Nieto, J., Alba, E.: Configuración Óptima del Protocolo de Encaminamiento OLSR para VANETs Mediante Evolución Diferencial. In: VII Congr. Sobre Metaheurísticas Algoritmos Evolutivos Bioinspirados (MAEB'10), Valencia-Spain, pp. 463–471 (2010)
5. Pinto, G., Sarmiento, D., Martínez, L.: Simulación y análisis de desempeño de protocolos unicast para Redes VANET. Tecnura: Tecnología y Cultura Afirmando El Conocimiento **15**(31), 66–75 (2011)
6. Fuentes Salazar, E., Valencia Enríquez, A.: Estudio de las Vanet para Control de los Vehículos en las Carreteras en el Ecuador. Tesis, Escuela Superior Politécnica de Chimborazo (2015)
7. Bradner, S.: Benchmarking terminology for network interconnection devices. https://tools.ietf.org/html/rfc1242. Accessed 20 Dec 2018

Design of a Competitive Intelligence System for the Meat Sector in Colombia Using Business Intelligence

Miguel Ángel Ospina Usaquén[1](✉), Víctor Hugo Medina García[2](✉), and Jorge Enrique Otálora[3](✉)

[1] Universidad Santo Tomas, Bogotá, Colombia
miguelospina@usantotomas.edu.co
[2] Universidad Distrital "Francisco José de Caldas", Bogotá, Colombia
vmedina@udistrital.edu.co
[3] Universidad Pedagógica y Tecnológica de Colombia, Tunja, Colombia
jorge.otalora@uptc.edu.co

Abstract. As the economy progresses, globalization and competitiveness in companies, there is evidence of the need to evaluate information, especially external, to transform it into knowledge and make decisions, this allows not only the application of knowledge but the identification of threats and early opportunities of a company, to this study, recognition and application is called competitive intelligence.

The proposed design of competitive intelligence system for the meat sector is developed from the research carried out at University, whose objective is to design competitive intelligence systems that respond to the business sector. Subsequently, the efforts made extend to develop a review of CI models, diagnose the sector, identify information needs, search for sources and collect input information and process the information that has validated sources, whose work generates the system design using Power BI, a well-known Microsoft business intelligence tool.

Keywords: Competitive intelligence · Knowledge management · Meat sector · Business intelligence · Decision making

1 Introduction

Through the research carried out there is a framework of what competitive intelligence is and how to take it into the context of today; in Colombia the knowledge of this tool is very low compared to other countries, when doing this research the utility of competitive intelligence in a sector of the economy, how it facilitates the identification of the environment and the decision making that helps to increase competitiveness of a sector or company and the importance of using this tool that is being recognized and used throughout the world in various projects and companies.

The in-depth implementation of competitive intelligence in Colombia would help the growth of the country's market sectors, allowing a competitive advantage and international recognition, in addition to this would increase employment, improve

© Springer Nature Switzerland AG 2019
L. Uden et al. (Eds.): KMO 2019, CCIS 1027, pp. 489–499, 2019.
https://doi.org/10.1007/978-3-030-21451-7_42

production, quality and create a relationship between companies and the state for national growth as do many countries today.

The objective of this research is to design a model of competitive intelligence system for the bovine meat sector that improves the competitiveness and efficiency of the sector through the study of the environment and timely access to information, facilitating decision making and solving the competitiveness problems that the sector has.

2   Competitive Intelligence

Competitive intelligence is the process of obtaining, analyzing, interpreting and disseminating information of strategic value on the industry and competitors, which is transmitted to those responsible for making decisions [1, 2].

Prescott, defines competitive intelligence as "the process of obtaining, analyzing, interpreting and disseminating information of strategic value on industry and competitors, which is transmitted to those responsible for making decisions at the right time" [3].

According to SCIP, the international association of competitive intelligence professionals, this discipline is based on an ethical, systematic and logical program to collect, analyze and manage external information that improves the strategic planning, decisions and operations of an organization [4].

According to studies conducted by Ching Seng Yap, it was found that the practice of competitive intelligence varies according to the type of strategic typologies and concludes that organizations practice competitive intelligence based on the perceived importance of the environment and use it in strategic decision making [5].

From the above it is concluded that competitive intelligence becomes an important tool to provide strategic business value from the external knowledge of competitors and the environment in general.

3   The Meat Sector in Colombia

The meat industry is one of the largest volume of sales in the country, this is responsible for producing, processing and distributing meat from different types of animals, especially beef from the hatchery point to centers of consumption, these consumption centers. Most of them tend to be in large markets in different cities of the country such as Bogotá. In the productive cycles there are the primary producers of complete cycle with production destined to the domestic market; primary producers conformed by breeders with production to the domestic market and producers of complete cycle-traditional exporters of fresh and refrigerated meat in integrated process [6]. Part of the meat is dedicated directly to human consumption and the other is taken to various sausage processing industries. The meat industry usually has as final products in the process of the production of frozen meat, minced meat, fresh meat offered in various cuts and various sausages.

There are types of meats that are handled in the industry depending on the type of consumption demanded:

- Canned meats: all meats are usually used for conservation, thus improving their distribution. Conservation techniques include canned and processed meats in different meats. The techniques for this go from drying to the air as it used to be done with a lot of salt, preparation of salted fish and the most frequent freezing.
- Processed meats: they are used for other uses such as the production of sausages. The minced meat is used, which is the noblest part of lean meat and sausages, sausages, instant broths, hamburger meat preparation and others are prepared.
- Fresh meat: this meat goes directly from the slaughter to its wholesale buyers such as supermarkets, restaurants, butchers where they are usually bought for normal daily consumption in families [7].

The meat industry also has other products or by-products that derive from what could be said waste such as meat flour, organ meats, bone meal, protein supplements, tallow among others.

The meat industry also tends to have many wastes causing environmental impacts, since it consumes a lot of energy in the centers such as refrigerators, slaughterhouses and cutting rooms, waste such as viscera and others, the water used to keep the meat in good condition is high, the hairs, the residual blood are almost not used and these are discarded in rivers or pipes and until now there is no definitive and effective solution for it [8].

4 Applied Methodology

To design the competitive intelligence system at a sectoral level in Colombia, we work with the following methodology, product of the review of several authors and the specific needs for design.

The methodology is focused in the area of identifying and establishing sectoral strategic needs and preparing the necessary information to design the system. The methodology worked is shown in the following phases (Fig. 1).

4.1 Review of Current CI Models

Currently the market and the whole world presents several processes of globalization, there is more competitiveness in the companies so that a constant search for the evolution of the companies is maintained.

A tool that has been used lately in different countries and has developed over time is the Competitive Intelligence, going from the evolution of the Surveillance Technology which has different ways of arriving at the planning of R & D to new and improved methodologies [9], thus reaching the Competitive Intelligence or also known as Strategic, Technological, Administrative, Economic Intelligence, depending on the place being examined, but based on the same objective of improving and increasing competitiveness among companies.

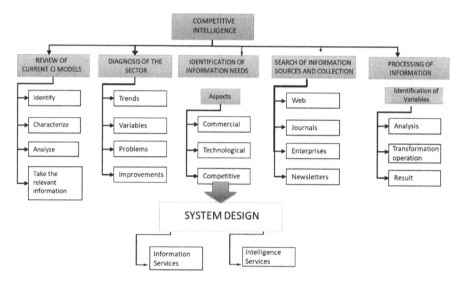

Fig. 1. Methodology. Source: The authors.

In this part of the research, we examined the literature of some of the most recent authors who speak and have knowledge about competitive intelligence, considering definitions, phases, functions and factors that apply in different countries.

Tools and Techniques: Prescott defines six key areas to which the design of an IC unit oriented to support decision-making has to respond: identify an approach or orientation of the CI unit, dimensioning and functions or responsibilities, definition of personnel profiles, definition of products and services to offer, organization of work and, finally, ethics [10, 11].

The stages of Competitive Intelligence configure a cycle that is defined as the process where information is retrieved, united, evaluated, analyzed and made available to those who make the decisions. Competitive Intelligence allows transforming traditional information into a real resource for the decision making [12]. In summary, educational opportunities for relatively young science professionals based on knowledge of management fields are not easy to define. Competitive intelligence (CI) has grown since the early eighties as the focus of information and knowledge management - Competition has increased. Although there has been a naturally healthy evolution of the available offer, not all of CI's educational developments have been positive.

Methodologies and Phases: The implementation of technological surveillance and intelligence usually follows a gradual process, both in companies and in other institutions. The commitment of senior management is essential for its success [13] (Fig. 2) and there is different fields of application in the different competitive intelligence concepts.

The Intelligent Competitor is not IC, but a part of it; the added value of the CI is that it takes the associated concepts of the Strategic Planning and the Smart Competitor [15, 16].

Management of external   Management of internal information

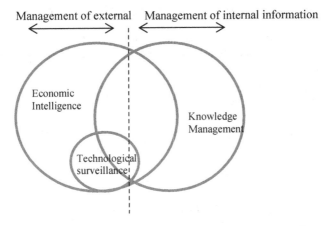

Fig. 2. Fields of application of the different intelligence concepts. Source: [14]

Competitive intelligence has evolved in recent years and has become a crucial point to integrate internal knowledge management of organizations and external knowledge management.

4.2   Diagnosis of the Sector

To carry out the diagnosis, the main variables with which the sector is measured are identified, as well as the national and international rankings.

An example of a variable is:

$$\text{Extraction Rate} = \frac{Cattle\ \ Sacrifice}{Bovine\ \ Inventory} \times 100$$

Where:
Bovine slaughter which equals the number of slaughter cattle heads in a period of time, usually one year.
Bovine Inventory: refers to the amount of animals in a given space at a specific time.

This indicator is productivity with excellence as long as its analysis is done in conjunction with other indicators such as age, slaughter weight, performance [17].

4.3   Identification of Information Needs

To develop the competitive intelligence system of the beef sector it is necessary to collect all the internal and external information of the sector in order to recognize the environment and identify all the necessary information variables for opportunities for improvement and identification of threats, which we managed to identify through these information needs, that allows us to assess the situation of the beef sector at a regional level, in the country, against competitive countries and in the world.

4.4   Search of Information Sources and Collection CI Inputs

Having defined the information needs, we continue with the search stage of this information, through this search we collect all the necessary information currently requested and existing about the sector.

4.5   Processing of Information

In the information processing stage, we sought to identify the most important information for the beef sector with respect to what was found in the needs and sources of information.

5   Design of Competitive Intelligence System

Thanks to the information collected and needs analysis, the competitive intelligence model of the beef sector began to be formed, which allows us to visualize the previously defined needs through the different variables presented in the previous table (Table 1).

The information that is within the design of the competitive intelligence system was made in the Power BI program where you can interact with all the information through tables, maps, images and graphics.

Below are some of the main boards that have the competitive intelligence system with information from the sector:

The following Table 1 shows the different actors where regulators are located at the national level and the different associations that exist in the beef sector.

Table 1. Actors of beef sector chain. Source: The authors.

The following Table 2 shows the per capita consumption of chicken, beef, pork and fish meat in the country and the growth rate from 2012 to 2016.

Table 2. Consumption per capita and growth rate of meats. Source: The authors.

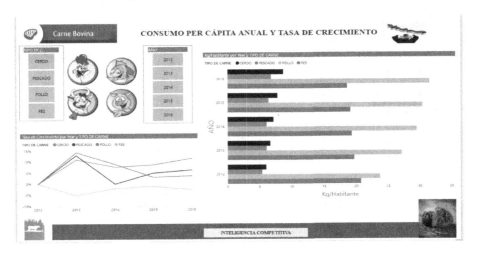

The following Table 3, shows the price of fat steer in the main countries producing meat and in our country and its value from 2012 until 2015, you can also interact with the world map depending on the country you want to see the figures and choose the year.

Table 3. Price fat bull in main producing countries and Colombia. Source: The authors.

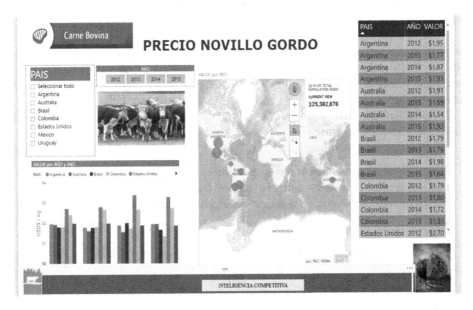

This board shows the bovine inventory in number of heads in the departments of the country and its variation from 2010 to 2016, it can also show the amount of slaughter heads from 2012 to 2016 and the data on the map according to the department that wants to review (Table 4).

Table 4. Cattle inventory in heads per year and department. Source: The authors.

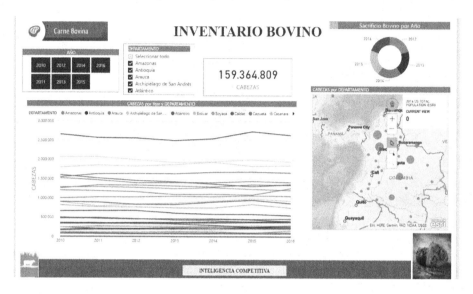

The inventory was also carried out by type of cattle (Males, females or calves) in the departments of the country from 2012 to 2016 (Table 5), in this you can also check the map and locate the department you want. watch.

Table 6 shows the import figures in CIF value (Cost, insurance and freight, port of destination agreed) and exports in FOB value (Port of freight agreed on board) from 2012 to 2016 and its variation, in addition shows the trade balance of these years, where a deficit is evident in all of them, since the value of exports is lower than that of imports in the country.

Throughout this investigation of competitive intelligence in the beef sector in Colombia and other countries we find that:

Regarding competitive intelligence:

- The different concepts of competitive intelligence were identified from the authors that define it and the studies that have been done in different parts of the world.
- We recognized the entire beef sector in Colombia and other countries.

Regarding the design of the competitive intelligence system for the beef sector:

- It is a project that can be replicated to the other sectors of the PTP.

Table 5. Inventory by type of beef in Colombia. Source: The authors.

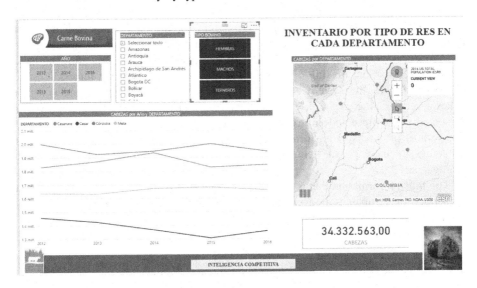

Table 6. Imports and exports 2012–2016. Source: The authors.

- The use of competitive intelligence systems will improve the competitiveness of the economic sectors of any country.
- It is a challenge for each one of the actors that make up a sector to understand and carry out processes and projects that adequately manage the knowledge of the sector [18] or an option can become competitive intelligence.

6   Conclusions

The creation of a competitive intelligence system for the beef sector will allow to identify in an agile and easy way the variables and elements that are affecting the environment of the sector not only nationally but also internationally, allowing easy access to information, making decisions more quickly and preventing threats.

The design of the system allows interacting with the different variables which makes it very graphic, clear, easy to understand and dynamic for any user, employer or consumer. This presented information is a contribution for the projects like PTP (Program of productive transformation) that allows to deepen in the sector, to detect problems, to increase the competitiveness, quality all through the competitive Intelligence.

Too much information that is currently on the web, organize it, filter it, and put it at the service of companies is a knowledge management process that can take a considerable time, but it is worth the investment.

References

1. Cavaller, V.: Fundamentos de análisis estratégico de la información (2008). http://www.raco.cat/index.php/QUICVECT_es/article/viewFile/122881/170153. Último acceso 2016
2. Gibbons, P., Prescott, J.: Parallel competitive intelligence processes in organisations (1996)
3. Prescott, J., Gibbons, P.: Global perspectives on Competitive Intelligence, Society of Competitive Intelligence Professionals, Alexandra, Virginia, USA (1993). http://files.paul-medley.webnode.com/200000023-97ce398c7e/Competitive%20Intelligence%20A-Z.pdf
4. Sanchez, Y.G.: De acuerdo con SCIP, la asociación internacional de profesionales de inteligencia competitiva, esta disciplina se basa en un programa ético, sistemático y lógico para recoger, analizar y administrar información externa que mejore la planificación estratégica, Diciembre 2012. https://riunet.upv.es/bitstream/handle/10251/18172/Memoria.pdf?sequence=1. Último acceso 2016
5. Yap, C.S.: Acquisition and strategic use of competitive intelligence. Malays. J. Libr. Inf. Sci. **16**, 125–136 (2011)
6. Errecart, V.: Universidad Nacional de San Martin - Análisis del mercado mundial de carnes. http://www.unsam.edu.ar/escuelas/economia/economia_regional/CERE%20-%20Mayo%20-%202015.pdf. Último acceso 2017
7. Rodriguez, F.J.: Industrailización del huevo y la carne, junio 2013. http://skrillexfernan.blogspot.com.co/2013/06/carne.html. Último acceso 2017
8. Falla, L.H.: Desechos de Matadero como Alimento Animal en Colombia. http://www.fao.org/livestock/AGAP/FRG/APH134/cap7.htm. Último acceso 2017
9. Pineda Serna, L.:Prospectiva Estrategica en la Gestión del Conocimiento: Una propuesta para los grupos de investigación colombianos, June 2013. http://www.scielo.org.co/scielo.php?script=sci_arttext&pid=S0121-32612013000100010. Último acceso 2016
10. Prescott, J.E.: The Evolution of Competitive Intelligence. Proposal Management. Spring (1999)
11. Medina, V.H., Rodríguez, L.H.: Model engineering research supported by knowledge management. J. Eng. Appl. Sci. **13**, 7045–7050 (2018). https://doi.org/10.3923/jeasci.2018.7045.7050. ISSN 1816949X (Print), 18187803 (Online)

12. Matilde Mier T.: Inteligencia competitiva: un factor importante para construir una tradicion tecnológica, 11–12 (2002) https://www.ineel.mx/bolDPATY02/tec2.pdf. Último acceso 2016
13. Herring, J.P.: Create an Intelligence Program for Current and Future Business Needs. Competitive Intelligences Magazine. SCIP, U.S.A (2005)
14. Escorsa, P., Lázaro, P.: INTEC Inteligencia competitiva factor clave para lo toma de decisiones estratégicas en las organizaciones (2007). http://www.madrid.org/bvirtual/BVCM001891.pdf
15. Wright, S., Pickton, D.W., Callow, J.: Competitive intelligence in UK Firms: a typology. Marketing Intelligence and Planning **20**, 349–360 (2002)
16. Guerra, J.L.M.: Inteligencia Competiviva. Bases teoricas y revision de la literatura (2006). https://works.bepress.com/jose_luis_masson_guerra/5/download/
17. Gomez, J.D., Rueda, R.A.: Productividad del Sector Ganadero Bovino en Colombia durante los años 2000 a 2009 (2011). http://repository.urosario.edu.co/bitstream/handle/10336/2629/1047396260-2011.pdf. Último acceso 2017
18. Medina, V.M., Medina L.M., Tarazona, G.M.: Investigación en Ingeniería apoyada por la gestión del conocimiento y la internet social, 1a Edn. Amadgraf Impresores Ltda., Bogotá, Colombia (2019). ISBN: 978-958-787-082-4

New Trends in KM and IT

Digital Readiness Frameworks

Current State of the Art and Research Opportunities

Franziska L. V. Voß[(✉)] and Jan M. Pawlowski

Computer Science Institute,
Ruhr West University of Applied Sciences, Bottrop, Germany
{franziska.voss,jan.pawlowski}@hs-ruhrwest.de

Abstract. Digital transformation requires major changes by introducing new strategies, processes and in particular information systems and technologies. However, enterprises and organization need to identify and assess their current status and transformation requirements. For this purpose, a variety of tools have been developed. We review those to better understand their scope, possible impact and credibility providing a threefold contribution by (a) structuring the research on digital readiness assessment models, (b) identifying gaps and (c) uncovering opportunities for further research.

Keywords: Digital transformation · Digital readiness assessment ·
Digital maturity assessment · Organizational change · Socio-technical

1 Introduction

These days, the notion of Digital Transformation seems to be omnipresent. No matter where we look, everyone seems to have an angle or a perspective on this issue. According to the benchmark study conducted by techconsult, already 47% of the small and medium enterprises say that digitalization is part of their new business strategy [1] acknowledging this as an investment into their future. Recently, also the German Government now instated a Digital Council with the aim, to identify the Chances and Challenges that come with the digital transformation process [2].

And, as "Digital Transformation means different things to different people" [3], the concept is not applied similarly in different contexts in IS literature. According to [4], definitions "range from software-based device control via online-based product offerings to changed business models through new IT-based solutions".

The Digital transformation framework [5] understands Digital Transformation as the interplay of the use of technology, changes in value creation, structural changes and the financial aspects, including *"changes to implications for products, services and business models as a whole"* [5], ultimately building up to some sort of organizational strategy. In this respect, their Digital Transformation Strategy can be used as a *"blueprint that supports companies in governing the transformations that arise owing to the integration of digital technologies, as well as in their operations after a transformation"* [5]. In 2017, the DESRIST conference dedicated the entire conference to the technical implications: *"Designing Digital Transformation"* [6]. Especially

© Springer Nature Switzerland AG 2019
L. Uden et al. (Eds.): KMO 2019, CCIS 1027, pp. 503–514, 2019.
https://doi.org/10.1007/978-3-030-21451-7_43

reports and studies regarding the advantages and potential pitfalls from a manager's perspective on DT and the companies' Readiness have received much attention, especially in the consulting world [7–13]. One reason for the success of popular assessments could be that the underlying concept allows the user to better understand and to reflect on one's own situation and blind spots as well as also getting a sense for the competitors' pitfalls and potentials. Also, the objectiveness and comparability make strategical decisions easier as assessments may also server as decision basis.

This paper provides a first overview of current research regarding the latest publications on Digital Maturity and its assessment, starting with the definition of the term 'Digital Transformation' found in IS literature and its implications and relations to other organizational topics such as change and employees as the force driving it. We then give an overview of the current models and conclude with the current gaps we found in this area of research.

2   Digital Transformation

2.1   Definition

Gimpel et al. [14] define Digital transformation as *"the managed adaptation of organizations as they capitalize on digital technologies to change business models, improve existing work routines, explore new revenue streams, and ensure sustainable value creation."* Based on the extensive literature review from Riasanow, Soto, Hoberg & Krcmar, who compared Digital Transformation to related organizational change philosophies, the term can be defined as *"probabilistic organizational change philosophy where digital technologies are used to fundamentally transform an organization's business model and value network"* [15].

Therefore, at least two factors are relevant: technical progress on the one hand and organizational change on the other. Hess puts it even clearer, stating that "[this] *means either the transfer of information from analogue to digital storage or the process of change caused by the introduction of digital technologies or the application systems based on them*" [16]. Therefore, Buhse concludes that companies are facing three upcoming challenges: faster reaction times towards change, increased complexity and finally expected easy-to-use solutions by employees and customers alike [17].

2.2   Digital Readiness (Maturity) and Change Readiness

In the following, we will outline approaches, which assess the readiness of organizations. As the term *"readiness"* refers to "*a state of being fully prepared for or willing to do something*" [18], respectively the *quality of being immediate, quick, or prompt,* it can be said that this describes a forward-looking state for something that is about to come in the future or has almost arrived. The term *"maturity"* on the other hand, describes "*a state of being complete, perfect or ready*" [19], implying a certain progress in the development. Consequently, "*maturing systems (e.g. biological, organizational or technological) increase their capabilities over time regarding the achievement of some desirable future state. Maturity can be captured qualitatively or quantitatively in a discrete or continuous manner*" [20] quoting [21].

From an **organizational point of view**, the consulting agency Deloitte defines Digital Future Readiness *"on the basis of four dimensions: organization, culture, employees and digital environment"* [9]. Here, navigating the waters of *current economic, technological, politically/regulatory and social challenges, as well as seizing new growth opportunities* is key for the further development of the company.

On an **individual level**, Digital Readiness can be described as a an interconnection of "digital **skills** [...] and, **trust**, that is the people's **beliefs**, about their capacity [...]. These two factors express themselves in a third dimension, namely **use** – the degree to which people use digital tools in the course of carrying out online tasks" [22].

The term *"Change Readiness"* was first introduced by Armenakis et al. [23], as the opposing concept of "Resistance". This concept drew from awareness, active involvement of employees and communication. Also, Dalton et al. [24] describe Change Readiness as a general conviction that the change is necessary and feasible. From a process perspective, "Readiness" describes activities recognizing the necessity and encouraging change, estimating the costs and benefits of implementing a change or scheduling a change. Researchers [23–26] agree, that Change Readiness generally manifests on two levels: (1) **individual** (e.g. motivation and competence) and (2) **organizational** (e.g. culture, climate and availability of resources). This indicates that Change Readiness and Digital Readiness are strongly related. One could say, that Digital Transformation Readiness is a form respectively a part of Change Readiness.

Although organizational change and transformation induced by technology have been a fascination for researchers of multiple disciplines since the late 1950ies [27], Bennet and Lemoine [28], Yoo et al. [29] and Berghaus and Back [30] point out that the nature of Digital Transformation has changed thanks to the influence of the rapid development on user behavior, organizations, and industries. Consequently, also Hess et al. [5], Gimpel et al. [14] and Hansen et al. [31] point out that this represents new challenges and may need an updated model.

3   Analysis of Digital Transformation Readiness Models

3.1   Method

As a first step, a structured literature review was conducted in order to assess the current knowledge level on the one hand and to identify potential research opportunities on the other. Therefore, we followed the established recommendations for a concept-based literature search [32] to find current models on Digital Readiness respectively Digital Maturity and their assessment. In the next phase, we then extended the databases and evaluated the sources depending on relevance. Also, we intended to compare and examine the contributions [33]. We therefore did not limit our search to certain journals and conferences of Information Systems [34] but also considered interdisciplinary search engines and databases (Google, Google Scholar, Science Direct, SpringerLink and WebScience) using combinations of "digital transformation" and "readiness" or "maturity" as well as "digital readiness assessment" or "digital maturity assessment". As the term "Digital Transformation Readiness" is still quite young, the time frame was limited to the past ten years. This way, about 20 promising publications were found. After scanning the titles and abstracts, publications that did not fit the scope were excluded. After examining the full text publications not fitting our criteria, respectively proposing a concept or a recommendation without not a model or a framework were excluded as well. In the end, nine publications were considered.

The classification and analysis of the literature was developed based on Urbach et al. [35], adjusting framework guides and categories for content and research approach. The main message of the publication was extracted using a coding technique proposed by Wolfswinkel et al. [36]. First, the relevant passages were highlighted and paraphrased. In a second step, we reclassified those aspects (if necessary) and mapped them respectively in the concept matrix below (see Fig. 1 Readiness and Maturity models).

3.2   Results of the Literature Review

It should be noted that besides reviewing the scientifically grounded models, we also considered consulting models respectively practice oriented models as they are used and implemented as well in practice and are therefore relevant for our research.

The categorization is based on Urbach et al.'s classification scheme [35] in the table below and illustrates the different approaches towards Digital Transformation Readiness Assessments and how they were developed, in which industry they find application and where the respective focus lies. The following sections give a content-wise description of the findings and the respective model.

The *Digital Maturity model* by Back and Berghaus [37] is based on Österle & Winter's Business Engineering landmark [42] and comprises of nine dimensions: "Customer Experience", "Product Innovation", "Strategy", "Organization", "Process Digitalization", "Cooperation", "Information Technology", "Culture and Expertise" and "Transformation Management". Each dimension is derived from literature analysis and validated through expert interviews and comprises of about three maturity criteria. The ongoing study, which is now in its fourth year, not only helps the organization to get a decision basis for strategical measures, their additional feedback also contributes to a further development of the underlying questionnaire. As the model itself is quite general, it can be adapted to a variety of contexts. However, Back & Berghaus remind the users that there is no one size fits all solution, and encourage their clients to decide based on their individual situation.

In 2016, Binninger et al. [38] proposed the *360° OmniSales model*, consisting of three layers: "Management", "Fields of action" and "Macro Environment". The model strives to explain how digital transformation affects almost every part of the business processes aiming to provide a holistic perspective on the organization (first layer) while offering more detail in the fields of action (second layer) to manage and monitor (third layer). For each layer, a comprehensive set of key questions is provided, assessing the organization's health and maturity. The first layer (light gray) is called "Management" and includes objectives and strategic orientation, the classic tasks of the management cycle consisting of planning, management and control – in the context of the resources available and the budget. The focus is on the "How do we do?" [38]. The second level (coloured), "Fields of Action", provides a framework that contains a large number of important action points assigned to the three sub-areas Product & Presentation,

Literature		Approach			Type					Industry			Focus					
Author(s) (alphabetical order)	Model	Qualitative	Quantitative	Non-Empirical	Conceptual	Literature Review	Case Study	Long-term Study	Survey	Productive industry	Service industry	Media industry	Organization	Technology/Infrastructure	Strategy	Management	Employees / People	Culture
Back et al. (2017) [37]	Digital Maturity Model	✓			✓		✓	✓		✓	✓		✓	✓	✓	✓	✓	✓
Binniger et al. (2017) [38]	360° OmniSales model			✓	✓						✓		✓	✓	✓	✓	✓	✓
Deloitte (2017) [9]	The transformation model	✓							✓	✓	✓		✓	✓	✓	✓	✓	✓
Gimpel et al. (2018) [14]	Digitalization requires mastering six action fields	✓							✓	✓			✓	✓	✓	✓		✓
Kahre et al. (2017) [39]	Concept Matrix	✓					✓			✓	✓		✓		✓			
Hess et al. (2016) [40]	Key Decisions for a Digital Transformation Strategy			✓			✓					✓	✓		✓	✓		
Lichtblau (2015) [41]	Readiness-Model	✓							✓	✓			✓	✓	✓	✓	✓	✓
Matt et al. (2015) [5]	Digital transformation framework			✓	✓					✓	✓	✓	✓		✓	✓		
Schumacher et al. (2016) [20]	Industry 4.0 readiness and maturity model			✓	✓					✓			✓	✓	✓	✓	✓	✓

Fig. 1. Readiness and maturity models.

508 F. L. V. Voß and J. M. Pawlowski

Infrastructure and Customer Experience. This system should aims to analyze and implement questions of the Digital Transformation as comprehensively and integrated as possible. Here the focus is on "What do we do?" [38]. The third level, "Macro Environment", aims at determining the position of the organization asking "Where are we?". The areas observed include classic strategical areas such as technological and cultural trends or legal and political developments [38].

Although the model puts a strong focus on e-commerce companies, it may serve as an initial draft for other industries, thanks to its multidimensional visualization and comprehensive questionnaire. So far, they appear to be the only ones trying to visualize the complexity and interdependencies of this issue: Integrating the strategic level (grey circle) as well as the managerial and the operative perspectives (inner circles) in one model. Unfortunately, neither their methodology, nor the basis for their data are available just yet [43]. However, the inquiry for more information is still ongoing.

When it comes to comprehensiveness, in 2017, Deloitte also presented *The transformation model* [9], based on an Digital future readiness study conducted in 2015 interviewing board and senior management members in Swiss manufacturing companies. The model consists of four dimensions, which are "Organization", "Culture", "Digital Environment" and "People", each one and its intersections comprising of two subcategories. The provided checklist for the transformation also offers first steps (approaches) and further explanations, if the question is either not understood or has to be denied. As some items are quite generic, this model also seems adaptable to non-productive industries.

For Gimpel et al., *Digitalization requires mastering six action fields* [14], namely "Customer", "Data", "Value Proposition", "Organization", "Operations" and "Transfomation Management". Each action fields includes four action items helping to provide a "holistic yet concrete perspective" on digital transformation aiming to reduce the risk of silo thinking in departments. The authors conclude that there is no there is no one-size-fits-all approach to digital transformation. As the action fields may vary in importance per industry, one needs to make an individual assessment of the situation before jumping to the solution. The included case study can be an inspiration for both the productive industry as well as the service industry since the customer is a significant factor in the model.

Adding to the collection of models taking into account organizational behavior, [14] followed the invitation of Matt [40] to consolidate partial analysis. They examined the skills and potential success factors as Action Items of Digital Transformation, stating that "what is missing is a fundamental redesign of organizational setups together with a change in employees' and managers' skills and mindset. Although the research rigor is undeniable, there was only a qualitative approach (expert and group interviews targeting management or skilled employees in various organizational functions, such as innovation, marketing or manufacturing). The final model however (see above), does not reflect an appreciative attitude towards employees, e.g. as part of the corporate culture [14], although Matt et al. found that the "companies [managers] believe that they need to develop their current workforce in new, digital technologies" [40]. Further, there is no clear definition to be found, what a "digital mindset" exactly comprises of or how it can be achieved.

The *Key Decisions for a Digital Transformation Strategy* by Hess et al. [40] focus on the managerial challenges one faces when preparing the organization for digital transformation. The described case study illustrates how the provided list of 11 strategical questions may assist in formulating a digital transformation strategy. The questions cover the technical perspective as well as the companies' attitude towards it while asking for their customers' digital needs. The questionnaire then moves on to the willingness to change in value creation as well as structural changes in the organization before asking for an outlook into the near future and finally assessing the financial aspects. As the case study outlines the journey of three media companies struggling to find their paths in the digital age, this may can also be an inspiration to other sectors.

As the comprehensive *Concept matrix* of Kahre, Hoffmann & Alemann has shown, not only do most Assessments in this field prefer a non-empirical approach [39], e.g. conceptual studies, editorials and research commentaries. Only a little proportion used an empirical approach and even less field studies were found. Most of them, focused on the organization's position in the economic environment and its strategical perspectives from an Information Systems perspective [44–46], by providing a concept based on non-empirical data [39]. Although [5] emphasize the need for a continuous reassessment of the underlying assumptions and the transformational process based on organizational outcomes, there is no concrete list of recommendations regarding its implementation. Only one [47] tackled the question of organizational behavior in an empirical, yet qualitative approach. Also, they found that also the impact of the related digital business strategy on *organizational* outcomes and *reciprocal feedback* mechanisms has not yet been examined thoroughly (cf. [44, 48] and may have been perceived as a paradigmatic shift. Here, Kahre et al. suggest that *"future research might employ organizational learning perspectives to explain how, when, and why organizations reconfigure their resource and capability base when confronted with technological disruption and – vice versa – how innovative technologies enable new dynamic capabilities"* [39].

Lichtblau's *Readiness-Model* [41] was developed in 2015 and puts a strong focus on the technological aspects of DT in mechanical engineering. This rather complex yet comprehensive model takes into account the entire manufacturing process as well as strategical, operational and managerial aspects. By taking into account, the employees current level of competency in the respective field of expertise, the model allows for a detailed analysis of the organization on would like to assess. The findings are presented in a clear and structured manner. However, the focus is very much on mechanical engineering, it seems that this model would be most useful to productive industries and less helpful for the service industry.

The *Digital Transformation Framework* [5] was first introduced in 2015 by Matt, Hess et al. and consists of four transformational dimensions and their dependencies, namely "Use of Technologies", "Structural Changes", "Financial Aspects" and "Changes in value creation". A simple model focusing on the interrelations of the four dimensions and its strategical implications for managers. As this model could be described as a rather high-level view DT and implementation strategies, the authors invite researchers to continue the research.

Schumacher et al.'s *Industry 4.0 readiness and maturity model* [20] partly builds on Lichtblau's findings, reducing the level of detail in favor of its usability.

The dimensions being "Products", "Customers", "Operations" and "Technology" to assess the basic enablers. Additionally, "Strategy", "Leadership", Governance, "Culture" and "People" allow for including organizational aspects. The questionnaire shall serve as basis for strategic management decisions. Concrete recommendations are not included. This model therefore takes a closer look at the "softer factors". Although Schumacher et al. focus on solely manufacturing enterprises, their approach seems to be quite sustainable as they understand the readiness assessment only as the first step before engaging in the *"maturing process, whereas the maturity assessment is capturing the as-it-is state whilst the maturing process"* [20], which allows for a finer distinction. The final section of this paper summarizes the research gaps and offers the conclusion.

4 Discussion and Outlook

4.1 Discussion

In the previous section, we reviewed the basic concepts we found in relation to Digital Transformation and Change as well as promising Readiness Assessments.

We want to acknowledge that the models of Back and Berghaus [37], Gimpel [14], Hess [40], Lichtblau [41] and Buvat et al. [49] are based on a comprehensive dataset and details about dimensions, items and the approach to assessment are offered. The models seem scientifically grounded and its structure and results explained in transparent manners. The other approaches of Hofert [50], Ganguly [47], Berman [51], Schumacher [20], Fischer et al. [38] or Deloitte [9] give less details regarding the development process, structure and assessment-methodology and therefore do not seem to fit as base for further investigation. Other models or tools we found did not offer sufficient details regarding structure, content, method or underlying theory and are therefore not listed.

As König [4], Matt et al. [5], Röglinger [14] and Ravichandran [52] have stated, the area of Digital Transformation Readiness, especially the interrelation of the mindset is still under researched and waits to be explored. This is not only beneficial from an academic perspective but also promising when it comes to the application in real business live situations as well.

Despite the multitude of published Readiness Assessments on Digital Transformation [9, 12, 13, 38, 49, 53], this topic seems not yet to have been assessed *empirically* from an *employee's perspective*. Here, we see an opportunity to develop a user-friendly framework comprising of the cognitive (e.g. digital skills) and the affective aspects (e.g. a specific mindset) that are needed for this organizational development. Such a comprehensive investigation may have a considerable impact on the employees' motivation (e.g. technical projects with a transformational impact on organizational change) and result in a more *comprehensive assessment of an organizations' digital readiness*.

4.2   Research Gaps

As the studies and mentioned research gaps, respectively suggestions for future research indicate, the issue of Digital Transformation and the Readiness for it have yet been examined neither empirically nor in a comprehensive manner. Here, a detailed operationalization of the different factors influencing the change process would be helpful to verify the items in the analysis categories.

In addition, although some models have proven to be relevant in practice, there is little long-term observation yet to be found. This is especially important, as longitudinal studies help understand the different phases and interrelations throughout the digitalization change process.

Finally, comparative studies would incorporate contextual aspects and influence factors by comparing countries, cultures, sectors or even hierarchical. Consequently, not only top and middle management play a major role in successfully transforming the organization at stake. Interestingly, although briefly discussed in the context of organizational change [54], there is little research to be found in this particular area of digital transformation when it comes to the interaction of digital change, ones mindset and the question how they may be interrelated. As mostly managers have been asked to assess their company's state [9, 14, 50, 55], it would be interesting to see the other side of the coin and invite the employees to let us know about their perspective on these developments.

4.3   Outlook

Future research activities may aim to assess the digital readiness of a group of specific organizations. In addition, it would be interesting to observe the increasing maturity in such a process and how the organizations' metamorphose will be carried out in practice. Further, those results could lead to an adaption of a holistic framework localizing the chances and challenges by examining, whether the peoples' attitude towards change has an impact on the efficiency and purposefulness with which the change programs (or projects) are carried out. On final note, an updated readiness model would significantly contribute to the current research on digital readiness.

References

1. Deutsche Telekom AG: Digitalisierungsindex Mittelstelstand 2018. Der digitale Status Quo in deutschen Industieunternehmen (2018). https://www.telekom.com/resource/blob/553614/f5786646c67b9487d86764caa812774d/dl-digitalisierungsindex-2018-logistik-data.pdf. Accessed 8 Jan 2019
2. Merkel, A.: Merkel: Neuer Digitalrat wird viele Ideen hervorbringen – YouTube (2018). https://www.youtube.com/watch?v=sPt26is9xFs. Accessed 18 Aug 2018
3. Solis, B., Li, C., Szymanski, J.: The 2014 state of digital transformation. Altimeter Group (2014)
4. Mertens, P., Bodendorf, F., König, W., Schumann, M., Hess, T., Buxmann, P.: Grundzüge der Wirtschaftsinformatik, 12th edn. Springer Gabler, Berlin (2017). https://doi.org/10.1007/978-3-642-30515-3

5. Matt, C., Hess, T., Benlian, A.: Digital transformation strategies. Bus. Inf. Syst. Eng. (2015). https://doi.org/10.1007/s12599-015-0401-5
6. Maedche, A., vom Brocke, J., Hevner, A. (eds.): DESRIST 2017. LNCS, vol. 10243. Springer, Cham (2017). https://doi.org/10.1007/978-3-319-59144-5
7. KPMG: Digital Readiness Assessment DRA 1492. https://de.slideshare.net/BernhardDrSchmalzl/digital-readiness-assessment-dra-1492. Accessed 19 Mar 2018
8. Management Circle: Digital Readiness Assessment: Sven G. Janszky & 2b AHEAD ThinkTank. https://www.ccw.eu/blog/mithilfe-7-dimensionen-an-die-digitalisierung-herantasten/. Accessed 19 Mar 2018
9. Deloitte: Digital Future Readiness. How do companies prepare for the opportunities and challenges of digitalisation? Deloitte (2017). https://www2.deloitte.com/content/dam/Deloitte/ch/Documents/consumer-business/ch-cip-en-swiss-transformation.pdf. Accessed 12 Mar 2018
10. FOSTEC & Company: Digital Readiness - Digitaler Reifegrad | FOSTEC & Company (2018). https://www.fostec.com/de/kompetenzen/digitalisierungsstrategie/digital-readiness/. Accessed 19 Mar 2018
11. NOVELDO GmbH: Digital Readiness Assessment. http://www.noveldo.com/en/digital-readiness-assessment. Accessed 19 Mar 2018
12. KPMG: digital-readiness-assessment 2015 (2015). Accessed 19 Mar 2018
13. Kienbaum: Digital Readiness Check – Demo (2018). https://websurvey.kienbaum.com/index.php/971517. Accessed 19 Mar 2018
14. Gimpel, H., Hosseini, S., Huber, R., Probst, L., Röglinger, M., Faisst, U.: Structuring digital transformation. a framework of action fields and its application at ZEISS. J. Inf. Technol. Theory Appl. 19(1), 31–54 (2018)
15. Riasanow, T., Soto Setzke, D., Hoberg, P., Krcmar, H.: Clarifying the Notion of Digital Transformation in IS Literature. A Comparison of Organizational Change Philosophies. Working Paper (2017)
16. Hess, T.: Digitalisierung. Enzyklopaedie der Wirtschaftsinformatik (2013). http://www.enzyklopaedie-der-wirtschaftsinformatik.de/lexikon/technologien-methoden/Informatik–Grundlagen/digitalisierung. Accessed 26 Mar 2018
17. Buhse, W.: Management by Internet. Neue Führungsmodelle für Unternehmen in Zeiten der digitalen Transformation; Unternehmen im Wandel, digitale Medien als Werkzeugkoffer für Veränderer, Vernetzung, Offenheit, Partizipation und Agilität als Werte einer neuen Unternehmenskultur. Plassen, Kulmbach (2014)
18. Oxford Dictionaries: readiness | Definition of readiness in English by Oxford Dictionaries. https://en.oxforddictionaries.com/definition/readiness. Accessed 25 July 2018
19. Simpson, J.A., Weiner, E.S.C.: The Oxford English dictionary, 2nd edn. Oxford University Press, Clarendon Press, Oxford, New York (1989)
20. Schumacher, A., Erol, S., Sihn, W.: A Maturity Model for Assessing Industry 4.0 Readiness and Maturity of Manufacturing Enterprises. Procedia CIRP (2016). https://doi.org/10.1016/j.procir.2016.07.040
21. Kohlegger, M., Maier, R., Thalmann, S.: Understanding maturity models. results of a structured content analysis. In: Proceedings of I-KNOW 2009 and I-SEMANTICS 2009 Graz, Graz, Austria (2009)
22. Horrigan, J.B.: Digital Readiness Gaps. Pew Research Center (2016). http://www.pewinternet.org/2016/09/20/digital-readiness-gaps/. Accessed 15 Mar 2018
23. Armenakis, A., Harris, S., Feild, H.: Making change permanent. a model for instiutuion-alizing change interventions. In: Research in Organization Change and Development, vol. XII, pp. 97–128 (1999)

24. Dalton, C.C., Gottlieb, L.N.: The concept of readiness to change. J. Adv. Nurs. **42**(2), 108–117 (2003)
25. Oakland, J.S., Tanner, S.: Successful change management. Total Qual. Manage. Bus. Excellence **18**(1–2), 1–19 (2007)
26. Weiner, B.J.: A theory of organizational readiness for change. Implementation Sci. **4**(1), 67 (2009)
27. Kane, G.C., Palmer, D., Phillips, A.N., Kiron, D., Buckley, N.: Strategy, not technology, drives digital transformation (2015). https://sloanreview.mit.edu/projects/strategy-drives-digital-transformation/. Accessed 26 Mar 2018
28. Bennett, N., Lemoine, G.J.: What a difference a word makes: understanding threats to performance in a VUCA world. Bus. Horiz. **57**(3), 311–317 (2014)
29. Yoo, Y., Boland Jr., R.J., Lyytinen, K., Majchrzak, A.: Organizing for innovation in the digitized world. Organ. Sci. **23**(5), 1398–1408 (2012)
30. Berghaus, S., Back, A. (eds.): Stages in Digital Business Transformation. Results of an Empirical Maturity Study (2016)
31. Hansen, A.M., Kraemmergaard, P., Mathiassen, L.: Rapid adaptation in digital transformation. a participatory process for engaging is and business leaders. MIS Q. Executive **10**(4), 175–185 (2011)
32. Webster, J., Watson, R.T.: Analyzing the past to prepare for the future: writing a literature review. Sci. Q. **26**(2), xiii–xxiii (2002)
33. Fettke, P.: State-of-the-art des state-of-the-art. Wirtsch. Inform. (2006). https://doi.org/10.1007/s11576-006-0057-3
34. Lowry, P., et al.: Evaluating journal quality and the association for information systems (AIS) senior scholars' journal basket via bibliometric measures: do expert journal assessments add value? MIS Q. **37**(4), 993–1012 (2013)
35. Urbach, N., Smolnik, S., Riempp, G.: The state of research on information systems success. Bus. Inf. Syst. Eng. **1**(4), 315–325 (2009)
36. Wolfswinkel, J.F., Furtmueller, E., Wilderom, C.P.M.: Using grounded theory as a method for rigorously reviewing literature. Eur. J. Inf. Syst. **22**(1), 45–55 (2013)
37. Back, A., Berghaus, S.: Digital Maturity & Transformation Report 2017. Über das Digital Maturity Model. Institut für Wirtschaftsinformatik, Universität St.Gallen und Crosswalk AG (2016). https://aback.iwi.unisg.ch/fileadmin/projects/aback/web/pdf/digitalmaturitymodel_download_v2.0.pdf. Accessed 12 Mar 2018
38. Binninger, F.-M., Fischer, K.P., Schöler, A., Steuernagel, A.: Digitalisierung im Handel – das 360-Grad-Omnisales-Modell als Lösungsansatz. In: Hildebrandt, A., Landhäußer, W. (eds.) CSR und Digitalisierung. MCSR, pp. 483–510. Springer, Heidelberg (2017). https://doi.org/10.1007/978-3-662-53202-7_35
39. Kahre, C., Hoffmann, D., Ahlemann, F.: Beyond business-IT alignment - digital business strategies as a paradigmatic shift. a review and research agenda. In: Proceedings of the 50th Hawaii International Conference on System Sciences (HICSS), Honolulu, HI (2017)
40. Hess, T., Matt, C., Benlian, A., Wiesböck, F.: Options for formulating a digital transformation strategy. MIS Q. Executive **15**(2), 123–139 (2016)
41. Lichtblau, K.: Industrie 4.0-Readiness. Impuls-Stiftung für den Maschinenbau, Frankfurt (2015)
42. Österle, H., Winter, R.: Business Engineering-Auf dem Weg zum Unternehmen des Informationszeitalters. Springer, Berlin (2003). https://doi.org/10.1007/978-3-642-19003-2
43. Fischer, K.P., Schöler, A., Binninger, F.-M.: 360-Grad-Omnisales. holistische Betrachtungsebenendes E-Commerce. unveröffentlichtes Arbeitspapier. (2016)
44. Bharadwaj, A., El Sawy, O., Pavlou, P., Venkatraman, N. (eds.): Visions and voices on emerging challenges in digital business strategy (2013)

45. Bennis, W.: Leadership in a digital world. embracing transparency and adaptive capacity. MIS Q. **37**(2), 635–636 (2013)
46. Collin, J., Hiekkanen, K., Korhonen, J.J., Halén, M., Itälä, T., Helenius, M.: IT leadership in transition. The impact of digitalization on Finnish organizations. Research Report, Aalto University (2015)
47. Ganguly, A.: Optimization of IT and digital transformation. strategic imperative for creating a new value delivery mechanism and sustainable future in organization. Eur. J. Bus. Innov. Res. **3**(2), 1–13 (2015)
48. Lucas Jr, H.C., Agarwal, R., Clemons, E.K., El Sawy, O.A., Weber, B.: Impactful research on transformational information technology. an opportunity to inform new audiences. MIS Q. **37**(2), 371–382 (2013)
49. Buvat, J., et al.: The Digital Culture Challenge. Closing the Employee-Leadership Gap (2017). https://www.capgemini.com/de-de/news/studie-unternehmenskulturelle-aspekte-behindern-die-digitale-transformation/. Accessed 1 Mar 2018
50. Hofert, S.: Das agile Mindset. Mitarbeiter entwickeln, Zukunft der Arbeit gestalten. Springer Gabler (2018). https://doi.org/10.1007/978-3-658-19447-5
51. Berman, S.J.: Digital transformation. opportunities to create new business models. Strategy Leadersh. **40**(2), 16–24 (2012)
52. Ravichandran, T.: Exploring the relationships between IT competence, innovation capacity and organizational agility. J. Strateg. Inf. Syst. **27**, 22–42 (2018)
53. Gimpel, H., Röglinger, M.: Digital Transformation. Changes and Chances. Insights based on an empirical Study (2015). Accessed 27 February 2018
54. Schein, E.H.: Organizational Culture and Leadership, 3rd edn. Jossey-Bass, San Fransisco (2004)
55. Steinhoff, I.: Digital Maturity & Transformation Report 2017 (2017). https://crosswalk.ch/dmtr2017-delivery. Accessed 18 Aug 2018

Hybrid Artificial Intelligence B2B2C Business Application – Online Travel Services

Eric Kin Wai Lau[1(✉)], Abel Zhao[2], and Anthony Ko[1]

[1] Lee Shau Kee School of Business and Administration,
The Open University of Hong Kong, Kowloon, Hong Kong
ekwlau@ouhk.edu.hk
[2] TravelFlan, Hong Kong, China
http://www.travelflan.com

Abstract. Expert systems are commonly used artificial intelligence AI applications in business. They aim to solve complex problems with expert-level knowledge and rule-based techniques. However, a narrowly defined scope and existing structured knowledge base are necessary for an expert system. The case study concerns the deployment of a hybrid AI model in a business application that tries to overcome the limitations of a predefined domain of knowledge stored in the expert system. In addition to the data set or the algorithm, the case illustrates the successful use of a hybrid AI application as an effective business solution in B2B2C industries.

Keywords: Hybrid artificial intelligence · B2B2C · Expert system

1 Introduction

AI is defined as "the ability of a computer or other machine to perform those activities that are normally thought to require intelligence. The branch of computer science concerned with the development of machines having this ability" (http://www.yourdictionary.com/artificial-intelligence [2]). Guerin (2011, p. 233) added that "AI systems which attempt to build their own knowledge and abilities autonomously (starting with little innate knowledge), and to develop continuously to reach increasingly higher levels of knowledge" [9].

It is estimated that the global artificial intelligence market is worth about US$7.35 billion in 2018 [25]. AI applications are expected to offer automated data storage, analysis, and execution without human interference. Dounis reviewed the advantages and disadvantages of the deployment of AI applications [6]. AI can fit well with well-specified goals in the system. The complexity of causation in decision making limits its power. Many AI paradigms, such as neural networks, have been criticized for the generalization power from the training data set.

© Springer Nature Switzerland AG 2019
L. Uden et al. (Eds.): KMO 2019, CCIS 1027, pp. 515–524, 2019.
https://doi.org/10.1007/978-3-030-21451-7_44

2 Business Applications Using AI Technologies

Hernandez-Orallo summarized the current successful AI applications as computer vision, speech recognition, music analysis, machine translation, text summarization, information retrieval, robotic navigation and interaction, automated vehicles, game playing, prediction, estimation, planning, automated deduction, and expert systems [11]. Sreedevi, Saravanan, and Subhamathi (2017) listed the following commonly adopted AI systems: robotics, expert systems, natural language processing (NLP), language translators, intelligent computer assisted instruction (ICAI), game playing, artificial neural networks, fuzzy logic, genetic algorithms, computer vision and scene analysis, and recognition [24]. Table 1 shows the previous business cases in AI, they indicating that the rule-based expert system is a common AI application in business [13, 14, 27].

Table 1. Previous case studies of business applications using AI

Authors and publication year	Business applications	AI contexts
Shim and Rice (1988) [23]	Several applications in managerial accounting, such as AUDITOR, Tax Advisor, TICOM, EDP Auditor, TAXMAN, CORP-TAX, Financial Advisor, Plan Power, Cash Value, Expert-Ease, AION Development System, GURU, Platinum Label, and EURISKO	Expert system
Schutzer (1990) [22]	The Trader's Assistant	Expert system
Martin, Jones, McWilliams, and Nabors (1991) [15]	Entrepreneurial assessment and financial statements – Potential Entrepreneurial Assessment (PEA) system in Texas Instrument's Personal Computer Plus	Rule-based expert system developmental tool
Chan and Jiang (2001) [4]	Flexible manufacturing system (FMS) design and analysis technologies	Expert system tool and simulation models, fuzzy logic, and neural networks
Bergmann and Cunningham (2002) [3]	E-commerce applications – elicitation systems	McSherry's approach to query specificity, Burke's FindMe approach, Shimazu's ExpertClerk system, Bridge and Ferguson's order-based retrieval, and Schmitt's simVar approach to question selection

(*continued*)

Table 1. (*continued*)

Authors and publication year	Business applications	AI contexts
Moreno and Kearney (2002) [16]	Customer-Orientated System for the Management Of Special Services (COSMOSS)	Activity templates and conditional processing controls
Reyes-Moro, Rodriguez-Aguilar, Lopez-Sanchez, Cerquides, and Gutierrez-Magallanes (2003) [21]	E-sourcing tools	Fuzzy matching scoring function in the RFQ offer matching module
Ragothaman, Naik, and Ramakrishnan (2003) [20]	ACQTARGET – Business M&A evaluation system	Expert system
Fernandez, Aler, and Borrajo (2005) [8]	Hybrid hierarchical and partial-order planners for manufacturing	Machine learning, rule-based system
Subramoniam and Krishnankutty (2005) [26]	EDSIM: Expert database system for inventory management	Expert database system (EDS)
Delisle, St-Pierre, and Copeck (2006) [5]	The Performance, Development, Growth (PDG) system	Expert system
Qi, Wu, Li, and Shu (2007) [19]	Network management expert systems	Machine learning and distributed AI
Haag and Riemann (2011) [10]	SAP Business ByDesign solution	Rule-based decision support system
Falkner, Friedrich, Haselböck, Schenner, and Schreiner (2016) [7]	Several applications, such as railway interlocking systems, telecommunication switches, and a European train control system	Constraint satisfaction techniques
Issa, Sun, and Vasarhelyi (2016) [12]	Auditing expert systems and artificial neural networks	Sensors, meta-controls/meta-processes, and automatic audit analytics
Anuradha and Sharma (2017) [1]	AI-enabled 5G cellular networks	Transfer learning (TL), RL, and dynamic programming (DP) used in network self-configuration AI sensing techniques such as logistic regression (LR) used in networks Automatic fault detection and recovery
Nega and Kumlachew (2017) [17]	Hybrid intelligent system for medical application	Case-based reasoning (CBR) module and rule-based reasoning (RBR) module
Ong (2018) [18]	Office automation system by 86 corporations in Metro Manila	Expert system

3 The Business Case

The business case, TravelFlan, is a one-stop travel platform that provides travellers with a personalized and hassle-free travel experience through the use of AI technology. Instead of being overloaded by information that is available on multiple mobile apps and websites, travellers can acquire the latest and most relevant travel recommendations and experiences from our service at any time and anywhere.

The business model of TravelFlan is B2C, whereby it provides online concierge services that allow users to ask questions regarding their upcoming trip, such as itinerary planning, flight tickets, and hotel bookings, as well as on-the-road requirements, like emergency support and instant transaction services (Fig. 1). Its business is targeted to people with all kinds of travel needs throughout the travel cycle. In the meantime, the company offers travel-related products, such as mobile SIM cards, WiFi eggs, local tours, and travel insurance.

The company is based in Hong Kong and integrates artificial intelligence technology into the travel eco-system (Fig. 2). The team consists of dedicate professionals with more than 40 years of experience in the travel and IT industries. It makes the most relevant, convenient, and efficient AI-powered travel services available at travellers' fingertips. With customized AI (i.e. an AI-powered virtual assistant chatbot) and big data technologies specifically designed for customer-centric industries, the company can provide a unique digital solution and marketing approach to its business partners and end customers (Fig. 3). They include TravelFlan's AI rating and recommendation systems, precision data machine training and learning, market data crawling, and market BI analysis, including price comparison and relevant pushing functions.

Fig. 1. TravelFlan's customer touch points

With the AI + human hybrid system, the company can maximize customers' satisfaction in the service session and coordinate better with its travel agents. Figure 4 illustrates the AI + human hybrid travel system adopted by TravelFlan.

Key words from each inquiry will be pulled into the backend database system. Based on the pattern of key words and specific algorithms, the AI system will search

Fig. 2. TravelFlan's AI chatbot solutions

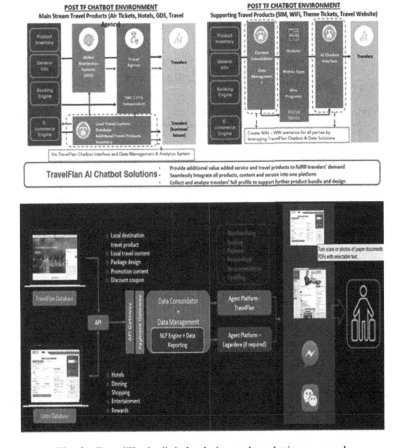

Fig. 3. TravelFlan's digital solution and marketing approach

for the best-matched replies; if insufficient data are found, this inquiry will trigger an indicator at the backend agent platform for a human agent to handle. Meanwhile, the AI system will provide a suggested response as a recommendation as well. This process aims not just to ensure service quality but also to train the machine learning engine accurately.

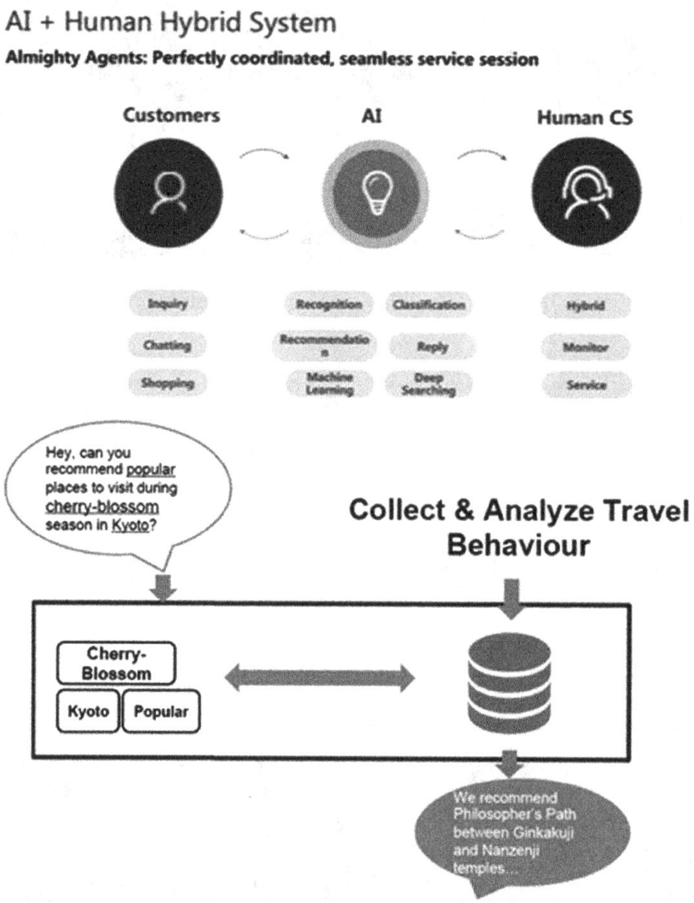

Fig. 4. AI + human hybrid travel system adopted by TravelFlan

In the case that the AI travel system cannot process the customer enquiry, it will switch to a human agent. Figure 5 shows the actual travel agent frontend solution used by TravelFlan. It can accept customer enquiries from different sales channels and assist the travel agent with the conservation records. The hybrid system increases efficiency and enhances the customer experience.

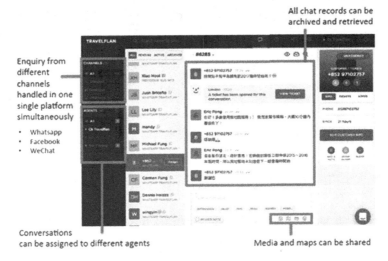

Enquiry from different channels handled in one single platform simultaneously

- Whatsapp
- Facebook
- WeChat

All chat records can be archived and retrieved

Conversations can be assigned to different agents

Media and maps can be shared

Fig. 5. TravelFlan agency platform technology

Based on the latest company statistics, the company processes 20–30 million pieces of data (data entries) per week (January–August 2018). The AI utilization ratio has reached 82% (Fig. 6). The company AI expert system consists of travel industry knowledge and expertise. In-house big data processing and management systems (Fig. 7) are constructed and based on the travel sector-focused AI algorithms and formula design shown in Fig. 8.

AI vs Human

Total Request 35572

82.93 %
■ AI

17.08 %
■ Human

Fig. 6. AI utilization ratio in TravelFlan with 35572 customer requests

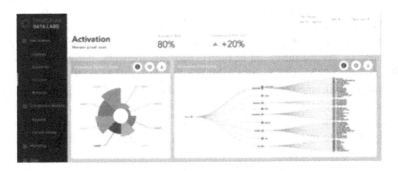

Activation   80%   ▲ +20%

Fig. 7. TravelFlan AI-based market analysis

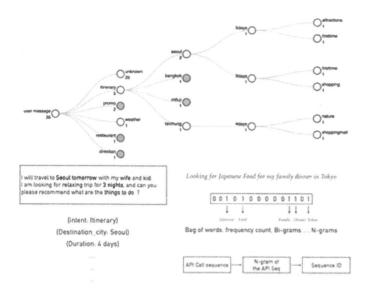

Fig. 8. AI Algorithms and formula design adopted

4   Managerial Implications and Limitations

Theoretically AI can replace human doing their intellectual jobs. However, as shared in the case study, it is difficult to 100% fulfil travellers' requests from the existing travel expert system and the human involvement is still a necessary component in the hybrid model adopted in the case. In addition, well written AI algorithms are important for the success of the travel system discussed in the case. They need frequent updates so that the system can cater for the new needs and changes in travellers' behaviour. It is also the significant investment and competitive asset for the company.

5   Concluding Remarks

The complexity of knowledge is always problematic and challenges the use of expert systems. It is impossible to build an "all-scenario" rule-based decision tree, especially to solve human problems without humans. Especially in business, the lack of standard problems raised by the end-users is one of the common commercial barriers to the development of AI business applications. Moving forward, unlike computer-aided decision systems in the past, hybrid solutions that can enable multi-intelligence (MI), such as human assistance and AI, can improve the problem-solving capabilities more than purely AI applications. The case study here presented the AI + human hybrid travel expert system to address the needs and benefits. The algorithms and travel knowledge base are important success factors in cases involving human interaction.

References

1. Anuradha, C.B., Sharma, P.: Empowering the future 5G networks: an AI based approach. Telecom Bus. Rev. **10**(1), 53–59 (2017)
2. Artificial Intelligence. http://www.yourdictionary.com/artificial-intelligence
3. Bergmann, R., Cunningham, P.: Acquiring customers' requirements in electronic commerce. Artif. Intell. Rev. **18**(3–4), 163–193 (2002)
4. Chan, F.T.S., Jiang, B.: The applications of flexible manufacturing technologies in business process reengineering. Int. J. Flex. Manuf. Syst. **13**(2), 131–144 (2001)
5. Delisle, S., St-Pierre, J., Copeck, T.: A hybrid diagnostic-advisory system for small and medium-sized enterprises: a successful AI application. Appl. Intell. **24**(2), 127–141 (2006)
6. Dounis, A.I.: Artificial intelligence for energy conservation in buildings. Adv. Build. Energy Res. **4**(1), 267–299 (2010)
7. Falkner, A., Friedrich, G., Haselböck, A., Schenner, G., Schreiner, H.: Twenty-five ears of successful application of constraint technologies at Siemens. AI Mag. **37**(4), 67–80 (2016)
8. Fernández, S., Aler, R., Borrajo, D.: Machine learning in hybrid hierarchical and partial-order planners for manufacturing domains. Appl. Artif. Intell. **19**(8), 783–809 (2005)
9. Guerin, F.: Learning like a baby: a survey of artificial intelligence approaches. Knowl. Eng. Rev. **26**(02), 209–236 (2011)
10. Haag, A., Riemann, S.: Product configuration as decision support: the declarative paradigm in practice. Artif. Intell. Eng. Des. Anal. Manuf. AI EDAM **25**(2), 131–142 (2011)
11. Hernández-Orallo, J.: Evaluation in artificial intelligence: from task-oriented to ability-oriented measurement. Artif. Intell. Rev. **48**(3), 397–447 (2017)
12. Issa, H., Sun, T., Vasarhelyi, M.A.: Research ideas for artificial intelligence in auditing: the formalization of audit and workforce supplementation. J. Emerg. Technol. Account. **13**(2), 1–20 (2016)
13. Keim, R.T., Jacobs, S.: Expert systems: the DSS of the future? J. Syst. Manag. **37**(12), 6–14 (1986)
14. Kennedy, A.J., Yen, D.C.: Enhancing a DBMS through the use of an expert system. J. Inf. Syst. Manag. **7**(2), 55–61 (1990)
15. Martin, W.S., Jones, W.T., McWilliams, E., Nabors, M.V.: Developing artificial intelligence applications: a small business development center case study. J. Small Bus. Manage. **29**(4), 28–32 (1991)
16. Moreno, M.D.R., Kearney, P.: Integrating AI planning techniques with workflow management system. Knowl. Based Syst. **15**(5–6), 285–291 (2002)
17. Nega, A., Kumlachew, A.: Data mining based hybrid intelligent system for medical application. Int. J. Inf. Eng. Electron. Bus. **9**(4), 38–46 (2017)
18. Ong, H.T.: The applications of expert system among the top corporations in Metro Manila and its perceived advantages and disadvantages. Rev. Integr. Bus. Econ. Res. **7**, 57–66 (2018)
19. Qi, J., Wu, F., Li, L., Shu, H.: Artificial intelligence applications in the telecommunications industry. Expert Syst. Int. J. Knowl. Eng. Neural Networks **24**(4), 271–291 (2007)
20. Ragothaman, S., Naik, B., Ramakrishnan, K.: Predicting corporate acquisitions: an application of uncertain reasoning using rule induction. Inf. Syst. Front. **5**(4), 401–412 (2003)
21. Reyes-Moro, A., Rodriguez-Aguilar, J., Lopez-Sanchez, M., Cerquides, J., Gutierrez-Magallanes, D.: Embedding decision support in E-sourcing tools: quotes, a case study. Group Decis. Negot. **12**(4), 347–355 (2003)

22. Schutzer, D.: Business expert systems: the competitive edge. Expert Syst. Appl. **1**(1), 17–21 (1990)
23. Shim, J.K., Rice, J.S.: Expert systems applications to managerial accounting. J. Syst. Manage. **39**(6), 6–13 (1988)
24. Sreedevi, E., Saravanan, K., Subhamathi, V.: A review of artificial intelligence systems. Int. J. Adv. Res. Comput. Sci. **8**(9), 418–421 (2017)
25. Statista: Revenues from the artificial intelligence (AI) market worldwide from 2016 to 2025 (in million U.S. dollars) (2018). https://www.statista.com/statistics/607716/worldwide-artificial-intelligence-market-revenues/. Accessed 25 Oct 2018
26. Subramoniam, S., Krishnankutty, K.V.: EDSIM: expert database system for inventory management. Kybernetes **34**(5), 721–733 (2005)
27. Yamasaki, L., Manoochehri, G.H.: The commercial application of expert systems. SAM Adv. Manag. J. **56**(1), 42–45 (1991)

Legal Aspects and Emerging Risks in the Use of Smart Contracts Based on Blockchain

Yeray Mezquita[1] , Diego Valdeolmillos[1] ,
Alfonso González-Briones[1,2(✉)] , Javier Prieto[1] ,
and Juan Manuel Corchado[1,2,3,4]

[1] BISITE Research Group, University of Salamanca,
Calle Espejo 2, 37007 Salamanca, Spain
{yeraymm,dval,alfonsogb,javierp,corchado}@usal.es
[2] Air Institute IoT Digital Innovation Hub (Spain),
Carbajosa de la Sagrada, 37188 Salamanca, Spain
[3] Department of Electronics, Information and Communication
Faculty of Engineering, Osaka Institute of Technology, Osaka 535-8585, Japan
[4] Pusat Komputeran dan Informatik, Universiti Malaysia Kelantan,
Karung Berkunci 36, Pengkaan Chepa, 16100 Kota Bharu, Kelantan, Malaysia

Abstract. Although the majority application of Blockchain Technologies (BT) are in the field of cryptocurrencies, they are gradually spreading to other services where a decentralized, reliable and immutable model makes sense. One of the fields where the use of Blockchain Technologies is spreading the most is in Smart Contracts, computer programs which are executed in the blockchains establishing a collection of clauses between the participating parties that agree to interact with each other and that are executed automatically at the moment in which these clauses are fulfilled. As it is a computer code, both the client and the service provider cannot misinterpret the agreed clauses, facilitating and verifying the agreement of the contract. This article will review existing applications and reviews the main vulnerabilities of Smart Contracts deployed within Blockchain Technologies. It also reviews the legal implications of the use of these technologies.

Keywords: Smart contracts · Blockchain · Legal aspects · Review

1 Introduction

The term Smart Contract arises in 1994 when the computer scientist and jurist Nick Szabo his work "Smart contracts: building blocks for digital markets" [35]. In it he defines a Smart Contract as a set of contractual clauses embedded in software and hardware. Before that work, he had defined protocols running on public networks, such as Internet, using cryptographic keys [33]. Behind those protocols, the clauses of the Smart Contracts could be automatically executed. In order to carry out this idea, he proposed in 2005 distributed and decentralized databases in his work "Secure property titles with owner authority" [34].

© Springer Nature Switzerland AG 2019
L. Uden et al. (Eds.): KMO 2019, CCIS 1027, pp. 525–535, 2019.
https://doi.org/10.1007/978-3-030-21451-7_45

The clauses of a Smart Contract must not be altered after the parties have signed them, that is why the only environment in which they can be kept unaltered is in a decentralized and distributed one in which every party that participates in an agreement knows exactly what is going on with the contract after signed it. Szabo in [34] tried to carry out his idea, but it has finally been Blockchain Technology (BT) the technology that allows the use of Smart Contracts, assuring no party has modified their clauses, by people in their daily life tasks.

Initially BT appears as the technology underlying Bitcoin [26]. Bitcoin arises in 2008 as an alternative to the centralized financial system with a financial asset that allows the exchange of value without the need of intermediaries such as banks. This kind of BT is called first generation blockchain.

In order to bring more functionality to this technology Buterin launch the Ethereum Blockchain, in which it is allowed not just the storage of transactions, but the execution of code thanks to the Ethereum Virtual Machine [6]. The code that can be executed is considered a Smart contract, due to being stored in the blockchain it is not possible to tamper it, also the execution is validated by all the network making it impossible to favor one of the parties that takes part in the Smart Contract. The possibility of developing Smart Contracts allows the execution of automatic commercial transactions between entities of a platform and the processes associated to them. The BT that give support to Smart Contracts is called second generation blockchain.

The Smart Contracts offer low legal costs due to the elimination of a central coordinator as an intermediary while reaching more public than traditional financial contracts because of their higher costs. Also, Smart Contracts get rid of the paper-based systems automatizing the execution of the agreements reached by the interested parties, improving the speed up to execution time in commercial processes.

Due to blockcahin's decentralized nature and its own cryptographic algorithms that ensures the security of the system, the Smart Contracts are autonomous and do not need an outside party to prove that the agreement is being fulfilled by those parties involved in it. The use of BT in order to store and execute a Smart contract avoid the possibility of being tampered or non-compliance by one of the parties involved in it, making them trustful [10, 14].

All of this is possible because it is maintained a backup copy inside each participant of the blockchain network. Also, the execution of a Smart Contract with given parameters is validated by the entire network, preventing the manipulation of the result by any of its participants. These features are the ones who give BT its decentralized nature.

Thanks to the intertwine of the blocks of the blockchain, the data stored in a block cannot be edited without edit all the subsequent blocks. So, after a block is accepted and distributed among the nodes of the network, the data of that block is irreversible and impossible to being manipulate afterwards. Which makes the terms of the Smart Contract safe from being altered after the signature is given by the parties involved [7–9].

This paper is organized as follows: the Sect. 2 is going to explain in detail the background of the Smart Contracts in its life time. Section 3 compiles some of the works that have been already implemented in the real life. Section 4 describes one of the conflicting points of the execution of Smart Contract regarding its data sources. Section 5 explain in detail the importance of audit the code before upload in order to avoid potential risks with the execution of the Smart Contracts. Section 6 Gives an understanding of how the legislation works regarding this topic in Spain. Finally, Sect. 7 closes this paper with the conclusions reached after finishing it.

2 Background

Bitcoin Script language is a simple, stack-based language in which code lines run from left to right. This language is not Turing-complete, does not support loops thus avoiding possible infinite loops in the verification of transactions [32]. In addition, because bitcoin makes use of the UTXO (Unspent Transaction Output) model it does not allow a fine grain control on unused transactions. In this model, it is stored in a database of unused transactions all the transactions unused by their owners, making it impossible to change their state [6].

Ethereum thus arises as an alternative to Bitcoin allowing the construction of decentralized applications on the blockchain and the representation of the business logic in the blockchain. In order to achieve this, Ethereum of a complete Turing programming language that allows the users of the blockchain to define their own rules. Unlike Bitcoin, Ethereum makes use of an account balance model in order to store the assets owned by the users. This model also allows the use of different formats and the transition between states of the assets stored.

In order to avoid excessive use of computing, network and storage resources, thus avoiding infinite loops, the one who wants to execute the code of a Smart Contract must make a proportional payment to the complexity of the code [6]. The payment is made in GAS, which is the internal price that is used to execute a contract or a transaction, being the miners the ones in charge of fixing it.

The Ethereum blockchain was the first to give support to Smart Contracts and allowing the development of decentralized Applications (dApps). The Smart Contracts deployed on the Ethereum Network are decentralized code based on clauses IF-THEN. Once agreed between parties, these clauses are immutable, automatic and binding allowing the execution of the contract without the need for a third party. After being developed, the code of a Smart Contract is distributed to all the participants of the blockchain network.

To be executed, a Smart Contract must receive a message. A message is a transaction originated by users, other Smart Contract or events with specific information through an external action. After being executed, all the blockchain network validates its result in order to prevent it from being falsified.

One of the first programming languages used to build dApps in Ethereum was Serpent, but an audit made by blockchain security firm Zeppelin Solutions discovered problems with compiler and some critical vulnerabilities [2]. Because of this, Solidity programming language has taken place, being now the most used programming language in the development of Smart Contracts for the Ethereum virtual machine [13, 23]. But although this programing language has none of the vulnerabilities discovered in its predecessor, it is still a very new one, not very know by developers which make them commit mistakes in the development of Smart Contracts and dApps.

One of the more famous exploits occurred in the history of Ethereum was the DAO exploit. This exploit occurred due to a vulnerability in the pattern of coding the Smart

Contract. It was known and it was being fixed by its creators, but while they were doing it, the hacker prepared the exploit in order to drain all the funds from the DAO [31]. The script consisted of calling recursively the "split" function inside of itself, collecting the Ether from it many times with one transaction [5].

The second largest attack to an Ethereum dApp, was the one called the Parity Wallet Hack [30]. In order to steal 150,000 Ether (ETH), the attacker sent two transactions to each contract with vulnerabilities. With the first transaction, the hacker gained ownership over the wallet, and with the second he transfers all the victim's funds.

In [27] it has been done a classification of Smart Contracts depending on the type of vulnerability they have:

- Greedy: This kind of Smart Contract is capable of lock the funds from their users and then holding them back indefinitely without release them. The errors more common in Greedy Smart Contracts are that they accept Ether but they lack the set of instructions that sends the Ether out.
- Prodigal: The Smart Contracts that can send Ether to an address that is not its owner address, nor one of the address that have sent Ether to the contract before and nor an address of someone that has given some kind of solution to it, are called Prodigal Smart Contracts.
- Suicidal: In order to let its owner close and kill a Smart Contract under critic circumstances like an attack or because a deprecated function it is often implemented suicidal functions in the Smart Contract. When an arbitrary account is capable of invoking these functions, the Smart Contract has a vulnerability and is called a Suicidal Smart Contract.

In order to make customized interchangeable assets, it has been defined some standards for their interface design and implementation. These standards are needed in for the sake of interoperability between Smart Contracts. The most famous one is the standard ERC20 [3] which is used for fungibility tokens. In the case of non-fungible assets, it has been defined the standard ERC721 [21].

Although Ethereum was the first blockchain in allow the development of Smart Contracts and the most accepted too, there exist other BT that allows the development of them. Also, it is being developing the third generation blockchain, in which we could group technologies such as Cardano, EOS and TRON. They want to improve the flawless BT such as Ethereum has, changing its conventional Proof of Work consensus algorithm for others faster, eco-friendlier with less resource consumption and more scalable, being the last try to bring to the daily lives of people the use of Smart Contracts. But these BT are yet to be more tested and to put under more pressure because they are still too young.

3   State of the Art

In recent years, most of the research in the field of Smart Contracts focuses on their integration with technologies such as smart power microgrids and e-commerce. For instance, in [1] the authors implemented a proof-of-concept for a decentralized trading system of energy based on BT. In this system agents negotiate between them the energy prices and securely perform trading transactions. In order to maintain the anonymity of the peers that interact in the system, while giving increased security, authors have used also multi-signatures and anonymous encrypted message propagation streams. They found in that work that with the use of those technologies together it can be implemented a truly decentralized Smart Grid energy trading system with higher security and privacy than the centralized ones [11, 19].

It has been demonstrated also in another work [24], taking the use case of the Brooklyn Microgrid project, that BTs are eligible technologies to operate decentralized microgrid markets. In that work and after a review of the state of the art of microgrid power markets, authors have found 7 market components for the efficient design of a microgrid energy market based on BT. They also implement six of the seven components they previously derived to evaluate the Brooklyn energy microgrid market based on BT. With the evaluation they found BTs are suitable systems that can facilitate localized energy markets. The downside is that most countries don't have a regulation that allows to run local energy market [16].

In the field of e-commerce, Yu Zhang in [36] propose a truly decentralized business model for the Internet of Things (IoT). In order to achieve it, they make use of BT to accomplish peer-to-peer transactions between devices. That work makes use of two types of assets implemented in Smart Contracts, the Smart Property and the paid data which devices exchange between them.

There are other fields where it is being implemented Smart Contracts in real life. That is the case of land registry in Sweden, has been testing BT in the field of real-state property transactions since 2016 [17]. The Sweden's land-ownership authority have been searching volunteers to test its BT based platform, in order to register the transactions of real-states between people [12, 15, 25].

Also, countries like Colombia, which in order to reduce the time it to process the land rights, is making use of BT in land rights transactions. In this case, Colombia record the transactions within Ethereum-based blockchains [28].

Ghana, Ukraine and Georgia are doing the same as Sweden and Colombia. The way they all are storing the real-state properties within the blockchain, is by giving them a unique identifier. Also, in order to make each transaction publicly available, it is being hashed the transaction. So, with a simple search, it can be terminated argues about which one is the owner of a given property.

In the case of countries such as Spain, where it is a right registry instead of document registry, it is difficult to use BT in the same way as the previously mentioned countries have done [22].

4 Oracles

Smart Contracts have a critical point, the data sources where they get the data their clauses work with. That's why they need reliable data sources that allow them to interact with the outside world without losing the trust that users have placed in them.

In order to allow users that trust the external data won't be falsified, arise the term oracles. The oracles are external agents that observe and validate external data of the real world [4]. Oracles are centralized and can be black boxes, which makes them a new trusted intermediary betraying the security and reduced-trust model of blockchain applications [29].

Regarding on how an oracle interacts with the Smart Contracts of a blockchain, there can be classified in [4]:

- Software Oracles: The oracles of this kind gather the information from sources like web sites or public databases. Thanks to this, they can provide Smart Contracts the most up-to-date information from Internet. Examples of their use is in temperature readings, current price of financial assets or public transport information.
- Hardware Oracles: This kind of oracles provides the Smart Contract with data directly from the physical world. These readings come from sensors that takes measurements from their environment.
- Outbound Oracles: These oracles do not provide the Smart Contract with data from outside, instead they provide another Smart contract with data from a previous one. For example, it can provide a wallet provider that the balance of a user has changed due to some conditions.
- Consensus based oracles: A possible solution to a centralized oracle model is to make use of a set of oracles and giving them the capacity of reach a consensus deciding the solution of a task in a decentralized way:

  a. The oracles provide a deposit in the intelligent contract.
  b. After that they send a vote with the result they have achieved independently.
  c. The result with the most votes is the one used in the execution of the Smart Contract.
  d. If a result given is not between acceptable and previously defined margins, the oracle in question loses the deposit.

The problem of the consensus-based solution is that the set of oracles that finds a true solution would need an economic compensation. This is needed because if there is no incentive, it would be very difficult to create a decentralize network of oracles where they put their resources for the network. Also, it is needed a predefined standard on data format.

In order to overcome the flaws exposed previously and use just one centralized oracle, Oraclize has developed a solution that demonstrate the data fetched from the original data-source is genuine and untampered [29]. In order to demonstrate it, the data fetched is accompanied with a document called authenticity proof.

Thanks to it, the developers and users doesn't need to trust Oraclize, maintaining its security model and, in order to be compatible with blockchain protocols, data providers doesn't have to modify their services. This solution allows Smart Contracts to access data from directly the data sources like Web sites or APIs.

5 Smart Contracts Audits

When BT is used to store data, it becomes immutable, the same occurs with the code of a Smart Contract deployed in it. Because of that, before deploys a new one in a blockchain network, it is needed to audit it with computer experts. They should know the best practices and patterns that identify vulnerabilities in the code of Smart Contracts, so they can read it correct them if it is found any vulnerability. An audit structure could be [20]:

- Exemption from liability: indicating that it is not a legally binding document, no one can ensure that no bugs will be found in the future that may take effect in existing contracts.
- Overview of the audit, indicating the good practices carried out.
- Attacks to a contract, where all the existing attacks to the contracts of the blockchain and their results, structured in serious, medium and low vulnerabilities will be covered.
- Line-by-line comments indicating possible safety and cost improvements for blockchain maintenance and execution.
- Summary of the audit with conclusions.

There has been developed tools capable of automatically checking some of the common vulnerabilities of Smart Contracts. For example, in [27] it is developed a tool called MAIAN which precisely specify and reasoning about the trace properties of the vulnerabilities in Smart Contracts: Greedy, Prodigal and Suicidal. With an average of ten second per Smart Contract analyzed, this tool found in 1000000 contracts 34200 with vulnerabilities. Also, from a subset of 3759 contracts they reproduce real exploits at a true positive rate of the 89%, yielding exploits for 3686 Smart Contracts.

This analysis shows the importance of have a well-tested code and make the proper audit for it, before deploying it in the blockchain network and putting at risk the funds of the users who would interact with it.

6 Legally Binding Contractual Effects of Smart Contracts

The underlying basis of the Smart Contracts allow the programming of agreements between parties. This programming implies that the agreement it is not left to interpretation and it is a way of getting an agreement to be fulfilled automatically. In this respect, the role of the programmer is fundamental in order to translate into code the clauses of a legal agreement.

Due to the complications that arise from the ambiguous interpretation of the law, a merely programmer could need the help of a legal person. In order to make a well-transcript Smart contract that has into account the interpretation of the laws that could affect it, a legal person should communicate the representation of each of the clauses of the laws to the programmer.

In the case of Spain, the very nature of the Smart contracts deployed within BT fulfill the 1256 article of the civil code which says: "the validity and performance of contracts cannot be left to the free will of one of the contracting parties". In the case when a Smart Contract is executed in a blockchain network, all the participants of the network validate and enforce the contract, which satisfies the previous clause.

From the article 1281 of the civil code, "If the terms of a contract are clear and leave no doubt as to the intention of the contracting parties, it is in the literal sense of its clauses", fulfill another basis of the implementation of Smart Contracts, their clauses are not left to interpretation, which means that all are clear to the parties that agreed to them.

Also, the 1261 article of the civil code says that there is no contract unless the following requirements are met:

1. Consent of the contracting parties.
2. Certain object which is the subject matter of the contract.
3. Cause of the obligation to be established.

Therefore, in a Smart Contract as long as the object is lawful, there exist a legal cause and there is consent between the parties involved, the execution of a Smart Contract should be contractually binding.

The only problem, in Spanish legislation, to this kind of contractual bindings is the 1290 article of the civil code: "validly concluded contracts may be terminated in cases established by law". The same goes for the rest of termination articles for contracts. That means, every contract should offer a way to terminate it, which thanks to the immutable property of Smart Contracts deployed in any blockchain network, makes them impossible to terminate.

The code and addresses of a Smart Contract are immutable, so the only way to update the clauses of an active Smart Contract or to terminate it after its conclusion is to deploy a new one. The old one should be capable of redirect the transactions sent to it by the parties to the new one.

Even with all that, in accordance with Article 34 of the European Directive on the Information Society and Electronic Commerce, all member states of the European Union must adjust their legislation with regard to requirements that may hinder contracts by electronic means [18].

It is only a matter of time before Spanish law picks up on the electronic contractual agreements that appeared with the deployment and implementation of Smart Contracts in blockchain networks.

Besides, right now it is being developing and deploying a great number of Smart Contracts in different blockchain networks with different BT. So, a developer of Smart Contracts, could be able of deploy a Smart Contract within a blockchain network, that every clause of it is adjusted to the Spanish laws. If he implements a "selfdestruct" function that allows to terminate or invalidate the Smart Contract, he would be capable of deploy already a contractual agreement completely legal, according to Spanish laws.

7 Conclusions

The use of BT as a disruptive technology and the deployment of Smart Contracts within it, is a topic of discussion in some sectors of the society, for example the inclusion of them in the legal field. Because of this, it is necessary the adaptation of the existent laws in order to legally collect the areas Smart Contracts covers.

Also, it is needed the emergence of specialized lawyers in new digital technologies capable to collaborate with computer experts in order to manage possible legal risks adjusting the implementation of Smart Contracts to the existing laws.

Another of the challenges the deployment of Smart Contracts within BT poses, is in which cases, its implementation is necessary, and its use is justified. Differentiating from which other cases the existing techniques already work in a practical way. Recalling that this technology is not suitable to everything.

It should not be forgotten that these technologies are going through their early stages and still need to mature, needing both technologically and legally supports.

Acknowledgements. This work is supported by the Salamanca Ciudad de Cultura y Saberes Foundation under the Atracción del Talento programme (CHROMOSOME project). The research of Yeray Mezquita is supported by the pre-doctoral fellowship from the University of Salamanca and Banco Santander.

References

1. Aitzhan, N.Z., Svetinovic, D.: Security and privacy in decentralized energy trading through multi-signatures, blockchain and anonymous messaging streams. IEEE Trans. Dependable Secure Comput. **15**(5), 840–852 (2018)
2. Castor, A.: One of Ethereum's earliest smart contract languages is headed for retirement. https://www.coindesk.com/one-of-ethereums-earliest-smart-contract-languages-is-headed-for-retirement, last accessed 2019/01/15
3. Anon, ERC20 Token Standard. ERC20 Token Standard-The Ethereum Wiki
4. Blockchain Oracles Explained. https://www.mycryptopedia.com/blockchain-oracles-explained/. Accessed 15 Jan 2019
5. Buterin, V.: CRITICAL UPDATE Re: DAO Vulnerability - Ethereum Blog. https://blog.ethereum.org/2016/06/17/critical-update-re-dao-vulnerability/. Accessed 15 Jan 2019
6. Buterin, V.: A next-generation smart contract and decentralized application platform. White paper (2014)
7. Casado-Vara, R.: Blockchain-based distributed cooperative control algorithm for WSN monitoring. In: Rodríguez, S., et al. (eds.) DCAI 2018. AISC, vol. 801, pp. 414–417. Springer, Cham (2019). https://doi.org/10.1007/978-3-319-99608-0_56
8. Casado-Vara, R.: New approach to power system grid security with a blockchain-based model. In: Rodríguez, S., et al. (eds.) DCAI 2018. AISC, vol. 801, pp. 418–421. Springer, Cham (2019). https://doi.org/10.1007/978-3-319-99608-0_57
9. Casado-Vara, R.: Stochastic approach for prediction of WSN accuracy degradation with blockchain technology. In: Rodríguez, S., et al. (eds.) DCAI 2018. AISC, vol. 801, pp. 422–425. Springer, Cham (2019). https://doi.org/10.1007/978-3-319-99608-0_58
10. Casado-Vara, R., Corchado, J.M.: Blockchain for democratic voting: how blockchain could cast off voter fraud. Orient. J. Comput. Sci. Technol. **11**(1) (2018)

11. Casado-Vara, R., Chamoso, P., De la Prieta, F., Prieto, J., Corchado, J.M.: Non-linear adaptive closed-loop control system for improved efficiency in IoT-blockchain management. Inf. Fusion **49**, 227–239 (2019)
12. Casado-Vara, R., de la Prieta, F., Prieto, J., Corchado, J.M.: Blockchain framework for IoT data quality via edge computing. In: Proceedings of the 1st Workshop on Blockchain-enabled Networked Sensor Systems, pp. 19–24. ACM(2018)
13. Casado-Vara, R., González-Briones, A., Prieto, J., Corchado, Juan M.: Smart contract for monitoring and control of logistics activities: pharmaceutical utilities case study. In: Graña, M., et al. (eds.) SOCO'18-CISIS'18-ICEUTE'18 2018. AISC, vol. 771, pp. 509–517. Springer, Cham (2019). https://doi.org/10.1007/978-3-319-94120-2_49
14. Casado-Vara, Roberto, Prieto, Javier, Corchado, Juan M.: How blockchain could improve fraud detection in power distribution grid. In: Graña, Manuel, et al. (eds.) SOCO'18-CISIS'18-ICEUTE'18 2018. AISC, vol. 771, pp. 67–76. Springer, Cham (2019). https://doi.org/10.1007/978-3-319-94120-2_7
15. Casado-Vara, R., Prieto, J., De la Prieta, F., Corchado, J.M.: How blockchain improves the supply chain: case study alimentary supply chain. Proc. Comput. Sci. **134**, 393–398 (2018)
16. Chamoso, P., González-Briones, A., Rodríguez, S., Corchado, J.M.: Tendencies of technologies and platforms in smart cities: a state-of-the-art review. Wirel. Commun. Mob. Comput. (2018)
17. Chavez-Dreyfuss, G.: Sweden tests blockchain technology for land registry. Reuters (2016). http://www.reuters.com/article/us-sweden-blockchain-idUSKCN0Z22KV
18. DIRECTIVA 2000/31/CE DEL PARLAMENTO EUROPEO Y DEL CONSEJO de 8 de junio de 2000. https://www.boe.es/doue/2000/178/L00001-00016.pdf. Accessed 13 Jan 2019
19. González-Briones, A., De La Prieta, F., Mohamad, M., Omatu, S., Corchado, J.: Multi-agent systems applications in energy optimization problems: a state-of-the-art review. Energies **11**(8), 1928 (2018)
20. Grincalaitis, M.: The ultimate guide to audit a smart contract + most dangerous attacks in Solidity. https://medium.com/@merunasgrincalaitis/how-to-audit-a-smart-contract-most-dangerous-attacks-in-solidity-ae402a7e7868. Accessed 16 Jan 2019
21. http://erc721.org/. Accessed 15 Jan 2019
22. del Moral, I.L.: Blockchain en el ámbito registral. https://www.lawandtrends.com/noticias/tic/blockchain-en-el-ambito-registral-1.html. Accessed 15 Jan 2019
23. Introduction to Smart Contracts—Solidity 0.4.23 documentation. https://solidity.readthedocs.io/en/latest/introduction-to-smart-contracts.html. Accessed 15 Jan 2019
24. Mengelkamp, E., et al.: Designing microgrid energy markets: a case study: the Brooklyn microgrid. Appl. Energy **210**, 870–880 (2018)
25. Zuckerman, M.J.: Swedish government land registry soon to conduct first blockchain property transaction. https://cointelegraph.com/news/swedish-government-land-registry-soon-to-conduct-first-blockchain-property-transaction. Accessed 15 Jan 2019
26. Nakamoto, S.: Bitcoin: a peer-to-peer electronic cash system (2008)
27. Nikolic, I., et al.: Finding the greedy, prodigal, and suicidal contracts at scale. arXiv preprint arXiv:1802.06038 (2018)
28. Oliver, A.: Colombia launches time-saving blockchain land registry pilot project. https://coinrivet.com/colombia-launches-a-time-saving-blockchain-land-registry-pilot-project/. Accessed 15 Jan 2019
29. Oraclize Documentation. http://docs.oraclize.it/. Accessed 16 Jan 2019
30. Palladino, Santiago. "The parity wallet hack explained.", https://blog.zeppelin.solutions/on-the-parity-wallet-multisig-hack-405a8c12e8f7. Accessed 15 Jan 2019

31. Daian, P.: http://hackingdistributed.com/2016/06/18/analysis-of-the-dao-exploit/. Accessed 15 Jan 2019
32. Script - Bitcoin Wiki. https://en.bitcoin.it/wiki/Script, Accessed 11 Jan 2019
33. Szabo, N.: Formalizing and securing relationships on public networks. First Monday 2(9) (1997)
34. Szabo, N.: Secure property titles with owner authority (1998). http://szabo.best.vwh.net/securetitle.html
35. Szabo, N.: Smart contracts: building blocks for digital markets. EXTROPY: J. Transhumanist Thought (16), 18 (1996)
36. Zhang, Y., Wen, J.: The IoT electric business model: using blockchain technology for the internet of things. Peer-to-Peer Netw. Appl. 10(4), 983–994 (2017)

Using Blockchain for Traceability in the Drug Supply Chain

Jennifer Cristina Molina$^{(\boxtimes)}$, Daniela Torres Delgado$^{(\boxtimes)}$, and Giovanni Tarazona$^{(\boxtimes)}$

Francisco José de Caldas District University, Bogotá, Colombia
cristil0523@gmail.com,
dtorresd@correo.udistrital.edu.co,
gtarazona@udistrital.edu.co

Abstract. The illegal trade of medication is a problem which has claimed lives all over the world. In spite of the efforts from different international institutions aiming to stop this situation, illegal sales continue to grow. The following article proposes the use of Blockchain technology as a solution to the traceability problems and lack of control in the drug trade, as well as the way different entities would participate in it.

Keywords: Blockchain · Counterfeit · Medication · Security

1 Introduction

The commercialization of medication in various Latin American countries is known to be decentralized [1], i.e., any organization that meets the legislation and regulations in force can become a pharmaceutical distributor. This leads to the uncontrolled trade of medicines from questionable sources which rapidly reach the hands of consumers due to their low costs. Under the pretext of false promises, these illegal medications can hinder legal treatments on a short-term basis, increase the resistance to other drugs and even cause death [2].

Globally, the incidents reported with medicines increased by 11% from 2016 to 2017. These incidents are related to pharmaceutical theft, counterfeited medication and illegal deviation which can cause that the end consumer to receive an illegal or adulterated product believing that is a genuine one [3] (Fig. 1).

The Pharmaceutical Security Institute is an organization created to report counterfeit, theft and illegal deviation of medications all over the world. It states that 1.378 people were arrested last year for such charges which indicates that arrests increased by 10% during the 2016–2017 period. The research also revealed which stages of the supply chain had more arrests: production, distribution, transportation and sales [4]. Figure 2 shows the arrests per region in terms of illegal activities regarding medications.

© Springer Nature Switzerland AG 2019
L. Uden et al. (Eds.): KMO 2019, CCIS 1027, pp. 536–548, 2019.
https://doi.org/10.1007/978-3-030-21451-7_46

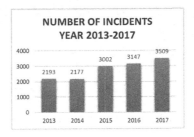

Fig. 1

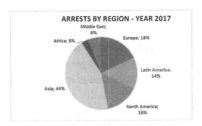

Fig. 2

Currently, different technologies and techniques have been implemented to reduce the arrival of illegal medicines to consumers. However, these have not been successful which is why this article proposes blockchain structure that allows the patient or the entity to determine the source of the medication and make decisions accordingly. Therefore, the actual functioning of the drug supply chain and its complications will be explained, a vision of the operation of a blockchain will be given later and the proposal will finally be developed.

2 Manipulation of Medication

An approximation to the worldwide pharmaceutical supply chain is described in this section. The supply chain seeks to offer a service to the end consumer through the provision of medications. An information system can be used by the user to report his needs often within the supply chain. The consumer informs the medical center or pharmacy that he needs a certain product, the pharmacy then requests said product to the distributor and so on.

The internal actors of the supply chain can be different according to the country where they operate since regulations and institutions change from one country to another. The general overview of the drug supply chain corresponds to the one described in Fig. 3. For instance, in Colombia the supply chain is mostly decentralized meaning that the people responsible for its operation are not reunited in a single entity since different tasks are split between public or private operators [5].

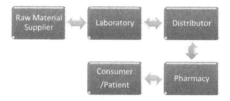

Fig. 3. Pharmaceutical supply chain

Depending on the type of product that is being commercialized, if it is sale-restricted or included in programs for the control of diseases and transmittable pathologies, its purchase and delivery can be performed in a centralized manner. If the product is used on a daily basis or in unsupervised treatments that do not require medical prescription, its commercialization is decentralized. However, the specifications of storage mechanisms, inventory management and transportation are the same regardless of the type of operator or entity that is in charge. The purchase of medication is carried out by the departments or city halls and the recollection is carried out by lower-level entities such as regional warehouses when the delivery or purchase is directly performed. This is all supported by policies that regulate the supply of medications, control prices and make sure that the establishments run proper trade and standard procedures for handling goods [5].

Nowadays, health entities are improving the information systems for medicines in their countries, in order to provide accurate and opportunistic systems, offering support in case of shortages or real-time reports of lacking medications [2]. However, in spite of the control policies in force all over the world, one of the main problems in drug trade are counterfeited medicines and how they reach the hands of patients.

Although some medications are distributed with special characteristics marked in their presentation so that consumers and pharmacies can distinguish the fake ones from the real ones, the producers of adulterated products rapidly change their own products to pass them as legit. Furthermore, elevated costs cause patients to purchase their pharmaceuticals in other places with no clear knowledge of their origin.

According to a 2017 report of the PSI (Pharmaceutical Security Institute), the types of pharmaceutical crimes are:

a. *Medication counterfeit:* Products are deliberately and fraudulently produced or even wrongly labelled in order to appear as genuine products whether they come from a brand or a generic source.
b. *Illegal deviation:* It occurs when a pharmaceutical product is approved and is meant to be sold in a certain country but is then illegally intercepted and sold in another one.
c. *Pharmaceutical theft:* It is the illegal handling of medication and involves the theft or embezzlement of goods. The people responsible can have privileged information such as employees, external staff or professional thieves. This can take place in any part of the distribution chain.

3 Blockchain

Blockchain is a consensus-based protocol created in 2009 by Satoshi Nakamoto [6], designed to support the transactions of the crypto-currency known as Bitcoin [7]. It only gained popularity until 2014 when it began to be used in different applications.

This technology is mainly constituted by a ledger or electronic account book where all the executed transactions are coded in the form of blocks in decentralized and open manner which is tolerant to the Byzantine failure [8] since the information is distributed to several independent nodes that validate it without a need for trust between them.

Each block in the chain has: two hashes, one for the preceding block (Prior Hash) and one for itself (Current Hash), the creation date of the block and the information of all transactions carried out (Fig. 4). Therefore, if the information is altered in one of the blocks, the information of the following block must also be altered. The blocks are linked with transaction codes and are cryptographically protected. The miners are in charge of validating the blocks that are being added to the chain, through of mathematical algorithms and whose result is lodged in the node without causing any type of affectation to the data (Nonce), in order to give legitimacy to the overall process.

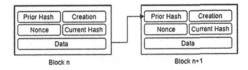

Fig. 4. Blockchain relation between blocks

The most relevant and interesting features of the Blockchain technology are [9]:

A. *Distributed database:* In Blockchain, there is no authority or entity that has a database in its power, since the information is distributed in many nodes. Copies are stored and updated in real time in all computers where the network is open.

B. *Peer-to-peer (P2P) transmission:* The communication between peers is carried out without the need of a middleman, which allows each node to store and forward information to other nodes.

C. *Transparency:* All transactions are visible for all network users. Each node has an address that identifies it and it can choose whether to remain anonymous or not.

D. *Inalterable records:* Once a transaction is inside the database and the information that cannot be modified has been validated, any changes must be approved or validated by various nodes. The transaction is then added as new block at the end of the chain.

E. *Computational logic:* All transactions must be programmed meaning that users can code and establish rules to activate automatic transactions.

F. *Auditable information* [10]: Since the information is stored and cannot be modified or deleted, the system allows anyone to check the traceability of previous records which can be achieved by arriving to the beginning of the chain.

Although one of the most predominant features of Blockchain technology is the public access to databases, many organizations have created structures that change this characteristic and allow block chains to adapt to any purpose or organization. The types of blockchain are [11]:

Public: This type of blockchain could be defined as the original one since one of its main platforms is Bitcoin and it is characterized for being global and always available. It has many nodes which powers its transparency and trust regarding data. It is open source, so anyone can easily build services with added value. Its main platforms are Bitcoin and Ethereum [13].

Private: Private blockchains are mostly used by companies that do not want that their information to be publicly divulged and want users that can make changes to be authorized. It offers better performance and confidentiality and the creating entity has more control over its behavior. Some platforms that offer this type of chains are Multichain [14], Ethereum and Hyperledger [15].

In the private blockchain scenario, it is also possible to create mixt chains (public-private chains) which allows an entity to restrict the users that can add information to the chain and allow certain transactions to be visible for all the other nodes.

4 Proposal

It has been proposed that the security of the consumer regarding the legitimacy of any product can be verified when working with the Blockchain technology [16]. However, although the information is being implemented in different applications it may not be the most convenient or efficient solution for current problems in different industrial or logistics environments. Hence, it is necessary to assess the area of impact and compare it with the Blockchain's own characteristics in order to validate that its implementation is logical and functional. The solution consists on offering information to the client that can be used to verify the authenticity of the drug and reduce the traffic of illegal and counterfeited products [17].

In first place, it is necessary to know if traditional database technologies can determine user needs. Currently, the traceability of medications is carried out with the e-pedigree system (2009). It is based on RFID technology and consists on making sure that documents store the information on the progression of drug properties throughout the entire supply chain, from the production stage up to the pharmacy sale [18]. The system includes chips that send a radiofrequency signal to the targeted antenna, sending the information contained in the cell [4] and a data storage system that saves traceability [19].

However, this type of system has not been widely spread all over the world. In 2012, e-pedigree was the only method know for the legislation of medication traceability in some states of USA and in Korea [19]. In other countries such as Colombia, this type of system does not exist, and the traceability of medications is lost causing them to arrive to healthcare centers which derives in bigger issues [20]. Additionally, the tags or labels that keep traceability information are easily forged which leads inaccurate information to be saved in the e-pedigree system [21]. This situation implies that this type of technology does not cover the real needs regarding the verification of the origin of medications.

Another inherent feature of Blockchain is that many participants of the supply chain add information. In the problem to solve it is understood that all the participants of the supply chain are independent and each one has its own information which would be impossible for a single entity to supervise at the same time. Furthermore, the data needs to be obtained rapidly so more than one participant has to be able to upload information.

As previously explained, all the participants are independent and each one has different tasks which are unbeknownst to other stages of the chain. Currently, mutual trust is mandatory so for instance if a patient acquires a medication from a healthcare center, he trusts that the product is original and complies with all the legislation, yet it can be adulterated up to a certain point. In the same manner, the medical center needs to trust the laboratory based on its brand or in previous contracts, but there is no real certainty of its production so there is no full trust between the agents of the supply system.

One of the properties of the Blockchain strategy is that the information is immutable. In the e-pedigree system, the information is separately stored in RFID labels according to the process stage of the medication (production, distribution, etc.). In between the stages, fraud can occur, and labels are copied causing the reader to identify two medications as identical. Additionally, records take some time to be ready, so they can remain incomplete [22]. Therefore, it is concluded that the database can be attacked in order to modify or steal information.

Currently, the entity in charge of health of medications is the WHO (World Health Organization) [24]. In Latin America, the institution in charge of the supervision of the health sector is the PAHO (Pan-American Health Organization) [23]. These institutions have the role to constantly supervise the participants of the supply chain to guarantee quality and effectiveness in their services. With the implementation of blockchain, the participation of a third 'top-level' agent that everyone would need to trust is no necessary, since it is a consensus-based system where all members are peers. Each one acts correctly since the other participants know their identities and hold them accountable for specific tasks [17].

By posing the idea of using Blockchain technology as a solution for the traceability of medications in order to offer security from the producer all the way to the consumer of the product's reliability, the information must remain open for any person or entity that wishes to look up.

Based on the previous explanation, a public chain does not need to control who makes changes in the network since a consensus-based model can be used to guarantee that any modifications to the code must be approved by other members of the chain. In contrast, the private chain grants access to specific entities to perform changes.

With this in mind, it is concluded that Blockchain technology can be applied as a solution to the problem of traceability of medications. In the following article, the structure that could be applied to the case study is proposed.

The only people who should alter the supplied information are the entities that participate and are responsible of the medications in the entire supply chain (raw material providers, laboratories, distributors, pharmacies and healthcare centers). The information stored by these institutions is public for any consumer or patient who wishes to review it.

Based on the Hyperledger platform, which can create authorized or private chains, the following structure is given (Fig. 5):

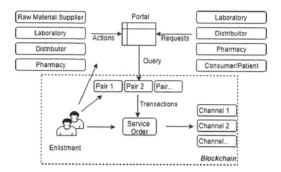

Fig. 5. Proposed structure of the medication supply chain

With the blockchain technology, each actor in the supply chain has a ledger or associated ledger where it registers the parameters associated with the process for which it is responsible. A web portal will be used as the center of the databases where each of the parts of the supply chain, you can enter with an ID or assigned serial, which would belong to the person in charge of the information contained in the block and also to the physical product that would be transferred.

Each transaction has two actors that perform simple operations, where the responsibility of the input is delivered to the next participant in the chain and the ledger of the operational flow of the transactions is fed.

The transactions that would take place between the different agents are now explained. Such agents are the suppliers of raw materials (Pmp), laboratories (L), distributors (D), pharmacies (F) and consumers (C). The process is described using a protocol with public (M_α) and private (M_α^{-1}) keys for a certain actor α.

1. Raw material supplier

- Company ID, Name, City

1.1. Transaction parameters.

- Insert ID of the distributor that receives the raw material.
- Upload information of the raw material, characteristics, quality, and quantity.
- Send information about the dispatch of the raw material (type and conditions of transport) to the designated laboratory.

$$Owner\ M_{Pmp}^{-1} \rightarrow M_L^{-1}$$

2. Laboratory

- Laboratory ID, City, Brand

2.1. Transaction parameters:

- Insert Id of the laboratory that receives the raw material to the supplier's serial number.
- Receive delivery order from the supplier, verify quality characteristics, quantity.
- Describe the raw material and supplies used to obtain the medicine.
- Describe the process used to manufacture the medication.
- Define batches by type of medication.
- Assign the distributor that will receive the finished product.
- To verify the origin of the raw material, the owner now does it with a public access key.

$$Check \rightarrow M_L \qquad Owner\ M_L^{-1} \rightarrow M_D^{-1}$$

3. Distributor

- Distributor ID, Name. City.

3.1. Transaction parameters:

- Insert ID of the distributor that receives the finished product after the ID of the laboratory.
- Receive a finished product relation.
- Sort by batch and type of medication and finally store.
- Assign delivery times.
- Assign to the correspondent pharmacy according to order.

$$Check \rightarrow M_D \qquad Owner\ M_D^{-1} \rightarrow M_F^{-1}$$

4. Pharmacy

- Pharmacy ID, Name, City.

4.1. Transaction parameters:

- Insert ID of the pharmacy that receives the finished product.
- Make the entry of medications by type and batch in the stock of the pharmacy.
- Enter request for medication delivery per user.
- Download medicines from the stock.

$$Check \rightarrow M_F \qquad Owner\ M_F^{-1} \rightarrow M_C^{-1}$$

5. Consumer/Patient:

- Consumer ID, Type of medication, City, Age, Sex, Type of disease, Safe

5.1. Transaction parameters:

- Enter the platform: the type and batch of the medication.
- Identify each of the links in the supply chain where the data that each participant leaved as public gives support to the traceability of the security in the chain is described, since the miners are responsible for directing the request to the channel where the selected drug is.
- Each of the aforementioned transfers of responsibility are automated in the system using the Smart Contracts or Chaincode, which are or scripts that are activated by directing us to a single address and allowing transactions in a virtual way (27), the foregoing would authorize that in each addition of information of transfer of responsibility initiate a new contract and it will be close when another element of the supply chain receives the medication.

For cases of fraud in the information of drug labeling, sabotage of fictitious actors in one of the links of the chain or extortion in the change of batches for the entry of falsified medicines or of doubtful precedence, will be controlled through the application of the blockchain technology, where each link executes transactions and defines them in the block assigned according to the criteria established in the architecture of the network.

Any batch of medications can be traced through the supply chain, identifying the type of transaction executed among the participants. If, when verifying a transaction is missing, the actor is identified and becomes responsible for the inconvenience presented. This base of transactions executed on distributed servers is fed from the nodes of the participants of the supply chain chronologically, that is, how the process is executed. Each node maintains the information that the person in charge has stored and allows to specify with the next node. The technology allows an efficient process in the case of suspicious transaction reports, that is, clearly identify the transaction executed by each actor. The information provided would be stored in a cryptographic hash that ensures that the information is true because it does not allow data manipulation.

5   Discussion

To confirm that the proposal contained in this article can be useful and accepted by the parts involved in the supply chain, a poll was chosen as a validation method.

The population used for the statistical analysis was established according to the INVIMA management report of the second semester of 2017 [26]. The report states that 938 establishments of producers and marketers of medications in Colombia are under the observation of this entity in charge of their inspection, supervision and control.

The study considers variables such as: certifications, records, inspection visits, measures of illegality measures and sanitary sanctions to establish the level of risk. According to the above, 155 establishments are under a high risk level, that is, they are those that require the most attention, therefore, we take this amount as the base population to determine the sample to which the surveys will be applied, and hence we use formula (1).

The constant of 0.5 is the expected probability or expected proportion of success, it is used when we assume that the population is distributed equally among each of the chain actors that know the Blockchain technology and the possibility of adapting its structure for controlling the falsification of medicines, as well as those who have never heard this new tool (Table 1).

Table 1. Values of the equation.

	Characteristic	Value
n	Calculated size of the sample	–
N	Size of the population	155
e	Maximum estimated error	10%
Z	Statistical parameter (level of confidence)	95%
α_C	Variance	1.96

$$n = \frac{N * (\alpha_C * 0.5)^2}{1 + (e^2 * (N - 1))} \tag{1}$$

$$n = \frac{155 * (1,96 * 0.5)^2}{1 + ((10\%)^2 * (155 - 1))} = 58,60 \cong 60 \tag{2}$$

According to the analysis, a sample size of 60 individuals was determined so the poll was personally and virtually applied to consumers of medications, pharmacy technicians, professionals in pharmaceutical production and commercial establishments.

The place chosen for the study was the city of Bogotá and the critical path of the medications was considered during the supply chain as well as the risks for each link (counterfeit, manufacturing errors, illegal deviation or theft) and the possible impact (toxicity, death, increase in costs, loss of trust and funding illicit activities).

The poll included the six following questions:

1. How would you rate the existing control policies to avoid the trade of adulterated/counterfeit medications?

2. How would rate the policy to have the database of the supply chain distributed in all its parts?

3. How would you rate the idea of knowing the traceability of medications before their trade or when you acquire them?

4. How would you rate the Blockchain technology as a mechanism that could regulate the origin and minimum attributes required for the trade of medications?

5. How would you rate a platform (Blockchain) that allows access to inalterable information from the entire supply chain, that can be fully trusted?

The purpose of this poll consists on validating the implementation of the Blockchain technology in the supply chain of medications as a solution to the problem of counterfeited drug trade. The answers received in the poll revealed the following insights.

- For the first question, 74% of the surveyed people agreed that the existing control policies were poor or average which indicates that there is an unconformity in terms of the way in which the control entities supervise the quality and legality of the products.
- For the second and third questions respectively, 60% and 77% considered to be good or excellent the distribution of the database between all the involved parties and the possibility of knowing with certainty the origin of a certain medication before its trade or at the moment of purchase. This shows that Blockchain features such as the management of public databases, their transparency and its auditability would be well received by the enquired population.
- For the fourth and fifth questions respectively, 85% and 88% of the surveyed sample considered good or excellent the Blockchain technology as a regulating agent on the precedence of medications and the information that it would store. This confirms that the inalterability feature would also be convenient based on the pharmaceutical sector's needs.

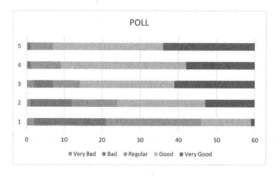

Fig. 6. Results of the poll

The previous exercise corroborates that the proposal of implementing the Blockchain technology is in fact feasible, since both the consumers and pharmacy owners see a weakness in the current management of medication security that could benefit from the discussed features regarding traceability control (Fig. 6).

6   Conclusion

With the global implementation of the Blockchain technology to store the traceability of medications, all the parties of the supply chain could know the origin of the acquired products thereby contributing to strike the groups that trade stolen or adulterated products. The number of patients that suffer from ailments due to the mismanagement of drugs would also be reduced. The success of this strategy depends on the commitment from countries to build a legislation that enables businesses and organizations to access the Blockchain platform and citizens to use it for information review.

References

1. INVIMA. Informe de gestión del desabastecimiento de medicamentos en Colombia 2013–2018 (2018)
2. Ebel, T., George, K., Larsen, E., Neal, E., Shah, K., Shi, D.: Strength in Unity: The Promise of Global Standards in Healthcare. McKinsey & Company, New York (2012)
3. Pharmaceutical Security Institute: Tendencias de Incidentes [Conjunto de datos] (2017). http://www.psi-inc.org/incidentTrends.cfm. Accessed 29 July 2018
4. Pharmaceutical Security Institute: Información de arrestos [Conjunto de datos] (2017). http://www.psi-inc.org/arrestData.cfm. Accessed 29 July 2018
5. USAID, & SIAPS: Caracterización de las Cadenas de Suministro de Medicamentos e Insumos Médicos en América Latina (2015). http://apps.who.int/medicinedocs/documents/s22392es/s22392es.pdf. Accessed 05 July 2018
6. Nakamoto, S.: Bitcoin: A Peer-to-Peer Electronic Cash System. https://bitcoin.org/bitcoin.pdf. Accessed 03 Aug 2018
7. Meunier, S.: Blockchain 101: what is blockchain and how does this revolutionary technology work? In: Transforming Climate Finance and Green Investment with Blockchains, pp. 23–34. Academic Press (2018)
8. Eyal, I., Efe Gencer, A., Gün, S., Van Renesse, R.: Bitcoin-NG: a scalable blockchain protocol. In: Symposium on Networked Systems Design and Implementation, pp. 44–59. USENIX (2016)
9. Lansiti, M., Lakhani, K.R.: The truth about blockchain. Harvard Bus. Rev. **95**(1), 118–127 (2017)
10. Viriyasitavat, W., Hoonsopon, D.: Blockchain characteristics and consensus in modern business processes. J. Ind. Inf. Integr. **13**, 32–39 (2018)
11. Sanchez, V., Cuenca, F., Puertas, M.: Cómo impacta Blockchain en la Logística 4.0. Indra, & UNO (eds). https://www.minsait.com/sites/default/files/newsroom_documents/informe_blockchain_logistica_uno_e_0.pdf. Accessed 10 Aug 2018
12. Bitcoin Blockchain. https://bitcoin.org/es/. Accessed 11 Aug 2018
13. Plataforma Ethereum Blockchain. https://www.ethereum.org/. Accessed 10 Aug 2018
14. Plataforma Multichain Blockchain. https://www.multichain.com/. Accessed 10 Aug 2018
15. Plataforma Hyperledger Blockchain. https://www.hyperledger.org/. Accessed 08 Aug 2018
16. Preukschat, A.: Blockchain: La revolución Industrial de Internet, 7th edi, Gestión 2000, Barcelona-España (2017)
17. Peck, M.E.: Blockchain world - do you need a blockchain? This chart will tell you if the technology can solve your problem. In: IEEE Spectrum, vol. 54, pp. 38–60, October 2017

18. Tu, Y., Zhou, W., Piramuthu, S.: Identifying RFID-embedded objects in pervasive healthcare applications. Decis. Support Syst. **46**(2), 586–593 (2009)
19. Rodríguez, N.A., Mora Carrión, S.: Diseño de un prototipo basado en la tecnología RFID para el monitoreo de equipos digitales. Universidad Libre. http://repository.unilibre.edu.co/handle/10901/10814. Accessed 01 Aug 2018
20. Kim, H., Jeong, H., Park, H.: A study on RFID/USN based e-pedigree system for cold chain management. In: International Technology Management, pp. 138–143. IEEE, Dallas (2012)
21. Casa Editorial El Tiempo. Este año han caído más de 2.6 millones de medicinas falsificadas. Comunicado de prensa, 27 abril 2018. https://www.eltiempo.com/justicia/investigacion/asi-operaba-red-de-medicamentos-falsos-judicializada-por-la-fiscalia-210386. Accessed 15 Aug 2018
22. Kamaludin, H., Mahdin, H., Abawajy, J.H.: Clone tag detection in distributed RFID systems. PLOS ONE **13**(3), e0193951 (2018)
23. Organización Panamericana de la Salud. https://www.paho.org/hq/index.php?lang=es. Accessed 07 Aug 2018
24. Organización Mundial de la Salud. http://www.who.int/es. Accessed 18 July 2018
25. Azaria, A., Ekblaw, A., Vieira, T.: MedRec: using blockchain for medical data access and permission management. In: International Conference on Open and Big Data (OBD), pp. 25–30. IEEE, Viena (2016)
26. INVIMA, Informe de Gestión segundo semestre del 2017. Colombia (2017)

Author Index

Printed in the United States
By Bookmasters